The Welsh National School of Medicine, 1893–1931: The Cardiff Years

The Welsh National School of Medicine, 1893–1931

The Cardiff Years

Alun Roberts

UNIVERSITY OF WALES PRESS
2008

www.uwp.co.uk

British Library Cataloguing-in-Publication Data
A catalogue record for this book is available from the British Library.

ISBN 978–0–7083–2174–4

The right of Alun Roberts to be identified as author of this work has been asserted by him in accordance with sections 77, 78 and 79 of the Copyright, Designs and Patents Act 1988.

Typeset by Mark Heslington Ltd, Scarborough, North Yorkshire
Printed and bound in Great Britain by CPI Antony Rowe, Wiltshire

Contents

Illustrations

between pages 220 and 221

Foreword

by Professor Stephen Tomlinson and Dr David Grant

The year 2008 commemorates the 125th anniversary of the establishment of Cardiff University, which officially opened on 24 October 1883 as the University College of South Wales and Monmouthshire. Many events have been held during this year to celebrate this achievement and it is a matter of no little satisfaction that the publication of Alun Roberts's book has coincided with these celebrations. For, although the Cardiff Medical School itself did not come into existence until 1893, one of the college's central objectives, from the start, was the provision of medical education in Wales the first clause in the college charter was quite specific on this point.

Since its establishment the medical school has experienced many changes. Until 1921 it was a preclinical institution; in that year it became, as the Welsh National School of Medicine, a full medical school, offering clinical as well as preclinical instruction. Ten years later, after a decade of controversy, the school divided into two, the preclinical part remaining within the University College of South Wales and Monmouthshire (often referred to in this book as University College, Cardiff), and the clinical part becoming an independent Welsh National School of Medicine within the University of Wales. In 1984 the school, now embracing dentistry and nursing as well as medicine, changed its name to the University of Wales College of Medicine (UWCM), achieving full constitutional parity with the other colleges in the University of Wales four years later. In 1995 the college further increased its range of academic disciplines with the addition of several professions allied to medicine. Finally, in 2004, in a spirit of harmony quite absent during the 1920s, the College of Medicine merged with what was formally known as the University of Wales, Cardiff, to become the present Cardiff University.

This book discusses the history of the medical school during the first four decades of its existence, as part of University College, Cardiff. It was commissioned by one of us, Professor Tomlinson, whilst vice-chancellor of UWCM. The proposal was strongly supported by the other vice-chancellor, Dr Grant. We were fortunate in having a one-time historian as a member of staff, Dr Alun Roberts, who enthusiastically took on the task. What emerges from this book is a splendid story of people and times that at first may appear remote. But those people cared about things we care about and needed to get things done at that time, including the establishment of a medical school within the newly established University of Wales. Why? Because in many ways the new University of Wales was the only visible and tangible expression of Wales's aspiration for self-recognition as a nation within the United Kingdom. As with other independent universities within the UK, the ability to offer instruction in medicine was deemed to be essential. In the story of the establishment of the Welsh National School of Medicine there are many elements which resonate with the times we live in now, not least creative tensions between the medical school and its parent, University College, Cardiff; differences of opinion between universities, medical schools and health services, and funding matters.

Great men emerge from these pages: Sir William Osler, Sir Isambard Owen, Principal Viriamu Jones, Sir Thomas Lewis, Sir William James Thomas and many others who laid the foundations for teaching and research in medicine in Wales. These people were dedicated to the health of the people of Wales, a commitment which has continued from then to this day. The history is not a dry chronology but a fascinating account of struggle, failure and success, innovation and progress. It catches the personalities (and in some cases lack of them!), the qualities and the foibles of the key players. After separation, though sometimes financially stretched, the Welsh National School of Medicine went from strength to strength, often 'punching above its weight' in academic excellence and led by men (and later women) of vision, energy and determination, including Professor Harold Scarborough, who produced fourteen professors, amongst them Sir William Asscher, Sir Netar Mallick and Sir Keith Peters, the current chairman of the Council of Cardiff University.

The separation of the medical school from its parent college, and its establishment as a constituent institution within the University of Wales was perceived by many to be right for its time in 1931. Today is a different time. The establishment of a Welsh Assembly government and other manifestations of nationhood have led to a reappraisal of the central role of the University of Wales. At the same time it is now recognized that to be globally competitive, modern universities must have academic and financial critical mass. The merger of University of Wales, Cardiff and UWCM has created the critical mass which enables Cardiff University to be not only a 'local hero' but also a global player contributing substantially to health, society and wealth for Wales, the UK and beyond.

If merger seems such a natural step to take now, one may ask why on earth a schism took place in 1931. This is one of the issues that Alun Roberts has tackled in his wide-ranging book on the history of medical education during the last decade of the nineteenth and early decades of the twentieth century. The separation of Cardiff from most of its medical school in 1931 took thirteen difficult years; reunification has been achieved in three remarkably productive years for Wales.

This important book describes, in a scholarly and entertaining way, the emergence of the Welsh National School of Medicine, while laying the foundation for today's world-class Cardiff University. It is a great story!

Cardiff University, October 2008

Preface

On 1 August 2004 the activities of the University of Wales College of Medicine and the body then known as the University of Wales, Cardiff merged. The legal merger of the two was confirmed on 1 December 2004, following the passing of the University of Wales, Cardiff Act. In March 2005 the Privy Council granted the merged university a supplemental charter in the formal name of Cardiff University, at which point the institution ceased to be a constituent of the federal University of Wales. Over seventy-three eventful years had elapsed since the Welsh National School of Medicine, or, to be strictly accurate, the clinical component, had split away from the University College of South Wales and Monmouthshire to become an independent institution within the federal University of Wales.

Confident that merger would take place, early in 2003 Professor Stephen Tomlinson, the vice-chancellor of the College of Medicine, invited me to write a history of the college so that its achievements, and failures, would be preserved for posterity. Whether one can trust the historical perspective of an author whose previous excursions into print have included a book on Welsh national heroes which failed to honour Wales's greatest rugby player, Gareth Edwards, is a matter for others to judge. However, I did originally train as a historian, and had some personal knowledge of, and involvement in, the recent history of the college, having served as its registrar and secretary between 1984 and 1996, and subsequently as director of its NHS Liaison Unit until my retirement in 2004. In the preface of his book, *The University of Wales, 1939–1993*, Professor Prys Morgan went so far as to describe me as the college archivist, a title which has never formally existed so far as I know, but one that I was pleased to accept from him, meagre though my efforts were in supplying information for his history. I have another, more personal reason for taking a special interest in the history of the Welsh National School of Medicine. A great-uncle, two uncles and a cousin, all on my mother's side, studied there, two of them during the 'Cardiff years'.

During my modest searches in relation to Prys Morgan's book, one thing became pretty clear: not much had been written about the Welsh National School of Medicine and (from 1984) the University of Wales College of Medicine. There were a few articles and other brief accounts of the school and some of its early pioneers, written notably by John Cule, Alan Trevor Jones (one-time provost) and Peter Thomas, to which reference is made in the bibliography. A former colleague of mine, Alan Parsons, wrote, in part-fulfilment of the requirements for the M.Ed. of the University of Wales, a short dissertation on 'The origins and subsequent development of the Cardiff Medical School into the Welsh National School of Medicine, 1894–1971', which recorded the main milestones. T. I. Ellis's book, *The Development of Higher Education in Wales*, published in 1935, covered the post-First World War history of the medical school in one paragraph of twenty-two lines. The school fared a little better in D. Emrys Evans's short but elegant work, *The University of Wales: A Historical Sketch*, published by the University of Wales Press in 1953, and a brief account of the medical school during its association with the University College of South Wales and Monmouthshire appeared in *A Short History of the College, 1883–1933*, written by A. H. Trow and D. J. A. Brown, to commemorate Cardiff's Golden Jubilee. S. B. Chrimes edited, and wrote nearly half of the volume *University College, Cardiff: A Centenary History, 1883–1983*, which contained some useful material on the early decades of medical education in Cardiff. Though never published, copies of the bound typescript remain accessible. Until the 1990s arguably the best published treatment of the early history of the Welsh National School of Medicine appeared in Arnold Aldis's concise but well-researched and splendidly illustrated *Cardiff Royal Infirmary, 1883–1983*, produced to commemorate the hospital's centenary. Apart from its other virtues, this book demonstrated how much the history of medical education in the United Kingdom is bound up with that of the health service in its many forms. With the appearance, in the 1990s, of Professor J. Gwynn Williams's and Prys Morgan's volumes on the history of the University of Wales, the first hundred years of the medical school, from its foundation in 1893, were given proper treatment for the first time. Those seeking a broad overview of the main phases in the school's development, from the modest Cardiff Medical School of the 1890s to the internationally acclaimed University of Wales College of Medicine of recent years will find no better introduction than is provided in these three volumes, supplemented by some splendid pictures included in Professor Geraint Jenkins's *The University of Wales: An Illustrated History* (1993), a few of which appear in the present book. Nevertheless, Professor Williams did suggest that the Welsh School of Medicine deserved a history of its own, and one hopes that this volume goes at least some way towards filling part of the gap.

Apart from being a contribution to the history of the University of Wales, the present book also seeks to contribute to the history of medical education in the United Kingdom during the late nineteenth and early twentieth centuries. This was a period of great significance in the development of academic medicine in the United Kingdom, during which the essential framework of the modern medical curriculum was defined, the pursuit of research began to be seriously embraced by the medical community, stimulated by the activities of the Medical Research Council, and new relationships began to be forged between universities and their associated hospitals, exemplified by the post-war introduction of the 'clinical unit'. It is fair to say that, until relatively recently, developments in medical education have been somewhat neglected. During the first half of the twentieth century those histories of medical schools that were produced, usually to commemorate a significant anniversary in their development, while providing useful facts and figures as well as vignettes of local medical worthies, tended to be unbalanced and selective in their coverage. Two examples of the genre were W. S. Porter's *The Medical School in Sheffield, 1828–1928* (1928) and G. Grey Turner's *The Newcastle upon Tyne School of Medicine, 1834–1934* (1934). In recent years the situation has substantially improved, owing in no small part to the generosity of the Wellcome Trust, which has made a major investment in the promotion of the history of medicine as an area of serious academic endeavour. Several university-based centres for the history of medicine, substantially funded by the trust, now exist in London, provincial England, Scotland and Wales, and while their research interests are broad, they do include studies of the development of medical education during the nineteenth and twentieth centuries. Journals such as *Medical History* have provided an important outlet for researchers in the field, whether from the centres or elsewhere – the work of Stella Butler and Steve Sturdy on developments in medical education at universities in the north of England during the late nineteenth and early twentieth centuries, and of Andrew Hull on more recent developments in Glasgow, immediately come to mind. Medical education in London has recently been well served by Elsbeth Heaman's *St Mary's: The History of a London Teaching Hospital* (2004) and by Keir Waddington's *Medical Education at St Bartholomew's Hospital, 1123–1995* (2003), which by no means confines itself to developments in that particular institution but provides insights across the metropolis and beyond. Indeed, he addresses a theme which has engaged the skills of several historians in recent years, the development of scientific medicine, exemplified by the work of Christopher Lawrence, author of *Rockefeller Money, the Laboratory and Medicine in Edinburgh, 1919–1930: New Science in an Old Country* (2005), Mark Weatherall, in his *Gentlemen, Scientists and Doctors: Medicine at Cambridge, 1800–1940* (2000), and Helen Valier, in her Ph.D. thesis for the University of Manchester, on 'The politics of scientific medicine in Manchester, c.1900–1960' (2002). The fruits of Jonathan Reinarz's research into medical education at a number of provincial universities from 1800 to 1948, which he has carried out at the Centre for the History of Medicine at the University of Birmingham, are eagerly awaited. Although my book concentrates on the Welsh scene, I have, where appropriate, sought to cast my eyes across Offa's Dyke, to see how far events in Cardiff matched or diverged from goings-on elsewhere.

It is hoped that my book may also be of some interest to those engaged in the study of history of health and medicine in its broadest sense, particularly in Wales, where these issues are receiving much attention at the present time. This has been nourished by a conviction, which certainly pre-dates the arrival of the National Assembly for Wales in 1999, that Wales has a distinctive story to tell. Many of Wales's, indeed Britain's, leading social historians have made notable contributions to two important volumes of essays addressing aspects of this theme. *Medicine in Wales, c. 1800–2000:*

Public Service or Private Commodity?, edited by Anne Borsay (2003), provides a multi-disciplinary perspective on aspects of medicine and health in Wales over the last two centuries. *Health and Society in Twentieth-Century Wales*, edited by Pamela Michael and Charles Webster (2006), while embracing a shorter timespan, is equally wide-ranging in its coverage, and includes a superb introductory overview by Pamela Michael, who provides an indispensable bibliography of books and articles relevant to the study of health and medicine in Wales during the last one hundred years. How does the present history of the Cardiff Medical School and the Welsh National School of Medicine during the late nineteenth and early twentieth century fit into this broad theme? The school's primary aim, that of training the medical workforce for Wales, was at least partly achieved, between 50 and 60 per cent of those who had spent some or all their student years in Cardiff settling in Wales to pursue their careers. In a real sense, the history of medical education in Cardiff is also the history of the hospital service in the city, particularly of the way a voluntary hospital primarily responsible for the people of Cardiff and the surrounding area, took on, not always comfortably, its enhanced role as a teaching and research institution. The influence of the medical school on health practice is also noted in other ways, through improvements in medical records systems initiated by the professorial clinical units, and the work of the pioneering academic departments of public health and tuberculosis in studying the condition of the industrial workers of Wales.

In their introductory essay to *Medicine and Health*, Anne Borsay and Dorothy Porter observe how

> In the past thirty years the historical study of medicine and health has undergone a revolution. From origins in the celebration of great medical men and their clinical achievements, it has tapped into social and cultural history, and pulled in concepts from the social sciences, to become a seedbed for interdisciplinary research.

Judged in those terms, some readers may regard my book as rather old-fashioned. It is, in a real sense, a biography of an institution, and, characteristically of biographies, it takes a broadly chronological approach, focuses on significant milestones and dwells on the importance of 'great medical men' in the origins and development, first of the Cardiff Medical School, and then the Welsh National School of Medicine. It is hoped that such an approach will be of interest to medical graduates of the University of Wales, curious to learn something of the early history of an institution of which they are justifiably proud, and of some of the men and women who were associated with it, as students, members of staff or both. At a practical level, the book may bring enlightenment to those who, during the course of their studies, have secured such accolades as the Alfred Sheen Prize, the Alfred Hughes Memorial Medal, the John Maclean Prize or one of the Willie Seager Prizes, or who have sat at the feet of successive David Davies professors of tuberculosis and chest diseases, Sir

Thomas Lewis professors of cardiology, or Mansel Talbot professors of epidemiology and public health.

When, during the 1970s, Dr William Price accepted the invitation to write the history of St David's University College, Lampeter, the initial plan was to produce a complete history of the college in one volume. In the event, two volumes appeared, separated by several years. I have to confess that it was also my original intention to produce a one-volume history of the College of Medicine in its various manifestations. The period between 1893 and 1931, in other words the period prior to the establishment of the Welsh National School of Medicine as a constituent member of the University of Wales, would be adequately covered in one or possibly two introductory chapters, with the bulk of the book being devoted to the period from 1931 to 2004. It soon became obvious, at least to me, that the pre-independence phase could not be adequately covered in a couple of chapters. Indeed, such was the excellence of the sources for the early period, and the importance of the early decades in explaining the more recent phases of the college's history, that the period until 1931 deserved a book to itself.

There were a number of things that made the history of the medical school during the period before 1931 of some interest. Established by its founder, Dr William Thomas Edwards, so that every Welsh boy (he did not mention girls) could have the opportunity to study medicine at home, the school soon acquired a reputation as an excellent training ground for high-quality doctors, some of whom went on to achieve great distinction in the medical profession. Those who spent their preclinical years in Cardiff, before proceeding to London for their clinical training, included Sir Thomas Lewis, the eminent cardiologist, Ernest Jones, disciple and biographer of Sigmund Freud, Sir Clement Price Thomas, surgeon to King George VI and later president of the Welsh National School of Medicine, Sir Tudor Thomas, pioneer ophthalmologist, and A. G. ('Pop') Watkins, the school's first professor of child health. Sir Daniel Davies, physician to King George VI and Aneurin Bevan, had been in the first cohort of students who obtained the MB B.Ch. of the University of Wales, having completed the whole six-year course in Cardiff, in 1924. It is little wonder that Lord Horder, the leading clinician of his day, could say, at the inauguration ceremony of the Welsh National School of Medicine, in October 1933: 'When I meet a graduate in medicine of the University of Wales, my attitude is one of entire respect.'

The school attracted the active support of some of the most influential doctors of the time as it developed. Indeed their contribution was decisive in making the medical school what it was in 1931. Six men deserve special mention. It was Dr (soon to become Sir) Donald MacAlister, president of the General Medical Council, and principal and vice-chancellor of Glasgow University, who wrote the report, in 1908, which was instrumental in persuading the government, not only that a clinical medical school in Cardiff was a desirable and practical proposition, but that it should provide state aid to set the wheels in motion. He remained a vigorous champion of the school within the portals of the General Medical Council, and for several years served on the Medical Board of the University of Wales; indeed from time to time its meetings were held at the headquarters of the Royal College of Physicians in London to suit his convenience. The structure of the clinical medical school in Cardiff was largely determined on the advice of Sir William Osler, regius professor of medicine at Oxford University, and arguably the most celebrated doctor of his day. He was the leading advocate of the introduction of university clinical units into the medical schools of the United Kingdom. He saw the new medical school in Cardiff as an ideal place to promote this almost revolutionary concept, and in view of the fact that he was the medical expert on Lord Haldane's Royal Commission on University Education in Wales, it was hardly surprising that in 1918 this body recommended the introduction of the clinical unit system into the Welsh National School of Medicine. The Rockefeller Foundation was so impressed by Cardiff's commitment to the clinical unit system that, on the advice of Dr Richard Pearce, director of the foundation's Medical Education Division, it agreed in 1924 to fund state-of-the-art laboratories for the school's professor of medicine, a significant milestone in the institution's progress to maturity. One of those consulted by Pearce was Sir George Newman, chief medical officer at the Ministry of Health, a man of immense knowledge and influence in the field of medical education. Though never underestimating the problems ahead ('agreement is a very rare quality in South Wales,' he once confided to a senior official in the Privy Council), Newman was a good friend of the Welsh National School of Medicine during all phases of its development, acting as an effective Whitehall trouble-shooter from time to time. Needless to say, his advice to Pearce was entirely positive. Sir Walter Fletcher, secretary of the Medical Research Council during the 1920s, was another good friend of the school. He played a significant role in enhancing its research profile, being particularly supportive of the work of the Department of Tuberculosis and a champion of the school in its dealings with the Rockefeller Foundation. The sixth eminent doctor to influence the development of the Welsh National School of Medicine was Sir Isambard Owen, who, despite many competing commitments as, in turn, dean of St George's Medical School, principal of Armstrong College, Newcastle upon Tyne, and, from 1909, vice-chancellor of Bristol University, always seemed to have time to offer guidance on matters relating to the proper development of the medical school. It was he who advised University College, Cardiff in 1913 that the school's new Institute of Physiology should be built near to the King Edward VII Hospital on Newport Road, and not a mile away in Cathays Park. Though he came to regret it later, it was also he who crucially advised the Haldane Commission that the Welsh National School of Medicine should be an independent college within the federal University of Wales, and not an integral part of University College, Cardiff (the name commonly used for the University College of South Wales and Monmouthshire from its earliest years, though the title was not formally adopted until 1972, by means of a special statute).

Another notable feature of the medical school during its formative years was the way it was able to attract the attention of a small number of philanthropists, without whose generosity the school would surely never have developed as it did. It was William Thomas Edwards's initial donation of £1,000 which encouraged other local worthies, mainly doctors, to dig into their own pockets with sufficient vigour to enable the Cardiff Medical School to open in 1893. Other generous benefactors included the Talbots of Margam, the Davies family of Llandinam, and, most remarkably of all, Sir William James Thomas, coal owner and railway company director, who donated the huge sum of £90,000 to provide buildings fit to house Wales's medical school.

Had the First World War not intervened, it is almost certain that Cardiff, and not St Bartholomew's Hospital, would have been the first medical school in the United Kingdom to introduce Sir William Osler's university clinical unit system. In the event, when the Welsh National School of Medicine did embrace the concept, in 1921, it did so without adequate planning and, crucially, without making quite sure that its partner, the King Edward VII Hospital, was ready to accept the implications. Personal animosity entered the equation. As a result, despite the existence of a formal agreement between the authorities of the King Edward VII Hospital (renamed the Cardiff Royal Infirmary in 1923) and University College, Cardiff, which, though commonplace today, is believed to be the first of its sort ever drawn up in the United Kingdom, the whole of the 1920s was characterized by conflict, often bitter, between the hospital and the academic authorities. This finally led in 1928 to the hospital closing its doors to the school's students, a situation without parallel in the modern history of medical education in the United Kingdom. While this was going on, an equally fierce battle was being fought between the University of Wales and University College, Cardiff over the implementation of the central recommendations of the Haldane Report concerning the status of the Welsh National School of Medicine. The arguments touched on some of the recurring themes in the history of higher education in Wales ever since the 1890s: the relationship between the constituent institutions and the federal university, the all-Wales role of the School of Medicine (apart from other considerations, important for maximizing its income base) and, indeed, the antipathy often felt for Cardiff by the rest of the country. Like most disputes, with Whitehall becoming increasingly irritated, and even Sir Harry Reichel, principal of University College of North Wales, Bangor muttering about the *perfervidum ingenium Celtorum*, the perfervid – or overheated – spirit of the Celts, this one finally ended in compromise.

Like those who only decide to research their family tree once all their closest relations have passed on, I wish I had taken a closer interest in the history of the School of Medicine several years ago, when there were still doctors around who could remember the early years. I once had cause to visit Doctors Rosentyl and Bryneilen Griffiths, Cardiff general practitioners, who wished to endow a student prize in obstetrics and gynaecology in the College of Medicine. Over a cup of tea, they spoke about their student days and the crisis of 1928, when all the clinical students, excluded from the Royal Infirmary, were forced to make other arrangements to continue their studies. I wish that I had had the presence of mind to encourage them to commit their recollections to paper, as any history of the Welsh National School of Medicine during the inter-war years would have been enriched by their reminiscences. Let this be a lesson to all of us who seek to preserve records of the past. Nevertheless I have been fortunate in the range and quality of the written material available to me in preparing this book.

Needless to say, the records held by Cardiff University provide the greatest single corpus of information. The university's central archives, housed in the main building in Cathays Park, contain the minute books of all the relevant committees, the Council, the Senate, and a multitude of subcommittees of University College, Cardiff, together with the main committees of the Welsh National School of Medicine during the 1920s. There are excellent collections of press cuttings dating from the earliest years of the college, and almost complete records of student registrations and progress covering the whole period of this study. This material is supplemented by many files of correspondence, most of it compiled by the excellent Daniel Brown, college registrar from 1913 to 1936, who, it seems, could hardly bear to throw anything away.

Much of the research for this book was undertaken while the University of Wales College of Medicine was an independent institution. At that time the college's own archives held sets of the minute books of the committees of the Welsh National School of Medicine and its successor, the College of Medicine, from 1921 until 2004, together with the usual runs of calendars, prospectuses, annual reports and other material. The Sir Herbert Duthie Library, embedded within the University Hospital of Wales, also had material of great value to my work, not least a full set of the printed minutes of the General Medical Council from 1858 until the 1990s, generously donated by Dr Derek Llewellyn. Most of this material has, since the merger, been transferred to the Special Collections Department of the main University Library, where it will be recatalogued and integrated in the university's historical collection, which already holds material which has been of great use to me, particularly the college's student magazine. Medical historians will, however, continue to cherish the Duthie Library for its first-class holdings of books and journals, especially bound volumes of the *British Medical Journal* and *The Lancet*, stretching back deep into the nineteenth century, and its excellent inter-library loan service. Apart from a few items concerning William Thomas Edwards, the university has no collections of personal papers relating to those prominent in the history of medical education in Cardiff from the 1890s to the 1930s. However, historians of the Welsh National School of Medicine in later decades will undoubtedly benefit from studying some of the wartime correspondence of John Duguid, professor of pathology from 1933 to 1948, and the archive, particularly the diaries, of Alan Trevor Jones, provost from 1955 to 1969, both kept in the university's Special Collections Department.

Three other Cardiff locations have been of much assistance in my studies. Although most of the archives of the University of Wales have been transferred to the National Library of Wales, the University Registry in Cathays Park still retains bound volumes of the minutes of the University Court and the University Council from 1920 onwards, together with a complete set of the University of Wales *Calendar*. The Glamorgan Record Office, at present next door, is particularly useful for the records of the Cardiff Royal Infirmary and the minute books of the Cardiff Medical Society. The Record Office also holds the rather disappointing papers of Professor Francis Davies, one-time Cardiff preclinical student, later to become professor of anatomy at the University of Sheffield. The Local Studies Department of the Cardiff Central Library is excellent for back numbers of the local newspapers, for the annual reports of bodies such as the Cardiff Royal Infirmary, and over the years it has built up a good collection of press cuttings on all manner of people and events.

The archives of the National Library of Wales at Aberystwyth have been of great value. Not surprisingly, the most useful records have been those relating to the University of Wales, particularly the files dealing with constitutional matters during the 1920s. As the bibliography will show, use has also been made of the personal papers of several leading figures in Welsh public life during the early decades of the twentieth century. Unfortunately the papers of Sir John Williams, perhaps the most eminent Welsh doctor of his time, offer no insights into the development of medical education in Wales, though his diary reveals that he was less than impressed with the Stepney Hotel, Llanelli. The fact was that he did not involve himself much in this issue, a conclusion perhaps confirmed by the entry in Sir George Newman's diary for 26 March 1916, on the occasion of a visit to Aberystwyth: 'The National Library. Sir John Williams – a delightful visit – discussed the Queen and her children; Drink; mysticism; ideals; medical heroes; National Library.' Not a word about the aspirations of the Welsh National School of Medicine, a cause which was taking up much of Newman's energy at that time. Although the papers of Sir Isambard Owen, in the archives of Bangor University, do contain some illuminating items, they are, in general, disappointing with regard to his involvement with the affairs of the medical school.

Last, but by no means least, reference must be made to two invaluable archives in London. The Wellcome Library, Euston Road, one of the great libraries for the study of the history of medicine, contains a number of collections of relevance to the present book, particularly the papers of the Cardiff Medical School's greatest alumnus, Sir Thomas Lewis, who, as his papers clearly reveal, maintained an active interest in the affairs of the Welsh National School of Medicine for many years. It need hardly be said that no historian of medical education during the twentieth century can afford to ignore the wide range of records in the National Archives at Kew, of government departments such as the Privy Council, the Board of Education and the Ministry of Health, of the Medical Research Council and the University Grants Committee.

I would like to thank the authorities of Cardiff University for contributing so generously towards the production costs of the book, and in particular Dr David Grant, the vice-chancellor, and Dr Chris Turner, the university secretary, for their encouragement and support, for giving me ready access to the archives of the University College of South Wales and Monmouthshire and for allowing me to quote from them. Ms Sarah Phillips, the university records and institutional archives officer, and Mrs Barbara Parry have been most helpful in navigating me through the relevant sections. Several members of the University Library, including Mr Peter Keelan, head of special collections and archives, Mr Stephen Pritchard, one-time College of Medicine Librarian, and the staff in the Sir Herbert Duthie Library on the University's Heath Park campus, particularly Mrs Christine Griffiths and Mrs Lindsay Roberts, have been generous in their support. I have much appreciated the interest shown, and assistance given, by members of the University of Wales Registry, particularly Dr Lynn Williams, Ms Alwena Morgan and Mrs Jenny Childs. I am grateful to the staff of the National Library of Wales, particularly Dr Maredudd ap Huw, Dr J. Graham Jones, Mr Gareth Parry and Mr Alwyn Roberts for guiding me through the University of Wales archive and other relevant collections. I would also like to thank the staff in the Bangor University Archive Department, the Glamorgan Record Office, and the Local Studies Department of Cardiff Central Library (particularly Ms Katrina Coopey) for their friendly assistance. I am also grateful to the officers of the Cardiff Medical Society for allowing me to quote from the society's minutes and publications. Thanks are also extended to the invariably helpful staff at the National Archives, the Wellcome Library and the Medical Research Council, and to Ms Olivia Sibley, Mrs Dee Cook, Ms Victoria Rea and Mrs Annie Lindsay, archivists at the British Medical Association, the Society of Apothecaries, the Royal Free Hospital Archives Centre and the University College London Hospitals NHS Foundation Trust respectively, who promptly answered various e-mail queries about the subsequent careers of certain Cardiff medical students. Mr Ben Griffith, at the General Medical Council, kindly sent me copies of material relevant to the conduct of medical examinations in the University of Wales during the 1920s. I am much obliged to Mr Ken Rose, assistant director, and Mr Tom Rosenbaum at the Rockefeller Archive Centre, Sleepy Hollow, New York, for arranging access to material relating to the grant awarded by the Rockefeller Foundation to the Welsh National School of Medicine in 1924. I also wish to thank Mr Paul Langmaid for allowing me to consult his father's papers. I have greatly benefited from discussions with Professor Neil McIntyre, emeritus professor of medicine at the Royal Free and University College School of Medicine, an authority on the London School of Medicine for Women and Sir Isambard Owen, and with Professor Owen Wade, emeritus professor of therapeutics at the University of Birmingham, and a member of one of Cardiff's most eminent medical families. I have also been most gratified by the keen interest shown in the developing project by many friends in the History of Medicine Society of Wales.

One of my aims in writing this book has been to put the history of the Welsh National School of Medicine into a wider context, looking particularly at what was going on in other medical schools at the same time. I am most grateful to many people for granting me access to relevant university archives, for sending me copies of key documents, or for willingly answering questions about developments in their own universities. At the University of Birmingham I would like to thank Ms Philippa Bassett and Dr Jonathan Reinarz; at the University of Bristol, Ms Hannah Lowery; at the University of Leeds, Mr Bill Mathie and Dr Malcolm Parsons; at the University of Liverpool, Mr Adrian Allan and Ms Gillian Bridgett; at the University of Manchester, Dr James Peters; at the University of Newcastle upon Tyne, the Lord Walton of Detchant, Emeritus Professor David Shaw and Dr Vanessa Hammond; at the University of Sheffield, Mr Matthew Zawadzki. Dr Keir Waddington, Cardiff University, wrote to me about a number of issues relating to the London scene. He, and the following authors, have kindly allowed me to quote brief extracts from their writings, thereby illuminating my own, Dr Stella Butler, Dr John Davies, Dr Tom Davies, Professor Christopher Lawrence, Dr Irvine Loudon, Professor John Pickstone, Dr Jonathan Reinarz, Dr Steve Sturdy, Professor Owen Wade and Professor J. Gwynn Williams. I am grateful to them all.

Inevitably, my warmest thanks are reserved for many friends and colleagues at what was, until the summer of 2004, the University of Wales College of Medicine, from whom I have been fortunate to receive much encouragement. I would particularly wish to thank Professor Stephen Tomlinson, himself an enthusiast for the history of medicine, who, when vice-chancellor of the college, not only asked me to take on the task of writing its history, but has maintained a close interest in its progress, reading the chapters as they have appeared and offering constructive advice on the way. Others who have given me much assistance and support include Professor Geraint Roberts, Professor D. P. Davies, Mrs Sue Williams, and Mr Steve MacAllister in the graphics unit. I would like to extend a special expression of gratitude to Dr Tom Davies, honorary senior clinical fellow in the history of medicine at Swansea University, a Welsh medical historian of great distinction, and himself a graduate of the Welsh National School of Medicine, who has read successive drafts of the manuscript. His detailed comments and suggestions for improvement, offered gently but persuasively, have been invaluable, as have those of the anonymous readers invited by the University Press to review the work. Any errors and misjudgements that remain are entirely my fault. I also wish to record my great appreciation for the patient, expert and friendly way in which members of the University of Wales Press have processed this book, especially production manager Siân Chapman, editor Dafydd Jones, typesetter Eira Fenn Gaunt, commissioning editor Sarah Lewis and her assistant Ennis Akpinar, and the book's typesetter Mark Heslington.

My final words of thanks are to two people who have been a constant source of encouragement during the years when this book has been in preparation, my sister

Margaret, whose computer skills have been of much assistance at crucial moments, and to my wife, Cynthia, to whom I owe so much.

Every effort has been made to trace all copyright holders for illustrations reproduced, but in some cases this has not proved possible. The co-operation of the following in agreeing to the reproduction of the illustrations cited is gratefully acknowledged:

Cardiff University: illustrations numbered 1, 3, 7, 15, 17, 21, 22, 28 (the final one originally appearing in A. H. Trow and D. J. A. Brown, *A Short History of the University College of South Wales and Monmouthshire, Cardiff, 1883–1933*, Cardiff, 1933).

Dr Arthur Hollman: illustration 4.

David Jones, who has granted permission for illustration 5 to be reproduced from his book *Corris Trwy Lygad y Camera/ Corris through the Eye of the Camera* (David Jones, Cardiff, 2003).

Media Wales, Ltd: illustrations 6, 13, 24 (originally appearing in the *Western Mail*), 12 (originally appearing in the *South Wales Daily News*), and 20 (originally appearing in the *South Wales News*).

Cardiff and Vale NHS Trust: illustrations 8, 25, 26 (the last two originally appearing in the annual report of the Board of Management of the Cardiff Royal Infirmary, 1933).

Cardiff University Students' Union: illustrations 10, 18, 19, 23 (originally appearing in issues of *The Leech*, the journal of the Cardiff Medical Students' Club, during the late 1920s).

Pathological Society of Great Britain and Ireland: illustration 9 (originally appearing in the *Journal of Pathology and Bacteriology*, vol. 27, 1924).

Cardiff Libraries and Information Service: illustrations 11, 14, 16.

Willmott Dixon Construction Ltd: illustration 27 (originally appearing in *Superb Buildings: E. Turner and Sons, Builders and Contractors, Cardiff,* published by the Red Balloon Co. Ltd, 1989).

Illustration 2 originally appeared in Sir D'Arcy Power (ed.), *British Medical Societies* (Medical Press and Circular, 1939).

This book is dedicated to generations of
medical graduates at the University of Wales,
and to their splendid teachers.

Origins of the Cardiff Medical School to 1893

The date 4 October 1893 marks a significant milestone in the development of medical education in Britain. That day saw the start (the official opening took place four months later) of the first medical school in Wales. It was not a full medical school in the sense that it would provide training in the clinical subjects – the time for that would come later. In the meantime the Cardiff Medical School would offer, close to home, a course of training in the basic science and preclinical disciplines, for Welsh boys – and girls – who would otherwise have had to enter medical schools across Offa's Dyke, like generations of aspiring doctors before them.

Why did Wales lag so far behind the rest of Britain in the provision of medical education? For most of the nineteenth century the social and economic conditions were less than ideal. In contrast, for instance, to the large urban communities created in provincial England by the Industrial Revolution, there were no comparable centres in Wales where medical schools could flourish. Furthermore, as the nature of medical education evolved, with what Thomas Neville Bonner has called 'the spread of laboratory teaching',[1] Wales, lacking institutions of higher education where such teaching could be pursued, remained incapable of rising to the challenge. Only with the establishment, in Cardiff, of the University College of South Wales and Monmouthshire, in 1883, after a fierce struggle with arch-rivals Swansea, did a Welsh medical school become a practical possibility, though ten more years would elapse before the dream of a few enthusiasts became a reality. Had the contest between Cardiff and Swansea taken place a decade earlier, the probability is that Swansea would have won, and Swansea, not Cardiff, would have become the home of Wales's medical school. How far such an outcome would have changed the subsequent evolution of medical education in Wales is an interesting matter for speculation, but not here.

THE DEVELOPMENT OF MEDICAL EDUCATION IN BRITAIN DURING THE NINETEENTH CENTURY

Neither is any attempt made here to provide a comprehensive account of the development of medical education in Britain during the nineteenth century, let alone to place that development in a wider European and transatlantic context. Works such as T. N. Bonner's, already cited, achieve that object more than adequately. It is, however, necessary for the origins of medical education in Wales to be placed in a wider, British context.

In the words of Keir Waddington, 'Until the nineteenth century, medical education [in Britain] was generally informal and unregulated, seldom rigidly confined within an institution.'[2] Though established centuries earlier, Oxford University (founded in 1167) and Cambridge (1209) had become moribund.[3] Apart from those who had qualified in Europe (Leiden was the leading medical school in eighteenth-century Europe) most doctors with formal qualifications were trained in the Scottish universities. Many practitioners had no qualifications at all. Some were simply quacks, while others were men of some education and standing who enjoyed the gift of healing which they chose to share with less favoured members of their community.[4] In Wales one such man was Thomas Morgan (1737–1813), the son of a Carmarthenshire weaver who became a schoolmaster and Unitarian minister in the Vale of Neath, acquiring on the way a reputation as a herbalist and country physician. He was reportedly the first person in Glamorgan to appreciate the value of cowpox as a preventive for smallpox, and he is said to have inoculated 101 children in the year 1784 alone. When he died his friends erected in Gellionnen chapel a marble memorial to him with the inscription: 'He died, not leaving many equals behind him'.[5] Other practitioners gained what knowledge they had from private anatomy schools or through attendance at hospitals, this latter route becoming increasingly popular by the end of the eighteenth century, particularly in London, where, unlike in the provinces, the teaching hospitals were recognized for the purpose by the Royal College of Surgeons.

Medical education made a major advance in 1815 through the passing of the Apothecaries Act, which represented the first step in the regulation of the medical profession in the United Kingdom. The Act required that all those practising as apothecaries (in effect general practitioners) had to be Licentiates of the Society of Apothecaries (LSA), which meant five years' apprenticeship, certificates showing that candidates had attended courses of lectures in anatomy and physiology, plus six months' hospital experience. From 1827 evidence was also required that a candidate had received some training in midwifery. Although it is not true to say that the Act effectively created the profession of doctor, it conferred on the profession a respectability it had not hitherto enjoyed, and despite the considerable expense involved parents were clearly convinced that the investment was worthwhile. By the 1830s more than 400 students were taking the LSA[6] and the demand for facilities offering systematic instruction in medicine soared. London, by far the largest and, in terms of hospitals, best-endowed urban centres in the United Kingdom, became the Mecca of aspiring doctors. To well-established medical schools like St Bartholomew's, Guy's, St Thomas's and the London were added, during the first quarter of the nineteenth century, new institutions such as Charing Cross and the Middlesex, with the

Westminster, University College and King's following in the course of the next decade.[7] The twenty years following the Apothecaries Act saw a significant expansion of private medical schools in the English provinces too, with at least ten created between 1824 and 1834, a development partly stimulated by the decision of the Royal College of Surgeons to recognize courses of instruction provided by medical teachers outside London, in 1824.

This expansion in the availability of medical training facilities was a direct consequence of the Industrial Revolution, which was changing the face of Britain, bringing about a substantial increase in the population. Between 1751 and 1801 the population of England, Scotland and Wales increased from 7,250,000 to 10,943,000, and by 1831 had reached 16,539,000; in other words it doubled. A particular feature of the expansion of the population was the growth of an urban society in provincial England, with dramatic changes coming about in centres such as Manchester, Birmingham, Leeds, Liverpool and Bristol. Rapid, large-scale urbanization inevitably created severe health problems which needed the attention of the medical profession. Such a development also created a new, and powerful middle-class elite, sophisticated men who, when not involved in the pursuit of business, involved themselves in local literary and philosophical societies and similar scientific and cultural organizations where they would rub shoulders with the leading doctors of the district. Men such as these expected for themselves and their families the best medical services that money could buy.[8] It was hardly surprising, therefore, that the medical profession, like the legal profession, was increasingly regarded as an eminently respectable pursuit for middle-class men to take up.[9]

The year 1825 saw the origin of a medical school in Birmingham, founded by William Sands Cox, a local surgeon who, shocked by the wild behaviour of the medical students in London, where he himself had trained, decided to set up a medical school in the town where, in the words of Ben Davis, a noted member of that rare breed of doctors, the forensic pathologists, and historian of the Birmingham Medical School, 'The pupils might be kept under the eye of their masters and probably of their parents as well, and consequently be more likely to behave themselves and apply themselves to their studies with diligence.'[10] The Birmingham Medical School began with a course of lectures given by Sands Cox in his father's house, 24 Temple Row, on 1 December 1825. This initiative developed into what he described in April 1828 as a 'proper school of medicine and surgery in Birmingham', reaching the point when, in larger premises, the king conferred on the school the title of the Birmingham Royal School of Medicine and Surgery in 1834. Frustrated by limited access by his students to existing clinical facilities, Sands Cox then determined to build a brand-new teaching hospital 'in order to provide the practical and efficient education of the students', and in June 1840 over 10,000 citizens of Birmingham, led by the mayor, attended the stone-laying ceremony for the new Queen's Hospital, the first patients being admitted the following year. In 1843 the medical school was renamed Queen's

College and, after various ups and downs, became part, first, of Mason College and finally, in 1900, part of the new University of Birmingham.[11]

The other nine medical schools opened in Manchester (1824), Sheffield (1828), Leeds and Hull (1831), Newcastle upon Tyne (1832), Bristol and Nottingham (1833), and Liverpool and York (1834), almost all of them centres being transformed by the Industrial Revolution. The first prospectus of the Sheffield Medical School assured prospective students that certificates of attendance at its course of lectures 'are received at Apothecaries Hall', while the Bristol prospectus proclaimed: 'The whole curriculum of study, both theoretical and practical, prescribed by the Society of Apothecaries may be completed in this city without repairing to London, except for the purpose of undergoing examination.'[12] The secretary of the Society of Apothecaries considered that the training offered at Manchester was surpassed at no other medical school.[13]

It should be noted, however, that the LSA was by no means the sole qualification available to the aspiring doctor, even for those, the overwhelming majority outside London, whose horizons were limited to the pursuit of general practice. By the mid-nineteenth century over half of those working in general practice also held the Membership of the Royal College of Surgeons (MRCS), a qualification which conferred extra respectability on its holders, and a handful were the proud possessors of a university degree (usually from Scotland), as well as, or instead of, the LSA/MRCS. Those practitioners described as physicians or surgeons, in other words enjoying special skills and experience, whether or not they worked in hospital practice, tended to have university degrees and/or qualifications from the royal colleges. Indeed surgeons invariably held the MRCS or FRCS qualification wherever they worked, whereas it was the physicians based in the metropolis rather than in the provinces who usually possessed the licence or fellowship of the Royal College of Physicians, at that time more akin to an exclusive London club than an examining body.[14]

By the middle of the nineteenth century there were nineteen separate bodies authorized to confer licences to practise in Britain, with wide variations in their detailed curricular requirements.[15] However, in important respects they all reflected a growing uniformity of practice. The apprenticeship system was everywhere becoming outmoded. Medical education was now becoming characterized by more formal hospital-based instruction in lectures and on the wards, taking account of important innovations in medical practice. The concept of diagnosis through the taking of case histories, or asking the patient, had been superseded by the concept of diagnosis through physical examination, using the latest technical advances, such as Laennec's stethoscope, a major landmark in the history of medical diagnosis.[16]

Alongside the increasingly well-trained licensed medical practitioners operated a large army of unqualified irregulars. Some enjoyed respect and affection within their communities, but many travelled from town to town, peddling their home-grown remedies to the gullible poor, and not-so-poor, much to the irritation of the genuine doctors. However, those who hoped that the Medical Act of 1858 would abolish the quacks were disappointed. The main purpose of the Act was contained in its preamble: 'Whereas it is expedient that Persons requiring medical aid should be enabled to distinguish qualified from unqualified practitioners: Be it therefore enacted ...'.[17] In other words, the Medical Act established, for the first time, a register of qualified practitioners. Some doctors, considering the plethora of licensing bodies unnecessary, given the steady convergence of medical training schemes, hoped that the Act would establish a single portal through which trainees could be licensed to practise. Their hopes, too, were not fulfilled because of the unwillingness of the various licensing bodies to give up their privileges.[18] Even so, the establishment of the General Medical Council (GMC) in 1858, one of the features of the Act, composed as it was of all the main vested interests including the licensing bodies involved in medical education, led to further progress in the standardization of medical curricula throughout the country; in 1867 the council made particular regulations defining the basic skills and knowledge that all medically registered practitioners should possess.[19] Moreover, reflecting what Charles Newman called 'the rise of laboratory medicine', the council gave guidance on how the curriculum, especially the basic and preclinical sciences, should be delivered, taking account of the latest thinking, much of it deriving from Germany and focusing on the use of practical classes in the laboratory.[20]

Arguably the most significant milestone in the rise of the preclinical sciences, especially physiology, in Britain was a decision made by the Royal College of Surgeons in 1870.[21] In that year the college amended its examination regulations by requiring candidates for its qualifying examination to have attended 'a practical course in anatomy and physiology', during which 'the learners themselves shall individually be engaged in the necessary experiments, and manipulations, etc.' This requirement was adopted by the University of London in the following year. As Charles Newman observed, the implications for medical education were profound: 'The provision and exploitation of laboratories is costly both in money and in time: it is difficult for a small, self-contained [medical] school to provide the facilities and it is difficult for part-time medical teachers, busy with private practice, to make the most of the facilities when they are provided.'[22] A few medical schools such as Hull, Nottingham and York fell by the wayside. In London the medical schools' response was initially uneven.[23] However, the general reaction among the provincial schools was positive.

The third quarter of the nineteenth century saw the origins of what later became the great civic universities of provincial England. During that period a number of the larger cities of England saw the establishment of colleges, primarily scientific in orientation, in order to meet the needs of local industry, and substantially funded by the businessmen of the district who also saw such developments as the erection of elegant town halls, museums and art galleries as graphic manifestations of civic pride. Owen's College in Manchester, established in 1851, was the first, to be followed by the

Yorkshire College of Science, Leeds (1874), Mason Science College, Birmingham (1875), University College, Bristol (1876), Firth College, Sheffield (1879), and University College, Liverpool (1882). The medical schools needed access to the scientific and laboratory facilities available in the new colleges. The colleges were more than happy to oblige, benefiting as they did from a regular supply of students attending preliminary studies in the liberal arts as well as science classes, and enjoying a status enhanced through contact with members of one of the elite professions. One by one the provincial medical schools became formally affiliated with their local science college, Manchester in 1873, Bristol in 1879, Sheffield in 1883, Leeds and Liverpool in 1884 and Birmingham in 1892.[24]

At the same time the medical schools, now secure in their science infrastructure, set about appointing full-time teachers in the preclinical disciplines, those in physiology usually being the first, as Stella Butler has shown.[25] The University of Cambridge saw the appointment of the first full-time professor of physiology, Michael Foster, in 1870, followed by Arthur Gamgee at Manchester (1873), John Burdon Sanderson at University College, London and William Rutherford at Edinburgh (both 1874). Other full-time professors of physiology appointed in the next few years included Alfred de Burgh Birch at Leeds in 1884 and Francis Gotch at Liverpool in 1891, while elsewhere full-time professors in anatomy took the lead, as at Bristol, where Edward Fawcett was appointed to the chair in 1893, continuing in post for the next forty-one years.[26] Curricular reform was not, however, confined to the preclinical phase of the medical course. The Medical Amendment Act of 1886 for the first time insisted that all final qualifying examinations should include midwifery as well as medicine and surgery. This requirement applied to a new licensing body, the Conjoint Board, created jointly by the Royal College of Physicians of London and the Royal College of Surgeons of England, in 1884.[27] Intended as a modest step towards rationalizing the plethora of medical qualifications on offer, the MRCS LRCP qualification proved to be instantly popular, its introduction proving to be the death knell of the LSA, by now regarded as an infinitely less prestigious reward for several years of hard work.

By the late Victorian period, the GMC had been able to bring about a considerable degree of standardization in the system of medical education in Britain, particularly in matters such as the minimum duration of study and essential course requirements. However, it shied away from enveloping the curricula of the several medical schools in a rigid straitjacket, taking its cue from the report of the Royal Commission on the Grant of Medical Degrees (1882):

> It would be a mistake to introduce absolute uniformity into medical education. One great merit of the present system, so far as teaching is concerned, lies in the elasticity which is produced by the variety and number of educational Bodies. Being anxious not in any way to diminish the interest which the teaching Bodies now take in medical education, or to lessen their responsibility in that respect, we desire to leave

to them as much initiative as possible … Nothing should be done to weaken the indi-viduality of the Universities and Corporations, or to check emulation between the teaching institutions of the country.

In other words, as Donald MacAlister, president of the GMC, told his listeners at the opening-of-session ceremony at the University of Manchester, in 1906, 'competi-tion between a multiplicity of teaching bodies, as such, tends to the advancement of education.'[28]

WALES LAGS BEHIND

By the 1880s, in addition to those at Oxford and Cambridge, there were no fewer than twelve medical schools in London, seven in the English provinces, eight in Scotland (including some which are now long forgotten, such as the Edinburgh School of Medicine for Women and Anderson's College Medical School, Glasgow) and five in Ireland. The *Medical Students' Register* for 1884, issued by the GMC, recorded that in that year 1,957 persons entered the official register for the first time as medical students, 896 in England, 617 in Scotland and 444 in Ireland. Edinburgh University saw the largest number of new registrations with 270, followed by Glasgow University with 141. In England, Cambridge came highest with 107, St Bartholomew's Hospital Medical School with 86 and Owen's College, Manchester with 67.[29] In Wales there was no medical school and there were no medical students.

The wheels of progress turned rather more slowly in Wales. The year 1817 saw the opening of the first in-patient infirmary in Wales, in Swansea. Built as part of the Bathing House it was known as 'The Swansea Infirmary, for warm and cold seawater bathing, and for the relief of the sick and lame poor from every part of the kingdom'. The sick wards contained sixteen beds, two of which were reserved for accidents. In the decades that followed, the infirmary prospered, attracting medical staff of high quality, not least Dr Thomas Williams (1818–65), a son of the vicar of Llandyfriog, Cardiganshire. After training in Guy's Hospital and becoming one of the University of London's first medical graduates he returned to Wales to pursue a distinguished career as a man of science and physician after some highly successful years in the teaching hospitals of London. There he came into contact with some of the greatest doctors of the day, Sir Astley Cooper, Richard Bright, Thomas Addison, Thomas Hodgkin, and dissected the body of the celebrated republican radical, Richard Carlile.[30] It was Williams who, in 1858, first seriously raised the possibility of estab-lishing a medical school linked to the Swansea Infirmary so that young men 'may be educated in their profession and be allowed to witness the many scientific operations performed there'.[31] Nothing came of this suggestion, as indeed nothing had come of an earlier plea by Benjamin Thomas Williams, a distinguished lawyer and Member of

Parliament. In 1853, when still a young student at Glasgow University, he had written a pamphlet, *The Desirableness of a University for Wales*, contrasting the position of Scotland and Wales in this respect, referring particularly to the need for a medical school in Wales, and stating a firm belief that the Welsh had an aptitude for this particular discipline.[32] Whether or not the Welsh had a special flair for medicine, the fact was that, in terms of size and resources, Wales in the middle of the nineteenth century was not yet ready for a medical school of its own.

Like England, Wales had experienced the effects of the Industrial Revolution. The population of the principality, some half a million in 1770, had doubled to over a million by 1851. The 1840s alone experienced an increase of 117,000, 80 per cent occurring in the coal-mining areas of south and west Wales.[33] However, although, as in England, industrialization brought hardship and squalor to large sections of the Welsh population,[34] and although there is good evidence to indicate that Wales was relatively under-doctored compared with England,[35] the process did not create large urban centres with infrastructures conducive to the formation of medical schools to meet the local need. In the census of 1861 Merthyr Tydfil was the largest town in Wales, with a population of 50,000, but few would claim this polluted industrial sprawl to be the centre of sophisticated Welsh life. Indeed, the Merthyr of the 1850s was said to be 'as destitute of civic government as the smallest rural village of the empire'.[36] A hospital had been erected there in 1853 as part of the workhouse, to minister to the needs of the destitute poor of Merthyr and surrounding parishes but, staffed by a house surgeon, a nurse and a porter, man and wife, and assisted by some of the female inmates of the workhouse, it hardly measured up as a possible centre for the training of medical students.[37] Swansea, the second largest town in Wales, with a population of over 40,000 in 1861, was, by contrast, in the words of Professor Gwyn A. Williams, 'a cultivated place, home of an accomplished middle class, a miniature social and intellectual capital'.[38] When the British Medical Association visited Wales in 1853, it was to Swansea that the delegates came, the only place in the principality which could possibly receive them. Even so, with only twenty-six beds by 1861, the Swansea Infirmary, though better resourced than the hospital in Merthyr, was hardly better equipped to serve as a focus for medical education at this time. Cardiff, one of eleven towns in Wales to have a hospital by 1860,[39] was, in the mid-nineteenth century, an even poorer prospect as a centre of medical education. The development of the docks during the first half of the century, to serve the needs of the growing coalfields of the south Wales Valleys, had transformed a community of fewer than 2,000 people in 1801 into a crowded and unhealthy town of some 18,000 by 1851, almost entirely devoid of the infrastructure required to sustain any sort of civilized existence, let alone a medical school. In short, if the young men of Wales wished to become doctors, they would have to cross Offa's Dyke to realize their ambition.

Benjamin Thomas Williams was right. There is much evidence to confirm his view that the Welsh had an aptitude for the medical profession. It is an undeniable fact that

Wales managed to produce its fair share of eminent doctors during the nineteenth century. We have already noted Dr Thomas Williams. There was David Daniel Davis (1777–1841) of Llandyfaelog, Carmarthenshire who, after qualifying in Glasgow and practising in Sheffield, went to London where he was appointed physician at Queen Charlotte Hospital and attended the Duchess of Kent when giving birth to the girl who later became Queen Victoria. By 1806 he had added 'Daniel', his father's name, and dropped the 'e' from his surname since his original name, David Davies, was commonplace in the medical profession.[40] Sir William Roberts (1830–99) of Mynydd-y-gof, Anglesey, after studying at University College, London and pursuing postgraduate studies at Paris and Berlin, became chief physician at Manchester Royal Infirmary and professor of medicine at Owen's College. He was a pioneer in the science that led to the discovery of penicillin fifty years before Alexander Fleming got the credit for it.[41] Sir John Williams (1840–1926) climbed even higher up the medical ladder. From humble beginnings in Blaenllynant, Carmarthenshire, and after an apprenticeship with two general practitioners in Swansea, he too graduated at University College, London, via the University of Glasgow and after a spell in Swansea, returned to London where he became one of the most prominent doctors of his day, enjoying the patronage of the Royal Family. After his retirement he played the central role in the foundation of the National Library of Wales, becoming its first president in 1907.[42] Other distinguished products of University College, London include Timothy Richards Lewis (1841–86), of Narberth, Pembrokeshire, who became a pioneer in the science of tropical medicine[43] and Sir Charles James Watkin Williams (1828–84), son of the rector of Llansannan, Denbighshire, who, having qualified in medicine became a successful lawyer and Liberal MP.[44] Hugh Owen Thomas (1834–91), of Bodedern, a descendant of the celebrated family of Anglesey bonesetters, having trained at Edinburgh and University College, London, set up in practice in Liverpool, becoming a pioneer of modern orthopaedic surgery.[45]

There was Dr William Price (1800–93), arguably Wales's greatest eccentric. Born in the parish of Rudry, the third son of the Revd William Price, after doing a medical apprenticeship to a doctor in Caerphilly he went to London, where he studied under such celebrated doctors as John Abernethy and Edward Grainger before securing the LSA and membership of the Royal College of Surgeons in 1821. Apart from pursuing all the interests for which he is renowned, William Price worked as a busy doctor in the Pontypridd area for much of his life.[46] Dr Henry Naunton Davies (1827–99), the first recipient of the British Medical Association's Gold Medal for distinguished merit in 1877, was probably the best-known member of a prominent family of south Wales doctors. Having trained at Guy's Hospital, qualifying in 1854, he lived and worked in the Rhondda valley, becoming surgeon to several collieries, and achieved lasting fame for his heroism during the Tynewydd colliery disaster of April 1877, when he led a team of doctors who remained on site for a period of ten days and nights.[47] No list of distinguished Welsh doctors of the nineteenth century can omit Sir Herbert Isambard

Owen (1850–1927). Born in Chepstow, the son of the chief engineer of the Great Western Railway and godson of Isambard Kingdom Brunel, Owen qualified at St George's Hospital and Cambridge University before pursuing a distinguished academic career which had a major impact on the development of university education not only, as we will see, in Wales, but also in London, Newcastle upon Tyne and Bristol.[48] Last, but by no means least in this survey of celebrated Welsh doctors, comes the first Welsh woman to graduate in medicine, Frances Elizabeth Morgan, from Breconshire, who received her MD from Zurich in March 1870 but was not admitted to the Medical Register until 1877.[49]

The one thing they all had in common was the fact that they had to leave Wales to train as medical practitioners. In the early decades of the nineteenth century the journeys were long and hard, as Dr William Thomas Edwards of Caerphilly would recall in an interview to the *South Wales Daily News* in 1910, on the occasion of his eighty-ninth birthday: 'Some seventy years ago, when I set out for London, the journey took me two days; I can do it now almost in as many hours! I had to go to Newport on foot; then by packet to Bristol; from there to London by coach.'[50] Fortunately for Wales, having qualified, many young men returned, to pursue fulfilling careers in communities which greatly needed their attention. Edward Davies, for instance, has written of the medical practitioners who worked in the slate-quarrying districts of north Wales during the nineteenth century, almost all of them natives of the area.[51]

THE EMERGENCE OF CARDIFF

The most important precondition for the creation of a medical school in Wales was the emergence of Cardiff as the largest and most sophisticated town in the principality during the third quarter of the nineteenth century, enabling it to bid successfully for the establishment of a university college in 1883.

At the beginning of the nineteenth century Cardiff, with a population of less than 2,000, was a small settlement of no real significance, 'an obscure and inconsiderable' place according to Edward Williams (Iolo Morganwg).[52] Fifty years later the population had multiplied tenfold, to 18,000, still less than half that of Merthyr and Swansea but a portent of things to come. The creation, initially of the Glamorganshire Canal linking Merthyr and Cardiff, and in 1840 of the Taff Vale Railway, and the opening of the first Bute Dock in 1839 at the initiative of the second Marquess of Bute, quickly transformed Cardiff into the coal-exporting capital of south Wales – and later the world. In 1841 87,170 tons of coal were exported out of Cardiff. By 1854 the annual tonnage was 1,051,748, and by 1880 over 5,000,000 tons, additional docks having been built in 1859 and 1874.

The rapid growth of Cardiff came at a price. By the middle of the century the town was in a distressing condition, some parts being squalid in the extreme. In 1848,

Parliament passed the Public Health Act, aimed at improving the living conditions in urban centres by empowering towns to set up local health boards to introduce ameliorating measures. Despite the reluctance of some, sufficient of the anxious ratepayers of Cardiff petitioned the corporation to commission a review of existing conditions by T. W. Rammell, the Board of Health inspector responsible for a similar survey of Merthyr Tydfil. Rammell's *Report on a Preliminary Inquiry into the ... Sanitary Conditions of the Inhabitants of the Town of Cardiff*, published in 1850, and following hard on a fearsome cholera epidemic which claimed nearly 400 lives, made sober reading. The report condemned the overcrowding in the warren of streets in the town centre, the inadequacy of the water supply, the condition of the graveyards and much else, and impelled the Cardiff Corporation to establish itself as the Local Board of Health. Its first task was to appoint Henry James Paine as the town's medical officer of health. Thanks to his efforts, those of the town corporation and the enlightened self-interest of the leading landed families of the area, not least the Butes, Cardiff, during the next thirty years, was able to respond positively to the demands placed upon it by the acceleration of the Industrial Revolution in the south Wales Valleys.[53]

The 1871 census revealed that, for the first time, with a population of nearly 60,000, Cardiff was now the largest town in Wales. Commentators were referring to Cardiff as 'the Metropolis of Wales' and comparing the town favourably, not only with centres like Liverpool and Bristol, but even with burgeoning towns and cities in America such as Chicago.[54] New buildings asserting the growing confidence of a new middle-class elite, were appearing: a new town hall, opened in St Mary's Street in 1854 by the radical mayor John Batchelor, hotels like the Royal Hotel, opened in 1866 and described by the *Cardiff Times*, as 'a really first class hotel, one worthy of the metropolis of Wales'. The incorporation of the pleasant suburbs of Roath, Canton and Cathays in 1875 further enhanced the town's ambience and its population, which in 1881 was recorded as 82,761, 20,000 more than that of Swansea.

The abolition of the Stamp Act in 1855, and the passing of the Second Reform Act in 1867, which gave the vote to the working men of urban Britain, led to the appearance of new daily newspapers in Cardiff, aiming not only at keeping the local citizens abreast of events but also at moulding their opinions on matters of national and local importance. The year 1869 saw the establishment, by the trustees of the Bute estate, of the *Western Mail*, the first daily newspaper in Wales, and the mouthpiece of radical Toryism. The *South Wales Daily News* appeared three years later to promote the Liberal point of view. Both newspapers would become essential sources of information and opinion on the development of medical education in Wales until 1928, when the *Western Mail* took over its rival.[55]

A further manifestation of Cardiff's growing importance was the decision to build a new hospital to replace the Glamorganshire and Monmouthshire Infirmary and Dispensary (to give it its full title). Originally built in 1837 with twenty beds, by the 1870s, despite a trebling of its bed numbers, the infirmary was generally considered incapable of meeting the needs of the local people on its existing site on Newport Road. The hospital, described by Neil Evans as 'the first charity in Wales', had, like all voluntary hospitals at this time, been dependent on the support of philanthropic donors from its inception, and its quest for funding for redevelopment came at a bad time owing to a trade depression in the late 1870s. Thanks, however, to the initiative of the third Marquess of Bute, who provided land for a hospital on Longcross Common, a little east of the existing infirmary, on an 850-year lease and at a peppercorn rent of £15 per year, sufficient funds were raised from local subscribers (including £1,000 from the marquess) to enable building work on a hundred-bed hospital to start in July 1882.[56] A significant landmark on the journey towards the establishment of a medical school in Cardiff had been reached.

Alan Trevor Jones, one of the great names in the development of medical education in Wales, and provost of the Welsh National School of Medicine from 1955 to 1969, linked the first serious stirrings with the establishment of the Cardiff Medical Society in 1870. Describing the society as 'a forum for lively discussions on medical subjects', Jones claimed that it 'continuously pressed for a medical school in Cardiff'.[57] Jones was mistaken. As we shall see, it was not until 1885 that the society first discussed the possibility of setting up a medical school in Cardiff. However, in January 1870 the medical staff of the Glamorganshire and Monmouthshire Infirmary issued an invitation to the medical profession of the town to meet for the purpose of forming a medical society for the town and neighbourhood, its object being 'to relate and discuss matters of professional interest'. Seventeen turned up and in March they agreed a constitution. As the first president they chose the senior medical practitioner in the town, Thomas Evans, who used to visit his patients on a white pony. William Thomas Edwards, the senior medical officer at the infirmary, to whom we have already referred, was appointed vice-president (he became its second president), and Alfred Sheen, a local general practitioner who became surgeon to the infirmary in 1871, took on the roles of secretary and treasurer. Other founder-members of the society included H. J. Paine, medical officer of health for Cardiff and chairman of the local Board of Guardians, who became the society's third president; William Taylor, surgeon, the society's fifth president and mayor of Cardiff in 1878; J. R. Reece, another surgeon; and David Edgar Jones, who was to become mayor of Cardiff in 1885.[58]

Despite the commitment of men like these, the early years of the society were difficult. By 1874 the membership had fallen to fifteen and prior to that year's annual general meeting the following notice was circulated to the members:

> Only five meetings have been held and three of these have been special. At other times though meetings were convened not sufficient members were present. The Committee regret exceedingly that the object of the Society – the meeting together to relate and discuss matters of professional interest – does not seem to meet with the cordial support which is its due. It would seem almost impossible to get a fair ordi-

nary meeting together without beating up each individual member, and it is hoped that during the present year the meetings will be better attended, if some of them end only in amiable small talk. For it is to be borne in mind that the Society exists, not only to meet and discuss professional matters but also to maintain an honourable and friendly feeling amongst its members, and it is not at all certain that this is not the more important objective of the two.

The Committee would suggest that at each meeting a subject should be proposed for discussion at the next meeting and they ask all members to take a deeper and livelier interest in the Society and its objects. It was never intended that we should be daily and hourly drudges all year round, surely, two hours a month, for seven or eight months in the year, is not too much to devote to semi-professional or more purely social communion with each other.[59]

Though things were to improve after that, it can hardly be asserted that the creation of a new medical school in Cardiff was uppermost in the thoughts of the members of the Cardiff Medical Society.

Indeed, Neil Evans has implied that the doctors of Cardiff were less than enthusiastic in advocating any expansion in the profession which might threaten their own livelihoods.[60] Some may have taken this view. The fact remained that the economic and social changes that were sweeping across south Wales during the late Victorian period – the population of the Rhondda grew from less than 1,000 to over 50,000 between 1851 and 1881 – were creating a real demand for more doctors, particularly ones who could converse in Welsh, still the first language of most inhabitants of the principality. Although the major expansion in the provision of hospitals in the south Wales Valleys did not come about until the 1890s,[61] the origins of the workmen's medical clubs in the south Wales coalfields, which provided medical services to their subscribers, can be traced back to the 1870s, with the establishment of organizations such as the Ocean Western Colliery Medical Aid Society (1872) and the Tredegar Medical Aid Society (1874).[62] The origins of medical clubs in the north Wales quarries go back even further.[63]

Notwithstanding the underlying demand for more doctors being created by the progress of industrialization in south, and indeed north Wales during the late nineteenth century, the immediate catalyst for the formation of a medical school in Cardiff was the decision of the Board of Education, in 1883, to support the establishment of a university college for south Wales in Cardiff capable of providing what medical education required during the late nineteenth century, a solid foundation in the biomedical sciences.

A UNIVERSITY COLLEGE FOR CARDIFF

The first reference to university education in Wales can be traced back to the celebrated 'Pennal Letter' of 1406, in which Owain Glyn Dŵr outlined his vision of two universities, *studia generalia*, in Wales, one in the north and one in the south. However, it was not until 1827, with the establishment of St David's College, Lampeter, that an institution of university status came to the principality. The aim of the college, according to its founder, Thomas Burgess, the bishop of St David's, was 'to provide an appropriate course of studies, for young men intended for Holy Orders, which should unite in some considerable degree the advantages of a University Education by combining a progressive method of Theology, Literature and Science with the regularity of moral discipline'.[64] As an Anglican foundation there was no possibility of the college emerging as a university institution serving the needs of an increasingly Nonconformist Wales, and in 1872, more by luck than judgement, Aberystwyth became the home of Wales's first university college. In the words of Professor J. Gwynn Williams, the college was founded there 'not because of deliberate choice, as in the case of Cardiff and Bangor, but because it was there that the wheel of fortune had spun to a standstill'.[65] One thing was certain. Though from the outset the college had academic departments in the main basic sciences, its size and location, relatively isolated in a rural environment, never made it a serious candidate as a base for a medical school.

Indeed, heroic as were the efforts of the University College of Wales, Aberystwyth to provide a measure of higher education to the people of Wales it its early years, they were never going to be enough to meet the needs of a rapidly expanding population. In the county of Glamorgan alone, the population increased by 113,574 during the 1870s. Whereas, at this time, the ratio of university students to the population in Scotland was 1:840, and in Ireland 1:3,121, the ratio in Wales was 1:8,200.[66] It is therefore hardly surprising that one of the first actions of the Liberal government in 1880 was to set up a departmental committee to inquire into the condition of intermediate and higher education in Wales and Monmouthshire. The committee's chairman was Lord Aberdare (1815–95) who, as Henry Austin Bruce, had served as home secretary in Gladstone's first administration, but, since his elevation to the peerage, had taken an increasing interest in social and educational matters. On 20 August 1881 the committee presented its report:

> We recommend that for the present only one college in addition to that already existing [at Aberystwyth] should be provided. It would, we believe, be almost unanimously agreed that such a college should be placed in Glamorgan, though there might be some difference of opinion as to the rival claims of Cardiff and Swansea to be regarded as the most suitable site. Cardiff and the places within reach of it supply, within a given area, the larger population, while Swansea and its neighbourhood are seats of more varied industries.[67]

The year 1882 saw both Cardiff and Swansea striving hard to persuade the government of the merits of their respective cases. The potential of each candidate to host a medical school was certainly referred to. At one of the public meetings held in Swansea the warden of Llandovery College, the Revd A. G. Edwards, 'assuming that the medical department in the new college would be an important one', cited the excellence of the facilities at the Swansea Hospital as a strong argument in favour of establishing the new college in Swansea.[68] Cardiff's supporters cited the brand-new hospital being planned in their town. The substantial 'memorial' submitted by the Cardiff Corporation to the Privy Council asserted:

> That the new Glamorganshire and Monmouthshire Infirmary about to be erected in Cardiff at a cost, including the site, of from £40,000 to £45,000, will be of such proportions as to entitle Cardiff to a School of Medicine – a claim, it is believed, that no other town in the principality can prefer.[69]

This statement was, however, merely one sentence in a memorial of fifty-eight clauses and twenty-two appendices, and it is clear that the crucial arguments between Swansea and Cardiff revolved around other issues: relative size, prosperity, accessibility and things of that sort. Whereas Swansea's memorial was 'a short document with no tabular appendices',[70] Cardiff's was, in the words of Gwyn Williams, 'a Statement of Facts which was a cannonade'.[71] One of the powerful arguments employed by Cardiff was that whereas the population of west Wales, the part that might look to Swansea, was about 300,000, that of east Wales, which would naturally look towards Cardiff, came to nearly 800,000 – including Monmouthshire, which for this purpose at least, was conveniently counted as part of Wales. Moreover, in the assessment of G. W. Roderick, Swansea seriously underestimated the financial support required for a new college, and while Swansea's fund-raising efforts realized £3,000, together with a site worth £20,000, Cardiff's subscribers were able to pledge £31,746.[72] However, not wishing to decide on his own, the responsible government minister, the Right Hon. A. J. Mundella, vice-president of the Committee of Council on Education, referred the matter to arbitrators (including himself), who in March 1883 pronounced unanimously in favour of Cardiff.[73]

It is John Davies's view that 'had the choice been made a decade earlier, Swansea, long Wales's most distinguished intellectual community, would undoubtedly have been the victor'.[74] In such circumstances Swansea, not Cardiff, would have become the home of Wales's medical school, for though the establishment of a medical school was not a major issue in the debate, it formed part of the 'package' for the winning side.

If the new University College of South Wales and Monmouthshire was to open, as planned, in October 1883, much had to be done in a short space of time. June saw the appointment of John Viriamu Jones, ironically a Swansea man who had become principal of Firth College, Sheffield, as college principal, at what would now be regarded as the astonishingly young age of twenty-seven. This was quickly followed by appointments to eleven further academic posts, including professors in the science subjects of chemistry, mathematics and biology (Principal Jones himself being a physicist). The securing of suitable accommodation took a little more time, the college authorities rejecting several locations offered by the town council, before finally opting, as a temporary arrangement, for the building on Newport Road which had hitherto housed the Glamorganshire and Monmouthshire Infirmary, and which would remain part of the college until its demolition in the 1960s.[75] Lord Aberdare, the college's first president, dismissed the fears of those who felt that a former hospital might constitute a health hazard to members of the institution. Writing to the newly-formed College Council he reported: 'I had the advantage of questioning Dr Sheen as to the alleged disadvantages of the Infirmary. He apprehends no danger whatsoever to the health of the students and supported that opinion by convincing reasons.' There might be some noise from the railway station nearby, but otherwise, its very proximity would, in his view, be beneficial to all.[76]

FIRST STEPS TOWARDS THE FORMATION OF THE CARDIFF MEDICAL SCHOOL

Though not a particularly prominent component of its case for a university college, a medical school was certainly part of Cardiff's development plan from the outset. As in England, no self-respecting university would wish to do without one, as Principal Viriamu Jones could attest from his time at Sheffield. Even if its formation was not its first priority, nothing could have signalled the college's aspirations more clearly than the first article of the college charter:

> The object of the College shall be to provide such instruction in all branches of a liberal education as may qualify residents in the six counties of South Wales, and in the County of Monmouth, and elsewhere, to take Degrees in Arts, Science, Law and Medicine at the University of Wales (whenever such University shall have been constituted) or at any of the Universities of the United Kingdom.[77]

The driving force for this development was William Thomas Edwards (1821–1915), south Wales's leading physician at that time and the man who, more than anyone else, deserves recognition as the founder of the Cardiff Medical School. Born and brought up in Caerphilly, he was the great-grandson of William Edwards, the celebrated pastor of the historic Groes-wen chapel and architect, in 1756, of the bridge crossing the river Taff at Pontypridd which had, at that time, the longest single span in Europe. His father had been a highly respected doctor with an extensive country practice which he conducted on horseback, and William, following a period of apprenticeship to his father, proceeded to train in medicine, like many other Welsh doctors, at University College, London, graduating MB BS in 1844. Returning to south Wales he eventually became physician to the Glamorganshire and Monmouthshire Infirmary in 1862, retaining his connection with this hospital, and its successor, until his retirement and beyond. He was a leading member of the Cardiff Medical Society from the beginning, and he involved himself with many areas of the public life of Cardiff. As a keen Congregationalist he was an active member of the Liberation Society, pledged to bring about the disestablishment of the Church of England, and was a prominent member of the local Liberal Association. Indeed, for many years Edwards was a close associate of John Batchelor, mayor of Cardiff in 1853 and the town's leading radical in the mid-Victorian period, hated and loved in equal part by the local people. After the death of his first wife Edwards married one of Batchelor's daughters. A long-standing supporter of a university college in Cardiff, Edwards immediately became involved in the work of the new college, subscribing £500 to its development fund and becoming a life governor. From the outset he served as a member of the College Council, a position he would retain until 1897.[78]

By 1885, little more than a year after the formation of the college, informed medical opinion in south Wales – perhaps more accurately a handful of enthusiasts – was only beginning to discuss the prospect of the early establishment of a medical school in Cardiff for the first time. On 11 February 1885, Thomas Wallace, the secretary of the Cardiff Medical Society and a surgeon at the infirmary, proposed to a poorly attended meeting that the 'desirability or non-desirability' of establishing a medical school in connection with the college, should be considered. In view of the small attendance, further discussion was deferred. At a special meeting, held on 27 February, attended by eight members (only two more than had attended the previous meeting), the society agreed, no discussion being recorded, to work with other bodies 'to consider the desirability of establishing a medical school in connection with the University College of South Wales and Monmouthshire'.[79] Lest it be thought that this became a burning topic for members of the society, it should be noted that the Cardiff Medical School was not referred to again at its meetings until October 1893. Meanwhile, however, the South Wales and Monmouthshire branch of the British Medical Association was pursuing the matter.[80] At its spring meeting in 1885, guided by William Edwards and Alfred Sheen, the branch expressed the view 'that it is eminently desirable to establish a partial medical school at Cardiff, which shall carry a student to the Intermediate MB Lond.', and nominated a number of its members to participate in any joint meetings that might be arranged with the college.[81] There are two points of particular interest here. All of those nominated were from outside Cardiff, three from Swansea, and one each from Aberdare, Brecon and Tredegar. Furthermore, the aims of those proposing a medical school were modest, indeed realistic. There was no suggestion that a full medical school should be established at this juncture. Apart from any other consideration, the clinical facilities in Cardiff were inadequate. Certainly the Glamorganshire and Monmouthshire Infirmary was brand-new, but funds were short and the number of beds, one hundred, was scarcely capable of supporting undergraduate clinical training to the extent expected of a teaching hospital. All of the London teaching hospitals were, in terms of beds, at least twice as large as the infirmary, some many times larger. In the provinces, the number of beds available for teaching in Birmingham was 400, in Bristol 460. At Leeds the General Infirmary had over 400 beds, while the Liverpool and Manchester Royal Infirmaries had 300 each, the same number as the Sheffield General Infirmary and Royal Hospital combined.[82] That aside, what the supporters of a medical school in Cardiff wanted was somewhere for aspiring doctors from Wales to train during the years when they were at their most vulnerable. Interviewed by the *South Wales Daily News* on the occasion of his eighty-ninth birthday in 1910, William Edwards explained his motivation: 'You were the pioneer of the Medical School, Dr Edwards? The doctor closed his eyes. I wanted every Welsh boy to get the fullest opportunity to study Medicine at home.'[83]

Edwards secured a perfect platform to promote the formation of a medical school in Cardiff when, in July 1885, the fifty-third annual meeting of the British Medical Association met in the town. As one of the most prominent medical man in south Wales he was elected president and, during a wide-ranging address to the delegates, touching on developments in medical science since the previous visit of the association to Wales (to Swansea in 1853), and landmarks in the recent social, economic and cultural history of Cardiff, he took the opportunity of mentioning his aspirations for a medical school in Cardiff: 'We hope at no distant time to see a medical school connected with our College, as there is at present not one in Wales, though it supplies a large number of medical students to the Irish, Scotch and London universities.'[84] To demonstrate his personal commitment to the cause, Edwards, who had already subscribed £500 to the college at its foundation, publicly pledged a further £1,000 towards the establishment of the medical school.

Meanwhile, the College Council, in conjunction with the local branch of the BMA and the Cardiff Medical Society, had set up a joint committee to take the project forward. At its first meeting on 7 May the essential shape of the proposed school was defined:

> In the opinion of the Committee the teaching of the School should be for the present limited to the preparation for the first MB Examination of the University of London, and the first two Professional Examinations of the Colleges of Physicians and Surgeons. To carry out the above scheme it will be advisable to found Chairs of Anatomy and Physiology, and to appoint demonstrators in those subjects. A dissecting room, physiological laboratory, museum and lecture theatre would be necessary.[85]

All of this required money, which, despite the personal generosity of William Edwards, the college did not have. It was at this point that Alfred Sheen (1839–1906), since 1882 the senior surgeon at the infirmary, took centre-stage. Born in Leicester, Sheen had commenced his medical studies in Madras – where he sang in the cathedral choir – before continuing his training at Guy's Hospital. He moved to Cardiff in 1864 to work for two years as house surgeon at the infirmary, before spending a few years in general practice. In 1871 he was appointed as an assistant surgeon to the infirmary, shortly afterwards becoming a full surgeon, a position he would retain until his retirement in 1900. He was mainly responsible for persuading the Marquess of Bute to provide a site for the new infirmary, reportedly over a game of chess, and for raising much of the money for the building. Indeed, Sheen's son William, later to become the first provost of the Welsh National School of Medicine, once wrote of Alfred's 'genius for secretarial work and organisation'. It was Sheen who, as secretary of the South Wales branch of the BMA at the time, was responsible for arranging the conspicuously successful annual meeting of the association in Cardiff in 1885, and incorporating, for the first time, dancing in the social programme.[86] In view of his organizational and fund-raising skills it was natural that Alfred Sheen should assume the role of fund-raiser for the cause of the medical school and, given his good relationship with one of the wealthiest men in Britain at that time, it was equally natural that he would try the Marquess of Bute first. When Sheen approached Sir William Thomas Lewis, the coal magnate and Bute's right-hand man, for £15,000, he must have felt optimistic.

> Dr Edwards has generously promised a donation of £1,000 towards the establishment of the medical school and I have no doubt that if Lord Bute would render the assistance which I have privately suggested to you it would give an impetus to the scheme which would very shortly ensure its successful start.

Lewis's reply was rather discouraging:

> I have no great hope of success at present, and more especially having regard to the number of matters which Lord Bute just now considers to have stronger claims for his sympathy and support, in the shape of Hospital arrangements in the Mining Districts.[87]

Fortified, however, by letters of encouragement from Lord Aberdare, the president of the college, and from the licensing bodies, Principal Viriamu Jones secured, in March 1886, the support of the College Council for the organization of a delegation to the government 'at the earliest opportunity' to seek state aid for the project.[88]

Despite the fact that Gladstone's Liberal government was preoccupied with the question of Home Rule for Ireland, on 14 April Earl Spencer, lord president of the Council, received an impressive delegation, representing the college, the Corporation of Cardiff, the South Wales branch of the BMA, the Cardiff Medical Society, and the medical staff of the infirmary. A memorial had been prepared, which set out the case for a medical school in Cardiff. The arguments included the following:

3. The convenience and advantages, material and moral, of residence near home during the first years of professional study, constitute a strong argument in favour of a medical school for Welsh students at Cardiff; and in such a school, each student will receive more individual supervision from the professors, and be stimulated by more personal association with them than is possible during the first years of study in a large metropolitan hospital.
4. The medical faculties are perhaps the most successful in the Scotch and Irish Universities; and a like result may be expected in Wales, in which at present there is no medical school.
5. The University College of South Wales and Monmouthshire already provides teaching in many of the preliminary scientific subjects of medical education, and students intending to enter the medical profession already avail themselves of the advantages offered at that institution.
6. In Cardiff there is a hospital, erected at a cost, including the site, of about £40,000 of such extent and dimensions as to entitle Cardiff to a school of medicine.

The case was presented by some of Wales's leading public figures. Lord Aberdare referred to the fact that of 1,585 medical men practising in Wales over 300 had been trained in Scotland, and felt that it would be 'a very great advantage for Welsh young men if they could receive a portion at least of this medical education nearer home and upon more economical terms'. Sir Hussey Vivian MP, Swansea's greatest industrialist, played the Welsh-language card for all it was worth: 'It was of vast importance that Welsh medical men should be Welshmen able to speak their own language.' The formidable Henry Richard MP, the so-called 'Member for Wales', suggested that the government had some catching up to do as far as Wales was concerned: 'The British Government owed to Wales long arrears to make up for ages of past neglect.'[89]

While the government representatives present at the meeting were polite, even sympathetic, the likelihood of success was remote. Quite apart from the fact that the Liberal administration was struggling to maintain its very existence during the spring and early summer of 1886, there were no precedents for the provision of special state funds to establish a medical school. The government's formal rejection of the college's request, three months later, while disappointing, was not unexpected.[90] Certainly there was little evidence of immediate indignation among the members of the college, and there would be virtually no reference to the establishment of a medical school at meetings of the Senate and Council for over three years. In reality the college was extremely short of money, scarcely able to meet its existing commitments, let alone engage in new, expensive, projects, desirable though they might be. Indeed, in the very presence of William Edwards, the Council, at its meeting on 7 March 1888, went so far as to resolve that consideration of the establishment of a medical school 'be postponed *sine die*'.[91]

Such a state of affairs could not be allowed to continue for ever. The Court of the college, always more likely than the council to 'speak out of turn', returned to the issue in the spring of 1890,[92] and although neither the Senate nor the Council immediately responded to the challenge, others did. At the annual dinner of the South Wales and Monmouthshire branch of the BMA in June the local president, Dr William Price (1845–1917), a prominent Cardiff general practitioner, who had once been apprenticed to William Edwards, pledged £1,000 to the cause, to augment the sum already pledged by his old mentor. Following Price's lead others, both doctors and laymen, donated lesser amounts (notably £250 from the local businessman and philanthropist John Cory) against a target of £20,000.[93] That evening a committee composed of some of the leading doctors in the region[94] was set up to launch an appeal for funds aimed not only at the medical profession but also the general public, for, as Dr Isambard Owen, dean of St George's Hospital Medical School, observed in a letter to Alfred Sheen, one of the honorary secretaries, 'The establishment of a medical school at Cardiff is a matter for the benefit of the public, and not especially for the advantage of the profession, and it is the public who ought to subscribe.'[95] A special appeal to the Welsh of London was launched by Owen who, in a memorandum to his compatriots, argued that although it was not intended at this time to offer a full course of training for medical students there was no reason why Cardiff could not provide training during the first three, crucial years. He emphasized one issue which people in the metropolis would well understand:

> Student life in a populous town necessarily offers many temptations to young men at the age at which medical studies are usually commenced. The evil is at its maximum when the student finds himself an unknown stranger in a distant city, among unfamiliar surroundings; it is minimised when he is within reach of the restraining influences of relatives, friends and home associations. I can well understand that many a parent in South Wales would be glad for his son to commence his studies in a town where such influences may be available, and to proceed to the metropolis at a later age, when some experience of life has been obtained and the character is more firmly established.[96]

Despite much good will, the money was slow to come in. Principal Viriamu Jones in January 1891 was still referring to the school of medicine as a 'castle in the air',[97] and by the autumn of 1891 the college treasurer was reporting that only £4,000 had been promised and, in his estimation, a further £12,000 was needed.[98] Once again, the members of the College Court, who came as close to representing the voice of informed public opinion as could be expected in those days, took the initiative. At its meeting in the autumn of 1892, rejecting a vague commitment by the Council to found a school of medicine 'as soon as financial circumstances permit' the Court adopted a motion which called on the Council to take whatever steps were necessary to open a school of medicine in October 1893.[99]

The *South Wales Daily News*, Cardiff's Liberal morning newspaper, praised the Court for its determination:

> It is a very unsatisfactory state of affairs that the Welsh medical student cannot receive his professional education in the Principality. Such a school must be situate in a town possessing a good hospital, otherwise the students would not have proper facilities for study; and Cardiff, where a first class infirmary exists, with over a hundred patients usually under treatment within its walls, furnishes just the place for study that is required. The Governors have, in the resolution of yesterday, demonstrated once again their intention to keep abreast of the requirements of the time. This has been their prevailing characteristic throughout; and they will, without doubt, receive hearty public support in the fresh endeavour to further extend the usefulness of the great and growing institution over whose destinies they preside with such conspicuous success.[100]

THE ESTABLISHMENT OF THE UNIVERSITY OF WALES

Meanwhile, during 1892 and the early months of 1893, the leading lights at the University College of South Wales and Monmouthshire were immersed in discussions with their colleagues at the University College of Wales, Aberystwyth and at the University College of North Wales, Bangor (established in 1884) regarding the terms on which a federal University of Wales should be created. The concept of a University of Wales, under discussion for several decades, had been gathering pace during the 1880s, notwithstanding the establishment of three separate university colleges covering the principality as a whole. Indeed, the principal of the University College of South Wales and Monmouthshire, Viriamu Jones who, in the words of Professor Gwynn Williams, 'had not returned to Wales simply to be Principal of Cardiff',[101] was a passionate advocate for the setting-up of a University of Wales embracing the whole nation. In his inaugural address to his own college, delivered in October 1883, Jones made his position clear:

> The various Colleges of Wales will be isolated units till the University of Wales exists, not in name, but in fact. The inauguration of the new Colleges is the first step towards it. When the University is founded it will, I believe, bring about a harmony

of sentiment and interest between the Colleges affiliated to it that cannot be attained in any other way.[102]

Such sentiments struck a chord with many prominent Welshmen and with bodies such as the London-based Cymmrodorion Society, enthused by any manifestations of Welsh national consciousness. The concept of a University of Wales as a degree-awarding body was attractive to many in the three colleges who regretted the fact that their students, while taught at Aberystwyth, Bangor and Cardiff, were required to take the degree examinations of external bodies such as the University of London. It was impracticable for each of the colleges to seek degree-awarding powers for themselves – the Privy Council strongly resisted the proliferation of degree-awarding institutions at this time. However, an arrangement in Wales such as that existing in the north of England at the Victoria University, incorporating university colleges in Manchester, Liverpool and Leeds, was surely attainable – notwithstanding the fact that for several years a significant minority of students at the Victoria University continued to take the examinations of the University of London in preference to their own.[103]

At important conferences of Welsh educationalists and patriots held in Shrewsbury in 1888 and 1891, the essential characteristics of a University of Wales were defined, notably that, unlike the University of London, it would be a teaching as well as an examining body, in the sense that those seeking a University of Wales degree would have to study at one of its constituent colleges first. The return of a Liberal government to power in 1892, susceptible to the influence of Welsh MPs, accelerated progress towards the establishment of a University of Wales.[104] At a further conference at Shrewsbury in January 1893 broad agreement was given to a charter, largely drafted by Isambard Owen, dean of St George's Medical School in London, which, in the words of Professor Gwynn Williams, 'he fashioned clause by clause in his Mayfair home during the early hours of the morning after a day in the hospital or consulting room'.[105] Having secured the endorsement of Parliament during the following months, the charter of the University of Wales received the royal assent on 30 November 1893.

With regard to the development of the medical school in Cardiff the university charter was significant in two particular respects. Under its first clause women were to be given complete equality with men, in relation to the holding of any office in the University and to admittance to any degree, which, as will be noted in the next chapter, placed prospective women medical students in Cardiff at some advantage over those at several other medical schools.[106] Secondly, the charter was significant for what it did not say. Although the charter of the University College of South Wales and Monmouthshire had explicitly looked forward to the time when its students could sit for the medical degrees of the University of Wales, the charter of 1893 did not give the university the power to confer such degrees. Isambard Owen, who knew as much about medical politics and practicalities as anyone in the country, firmly advised against pursuing the matter at that time:

> He had no hesitation in saying that at the present moment they might just as well ask for powers to confer baronetcies as for powers to grant degrees in medicine. Next October at Cardiff he hoped they would teach anatomy, but to get a complete medical school for Wales they could not for the next ten years at least.[107]

To insist on including in the charter the right for the University of Wales to award degrees in medicine, when Wales did not even have the semblance of a medical school, could put the whole charter at risk and for the time being the issue was dropped.[108]

THE CARDIFF MEDICAL SCHOOL BECOMES A REALITY

Notwithstanding his advice on degree-awarding powers, Isambard Owen was more than happy to offer whatever practical assistance he could in getting the Cardiff Medical School off the ground. At its meeting on 7 November 1892 the Cardiff College Council responded to its Court's demand that a medical school be set up without further delay by instructing its finance committee to come up with practical proposals. Lacking up-to-date expertise in this matter the committee invited Owen, who was a member of the College Court, to advise it. At its December meeting, after extending its cordial thanks to Isambard Owen for his valuable assistance, the Council proceeded to adopt the recommendations of its finance committee, namely that advertisements be placed immediately for professors of anatomy and physiology, at the standard college professorial salary of £350 per annum. It was stipulated that the professors, when appointed, 'shall be required to devote all their time to their professorial duties, and shall not be allowed to engage in private or consultation practice'.[109] The college's insistence on full-time professors was in accordance with the practice then being adopted by medical schools throughout the country, reflecting, as has already been noted, their determination to align their biomedical departments as closely as possible with the mores prevailing elsewhere in the university communities to which they were becoming affiliated.

Despite the fact that, during this period Cardiff, indeed all the Welsh university colleges, paid their professors less generously than equivalent institutions elsewhere in Britain,[110] the response to the advertisements was reasonably encouraging. The chair of anatomy attracted eleven applicants, ten from the United Kingdom and one from the University of Texas. Five candidates applied for the chair of physiology. Having sought the opinion of the Senate on the candidates' relative merits, the Council, on 15 March 1893, fittingly chaired by William Edwards, interviewed three applicants shortlisted for the chair of anatomy, and two for the chair of physiology. After four hours the proceedings concluded with the appointment of the two candidates particularly favoured by the Senate, Alfred William Hughes (1861–1900) as professor of anatomy, and John Berry Haycraft (1857–1922) as professor of physiology. Hughes was the perfect candidate. Aged thirty-one, he was a Welsh-speaker from Merionethshire. Having graduated in medicine at Edinburgh in 1885, he had since 1889 been a lecturer in anatomy at that university, pursuing research on the rotatory movements of the human vertebral column. Haycraft, aged thirty-five, had also graduated in Edinburgh (1878) and after periods in Leipzig, Edinburgh and elsewhere he had in recent years served as a research scholar at University College, London.[111] *The Lancet* was pleased with the appointments:

> We congratulate South Wales on obtaining the services of such well-trained professors for their new chairs; but we cannot avoid pointing out that salaries of £350 per annum, without a share of the fees paid by their students, are quite insufficient to retain their services for any period of time should they be offered similar chairs in other medical schools.[112]

Time would tell how far the journal's prediction proved to be accurate.

As the college's memorial of 1886 to the government had stated, the science departments of the college were already accredited by the several medical licensing bodies as offering suitable one-year courses of study in preparation for the London Matriculation Examination, the Preliminary Scientific Examination of the University of London, the First Examination of the London Conjoint Board (established in 1885) and the First Examination of the Scottish Triple Qualification, among others. Indeed, so proud had been the professors of chemistry (Professor C. M. Thompson) and biology (Professor W. N. Parker) that certain of their courses had been recognized in 1886 by the University of Edinburgh as qualifying for its MB degree, that they wrote a special article on the matter for the newspapers.[113] Alfred Sheen's son William had, at the tender age of sixteen, enrolled as a Cardiff student in October 1885, and, having passed the London Matriculation Examination, had proceeded to Guy's Hospital Medical School, for his preclinical and clinical training, before qualifying MB and MRCS LRCP in 1892. In fact, five students having enrolled at Cardiff in 1883/4, the college's inaugural year, went on to qualify as doctors, including Herbert Herbert, a farmer's son from Ammanford, born in 1864. He did his preclinical and clinical training at the London Hospital Medical School, becoming a Licentiate of the Society of Apothecaries in 1889. This achievement identifies Herbert as the first former student of the University College of South Wales and Monmouthshire to qualify as a doctor, later practising in Tumble, near Llanelli. Another of the five students, Abel Christmas Davies, born in 1863, the son of a retired butter merchant from Llandysul, Cardiganshire, came to Cardiff from University College of Wales, Aberystwyth, and went on to train at University College, London, obtaining the MRCS LRCP in 1890. He was thus the second student to qualify as a doctor, having had some of his preliminary training in Cardiff. He would become a medical officer to a number of steelworks and collieries in the Swansea area.[114]

In 1892/3 there were already several first-year students working in the college's science departments in preparation for their first qualifying examinations, who were hoping to enter the inaugural preclinical year in Cardiff, given the opportunity to do so. If the medical school was to open in October 1893 there was no time to lose. The first task for the two new professors was to work with their science colleagues to draw up a detailed medical school prospectus, not only for publicity purposes but also for submission to the Senate of the University of London, the Conjoint Board, the Apothecaries Hall and other medical licensing bodies. For there was no purpose in establishing a preclinical school whose students could not subsequently proceed elsewhere for their clinical training. The task of compiling a curriculum was fairly straightforward. The basic requirements of the General Medical Council were, by the 1890s, clearly established throughout the university system, and Hughes, Haycraft and their science colleagues were obviously well aware of the main issues. Of particular relevance to Cardiff were the three years of training prior to clinical studies in London or elsewhere, the first year primarily devoted to the basic sciences, the second and third to anatomy, physiology and materia medica (the theory and practice of pharmacology).[115]

By early May the prospectus, having received the Council's approval, was dispatched to the various licensing bodies and publicized in the local press. The *Western Mail* was impressed:

> Parents who desire to keep their children as long as possible under the parental roof, or in surroundings where they can be in touch with them will welcome this new effort on the part of the council of the University College, Cardiff. This first attempt to educate Welsh students in Wales itself will, in addition, be welcomed by everyone connected by the Principality and interested in the progress of Welsh education.[116]

The college's next priority was to find room to accommodate the medical school. There was no existing space to spare, and the decision was soon made to provide purpose-built accommodation by adding a new storey on top of the existing college building, at a cost of under £6,000, to incorporate two lecture theatres, a dissecting room, a museum, a physiological classroom and offices for the professors. The building work commenced in July, but had not been completed by the time that the medical school opened in October, so that until Christmas the anatomy and physiology classes had to be conducted in the students' gymnasium.[117] Indeed, the editor of the Cardiff students' magazine complained about the disruptive effects that the building work was having on the whole college. The medical school 'will certainly be good, when finished, if we are to judge by the time it is taking and the deafening noise which we have been entertained with, during the term, to the great discomfort of both professors and students'.[118]

Nevertheless, the licensing bodies were sufficiently satisfied with the progress being made to notify the college authorities in August that Cardiff's preclinical course would be recognized as suitable preparation for the pursuit of clinical studies. The notification from the University of London was typical (and gratifying):

> I have the honour to inform you that by a resolution of the Senate passed on June 29th last, which has since been approved by the Secretary of State. The Medical School of the University College of South Wales and Monmouthshire is recognised as an institution from which the University of London will receive certificates for the Intermediate Examination in Medicine.[119]

Those planning a medical school had referred to costs in the order of £14,000 or more. Lacking government assistance, the college had, as has been seen, placed its hopes on the success of a public appeal. In fact, the appeal had fallen short of expectations. Even in 1895, two years after the school had opened, the appeal fund had realized only £6,696 in donations or promises, from a total of thirty-two donors from south Wales and a handful of London-based donors, stimulated by Isambard Owen's appeal to the Welsh of London.[120] The largest single donation, of £2,000, came from the estate of the late Charles Jones MD of Pontypridd. Donations of £1,000 were promised from William Edwards, William Price and Arthur H. Thompson of London. Other major donors included the shipping magnates John Cory (£250) and Richard Cory (£200), James Howell, the retailer (£125), and the Lords Aberdare and Tredegar, who promised £100 each. Most of the other donors were doctors from south Wales, by no means all of them from Cardiff. This rather disappointing outcome bears out the assessment of Michael Sanderson that the higher educational institutions of Wales, particularly Cardiff, were poor at engaging the active support of local industry and commerce during the late nineteenth century.[121] Nevertheless, Cardiff had grasped the nettle, and at least one donation was safely banked by the date of the school's opening. At the meeting of the council on 29 September a letter was read from William Edwards: 'I enclose my cheque for a thousand pounds … The only condition I attach to it is that in the event of the Medical School ultimately proving a failure the Council shall invest the capital for maintaining a scholarship or scholarships in my name.'[122] William Edwards was essentially a modest man. He had, at the time of the launch of the appeal, refused to countenance the proposal, seriously made by others, that the chair of anatomy should be named after him. In making such a suggestion in his letter to the council he, at least, did not expect his beloved medical school to fail.

The Cardiff Medical School

Towards the end of his life Sir Isambard Owen said of the early years of the Cardiff Medical School: 'It may not be far wrong to say that it was the most brilliant single piece of work ever done in the University of Wales.'[1] There is no doubt that, during the first quarter-century of its existence, the school achieved much about which it had good reason to be proud. Despite difficult financial circumstances, its small complement of dedicated staff provided courses of instruction fully in accord with contemporary best practice, and succeeded in producing cohorts of well-trained students for the clinical schools of London and elsewhere, several of whom went on to achieve great distinction in their chosen profession. Reflecting the ethos of the University of Wales, the Cardiff Medical School's policy on the recruitment of women students was enlightened, in contrast, for instance, with the situation in London. As is noted in a later chapter, the school's research reputation was not particularly high, but was certainly no worse than that of most medical schools in provincial England at that time.

LAYING THE FOUNDATIONS

The medical school opened on 4 October 1893 when, at 8 p.m., before what the *Western Mail* described as 'a goodly audience', the new professor of physiology, John Berry Haycraft, delivered an introductory lecture on 'Some of the present aspects of medical education'. Well covered in the pages of the *British Medical Journal*,[2] the lecture represented a vigorous critique of how medicine was taught, or indeed overtaught. As far as he was concerned, the most important thing for students to acquire was the ability to sort out the wheat from the chaff:

> The minute geography of the bones and muscles, the details of posture crammed up for examination are forgotten as useless by the practising physician or surgeon. They pass out of his life as facts having no practical importance nor scientific interest. He might just as well have crammed up the exact position of every gas lamp and drain pipe in the metropolis … My advice to you tonight is to get the big ideas and principles, and then fill in the details.

Principal Viriamu Jones was there; so was William Edwards, who proclaimed the day to be a historic occasion. A visitor from Edinburgh University, admittedly with little evidence on which to base his opinion, stated that Edinburgh was convinced that it had a serious competitor in Cardiff.[3]

Also in the audience were no doubt most, perhaps all, of the eleven students who, having entered the college in 1891 or 1892, had pursued foundation courses in the basic sciences before progressing in 1893/4 into the preclinical stage, to be exposed as 'guinea pigs' to instruction from the newly appointed professors of anatomy and physiology.[4] In addition, Professor Haycraft's audience probably included several of the seventeen aspiring doctors who would register as first-year students in the 1893/4 session, as a prelude to proceeding to the preclinical phase in due course. These two dozen or more pioneers were overwhelmingly solid middle-class boys from the south-eastern corner of Wales. The majority had been educated in what later became known as grammar schools, though a few attended minor public schools such as Brecon, Llandovery and Kingswood School, Bath. One-quarter were sons of doctors and dentists, two were 'sons of the manse', and the fathers of most of the others were merchants of various descriptions.

Two of the new entrants to the college were women. As Carol Dyhouse has shown, access by women to higher education at this time was patchy, and even where women were generally admitted, they did not always enjoy the right to pursue medicine. Indeed, with the obvious exception of the London School of Medicine for Women, the doors of the London medical schools were firmly shut to women until the First World War.[5] By contrast, from the outset, the charter of the University of Wales proclaimed the equality of the sexes, eliciting a handsome accolade from a London doctor who wrote as follows to the *British Medical Journal* in 1895:

> In the University of Wales every post is expressly open to women – even to that of the Chancellor. Sex is no bar to any professorship, or examinership or office of any kind. And the Cardiff Medical School throws open all its classes, and offers all its advantages to men and women on equal terms. Both Professor Hughes and Dr Haycraft will heartily welcome women medicals, and having determined to send my own daughter to be under their able teaching I thought that other fathers might like to know that such a medical school exists for their girls, and so make further and fuller inquiries for themselves.[6]

The two women who registered as medical students in 1893/4 were Victoria Evelyn May Bennett and Mary Elizabeth Phillips. Bennett, a relatively mature twenty-seven-year-old student at enrolment, was to qualify from the London School of Medicine for Women with the LSA in 1903; Mary Elizabeth Phillips (she signed her name 'Bessie' in the college matriculation book) was a farmer's daughter from Merthyr Cynog, near Brecon. She too went to the London School of Medicine for Women for her clinical training and qualified MB in 1900, thereby becoming the first woman student to qualify in medicine having pursued her initial training in Cardiff. During the First World War she served with great distinction with the Scottish Women's Hospital in Belgium, Corsica and the Dardanelles.[7]

By Christmas 1893 the work on the top floor of the college had been finished, enabling the official opening of the medical school to take place on 14 February 1894. The guest of honour was Sir Richard Quain, president of the General Medical Council. At the opening ceremony, presided over quite fittingly by William Edwards, Quain congratulated 'gallant little Wales' on its achievement before inspecting the school's new laboratories and lecture theatres. By now some £6,000 had been donated by doctors and laymen in south Wales, with an additional sum of £500 collected by Isambard Owen's London committee. Though nowhere near the target of £16,000, this was enough to provide premises which, in Quain's opinion, were 'as perfect as could be made'. The *Western Mail* described the facilities thus:

> In Professor Haycraft's department there is a lecture theatre, seating 135 students, on raised galleries, overlooking the lecture table, with apparatus and diagram rooms adjoining, and in connection therewith large well-lighted classrooms for chemical physiology and histology and for practical study. All the rooms are fitted with every requisite appliance for their special uses. In Professor Hughes's department there is also a lecture theatre, seating 100 students, on raised galleries, an admirably lighted and arranged museum, dissection and injection rooms, fitted with all necessary appliances. These schools are approached by their own special staircase, and are separated from the college buildings, of which they form the top storey, by a sound-proof and fire-proof floor over the entire area. The whole of the rooms are thoroughly well lighted, and an examination of them makes it manifest that the most rigid economy, consistent with sound and durable work, has been exercised throughout.

In the evening some 150 guests attended a celebration banquet in the town hall which included not only salmon, saddle of mutton and sirloin of beef, but also such delicacies as fried smelts, stewed eels and curried prawns, all consumed to the accompaniment of Mr Fred Roberts's band. The whole occasion was a great success and in an editorial the *Western Mail* was fulsome in its praise for the new school: 'With all sincerity we wish it every prosperity, and commend to the uttermost the noble generosity of those Welsh medical practitioners and others who have made its existence feasible.'[8]

A month later, the school made an important new appointment, that of Donald Rose Paterson (1862–1939) to the post of part-time lecturer in materia medica and pharmacy, in time to instruct the first-year students during the summer term. Paterson, a

Scotsman from Inverness, having trained at Edinburgh, came to Cardiff in 1884 to become house surgeon at the Glamorganshire and Monmouthshire Infirmary, and, after a short spell of postgraduate training in Vienna and Berlin, became honorary pathologist at the infirmary in 1891, the first person to hold such a post in the hospital.[9] He was to become one of Wales's most eminent doctors in due course, but in the 1890s he contributed much to the rapidly growing reputation of Wales's infant medical school.

It was a sign both of the school's growing self-confidence and of the complexity of co-ordinating the medical teaching arrangements that by the autumn of 1894 the Senate was calling upon the College Council to establish the post of dean of the Faculty of Medicine. The following duties were identified:

i. To interview students, their parents or guardians, at the commencement of each term, and to report progress of students to their parents or guardians; to conduct correspondence with intending students, their parents or guardians;
ii. To arrange for the registration of medical students;
iii. To become thoroughly in touch with the requirements of the various Universities and Examining Boards, and to receive official notice of any change in these;
iv. To arrange with members of the Faculty for due compliance with these;
v. In conjunction with the office, to check the payment of fees by students;
vi. To ascertain from other members of the Faculty the attendance of students and their efficiency, and to sign their schedules if their conduct and progress have been satisfactory;
vii. To superintend with the office the advertisement of the school in the daily and medical press.[10]

In March 1895 John Berry Haycraft thus became the medical school's first dean, to be reappointed annually until 1898, when ill health forced him to stand down.[11] A study of successive editions of the University of Wales *Calendar* shows that for several years the dean of the medical school – who received an annual honorarium of £25 – was formally listed among the senior officers of the college, alongside the president, the vice-presidents, the principal, the treasurer and the registrar. Indeed, not until 1903 was the dean of medicine joined for the first time by deans in the Faculties of Arts and Science.

THE SHAPE OF THE MEDICAL COURSE

The co-ordinating and advisory role of the dean of medicine in Cardiff becomes clear when one considers the nature of the curriculum that the medical school was required to cover. In contrast with other university courses which were primarily organized and taught by a single academic department, the first three years of the medical course in Cardiff and elsewhere depended on the contributions of several academic departments, not only the medical school Departments of Anatomy, Physiology and Materia Medica, but also the basic science Departments of Physics, Chemistry and Biology, all six of which were grouped within the college's faculty of medicine. As deans of the faculty, John Berry Haycraft and his successors had the task of ensuring that the contributions of the several departments were effectively co-ordinated. The dean's organizational role was further complicated by the fact that the medical faculty was, of necessity, required to teach more than one syllabus. As the Cardiff college was not in a position to provide a course leading to the medical degree of the University of Wales, it had no alternative but to provide a range of courses which satisfied the examination requirements of several licensing bodies. The educational numbers produced annually by the *British Medical Journal* and *The Lancet* for the guidance of prospective medical students, not only provided a general outline of the essential features common to all the medical curricula throughout the United Kingdom, but were also anxious to point out the often subtle differences between the requirements of the various licensing bodies at that time. The Cardiff College *Calendar* for 1895/6 listed the requirements of the University of London, the Scottish Universities, the Conjoint Board, the Scottish Triple and the Society of Apothecaries. All of them required students to pass a preliminary (London) or first (Conjoint Board and Scottish Triple) examination in physics, chemistry and biology, normally after one year of study, though the course content varied, depending upon the regulations of the licensing body. For example, to take the first professional examination of the Conjoint Board, students had to attend courses in theoretical and practical chemistry, whereas those wishing to take the London preliminary scientific examination were required to attend classes in theoretical chemistry, chemical philosophy and a different, and longer, course in practical chemistry. As the *British Medical Journal* commented in its educational number of 1895, 'the preliminary examinations of the various corporations are not in all cases interchangeable. It is desirable therefore, that an early decision should be arrived at as to the degree or diploma which the intending student hopes to attain.'[12] It was the dean's responsibility to keep abreast of the various examination regulations, as well as ensuring that the whole of the premedical and preclinical curriculum was efficiently managed. Fortunately it is clear that the college's basic science departments and the departments of anatomy, physiology and materia medica were fully capable of meeting the needs of Cardiff's medical students during the first few years of the school's existence.

By the late nineteenth century, thanks to the way that science had become internationalized, owing, to no small degree, to advances in communications, medical education had acquired similar characteristics in Britain, major parts of mainland Europe and the United States. Nevertheless, as T. N. Bonner has reminded us, in important respects national differences persisted.[13] For example, whereas in parts of Europe a debate continued to rage as to the nature of the basic education required of those seeking to train as medical students (such as the relevance of a sound grounding in the classics), medical schools in the United States tended to take a more relaxed view of such matters. There were differences regarding the order in which the subjects in the medical curriculum should be taken, with the French placing great stress on early student exposure to the clinic, in contrast to the German emphasis on an initial solid grounding in the basic medical sciences. There were also differences between the European and American medical schools in relation to the duration of medical training: whereas the Europeans were increasingly expecting medical courses to last at least five years, in America, in 1895, only a third of students were enrolled on courses of even four years' duration.

In the United Kingdom, notwithstanding certain subtle differences, as noted above, in the regulations of the various licensing boards (of which there were some thirteen), by the early 1890s the curricula of all the universities and conjoint boards were governed by the requirements of the General Medical Council, and therefore followed a broadly standard format. The GMC regulations required that undergraduate training as a registered medical student should last a minimum of five years. The first year would primarily be devoted to the basic sciences, the second and third years to the continued study of the basic sciences and the core preclinical subjects, anatomy, physiology and materia medica and pharmacy or pharmaceutical chemistry. The fourth and fifth years would be devoted to clinical studies in a medical school recognized by the GMC for the purpose. The Cardiff Medical School was recognized by the GMC and the various licensing boards as suitable for medical training for the first three years of the course.

At Cardiff, the first-year courses, in physics, chemistry and biology, consisted of lectures and practical, laboratory-based, instruction, involving, in the case of biology, dissection and microscopic examination of various animals, ranging from earthworms to mammals such as frogs and rabbits. During the summer term botanic field excursions were made, 'weather and other circumstances permitting, to various places of interest in the locality'.[14] That the first-year students were keen to be identified with their future preclinical colleagues may be inferred from the following poem, written by 'Old Stager Medical', which appeared in an issue of the student journal, *The South Wales and Monmouthshire University College Magazine*:

The First Year Medical

When in the Common Room, while waiting some day,
You hear a *very* young student 'gassing' away
And describing most vividly some gruesome sight,
And endeavouring to upset you with all his might;

You will know then that you've really met at last
The First year Medical! He's going too fast.

This Medical (in embryo) takes delight in reciting
To a few lady freshers, some events most exciting.
They must think from his speech that he spends all his time
Midst the horrors he speaks of in a manner so fine;
But it's interesting to know that inside he's not been,
For it's worth more than his life in that *Room* to be seen.

But, fairplay, we will add that if he's been lucky
And evaded our 'Alec' [Alick MacIntosh, anatomy technician] in a
manner quite plucky,
He may, then perhaps a short glimpse obtain,
To be straightway ejected with no little pain.[15]

Most students, in Cardiff, as elsewhere, successfully negotiated the end-of-year examinations and proceeded into the second (first preclinical) year, though a few left to continue their medical training in London. One such student was Thomas John Carey Evans (1884–1947), son of a doctor from Blaenau Ffestiniog, who, having studied in Cardiff for one year, during the 1900/1 session, undertook his medical education at Glasgow and St Bartholomew's Hospital before qualifying at the early age of twenty-one. He later pursued a distinguished career in the Indian Civil Service, culminating in his appointment as medical adviser to Lord Reading when he was viceroy of India, an advancement which was probably influenced by his father-in-law, David Lloyd George, and brought him a knighthood.[16]

T. N. Bonner has described how, from the 1870s, instruction in the preclinical subjects became more laboratory-based, primarily because of the requirement, laid down by the Royal College of Surgeons in 1870, that all candidates for their examinations had to attend 'a practical course of general anatomy and physiology' in which 'the learners themselves shall individually be engaged in the necessary experiments, manipulations etc.'[17] The University of London itself soon adopted this requirement, as did most of the provincial medical schools; indeed, those slower off the mark, such as Sheffield, suffered a temporary decline in their fortunes.[18] Fortunately, the preclinical departments at the Cardiff Medical School were well placed to benefit from the experience of longer-established schools. According to the college *Calendar*, the Department of Anatomy consisted of 'a Lecture Room, Museum, and Bone Room, Dissecting Room, Preparation and Private Room. A large number of dried and moist preparations are accessible to Students.' The anatomy course in years two and three comprised not only series of systematic lectures but demonstrations on recently dissected parts, preparations and models, together with a few demonstrations of surface anatomy on the living subject. Students not otherwise committed to timetabled classes were expected to attend the dissecting room, where they would be directed and assisted by the professor of anatomy. To assist the medical students further in their studies, free access was granted to the department's well-stocked museum, where 'bones with the muscular attachments painted upon them can be studied in revolving glass cases, and unpainted specimens are placed where students can examine and freely handle them.' Dissections and preparations of the brain were placed in basins, open for study and inspection, and there was a large collection of wax and plaster models in the cabinets. As Jonathan Reinarz has observed, in a review of the place of medical museums in medical education, 'For medical students, the museum was the site where theory first encountered practical learning, as ideas first introduced in lectures were explained and illustrated with the help of preserved specimens.'[19]

The physiology department was provided 'with a Lecture Room, Practical Class Room, Research and Advanced Students' Laboratory, Instrument and Photographic Room'. In addition to lectures on physiology and histology, students attended the practical classroom on certain days of the week, the emphasis throughout being on student participation. As the great Cambridge physiologist, Michael Foster wrote in the 1870s, 'the student will gain but little good if he simply listens to lectures, however well-illustrated with experiments, or merely reads books.'[20] In the chemical physiology classes, for instance, as explained in the college *Calendar*, 'the student will himself experiment with the properties of albumen and its allies, the carbohydrates and fats of the food, blood, milk, the digestive juices, glycogen, and urine. He will be shown the more useful methods of qualitative testing and quantitative estimation.' In the experimental physiology classes 'the student will perform for himself experiments upon the dead animal, and learn the use of the physiological apparatus used for the study of nerve, muscle, circulation, respiration, and organs of sense.' In Histology 'the student will himself prepare and examine the tissues and organs of the body, and learn the method of fixing, hardening, staining, section cutting, injecting etc. He will make for his own use some fifty microscope preparations.' For a nominal extra fee, students judged by the professor to be particularly able could secure access to the research and advanced students' laboratory to pursue supervised research projects. As we shall see later, Thomas Lewis was one such student.

The hour from nine to ten o'clock each day during the summer term was devoted to lectures and demonstrations given in the college by the lecturer in materia medica and pharmacology. Two main areas were covered, materia medica and pharmacy, dealing with the nature and composition, and the most important physical and chemical properties of drugs, with their preparation and doses; and pharmacology and therapeutics, dealing with the mode of action of medicinal agents. There was a small museum of materia medica which contained a collection of drugs, in preparation jars and bottles, and a series of models, illustrative of the more important medicinal plants, all open to inspection by the medical students. In addition, a class for practical dispensing was held in the dispensary of the Cardiff Infirmary, when students were given practical instruction in pharmaceutical processes, and were taught the principles of writing prescriptions and methods of dispensing.

This was by no means the only exposure to the hospital experienced by the preclinical students before the First World War. Within a year of the school's opening it entered into an arrangement with the Glamorganshire and Monmouthshire Infirmary whereby suitable preclinical students would spend time in its wards and clinics to gain experience of the hospital environment. The scheme was overseen by a body known as the Clinical Board, set up jointly by the College Council and the governors of the hospital, and composed of the college principal, the heads of the medical school departments and the senior medical staff of the hospital. Judging by an enthusiastic report from the College Senate to the Council, the scheme worked well from the outset, with satisfactory arrangements made for the teaching of the students 'and we were fortunate enough to obtain important concessions on the part of the Hospital Staff, involving a complete change of their existing visiting hours to such times as best suited the convenience of students'.[21] For an additional annual fee of £3. 3s. 0d. over and above their normal composition fees, students not otherwise engaged in lectures and other classes could attend out-patient sessions during the afternoons, and obtain, in the words of the college *Calendar* 'experience in surgical dressing and clinical clerking from 9 a.m. till 11 a.m. under the superintendence of the surgeons and physicians and the resident medical officers'. Students were also entitled to attend ward rounds (what the *Calendar* described as 'bed-to-bed visitations') and operating sessions, details of which were posted on the college notice boards. The regulations laid down that 'in most cases it will be inadvisable for students to attend the Infirmary until after the completion of their second winter session',[22] though it is known that first-year students surreptitiously gained access to the hospital corridors on occasion. Clement Price Thomas, a medical student immediately before the First World War, for instance, described how

> Quite against the rules, during the year of my premedical studies, I used on every available opportunity to go to the operating theatre in the Infirmary. I well remember how clearly [William Sheen] explained to our untutored minds the reasons for and the anatomical features of the operation he was performing. I was, I remember, a little disappointed, though very impressed by the small amount of blood which was lost. He was obviously a very good clinical teacher, aiming at the fundamentals and striving always to make the student think for himself.[23]

Although it was hoped that Cardiff's medical students would ultimately wish to obtain a medical degree from a university such as London, Edinburgh or Glasgow, because of the greater prestige such a qualification was thought to confer, in reality most chose to study for the Conjoint Board diploma, the widespread perception being that this qualification was somewhat easier to obtain than a university degree. Indeed, the fact was that during the last years of the nineteenth century, most internal students at the London medical schools themselves opted for the Conjoint Board diploma rather than the London MB.[24] One of the effects of studying for the Conjoint Board diploma, compared with the MB of the University of London was that, whereas the intermediate examination in medicine of the latter normally took place in the summer term of the third year, the second examination of the Conjoint Board took place in the spring. As the college *Calendar* declared, 'a student who has passed his Second Examination in the spring, may remain in Cardiff during the forthcoming summer, putting in hospital work as a Surgical Dresser.'

Scrutiny of the biographical details contained in volumes of the *Medical Directory* reveals that while about 15 per cent of Cardiff's preclinical students chose to pursue their clinical studies in the Scottish universities, the overwhelming majority went east to London. It is a fact that the nearest medical school to Paddington station, the end of the line for trains from Cardiff, was St Mary's Hospital Medical School, and, coincidentally or not, more of Cardiff's London-bound medical students went there before the First World War than anywhere else – nearly 20 per cent. Marginally, the second most popular was the London, closely followed by St Bartholomew's Hospital, the Middlesex and University College Hospital, with lesser numbers going to the others. The women, of course, all went to the London School of Medicine for Women and its associated hospital, the Royal Free.

SETTLING DOWN NICELY

By February 1895, according to the report given by Principal Viriamu Jones to the College Court, there were upward of thirty students in the medical school. A year later, enrolments totalled forty and, according to a report in the *South Wales Daily News* in July 1896, 'Owing to an unprecedented entry during the present summer that number has increased to 48.'

Probably the most outstanding of the early crop of Cardiff medical students was Herbert Sherwell Clogg (1874–1932). At the autumn meeting of the Court in 1896, Dr A. Garrod Thomas, honorary physician at, and generous benefactor of the Newport and Monmouthshire Infirmary,[25] having congratulated the school on its success, referred to the:

> unique position of one of the candidates for the intermediate MB of London University. That was carrying away what he might call the 'blue ribbon' in anatomy for the year. Not only did Mr Clogg take the Exhibition and the gold medal, but he appeared alone in first class honours; so that it was not a snatched prize, but one fully earned.[26]

This was only the second occasion in fifteen years on which a student from a provincial university had achieved such distinction,[27] surely an indication of the quality of the preclinical teaching in Cardiff during the early years. It was therefore a matter of great regret that, early in 1897, Professor Hughes left to take up the chair of anatomy at King's College, London and reside in the drier air of south-east England, more congenial to his ailing wife than the damp climate of south-east Wales. Hughes had been a popular member of the Cardiff Medical School, earning, on his departure, the following tribute from the editor of the college's student magazine:

> Everybody regretted his departure, from his many friends in the town outside to his students and colleagues, who miss his pleasant nod and warm grip of the hand in the corridor of the Medical School.
>
> As a teacher he was such a delightful departure from what we are accustomed to consider as professional. Sharp at half-past nine the dissecting-room door opened, and in he came resplendent in cords, a well-cut coat, and a flower in his button hole, bringing with him all the freshness of a country man and of country air, wherewith to freshen up for the day our heavy town atmosphere.
>
> When surrounded by a dozen students he was in his element, and every one could feel that he enjoyed his work, and as a natural consequence those who worked with him were so subtly influenced, they forgot the difficulties in realizing the pleasure of their occupation. We are all creatures of sympathy – even the orthodox professor – and the dullest student could not but take interest in even the driest details of his work when these were presented to him with a kindly and encouraging smile, and in a tone that made him feel that for the moment they were details of the greatest importance.[28]

Gifted though he was, Hughes has been characterized by Professor S. B. Chrimes as a rather restless man who as early as January 1895 had indicated his wish to resign his chair in order to run for Parliament as a Conservative candidate in the north Wales constituency of Arvon. He was persuaded not to resign on the understanding that he would inform the Council if he found that his political activities were interfering unduly with his academic work, and in the event he was unsuccessful in the general election held later that year.[29] On his departure to London, Hughes took with him his valuable personal collection of anatomical preparations, but gave Cardiff £350 to replace the stock. He was immediately succeeded by Dr Andrew Francis Dixon (1868–1936), aged twenty-nine, a graduate of the University of Dublin and chief demonstrator in anatomy at Trinity College, Dublin.

Thanks mainly to the efforts of the distinguished Welsh royal *accoucheur,* Sir John Williams, the standing of Welsh medicine was enhanced in 1896 when the *Medical Directory* decided to treat Wales for the first time as a separate country within the United Kingdom, as Scotland and Ireland had always been treated, with information provided about the University of Wales and its facilities for the study of medicine.[30] Two years later, the educational number of the *British Medical Journal* was referring for the first time in its editorial to the University College of South Wales and Monmouthshire, where 'the patriotic native of the Principality will find an institution which will provide him with excellent opportunities for obtaining instruction during the first three years of his curriculum.'[31]

In November 1900 members of the college and the wider medical community in south Wales, were saddened to learn of the untimely death of their former colleague, Alfred Hughes. Though he had left Cardiff in 1897, he had kept in touch with the college (he had given the inaugural address at the opening of the medical school session in October 1899) and his demise, from enteric fever contracted while organizing the Welsh Hospital in Springfontein, South Africa, during the Boer War, was widely lamented. Professor John Viriamu Jones, himself to pass away at the early age of forty-five a few months later, paid Hughes this handsome tribute:

> His patient devotion and rare vigour as a teacher, his sweet temper and helpful presence, his force of character, the pleasantness and strength of his whole personality, won for him the most sincere and grateful affection of his colleagues and students; and no Welshman could be with him long without a quickening sense of kinship, for he had a great love for Wales and a vivid desire to do it service.[32]

Scarcely had his body been laid to rest in Corris churchyard in his beloved county of Merionethshire than a meeting was held at University College, Cardiff, chaired by its vice-president, the now venerable William Edwards, and attended by all the leading academics and doctors of the area, to launch a fund to commemorate Hughes's contribution to the early success of the medical school.[33] John Lynn Thomas, Cardiff's leading surgeon, who had been over in South Africa with Hughes, immediately donated £100 and William Edwards himself added £100. Within a short time £1,775 had been collected, nearly twice as much as had been expected, resulting in the official opening, in the medical school, of the Alfred Hughes Anatomical Museum by William Edwards in June 1902, and the formal establishment of the Alfred Hughes prize medal for anatomy (designed by the celebrated sculptor William Goscombe John). After presenting the second medal to R. K. Shepherd, the year's best anatomy student (the first had been given to Hughes's widow), William Edwards took the opportunity to refer to the future development of the medical school:

> He hoped that the medical school would soon be removed to larger premises, and that they would never rest satisfied until they had brought the school to that state of completion which would make it unnecessary for any of their students to go elsewhere to finish their course. Some of the best students of London during recent years had been drawn from the Cardiff school, and many of their old students were already filling positions of high distinction all over the Kingdom.[34]

He might have had in mind the already cited Herbert Sherwell Clogg who, after a brilliant undergraduate career in Cardiff and London, went on to win the gold medal for his London Mastership in Surgery (MS) in 1902, only the ninth student to secure such an accolade in sixty-four years, and was now assistant surgeon at Charing Cross Hospital. Or he could well have been alluding to the six Welsh students, all initially trained in Cardiff, who had passed their final examinations in London the previous November.[35]

One of them was Alfred Ernest Jones (1879–1958), son of an aspiring colliery clerk from Gowerton who, having been educated at Llandovery College, went to University College, Cardiff in 1895, at the age of sixteen. His three years there were not marked by any particular distinction. In the opinion of Tom Davies, one of Jones's biographers, 'It may well be that the powerful psychological conflicts which devastated him at the time, and which arose mainly from his religious doubts, were partly responsible for this.'[36] However, Jones looked upon his teachers with affection and respect and, in his subsequent memoirs, he admitted that it was during his student days in Cardiff that he began to develop his lifelong interest in the working of the mind.[37] Jones's student career blossomed during his clinical years at University College Hospital, London and after qualifying MRCS LRCP in 1900 he obtained the University of London degree in 1901, with honours in medicine and obstetrics, the University Gold Medal in both subjects and a university scholarship in obstetrics, on the recommendation of none other than the great Sir John Williams himself. Ernest Jones would, in time, achieve international recognition as the greatest proponent of the science of psychotherapy after Sigmund Freud, whose three-part biography he wrote in the 1950s.

Equally Edwards could have been thinking of that precociously talented student, Thomas Lewis (1881–1945), son of a Cardiff mining engineer who had enrolled for the First MB in 1898 at the tender age of sixteen. After a brilliant preclinical career in Cardiff, during which he managed to publish two scientific papers on the proteins of unstriped muscle in the *Journal of Physiology*, in association with his physiology lecturer, Swale Vincent, he passed the London Second MB examination with first-class honours in anatomy and physiology, winning the gold medal, in July 1902, and proceeding to London for his clinical studies. An exact contemporary, Ivor J. Davies (1880–1958), later to become a leading physician at the Cardiff Royal Infirmary, remembered Lewis well:

> Thomas Lewis was aloof and reserved but would relax to any of us who could join him in country pursuits around his old home at Tynant, Taff's Well. He was a skilful photographer, especially of birds. We foresaw, as fellow students, that he was predestined for a great future and did not take it amiss that he seldom came to the common room.[38]

A book of sketches, elegantly drawn by Lewis while attending biology classes in the museum of the Medical School between 1898 and 1900, is kept among the archives of the Sir Herbert Duthie Library, Cardiff University.

The academic achievements of Cardiff's preclinical students at this time were indeed noteworthy, bearing in mind the limited resources available to them. It should not be forgotten that only in 1898 were the departments of anatomy and physiology transformed from being 'one-man bands' by the establishment of a post of assistant lecturer/demonstrator in each, and it would not be until the second decade of the twentieth century that additional academic staff were appointed, funded by new money from the government, on the advice of the president of the General Medical Council. Meanwhile, the academic staff of the medical school were fully stretched. It is recorded that in the 1902/3 session all the anatomy teaching was conducted by Professor Dixon and his assistant, Dr John Evatt, Dixon giving one hundred formal lectures and forty demonstrations, with Evatt (who, in 1909, would be appointed to the chair of anatomy at Winnipeg University, Canada) giving a further fifty informal lectures and forty demonstrations. Either one or the other was expected to be on hand in the dissecting room, open from 9 a.m. to 5 p.m., apart for an hour for lunch (9 a.m. to noon on Saturdays). At the end of each term there were examination scripts to mark, occupying both of them for 'at least two nights', in Professor Dixon's estimation, and in the weeks before the Conjoint Board and London Second MB examinations they were heavily engaged in marking the students' test examinations. In addition Professor Dixon had deanly responsibilities to discharge, and it is hardly surprising that he considered the opportunities for engaging in research to be extremely limited.[39] Dixon took his obligations as dean very seriously. According to a writer in the college student magazine, 'Never were the students' forms filled up with such scrupulous care, nor the little troublesome details involved in the drawing up of the Medical Prospectus more ably done.'[40] His resignation in 1903, to return to Trinity College, Dublin as professor of anatomy in succession to his great mentor, D. J. Cunningham, though regretted, came as no surprise. He was succeeded as head of department by David Hepburn (1859–1931). A distinguished graduate of the University of Edinburgh and previously lecturer in regional anatomy at his alma mater under Sir William Turner, Hepburn was immediately appointed as dean of the medical school on his arrival, a position he would continue to occupy without interruption for the next nineteen years.[41]

The medical students were fortunate to encounter equally skilled and dedicated teachers in the Department of Physiology. Though indisposed for much of the 1898/9 session after an attack of hemiplegia, from which he made a remarkable recovery, John Berry Haycraft was regarded as a brilliant teacher and, time permitting, an able researcher. His attributes in this regard had been acclaimed at the time of his appointment to the chair, and in the following year he gave the prestigious Milroy Lectures of the Royal College of Physicians of London, on the controversial subject 'Darwinism and social progress'. Haycraft contributed articles on animal mechanics, the sense of taste and the sense of smell in Schafer's celebrated *Textbook of Physiology* (1900) and was, particularly during the 1890s, a regular contributor to the *Journal of Physiology* and other periodicals on a wide range of topics, including colour vision and the activity of the heart muscle. In this last sphere of research he worked closely with Donald Rose Paterson, who was not only a part-time lecturer in the medical school, but a busy clinician in the hospital, thereby representing an early example of the sort of preclinical/clinical collaboration which would later become commonplace in the full medical school.[42] The department's first assistant lecturer, appointed in 1898, was Mr (later Professor) S. C. Mahalanobis, who returned to Calcutta in 1900, where he founded Presidency College, the first science college in India.[43] He was succeeded, for three years, by Thomas Swale Vincent, a pioneer in the study of the function of the endocrine glands, who made a great impression on the young Thomas Lewis, and went on to become professor of physiology at the Middlesex Hospital, London.[44]

The beginning of the next decade saw a modest increase in the academic strength of both the departments of anatomy and physiology, the result (as will be noted in the following chapter) of new Treasury funding, a clear indication that the Cardiff Medical School was achieving its main objective after less than twenty years' existence. Indeed, the year 1910 represented something of a milestone in the development of the medical school, for in that year one of the three members of the academic staff of the Department of Physiology, R. L. Mackenzie Wallis, acquired an additional title, that of lecturer in physiological chemistry. Although the essence of what later came to be known as biochemistry had been taught in the department's chemical physiology classes from the outset, Wallis's new title showed that in the context of the history of biochemistry as an academic discipline, Cardiff was very much in the mainstream of universities and ahead of schools such as Sheffield and Leeds.[45]

Information gleaned from the college *Calendar* for the 1909/10 session indicates that by then some 102 students of the school had received their preclinical training in Cardiff before proceeding elsewhere (mainly to London) to receive their clinical training. Most (sixty-two) had obtained a medical qualification from the Conjoint Board of the Royal Colleges of Physicians and Surgeons (MRCS LRCP) or from the Society of Apothecaries (LSA) alone. Twenty-two had obtained a university degree alone, and a further eighteen had obtained both. Of the forty students possessing a university degree, twenty-eight had the London MB BS, seven had qualified in Edinburgh and two in Glasgow, one in Cambridge, while two appear to have secured a degree from mainland Europe.

In December 1910, on the occasion of his eighty-ninth birthday, the venerable Dr W. T. Edwards, still an active vice-president of the college, gave an interview to the *South Wales Daily News*:

> 'You were the pioneer of the Medical School, Dr Edwards?' The doctor closed his eyes. 'I wanted every Welsh boy to get the fullest opportunity to study medicine at home.'[46]

It is hardly surprising therefore that virtually all Cardiff's aspiring medical students had originated in Wales (as did 96 per cent of all of the college's students in those days). The college *Calendar* for 1909/10 contains a list of nineteen Cardiff preclinical students who had obtained certificates of merit for distinguished work during the practical anatomy course in 1907/8, a fair cross-section of the whole cohort. Only two of these students came from outside Wales (from Tunbridge Wells and Portrush); the other seventeen all hailed from south and west Wales (including the author's great-uncle, David Henry Griffiths of Lletycaru, a farm near Carmarthen, later to become a respected general practitioner in Cross Hands).

What the college *Calendar* for 1909/10 also reveals is that 63 per cent of Cardiff's ex-medical students had returned to practise in Wales, with 16 per cent choosing to work in London, 14 per cent working elsewhere in England and the remaining 7 per cent working overseas, mainly in South Africa. A study of their subsequent careers, as shown in later editions of the *Medical Directory*, indicates that in the longer term nearer 50 per cent of Cardiff's preclinical students settled permanently in Wales, 30 per cent in provincial England and 20 per cent in London. The *Calendar* also shows that, despite the optimism expressed in the mid-1890s, only five of Cardiff's ex-students were women, and it is worth listing these intrepid pioneers here:

> Phillips, Mary Elizabeth MB BS Lond, 1900
> Williams, Henrietta Leila Delfield MB BS Lond, 1903
> Bennett, Victoria Evelyn May MB BS Lond, 1904, LSA 1903
> Shields, Ida Russel MB BS Lond, 1905
> Powell, Laura Gertrude MB BS Lond, LSA 1908.

All pursued their clinical training at the London School of Medicine for Women, the only school in the metropolis open to women medical students at that time.[17]

FROM CARDIFF TO LONDON

The departure of Cardiff's preclinical students to pastures new did not mean that the college lost interest in their subsequent progress. Each year the college *Calendar* would devote several pages to recording the successes of ex-Cardiff students in the clinical examinations of the University of London, the Scottish universities, the Royal Colleges of Physicians and Surgeons and the Society of Apothecaries. Notable achievements were given due prominence, the *Calendar* for 1900/1, for instance, announcing:

> T. L. Llewellyn has gained the Tuke Silver Medal in Pathology and Bacteriology at University College, London.

A. E. Jones has gained the Fellowes Silver Medal in Clinical Medicine at University
College, London.

C. J. Thomas has gained the Lawrence Gold Medal and Scholarship at St
Bartholomew's Hospital.

R. B. Kinloch has obtained a college prize in pharmacology at St Thomas's Hospital.

The clinical students, primarily London-based, were similarly keen to retain their
links with their alma mater. By 1899 there were about forty 'Old Cardiffians' studying
in the metropolis, and the autumn of that year saw the establishment of an annual
dinner, held at the Horse Shoe Hotel at the corner of Tottenham Court Road, and
presided over by Professor Alfred Hughes. According to one of those who attended,
'one of the chief features was the entering of the names of all present in a very hand-
somely got-up Album, which Professor Hughes bought for the purpose, and which is
to be produced every year at the dinner.'[48] The second 'annual dinner of Cardiff
medicals in London', postponed until March 1901 because of the death of Professor
Hughes, attracted thirty-six participants, including six members of the resident staff
of the London teaching hospitals, and Professor A. F. Dixon, dean of the Cardiff
Medical School. In November 1901, a correspondent to the Cardiff students' magazine
wrote with eager anticipation about the imminence of the third annual dinner:

> The Annual Old Cardiff Medicals' Dinner is already being talked about, and is
> expected to come off sometime during the beginning of December, when there will
> be the usual discussions. Firstly – Which hospital is going to win the Footer Cups? –
> Cardiff men playing a prominent part in football at their respective Hospitals, this
> being especially so at Mary's, three old Cardiff men being in the Soccer XI, and two
> in the Rugger XV; and, Secondly – which is the best Hospital? – Each man sticking up
> for his own, of course.[49]

Indeed, the Cardiff students' magazine was, for several years round the turn of the
century, a useful source of news about the activities of ex-Cardiff students based in
London, many of whom apparently lived in the vicinity of Russell Square: 'That
neighbourhood swarms with us, and a caller at Doughty Street or Grenville Square
would hear a good deal of Medical gossip.'[50] Some of the most prominent clinical
students, including Ernest Jones, and two former presidents of the Cardiff Students'
Representative Council, B. G. Fiddian and Herbert Septimus Ward, would send occasional letters to the magazine, reporting on the academic and sporting achievements
of their London colleagues and on their perspective on life as clinical students.
January 1899 found Ward, a fourth-year student at St Bartholomew's Hospital,
reporting on the events of Christmas and the New Year:

> If there's one thing that makes one long for the old times at Cardiff, it is the length –
> or rather shortness – of our Christmas vacation. In place of a leisurely three weeks or

so, we are lucky if we are able to get as many days. If you cannot get any 'keen' man to do your work for you, you get no holidays at all, as one appointment ends on December 31st, and the next one begins on January 1st. Of course, if you do stay up, you get some fun at the Hospital.

On Christmas Day, but on Boxing Day this year, the patients are regaled with tea in the wards, which are generally decorated for the occasion. I mean of course a special tea. They are also entertained with songs and 'bigaphone bands', more or less musical. Then in the New Year, the Hospital entertainment takes place. This, at Barts, is given by the Dramatic and Orchestral Societies. Three performances were given, on the 4th, 5th and 6th of January. The first to the patients, the others to the medical and nursing staffs and visitors. These were given in our Great Hall, of which we are very proud. On the staircase the entire wall is covered by two paintings of Hogarth, which are very famous.[51]

A year later, Ernest Jones was pleased to report that 'the Cardiff men at the hospitals are holding their own well'. His own, University College Hospital, although among the smallest of the London teaching hospitals,

has the largest number of Cardiffians and is rapidly becoming the centre for old Cardiffians in London. The cosmopolitan character may be illustrated by the fact that only yesterday I was at a class in which the teacher and seven students were Welsh, five Americans, three Hindoos, and no member of any other country.[52]

On the other hand, six years later, Barts appeared to be the most popular destination for the Cardiff students. The fact was, as another correspondent reported in 1901, 'There is not a hospital now which does not claim one of us, and scarcely a hospital – certainly not of note – which is not represented on the resident staff, by at least one alumnus of Cardiff.'[53]

While it was natural for the correspondence published in the students' magazine to concentrate on the social and sporting aspects of life in the metropolis, it was equally predictable that students' letters home tended to emphasize more scholarly pursuits, particularly those from Thomas Lewis, a clinical student at University College Hospital. 'Every day is more or less the same; one or two lectures and the rest of the time wards and operations. I saw Victor Horsley do two of his famous brain operations last week; he is exceedingly smart, using both hands equally well.' A few weeks later he told his mother of a good term's work: 'I have managed to pick up a good deal this term, more particularly of Medicine', adding, sadly, 'Two of our patients died the other night, and three more will not last long. So many hopeless cases come in.'[54]

IN TIME OF WAR

It is a truism that the First World War had a profound impact on all aspects of British life, not least on the place of women in society. As men in their millions answered the call to arms, initially as volunteers, later as conscripts, women stepped into the breach on all fronts. In July 1915 Whitehall witnessed the impressive sight of 30,000 women on parade chanting 'We want to serve', and in a short while women were taking their place in offices and factories all over the land. A. J. P. Taylor records how 200,000 entered government departments, while over twice as many secured work in private offices. Women became conductors on buses and trams and a quarter of a million found employment on the land. Nearly 800,000 were recruited into the engineering trades. As Taylor would later conclude, the coming of the war 'was a decisive moment in women's emancipation'.[55] The desire to serve manifested itself in other ways too. Women determined to 'do their bit' flocked in their thousands to join organizations such as the Women's Army Auxiliary Corps, the Women's Royal Naval Service and the Voluntary Aid Detachment, also demonstrating that women could contribute far more to the life of the country than men had hitherto been prepared to concede.[56] Indeed, as early as December 1914 a group of men as conservative as the Medical Board of Cardiff's King Edward VII Hospital were recorded as voting unanimously in favour of the principle 'of the employment of Women Residents as a temporary measure in the present Emergency'.[57]

This resolution reflected the prevailing concern that the country was facing a serious shortage of doctors. *The Lancet* articulated this concern in the spring of 1915:

> Among the cataclysmic results of the war is a shortage of doctors necessary to meet the needs not only of the army and navy, but of civil practice, hospital work, the health department, and other non-military public services. Moreover, the shortage in the immediate future is likely to increase rather than to diminish, for not only are many junior students interrupting their curriculum to go to the front in various capacities, but there is also a marked fall in numbers of those entering for a medical career, so that there will necessarily be a falling off of graduates some six years hence. This future shortage, even more than the present deficiency, forms a powerful justification for an increase in the number of women students of medicine.[58]

A changing perception of the role of women, combined with fears of a shortage of doctors, led to a significant increase in the number of women students in medical schools as the war progressed. For the first time, even some of the London medical schools, albeit rather tentatively, joined the London School of Medicine for Women in opening their doors to women students.[59] In Cardiff, after a decade during which the annual number of new female registrations had averaged no more than one or two, five women registered for the first time in 1915, fourteen in 1916 sixteen in 1917 and twenty in 1918. In the 1917/18 session, one-third of Cardiff's medical students were women. Indeed, early in 1917, Cardiff's principal, E. H. Griffiths, was reported as attending a meeting of the City of Cardiff building and sites committee in order to encourage the authority to improve the facilities for teaching practical elementary physics at the Cardiff High School for Girls. 'He said the matter was urgent because the number of girl students intending to enter the medical profession was steadily increasing.'[60]

It was hardly coincidental that February 1916 saw the establishment, in Wales, of a General Committee for the Promotion of Medical Training of Women. Consisting of representatives of the University of Wales and its constituent colleges and other educationalists, its prime aim was to help women medical students who had pursued their preclinical studies in Cardiff and who might need financial help during their clinical years of training, wherever these were pursued. While the president of the committee was Lord Kenyon (1864–1927), senior deputy chancellor of the University of Wales, the chairman of the executive committee and driving force was Daniel (later Sir Daniel) Lleufer Thomas (1863–1940), junior deputy chancellor of the University, stipendiary magistrate for Pontypridd and the Rhondda (he was a central figure during the Cambrian Combine strike of 1910) and a major force in Welsh public life. The honorary secretary of the committee was Miss Mabel Howell, a niece of the founder of Howell's Stores, Cardiff's leading department store, and honorary treasurer of, and generous benefactor to, Cardiff College's women's hall of residence, Aberdare Hall.[61]

The concern expressed in some quarters regarding a serious fall-off of medical students during the war was not, in fact, entirely borne out in Cardiff. To be sure, a number of men students left their studies to serve in the armed forces, but nowhere near the fifty reported in the local press in 1915. The number of men entrants to the first year, twenty-three in 1914, rose to thirty in 1915 and thirty-one in 1916, so that in December 1916 the number of medical students in Cardiff, men and women, stood at over seventy, a number larger than in almost any other medical school in the country.[62]

Some of the students of this period would later achieve great distinction in their profession. There was Clement Price Thomas (1893–1973), a merchant's son from Abercarn, Monmouthshire. Having completed his first year in Cardiff during 1913/14, he was one of those who interrupted his studies to join the army, serving as a private in the Thirty-second Field Ambulance of the RAMC in Gallipoli, Macedonia and Palestine, before resuming his course in Cardiff in 1917/18. In 1919, having won the Alfred Hughes Memorial Prize Medal, he went to the Westminster Hospital Medical School for his clinical training, qualifying in 1921. He would later win recognition as one of the world's finest thoracic surgeons. In 1951, after performing a successful thoracotomy on King George VI, he was created KCVO, and in 1958 he was appointed president of the Welsh National School of Medicine, a position he would hold until 1970. Another talented wartime student was Francis Davies (1897–1965), a

Merthyr boy who, having spent two years as a pupil teacher, when he received 'training in the art of teaching', pursued his preclinical studies in Cardiff from 1917 until 1920, winning the Alfred Sheen Prize in 1919. He qualified from University College Hospital, London in 1922, beginning a university career which culminated in his appointment as professor of anatomy in the University of Sheffield in 1935. There he would gain much satisfaction as co-editor of the thirty-second (centenary) and thirty-third editions of *Gray's Anatomy*. Another wartime Cardiff student, who would later achieve great success as a surgeon, was Ivor Lewis (1896–1982), a farmer's son from Llanddeusant, Carmarthenshire. Having studied at Cardiff between 1915 and 1918, he too undertook his clinical training at University College Hospital, and after distinguished service in London he returned to Wales where he established a formidable surgical reputation at the Royal Alexandra Hospital, Rhyl and at other centres in north Wales. He served for many years as an influential member of the Welsh Regional Hospital Board and became founder president of the Welsh Surgical Society, as well as gaining admission to the Gorsedd of Bards of the National Eisteddfod of Wales.[63]

Professor David Hepburn had an extremely busy war. He continued to fulfil his teaching commitments. Furthermore, not only was he dean of the medical school; he was also, as Lieutenant Colonel Hepburn, the commanding officer of the Third Western General Hospital, which was what elements of the King Edward VII Hospital plus several converted schools became in order to care for wounded soldiers.[64] Only in respect of his attendance at Senate did Hepburn allow his dedication to duty to flag somewhat. In the pre-war years his attendance record, 83 per cent, had been exemplary, demonstrating a laudable commitment to the wider affairs of the college, the vice-principal of which he had been in 1908/9. During the war years, however, Hepburn managed to attend only five out of a possible sixty-six meetings of the Senate. War service ensured that Professor Emrys-Roberts, another regular attender of Senate before the war, did not attend once between 1915 and 1918, though John Berry Haycraft managed to put in an appearance on twenty-one occasions, thereby ensuring that the voice of the medical school was not entirely silent. However, it is worth adding that the affairs of the medical school by no means dominated the proceedings of the Senate, either before or during the war. Apart from presenting a brief report on student admissions to the medical school each autumn, and addressing occasional acts of indiscipline performed by the medical students, the dean rarely had anything else to say. Unlike the deans of the Faculties of Arts and Science, who regularly presented formal reports from their faculties, the dean of medicine hardly ever submitted a report to the Senate from the Faculty of Medicine as such, the first occasion being as late as 6 November 1914, when matters of a wholly routine nature were communicated.

From time to time during the war years, the local newspapers would report on the successes of former students of the medical school, notably the award of the London

MD to Dr Laura Gertrude Powell, who, with Dorothy Cochrane Logan, became, in 1916, the first ex-Cardiff woman doctor to hold this qualification. Having done her preclinical training in Cardiff, Powell had proceeded to the Royal Free Hospital, qualifying with the London MB in 1908. Described by the *Western Mail* as an ardent Welsh nationalist, she was, at the beginning of 1917, working as a medical inspector with the Monmouthshire Education Committee.[65] Another ex-Cardiff woman student, indeed the first woman medical student from the college to qualify as a doctor, Mary Elizabeth Phillips, was hailed for the distinction of her war work, serving as a doctor with the Scottish Women's Hospitals (SWH) on the Western Front, in Serbia, Salonika and Corsica (acting for several months as the organization's chief medical officer there), in between visits home to engage in fund-raising speaking tours. At the end of the war it was reported in the *British Medical Journal* that King George V had granted her 'unrestricted permission' to wear the insignia of the Fourth Class of the Order of St Sava, conferred upon her by the king of Serbia in recognition of her services with the SWH in Serbia. After the war, as Mrs Eppynt-Phillips, she served for several years as assistant medical officer of health in Merthyr Tydfil, among other things initiating a nurse training scheme for Serbian girls.[66] Charles Jennings Marshall, who had enjoyed an outstanding undergraduate career in Cardiff and at Charing Cross Hospital before the war, before becoming surgical registrar at that hospital, spent much of the first half of the war in the Anglo-Russian Field Hospital on the Lutzk front. Returning home on leave in late 1916, he spent his leisure time studying for the London Mastership in Surgery, securing the All-England Gold Medal in the process. In later life he would become one of London's leading surgeons, with an address in Harley Street.[67]

Pride of place, however, must go to the quite brilliant Thomas Lewis, by now head of the Department of Clinical Research at University College Hospital, whose pioneering cardiological research earned him the Fellowship of the Royal Society while the war was still in progress. The award of the FRS delighted Principal E. H. Griffiths, as can be seen in a letter he wrote to Professor Hepburn:

> I wish through you to convey to the Medical School my congratulations on the high honour conferred on the School by the selection of Thomas Lewis by the Council of the Royal Society for election into that body. Not only is Lewis the first student of this College to receive this honour, but I believe I am correct in saying that he is the first graduate of the University of Wales … You know what such an election means, and that it is an extraordinary high honour to be conferred on so young a man.[68]

It was right that the Cardiff Medical School should bask in the reflected glory of Thomas Lewis, for, as we have seen, it had a solid record of achievement to proclaim. However, as the next chapter will describe, its ambitions were by no means confined to the preclinical sphere.

3

Towards a Full Medical School

Though initially established in 1893 as a preclinical school, it was always envisaged that the Cardiff Medical School would eventually become, in the parlance of the time, a 'full medical school', offering clinical as well as preclinical instruction. As has been described in the previous chapter, within a year of the school's opening it had entered into an arrangement with the Glamorganshire and Monmouthshire Infirmary whereby suitable preclinical students would spend time in its wards and clinics to gain experience of the hospital environment. When asked by the hospital authorities, in 1898, whether there was an early intention to establish a full medical school, the College Council responded positively, attributing any delay to a lack of funds.[1] Funding was undoubtedly an issue, and one which was addressed with some success in the years leading up to the outbreak of the First World War, thanks partly to the intervention of a remarkably generous local benefactor and partly to the decision of the government, in 1908, to provide state funding to medical schools for the first time. Thanks to Sir Donald MacAlister, president of the GMC, the Cardiff Medical School became an early beneficiary of this new policy.

Identity was another issue. Traditionally, most medical students in England and Wales, wherever they were trained, eventually qualified with the Conjoint Board qualification or the London medical degree. In their formative years the university colleges cherished their close association with London University, but as they matured they sought to lessen their dependence on this institution.[2] During the years around the turn of the century university colleges in the English provinces trans-formed themselves into universities with the right to award their own medical degrees. It was in this context that steps were taken to ensure that students at the full medical school in Cardiff, when established, would be able to graduate with the MB B.Ch. of the University of Wales. Sir Isambard Owen, senior deputy-chancellor of the University of Wales, deserves the credit for this, and for the decision to develop the expanding medical school as close as possible to the King Edward VII Hospital rather than a mile away with the rest of the college.

What sort of school would the full medical school be? To the leading medical educa-tional reformer of the day, Sir William Osler, regius professor of medicine at Oxford University, the exciting thing about the Cardiff Medical School was that it was new, and lacked the traditions and vested interests which surrounded all the other schools in the United Kingdom. Cardiff would be the perfect place to establish a central feature of his beloved Johns Hopkins School of Medicine, the 'clinical unit' system, in this country. Flattered to receive the close attention of such a distinguished man, those planning the introduction of the full medical school in Cardiff were unlikely to take a different view.

THE SCHOOL BROADENS ITS REMIT

In the spring of 1900 University College, Cardiff and its medical school took a significant step in bringing their activities directly in touch with the health and welfare of the local community with the establishment of a new department of hygiene and public health, and appointing as part-time lecturers Edward Walford, medical officer of health for Cardiff, and William Williams, who held the same post in the county of Glamorgan. As has already been noted, the local authorities in Cardiff, led by men like H. J. Paine, had, during the second half of the nineteenth century, achieved much to transform Cardiff from the wretched town of the Rammell Report to a more comfortable, indeed elegant, town. The death toll fell by half during this period, with particularly dramatic improvements in the incidence of infant mortality, with Cardiff ranked fourth lowest of any town of comparative size in the United Kingdom.[3]

However, there was much more to be done. Though Cardiff's achievements in the field of public health were a cause for satisfaction it could hardly rest on its laurels. Its position as a rapidly expanding seaport, enjoying trading links with all corners of the world, also made it vulnerable to potentially serious challenges requiring a rapid local response.[4] As Professor John Berry Haycraft, then dean of the medical school and a keen supporter of the cause of public health, once reminded a sceptical member of the Cardiff Corporation who believed that the needs of south Wales could be perfectly well handled from London, 'Suppose a vessel comes into dock from an infected district, we could have a thorough examination without causing any delay. This would be of much advantage to the port.'[5] As far as Haycraft, wearing his academic hat, was concerned there was an urgent need for proper facilities in Cardiff, which would not only enable the routine public health work of the district to be carried on, but which would also provide opportunities for study and training, a sentiment which attracted the strong endorsement of Joseph, Baron Lister, the eminent surgeon and pioneer of antisepsis.[6] Though it took over twenty years for state-of-the-art academic facilities to be funded and built in Cardiff, a start was made in 1900, as the education issue of the *British Medical Journal* for that year proclaimed:

> The Cardiff Corporation and the Glamorgan County Council have placed their public health laboratory at the disposal of the College for teaching purposes. Medical men from Cardiff and the neighbourhood wishing to prepare for a Diploma in Public Health can now take complete courses of Lectures and Laboratory work in

this department and study outdoor sanitary work under the Medical Officer of Health, Cardiff Urban and Port districts, or under the Medical Officer of health to the Glamorgan County Council.[7]

As we shall shortly see, not many years would elapse before the department offered its own postgraduate diploma under the aegis of the University of Wales.

In the autumn of 1904 the medical school further demonstrated its commitment to serving the health needs of the local community by responding positively to a plea from the Cardiff branch of the BMA that the college should provide facilities for the training of midwives in compliance with the terms of the Midwives Act of 1902. The local authorities, which were legally responsible for ensuring that the act was being properly implemented, were only too willing to support the provision of suitable training facilities and established a number of student grants (seven by Glamorgan County Council, three by the Cardiff Corporation, later increased to twelve), and agreed to meet some of the running costs. Thirty-eight students enrolled for the inaugural course in October 1904, the principal lecturer being Dr Ewen Maclean, the senior gynaecologist at the Cardiff Infirmary. In the following years numbers would average about eighty, a third of the students residing in Cardiff, as Edward Walford would observe in his annual report to the Cardiff Corporation as medical officer of health.[8]

Encouraging though these developments were, a number of steps had to be taken before a full medical school could come into existence in Cardiff, four in particular. The charter of the University of Wales had to be amended to enable the university to confer degrees in medicine and surgery; suitable clinical facilities would be required to enable students to be trained in Cardiff beyond the first three years of the medical course; thirdly, adequate resources would need to be provided, both in terms of funding and accommodation; last, but by no means least, agreement would be necessary on the status of the school, when finally established. The rest of this chapter deals with the first three of these issues.

THE QUEST FOR DEGREE-AWARDING POWERS

It has already been noted how Isambard Owen, main architect of the charter and statutes of the University of Wales, had advised in 1893, that it would be fruitless, at that stage, when no medical school of any sort was in being for the university to apply for degree-awarding powers in medicine. However, by 1904, some twenty years after the opening of the medical school, Sir Isambard (he had been knighted in 1902 for his services to the university) believed that the time was now right to take the matter forward. One of Sir Isambard Owen's less onerous but clearly pleasurable tasks as senior deputy chancellor of the University of Wales during this period, was to write regularly to the private secretary of the Prince of Wales, in his capacity as chancellor of the university, to keep him informed of university matters. Most of the letters dealt with matters of little real consequence: student numbers, staff distinctions, resolutions passed at meetings of the Court and other committees. Occasionally he would mention Cardiff's excellent medical students, 'who have already carried off several high honours in the University of London and gained a number of Open Scholarships at the London hospitals'.[9] However, in May, 1904 Owen wrote to inform Sir Arthur Bigge (and through him the Prince of Wales) that he now considered it appropriate for the University of Wales to seek, via a supplemental charter, power to confer degrees in medicine and surgery, 'whether we have immediate need to use it or not',[10] a move which the influential Sir John Williams fully endorsed: 'It is not fair to students that they are obliged to go elsewhere for a degree in medicine, and it is not fair to the University, for it is deprived of the credit which would accrue to it from a distinguished body of medical graduates.'[11] It should be remembered that in the very recent past a number of provincial universities had secured charters granting the right to confer medical degrees on their own students, including Birmingham in 1900, and the universities of Leeds, Liverpool and Manchester following the dissolution of Victoria University in 1903.

On 13 August 1906 the Privy Council approved the supplemental charter which gave the University of Wales the right to confer degrees in medicine and surgery. It took a further year for the university, led by Sir Isambard Owen and advised by Dr Donald MacAlister, president of the General Medical Council, to draft supporting statutes, but when these were submitted by the Privy Council for the GMC's endorsement, in November 1907, MacAlister could not have been more complimentary. 'Liverpool has sometimes been described as the English metropolis of Wales. But signs are not wanting that, in the matter of medical education, at least, Wales may soon be ready to establish a national centre on its own soil.' He drew particular attention to the fact that the medical degree of the University of Wales would only be awarded after six years' study, during the course of which all candidates would be required to obtain an appropriate qualifying science degree from the University of Wales or another approved university. Taken together, these features made the Wales medical degree unique in the United Kingdom. MacAlister summed up: 'The ambition of the University of Wales to establish for its alumni professional degrees implying not only qualification, but distinction in medicine, deserves, in my opinion, our official encouragement.'[12]

MacAlister rightly referred to the uniqueness of the Wales medical degree regulations. At six years in length the Wales degree course, when implemented, would be the longest in the country, a year longer than the minimum laid down by the GMC. Moreover, to be eligible to sit the final examinations, Welsh degree students had to obtain a Wales B.Sc. degree on the way. Sir Isambard Owen, chairman of the university committee which had formulated the regulations, was determined to steer as many Cardiff students as possible away from opting for the London degree qualification by offering an alternative qualification which was quite distinctive. He robustly defended the university's scheme in the face of some opposition from members of the University Court who considered the B.Sc. hurdle to be an unnecessary imposition. He made his position clear in a letter to the university registrar:

> There was, of course, a view, which found expression in the Court when the matter was discussed, that the University of Wales should aim at establishing not a first class degree, but a 'cheap' degree for the 'ordinary man'. Such a course, I need hardly point out, would be suicidal and the result would inevitably be that the good Cardiff student would wish to take the London degree, and leave the Welsh degree to be the badge of the inferior man.[13]

However, possession of a medical degree from the University of Wales did not, of itself, confer the right of registration with the GMC. This required a separate Act of Parliament. Here too, despite his many competing commitments, Sir Isambard's practical advice to a university registrar, sorely in need of help, was invaluable. By now vice-chancellor of Bristol University, Owen wrote to Dr Mortimer Angus at the end of 1910:

> I think you have a copy of the University of Bristol calendar? On page 99 etc you will find the University of Bristol Act. Clauses 7 and 8 are those which would be embodied in the University of Wales Act, and I think clause 12 ought also to be inserted ...[14]

Within a year the University of Wales (No. 2) Bill 'to define and enlarge the rights of graduates in medicine in the University of Wales' had been passed (piloted through the House of Commons by Sir D. Brynmor Jones MP, the brother of Viriamu), which made the medical degrees of the University of Wales qualifications registrable with the GMC. Dr Angus explained the significance of this in a letter to the fourth Baron Kenyon of Gredington, who had recently succeeded Sir Isambard Owen as senior deputy chancellor of the University of Wales, and one of the sponsors of the bill in the House of Lords:

> Medical degrees are conferred not only by the older Universities of Oxford and Cambridge, Durham and London, and the Scottish Universities, but by the newer English Provincial Universities, Manchester, Liverpool, Leeds, Birmingham and Bristol, and in all these cases the degrees carry registrable qualification. The University of Wales stands alone in having power to grant degrees which do not entitle this privilege. The Parliamentary Bill is for the purpose of removing this disability. I think it might fairly be urged that, subject to due safeguards being secured as to the standard of the degrees, registrable qualification should be

attached to them on the ground that it is only fair (1) to the student that he should receive this substantial reward for his work and that the degree should not be reduced to an empty honour; and (2) to the Medical School, that its development should not be hampered by having to compete at such disadvantage with other Medical Schools.[15]

Passage of the Act also enabled (by now) Sir Donald MacAlister, at the opening of the ninety-fifth session of the GMC on 4 June 1912, to welcome Professor David Hepburn, dean of the medical school in Cardiff, to his first meeting as the representative of the University of Wales: 'The Council will follow with interest the progress of the movement towards higher professional education to which, with a laudable ambition to excel, the Welsh nation has thus committed itself.'[16]

Hepburn's appointment to the GMC was made by the Court of the University of Wales on the recommendation of the University Medical Board, a body established in the university statutes to advise the university authorities on all matters pertaining to the University of Wales degrees in medicine and surgery and any other medically-related qualifications. With practical medical expertise in the university largely confined at this time to the professors of anatomy and physiology (and from 1910 pathology) at University College, Cardiff, the Medical Board, chaired by the vice-chancellor of the day, was augmented by such distinguished knights of the realm as Isambard Owen, John Williams and Donald MacAlister and, to suit their convenience, the board met, on occasion, at the offices of the Royal College of Physicians in London.[17] However, during most of its existence, from 1908 to 1919, the board usually met, once a year, in Cardiff, its meetings attended by the professors of anatomy, physiology and pathology and one or two others, to transact fairly routine business, principally the appointment of examiners for degree schemes and the drafting of detailed regulations for the MB B.Ch. degrees and for the university postgraduate Diploma in Public Health, initiated in 1908. Very occasionally controversial issues were addressed, such as the time when Sir Isambard Owen intervened to block a move to amend the MB B.Ch. regulations by rescinding the requirement for candidates for the Wales degree to obtain a B.Sc. degree on the way.

In reality, this issue was more or less academic. During the first years of the existence of the Wales medical degree, very few students considered becoming candidates for it. It only became a registrable qualification in 1912 and, in the years that followed, virtually all Cardiff preclinical students chose to sit for the qualification offered by the medical school where they were pursuing their clinical studies. Indeed, the first occasion that anyone resolved to attempt the final medical examination of the University of Wales was in 1916, right in the middle of the war. Everyone was being urged to minimize unnecessary expenditure, as Professor E. H. Griffiths, in his capacity as vice-chancellor, explained to John Lynn Thomas, the eminent Cardiff surgeon, who was then junior deputy chancellor of the University of Wales:

Two students, G. F. Randall and W. Tudor Thomas, have signified their desire to sit for their examinations, the former probably in medicine only, the latter in all three subjects. As you are aware, the Lords Commissioners of the Treasury have urged upon the University the necessity for economy and suggested the cutting down of our expenditure in the coming Session. In these circumstances it is a very serious matter to face an expenditure which would probably exceed £150 for the sake of these two students. On the other hand, it would have a bad effect if the University at this stage in the history of the Medical School, declined to hold an examination; in fact I think we might possibly expose ourselves to legal proceedings.[18]

Lynn Thomas was a well-connected man, and at the meeting of the University Medical Board, in December 1915, the vice-chancellor was able to report that Thomas had recruited a galaxy of stars to serve as honorary (in other words, unpaid) external examiners in the final examinations, Sir James Kingston Fowler KCVO (medicine), Sir Alfred Pearce Gould KCVO, vice-chancellor of the University of London (surgery), and Sir Francis Henry Champneys Bt (obstetrics). Both G. F. Randall and J. W. Tudor Thomas took the whole examination. Although Randall managed to fail all three subjects, the other candidate passed, a result which made James William Tudor Thomas (1893–1976) the first person to obtain the MB B.Ch. of the University of Wales, several years before the establishment of a full medical school in Wales. This pioneer, born in Ystradgynlais and brought up in Carmarthenshire, had pursued his preclinical training in Cardiff, where he had won the Alfred Sheen prize before proceeding to the Middlesex Hospital for clinical studies, obtaining the Conjoint Board diploma in 1915. He was to serve as ophthalmic surgeon at the Cardiff Royal Infirmary from 1921 until 1958, during which time he established himself as one of the world's foremost authorities in the field of corneal grafting, for which he was awarded a knighthood in 1956.[19]

Four other students, three of them women, graduated with the degrees of MB B.Ch. of the University of Wales, after pursuing clinical studies in London, before 1924:[20]

1921	Florence Janetta Humphreys
	Helena Webster
1922	Eroica Rowe Lewis
	David John Jones

By this time the other medically related qualification offered by the University of Wales, the postgraduate Diploma in Public Health, was well established. After several years during which Cardiff College's Department of Hygiene and Public Health had provided training to enable public health doctors to obtain one of the several diplomas offered elsewhere in the country, in 1908 the University Medical Board approved a scheme for a diploma offered by the department itself. The course was highly regarded by the students,[21] and June 1910 saw the award of the DPH (Wales), for the first time, to three students: Elizabeth Fleming Elder, Evan John Griffiths and Manec Bujorji Patel. Unfortunately, again displaying some unfamiliarity with medically related procedures, the university registrar omitted to have the diploma accredited by the GMC and it took two years of anxious correspondence between Dr Angus and the registrar of the GMC to regularize matters, by which time there were five holders of an essentially useless qualification. One can only imagine Mortimer Angus's relief to receive Norman King's formal letter confirming the registration of the diploma by the GMC in June 1912: 'This decision is retrospective so that Diplomas granted before the passing of this Resolution are also registrable'.[22]

For completeness, it is worth noting that in 1912, the University of Wales, or at least its Medical Board, at the instigation of the dean of medicine, David Hepburn, briefly looked into the possibility of setting up a postgraduate Diploma in Psychological Medicine for registered medical practitioners. Hepburn argued that in its Departments of Anatomy, Physiology and Pathology the Cardiff College already possessed adequate expertise covering most of the course. All that was needed was to negotiate clinical placements with the authorities of the Cardiff Mental Hospital at Whitchurch. Doubtless conceding that such a venture was probably premature bearing in mind that a full medical school was not yet in existence, the Medical Board wisely decided to shelve the idea for the time being, and many decades were to elapse before such a proposal re-emerged.[23]

THE MEDICAL SCHOOL AND THE CLINICAL DIMENSION

Of all the preconditions necessary for a full medical school, access to appropriate clinical facilities was among the easiest for University College, Cardiff to demonstrate. In 1883 a brand-new state-of-the-art hospital was opened to replace the original Glamorganshire and Monmouthshire Infirmary which, as has already been noted, had, by the late nineteenth century, become incapable of satisfying the needs of a rapidly expanding, and increasingly sophisticated town. Using land leased from the third Marquess of Bute at a peppercorn rent of £15 per year the hospital opened with an initial complement of one hundred beds, with the capacity to expand as further resources came available. In the brochure produced for the foundation stone-laying ceremony, by the Marquess of Bute, on 31 January 1883, the architect described the building thus:

> The main building will consist of three blocks, connected by a central corridor, from which the two ward blocks for male and female patients will project north and south. Space for two smaller blocks is reserved on the eastern side of the site. Accommodation will be provided in the first instance for 102 beds in four chief

wards, two smaller and four special wards, each of which is to be ventilated and warmed by the most modern appliances. The administration block will form the chief front of the building parallel with Adamstown Road and the foundation stone which is being laid today will form the base of a buttress of the north side of the entrance doorway. The north wing of the upper floor of this block will be occupied by the apartments for the resident officers. The ground floor of the south wing will be occupied by the dispensary and the outpatient department. The architecture is that of the late Gothic period with a semi-domestic character.

The hospital continued to be known as the Glamorganshire and Monmouthshire Infirmary until 1895, when its name was changed to the Cardiff Infirmary, in acknowledgement of the fact that, three years earlier, the Newport and County Infirmary (the forerunner of the Royal Gwent Hospital) had adopted the name of Newport and Monmouthshire Infirmary, reflecting an expansion in its own catchment area.[24] The name of the hospital would change twice more in its history. Following the death of King Edward VII in 1910, the lord mayor of Cardiff launched a King Edward VII Memorial Fund in order to clear the hospital's debts and to raise money to extend the building. At the same time, King George V consented, in 1911, to the renaming of the hospital as the King Edward VII Hospital. In 1923, as a device for relieving its honorary treasurer of personal liability for the debts of the hospital, the institution became incorporated by royal charter and adopted the name of Cardiff Royal Infirmary.

As the years passed extensions were added to the Cardiff Infirmary in all directions, as finances, always tight, allowed. By the turn of the century the number of beds had increased to 188. By this time the hospital received an annual grant from the Cardiff Corporation, and benefited from a workmen's contributory scheme, whereby participating mines and factories deducted, first one, then two pence a week from their employees' wages, as well as receiving subscriptions from the public. However, the generosity of a small number of well-to-do philanthropists was crucial. Those donating £1,000 had wards named after them – Bute, Gwendolyne, Insole, Shand, Ware and Windsor. The greatest of them all was William James Thomas (1867–1945), arguably south Wales's most celebrated philanthropist before the First World War.[25] He had made a fortune in the coalfields of south Wales and, in many ways a humble man (he maintained a close connection with Saron Welsh Congregationalist chapel, Ynyshir for much of his life), he was determined to use his wealth to do good. Many hospitals throughout south Wales benefited from his generosity, not least the Cardiff Infirmary, where he endowed twenty beds at a cost of twenty guineas each, enabling the total number of beds in the hospital to reach 260 by the end of the decade. In May 1908 a notable milestone was reached in the development of the hospital with the opening, by Professor William Osler, regius professor of medicine at Oxford University and the most celebrated clinician in Britain at that time, of a new, state-of-the-art, out-patient department, and X-ray facility (quaintly known as the 'electrical pavilion'), financed in large part by another local benefactor, John Cory, the shipping magnate. This was not the first time that Osler had been among the members of the Cardiff medical community. In November 1905, not long after his appointment to Oxford, he had been guest of honour at a meeting of the Cardiff Medical Society, when he struck up a friendship with John Lynn Thomas, the society's president that year, which would last for many years. During his talk on the history of the Johns Hopkins Medical School, founded by a Welshman, Osler looked forward to the day when a full medical school was established in Cardiff. Three things were necessary: 'enthusiastic teachers, the true university spirit, and a good understanding between the men in the medical school and the medical men in the neighbourhood'.[26] Speaking at the opening of the out-patient department two and a half years later, when emphasizing the central importance of a good out-patient department in medical education, Osler observed with satisfaction that a room in the department had been specially devoted to teaching, demonstrating a good local spirit. He looked forward to the day when a full medical school was established in the city: 'There was no reason why in Cardiff, with its 180,000 inhabitants, they should not have in a few years as good a medical school as there was in the United Kingdom.'[27] In parallel with this development was the decision by the hospital to build, at the eastern end of the site, beyond the wards, a new three-storey pathology block consisting of a mortuary, autopsy room, a lecture theatre, clinical laboratories, a pathology museum and offices.[28]

Supporters of the establishment of a full medical school could only have been encouraged therefore by a report, written in 1909 by Sir Donald MacAlister, as part of a review conducted by a special Treasury committee, chaired by the distinguished lawyer Sir Thomas Raleigh, into the question of university funding in Wales. The significance of this review will be considered in more detail later, but relevant here is what MacAlister wrote about the clinical teaching facilities available in Cardiff to support a full medical school:

> In Cardiff the existing hospital accommodation is already quite sufficient to furnish forth such a Medical School, and it is in the process of enlargement. The arrangements are modern, and in many respects in advance of those in other provincial schools with which I am acquainted. The staff includes physicians, surgeons and specialists of distinction, who are fully qualified to instruct a large body of students in the several subjects of the final or qualifying examination. Provision has been made for the scientific study of morbid anatomy in connection with the hospital, which would be of great use to the Professor of Pathology in the College, if it were made accessible to him, as it doubtless is intended to be.
>
> Thus Medicine and Surgery might be taught, and well taught, to university students in an institution close to the college, so soon as the teaching staff is organised in connection with the latter. Eligible teachers and the needful material and equipment are at hand. I learn that the means for teaching to medical students the

final subject, namely Midwifery, are available, though at present these are used chiefly for the instruction of midwives. I understand that at Newport, which is within easy reach of Cardiff, further clinical facilities might be obtained in supplement of those I have mentioned.[29]

Such a glowing testimonial from a man with such influence was indeed gratifying, not least his observation about the high calibre of the hospital's clinical staff. As in all large voluntary hospitals at that time, the clinical staff were classified in three broad categories. At the head of the tree were the honorary physicians, honorary surgeons and honorary gynaecologists, below whom were the honorary assistant physicians, and so on. As their title suggests the holders of these appointments worked in the hospital in an unpaid capacity, for a defined period of time each week. Each of the honorary physicians and surgeons had control of a defined number of beds and an assistant was attached to each of them, to serve as their deputies when their chiefs were absent. Some of the assistants were responsible for running the out-patient department; indeed, until 1895 the assistant physicians and assistant surgeons had been known as medical officers for outdoor patients. For the remainder of the week the honorary clinical staff and their assistants worked in their consulting rooms (as likely as not located in their homes), as general practitioners, not in the modern sense of the term, but as generalists, the concept of specialization being in its infancy at that time. They received fees for these and other services provided for the local community, including the local courts where the doctors acted as medical referees. It was length of service that tended to differentiate the honorary physicians and surgeons from their honorary assistants; advancement was usually based on internal competition as vacancies occurred through death or retirement. It was therefore by no means unusual to find highly qualified and experienced doctors, with a substantial private practice, working as assistant physicians and surgeons well into their fifties. Below the honorary clinical staff and the honorary assistants were the resident medical staff, the house physicians and house surgeons, whose role has been defined thus by Arnold Aldis:

> He was in full-time employment and forbidden to engage in private practice or to receive any fees; and while he was responsible to the honorary physicians and surgeons to the Infirmary, within these restrictions he was monarch of all he surveyed, being in charge of the matron, the nurses, the domestics, porters and patients.[30]

At the time of the opening of the infirmary in 1883 there was only one resident medical officer, a house surgeon. By 1913 the number had grown to six and by 1923 to nine. In addition to the clinical staff already defined, the hospital had a number of 'elder statesmen', consulting physicians and surgeons who had left active service in the hospital, the retiring age at that time being defined in two ways, by reaching the age of sixty, or by serving as a full physician or surgeon for a period of twenty years.

Who were some of the infirmary's clinical staff who had made such a favourable impression on Sir Donald MacAlister? Undoubtedly the most distinguished among them was John Lynn Thomas (1861–1939), one of the hospital's three honorary surgeons. The Welsh-speaking son of a Llandysul farmer, Thomas was, at this time, both literally and metaphorically, a giant among the medical fraternity of Wales, massively built with a large head and a great shock of hair. Having trained at the London Hospital, he had returned to his homeland, becoming honorary surgeon at the Cardiff Infirmary in 1901, while enjoying a thriving practice in his rooms in Charles Street, specializing in the surgery of the thyroid and the prostate. Though capable of inspiring friendship, he was a combative character, with a penchant for engaging in litigation in connection with his professional work. In 1905 and 1906 he became embroiled in a costly, and celebrated, court case (Southern *v.* Lynn Thomas and Skyrme) when one of his patients, T. A. Southern, a Cardiff mining engineer, dissatisfied with his treatment for a broken arm two years previously, sued for damages and won, despite the best efforts of two of the leading barristers of the day, Samuel T. Evans and Rufus Isaacs. The medical community was outraged. Dr Hugh Jones of Dolgellau expressed the sentiments of many when he wrote: 'The feeling in North Wales amounts to a sense of horror at the result of this abominable persecution to which you have been subjected. I hardly know what things are coming to. We are all living at the edge of a precipice.' *The Lancet* took up the cudgels:

> Many of our readers have no doubt already received a statement of the case in which the pertinent question is asked: 'is a surgeon to be held culpable if after careful investigation he advises treatment which he considers the best even if different from all other methods previously adopted. The answer to this question is loudly and clearly 'No'. Such a surgeon must be held blameless whatever the issue. Every method of treatment embodying an advance must differ from methods either in usual practice or recommended in text-books, and to punish the surgeon for intelligent and thoughtful modifications of existing routine, or traditional technique, is simply to punish him for making progress in his science.

There was, as far as the medical profession was concerned, an important issue of principle involved here, and a national appeal was launched in 1908 to raise funds to meet the defendants' costs (£3,197, the Medical Defence Union having found the other £928). Among those signing the letter of appeal were the president of the BMA, the directors-general of the Army and Royal Navy Medical Services, William Osler, Sir John Williams, Sir Isambard Owen, the presidents of two royal colleges of surgeons, twelve professors of surgery, over two score senior surgeons from the London and provincial hospitals, seventeen leaders of the BMA in Wales and representatives of the four leading medical societies in Wales. The honorary treasurer of the appeal was Thomas's infirmary colleague, William Sheen. With such powerful support, which says much for the high esteem in which Lynn Thomas was held in the medical profession, it came as no surprise that the requisite funds were easily raised, *The Lancet* publishing lists of donors from time to time. He was regarded at home and abroad, particularly in the United States, as one of the finest 'provincial' surgeons in the United Kingdom, being ranked with such giants as Sir Berkeley Moynihan and Sir Robert Jones. The award of a knighthood in 1919 was greeted with general acclaim.[31]

Brief reference has already been made to Donald Rose Paterson, who had served the medical school well as part-time lecturer in materia medica from 1894 until 1906, while at the same time gaining recognition as one of Wales's most versatile clinicians. Appointed in 1891 as the infirmary's first honorary pathologist, four years later he became an assistant physician in the out-patient department. In the next few years Paterson developed an interest in laryngology and otology, and by the time of MacAlister's review he was establishing himself as an accomplished and indeed pioneering specialist in the discipline, with a growing international reputation. Indeed, having studied at the feet of Professor Killian at Freiburg, Paterson became, according to his obituarist, the first man in Britain to employ Killian's techniques in oesophagoscopy, bronchoscopy and other endoscopic procedures.[32] At this time the hospital's senior physician was Herbert Redwood Vachell (1853–1938), president of the Cardiff Medical Society in 1898, sometime chairman of the infirmary's Medical Board, and the last member of one of Cardiff's most distinguished medical families which had served the citizens of Cardiff for well over a century.[33] His place as senior physician at the hospital in 1913 would be taken by William Mitchell Stevens (1868–1944). Hailing from Cornwall, Stevens had enjoyed a brilliant undergraduate career at University College, London. Following junior hospital posts in Bristol and London, he settled in Cardiff in 1896, and, having become an honorary assistant physician in 1902, he steadily progressed up the tree of advancement. In 1906 he was appointed part-time lecturer in materia medica in the medical school in succession to Paterson (he had also applied in 1894 but missed the train on the way to the interview), not long afterwards demonstrating some of the angularity which characterized his later dealings with the academic authorities by attempting, unsuccessfully, to claim membership of the Senate of University College, Cardiff. In 1914 he would become the first member of the staff of the hospital ever to be elected a Fellow of the Royal College of Physicians of London.[34]

The senior surgeon in the hospital in the years before the war was Philip Rhys Griffiths (1857–1920), a passionate supporter of all things relating to the history and culture of Wales, a leading member of the Cardiff Naturalists' Society, sometime president of the Cardiff Medical Society and a warm supporter of the Cardiff Medical School.[35] The third honorary surgeon at this time was Alfred William Sheen (1869–1945), son of Alfred, one of the pioneers of the medical school. Appointed honorary surgeon to the infirmary in 1900, he would serve in that capacity until 1919.

In that year the hospital's rigid retirement rules would force him to seek alternative employment in London aged just over fifty years old, only to return to Cardiff two years later in another capacity.[36] The hospital's senior gynaecologist was Ewen Maclean (1865–1953). Born in Carmarthen and trained in Edinburgh, he had joined the staff of the infirmary in 1901, three years later demonstrating his commitment to education and training by initiating a highly successful course for midwives. Maclean was also a prominent member of the BMA nationally, and within a year of MacAlister's report, would be found leading the negotiations with the government over the introduction of its National Insurance Bill.[37]

Sir Donald MacAlister was right. The Cardiff Infirmary, during the early years of the twentieth century, was well served with talented, even distinguished, medical men well capable of supporting a full medical school in Cardiff. Moreover, relationships between them and the existing members of the medical school were amicable, as exemplified by the activities of the Cardiff Medical Society during the late Victorian and Edwardian period. It is fair to say that the society had not proved to be a particularly vigorous promoter of a medical school in Cardiff, no reference being made to the project in the minutes of the society's proceedings between 1886 and the autumn of 1893. However, at the opening of the school in October 1893 the society did invite the new professors of anatomy and physiology to become members, and although Professor Hughes seems only to have attended on one occasion, when he gave a demonstration of the movements of the spinal cord, Professor Haycraft proved to be a fairly regular attender. He gave lectures and demonstrations from time to time, and, as we shall see, he used the forum of the Cardiff Medical Society in 1911 to launch his campaign for a new Institute of Physiology by delivering a widely reported lecture on 'The Cardiff Medical School, a critical time'. On one occasion he shared the stage with Donald Rose Paterson, a notably prolific contributor to the society's proceedings over the years, presenting their joint research on the movement of the heart within the chest cavity. The minutes of the meeting recorded that 'several lantern slides were shown and the movements of the living frog's heart were also projected on the screen, thereby showing the alterations in the heart during systole and diastole and also the action of gravity on the apex movements'. Alfred Hughes's successors as professors of anatomy, Francis Dixon and David Hepburn, were regular attenders and presenters at meetings of the society, Dixon briefly serving on its executive committee and Hepburn as president during the 1910/11 session. The non-professorial academic staff also contributed to the activities of the society, among them Swale Vincent and R. L. Mackenzie Wallis from the Department of Physiology, and E. J. Evatt from the anatomy department. Although most of the society's meetings were held at its rooms in Queen Street, several took place in one or other of the medical school's lecture theatres, especially when large audiences were expected. In other words, the members of the Cardiff Medical School worked hard, in the years before the war, to follow the advice of William Osler, given at a meeting of the Cardiff Medical Society in 1905, to develop 'a good understanding between the men in the medical school and the medical men in the neighbourhood'.[38]

This did not mean that all of the hospital clinicians welcomed the prospect of being associated with a full medical school with equal enthusiasm, as was seen in an acrimonious debate in November 1913 about the professional qualifications that should be expected of future clinicians in an institution with aspirations to be a teaching hospital. In July of that year, by a majority, albeit narrow, of 8 to 6, the hospital's Medical Board, the body representing its senior clinicians, had voted in favour of the proposition that with effect from 1 January 1916, physicians and assistant physicians in the hospital should hold the membership or fellowship of the Royal College of Physicians of London, and the surgeons and assistant surgeons the fellowship of the Royal College of Surgeons of England.[39] As dean, David Hepburn strongly endorsed this step. London and many of the provincial teaching hospitals had already adopted such a rule. Why should Cardiff 'be the dumping ground for men whom the London hospitals won't take?'[40] Such a remark was bound to raise the hackles of traditionalists in the hospital, both professionals and laymen, and at a heated meeting of the hospital governors in November, they, led by the gynaecologist Tenison Collins, chided by Lynn Thomas as a man unable to pass his own professional qualifications,[41] rejected the proposal by a small majority, so that it took another twelve years for the rule to be adopted.

The meeting was chaired by Colonel Edwin Montgomery Bruce Vaughan (1856–1919), deputy chairman of what was now called the King Edward VII Hospital. Cardiff-born, he was one of Wales's most prolific architects, responsible for the design or restoration of over thirty churches, mostly in south Wales, and several other public buildings such as Llanelli Hospital and Aberystwyth Infirmary. As chairman of its house committee from 1903, he was a major figure in the expansion of the hospital, his persuasive tongue raising well over £100,000 for the purpose; indeed he revelled in the self-imposed title of 'beggar'. Appealing for funds to maintain the hospital during the ceremony at the opening of the out-patient department in 1908, he had proclaimed: 'May I once more appear in the role of beggar? I am proud of the title, as I have once before said, "for the Lord loveth a cheerful giver, and He also loveth a cheerful beggar".'[42] He was an enthusiastic supporter of the establishment of a full medical school in Cardiff, with his hospital playing a central partnership role and enjoying enhanced status as a result. Dismissing those of his hospital colleagues who seemed to be standing in the way of progress as motivated by 'selfish self-interest'[43] he, with John Lynn Thomas and Philip Rhys Griffiths, assisted David Hepburn to write a memorandum, 'Proposed completion of the Medical School', in preparation for a meeting between David Lloyd George, chancellor of the Exchequer, and representatives of the University of Wales, in the spring of 1914.[44]

Having described the history of the medical school hitherto and the glorious achievements of its past students ('it is claimed that no other medical school can show such a distinguished record'), the memorandum outlined the excellence of the clinical teaching facilities available in Cardiff: not only the King Edward VII Hospital, now accommodating 283 beds, but also the Seamen's (Royal Hamadryad) Hospital (56 beds), the Poor Law Hospital (200 beds but soon to be upgraded), the Glan Ely Hospital (tuberculosis, 120 beds), the Cardiff Mental Hospital (at Whitchurch, 750 beds), and the Cardiff Fever Hospital (168 beds). The memorandum quoted extensively from Sir Donald MacAlister's report of 1909 to the Raleigh Committee, as authoritative confirmation that the clinical facilities required for a full medical school were in place.

However, the memorandum went further: 'The new Medical School should be developed on what is sometimes called the "unit" system in general harmony with the unanimous recommendations of the Royal Commission on University Education in London.' In this respect the full medical school in Cardiff was offering something new, something which the existing medical schools in the United Kingdom, 'whose methods of organisation have for so long been established on different lines', would find it more difficult to introduce.

CARDIFF EMBRACES THE 'CLINICAL UNIT' SYSTEM

In the early years of the twentieth century concern had increasingly been voiced about the administrative structure of the University of London and its relationship to the several colleges affiliated to it. In 1909, the minister in charge of the Board of Education appointed a Royal Commission on University Education in London under the chairmanship of Richard Burdon Haldane (soon to become the Viscount Haldane of Cloan). During the course of its work the commission conducted an examination into the working of the London hospitals and the way clinical teaching and research was conducted. Among those who gave evidence was Abraham Flexner of the Carnegie Foundation for the Advancement of Teaching in the United States, who was well versed in new approaches to undergraduate teaching and research, not only in America but also in France and Germany. Whereas clinical teaching in the London hospitals was conducted, often poorly, by physicians and surgeons whose main interest was the pursuit of private practice – 'clinical teaching remains an incident in the life of a busy consultant' – the arrangements in Germany were infinitely better. There, the hospital-based clinical teaching was directed by professors of medicine, surgery and obstetrics, with control over large numbers of beds, and enjoying ready access to well-equipped laboratories in which to prosecute research. Flexner's approach was confirmed by Sir William Osler, who, informed by his experience at the Johns Hopkins University which had imbibed the 'German' model, argued that 'In a University Medical School, the principal teachers of clinical medicine and surgery in all their branches ought to be University professors in the same sense as the principal teachers of chemistry or physiology in a University.'

Haldane, a Germanophile who had been educated at Göttingen University, needed little persuading about the strengths of the German educational system, which he had already studied in some depth. Given the persuasiveness of the evidence presented to it and the predilections of its chairman, it was hardly surprising that, in respect of medical education, the Royal Commission, in its report of 1913, concluded that professors of medicine and surgery should be established in each of London's teaching hospitals, 'who would be willing to devote themselves mainly to teaching and research and to give up most of their time to professorial work'. Furthermore, the report promoted the concept of the 'clinical unit', being a department either under the complete control of the medical school or at least jointly controlled by the school and the teaching hospital. The report quoted Sir William Osler's views with particular approval:

> A professor of medicine requires the organisation of a hospital unit, if he is to carry out his three-fold duty of curing the sick, studying the problems of disease, and not only training his students in the technique of their art, but giving them university instruction in the science of their profession.[45]

Whereas the immediate reaction of the London medical schools to Haldane was mixed,[46] the view in Cardiff, with no previous customs and practice to address, was much more positive. It is generally accepted that Sir William Osler, already a good friend of the Cardiff Medical School and the hospital, and of the hospital's strongest advocates of a full medical school, Bruce Vaughan and Lynn Thomas, asserted his influence. Mitchell Stevens, in his warm tribute in the *British Medical Journal* to Osler following his death, said as much: 'Osler perceived that our medical school would not be hampered by preconceived ideas or old traditions, and that a virgin soil was presented for establishing a great medical school on the newest lines.'[47] An anonymous member of the clinical staff of the King Edward VII Hospital (possibly Lynn Thomas) writing in the *Western Mail*, echoed Osler's views entirely. As far as the writer was concerned, the Haldane Report provided the blueprint for Cardiff:

> If a full Medical School be established in Cardiff it behoves us to see that we start properly, and now we have the opportunity of being first in the field. It is better to have no medical school than to begin on the old lines. If Cardiff begins on the new lines, the old-established schools will, doubtless, laugh, will deride us, and even some of our own people may be unsympathetic. That does not matter. We shall succeed, and Little Wales will lead the way.[48]

Moreover, those centrally responsible for the strategic planning of medical education in Great Britain were equally keen to see the 'unit system' adopted in Wales. The Board of Education's Advisory Committee on University Grants (the forerunner of the University Grants Committee), chaired by Sir William McCormick, visited the University of Wales and its colleges in 1913. In its subsequent report regarding University College, Cardiff the committee referred to the college's plan to establish a full medical school:

> If such a complete school is to compete successfully with the large and well-equipped Schools of Medicine already in existence elsewhere, and if it is to provide a fitting medical education for students of the Principality, it must, in our opinion, be conceived on the most modern lines and be based on the 'unit' system as described in the recent report of the Royal Commission on University Education in London, with salaried heads, graded assistants, and well-equipped laboratories.[49]

In one particular respect Cardiff was determined to trespass into totally uncharted territory as far as the United Kingdom was concerned, by pioneering the employment of clinical professors on a full-time basis. This intention was explicitly stated in the memorandum compiled for the meeting with Lloyd George. The medical and surgical units would be staffed by full-time professors who, while having access to patients, would be debarred from engaging in private practice. 'This would prevent the time devoted to teaching being curtailed by the competition of private practice, and would, at the same time, allow the professor to retain that breadth of view which is so essential to the teacher of such a subject as medicine.' While gynaecology and obstetrics would also be organized on the unit system, the teaching requirements would be less demanding and 'For the time being, a whole-time professor would not be necessary.'

This approach was undoubtedly bold, for it actually went further than the Haldane Commission and Wales's good friend Sir William Osler proposed. The furthest that Haldane would go was to advocate, as we have seen, the appointment of professors who would devote most of their time to university work. As far as Osler was concerned 'he considered that it was not to the benefit of the professor to abstain from private practice, but that the assistants be whole time'.[50] Moreover, in a 'Memorandum on clinical units in medical schools' issued in 1920 the University Grants Committee, drawing on the conclusions of the Haldane Report, stated:

> Whether the Head of the [Clinical] Unit be occupied in his professorial duties whole-time or the major part of his time, whether he be allowed private practice or not ... these and many other points are relatively matters of detail if he be paid an adequate salary ...[51]

Why did Cardiff 'go out on a limb' in this matter? There is no doubt that the local hospital clinicians, jealous of protecting their private practice income (which in reality represented the bulk of their annual income), were keen to prevent additional clinicians, particularly those holding the prestigious title of professor, from drinking from this particular pond. During the hearings of the Royal Commission on University Education in Wales two years later, Lord Haldane, the chairman of this body too, asked Philip Rhys Griffiths, the senior surgeon at the King Edward VII Hospital, what he meant by 'whole-time'. Was the proposed new professor of surgery expected to devote himself entirely to research and teaching or have an opportunity to engage in some private practice? 'Do you think "whole time" necessarily excludes all private practice?' After Griffiths had replied in the affirmative, Haldane observed: 'I doubt whether you will find any whole time Professor of Medicine anywhere in the world just now who does not do a little private practice.' Griffiths's response was unequivocal: 'I have made this statement because I happened to know the feeling of my staff at the hospital at the present time.'[52] The plan to appoint clinical professors on a full-time basis was, however, not solely determined by reasons of self-interest. The 'clinical unit', as defined by Abraham Flexner, Haldane and Osler, was the way of the future. Everyone agreed that the heads of the units needed time to direct and provide undergraduate teaching and research properly, without being distracted by other demands on their time. That was what the memorandum asserted; the appointment of full-time staff was the logical solution. 'We shall succeed, and Little Wales will lead the way.'

STATE FUNDING SECURED FOR THE FIRST TIME

In addition to degree-awarding powers and access to good clinical facilities, a further prerequisite for a full medical school was the provision of adequate resources, both in terms of secure funding and suitable accommodation. Despite its undoubted success, the school was not paying its way. The Cardiff Medical School had started in 1893 on the basis of generous donations by a few benefactors and an appeal which, as has already been noted, fell somewhat short of the hoped-for target. By 1901 the Medical School Fund Capital Account stood at £7,077 in terms of contributions, of which £4,848 had already been spent on new accommodation and £1,996 on furniture and equipment. Most of the school's running costs, which, by 1904/5 showed a recurrent deficit of £479, were charged against the college's general funds.[53] The school attracted not a penny from the Treasury. Indeed the government's annual grant to University College, Cardiff, £4,000, had not been increased since 1883/4.

In March 1904 a delegation from the University of Wales and its colleges went to the Treasury to plead for additional state funding for their institutions and, in particular, to receive some funding specifically to support the development of the medical school. Despite glowing testimonies from Ernest Howard Griffiths (1851–1932), Viriamu Jones's successor as principal of University College, Cardiff, and Sir Isambard Owen about the excellence of the medical school and the high calibre of its students as judged by their performance in the London University examinations, Austen Chamberlain, the chancellor of the Exchequer was decidedly cool.

Let me say with reference to one branch of which you have spoken, viz. Medical Schools, no account is taken in any English College of any of the work done in the medical schools; that has to be provided entirely out of the local funds, and local funds devoted to that purpose are not included in the total local income on which the Government grant is based.[54]

That government policy was clear on this point was confirmed by its action, in the same year, of turning down an appeal for state funding from St George's Hospital Medical School to augment depleted resources from philanthropic sources. Grants-in-aid were for 'general purposes' and not to support special initiatives such as medical education.[55]

The authorities of the University of Wales and its colleges hoped for rather more sympathetic treatment from a Liberal government which had enjoyed an over-whelming victory in the general election of January 1906, with the Liberals dominating the Welsh parliamentary constituencies. After a good deal of tough argu-ment, which, among other things, exposed tensions between University College, Cardiff on the one hand and the University of Wales and the other two colleges on the other, the chancellor of the Exchequer, Herbert Asquith, was, as has already been noted, persuaded, in July 1907, to establish a committee, chaired by Sir Thomas Raleigh, to look at the quality of the educational provision in the University of Wales and the state of its finances, and to assess what funding the university needed to func-tion properly.[56] In the light of a generally favourable report, the Treasury agreed, in the spring of 1909, to make an additional annual sum of £15,000 available to the University of Wales and its colleges for a period of five years, with effect from 1909/10.

As has also been noted, one of the members of the review committee was Sir Donald MacAlister, the president of the General Medical Council, who wrote a highly compli-mentary report on the work of the Cardiff Medical School, and, in terms of future potential, the excellence of the clinical teaching facilities available in the nearby Cardiff Infirmary. His general conclusions were as follows:

The general result of my enquiry is, therefore, that given new buildings for the Medical School, and Chairs in the subjects posterior to the course to anatomy and physiology, Cardiff possesses all the requisites for a school of medicine, capable of instructing to a high degree of proficiency the aspirants to the medical degrees of the University of Wales, and thus of taking an eminent place among the professional institutions of the country. In at least one department of postgraduate work it might, moreover, develop a special school of national importance. I refer to Tropical Medicine and Hygiene, already pursued, with obvious advantages to the Empire at large, in Liverpool and London. The large international shipping trade of Cardiff, as of these other seaports, makes it a national centre for such studies. If such Tropical

School were organized in connection with the completed medical department of the College, it might well hope to attract students and practitioners from distant parts of the country, who were preparing to exercise their profession abroad.[57]

Sir Donald's report could not have been better timed, for it coincided with a change of policy at the Treasury. Ever since 1889 the Treasury had had a policy of giving state grants to finance technical education, but it had not, hitherto, regarded medical education as eligible. Finally, in 1908, the Treasury resolved to authorize the Board of Education to give grants in aid of education to the medical schools of England and Wales,[58] and in that year, after earlier rebuffs, St Mary's Hospital Medical School, teetering on the brink of insolvency, applied successfully to the Board of Education, securing a state grant of £1,037,[59] an outcome which established for the first time the principle that medical education was eligible for state funding.[60]

On the strength of Sir Donald's persuasive advocacy the Treasury determined that, of the £15,000 awarded to the University of Wales, £1,500 should be earmarked to support the development of the Cardiff Medical School, a significant landmark in its history, confirming the principle recently conceded by the government in relation to London, that the venture was entitled to state support as well as private philanthropy. Some of the new money would be used to strengthen the preclinical departments, by increasing the salaries of the senior staff, by creating additional lectureships in anatomy and physiology, and by establishing a new lectureship in physiological chemistry (the precursor of biochemistry). The remainder would enable the college to move decisively into the clinical domain, through the establishment of a chair in pathology and bacteriology, able to take advantage of the new pathology block being built at the Infirmary.

A CHAIR IN PATHOLOGY AND BACTERIOLOGY

As an academic discipline pathology was a relatively recent development in British medicine. Although the first chair in pathology had been established at Edinburgh in 1831, over fifty more years elapsed before the second was founded, at Aberdeen, in 1882. However, by the early years of the twentieth century, chairs in pathology had been set up in most provincial medical schools.[61] The advance of the discipline was part of the general enhancement in the status of the preclinical and laboratory sciences during the late nineteenth century. Pathology, originally, as morbid anatomy, the study of dead tissue in the mortuary, had, by the beginning of the twentieth century, developed into a laboratory-based scientific discipline, contributing to the diagnosis and treatment of disease, the branch of pathology known as bacteriology coming into particular prominence.[62] By 1906 its practitioners had become sufficiently self-confident to establish the Pathological Society of Great Britain and Ireland.[63]

In Cardiff, the advance of pathology as a discipline reflected the national pattern. Traditionally it had been regarded as little more than a useful early stepping-stone in a clinician's career. Indeed, during the 1890s the post of pathologist lacked sufficient status to be included among the list of infirmary staff printed in the University College, Cardiff *Calendar*. The first holder of the post, Donald Rose Paterson, appointed in 1891, had combined this role with that of assistant physician, as had his successor, from 1899, William Mitchell Stevens. The appointment of Harold Alfred Scholberg, previously bacteriologist to the joint Cardiff and County laboratory, as the infirmary's first full-time pathologist in 1908, and the simultaneous decision, by the hospital authorities, to build a new pathology department on site, indicated an encouraging determination to keep abreast with the best in current thinking. When, early in 1909, the Cardiff College announced its intention to appoint a professor of pathology and bacteriology, Colonel Bruce Vaughan, on behalf of the infirmary authorities, pledged the hospital's commitment to make the facilities of the new department available to the new professor, whoever it turned out to be.[64] In fact, the honorary clinical staff in the hospital fully expected Harold Scholberg to be appointed to the chair. Born in Chile of Scandinavian and Scottish parents, Scholberg, after qualifying at St Bartholomew's Hospital Medical School in 1898, had spent his early postgraduate years pursuing research in pathology before moving to Cardiff in 1903. He had, as his later career would demonstrate, an interest in and aptitude for research, which in many ways suited him for an academic career.[65] Certainly his hospital colleagues thought highly of Scholberg, as can be seen in the following resolution, passed by the hospital's Medical Board in March 1910:

> His enthusiasm and energy have been instrumental in greatly enlarging the scope and usefulness of his department whilst his keen scientific interest has made him a most valued colleague in the investigation of disease in the institution. The Board believes that in Dr Scholberg the Cardiff Medical School will find a leader who will add greatly to the strength of its staff and one who by his scientific attainments and original researches will add honour to its name.[66]

Unfortunately for Scholberg and his colleagues, the college authorities saw things differently. Without having any previous experience of making appointments to clinical academic posts, the college simply proceeded to appoint the professor of pathology and bacteriology in exactly the same way that they appointed any other professor, though the principal did discuss the arrangements with the infirmary authorities beforehand. Having approved the draft job description drawn up by Professors Hepburn and Haycraft, the council referred the details of the five applications received to the Senate which, advised by a small subcommittee comprising the principal and the professors of anatomy, physiology and chemistry, recommended that three candidates be interviewed by the Council. To be sure, Harold Scholberg was one of those seen by the Council on 13 July 1910, but, having concluded the interviews, the Council (with, it should be noted, Colonel Bruce Vaughan, John Lynn Thomas, the chairman of the infirmary governors and Dr A. Garrod Thomas being present) unanimously resolved to offer the post to one of the external candidates, Edward Emrys-Roberts (1878–1924). Emrys-Roberts was undoubtedly well qualified for the post. Born in Dawlish, a graduate of the University of Liverpool, and at the time of his appointment demonstrator in pathology at the University of Bristol and pathologist with the Bristol General Infirmary, he was regarded as one of the up-and-coming pathologists in the country.[67] Nevertheless, his appointment, in the summer of 1910, caused much resentment among the clinical staff of the Cardiff Infirmary, not least Harold Scholberg. Nearly a year would pass before the Medical Board agreed to recommend that the new professor be granted an honorary clinical contract. In the meantime Scholberg, who, quite reasonably, continued to regard himself as the head of the hospital's pathology service, competed with the professor for clinical work, pleading with the hospital authorities to arrive at a solution 'in the interests of the patients of the Infirmary'. Finally, a year after Emrys-Roberts's appointment, arrangements were agreed whereby half the clinical staff would be served by him and half by Scholberg.[68] As Ivor Davies would later record in his memoirs, 'The pathological work of the hospital was divided between these two individuals who were not even on speaking terms. The new professor had received a cold reception from a majority of the staff and thus a canker arose and persisted.'[69] The opening, by William James Thomas, of the new pathology department, on 1 June 1912, did little to improve relationships between the two men, and later, in his memoirs, Ivor Davies would take the view that in the appointment of the professor of pathology 'lay the *fons et origo* of the subsequent disagreement between the hospital and the college' during the 1920s.[70]

Even with the benefit of hindsight, it is hard to see how, in the context of the period, the appointment to the chair could have been handled much differently. The hospital authorities had indicated beforehand their willingness to accommodate the new professor within the hospital laboratories – the post was not being foisted on a resistant hospital. The principal had, according to the minutes of the council, discussed the arrangements for the appointment to the chair with the hospital beforehand. It is accepted that there is no evidence that the hospital authorities were involved in the formulation of the further particulars or the drawing-up of the shortlist, but those who were, including the professors of anatomy and physiology enjoyed, as we have already noted in this chapter, good relationships with their medical colleagues in the city. The College Council, which made the appointment, included among its members both senior hospital managers and eminent clinicians. Its only 'error' was to appoint the 'wrong' man, an outsider (though one with a Welsh wife and a Welsh mother) rather than the 'local favourite' – a man who, in years to come, would show himself to be a somewhat difficult, not to say vindictive, colleague. This may have been the first, but it was by no means the last occasion on which the college authorities would, at least in the eyes of the hospital clinicians, behave in an insensitive manner, whether over appointments or other matters of mutual concern.

Within a year of Emrys-Roberts's appointment, at a salary of £450 a year, mischievous anonymous correspondence was appearing in the *Western Mail*, suggesting that the post was a waste of money: 'So far he has not had a single pupil! In view of this fact the Treasury might allow the College to appropriate this sum to meet the general expenses.'[71] It was true that to be wholly effective the professor had to operate within the environment of a full medical school but, in all fairness, his appointment was the natural next step in the journey towards achieving this objective. After all, pathology came after anatomy and physiology and before clinical medicine in the medical curriculum. Moreover, as he reminded the audience at his college inaugural lecture, given in October 1910, his department had an important role to perform in prosecuting research relevant to the needs of the people of Wales. Shrewdly he spoke of the contribution his department could make in support of the campaign launched, less than a month earlier, to combat Wales's most dreaded affliction, tuberculosis.[72]

At the beginning of the twentieth century tuberculosis remained the commonest single cause of death in Wales. Indeed, seven of the fifteen counties in England and Wales with the worst mortality rate from tuberculosis were in Wales, with the death rate in Cardiganshire being nearly twice the national average. Instead of erecting memorial clocks and fountains all over Wales, as had happened on the death of Queen Victoria, David Davies, the independent-minded Liberal MP for Montgomeryshire (grandson of the great industrial tycoon, and later to become Lord Davies of Llandinam), proposed, in 1910, a rather more practical way of commemorating the death of King Edward VII. He convened a national conference involving a wide range of Welsh public bodies (assembling for convenience, as did many Wales-focused meetings in those days, in Shrewsbury) on 30 September 1910, at which it was agreed that a fitting memorial to the late king (who had once remarked: 'If curable, why not cured?') would be a campaign to eradicate tuberculosis from Wales. This initiative, towards which Davies and his celebrated sisters Gwendoline and Margaret contributed the colossal sum of £125,000, led to the establishment of the King Edward VII Welsh National Memorial Association for the prevention, treatment and abolition of tuberculosis, obtaining a royal charter in 1912. David Davies became president, and Thomas Jones, later to become cabinet secretary to four prime ministers, accepted Davies's invitation to become its first full-time secretary: 'The movement is really a chance of doing something for Wales, something really practical ... Don't hesitate to take on the job *at once*.' Sir William Osler and another prominent medical man, Christopher Addison, later to become minister of health, served as members of a committee to advise the association on its strategy.[73]

At the official opening of the pathology department at the King Edward VII Hospital, the guest speaker, Sir Isambard Owen, spoke enthusiastically about the important contribution he believed that the department could perform in the diagnosis and treatment of disease, particularly 'that terrible white scourge, tuberculosis', a sentiment echoed by the *Western Mail*, which expressed the hope 'that a fruitful co-operation will be set up between the King Edward Memorial Association and the Medical School of Cardiff'.[74] In fact, there is little evidence that the department diverted much of its energy into the pursuit of research into tuberculosis in the years that followed. Indeed, the professor spent most of the First World War with the First Army in France, where he commanded the Welsh Mobile Pathology Laboratory, his research activity primarily focused on the treatment of sepsis.[75] Nevertheless, a bond was forged between the association and the medical school which, less than ten years later, led to the endowment of the David Davies chair of tuberculosis at the medical school by David Davies and his sisters, in memory of their grandfather.

CATHAYS PARK OR NEWPORT ROAD?

The former infirmary building had never been intended as other than a temporary site for University College, Cardiff. The purchase, by the Cardiff Corporation, of thirty-eight acres of Cathays Park from the Marquess of Bute in 1897 provided the ideal development solution for the college, located, as it would be, in arguably the most prestigious site in Wales. The corporation, equally keen to have the college as one of the park's occupiers, made a free grant of five acres to the college in 1900 and three years later four architects were invited by the college to design buildings worthy of both their purpose and their setting. Basil Champneys, already experienced in designing educational buildings (Mansfield College, Oxford and Newnham College, Cambridge), was regarded as the front runner, but he produced a prohibitively expensive concept, and the contract was awarded to William Douglas Caröe, son of the Danish consul at Liverpool, whose main expertise hitherto had lain in ecclesiastical architecture. His concept, of producing elegant buildings in the traditional style, combining 'the charm and quiet dignity and scale' of Trinity College, Cambridge with the 'picturesque balance and delightful proportions' of some of the Oxford colleges, captivated the authorities of the Cardiff college. The first phase of the building work, initiated in 1904, took five years, leading to the opening of the 'New College' on 14 October 1909, initially consisting of the administrative and arts block, the magnificent Drapers' Library and the Viriamu Jones Memorial Physical Research Laboratory.[76]

Faced in white Portland stone the edifice was extremely pleasing to the eye. Dewi-Prys Thomas, the college's first professor of architecture, once wrote of his first visit to Cathays Park as an eighteen-year-old northerner in the mid-1930s, by which time, of course, the college had been much extended:

> The impact of that magical first impression is indelible. It was all so much the antithesis of England's satanic mills as to bring a lump to my adolescent throat. All

these noble buildings shone in mellow harmonies of white. Of differing styles, they sang united in concord of tone values – the pure tones of the innumerable white-washed Welsh cottages I had seen during that halcyon summer in Wales.[77]

The intention of the college authorities was that the Cardiff Medical School, and other departments, would be relocated to Cathays Park from their cramped accommodation on Newport Road as funds became available. As Professor E. H. Griffiths, the college principal, once explained to Colonel Bruce Vaughan, the incorporation of the medical school had been included in the architects' brief, and Caröe's plans had been framed with this in mind. Moreover, in Griffiths's view there were sound educational reasons for moving the medical school to Cathays Park:

> I have strongly held in the past the view that the College should be regarded as one unity, and I very much regret the partial separation which always exists between the social life of the medical students and of the others. I believe that the segregating of professional students during their University career is a mistake; one of the greatest benefits they derive from University life is associating with those entering on different professions. They thus escape that narrowness which is visible in all professional colleges, whether medical, training or theological.[78]

Griffiths's problem was that, with the best will in the world, the college did not have the resources immediately available to enable his strategy to be implemented. A public building appeal, launched in 1905 with the aim of raising £160,000 to develop the Cathays Park site, had raised less than half of that figure by 1909. In the words of S. B. Chrimes, 'New College was built, not indeed on sand, but on a pile of debt (equal to about four times the then annual general income) which was to burden the College finances for many years to come.'[79]

Meanwhile, some members of the medical school were expressing extreme dissatisfaction with the inadequate conditions in which they were expected to work. Having initially voiced his concerns to the College Council in 1908 to no avail, the other science departments claiming to be as hard-pressed as physiology, John Berry Haycraft resumed his attack in the spring of 1911 in an address to the Cardiff Medical Society. Whatever Dewi-Prys Thomas might think some years later, Haycraft was less than enamoured of the new college buildings in Cathays Park, which 'conformed to ancient, not modern ideas', aping the medieval concepts prevailing in the quadrangled Oxford and Cambridge colleges, in contrast with what he regarded as the excellent arrangements at Bristol: 'Unless care was taken the Bristol Medical School might tap the recruiting grounds for medical students of the University of Wales and thus prove a formidable rival to its medical school.' The plans for Cathays Park allowed no room for expansion, with his own department being hemmed in on all sides by other medical and engineering departments. There was another, powerful argument for leaving the medical school where it was: its proximity to the place where the medical students would obtain their clinical instruction, rather than a mile away in Cathays Park.[80]

Haycraft's position was immensely strengthened by the offer, by William James Thomas, to fund, from his own fortune, a new, state-of-the-art physiology block, on condition that it was built on the Newport Road site. Thomas had been persuaded to make this offer by Colonel Bruce Vaughan, who was not only convinced by Haycraft's arguments,[81] but was also quietly confident that he would be invited to act as architect for the project. The offer, by someone who was initially simply referred to as an anonymous donor, was announced by Bruce Vaughan during a royal visit to Cardiff by King George V and Queen Mary at the end of June 1912.[82] Needless to say, the heads of the science departments, located in equally inadequate accommodation on Newport Road, with no immediate prospect of any amelioration in their circumstances, were less than happy with the prospect of having a brand-new physiology department shoe-horned into an already congested site. One by one they protested to Principal Griffiths. 'I wish again to urge most strongly that the department is very cramped for room, both for the students' work and for material,' complained the professor of geology. Professor A. A. Read considered 'the Metallurgy Department to be the worst housed of all the departments in the College'. The professor of chemistry begged to differ: 'As far as I can judge the need of my department for new buildings is greater than any other department in the College.' Writing as professor of anatomy, David Hepburn considered that too much attention had been paid to the needs of physiology: 'The existing Department [of Anatomy] affords no possibility of expansion, provides no arrangements of a satisfactory kind for research as properly understood, and merely provides the barest minimum of the facilities required for teaching.' In his capacity as dean of the medical school he added his view that simply to address the immediate needs of the Department of Physiology would be a mistake. The needs of the medical school as a whole should be considered: 'I am convinced that it would be false economy and a fatal policy to proceed by a series of makeshifts.'[83] In fact, as the principal revealed in a letter to a lay member of the College Council, Hepburn himself wanted the medical school to be relocated to Cathays Park:

> I may say that he reports very strongly against the erection of the buildings on the old site. In his opinion it might lead in the future to an entire separation of the Medical School and the College, and the setting up of a National Medical School independent of the University.[84]

What was Griffiths to do? On the one hand, the proposal to build a new Department of Physiology on Newport Road was deeply unpopular among most of his professorial colleagues and offended his own judgement. On the other hand, here was an opportunity for an otherwise financially embarrassed college to make a major advance in the development of the medical school at no cost to itself. Wisely he persuaded the college's accommodation committee to seek the advice of an outside expert. Sir William Osler was first approached but he was too busy, and Sir Donald MacAlister was discounted for the same reason. At the meeting of the committee on 4 November 1912, Griffiths proposed that the views of Sir Isambard Owen be sought. He knew as much as anyone about medical schools, he was a member of the College Council and he knew the local scene. Griffiths was prepared to be guided by Owen's report.

> If he says that contiguity to the Infirmary is of the highest importance, other considerations must take a second place. But if he is of opinion that such contiguity is not an important matter, I have no doubt in my own mind that the right policy is the erection of a Medical School in Cathays Park.[85]

Sir Isambard Owen gladly accepted the college's invitation and by mid-January 1913 his report was ready, which was fortunate as Thomas, irritated by the college's apparent procrastination, was threatening to withdraw his offer.[86] In a well-argued report, submitted to the accommodation committee on 18 January, Owen suggested that, from the point of view of the corporate life of the college, it did not much matter where the medical school was located: 'There is a general tendency in our modern universities for the students of a technical faculty to keep themselves rather to themselves, forming their own especial clubs and societies, and holding more or less aloof from others.' However, having reviewed what students were expected to do during the various stages of the medical course, and looking forward to the time when the school would be offering a full medical course, involving clinical as well as preclinical instruction, Owen's main conclusions were quite clear: 'These considerations weigh on the whole in favour of locating Anatomy and Physiology, as well as the classrooms and laboratories for the final stage of the curriculum, as near to the Infirmary as circumstances allow.' Owen was also mindful of the timescale within which everyone was working: 'I am informed that the prospects of proceeding further with the erection of the Cathays Park buildings are at present indefinite. I have assumed, I think correctly, an intention on behalf of the College to have a complete medical school in Cardiff as soon as practicable.' Owen's final advice to the College was unequivocal:

> If a satisfactory scheme for the erection of College buildings on the Newport Road site can be devised … and if private benefaction is ready at once to erect so much of them as would provide a satisfactory Department of Physiology, and thus leave space vacant in the existing buildings for the concurrent extension of the Anatomical department, I should strongly recommend the College to accept the very generous offer made to it.[87]

At its next meeting the Council accepted Owen's advice. After several months of uncomfortable silence it also finally expressed its formal gratitude to William James Thomas for his generosity, whereupon he dug his hands deeper into his pocket. He undertook to meet the cost of building not only the physiology block, but also the grand entrance hall and main staircase for the use of the entire medical school when completed, at a total cost of some £30,000. Recognizing that the building of the physiology block would require the destruction of a number of houses along Newport Road which accommodated other college departments, the college resolved to buy other properties in the immediate vicinity to assuage the feelings of a number of aggrieved professors.

W. D. Caröe had also to be pacified. Not only would the medical school no longer be incorporated into his grand plan for Cathays Park; he would not be invited to design the physiology block in Newport Road. William James Thomas had decided that nobody but his good friend Bruce Vaughan was worthy of such a commission. The College Council had no alternative but to compensate Caröe, assure him of its full confidence and explain that the college was commissioning no one to build the physiology block. This would be a matter between Thomas and Bruce Vaughan. They would be responsible for erecting the buildings and, as Principal Griffiths explained to Lord Merthyr (formerly Sir William Thomas Lewis), the college president, they would 'make a present of them, when complete, to the College'.[88]

So, in the face of the reservations of other aggrieved heads of departments, not to mention those of the college principal and even the (not entirely dispassionate) dean of the medical school, the professor of physiology had his way. He was fortunate to have secured the support of influential and wealthy local champions at a time when advocates of an alternative strategy lacked funding of their own. However, there were sound academic arguments for Berry Haycraft's preferred solution. He was professor of a subject which was, at this time, establishing itself as an important bridge between the basic sciences and the clinical disciplines. As Stella Butler has written, 'The bedside and the laboratory were beginning to be seen as analogous spheres … Within clinical medicine there was greater emphasis on the functional nature of disease. It was therefore important for doctors to understand the normal functions of the body's organ systems.'[89] This was a central role of departments of physiology, and those at Cambridge, Oxford and at University College, London had established formidable reputations in this respect.[90] The second decade of the twentieth century was not the time to relocate the department in Cardiff 1,600 yards (Haycraft had measured the distance) from the King Edward VII Hospital. Even on a purely practical level, before a full medical school had come about, the hospital and the department needed each other. As part of a memorandum prepared for the principal, Professor Haycraft explained:

> Every year there must be a considerable interchange of material, and instruments between the Physiological Department and the Hospital. Every year I am continually sending over to the Hospital for specimens to shew my class, and they, in the Hospital, as often ask me for the loan of instruments etc.[91]

Though the right decision had been taken, the negotiations over the location of the physiology block had caused Principal Griffiths much anxiety, leading, as he confessed to Lord Merthyr at the end of March 1913, to 'insomnia, which is always a danger signal for me. My medical man enjoins three weeks' rest; I am willing to try a fortnight and hope to get away at the end of this week.'[92] He admitted that his anxiety had been compounded by additional work imposed on him following the departure of Percy Watkins, the college registrar, to the post of assistant secretary to the Welsh Insurance Commissioners. Although he had only been registrar for two years Percy Watkins (1871–1946) was undoubtedly an able administrator who would, in time, succeed Sir Alfred Davies as permanent secretary of the Welsh Department of the Board of Education, receiving a knighthood in 1931. While he maintained an interest in the fortunes of the medical school for some years, and would give evidence to the Haldane Commission on the subject, his memoirs offer no useful insights into the development of medical education in Wales during this period, which is rather surprising considering that his son, Arthur G. ('Pop') Watkins, would later become the first professor of paediatrics in the Welsh National School of Medicine. However, Watkins senior did refer with great affection to his successor as registrar at Cardiff, Daniel James Arthur Brown, previously deputy registrar, 'a real "white man" of the highest integrity and efficiency' who would continue in the post for twenty-three years until his retirement in 1936.[93]

FUNDING A FULL MEDICAL SCHOOL

With excellent clinical facilities and a professor of pathology in place in the King Edward VII Hospital, and impressive evidence of local beneficence, the time was thought ripe for an approach to be made for further government funding to enable the establishment of a full medical school in Cardiff. Arrangements were made for a delegation representing the University of Wales, University College, Cardiff and other stakeholders to meet David Lloyd George, the chancellor of the Exchequer, on 12 February 1914. Two issues needed to be addressed before the meeting. The first, concerning the nature of the delegation, which interests it purported to represent, will be considered in the next chapter. Suffice it to say here, that its leader was Lord Kenyon, senior deputy chancellor of the University of Wales, and a good friend of Lloyd George. The second matter to be addressed was the content of the background memorandum that had to be prepared prior to the meeting. Much of the content, dealing with the progress of the Cardiff Medical School hitherto, and the clinical aspects of the case, have been referred to earlier in this chapter. What the Treasury wanted to know above all else was what a full medical school was expected to cost. The authors of the memorandum not only indicated the intention for the full medical school to adopt the 'clinical unit' system; the medical and surgical units would be staffed by full-time professors, who, while having access to patients, would be debarred from engaging in private practice. As a matter of fact the principal had, a few weeks earlier, expressed his private opinion that the Treasury would be unwilling to fund professors of medicine and surgery on a full-time basis, on the grounds that, at least during the earliest years of the full medical school, 'The number of students in their third to fifth years would be small, and such whole-time professors would have very little to do.'[94] Nevertheless, for estimates purposes, the salaries of full-time professors of medicine and surgery were included (£1,500 each), with part-time salaries assumed for the remaining clinical academic staff, including the professor of obstetrics and gynaecology. Altogether, taking into account additional costs required in the existing departments of anatomy, physiology and pathology, together with other essential recurrent maintenance costs, the memorandum concluded that once the full medical school was up and running, the extra annual income required, over and above existing expenditure, would amount to £12,715 per annum. The authors conceded that the cost was considerable, especially since, during its infancy, the number of students in the later years of the course would be comparatively small. On the other hand,

> A vast amount of organisation will be necessary during the initial stages, and it is of the utmost importance that the Professors should at the very outset be given opportunities to acquaint themselves with the latest developments in laboratory equipment and educational methods. In short, everything should be done that is calculated to ensure that the new Medical School shall be the very best that experience and investigation can suggest.[95]

Despite the fact that in early February 1914, the government was preoccupied with the problems of Ireland and a deteriorating European climate, with the chancellor of the Exchequer embroiled in a struggle with Winston Churchill over the naval estimates, Lord Kenyon and his colleagues were given a warm welcome by Lloyd George. He indicated that the government would make a substantial contribution towards the cost of establishing a full medical school in Wales provided Wales itself made a significant financial commitment. At this point, and out of the blue as far as Principal Griffiths was concerned, Colonel Bruce Vaughan announced that a gentleman who wished to remain anonymous had agreed to donate £60,000 to build a school of public health on or near Newport Road.[96] The anonymous donor, who soon turned out to be the now knighted Sir William James Thomas, laid down a number of conditions, the most important of which was that 'the grant made by the Treasury, in addition to the present grant of £1,500, should be an adequate one for a first-rate full medical school', the judge of that to be Sir William Osler.[97] Following the meeting on 12 February, the Board of Education set up a special departmental committee to advise the Treasury on the amount of any grant that should be made, and on what terms.

Sir William's generosity (£90,000 before the First World War equates to some £5,000,000 today) may have impressed the government and its advisers, but it caused some short-term perturbation in Cardiff, with Principal Griffiths briefly threatening to resign. First, neither he nor his registrar, D. J. A. Brown, had been told about the donation of £60,000 – 'one of the most important communications ever made to the college'[98] – prior to its announcement to the chancellor. Secondly, Thomas had stipulated that his building should be erected in an area already earmarked by the College for a metallurgy department following a donation from local coal owners. Griffiths was forced to devote much time agreeing alternative arrangements with the coal owners, while being subjected to criticism from Thomas, and in particular his mouthpiece, Colonel Bruce Vaughan, for seeming less than overwhelmed by their own beneficence. In a state of some despair Griffiths complained to David Davies MP that he was being accused

> of trying to rob the College of a great benefaction, whereas, from my point of view, I am endeavouring to see that equal justice is being done to all interests … We are in the hands of one [Bruce Vaughan] whose interests are confined to the Medical School and the Hospital and who, as in a sense the self-appointed architect, naturally thinks chiefly of a great pile of buildings which will redound to his credit.[99]

Fortunately, by the time of the meeting of the College Council in May, Griffiths had managed to satisfy all interests, enabling the anonymous donor's generosity to be formally accepted. The point was, however, emphasized that full compliance with the donor's wishes lay outside the college's hands, depending, as it did, on the response of the Treasury to its request for adequate funding to initiate a full medical school.

The departmental committee set up to assess the funding needs of the full medical school was impressively high-powered in its composition.[100] Its chairman was Sir William McCormick, and its members were Dr Christopher Addison MP (later to become Britain's first minister of health in 1919), Sir George Newman, medical adviser to the Board of Education, Dr (later Sir) Frank Heath, head of the universities section at the Board of Education, C. L. Stocks from the Treasury, and A. T. (later Sir Alfred) Davies (1861–1949), head of the Welsh Department at the Board of Education. From the outset the committee was confronted with irritating procedural quibbles raised by the Cardiff College, but it worked hard to arrive at some credible financial estimates of the full medical school's needs. Not only did it rely on the figures submitted with the memorandum prepared for the earlier meeting with Lloyd George; it also sought the advice of Sir William Osler, who, after consulting senior members of the medical school, offered his own calculations, observing: 'For a first-class Medical School it is not excessive.' That Osler's estimate of annual expenditure was some £1,500 less than that of the Welsh delegation was almost entirely due to the fact that he projected annual salaries of £700 for part-time professors of medicine and surgery, whereas the calculations accompanying the memorandum included full-time salaries of £1,500.

To those hoping for a speedy decision, the outbreak of the First World War on 4 August 1914 caused much dismay. Writing to Principal Griffiths on that very day Lord Kenyon could only observe that 'like most of the fruits of peace, the Medical School will now have to wait some time,' a statement which elicited an equally gloomy response from Griffiths: 'One cannot suppose that the Treasury will be in a position to give additional grants for some time to come.'[101] Their despondent mood was scarcely lifted by the instruction of the Board of Education that no steps should be taken to commence work on the physiology block until it was authorized, a ruling which caused Bruce Vaughan much offence: 'It is deplorable to think that under the circumstances when *employment is very urgently needed* for men in the building trade that the work should be held up.'[102]

Nevertheless, the committee continued to do its work, submitting an interim report to the president of the Board of Education on 10 August, and a final report in mid-December. On the question of funding, the committee concluded that, excluding student fees, the estimates as submitted by the Welsh delegation were reasonable, indicating that, when fully operational, the additional annual funding required to support the complete medical school would be in the order of £10,000. While this amount might seem high in comparison with the expenditure incurred in some other provincial medical schools, the committee, in its final report, made the following observation: 'We realise that due allowance should be made for the fact that the School is to be organised on the "unit system", the expenses of which may be expected to be greater than those entailed by the organisation which at present prevails in the Medical Schools in England.'[103] On the other hand, the English medical schools secured a significant proportion of their income from endowments of various sorts and other locally generated sources such as the local authorities, and the committee took the view that the Welsh medical school should do so too. The committee concluded that half of the additional income required by the full medical school should come from the Exchequer, the remainder coming from local sources, from the local authorities, from endowments and from donors.

Furthermore, for Treasury funding to be forthcoming, all parties would have to agree a constitution for the complete medical school which reflected its all-Wales dimension. This issue will be addressed in the next chapter.

Whose Medical School?

In terms of structure there were broadly two categories of medical school operating in the United Kingdom in the years before the First World War. There were twelve free-standing medical schools in London, which were managed by boards of governors, and, in respect of such state funding that they received, they were directly funded by the Board of Education. With the exception of the Durham College of Medicine, which, for historical reasons also received its state funding direct from the Board of Education, all the other medical schools in the United Kingdom were integrated, as faculties of medicine, within multidisciplinary universities.[1] The Cardiff Medical School certainly came into this category, being one of three faculties, with Arts and Science, making up the University College of South Wales and Monmouthshire.

What made the Cardiff Medical School different from other medical schools was the perception that, on joining the ranks of the full medical schools, it would be expected to serve the needs not only of its local community, but of a whole nation. It was not just Cardiff's medical school; it belonged to the whole of Wales. That being the case, the challenge to all those interested in the future of the school was how to ensure that the whole of Wales acquired 'ownership' of the institution – and contributed to its running costs. No less a body than a Royal Commission was asked to form a view. In their wisdom the commissioners concluded that as a national institution the medical school should stand alone, independent in particular from the University College of South Wales and Monmouthshire. While in an ideal world this might have been an entirely reasonable conclusion to reach, the commissioners were living in anything but an ideal world. As Lord Haldane, the chairman of the Royal Commission once ruefully observed, 'Cardiff is a great centre, but a difficult place to deal with.'

CARDIFF'S OR WALES'S? THE ISSUE OF OWNERSHIP CONFRONTED

When the Cardiff Medical School was first established in 1893, there was no doubt in anyone's mind that it was, and would continue to be, an integral part of the University College of South Wales and Monmouthshire. That is not to say that people envisaged the school as primarily serving the needs of the community in the south-eastern corner of Wales. As far as the school's founder, William Thomas Edwards, was concerned, 'I wanted every Welsh boy to get the fullest opportunity to study medicine at home,'[2] and, as has already been noted, those actively engaged in campaigning for a medical school during the mid-1880s were drawn from much further afield than in and around Cardiff. Twenty years later, Samuel Thomas Evans, MP for Mid Glamorgan, a leading member of the Welsh Liberal establishment, and with strong roots in the Neath area, referred, at a London Welsh function, to the objective of establishing 'a real Welsh medical school. There were all the elements of it at Cardiff, which was not a South Wales town merely, but the metropolis of Wales, and he hoped it would be developed by the aid of the medical fraternity throughout the country.'[3]

Evans was being practical. He recognized that there could only be one medical school in a country the size of Wales, but he was also tapping into what was, at this time, a strong sense of Welsh identity. This had many manifestations, supremacy of the national Fifteen on the rugby field at one level, the advance of the National Eisteddfod of Wales and the establishment of national institutions like the National Library of Wales and the National Museum, both of which received their charters in 1907, not to mention the creation of the University of Wales, at another.[4] The idea that the Cardiff Medical School might profess an all-Wales role was not only attractive to those who saw the school as a further expression of national pride. There were influential voices in Whitehall who believed that a medical school enjoying the allegiance of the whole of Wales, rather than its south-eastern corner, would be better positioned to maximize its funding opportunities within the principality. Indeed, Sir William McCormick's departmental committee was quite specific on this point, on one occasion telling a delegation comprising Sir William James Thomas, David Davies MP and Colonel Bruce Vaughan: 'It would be practically impossible to enlist the practical sympathy of Local Education Authorities in North and Mid-Wales unless the School were really national in character.'[5]

David Lloyd George, who, as chancellor of the Exchequer, was well placed to influence funding discussions,[6] strongly favoured the full medical school assuming an all-Wales dimension. Despite his north Wales background, he was not hostile to the pre-eminent position of Cardiff in Wales. Indeed, as early as 1896 he had acknowledged that town's claim to be the natural capital of the country, and in 1908 he accepted, with pride, the freedom of the City of Cardiff, two months before receiving the freedom of Caernarfon.[7] Nevertheless, writing at the beginning of January 1914 to David Hepburn, who was making the detailed arrangements for the meeting with the chancellor, Lord Kenyon reported: 'I have seen Mr George and he would like a deputation of from 12–18. He wishes it to be non-party and thoroughly representative of N. and S.' Kenyon believed that ideally the delegation should include two lords lieutenant and two county council chairmen, and should not have 'a preponderance of Cardiff medical men. I think we must avoid making the application too local in appearance.'[8]

Apart from determining what a full medical school in Cardiff would cost to run, therefore, the departmental committee's other main task was to secure agreement on a structure for the medical school which would reflect the all-Wales context in which it was expected to operate. The memorandum prepared in advance of the Welsh delegation's visit to Lloyd George in February 1914 had been totally unilluminating in this respect. Apart from referring once to the 'National Medical School for Wales', and twice to the 'Welsh Medical School', the authors of the memorandum, all Cardiff-based, had not addressed this issue, their assumption clearly being that, whatever its title and vision, the school would continue to be an integral part of University College, Cardiff. For several weeks during the spring and early summer the college authorities resisted any suggestion that anything more was required. By virtue of the fact that, by common consent, there was room for only one medical school in Wales, the medical school in Cardiff would, by default, be the national medical school. Furthermore, the college had established and nurtured the medical school, and it had been to the college, that Sir William James Thomas had promised funding to enable a complete medical school to be erected. To a frustrated David Davies MP the solution was obvious. 'If the College people are so difficult to deal with' someone should persuade Thomas to make his gift to the University.[9] A memorandum prepared for the committee by its secretariat acknowledged how difficult it would be to arrive at a generally acceptable solution:

> The question of the future government of the Medical School is a difficult one. The University of Wales is a federal University, the constituent Colleges of which are financially independent and, owing to historic reasons, the University has little or no power over its Colleges under its Charter. Any question therefore, of making a 'National Medical School' governed by the University will need careful consideration. The Medical School as existing at present is managed entirely by the College Authorities and in its administration the University takes no part'.[10]

Three months elapsed between the committee's first meeting and its second, on 18 June, when the members' irritation with the failure of the authorities of the university and the Cardiff College to propose a way forward, was only too evident. Writing to Lord Kenyon after the meeting, the committee secretary, A. L. Hetherington, expressed the committee's concern at the considerable delay caused 'by the apparent difficulty in securing co-operation between the several persons and bodies concerned'. Thomas Jones, who was close to many of the key players, confided to David Davies: 'Unless someone like Kenyon or yourself take hold of the situation and push things through during the next two months, the thing will be badly bungled.'[11]

Jones's observations and Hetherington's strictures clearly had the desired effect for, at the next meeting of the departmental committee, on 14 July, most of the leading players attended, Lord Kenyon, Principal Griffiths, Sir William James Thomas, David Davies and Colonel Bruce Vaughan. During the course of the meeting Sir William McCormick and his colleagues made it quite clear that the issue before them was the creation and funding of a national medical school for Wales, and that 'it would prob-ably be difficult to institute a National School of Medicine and to enlist the sympathy of the whole Principality in it, unless arrangements were made for its government and administration other than by means of the Authorities of Cardiff University College only'. As far as Sir William James Thomas was concerned, although he had made his gift to the college, what he wanted was a 'first-rate and up-to-date medical school for Wales', in a position analogous to the National Library of Wales and the National Museum of Wales, and if arrangements could be agreed 'for the proper national organisation of the School, he would be content'. Lord Kenyon and David Davies both expressed support for the creation of an organizational structure which reflected the school's national character. Bruce Vaughan, whose overriding interest was in securing the contract for the building work, said nothing of note. Principal Griffiths was clearly put out by the flexible attitude being adopted by Sir William James Thomas, empha-sizing that the donation had unequivocally been made to, and accepted by the Cardiff College Council. However, he had already secured the permission of his council to entertain the idea of setting up an advisory board to run the medical school, subject to the supremacy of the College Council itself. He indicated to the departmental committee that such a body might consist of representatives of the university, the hospital, the Crown and the county councils, and would serve as the governing body of the medical school, but ultimately responsible to the Cardiff College Council.

The departmental committee, feeling that real progress had been made, invited all interested parties, including the university colleges at Aberystwyth and Bangor, to submit suggestions for a suitable organizational structure for a national medical school, with a view to holding a conference, representing all interests, on 31 July. In the event, only one scheme was submitted, from the authorities of the Cardiff College, and this was subjected to some last-minute amendments during an awkward pre-conference meeting of the Welsh delegation, at the Westminster Hotel, at which the Cardiff principal 'had a long struggle with Lord Kenyon, as he had evidently made up his mind that this was to be a University affair'.[12]

Sufficient show of unity among the Welsh delegation during the conference led the departmental committee to accept Cardiff's modified scheme as the basis of a scheme for the government of the national medical school. In its interim report to the presi-dent of the Board of Education:

> The committee are glad to find that there is a general recognition of the necessity for the inclusion in the local governing body of something more than merely local inter-ests and for some wider and more representative method of control than would be possible if the sole responsibility for the administration of the School were dealt with, like other departments of collegiate study at Cardiff, by the Council and the Senate of the College.[13]

The Medical Board would consist of twenty-one members, three nominated by the Crown, four each by the University of Wales, the Cardiff College and the King Edward VII Hospital, two each by the colleges at Aberystwyth and Bangor, and one each by the Welsh National Memorial Association and the Welsh Insurance Commissioners. The Medical Board would also have wide powers with regard to the allocation of funds and the employment of staff, but, at the end of the day, the Council of University College, Cardiff would remain the supreme governing body. The members of the departmental committee had had ample opportunity to observe the tensions between Cardiff and the University of Wales, and it was not surprising that the committee's interim report contained a less than wholehearted endorsement of the scheme that had emerged after six months' deliberations.

> The committee are aware that the proposals do not constitute an ideal organisation for a teaching institution of University rank in Wales, designed to serve the whole Principality rather than one particular part of it, but short of a reconstruction of the University and of fundamental changes not only in the University Charter but in those of the constituent Colleges, it would be impossible, in the opinion of the Committee to devise a completely satisfactory scheme. The Committee have decided to avoid making more radical proposals in view of the natural desire of the anonymous donor to see as rapid progress made as possible in the fulfilment of the scheme.

However, while the committee was prepared to recommend that 'a substantial grant' be made available to the new school on the basis of the existing proposals, it would quite understand if the Treasury required 'a stronger and more logical organisation' to be devised, perhaps in the context of a fundamental review of the structure of the University of Wales.

It so happened that the Advisory Committee on University Grants, also chaired by Sir William McCormick, was simultaneously conducting a review of the University of Wales and its colleges, five years after the implementation of the recommendations of the Raleigh Report. While this committee concluded that the University and its colleges needed more money, it was concerned that, as presently structured, higher education in Wales was unable to provide outcomes in an efficient and properly co-ordinated manner. The university authorities did not enjoy a central co-ordinating role which, among other things, could ensure the avoidance of wasteful duplication among the colleges. As currently constituted the federal university was not in a position to negotiate funding from the local authorities to support the activities of its colleges. In short the structure of the university and its relationship to the colleges needed to be reviewed.[14]

The Treasury could hardly ignore advice offered by two such influential bodies and, in a celebrated Treasury minute dated 9 February 1915, while accepting that the university and colleges should receive more money, it expressed doubt 'whether a mere increase in the amount of financial assistance will by itself be sufficient to effect all that is required to put University Education in Wales on a permanently satisfactory basis'. The Treasury advocated a 'competent enquiry into the whole question of the constitution of the University of Wales'. This would, of course, delay the implementation of a full medical school in Cardiff, but at least the Treasury gave permission for work to begin on the physiology block, 'on the distinct understanding that the buildings when erected will form part of the new National Medical School'.[15] Accused by the Cardiff College authorities of interfering in their internal affairs, the Treasury, understandably, refused to be drawn.[16]

BUILDING PLANS CONFIRMED AND DEFERRED

At least Sir William James Thomas and Colonel Bruce Vaughan could, at last, proceed with the building of the physiology block, and, nearly six months later, the *British Medical Journal* carried a substantial report of the official stone-laying ceremony for the new buildings on Newport Road, performed by Lord Pontypridd on 12 August 1915.[17] At the head of the report was the design of a most handsome building, from a sketch provided by the architect, Colonel Bruce Vaughan, much praised by Lord Aberdare, president of the college, who presided over the stone-laying ceremony: 'No one had done so much for the medical school and for the King Edward VII Hospital than he.' The crucial role of Sir William James Thomas was, of course, recognized, as well as the contributions of such pioneers as William Thomas Edwards, 'one of the best friends the College had ever had', having died a few weeks earlier at the ripe old age of ninety-two.

After singing the doxology the assembled guests, some 250 in all, made their way to the Cardiff City Hall where they were entertained to lunch by Sir William James Thomas. Sir William Osler, most appropriately, was called upon to propose a toast to 'the Welsh National School of Medicine'. This title for the future full medical school had emerged during a conference, held in April 1915, and involving all interested parties in the university, with the purpose of trying to devise a constitution for the medical school which would satisfy all parties. The stone-laying ceremony in August served to establish in everyone's minds, 'the Welsh National School of Medicine' as the title for the new institution, however it might finally be constituted – and Sir William Osler, during the course of his speech , acknowledged that this particular issue was still causing difficulties. He offered no particular solution other than to observe that Wales could only support one medical school, in Cardiff, 'the only town of sufficient size in Wales in which a medical school could have a proper existence'. In fact, the core of Osler's speech was a spirited defence of the 'clinical unit' system, which the school was planning to introduce:

You have got to face the problem of organising departments in the Hospital on University lines. That is to say, you have to recognise that medicine, surgery, obstetrics, pathology, gynaecology and the specialties are departments which have to be organised in the same way as the chemical, physical or physiological laboratories. They must be units in the university scheme, and means must be devised by which the University and the hospital will work in co-operation in furthering these vital interests of a medical school. Believe me, you may just as well not have laid the foundation stone of the physiological laboratory today if you do not go on to equip other departments, in connection with the school, on the same scientific lines.

Those responsible for promoting the early establishment of a full medical school in Cardiff could only have been encouraged by the words of the last speaker at the lunch, Professor E. H. Starling FRS of University College, London, perhaps the country's leading professor of physiology at that time. Science and medicine were allies in the wartime struggle against the Germans, and Wales had not yet played its full part, despite 'the peculiarly Welsh qualities of imagination and courage which have enabled our Minister of Munitions to do so great a work in the war against Germany'. The message was clear. The sooner the medical school was completed, the sooner Welsh medicine would contribute fully to the Allied cause.

It therefore came as a severe blow for the university and college authorities to receive a fairly uncompromising memorandum from the Treasury a month after the stone-laying ceremony. During the early summer a series of Welsh university conferences had been held to consider a response to the Treasury minute of 9 February 1915. Apart from proposing a structure for the medical school which, in the words of Professor Gwynn Williams, 'gave the Cardiff College far more general authority over a National School of Medicine than the Treasury would ever have considered desirable',[18] the conferences failed to offer any proposals for a radical reconstruction of the university, as also required by the Treasury. As far as the university and its colleges were concerned, their immediate priority was to secure enough funding to keep them solvent at a very difficult time. While the Treasury undertook to provide some interim funding, it was on condition that the university and colleges agreed to the 'immediate appointment of a Royal Commission on the University and to accept the decision which His Majesty's Government may arrive at, based on the findings of the Commission, with regard to the reform of the University, including the government of the National Medical School'.

A substantial part of the memorandum dealt with the building of the medical school, in particular the proposed Institute of Preventive Medicine, which, just before the outbreak of war, Sir William James Thomas had undertaken to provide in order to complete the Welsh National School of Medicine. Though fully mindful of Sir William's munificence, the Treasury was not prepared to agree to the completion of the medical school at that time, 'not only on financial grounds but also having regard to the special request that has been made for the deferment of all building and other work giving employment to men who could otherwise be used for military purposes or production of munitions'. The Treasury believed that the physiology block and existing buildings would provide enough accommodation for the school's medical students for the time being.[19]

Sir William accepted the position with an air of resignation:

> Candidly, it is a very great disappointment to me that this question had not been settled before the war started, and now my cherished hopes of seeing at once the establishment of a Welsh National School of Medicine are in danger of being frustrated for some years to come, on the plea which I cannot resist, that is a question of Patriotism.[20]

Colonel Bruce Vaughan was less conciliatory and devoted much time to attacking the Treasury's decision in the local press, and securing its support for his point of view. Having failed privately to persuade the government to relax its position, John Herbert Lewis, a prominent Welsh Liberal MP and parliamentary secretary to the Board of Education, finally wrote in exasperation to the editor of the *Western Mail*, urging the newspaper, and those who agitated in its columns, to moderate their attacks. There was no immediate need for the medical school to be completed. Current student numbers were relatively small:

> It must be some time, even under the most favourable conditions, before the Medical School acquires a prestige which will attract a large number of students. This prestige can only be gained by the excellence of the teaching provided and cannot be produced by overbuilding, the curse of so many educational institutions.[21]

Unfortunately, Lewis's blunt statement did not end the local discontent, forcing the chancellor of the Exchequer himself, Reginald McKenna, who also happened to be MP for North Monmouthshire, to become involved. He met and wrote to Sir William James Thomas to assure him of the government's commitment to see the remaining medical school buildings constructed as soon as the war was over, and sent Sir George Newman to Cardiff to convince the local leaders of the government's good faith.[22] In fact, when he got there Newman was 'agreeably surprised and pleased with the appearance of the physiological block (so far built) which seems to me to promise well'.[23] After meeting Professors Hepburn and Haycraft and Colonel Bruce Vaughan, and eliciting from them, particularly the colonel, an undertaking 'that there should be complete cessation of all public agitation', he was almost persuaded to recommend an immediate start on the rest of the school, having been told that Sir William James Thomas would not only pay for the capital cost, but also the full maintenance costs 'until such time as the Treasury may be able to make the promised grants'.[24] However, the Treasury could not be moved from its position that, apart from the physiology block, no new building in association with the medical school should begin until after the war. As Reginald McKenna explained to Sir William James Thomas, as his last word on the matter, 'All able-bodied men, whether of military age or not, are now required for munition work or for building munition factories or other urgent work'.[25]

THE WORK OF THE HALDANE COMMISSION

The chancellor's letter to Sir William James Thomas more or less coincided with the announcement on 12 April 1916 that the king had approved the appointment of a Royal Commission on University Education in Wales

> To inquire into the organisation and work of the University of Wales and its three Constituent Colleges, and into the relations of the University to those Colleges and to other institutions in Wales providing education of a post-secondary nature, and to consider in what respects the present organisation of University Education in Wales can be improved, and what changes, if any, are desirable in the constitution, functions and powers of the University and its three Colleges.

Although there were some in the principality who regretted that the University of Wales was being expected to subject itself to the humiliation of an external review, most acknowledged that such an approach was now fashionable and had been adopted with success elsewhere, as in London and Scotland.[26] All interests within the university had, by the end of the previous year, endorsed the proposal that a Royal Commission should be set up and by the spring its formal establishment was awaited with some impatience, and certainly less annoyance than might have been the case had a suggestion from a senior Treasury official been adopted. C. L. Stocks had wondered whether the words 'without any material increase of cost' should be added to the terms of reference after 'improved'. A. H. Kidd, secretary to the Haldane Commission and later secretary of the University Grants Committee, strongly advised against it:

> There can be no doubt that in Wales the phrase would be resented and would give rise to suspicion and ill-feeling. With recent experience of the unscrupulous agitation about the Medical School I really do not think it worth running the risk of starting the Commission under more hostile conditions than we need.[27]

Bearing in mind the important part he would play in the affairs of the Welsh National School of Medicine in the years to come, it was a little unfortunate that Kidd had, it seemed, already formed a poor opinion of some of the Cardiff promoters of the cause.

The appointment of Viscount Haldane of Cloan as chairman was widely welcomed. Both a former and a future lord chancellor, his role as chairman of the Royal Commission on university education in London (which had, among other things, made important recommendations regarding medical education) had been generally praised. The appointment of Sir William Osler as one of the members was welcomed even more. Although there was no specific mention of medical education in the Commission's terms of reference, as the *Western Mail* observed:

> The Medical School will require a large share of the attention of the Commission, and medical instruction, it is to be feared, is a subject which is little considered and less understood among those who are concerned with educational administration in the widest sense of the term.[28]

The general work of the Haldane Commission has been more than adequately covered by Professor Gwynn Williams in his history of the University of Wales, so the paragraphs that follow concentrate on the debate about the future shape of medical education in Wales. Despite Sir William Osler's very many commitments, this distinguished man was pleased to be involved. On the day that his appointment was announced he wrote to his nephew: 'I am on the Welsh University Royal Commission – for my sins – and will have a job in settling the new medical school at Cardiff. It is interesting work, and with such nice men.'[29] One of the nice men he looked to for local assistance was John Lynn Thomas, to whom he wrote not long after the commission had been set up: 'The Commission will visit Wales in June (end of) and I should like to hold meetings of the profession at Bangor, Aberystwyth and Cardiff. Please help in this when the time comes.'

Osler quickly made his mark. Speaking to the North Wales branch of the British Medical Association in Bangor at the end of June he made a powerful appeal to the patriotism of Welsh doctors to support the new medical school in Cardiff. Alluding to the traditional north/south rivalry, their inclinations might be more in the direction of the medical schools in the north of England; but, he asserted, they were Welshmen and though based in Cardiff, the medical school was to be a national one. Cardiff already had all the requisite clinical facilities; there was nowhere else in Wales which had comparable resources. He hoped that Cardiff would embrace the 'clinical unit' system, and went so far as to speculate on the sort of person who should lead the new school:

> He ought to be comparatively young, well trained, with a wide outlook, know a certain amount of science, appreciate a great deal more, be a good, practical man, should love his patients, get on with professional brethren, treat his nurses decently, and, above all, have a keen sympathy with his students.[30]

He did not, however, venture an opinion on the most appropriate constitutional arrangements for the medical school. That was a matter for the commission to consider.

The commissioners paid a preliminary visit to Cardiff from 20 to 22 June, when they visited the University Registry, the University College, the medical school and the King Edward VII Hospital. They met senior representatives of these institutions, and posed for a splendid group photograph, in which John Lynn Thomas and David Hepburn can be seen wearing the military uniform appropriate to senior officers of the Third Western General Hospital.[31] The commissioners heard all their evidence, however, in private, in the offices of the Board of Education in London, commencing on 4 October, when they met officers of the Cardiff College Council. On the following day it was the turn of representatives of the Cardiff Senate, and on the day after that, a delegation from the King Edward VII Hospital. The commissioners heard evidence from a wide range of other representatives of the university and the colleges regarding all aspects of higher education in Wales, on seven further days, thirty-one sittings altogether, ending with Sir Isambard Owen on 30 November 1916, the last of 156 witnesses to give evidence.[32]

David Hepburn, still dean of the faculty of medicine, the commanding officer of the Third Western General Hospital and an extremely busy man, chose not to submit tailor-made written evidence to the Commission:

> Under existing circumstances it is quite impossible for me to formulate a new state-ment for submission to the Royal Commission upon the question of Medical Education. I enclose a statement with which the Commissioners are already familiar [the memorandum written for Lloyd George in 1914] one that I had a considerable share in producing, and one that was to some extent the starting point of the present enquiry.[33]

However, the governors of the King Edward VII Hospital submitted a most impres-sive and comprehensive statement to the commission, setting out in detail the facilities that the hospital would provide for teaching and research purposes, 'if and when the Welsh National School of Medicine is constituted in Cardiff, in connection with the University College of South Wales and Monmouthshire'.

During the hearings, three main issues emerged with regard to medical education in Wales. The woman member of the Commission, Emily Penrose, principal of Somerville College, Oxford, asked David Hepburn whether women medical students would be treated on exactly the same footing as men. 'Absolutely; no distinction of sex,' a response later confirmed by Daniel Lleufer Thomas, junior deputy chancellor of the university and chairman of a committee aimed at promoting the medical training of women in Wales. The second issue concerned the introduction of what Lord Haldane termed 'the hospital unit' system in Cardiff, a development close to the heart of the former chairman of the Royal Commission on the University of London. David Hepburn was happy to confirm that it was very much the school's intention to introduce a system that did not exist anywhere in Great Britain at that time: 'We are not anxious to begin 50 years behind; we would like to begin 50 years ahead.' He believed that the 'hospital unit' system would be attractive to students not only from Wales, but well beyond. Bruce Vaughan, referring to the hospital's written submission, was able to confirm that as recently as 25 April its Medical Board, consisting of the hospital's honorary clinical staff, had supported the appointment of professors of medicine, surgery and obstetrics and gynaecology, with appropriate bed allocations. Both he, and David Hepburn, stated their intention that the clinical professors should be appointed on a full-time basis, though evidence from some of the honorary staff revealed some difference of view on this matter. Lord Haldane refused to be drawn into the argument: 'I feel myself quite unable to solve it, knowing the conflict of opinion there is; but no doubt when the critical moment comes, you will decide it somehow down in Wales through a competent body.' It is interesting to note that Sir William Osler happened to be absent for these exchanges. Had he been uncertain as to Cardiff's views on the clinical unit system it is inconceivable that he would have failed to attend, though Haldane himself was perfectly able to address the key issues in this area.

The third, and central, issue concerned the constitutional position of the Welsh National School of Medicine. Here, the weight of opinion among those giving evidence was overwhelmingly in favour of the medical school remaining an integral part of University College, Cardiff. This was certainly Principal Griffiths's view. Sir William James Thomas's buildings were intended for the college, they would be built on college land, and the college had already made financial sacrifices to develop the school. As far as Griffiths was concerned, the school's all-Wales dimension was adequately covered by the creation of a University of Wales Council of Medicine, as proposed by the Welsh university educational conferences in the previous year. Colonel Bruce Vaughan shared Griffiths's point of view. The college had to manage the school 'because they are on the spot'. The role of the university was as a guarantor of academic standards. Sir Owen M. Edwards, surely the leading advocate of Welsh nationalist aspirations on the commission, probed Vaughan on his vision of the medical school as a national institution. Why were they not looking to local authorities in north and mid-Wales for support? Vaughan's response might have been more sensitively expressed, in the circumstances: 'I did not think it was necessary. We in Cardiff have practically made the School.' In fairness, Professor T. F. Roberts, principal of University College of Wales, Aberystwyth, was entirely relaxed about Cardiff running the medical school, though, as that college's former professor of Greek, he could be forgiven for being well disposed to the place. Sir William Osler put it to him: 'You see an objection to the national medical school being part of Cardiff College?' 'No; in fact, I see it as a necessity that it should be part of the College.'

Percy Watkins, former registrar of the Cardiff College and still a member of its council, was one of only two who took a different view. He thought that the medical school should become a school of the University of Wales, and if the Cardiff College had to be compensated for loss, so be it. The last person to give evidence to the commission about the medical school was Sir Isambard Owen, still vice-chancellor of the University of Bristol. When invited by Lord Haldane (who happened to be chancellor of the University of Bristol) to comment on the constitutional position of the medical school, Sir Isambard confessed that the various schemes devised for its future seemed to him rather complicated. He went on: 'It has been in my mind whether the better plan would not be to organise the medical school as a separate corporation and make it in itself a constituent college of the University.' He saw no problem in a single-faculty institution becoming a separate constituent college of the university. As far as he was concerned, a constituent college needed 'a substantial foundation and is under really responsible government'. The last commissioner to question Sir Isambard was Sir William Osler. Among the issues he raised was the matter of the medical school buildings, donated to the Cardiff College by a benefactor. Surely it was not unreasonable for the local academic community to expect the school to be directly affiliated to their college, rather than to the university? In reply, Sir Isambard said:

> The original intention of the donor was unquestionably that it should be attached to the College; but I have been told lately that he is willing to accept the view, if that is arrived at, that it should be under the University instead of under the College.

As has already been noted, the Royal Commission took its evidence in private and it was only with the publication in June 1917 of the commission's minutes of evidence, that what had been said about the medical school became widely known. The *Times Educational Supplement* noted:

> Opinion seems to have been divided as to whether the Welsh National School of Medicine should become a department of the university college at Cardiff or become a self-contained and independent organization acting directly under the authority of the University. Happily, the evidence shows that the donor of the School has refrained from influencing the decision on this point.[34]

Nevertheless, as the influential monthly periodical, *The Welsh Outlook*, was to caution, how to reconcile the need for the medical school to retain its national character, while safeguarding the interests of the Cardiff College and the hospital, was a problem 'which requires careful handling'.[35]

Another nine months would elapse before the Royal Commission announced its recommendations, by which time permission had finally been obtained from the War Cabinet War Priorities Committee to proceed with Sir William James Thomas's

Institute of Preventive Medicine. Despite his earlier undertaking to Sir George Newman not to engage in public controversy in the matter, Colonel Bruce Vaughan had maintained an ongoing campaign against what he called the government's 'circumlocution office',[36] but what made the government finally relent was not Bruce Vaughan's tiresome complaining but a generous endowment to the Cardiff College from Miss Emily Charlotte Talbot of Margam Park, Port Talbot, announced in December 1917. This was, in fact, only the latest in a number of benefactions to be received by the college in 1917 to support the work of the medical school. Mrs John Nixon, widow of the coal magnate and a leading benefactor to the hospital resolved to endow research scholarships in medicine and medical pathology, and Lord Merthyr one for research in cancer; while the will of William Price, a generous supporter of the Cardiff Medical School from its earliest days, included a legacy of £20,000 (the equivalent of over £600,000 today) for the benefit of the medical school.[37]

Emily Charlotte Talbot was a member of one of the great landed families of south Wales, being a daughter of C. R. M. Talbot, sometime 'Father' of the House of Commons and the man after whom Port Talbot was named. Her wish was to endow the sum of £30,000 for the establishment of a professorship in preventive medicine, in connection with University College, Cardiff, the post to be known as the Mansel Talbot Professorship of Preventive Medicine, in memory of her father. Lord Haldane believed that Sir William Osler himself had been instrumental in persuading Miss Talbot to endow the chair.[38] Osler was certainly designated as the main trustee responsible for giving effect to the endowment, and it was to him that the secretary to the Works Construction Sub-Committee of the War Cabinet War Priorities Committee wrote in February 1918. The subcommittee had considered the representations made by Osler regarding permission to start work on Sir William James Thomas's Institute of Preventive Medicine: 'I am instructed to inform you that the sub-committee would be prepared to approve of the construction of such a building proceeding on condition that no war priority was granted to it, with reference either to materials or labour.'[39] Colonel Bruce Vaughan was naturally delighted. Writing to Principal Griffiths, he was clear 'that this committee has thought it advisable to grant this permission because of Miss Talbot's foundation of a Chair in Preventive Medicine'. He continued:

> I think that you and the Members of the Council will agree with me that Sir William Osler has placed not only the Council of the College deeply in its debt but the whole of the Principality as well, for the addition of this building together with Miss Talbot's great gift will do more to promote the happiness, the health and prosperity of its inhabitants than any other institution I can think of; and it will also teach the coming generation of medical men and inspire them not merely to practise the best that is known, but also themselves to advance knowledge which is the most important function of such a department.[40]

HALDANE: RECOMMENDATIONS AND RESPONSE

On 19 March 1918, the long-awaited report of the Haldane Commission was published. The final conclusion regarding the medical school was as follows:

> The proposed National Medical School should be organised as an independent Constituent College of the University, governed by a Council and Senate of its own. The special interests of the University College of South Wales and Monmouthshire should be recognised in the constitution of the Council. The hospital side of the College of Medicine at the King Edward VII Hospital should be worked upon the 'hospital unit system' under full-time professors.

The commissioners confessed that they, like others, had found it difficult to reconcile the existence of the medical school as a national institution on the one hand, and as an integral part of University College, Cardiff on the other. They preferred the simplicity of Sir Isambard Owen's solution, to have a medical school as a constituent college of the university. The quite reasonable views of the Cardiff College could be addressed by giving it strong representation on the medical school Council. A council of thirty-two members was proposed, two appointed by the University of Wales, ten by University College, Cardiff, six by the King Edward VII Hospital, two each by the university colleges at Aberystwyth, North Wales and, when constituted, Swansea, three by the medical school Senate, and one each by the Welsh National Memorial Association and the Welsh National Health Insurance Commission, with up to three co-opted members. While medical students would continue to be instructed in the basic sciences in the first year at Cardiff College, they would then proceed to the jurisdiction of the medical school for the following years, meaning, among other things, the transfer of staff in the preclinical subjects from Cardiff to the medical school. The commissioners considered that clinical training should be conducted according to the 'hospital unit system'. Paragraph 219 stated:

> For this purpose the Hospital should be organised so as to be brought directly within the sphere of the University and adapted to the scientific study of disease and the training of students on a scientific basis comparable to that afforded in other branches of University study. The Professor in each clinical subject will have a definite number of beds in the hospital assigned to him with the proper staff on both the clinical and the educational side, and with laboratories and lecture rooms and all that is required for teaching and research.

Although not specified in this paragraph, the commission's final conclusions, quoted above, clearly referred to the appointment of 'full-time professors' to head the units.

With regard to the headship of what the report called the 'University College of Medicine', while acknowledging that he might not be as busy in his administrative duties as the head of one of the other colleges, he would probably have academic duties. In any case he would have responsibilities in connection with the hospital. The head of the college should therefore hold the title of principal, but, because of his range of commitments, 'We do not think it is desirable that he should be on the rota for periodic service as Vice-Chancellor of the University.'[41]

The blueprint for the future Welsh National School of Medicine carried the unmistakable imprint of arguably the two leading medical educationalists in the United Kingdom at that time, Sir Isambard Owen and Sir William Osler. The immediate reaction of the *Western Mail* was positive, as was, in general, that of Colonel Bruce Vaughan. His main complaint was that there was not parity of representation on the medical school council as between the hospital and the Cardiff College. In his view 'the hospital is practically the School of Medicine.' Professor Haycraft thought the scheme proposed by Haldane to be 'a very fair and equitable arrangement, taking it as a whole'.[42]

The overwhelming reaction, however, to the report, as it concerned the future of the medical school, was hostile. The other Cardiff daily newspaper, the *South Wales Daily News*, considered the proposal to be 'impracticable or at least inimical to the best interests of the institutions concerned'.[43] Those associated with University College, Cardiff, naturally found the proposals quite unacceptable. Hugh Ingledew, a leading Cardiff solicitor and a long-serving member of the College Council, articulated the feelings of many in a letter to Registrar Brown:

> The proposals of the Commission practically mean that the Cardiff College should endow the new Medical School to the extent of an amount which is equivalent to something between £50,000 and £100,000, while at the same time the whole of the work, which has been so zealously and efficiently carried out by the Cardiff College in the direction of Medical Education during the last 15 or 20 years, is to be taken out of their hands and handed over to another body. This seems most unfair as there is not and has not been the slightest suggestion that the Cardiff College have not properly and efficiently carried out their medical work during the period they have been engaged upon it. The proposals also raise important legal questions as to the position of the College with regard to the benefactions which they receive such as those from Dr Edwards, Dr Price and the Talbot Trustees.[44]

The fact that Principal Griffiths had just announced his intention to retire at the end of the session did not inhibit him from launching a robust attack on the Royal Commission's recommendations concerning the medical school at a special meeting of the College Senate on 7 May. He referred at one point to the way the medical school had been identified with the college by the public of south Wales, and

> When the old accusation of our being engaged in producing only 'teachers and preachers' has been made, the most effective reply has been the excellence of the

work done for the medical profession. Separate that School from the College and much of the claim we have, both on the respect and affection of the people of South Wales, will cease to exist.

He referred to the harm that would follow the separation of medicine from the other scientific disciplines, to the administrative chaos which would result from two separate colleges occupying one piece of land, and deplored the wresting from the college of departments 'on which they had spent much money, much energy, and of which they were specially proud'.[45] Needless to say, the Senate roundly rejected the commissioners' recommendations, as, a week later, did the board of governors of the hospital, notwithstanding Bruce Vaughan's earlier, and clearly off-the cuff, reaction. It was hardly surprising that Lord Haldane would later observe, rather ruefully, 'Cardiff is a great centre, but a difficult place to deal with.'[46]

Sir William Osler was not entirely surprised by the generally adverse reaction given to the medical school aspects of the report. Writing to Principal Griffiths he observed: 'I always knew there would be a kick-up when the time came ... I suppose the Treasury will do what Wales wishes, so get these wishes quite clearly expressed.' In reply Griffiths stated that his position was:

> Not that I want Cardiff to 'run the show' but that I am anxious that the medical school shall not be separated from the College. Remember the College Council is a very different thing from Cardiff, in fact it is ten to one against Cardiff, and there is less danger of the school being made a purely local institution if it is in close connexion with the College.
>
> As for the views of Wales, the practically unanimous resolution of the University Senate is, at all events, some indication, and I believe it probable that the University Court at its meeting on July 19th next, will take the same line. I know that Glamorgan, Monmouthshire and Cardiff will; the hospital itself does. If my predictions are carried out this will be a fairly unanimous expression of feeling.[47]

Griffiths's predictions were soon proved accurate. He did not, however, predict Sir Isambard Owen's volte-face. Bearing in mind that those giving evidence to the commission had overwhelmingly favoured the medical school's continuing integration with the Cardiff College, the evidence given by Owen had, undoubtedly, been crucial. This was his response to a straightforward question from Lord Haldane: 'I gather that your mind, on the whole, leans to the notion of an independent organisation?' 'That seems to me to be the simplest solution of the difficulty.' While Owen admitted to the Cardiff president, Lord Aberdare that 'I had no opportunity of discussing the suggestion with anyone before I made it to the Commission,'[48] the fact remains that he had plenty of time afterwards – months – to clarify his opinion, in private, to its chairman. After all, Lord Haldane was the chancellor of the university,

Bristol, of which Owen was still vice-chancellor. Is it credible that conversations would not have taken place between them while the report was being compiled to make sure that there was no misunderstanding about one of its central recommendations? Indeed, in preparation for a meeting between Sir Isambard and members of the Cardiff College Council, following the publication of the report he was at pains to ensure that those at the meeting were fully aware of what he had said to the commissioners. In a letter to the Cardiff registrar he wrote:

> I do not know whether the members of the Council are quite clear as to what the terms of my suggestion to the Commission on the matter actually are. They are recorded in questions and answers 4592–6, on page 264 of the appendix to the Commissioners' first report. I think it might be as well to have this appendix at the committee on Tuesday; possibly it might be useful to have the extract manifolded and circulated to the members of the committee in advance.[49]

Nevertheless, by the time the meeting had finished, Sir Isambard was in full retreat. As Principal Griffiths would later report, Sir Isambard explained that he had made his suggestion to the commission as an alternative to what he had regarded as a 'hybrid' scheme for dual control of the medical school as proposed by the university conference in 1915. Clearly unnerved by the overwhelmingly hostile reaction to the commissioners' recommendation, Sir Isambard was now going out of his way to favour the continuance of the existing link between the medical school and the college, and offering to join any delegation to the prime minister to say so.[50]

On 14 August 1918 a deputation from the University of Wales, led by Lord Kenyon, did indeed visit David Lloyd George at 10 Downing Street, to discuss the Haldane Report, though, perhaps prudently in the circumstances, Sir Isambard Owen was not among the delegates. Although much involved with matters relating to the conduct of the war on the Western Front at this time, Lloyd George was still able to find time for issues nearer home. Indeed, his engagements immediately prior to his meeting with Lord Kenyon and his colleagues had included attending the National Eisteddfod at Neath, where he also received the freedom of the borough.[51] Addressing the university deputation, he declared his view that the Haldane Report was one of the most important documents in the history of Wales.[52] He supported its main conclusions, and provided the commissioners' recommendations were, in the main, accepted, he believed that the government would agree to fund the university and its colleges by giving a pound for every pound raised in Wales. He invited the university authorities, including those of the constituent colleges, to submit a scheme to the government on how they proposed to carry out the recommendations.

At that point Lloyd George was reminded by Principal Griffiths, who tended to irritate him, that the Haldane Commission's recommendations regarding the status of the medical school had secured virtually no support in Wales: 'I think you will find, Sir, that there is no piece of evidence in favour of separation, except the statement of Sir Isambard Owen, which seems to have been misapprehended.' Lloyd George refused to be drawn.

> I propose that the question of the Medical School should be included in that scheme. I am not going to lay down any condition on that head. Let Wales as a whole consider the matter; let us hear what are the views of those concerned in education as a whole throughout Wales, what they will do with regard to the Medical School.

In reality, no one was, at this time, particularly inclined to confront the Cardiff College in its resistance to the report's recommendations regarding medical education in Wales. No doubt this was partly because there was some sympathy for the college's specific arguments. Moreover there was a feeling that it would be unfortunate to allow the medical school issue to impair the hitherto cordial relationships existing between the three colleges. This was a point forcibly put, amidst applause, by Lord Kenyon, wearing his hat as president of the University College of North Wales, Bangor, to its Court in October 1918.[53] Even Lord Haldane, speaking in Cardiff, was forced to admit that he saw no inconsistency between making the school the National School of Medicine for all Wales, while at the same time keeping up its organic connection with Cardiff and its college, to which it owed so much. 'That was a problem they [the people of Wales] would have to solve.'[54]

When, in November 1918, the Cardiff College Council submitted a draft scheme addressing the future constitutional position of the Welsh National School of Medicine to a meeting of the University Court,[55] it is not surprising that the Court confirmed the view it had taken at its July meeting, in favour of the continuing integration of the school with the college. The draft scheme was presented by Albert Howard Trow (1863–1939), a Montgomeryshire man, head of physics, acting principal at the college following the retirement of Professor Griffiths and a 'tough and tenacious man, well-versed in university politics'.[56] He suggested that the union of the college and the school of medicine could be maintained without deviating very widely from the proposals of the commissioners. The essential feature in Cardiff's scheme was that, subject to the supremacy of the university, the Council of the Cardiff College should be the chief governing authority of the school of medicine, but that it should delegate to a Board of Medicine wide administrative powers and functions. The constitution of the Board of Medicine followed closely that earlier proposed by the commission (paragraph 217) in relation to the council of the independent medical college, except that two additional representatives were given to the University of Wales, and two representatives were allotted to the Cardiff and County Public Health

Laboratory Committee in acknowledgement of the close co-operation of this committee in the work of the future school's Department of Public Health and Institute of Preventive Medicine. Provision was also made for the representation of county councils, county borough councils and women. Having explained the scheme in detail, Trow maintained that if the scheme was accepted, Wales would have the most progressive medical school in the United Kingdom.[57]

Despite outward appearances that the Cardiff College's blueprint for the medical school enjoyed universal support, there remained in Whitehall circles, and among some of the academic community in Wales, a belief that the matter had not been subjected to adequate scrutiny. Sir Harry Reichel, principal of Bangor and, at the time vice-chancellor of the University of Wales, admitted to the Hon. William Napier Bruce (1858–1936) that he did not think that 'the details of the scheme have been sufficiently worked out by the University'.[58] Seemingly preoccupied with one of the commission's recommendations relating to agriculture which impinged upon Bangor's development plans, Reichel had not given enough thought to the potential risk of a Cardiff College owning a strong medical school choosing, sooner or later, to leave and therefore weaken the University of Wales. By the time that he and J. M. Angus, the university registrar, remembered the existence of the University Medical Board, and referred Cardiff's scheme to it, in July 1919, it was too late to do other than make a few inconsequential amendments to Cardiff's scheme. It was a rather embarrassed Dr Angus who explained the late involvement of the University Medical Board in the consultative process:

> The Medical Board has found it difficult to hold meetings during the war period – several of its members being unable to attend – and on the other hand there has been little for it to do, apart from this one matter, as the examinations have been mostly suspended. Hence the omission (for which I take whatever blame there is) to call a meeting of the Board to advise the Court on this matter.[59]

As far as Whitehall was concerned, William Bruce, who had not only been deputy chairman of the Haldane Commission, but was principal assistant secretary at the Board of Education, and A. H. Kidd, secretary to the Commission, were wholly unconvinced by the apparent show of unanimity in favour of Cardiff's scheme. In Bruce's view, 'the medical staff at Cardiff are anxious not to start a quarrel with the S. Wales College, and the other Univ. Colleges share this anxiety especially as they want the goodwill of Cardiff in other matters which more closely concern themselves.'[60] Kidd agreed:

> The show of unanimity in favour of altering the Royal Commission's scheme is one to which I attach very little importance. Cardiff and the South Wales authorities want to retain control of the School of Medicine, and Bangor and Aberystwyth do not feel their own special interests sufficiently affected to make it worth while to oppose Cardiff.[61]

However, both Bruce and Kidd conceded that, faced with such an apparent show of unity in Wales, there was nothing more they could do to save one of the central recommendations of the Haldane Report, whether it had been properly debated on its merits or not. When, therefore, the University of Wales's formal response to the report was submitted to the government in May 1919, incorporating Cardiff's scheme for the constitution of the National School of Medicine as an integral part of the college, as endorsed by the University Court, Whitehall conceded defeat. On the advice of his officials, H. A. L. Fisher, president of the Board of Education, wrote, with some regret, to David Lloyd George:

> My own view is that this recommendation [in the Haldane Report] was the right one both in the interests of the National character of the School and in that of medical education, and I shall be ready to give you my reasons for that view if you wish to have them. But it must be recognised that the recommendation has received no support from the College Authorities, the Medical Profession, or the general public, and it is very strongly opposed by the University College of South Wales and Monmouthshire and by the City of Cardiff. It cannot be said to be an essential element in the plan of the Royal Commission, and I think, therefore, you would be well advised to say that you are willing to concede this point, though not without reluctance.[62]

A deputation from the University of Wales and the local authorities met the prime minister again on 19 March 1920, to hear the government's decision. Lloyd George reminded those present of the government's expectation that, in return for pound-for-pound funding, the university should comply with the recommendations of the Haldane Commission: 'With regard to that Sir Harry [Reichel] has indicated quite clearly in his statement that you are prepared to do that with one or two exceptions which you have outlined well. So far as those are concerned, we raise no obstacle at all.'[63]

So, for the time being at least, the Cardiff College had won its struggle for control of the Welsh National School of Medicine. For a short time the General Medical Council, or at least its registrar, appeared to be confused about the status of the medical school. 'Am I to understand that the Welsh National School of Medicine is a new body? If so what is its address?' The reply of the Cardiff College registrar, by return, was short and to the point:

> In reply to your letter of the 24th instant, I have to state that the Welsh National School of Medicine is an integral part of this college. As the result of the Report of the Royal Commission on University Education in Wales it is hoped to establish a complete Medical School here in the near future. The address will be the same as before.[64]

In September 1920, the Privy Council formally approved a supplemental charter for the University of Wales, giving effect to most of the recommendations of the Royal Commission. In this charter a fourth college – at Swansea – was declared to be a constituent college of the university. No reference was made to the Welsh National School of Medicine; it was accepted by everyone (at the time) that the school was an integral part of the University College of South Wales and Monmouthshire. One important constitutional issue had not, however, been satisfactorily resolved, the relationship between the Welsh National School of Medicine and the King Edward VII Hospital.

THE DEVELOPMENT OF UNIVERSITY/HOSPITAL RELATIONSHIPS IN THE UNITED KINGDOM

The first two decades of the twentieth century were a time of change in university/hospital relations in general, characterized by Keir Waddington as 'the rise of academic medicine'.[65] They were a period during which Academe came to play a much greater role than hitherto in the organization and provision of clinical teaching. William Osler referred to the phenomenon as 'the active invasion of the hospitals by the universities'.[66] By the early years of the century 'academic medicine' was already the norm in the preclinical disciplines. As Christopher Lawrence has written,

> The basic medical sciences, especially physiology, were taught by men, and latterly also women, who were employed by universities and medical schools as full-time professional scientists. When they were not teaching, they would be in the labs on experimental research.[67]

In disciplines which bridged the preclinical and the clinical, subjects such as pathology and bacteriology, full-time academic posts were also created – as in Cardiff – where the incumbents held not only university appointments but also honorary hospital appointments, and took their share of the routine clinical work of their hospitals.

However, in the hospital-based disciplines, old habits died hard, indeed flourished. The medical students progressed from the preclinical, laboratory-orientated departments of the university medical school into a totally different hospital environment, in which clinical teaching demanded 'the ineffable wisdom and experience that came only with advanced years, a classical education and the bearing of a gentleman'.[68] Here the teachers were part-time physicians and surgeons, essentially suspicious of the laboratory, which was regarded as a challenge, even an insult, to their sound judgement and authority, attributes considered to be central to one of their main aims in life, the successful pursuit of private practice, which was, after all their main source of income.[69] Lord Platt, recalling his years as a medical student in Sheffield at the end of the First World War, once wrote: 'I must remind my readers that all staff appointments to teaching hospitals were literally honorary, in the sense that there was no pay attached to them and you had to make your living through private practice.'[70] They would receive modest payment for their teaching duties, not from the university but from the hospital, which would recoup their outlay from the students. Those clinical teachers holding the title of professor were cut from the same cloth as the rest, though they would receive some payment for their academic duties from their medical school or university; otherwise they too depended on private practice to earn their living.

Not everyone considered the British way as the best for the provision of undergraduate clinical training. There were those – notably William Osler, who had become regius professor of medicine at Oxford University in 1905 – who considered the sort of medical education given at the Johns Hopkins School of Medicine at Baltimore to be infinitely superior. As has been noted in chapter 3, Osler and others took the opportunity to make their views known to the Royal Commission on University Education in London, advocating the adoption in the London medical schools of the teaching arrangements which had proved to be so successful at Johns Hopkins.

Convinced by the evidence of Osler, Abraham Flexner and Professor E. H. Starling, professor of physiology at University College, London, the commission recommended that a new system for the provision of medical education should be adopted in the London medical schools. This would entail the establishment of clinical units in medicine and surgery, directed by professors and supported by assistants, all paid by the university. While the pursuit of private practice was not precluded it was expected that the members of the units would devote most, if not all, of their time to clinical teaching and experimental research.

The outbreak of the war delayed implementation of the clinical unit system in London, but the reformers did not let the matter drop. As we have already seen, Sir William Osler had been keen to see the unit system adopted in Cardiff, a new clinical school, indeed virgin territory, where new concepts could be tried without challenging existing practices. The adoption of the clinical unit system in Cardiff was confirmed by the Haldane Commission on University Education in Wales in 1918. Moreover, in the metropolis, clinicians influenced by the so-called German model (on which the Johns Hopkins system had been based), men like Archibald Garrod and Wilmot Herringham at St Bartholomew's Hospital, and Sir George Newman, chief medical officer at the Ministry of Health, continued to promote the clinical unit system. In particular, Newman commended it in his influential memorandum, *Some Notes on Medical Education in England* (1918), receiving the strong endorsement of Sir Clifford Allbutt, regius professor of physic at Cambridge University, who advocated the establishment of clinical units 'in every adequate clinical school'.[71] In the event, the first clinical units were established at St Bartholomew's Hospital Medical School in the autumn of 1919 but by 1923 only seven centres in Britain had adopted this system, hardly the 'active invasion of the hospitals by the universities' that Osler had called for. Nevertheless, the introduction of the clinical unit did represent a real advance in the progress of academic medicine at this time.

If one model for the organization and provision of clinical training was being formulated in London, another was evolving in the English provinces where, in one centre after another, the university authorities were taking responsibility for the clinical teaching programme from the hospitals with which they were associated. Care was, however, taken to ensure that the hospitals and the clinical teachers remained integral to the management process. In Liverpool, a body known as the Hospitals Board of the University of Liverpool Clinical School was established in 1906 to co-ordinate the school's clinical teaching. On the board sat doctors representing each of the participating hospitals. In addition, the university's Faculty of Medicine included representatives of the several clinicians involved in the teaching programme.[72] The decision of the Board of Education, in 1908, to award grants, for the first time, to universities in support of medical education, an action briefly noted in chapter 3 in connection with St Mary's Hospital Medical School, was a catalyst for change. In return for the grant, the universities were expected to take closer control of the teaching being undertaken on their behalf in the hospitals. In particular, universities should take on formal responsibility for the appointment and payment of the clinical teachers – indeed some of the state grant would be used for that purpose.[73] As a quid pro quo the clinical teachers could expect to be awarded university titles, and the hospital and its clinical staff granted membership of relevant university committees. The effect of the Board of Education's new policy was immediate. In Leeds responsibility for the organization of clinical teaching was transferred from the Leeds General Infirmary to the university in 1910, but all the hospital staff involved in the teaching programme became members of the university's Board of the Faculty of Medicine.[74] A similar process occurred at Sheffield. The university took over formal responsibility for organizing the clinical teaching at its medical school from the staff of the participating Sheffield hospitals. The hospitals' Clinical Studies Committee became a subcommittee of the University Council, an arrangement which ensured that the hospitals' clinical staff continued to carry great influence in the detailed organization of the medical school's clinical teaching programme.[75] Meanwhile in Bristol, the main governing body of the medical school, the Medical Board, included among its members not only the vice-chancellor, the dean of medicine and the professoriate, but also the senior clinicians at the Bristol Royal Infirmary and the Bristol General Hospital.[76] The concept of partnership between university and hospital in the provision of undergraduate medical education was articulated nowhere better that in Birmingham. In 1911 the University of Birmingham Clinical Board was reconstituted to comprise the dean of the Faculty of Medicine, four members of the Faculty of Medicine who held appointments in the two principal teaching hospitals, together with two members of the clinical staff from each of the two hospitals. The Clinical

Board had 'the general direction of the clinical teaching at the two hospitals, and in particular shall arrange that students must attend twelve months alternately at the General and Queen's Hospitals, as directed at time of registration'. The new regulations added: 'All the present members of the Clinical Staffs shall be appointed as University Clinical Teachers, their names to be printed in the University Calendar, and they shall be counted among University officials.' The University Clinical Board would report its proceedings to the Faculty of Medicine, on which the clinical teachers would have two representatives.[77]

COLLEGE AND HOSPITAL: AN UNEASY RELATIONSHIP IN CARDIFF

In spite of developments in England during the previous decade or more, as a result of which universities were taking greater control over the organization and provision of clinical teaching, it was never likely that the proposals drafted by the Cardiff College authorities for the governance of the medical school, would be acceptable to the hospital authorities. As far as Bruce Vaughan was concerned, 'the hospital is practically the school of medicine.' The Cardiff College authorities did not go as far as the Haldane Commission in advocating that the hospital should so organize itself as to be 'directly within the sphere' of the university. However, in their draft scheme for the governance of the Welsh National School of Medicine, devised during the autumn of 1918, they did accept Haldane's proposal that the Cardiff College should have ten representatives on the governing body of the medical school, with only six from the hospital. Furthermore, there would be no hospital representation at all on the College Council, or on the medical school's supreme academic authority, the Faculty of Medicine, or even on appointments committees set up to select members of the clinical academic staff. To add insult to injury, the college authorities, with crass insensitivity, sent their draft scheme for discussion at the meeting of the University Court in November 1918, without considering the hospital's objections, pleading pressure of deadlines. Needless to say, Bruce Vaughan was upset, as he admitted to the College registrar:

> I am sorry to hear that you have sent on to the University the draft scheme of the constitution of the medical School without having the views of the Hospital; for the Hospital certainly does not accept the scheme except for those branches of the School who will not work in the Hospital. We must have an equal share in the control of the School and in the appointment of men in the School who are to be teachers in the Hospital. This is reasonable and should be arranged by mutual consent and it should be done in the early stages of the organisation as it will save endless trouble in the future. Some members, indeed the senior members of the Medical Board of the Hospital, will not look at the draft scheme and I am doing my best to get them to

agree to something and the notes and suggested amendments which are numerous and important will be submitted to the Emergency Committee in January.[78]

In the light of university/hospital liaison arrangements elsewhere, particularly in the English provinces, Bruce Vaughan's pleas on behalf of his hospital were not unreasonable, and it was not surprising that he decided to appeal to Sir Isambard Owen for support. Owen, whose advice was clearly being studiously avoided by the college and university authorities during this time, replied to Bruce Vaughan that he had been, 'of late, very little cognisant of the discussions and negotiations that have taken place, and many questions may have cropped up of which I am altogether ignorant'. Nevertheless he was prepared to make some general observations. As far as the role of the hospital was concerned, 'It cannot be said that its contribution under the proposed scheme will be of any less importance than that of the College.' There should certainly be hospital representation on committees appointing the professors of medicine, surgery and obstetrics, and 'The hospital must clearly retain its full rights of regulating the conduct of students during such time as they are within its walls.'[79] In giving his opinion, Sir Isambard was able to draw on his extensive knowledge of the medical education scene nationally, and, relating to recent years, Bristol, where he continued to serve as vice-chancellor.[80] Armed with support such as this, it was entirely to be expected that when the hospital's Emergency and Reference Committee (in effect its executive committee) met early in the new year, it resolved to press for the College Council and the hospital Board of Management to have eight members each on the Board of Medicine, and for the hospital to have formal representation on the College Council itself.[81]

Nothing, however, was done to take the matter forward in Cardiff, and no amendments were made to the draft scheme for the medical school formulated the previous autumn. The explanation is fairly clear. At a crucial stage in the discussions the formidable colonel fell ill and died. One of his last letters was to Sir Isambard Owen:

> I was too unwell on Thursday to go out with the chance of having a word with you at the meeting of the University Court, and I have not been well since. One thing and another has been a bit too much for me and I do not seem to get over my last illness as quickly as I ought to have, but I am hoping that with the warmer weather I shall soon be myself again … I can assure you, were it not for your help and practical sympathy I should feel inclined to let the whole thing slide. No-one here has more than a very superficial grasp of the subject. Professor Trow and Ingledew are possessed with the idea that they know all about it, and the Hon. Staff are quite indifferent and General Lee [the hospital chairman] is too old to grasp the importance of having a scheme at the start so as to save friction and endless trouble in the future.[82]

This letter shows how crucial Bruce Vaughan was in driving the project for a full medical school forward, and two months later he had died, at the age of sixty-three, a devastating loss at an absolutely critical time. Though there is little doubt that Bruce Vaughan, a bachelor who devoted all his time to his work, enjoyed being in the lime-light and relished the plaudits and friendships he managed to attract, it is recorded that he waived professional fees worth thousands of pounds in relation to many of his most cherished projects. Perhaps this explains why his estate was subsequently assessed at only £8,251. The *Western Mail* paid the colonel a handsome tribute:

> Seldom has the public life of any community been impoverished by the decease of one man as the public life of Cardiff is impoverished by the death of Colonel E. M. Bruce Vaughan … In a somewhat sordid age, when greed and extravagance are everywhere manifest he was a burning and a shining light, a steadfast and unfailing exemplar of the gospel of unselfish labour for the public good.[83]

Many of the leading figures of Welsh public life attended his funeral, and among those who accompanied him to his last resting place in the Old Cemetery, Adamsdown were Professors Hepburn and Haycraft and a throng of bareheaded medical students. Sadly, the Old Cemetery no longer exists. In 1948 it was grassed over, becoming, in recent years, a rather run-down public park, with some of the headstones ranged round the perimeter wall. Against the north wall were the diminished remains of the colonel's memorial stone, daubed with red paint. By 2008 even that relic had disappeared, further landscaping having been carried out. Fortunately, other memorials to this dedicated man remain, not least the façade and main entrance of the physiology block on Newport Road, now Cardiff University's School of Engineering.

With the formidable colonel off the scene, the challenge presented by the establishment of a full medical school drifted off the hospital's immediate agenda. Indeed, the hospital's annual reports for 1919 and 1920, which in previous years had made much of the issue, made no reference to the matter at all. As has been noted, the honorary clinical staff appeared to be 'quite indifferent' whether their hospital became a teaching hospital or not. With Bruce Vaughan dead and the medical school's leading champions among the clinical staff, Sir John Lynn-Thomas and P. R. Griffiths, either retired or on the verge of becoming so, other voices, nervous of the impact that a full medical school might have on the working of the hospital, were coming to the fore.

There were, indeed, a few at this time who were questioning whether the existing King Edward VII Hospital was suitable to serve as a teaching hospital at all. Alderman D. J. Robinson, chairman of the Cardiff City Health Committee, and himself a well-respected general practitioner, advocated the conversion of the hospital into a casualty clearing station, a brand-new hospital being built 'somewhere outside the town'.[84] The eminent Welsh orthopaedic surgeon Sir Robert Jones voiced similar sentiments. Speaking at the inaugural meeting of the scientific section of the Cardiff Medical Students' Club in April 1920, he said that, splendid though the hospital was in many ways, he judged it incapable of meeting the needs of a modern teaching hospital. Four hundred beds were nowhere near enough; there should be at least 1,500, and the centre of a large city was an unsuitable environment in which to treat children.[85] In an ideal world Sir Robert might have been correct, but in reality there were no teaching hospitals in the United Kingdom which satisfied his criteria in 1920. The largest general hospital in London, The London, had 950 beds, with St Bartholomew's Hospital second with 757, and Guy's third with 644, closely followed by St Thomas's (630). Several of the most celebrated teaching hospitals had 300 or fewer. All were in highly populated parts of the metropolis, as they would discover to their cost during the London blitz.[86] The largest teaching hospitals in the English provinces, all located near to the city centres, were the Manchester Royal Infirmary and the Leeds General Hospital, each with some 620 beds, followed by the Royal Victoria Infirmary, Newcastle with 550. The Royal Infirmaries at Edinburgh, Glasgow and Aberdeen were comparable with the largest teaching hospitals in London,[87] but none matched Sir Robert Jones's ideal, and, one has to say, no one seriously stopped to ponder whether the establishment of a full medical school in Cardiff should be delayed because the King Edward VII Hospital was too small or in the wrong place.

Nevertheless, by the beginning of 1921, Cardiff's Principal Trow (he had been appointed to the post, to great acclaim in May 1919) was becoming anxious about the slow progress being made towards achieving this goal. The intention was to commence the full medical school in October 1921, and the senior preclinical students were beginning to ask about the prospects for clinical training in Cardiff later in the year. Discussions with the hospital authorities had achieved little, the matter of representation dominating their minds to the virtual exclusion of everything else, and Trow was concerned lest an impatient government might decide to divert their grant elsewhere. Invited to a meeting of the hospital's Emergency and Reference Committee on 12 January, Trow demanded answers to two questions. Would the hospital provide facilities by October 1921 for thirty, twenty or ten students? Would the hospital accept as members of its honorary staff professors in medicine, surgery and gynaecology, duly elected by the College Council on the recommendation of the committees of selection? 'If the Hospital cannot meet the College in these respects, circumstances will compel them to reconsider the position.' Predictably the members of the committee persisted with the concerns that they had always expressed. Would the hospital receive increased representation on the Board of Medicine, and some representation on the College Council? Would it be represented on the appointments committees for the clinical professors? Would the college ensure that the professors of medicine, surgery and obstetrics and gynaecology held full-time appointments?[88]

Principal Trow did his best to address at least some of the hospital's concerns. There was nothing the college could do at this stage about hospital representation on the Board of Medicine and the College Council; these matters had now been enshrined in statutes and regulations which could not easily be amended. However, the College Council readily agreed to allow the hospital to be represented on college appointments committees in which it had an interest. Furthermore, as Trow stated to the College Court, 'The men who were appointed as professors would not enter into competition with existing medical practitioners in Cardiff, for they would not be permitted to undertake private practice.'[89]

Apart from concerns over hospital representation on college bodies, the question whether the professors being appointed to head 'clinical units' in the hospital should be full-time or part-time was a serious issue for the honorary clinical staff, fearful that the professors might fish in a relatively small pool of private practice in the city to the disadvantage of existing practitioners. Their views on this matter had been made clear by the hospital's senior surgeon at the hearings of the Haldane Commission. The college authorities had no difficulty in assuaging the fears of the honorary clinical staff on that score. As has been noted earlier, the college authorities had, from the time of the Haldane Report on London University, declared their intention to appoint full-time professors, if they could afford them, for sound academic reasons. The report of the Haldane Commission had itself advocated the appointment of full-time clinical professors in Cardiff, and had the First World War not intervened, Cardiff might have become the first medical school in Britain to adopt the clinical unit system, employing full-time clinical professors. In the event, as has already been noted, this distinction fell on St Bartholomew's Hospital Medical College, where the first full-time professors of medicine and surgery in the United Kingdom were appointed in the autumn of 1919.[90]

Notwithstanding the college's assurance that the hospital would be involved in the appointment of the clinical professors, and that they would be appointed on a full-time basis, the honorary clinical staff remained disaffected. Led by the senior physician, William Mitchell Stevens, the senior surgeon, H. G. Cook, and the gynaecologist, Tenison Collins, the hospital's Medical Board, on 5 April 1921, unanimously resolved that the commencement of the full medical school be postponed. Neither the school nor the hospital was in any way ready to take the next major step in the development of medical education in the principality. Such a postponement would, it was suggested, 'lead to a better knowledge and understanding of the scheme by all the parties concerned and provide for the reasonable conservation of the interests of the existing members of staff'. Postponement would also enable the hospital to provide suitable facilities for the staff and students of the school, 'at present non-existent', and to formulate or revise various regulations within the hospital. In short, postponement would, in the view of the hospital's honorary clinical staff, result in 'the establishment of a measure of efficiency and prestige with harmony of co-operation unobtainable in the short period now proposed, which must prove of profound significance to the medical school'.[91]

Despite his national prominence, Thomas Lewis, by now full physician and director of the Department of Clinical Research at University College Hospital (and shortly to become a knight of the realm), still retained an interest in the goings-on in his alma mater. He took the same view as the Cardiff clinicians. As he confided to Sir George Newman, if the college proceeded to appoint clinical professors without proper facilities having been negotiated, it would mean that

> Cardiff will appoint professors of a very second-rate stamp, and once they are appointed the future of the school will be partially crippled. I very much question the advisability of proceeding with the final subjects until affairs have been thrashed out and proper accommodation is available.[92]

One must have some sympathy with the views of the medical staff and Thomas Lewis. Although the University Council, assured by the Cardiff principal that all was in hand, had agreed to allocate £12,830 to the College Council to make possible the establishment of a full medical school in the autumn,[93] there was much to do in very little time. Nevertheless, the hospital authorities quickly concluded that it was far too late to go into reverse. Fortunately, the hospital chairman, the ineffective General Lee, had been succeeded in 1920 by a bluff, no-nonsense businessman, experienced in handling crises. Sir William Diamond (1865–1941) was managing director of a large ship-repairing business at Cardiff's Bute East dock, and had during the First World War served as president of the Engineers' and Shipbuilders' Employers' Association. He persuaded the hospital's board of management, dominated by laymen, to set aside the resolution of the doctors and enter into detailed discussions with the college authorities, with a view to commencing a full medical school in six months' time.[94] In fairness, despite the somewhat negative attitude of the clinical staff, the hospital authorities had not been wholly inactive. They had already commissioned Colonel D. J. Mackintosh, superintendent of the Glasgow Western Infirmary, and acknowledged as one of the leading hospital planners of his day, to advise them on the practical implications of teaching hospital status, while emphasizing the 'importance of spending as little money as possible'.[95] In his subsequent report, Mackintosh, having consulted the college authorities, proposed an appropriate number of hospital beds to be allocated to the clinical professors, when appointed, and indicated the sort of facilities that the medical school should be offered in the hospital.

Showing a sense of urgency hitherto lacking on both sides, a high-powered joint committee, representing the interests of the college and the hospital, spent the period between mid-April and mid-July identifying the main issues at stake, and referring them to relevant hospital and college bodies for agreement and implementation. In all the circumstances, the joint committee, which included Mitchell Stevens, H. G. Cook and Ewen Maclean on the hospital side, and Sir John Lynn-Thomas as one of the college representatives, worked well.[96] Taking note of the advice of Colonel Mackintosh, the hospital undertook to make the following hospital facilities available to the medical school:

> The accommodation proposed is as follows: Lecture Rooms and Laboratories will be provided for the students in the place at present used for the admission of patients

> ... It is also proposed that the Matron's present room – on the left hand side of the entrance to the Hospital – is to be used for the Medical School Professors. This is one of the finest rooms in the Hospital and in the best position.[97]

Finally accepting that nothing could be done to amend the constitutions of the College Council and the Board of Medicine, fixed as they were by statute, the hospital authorities nominated their six representatives on the Board of Medicine, while, as a concession to the hospital, the College Council agreed that the senior administrative officer of the hospital could attend the board's meetings without voting rights. The council further agreed, on the recommendation of the joint committee, that the hospital chairman, together with the senior member of the honorary clinical staff in the relevant discipline, should sit on the selection committees for clinical professors. Bearing in mind what the Haldane Report had said, it was important to allay the fears of the hospital that the introduction of the 'clinical unit' system would result in the take-over of the hospital by the college. It was therefore accepted that the hospital authorities were fully entitled to formulate rules governing the conduct of students on hospital premises. Furthermore, agreement was reached over the ratio of professorial to other beds in the hospital, to prevent dominance by the professorial units of the clinical facilities of the hospital.

The various understandings and undertakings entered into by both sides were brought together in a document entitled 'Heads of the proposed agreement between the college and the hospital', drafted by the hospital's senior administrative officer and Daniel Brown, the college registrar. This agreement, governing the future relationships between the hospital and the college, is thought to be without precedent in the United Kingdom, probably because, elsewhere, such relationships were based on fairly loose, informal understandings which had evolved over the decades. Certainly, when the hospital authorities in Cardiff had cause, some years later, to ascertain practice in England, they discovered that 'there appeared in almost every instance to be no Agreement between the Hospital and the Medical School'.[98] It is clear from the minutes of a number of hospital committees during the first half of 1921 that the initiative for drawing up an agreement with the college came from the hospital authorities. Indeed, it was at a meeting of the hospital's Revision of Rules Committee in April that the hospital's general superintendent was asked to seek the views of Colonel Mackintosh on the content of the agreement 'so as to best safeguard the interests of the hospital'.[99] The document was placed before the joint committee on 11 July 1921, when it was approved, for tidying up and onward endorsement by the respective governing bodies. There were ten main clauses in the initial draft (fourteen in the final version drawn up by the lawyers). The hospital undertook, so far as was possible, to give 'such facilities as the college may require for the teaching, examination and research purposes of the Medical School in the building now existing at the hospital or any extensions thereof or additions thereto'. There was an agreement to apportion costs for capital, equipment and recurrent requirements to reflect usage. The number of beds to be allocated to the professorial units was confirmed (twenty to the professor of medicine, forty to the professor of surgery and eight to the professor of gynaecology). Moreover,

> In order to enlarge the teaching facilities of the professors of medicine, surgery and gynaecology they may, with the co-operation of the members of the Medical Staff concerned, have access to the cases under the charge of the Honorary Physicians, Surgeons and Gynaecologists on the Hospital Staff … Any additional beds which may become available in future for medical, Surgical and Gynaecological cases shall be allocated in the same proportion to the respective University Professors as to the other members of the staff.

The agreement would last for an initial period of five years, to continue thereafter, 'until altered by agreement between the parties'.[100]

As will be noted later, this agreement, or at least the interpretation of some of the clauses, would be the cause of much dissension between the academic authorities and the hospital. However, for the time being, a concordance, for some time a highly elusive commodity, had been reached between the college and the hospital, and not a moment too soon if the full medical school was to be launched in three months' time.

A Full Medical School at Last

Like most new ventures, the Welsh National School of Medicine experienced its fair share of high and low points during the first few years of its existence. On the positive side, the fund-raising efforts of Gwilym Hughes did much to underline the all-Wales context in which the school professed to operate. Thanks to the generosity of external benefactors, the school became the proud possessor of a much-admired Institute of Physiology building, intended as but the first phase of an exciting new complex, and two pioneering clinical chairs, in preventive medicine and tuberculosis, disciplines which immediately gave the institution a certain distinctiveness among British medical schools. The school's adoption of the clinical unit system led to its winning the favour of no less a body than the Rockefeller Foundation, the greatest medical charity in the world. The clinical unit system also made a positive contribution to the school's provision of an excellent medical course, which produced men and women students of high calibre.

On the negative side, it is clear that the establishment of the full medical school in October 1921 was rushed, and the failure of the college and school authorities to carry their hospital colleagues wholeheartedly with them into uncharted waters created an atmosphere of mutual antagonism, which would handicap the progress of the Welsh National School of Medicine for the rest of the decade and frustrate such aspirations as it may have had to expand in other directions.

THE WELSH NATIONAL SCHOOL OF MEDICINE BECOMES A REALITY

The year 1919 saw the final completion and occupation of the new physiology block, much to the relief of the college authorities. Cardiff, like other medical schools in the United Kingdom, had, at the end of the war, experienced a dramatic if short-lived surge in student numbers. The number of students enrolled in the first, second and third years of study at Cardiff rose from ninety-five in 1917/18 to 165 in 1918/19, three times the number registered before the First World War. As Professor Hepburn, still dean, explained, 'Some of them are men who are now coming back to complete courses which were broken by the war, and, in addition, there are a large number of women students.'[1] The medical students were encroaching on the already inadequate accommodation of the pure science departments on Newport Road, a situation which caused Acting Principal Trow to write a desperate letter to Colonel Bruce Vaughan. 'Our pure science departments, owing to a further great influx of medical students, are getting into a very serious condition for want of suitable accommodation. I hope you may be able to quicken the rate of construction so that the new physiological buildings may be ready for use almost at once'.[2] Finally, and not a moment too soon, with over a hundred new medical students joining the course at the beginning of the session, the physiology block opened for use in the autumn of 1919.

Nearly two years were to elapse before the building was officially opened. In Cardiff, on 8 June 1921, amidst much ceremonial, the Prince of Wales was installed as the new chancellor of the University of Wales. Two men with particularly close associations with the history of the University of Wales and its medical school, Lord Haldane and Sir William James Thomas, were each awarded the honorary degree of LL.D. After the ceremony, having passed through an arch of thigh bones held up by men and women medical students, the Prince of Wales accepted, from Sir William a gilded bronze key with which he opened the door of the handsome new physiology building. Prominent in the proceedings was Professor Thomas Graham Brown (1882–1965), successor as professor of physiology to John Berry Haycraft who had retired in 1919. Brown, a Scotsman, and son of a former president of the Royal College of Physicians of Edinburgh, had qualified in medicine at Edinburgh University. After appointments at the Universities of Glasgow and Liverpool (where he worked with Sir Charles Sherrington, the finest neurophysiologist of his time), he had become a lecturer in experimental physiology at the University of Manchester, from where he successfully applied for the chair of physiology at Cardiff in 1920.[3]

Immediately before the opening ceremony, the Prince of Wales had officiated at an even more glittering event, the laying of the foundation stone of the Department of Public Health and the School of Preventive Medicine on the Parade, behind Newport Road. All the leading figures of Welsh public life, and many other VIPs, were there, and Sir William Osler would have been there too, had he not passed away eighteen months previously. For, as has already been noted, he had been largely instrumental in bringing about the establishment of a school of preventive medicine in Cardiff during the closing months of the war, a development which would immediately place the infant Welsh National School of Medicine in the forefront of medical schools in the United Kingdom. As one of the trustees of the Emily Charlotte Talbot Fund, Osler had chaired a conference in Cardiff in March 1918, to set the process moving, and had spoken with great enthusiasm of the future. 'I think we may look forward with hope to the inauguration here in Cardiff of a really great School of Preventive Medicine which will be helpful to the city and an example to the world.' He knew what was needed. 'The Professor must be young, enthusiastic, a good organiser, a good "mixer", and must have a burning enthusiasm for research.'[4] Osler, and a distinguished advisory committee, proceeded to seek a suitable candidate, the choice of Edgar Leigh Collis (1870–1957) as Mansel Talbot professor in preventive medicine being announced in May 1919. Collis, an Oxford Blue, spent his early years as a general practitioner in his native Stourbridge, before joining the Home Office in 1908 as a medical inspector of factories. He soon became a leading authority on pneumo-coniosis, the subject of the Milroy Lectures he delivered to the Royal College of Physicians of London in 1915, two years before his appointment as director of welfare and health at the Ministry of Munitions. His appointment to the chair at Cardiff was both a privilege and a challenge, as he admitted in his inaugural lecture at the College in December 1919:

> I personally am undertaking a heavy responsibility in that today I am the first occu-pant of the only chair in the country devoted entirely to the subject of preventive medicine. There is no tradition to guide, no precedent to refer to; all must be wrought *de novo*.[5]

Collis was not, in fact, the advisory committee's first choice, the chair having initially been offered, in October 1918, to Andrew (later Sir Andrew) Balfour, at the time director-in-chief of the Wellcome Bureau of Scientific Research in London. Balfour admitted to Sir William Osler that he had been greatly impressed by what he had seen on a recent visit to Cardiff:

> My previous visits there were paid in connection with football and my recollection of the place is chiefly one of mud and enthusiastic Welsh crowds. Now the enthu-siasm seems to have found another outlet and there would seem to be no limit to the progress that can be made there in many directions.

However, for the time being he preferred to stay at the Wellcome Bureau where he was 'bound by many ties to Mr Wellcome'.[6] Five years later, Balfour would be appointed as the first director of the London School of Hygiene and Tropical Medicine.

Sir William Osler's work in relation to the chair in preventive medicine was to be his last great service to the development of medical education in Wales, for, at the end of December 1919, he died after several weeks' illness. It is perhaps an indication of the breadth of Osler's contributions to medical science that neither the *British Medical Journal* nor *The Lancet* found space to mention his role in the advancement of medical education in Wales. However, the *British Medical Journal* did at least publish a hand-some tribute, from a Welsh perspective, written by Mitchell Stevens, Cardiff's senior physician, in which he praised the great man's role in the development of the medical school. 'By the passing of Sir William Osler, gallant little Wales loses one of her best friends.'[7]

That year saw another important milestone in the progress of the Welsh National School of Medicine, and one which complemented neatly the recently-established chair in preventive medicine. Reference has already been made in chapter 3 to the establishment, in 1910, of the King Edward VII Welsh National Memorial Association for the prevention, treatment and abolition of tuberculosis (WNMA), under the presidency of David Davies, coal magnate, Member of Parliament and benefactor. This body was by no means the first in Britain to campaign for the eradication of a disease which, in the first decade of the twentieth century, caused the death of one person in eight, and was the greatest single killer of males and children. The National Association for the Prevention of Consumption and Other Forms of Tuberculosis had been founded in 1898, and at its launch the Prince of Wales (soon to become King Edward VII), when told that the terrible loss of life from tuberculosis was preventable, responded with the penetrating question, 'If preventable, why not prevented?' Bad though the incidence of tuberculosis, this classic disease of poverty and bad housing, was in England, the problem was even worse in Wales, with a death rate of 1.62 per 1,000 population in the immediate pre-war years, compared with a death rate of 1.56 in England. So David Davies and his supporters resolved to commemorate the passing of Edward VII with a Wales-focused campaign, and when, in 1911, the National (Health) Insurance Act made provision for the state funding of treatment for tuberculosis, the Welsh chancellor of the Exchequer made the WNMA responsible for providing a unified anti-tuberculosis service throughout Wales. In the next few years the association made considerable progress in Wales, as table 5.1 shows.[8]

Table 5.1

	1912	1915	1920
Total attendance at clinics	3,240	9,155	12,616
Hospital beds owned by WNMA	200	603	1,128
Number of whole-time medical staff	20	25	28
Net annual cost of WNMA Scheme	£21,196	£86,306	£132,997

It was not surprising, therefore, that by 1919 David Davies considered the time opportune to strengthen the association's research profile. In a letter to D. W. Evans, the association's general director, he wrote:

> I have been considering the question of research work in connection with the Welsh National Memorial, and have had the opportunity of consulting Sir Walter Fletcher, Secretary of the National Medical Research Committee with regard to this important matter. We are both of opinion that the time has arrived when a scheme should be prepared for organising the work of Research in connection with the campaign against tuberculosis in Wales, and placing it on a satisfactory basis.[9]

The involvement of Sir Walter Fletcher (1873–1934) was important because of his influential position as secretary of the Medical Research Committee, soon to become the Medical Research Council. It has already been noted how the 1911 National Insurance Act had paid particular attention to the problem of tuberculosis, and one of its clauses allowed for an annual sum of £57,000 to be earmarked for funding research into the disease's prevention and cure. The Medical Research Committee was established in 1913 to manage this fund, and although the outbreak of the First World War would lead to a broadening of the committee's remit, it, and in particular its secretary, continued to be an important source of guidance on tuberculosis matters, on which it was advised by a council, one of whose members was David Davies.[10]

Encouraged by Fletcher's support, the association set up an advisory committee, the members of which included Sir Walter Fletcher , who assured it of 'the cordial co-operation of the Medical Research Committee in any research work that might be undertaken by the Memorial Association'. Another member, Professor Leigh Collis, suggested that the post of chief medical officer of the association, which happened to be vacant, should be filled by someone who would also direct the association's research programme. He further advised that the holder of the post should hold a chair in the Welsh National School of Medicine, believing that 'great advantages both to the Medical School and to the Association would result from close co-operation'.[11]

It thus came to pass that on 26 May 1920, a deputation from the association attended a special meeting of the Council of University College, Cardiff, and offered the college an endowment of £12,500, donated by David Davies and his two sisters, Gwendoline and Margaret, to establish the David Davies chair of tuberculosis, named after their celebrated grandfather, the industrialist and founder of Barry docks. The sum would provide an annual salary of £1,250 to which the association would add an annual sum of £750 in payment of the professor's duties as its chief medical officer. The only proviso was that the Council would appoint to the chair the person nominated by the association. The Council accepted the offer with unanimity. In fact, the task of finding a suitable candidate was not an easy one. A number of prominent names were suggested for the chair of tuberculosis, none of whom would be remotely interested in taking the post, in Sir Walter Fletcher's view. Fletcher did, however, come up with the name of Colonel Stevenson Lyle Cummins (1873–1949), who was, at the time, professor of pathology at the Royal Army Medical College, Millbank. Though short of practical clinical experience, Cummins had compensating qualities which made him the ideal candidate: 'I think I have never made a suggestion with more confidence than I make this, and I think you will be very lucky if you can get him.'[12]

As we shall see, the leading physician at the Cardiff Royal Infirmary would, a few years later, pour scorn on Cummins and his 'fancy department', but for the time being, Sir Walter Fletcher's opinion was good enough for the Memorial Association. Having first been appointed as the association's chief medical officer, Cummins was appointed to the new chair of tuberculosis by the Council of University College, Cardiff on 10 December 1920, to take effect from February 1921.[13]

Welcome and innovative as the chairs in preventive medicine and tuberculosis may have been, they could hardly be considered fundamental to any medical school. However, having achieved a *modus vivendi* with the King Edward VII Hospital, the college was able to make the core appointments necessary to give the Welsh National School of Medicine a degree of credibility. The chair of surgery was the first to be filled, in June 1921, with Sir William Diamond and H. G. Cook serving as representatives of the hospital. The two shortlisted candidates were both good prospects. Ernest William Hey Groves had a first-class record of academic achievement, and would later become professor of surgery at Bristol University and vice-president of the Royal College of Surgeons. However, the 'local' candidate, William Sheen, inevitably had the edge. He had been one of Cardiff's leading surgeons before the war, and for some years had served as president of the Association of Past Students of University College, Cardiff. During the war he had distinguished himself in command of the 34th (Welsh) General Hospital, serving mainly in India and earning the CBE for his endeavours. The rules of the King Edward VII Hospital, requiring retirement from the hospital at the age of sixty, or after twenty years' service on the full staff, prevented Sheen from resuming his surgical career in Cardiff, and for a short time he practised in London. Fortunately the hospital rules did not apply to clinical academic staff, making it possible for Sheen to be appointed, though not without some misgivings, as the University of Wales's foundation professor of surgery. Three eminent surgeons, Sir John Lynn-Thomas, Sir Robert Jones and Thelwell Thomas, professor of surgery at Liverpool University, all complained to Sir Alfred Davies, permanent secretary of the Welsh Department of the Board of Education, that undue favour had been shown to the local man by those responsible for the appointment:

> Their condemnation at what they were unanimous in regarding as a very unfortunate appointment (brought about no doubt by local influence) was painful to listen to. It has been made apparently by the College Council in the teeth of the available expert opinion on the subject.[14]

The appointment of the professor of medicine, on 15 July, did not command universal acclaim either. Both shortlisted candidates were 'outsiders', which in itself upset Mitchell Stevens, the representative of the hospital physicians on the committee, who would have preferred a local man such as Ivor Davies. One of the shortlisted candidates, Sydney Wentworth Patterson, 'a proud Australian' according to his entry in *Munk's Roll*, could not turn up on the day. His candidature was therefore considered in his absence, with Professor Lyle Cummins, one of the College Council representatives on the panel, deputed to deal with any questions on his behalf as best he could. The other candidate, Alexander Mills Kennedy (1885–1960), a Scotsman in his mid-thirties, did attend. A graduate of Glasgow University, he was senior assistant to the Muirhead professor of medicine at that university. Although he had the MD qualification, he held neither the MRCP nor the FRCP, qualifications which Mitchell Stevens FRCP considered *de rigueur* for an honorary physician in a teaching hospital, not to mention a university professor of medicine.[15] Despite Stevens's objection Kennedy was appointed, and thus began a very difficult period in the professor of medicine's relationships with his hospital colleagues, which, as we will see, lasted several years. Indeed, his obituarist in *The Lancet* many years later would record that Kennedy 'spent his first weeks in a frigidly hostile atmosphere making what arrangements he could to find space and facilities to start teaching'.[16]

The salaries of the full-time professors of medicine and surgery were determined as £1,500 per annum as allowed for in the arrangements approved by the University Council in January 1921. At that meeting the Council had endorsed a resolution of the University Academic Board, proposing minimum salaries for professors of the University of Wales in order to make them comparable to those paid 'by institutions of similar rank'.[17] In the arts and pure science departments the minimum salary proposed was £800, with those in certain applied sciences being a little larger. However, 'the Board recognises that some salaries much higher than those included in the foregoing scales will be necessary in the new departments of the National School of Medicine, where whole-time Professors of Medicine, Surgery and Gynaecology will be appointed.' In fact, the salaries of the professors of medicine, surgery, gynaecology and preventive medicine had already been proposed in the draft scheme for the constitution of the National School of Medicine prepared in 1918. At £1,500 the rate was somewhat lower than that prevailing for similar full-time posts in London in the early 1920s, if the £2,000 annual salaries paid to the full-time professors of medicine and surgery at the London Hospital Medical School were typical.[18] In fact, the highest-paid member of the Welsh National School of Medicine at this time was Professor Lyle Cummins who, in addition to his annual college salary of £1,250, received an additional annual stipend of £750 from the Welsh National Memorial Association in his capacity as its chief medical officer.[19] Meanwhile, the professor of physiology was paid £900 a year and the professor of anatomy £800, the same as the professor of pathology and bacteriology. Proper recognition of this post as a clinical one in salary terms was not granted until 1924 with the appointment of Emrys-Roberts's successor. For comparative purposes it should be noted that at the University Council meeting in January 1921 it was also agreed that the minimum salary for college principals in the University of Wales be £1,500.

It is interesting to note that, not long after he had taken up his appointment in Cardiff, Professor Graham Brown had drawn the attention of the Faculty of Medicine to a letter he had received from Professor E. H. Starling of University College, London urging the new school at Cardiff to pay all its professors, preclinical and clinical alike, the same salary: 'The trained man of ability should be directed to Anatomy, Physiology and Medicine according to his taste and temperament, and should not be diverted by the existence of different scales of remuneration.'[20] Professor Starling no doubt hoped that the Welsh National School of Medicine would, perhaps in its innocence, set a precedent from which preclinical professors everywhere might, in time, benefit. However, nothing was done about it then or later. The differential between the salaries of the clinical and preclinical professors remained, a state of affairs accepted with apparent equanimity on all sides. In fact, salary differentials between preclinical and clinical chairs continued to be the norm in universities throughout the United Kingdom during this period, as a memorandum prepared by the Academic Board of the university in 1931 would clearly demonstrate.[21] Indeed, the position remains the same to this day.

In fact, the salaries of the academic staff of the school, both clinical and preclinical, were well in line with those of academic staff elsewhere in the United Kingdom, as a survey conducted by the UGC in the late 1920s showed. Only some 5 per cent of university professors earned £1,500 or more, the average professorial salary, including those in London, which tended to be higher than the norm, being £1,082.[22] Indeed, the salaries of the school's clinical professors placed them very much among the wage-earning elite, being twice that of the average general practitioner, over four times that of a qualified male teacher, and very much higher than the average income of an occupied man in the mid-1920s, some £180 per year.[23] It is salutary to note that in 1923, the post of night sister at the Cardiff Royal Infirmary was filled at an annual salary of £70, while the sister to the Bute ward earned the princely sum of £60 a year.[24]

Whatever had been the college's initial intention, when the time came to appoint a professor of obstetrics and gynaecology, it was decided that it would be more appropriate, at the current stage of the school's development, to make a part-time rather than a full-time appointment. Not only would money be saved, but a full-time appointment could hardly be justified in terms of the academic duties such a post would be expected to carry. A part-time appointment was entirely acceptable to the hospital authorities, provided its holder was chosen from among the existing members of the hospital. Thus it came about that Ewen John Maclean was appointed for an initial period of five years – subsequently extended - with the rather odd title 'professor extraordinary' of obstetrics and gynaecology, at a salary of £750 per annum, and it was further agreed that the question of formally establishing a 'clinical unit' in the discipline should be postponed until towards the end of that time.[25] In fact, Maclean was the obvious choice. He was the senior gynaecologist at the hospital and had enjoyed a long working relationship with the college as lecturer in midwifery since 1904. One of Wales's most distinguished doctors, Maclean, knighted in 1923, would later serve as president of the British Medical Association. His nephew in due course achieved notoriety as the spy Donald Maclean.

By the date of Maclean's appointment, the Welsh National School of Medicine had been operating as a full medical school for over two months, but its inception had been a fairly close-run thing. Not only had the clinicians at the King Edward VII Hospital sought a year's postponement; the University Grants Committee (UGC) too had come to the conclusion that it was premature for the medical school to open as a full medical school in October.

Established in 1919 to advise the government on the funding needs of universities, and to distribute the annual government grant as fairly as possible among eligible recipients, the committee played an important role in the development of medical education from the outset. Chaired by Sir William McCormick, who had previously chaired the Board of Education's Standing Advisory Committee on University Grants, the UGC included, as its medical member, Sir Wilmot Herringham, a distinguished physician who declined the opportunity to succeed Sir William Osler as regius professor of medicine at Oxford University, and Sir George Newman as assessor for the Ministry of Health. The committee did not operate in an ivory tower, taking great pains to inform itself, in various ways, regarding the needs of universities; indeed, in 1918 and 1919 Sir George Newman made it his business to visit most of the provincial medical schools to ascertain their principal requirements.[26] McCormick and Newman were well aware of developments in Cardiff; both had served on the Board of Education's Departmental Committee on the Cardiff Medical School in 1914, and Newman had been involved in discussions over the provision of buildings for the school during the war. As recently as March 1921, Thomas Lewis had been telling Newman that all was not well at Cardiff.[27]

Concerned about the premature opening of the full medical school, the UGC sent its medical subcommittee (in fact, Sir George Newman, Sir Wilmot Herringham being indisposed) to Cardiff on 16 and 17 June to assess the situation. In his diary Newman recorded his movements:

> 16 June 1921: Off to Cardiff. The Medical Scl. Cummins, Collis, Graham Brown, Emrys-Roberts, the Hospital. Joint Conference. Dinner at the Park Hotel. Sir W. Diamond, Sir W. J. Thomas, D. W. Evans, Maclean, Stephens [sic], Sir J. Lynn Thomas. Walk in Cathays Park midnight.
> 17 June 1921: Prince of Wales Hosp. with Sir John Lynn Thomas. Retd. to London.[28]

The subcommittee's report to the main committee concluded that the school was not yet ready to open. Neither of the bodies directly concerned with the running of the school, the Board of Medicine and the Faculty of Medicine, were yet in place; the Cardiff College appeared to have too much and the university too little influence on the direction of the school. Moreover the subcommittee had serious doubts whether the income available to the school was sufficient, notwithstanding the grant of £12,830 (the amount asked for by the Cardiff College) allocated by the University Council.[29] Professors Graham Brown and Collis, both of whom had met Newman during his visit (and Collis saw him again, privately two days later), were both of the view that it was madness to start clinical training so soon after the appointment of the professors of medicine and surgery. Graham Brown found it 'almost impossible to believe that the newly-elected professors of medicine and surgery were actually expected to commence their duties within a week of their date of appointment, without laboratories, without any scientific instruments, and without previous organisation of the medical course'. Collis, also recalling the situation six years later, was equally critical: 'An extremely complicated and intricate course, extending over three years, was embarked upon precipitately... The protests of existing professors, who asked for a period of preparation, were disregarded; utterly inadequate provision was made; clinical professors were appointed and called to teach immediately.'[30]

It will have been noted that neither the Cardiff principal, nor any other of the college's chief officers, had been seen by Sir George Newman during his visit. Nor had they been involved in a separate meeting between Sir Wilmot Herringham and senior officers of the university regarding the finances of the medical school, an omission which was furiously denounced by Principal Griffiths at the College Council on 15 July and the University Council four days later. Nevertheless, in the light of the UGC's reported concerns the University Council resolved to meet again in August to give further consideration to the timing of the opening of the full medical school.

The Cardiff College authorities were not prepared to wait that long. They had no intention of postponing the opening of the school, and the hospital authorities were equally unhappy at the prospect of putting off an event for which they had exerted much effort in preparation. The issue came to a head at the inaugural meeting of the school's Board of Medicine on 26 July. Chaired by the university pro-chancellor, and attended by an impressive gathering of the great and good of Welsh public life, its proceedings could not have got the Welsh National School of Medicine off to a less auspicious start. Lord Kenyon began by informing the meeting of the resolution of the University Council and the reasons for it, adding that Sir Wilmot Herringham was advising the postponement of undergraduate clinical training in Cardiff for a year. This course of action was immediately supported by the professors of physiology and pathology, whose speeches, according to the report in the *Western Mail*, 'gave rise to a brisk discussion which embraced some plain speaking'. The representatives of the hospital were especially put out, its chairman, Sir William Diamond (who had, with some courage, stood out against his own doctors who had been calling for a postponement some months earlier) pointing out how much trouble the hospital had taken in readiness for the reception of clinical students in October. 'It would be hopeless to expect the hospital to make similar provision for the students a year hence.' None of this furore was reflected in the minutes of the meeting, which simply record the decision:

> That this Board recommends to the College Council that the Medical School be started in October 1921. The Board is of the opinion that the budget should be reconsidered and amplified, and recommends that an appeal for funds toward the Medical School be issued without delay.[31]

On the afternoon of the same day, the Cardiff College Council met, and was addressed by Lord Kenyon, who had some fences to mend. He was anxious to emphasize that the University Council's only interest was in ensuring that the medical school got off to the best possible start, adding his personal support for the decision finally taken by the Board of Medicine. Needless to say, the College Council agreed unanimously that clinical training should start in October as arranged, and that an appeal be launched for funds to aid the school. Not for the last time, the Cardiff authorities chose to put aside the advice of the UGC, and the University Council abandoned plans to hold a special meeting in August to determine a way forward. As far as Cardiff was concerned, the die was cast.[32]

Of the seventy-three students who had been in the third year, a few, as always, failed the senior preclinical examinations, but at the beginning of October the majority proceeded to one of the London medical schools, undoubtedly the safe option for those either discouraged by the delays in the decision-making process or reluctant to be guinea pigs on a hurriedly prepared clinical course in Cardiff. One of those who took the London option was Alan Trevor Jones (1901–79), son of the headmaster of Lewis School, Pengam and much later to become the provost of the Welsh National School of Medicine, who went to University College Hospital to pursue his clinical studies. However, twenty-two of the school's preclinical students 'grasped the nettle', fourteen of whom were intending to study for the Wales degree, and the King Edward VII Hospital put some temporary arrangements in place to receive them.[33] The men's student lavatory would be found in the hospital's Insole corridor, and the men students' common room was in the recess of the same corridor. The women students' lavatory and common room (of the twenty-two students, six were women) were to be found in the corresponding rooms on the floor immediately above. Professor Sheen would use the sister's room in the Eliza Nixon ward for an office, while Professor Kennedy was allocated an office in the recess on the upper corridor, though, as has already been noted, the welcome afforded to him left much to be desired. As his obituarist would recall in the *British Medical Journal* many years later, 'When he arrived in Cardiff Professor Kennedy had a bare dusty room and no furniture. With the help of a porter he collected a table and a few chairs which were brought to the [hospital] as his initial equipment.'[34]

The Cardiff College prudently appointed the vastly experienced David Hepburn to serve as dean of the enlarged Welsh National School of Medicine for an initial period of one year, an appointment warmly welcomed by *The Lancet*: 'The honour given is great, but greater still is the responsibility, for the work of organising the new National School so as to ensure complete success will be no mean task.'[35] Hepburn and his colleagues had two immediate priorities, to ensure the financial stability of the school, and to secure academic recognition for its medical course from external licensing authorities, without which the course would be virtually worthless.

THE QUEST FOR FINANCIAL STABILITY

In August 1921, the UGC, having to accept the reality of a full medical school, whatever their reservations, indicated that, in accordance with Lloyd George's pound-for-pound formula, and with the conclusions reached by the Board of Education's departmental committee in 1914, the Treasury would make an additional grant of up to £5,000 available to the school on an annual basis, on condition that the school would find an equivalent amount from other sources. Reflecting the concern expressed by its medical subcommittee in June, the UGC also wished to be satisfied about the final constitutional position of the school, particularly with regard to its all-Wales dimension.[36] To that end, a scheme was devised by the University Council, following consultation with the Cardiff College, which created a body quite outside the Cardiff College framework, known as the University Advisory Board of Medicine. In some respects a successor to the ineffective and now defunct University Medical Board, the University Advisory Board was intended to provide advice to the University Council 'upon all matters affecting the National School of Medicine in the University'. Its membership would not only include the most senior officers of the University of Wales but also members nominated by such august bodies as the GMC, the Royal Colleges of Physicians and Surgeons and the British Medical Association.[37] The existence of such an ostensibly powerful body supervising the affairs of the Welsh National School of Medicine outside the control of University College, Cardiff was sufficiently impressive to address the immediate concerns of the UGC, although, as will be seen in chapter 7, the UGC would soon be agitating for the separation of the medical school from the college as the best means of securing its long-term viability. In the event, the Advisory Board turned out to be one committee too many, even for the University of Wales. This elaborate, even grandiose body never met once during the whole decade, and University Statute XXXVI was finally repealed by the University Court in 1929.

If constitutional concerns were, for the time being, dealt with, the funding issue was all the more difficult as, at exactly the time when the University Council launched its national appeal for £100,000 on behalf of the National School of Medicine, the authorities of University College, Cardiff were choosing to launch a separate appeal for £250,000 to fund new developments in Cathays Park. The college's action caused some concern among those who questioned the sincerity of its commitment to its medical school. Lord Kenyon, the university pro-chancellor, and Principal Trow (who was, at the time vice-chancellor of the University as well as principal of Cardiff) were forced to issue a press statement to explain the situation, 'for there is, we find, some confusion in the public mind as between the two appeals for university education purposes in Wales'. They attempted to draw a distinction between 'the special and immediate needs' of the Cardiff College, particularly for new science laboratories, and the urgent need of the medical school

> for a fund of £100,000 (or its equivalent in annual income), before August 1922 ... in order that the school may qualify for the Treasury grant of £5,000 *per annum*. That grant is absolutely dependent on the success of the appeal now being made on behalf of the Welsh National School of Medicine.[38]

Whatever view may be taken of Cardiff's action, by taking the lead on the appeal in support of the National School of Medicine, the commitment of the University of Wales to the school's successful development could hardly be doubted. Tactically, of course, to work through the University of Wales was eminently sensible as a means of maximizing the success of the appeal on an all-Wales basis. The appeal's prospects of success were enhanced through Lord Kenyon's securing of David Lloyd George's personal endorsement via an open letter which was widely publicized in the national and local press.[39]

The university was fortunate to secure, at a salary of 8 guineas a week, the services of Gwilym Hughes as the organizing secretary of the appeal. This able and energetic man had served for five years as chartered secretary of the Welsh National Memorial Association and, as a paragraph in the *Western Mail* noted, 'Mr Gwilym Hughes has been intimately connected with all Welsh national movements... A lifetime associated with the daily journalism of Wales has brought him into intimate touch with the leaders in all phases of national activities.'[40] Hughes's mission was to raise an annual sum of at least £5,000 for the medical school by persuading the seventeen local authorities of Wales to contribute the equivalent of one-eighth of a penny rate to the appeal fund. This would undoubtedly be a challenge in view of the fact that each of the local authorities had already undertaken to contribute the equivalent of a one penny rate on an annual basis towards the general upkeep of the university and its constituent colleges. However, Hughes did so well that, much to his disappointment, by the end of 1924 he had worked himself out of a job, with all the local authorities either contributing or promising to do so. His success was not achieved without a great deal of hard work on his part, both in his office, located in the medical school, and on the highways and byways of Wales, visiting local councillors and council officials and attending innumerable committee meetings. He was usually accompanied on his travels by Lord Kenyon or another senior member of the university or the medical school.

His dealings with the county borough of Merthyr Tydfil well typify his thorough approach. He first wrote, on 17 May 1922, to Isaac Hughes, an auctioneer and a prominent member of the local community, whom he already knew:

I know that Merthyr is very hard hit in the matter of rates at present, but I do not think that Merthyr would refuse us one-eighth of a penny rate if it realised how much is at stake for Wales in this matter. I do not care to apply direct to the Town Clerk without feeling some assurance that an application would receive favourable consideration. Possibly a day spent in Merthyr under your guidance in calling upon principal members of the Finance Committee would be helpful.

A week later, Hughes wrote individual letters to the mayor of the borough and to members of the finance committee. Having done his homework, Hughes, accompanied on this occasion by Professor Ewen Maclean, met the finance committee, and secured its unconditional promise of a subscription. After the meeting, Hughes took the trouble to write personal letters to half a dozen Merthyr people because, as he modestly told each of them, 'I am sure that for the great success we achieved great thanks are due to your good self.'[41]

The national appeal had, in fact, been launched on 25 January 1922 at the Cardiff City Hall, hosted by the lord mayor and attended by such prominent public men as Sir Charles Sherrington, president of the Royal Society, and Sir George Newman, both men of immense influence in the field of medical education at that time. Newman, of course, had been a member of the departmental committee in 1914 which had proposed that the full medical school should look to the local authorities of Wales for some of its financial support, so he had a personal interest in being present at the launch of the scheme. Within a month the Cardiff Corporation had agreed to levy an eighth of a penny rate in aid of the medical school, amounting to £650 per annum, and two months later the Glamorgan County Council, by far the largest local authority in Wales, had pledged a further £1,600. Other councils, Merthyr excepted, were slower to respond, and Hughes was frequently forced to employ his most persuasive skills to overcome the reluctance of councils such as Newport, who would only contribute provided that everyone else did so too. One by one, the local authorities of south Wales fell into line, the last to do so, perhaps not surprisingly, being Swansea, which resented the pre-eminence of Cardiff, and whose councillors were unconvinced that the medical school was truly a national institution. Only in April 1923, after a plea by Professor T. F. Sibly, principal of the new University College, Swansea, did the Swansea Corporation finally agree to subscribe to the appeal fund, but only for one year in the first instance.

With south Wales secure, at least for the time being, Hughes switched his attention to the north, which he had always regarded as the more difficult region to win over:

In North Wales the County Councils feel that the medical students from that area may, for some years, as in the past, proceed to the medical schools in Dublin, Liverpool and Manchester, which are more conveniently situated to North Wales than Cardiff, but we have every hope that if we can get the South Wales Councils to support the School, North Wales will not long lag behind.[42]

Gwilym Hughes was therefore pleased to report to Jenkin James, the secretary of the University of Wales,[43] of the 'splendid reception' he had received from the Caernarfonshire County Council at the end of June, but, as his letter shows, this was the result of much careful preparation:

> I had spent the week in interviewing nearly every member (25 out of 28) in various parts of the county and I secured an actual attendance of 20 members today, several of them attending specially at my request. Those who were really hostile had an opportunity of blowing off steam when I saw them at their homes and some of them were very pugnacious. When I addressed the Committee today, however, the number of hostile questions were very few, and after a brisk discussion, a motion to contribute one-eighth was carried unanimously, no amendment being moved. Had there been an amendment the motion would have carried, I think, by two to one … This is the first of the six North Wales counties to agree to the one-eighth, and the success today is, I hope, a fine augury of a similar success in the other five counties.[44]

It took another year for the last two Welsh counties, Montgomeryshire and Merionethshire, to fall into line but at the meeting of the University Council, on 27 November 1924, Gwilym Hughes, whose position as organizing secretary had been terminated a few weeks earlier, much to his disappointment, was able to report that all the county councils and county borough councils in Wales had agreed to contribute an eighth of a penny rate, which realized approximately £6,500 per annum in support of the Welsh National School of Medicine. Hughes had done well, and the council voted him a gift of 10 guineas as a 'special mark of appreciation for his services'. However, the income was decidedly vulnerable, as Hughes, hoping for an extension, had pointed out in a paper to the university secretary, in which he had reminded him of an earlier conversation:

> We realised that several counties required careful nursing and watching, as their contributions were strictly limited to one year only, and that the annual renewal of the grants in their case could be secured only as the result of discreet propaganda and constant vigilance. These counties include Anglesey, Carnarvon, Flint, Merioneth, Cardigan, Radnor, Monmouthshire and Swansea.[45]

The accuracy of Gwilym Hughes's warning would soon become only too apparent.

Important though the national appeal was to the financial well-being of the medical school, it was by no means the only component of the balance sheet. As has already been noted, the full medical school had been launched, perhaps precipitately, without a total understanding of its financial condition. It was prudent, therefore, of the University Council to decide in May 1922 to set up a committee to report on the financial position of the medical school, and secondly to advise on 'the provision which still requires to be made to make it efficient in every respect'. The committee members were impressive, the Hon. W. N. Bruce and two experts from outside the university, Sir George Newman, and Sir Humphry Rolleston, president of the Royal College of Physicians. In view of his position as dean Professor Hepburn declined the invitation to be a member, preferring to act as an 'accessor' to the committee. The committee worked quickly, perhaps too quickly, visiting the several heads of department in the school and the authorities of the main hospitals in Cardiff, but unfortunately failing to see the Cardiff principal, who happened to be away. The 'Report of the Special Committee' was considered by a special meeting of the council on 19 July 1922. The tone of the report was friendly, the committee acknowledging that the Welsh National School of Medicine was still in its infancy. However, the authors had to remind the university that the school was developing in a difficult financial climate and should accept that it could not achieve all its aspirations at once. Priority had to be given to those parts of the medical school which were central to the accomplishment of its core mission, undergraduate medical education. While praising the excellence of the new physiology building, the report warned against giving a disproportionate share of the school's resources to the Department of Physiology, particularly as the accommodation available to departments such as anatomy was so poor. The report was especially generous in its praise of Professor Hepburn, head of the Department of Anatomy and the dean, who 'has set an admirable example to his colleagues in the determination he has shewn to adapt his demands to the financial conditions'. The report pointedly added: 'There seems no adequate reason why the salary attached to this Chair should be lower than that of the Chair of Physiology.' With regard to the 'Hospital Units' the report considered that they appeared to have made a fair start, their financial aspirations were reasonable 'as compared with those of other Schools of the same type' and their plans to make full use of the clinical teaching facilities available to them were to be encouraged. In the current financial climate the committee believed 'that the University will not be justified in making any considerable grant to [the departments of preventive medicine and of tuberculosis] to supplement the endowments so generously provided by the late Miss Talbot and by Mr David Davies, MP'. Indeed, the committee made certain suggestions as to where the school's estimates could be reduced, particularly in the departments of physiology, preventive medicine and tuberculosis, and in the use of secretarial support, which was clearly regarded as a luxury in times of financial stringency. Even so, and assuming that the national appeal fully achieved its objectives, the school was still facing a deficit of several thousands of pounds.[46]

Interesting though the document was as a progress report on the infant Welsh National School of Medicine, offering an opinion by eminent outside experts on the school's immediate priorities, it was less useful as an authoritative statement of the school's true financial position. Its authors had misleadingly drawn conclusions about the school's deficit, and its consequent need to make economies, without making any assumptions at all regarding the amount of recurrent funding the school was entitled to expect from the university general pool. Both the Cardiff College Council and the school's Faculty of Medicine reacted sharply, pointing out that the council had already given £12,830 from the pool to the school for 1921/2 and there had never been any suggestion that a similar level of support would be denied in subsequent years. Assuming continuing support from that source, and given appropriate levels of income from endowments and tuition fees, and provided the national appeal bore fruit, then the financial stability of the Welsh National School of Medicine in the next few years should be assured. Embarrassed by what was clearly a flawed report, the University Council, in particular its finance committee, spent several weeks considering to what extent the medical school was entitled, on a recurrent basis, to a share of the funds from the university general pool. As far as the senior officers of the UGC were concerned, there was no problem, though the amount would depend on 'the claims of the other parts of the University upon the pooled funds'. Ironically the inadequacies in the 'Special report' achieved what the medical school had always wanted: a degree of clarity and stability in its funding; for during the course of 1923 the University Council agreed that from its general pool the Welsh National School of Medicine would be allocated £12,500 in 1922/3 and £14,570 per annum for the following three years.[47]

THE CHALLENGE OF SECURING EXTERNAL RECOGNITION FOR THE MEDICAL COURSE

In parallel with achieving a measure of financial stability, the school needed to secure recognition for its medical course from licensing bodies external to the University of Wales, not only the General Medical Council but also the Conjoint Board and the University of London. Apart from the 'respectability' such recognition would confer, the fact was that many of the school's students were, as in the past, choosing to study for the examinations of the Conjoint Board and the University of London, as well as, and instead of, those of the University of Wales. As Professor Hepburn stated in a wide-ranging interview to the *South Wales News* in December 1921, of the 241 medical students in regular attendance in the 1921/2 session, eighty-three were entered for the degrees of the University of Wales, eighty-three were pursuing courses of study for the medical and surgical degrees of the University of London, and a further seventy-five were pursuing courses of study for the Conjoint Board examinations.[48] The road to recognition was by no means as easy as the college authorities expected, for two main reasons. First, as has already been noted, the introduction of the clinical course had been made in haste, with reservations being expressed by members of the school, of the hospital and of the university. It is true that the essential content of the clinical curriculum was defined in general terms by the GMC, but it was still necessary for Professors Kennedy and Sheen and their colleagues to draft a three-year clinical course from scratch in the course of a few weeks, inevitably devoting the greatest attention to the course of study in the first clinical year. Despite their best endeavours, 'An addendum to the prospectus for the session 1921/22' covering schemes of study for students after the third year, did not reach the printers until the end of the first term, and reflected the haste with which it was produced. It was hardly surprising that in due course, the assessors from the University of London would be critical that not all the necessary arrangements for giving the course were in place.

A more serious obstacle to recognition was dissension between the authorities of the school and the hospital's clinical staff at a time when it was surely essential to demonstrate a sense of common purpose to the outside world. The root cause was the introduction (imposition may be a better word) of the 'clinical unit' system on a hospital which was ill prepared to accept it. Despite the initially strong encouragement of the UGC and Sir George Newman,[49] the concept of the clinical unit as the foundation of clinical undergraduate education in medical schools was extremely slow to take hold. By 1923, Newman was able to identify the clinical unit system in operation in only seven centres in the United Kingdom: St Bartholomew's Hospital (medicine and surgery), the London Hospital (medicine and surgery), St Mary's Hospital (medicine and surgery), St Thomas's Hospital (medicine and surgery), University College Hospital (medicine and surgery), the London School of Medicine for Women (obstetrics and gynaecology) and the Welsh National School of Medicine (medicine and surgery), most of the posts identified being held on a full-time basis.

There remained, during the 1920s, a strong preference among many clinicians, for the way in which hospitals had always operated, valuing, in the words of Christopher Lawrence, 'private practice, voluntary service in hospitals, and a system of appointment to hospital posts by seniority',[50] arrangements challenged by the clinical unit system which was characterized by the existence of full-time academics appointed because of their skills and experience, and their recognition of the key role of the laboratory in teaching, research and patient care. As John Pickstone and colleagues have observed, British hospitals remained 'generally unsympathetic to experimental, academic, medicine, at least when it encroached on the clinical'.[51] Christopher Lawrence cites the observations of an American professor of surgery, made in 1922, following a survey of British medical schools for the Rockefeller Foundation: 'Functional tests and the newer blood chemistry which are so commonly used in America, especially with reference to the kidney, seem to be almost unknown to the British surgeons … There seems to exist among the surgeons a feeling that laboratory examinations are unnecessary.'[52]

In such a climate of distrust, where long-established vested interests continued to hold sway, the concept of clinical units, directed by full-time professors, struggled to make headway among the elite clinicians of London, even in the hospitals where the concept had been established,[53] and made virtually no headway in provincial England during the inter-war years, with the exception of Bristol. In 1925, the authorities of the University of Bristol, advised by Sir Berkeley Moynihan, president of the Royal College of Surgeons of England, did consider the establishment of full-time chairs in medicine and surgery, but failed to make progress, mainly because of the unwillingness of the Bristol Royal Infirmary and the Bristol General Hospital, suspicious of the unit system, to co-operate. A further ten years elapsed before Bristol's first full-time professor of medicine, Charles Bruce Perry, was appointed.[54] An early attempt by the medical school authorities at Sheffield to create a full-time clinical chair in medicine failed to overcome the vested interests within the local hospitals, forcing them to establish a full-time, and, in research terms, highly successful clinical chair in pharmacology, held by Edward Mellanby, instead.[55] This was in 1920. Also in 1920, those members of the Faculty of Medicine at Manchester who wished to establish clinical units on the London model were confronted with a total lack of enthusiasm for what was dismissed as an untried experiment.[56] When, in the same year, the Faculty of Medicine of the University of Birmingham was sent its allotted copies of the UGC Memorandum on 'Clinical units in medical schools', it simply received the document, with no discussion. When, eight years later, in the context of discussions about the establishment of a brand-new teaching hospital for the city, the faculty's views were sought on the creation of full-time clinical professors, little interest was shown in the matter: 'The Faculty is of opinion that it is not advisable at present to establish full-time professorships in the clinical subjects.'[57] The very prospect of securing government funding to develop the clinical unit system appalled Dr George Adami, vice-chancellor of the University of Liverpool, declaring that any medical school which accepted state funds for such a purpose would find itself 'drifting into a mean and miserable servitude'.[58]

Some of the blame for the slow development of the clinical unit system in the provinces must be laid squarely at the door of the UGC itself. Despite issuing its pioneering memorandum in 1920, the committee quickly realized it was in no position to fund the system's widespread adoption. A few London medical schools were receiving special grants of up to £6,000 a year to support full-time clinical professors, but outside London only Edward Mellanby's unit at Sheffield received a special grant, the clinical units in Cardiff being funded out of general income. In December 1922 A. H. Kidd, who had recently succeeded W. B. Riddell as secretary of the UGC, confessed to Sir George Newman, one of the committee's medical assessors,

> Even if the Grants Committee thought it desirable to approve any more clinical units, they certainly have not got the money for it now, and in any public statement it is important to avoid giving the impression that any school that sets up units and fulfils the University of London's requirements can come to the Committee and demand a grant for their upkeep.[59]

Money was not, however, the only consideration. After its initial enthusiasm for the concept of clinical units, the UGC had become somewhat lukewarm, not least Sir Wilmot Herringham, who had been the main author of the celebrated memorandum. By 1924 he was seriously questioning the unique value of special clinical units, headed by full-time professors leading what he referred to as 'monastic lives', in the provision of high-quality clinical teaching:

> When you have the right man it is a good thing to set him free to pursue medicine in this way. But it is not ever the whole of teaching, it is not even the teaching which is most immediately requisite for the patient, and it never ought to be thought that students cannot be taught to think except by a medical monk.[60]

By the end of the decade, the UGC appeared to be taking so little interest in policy matters relating to clinical units that the committee's medical assessors, Sir George Newman and Sir Walter Fletcher, who was a strong supporter of the unit system, began seriously to question whether they still had a useful role to perform in the work of the committee.[61]

Some progress with the establishment of clinical units, led by full-time clinical professors, was seen during the 1930s, notably in Scotland,[62] and the Manchester Medical School went so far as to approve the creation of a full-time clinical chair in medicine in 1939, only for the Second World War to intervene.[63] However, it took the *Report of the Interdepartmental Committee on Medical Schools* (1944), better known by the name of its chairman, Sir William Goodenough, to bring about the wholesale adoption of full-time clinical chairs by the provincial medical schools of England. Set up during the Second World War 'to enquire into the organisation of medical schools, particularly in regard to the facilities for clinical teaching and research', one of the committee's central recommendations read as follows: 'In harmony with the general body of evidence it is recommended that, at the earliest possible date, the staff of every medical school should include a whole-time professor in each of the departments of general medicine, general surgery, and obstetrics and gynaecology.'[64] The report had an immediate, and dramatic effect. The establishment of full-time clinical chairs became the norm, to be held by some of the giants of British medical education during the second half of the twentieth century.[65]

However, at the beginning of the 1920s, the Welsh National School of Medicine was engaged in an experiment, involving as a partner a voluntary hospital with no tradition of operating in a serious way as a teaching hospital. There was, as we have noted in the previous chapter, no burning enthusiasm for the unit system among the hospital clinicians: we have as evidence Bruce Vaughan's own testimony, given shortly before his death, as well as the subsequent actions of the members of the

Medical Board during the spring and summer months of 1921, leading to the formulation of a written agreement with the college in order to protect the hospital's interests. There was certainly no acceptance, despite the recommendation of the Haldane Commission that the hospital should be 'directly within the sphere' of the university, that the clinical units should indeed have a leadership role within the hospital. The full-time professors and the students were, in fact, widely regarded as 'guests', with all that this implied.[66] In the circumstances prudence would have demanded that the professors of medicine and surgery should reach a *modus vivendi* with their hospital colleagues.

There is no actual evidence to show that the early problems between the professors and the hospital staff arose from different approaches to the management of patient care. However, what was apparent was a resentment among the hospital clinicians at what they perceived as a tendency of the professorial units to 'do things differently' in other ways when it was incumbent on the school authorities to secure the co-operation of their hospital colleagues. The first thing that upset the hospital staff was the action of the professors of medicine and surgery to have themselves designated as 'directors' of their respective clinical units by the University of Wales.[67] Although this term was commonplace in the London clinical units its adoption in Cardiff caused resentment among the honorary clinical staff. They considered the move as elitist, tending to drive a wedge between the professorial units and the other hospital firms, and certainly one which was quite inappropriate for guests to take.[68]

When it came to the question of organizing and carrying out the clinical teaching programme, the directors of the medical and surgical units acted in a most 'un-guest-like' manner. It has already been noted in chapter 4 how, with the first involvement of the Board of Education in the funding of medical education in 1908, the university medical faculties and their clinical professors had begun to assume greater control over the organization of clinical teaching up and down the country. In Sheffield, for instance, the somewhat uncoordinated clinical teaching provided by the hospital clinical staff was superseded in 1919 by more structured teaching arrangements imposed by the university Faculty of Medicine, with the university professors of medicine and surgery assuming a central co-ordinating role in the teaching process and providing systematic instruction to student groups.[69] Similar developments had taken place at Manchester,[70] and, of course, one of the main reasons for introducing the clinical unit system into the main London teaching hospitals was to bring the control of the curriculum into the hands of the full-time professors. Nevertheless, whether in London or elsewhere in the United Kingdom, the delivery of the clinical teaching programme had, of necessity, to be a shared activity, involving university academic staff and hospital clinicians, who, after all, controlled most of the beds used for teaching. At Edinburgh, for instance, most students received their clinical instruction from the hospital staff, a fact which attracted the observation of one of the professors that 'Whilst the professor has direct control over didactic or theoretical teaching, he has only indirect control over the clinical instruction of the majority of students.'[71] The same applied in the London teaching hospitals too, such as St Bartholomew's Hospital where, according to Keir Waddington, 'The professorial units were seen to provide the science, and the non-professorial units the bedside instruction and clinical medicine that had come to typify medical education in Britain.'[72] In short, in the provision of clinical teaching at the medical schools of the United Kingdom, the essential ingredient was co-operation between the university staff and the hospital clinicians.

Cardiff's circumstances were different from those elsewhere in the country in that the clinical course at the Welsh National School of Medicine was introduced simultaneously with the establishment of the clinical units. Apart from a small amount of clinical exposure granted to students during their preclinical years, there was no tradition of clinical teaching being organized and provided by the hospital doctors, and from the outset the directors of the clinical units, the professors of medicine and surgery, assumed total control over the process. Although they did at least send the clinical teaching timetable to the Medical Board for comment, they did nothing to involve their clinical colleagues in the fulfilment of the teaching programme. Certainly the hospital staff had shown themselves to be less than enthusiastic partners, and in the early months of the full medical school there were relatively few students to be taught. Even so, some sort of embrace with their hospital colleagues by the professors of medicine and surgery at that time might have paid dividends later.

Instead, at the beginning of January 1922, Professor Kennedy and Professor Sheen decided to share with the Medical Board their intention to appoint a number of part-time assistants in their units to assist them in the performance of their academic duties. The hospital staff considered such a step unnecessary at that time; if the professors needed help with the teaching, the existing clinical staff were available. Moreover, members of the Medical Board were concerned that five new assistants, two in medicine and three in surgery, would upset the balance of clinical staff in the hospital to the advantage of the new units. Furthermore, for reasons of economy, the assistants would be appointed on a part-time rather than a full-time basis. The fact that those appointed were all already working in the hospital in various capacities did not entirely compensate for the creation of a group of additional clinicians who, by virtue of their part-time status, were free to 'fish' in the local private practice pool, their curricula vitae enhanced by their association with the professorial units. Although the Medical Board was in no position to veto the professors' plans, it did attempt to control the status of the assistants by making their appointments subject to annual review, and their clinical responsibilities restricted to those delegated to them by the professors.[73] However, during the early months of 1922, meetings of the board were soured by accusations by the honorary clinical staff that the assistants in the clinical units, encouraged by their chiefs, were undertaking duties beyond those that had been sanctioned.[74] It was not, perhaps, surprising that when D. R. Paterson stood down as chairman of the Medical Board in March 1922, Mitchell Stevens proposed a vote of thanks for his services 'during a time when so many changes had taken place, and so many difficulties had to be contended with in connection with the development of the Medical School'.[75] At least Professor Sheen was well known to his clinical colleagues and, to a degree trusted, notwithstanding his new role in the hospital. The same could not be said of Professor Kennedy, whose appointment had been less than welcomed by the local clinicians. Having, reportedly, been told at his first attendance at the Medical Board, 'We view with great suspicion you outsiders coming here',[76] Kennedy was more than happy to turn his back on his clinical colleagues, barely ever attending meetings of the Medical Board even when matters germane to his activities were under discussion.

Though, at the insistence of the hospital authorities, precluded from testing the external market for assistants, the professors were able to make some excellent appointments from within the hospital. Ivor Davies, appointed as part-time assistant in the medical unit at an annual salary of £200, was already working in the hospital's out-patient department for two days a week, and serving as visiting physician to several district hospitals in the south Wales Valleys. Herbert Evans, the second assistant in the unit, was also an assistant physician in the hospital and a part-time demonstrator in the Department of Anatomy. Of the three assistants appointed to the surgical unit, J. W. Geary Grant (1866–1947) was a highly respected and long-established surgeon with a substantial practice in the cottage hospitals of the mining valleys; while John Berry Haycraft (1888–1969), son of the late professor of physiology, would, much later, become the hospital's senior surgeon. Although not established as a new clinical unit, Professor Maclean's Department of Obstetrics and Gynaecology also benefited from the appointment of a part-time assistant, in the person of Gilbert Innes Strachan (1888–1963), a research pathologist at the hospital, who, ten years later, would succeed Maclean in the chair.[77]

In view of the tensions described above it was hardly surprising that when the licensing bodies were invited by the Cardiff College to grant recognition to the full medical course of the University of Wales, they did not entirely like what they saw. The General Medical Council, it must be said, had declared itself entirely content, in November 1921, no doubt owing to the benevolence of its president, Sir Donald MacAlister,[78] but the assessors from the University of London and the Conjoint Board were made of sterner stuff. Having conducted a rigorous assessment, including on-site visitations involving meetings with the hospital authorities and clinicians, these two bodies, at the beginning of May 1922, pronounced themselves dissatisfied, their concerns summarized in a report from the University of London.[79] Although the teaching arrangements regarding obstetrics and gynaecology were 'satisfactory', those with regard to medicine and surgery were not, in three main respects. First, arrangements for the teaching of anaesthetics, dermatology and the diseases of children were not yet in place, an indication of the hurried introduction of the clinical course, the previous autumn. Secondly, the professorial medical and surgical units had made no attempt to maximize the clinical teaching opportunities in the hospital by involving their clinical colleagues on the honorary staff in the teaching programme, or to acknowledge their role with formal university titles. Thirdly, not only was the number of medical beds directly under the control of the professor inadequate, but the total number of medical beds in the hospital was significantly smaller than recommended by bodies such as the UGC. Although the London University assessors had been told that efforts would be made to find extra medical beds at other hospitals, they were insistent that the central teaching role of the King Edward VII Hospital should not be diminished.

Though disappointed with the criticisms, which the college authorities considered unfair, given the fact that the medical school was still in its infancy, there was no alternative but to address the criticisms. By the autumn term of the 1922/3 session eight of the eleven fourth- and fifth-year students who were working for the London qualifications, concerned that their Cardiff-based training might not be recognized, were 'voting with their feet', and transferring to the London medical schools.

In discussions between the college authorities and those of the Conjoint Board and London University clarification was obtained, during the autumn of 1922, as to exactly what had to be done in order for the medical course of the University of Wales to receive the necessary recognition. While noting that the college authorities had negotiated access, for medical teaching, to the City Lodge Hospital, an institution under the control of the Cardiff Board of Guardians, the total number of medical beds at the King Edward VII Hospital had to be increased to eighty, and thirty of them had to be in the medical professorial unit. Moreover, in line with normal practice elsewhere in the United Kingdom, all the honorary clinical staff of the hospital had to be formally recognized as teachers of the University of Wales and be required to undertake clinical teaching as part of their duties. Access to all the beds at the King Edward VII Hospital was regarded as of particular importance because the number in the medical and surgical professorial units (seventeen plus two cots and forty respectively) fell well short of the GMC's recommendation, that the number of beds controlled by professorial units should range between fifty and one hundred.[80] In this regard, the position in the London professorial units at this time is worthy of note:[81]

Table 5.2 The number of beds under the control of the professorial units (1923)

	Medicine	Surgery
St Bartholomew's Hospital	56	60
The London Hospital	70	97
St Mary's Hospital	111	113
St Thomas's Hospital	60	69
UCH	34	41

It took nearly two years for the medical course of the Welsh National School of Medicine to receive final recognition from London University and the Conjoint Board, during which time temporary recognition for one year at a time was conceded, lest the affairs of the school be thrown into complete chaos. The agreement by the hospital authorities that out-patient facilities for dermatology and the diseases of children should be provided, was negotiated with relative ease, thereby enabling comprehensive teaching in these disciplines to be undertaken.[82]

Securing the agreement of the disgruntled honorary clinical staff to participate in the clinical teaching programme took more effort, the matter being thrashed out in a number of meetings of the Medical Board in late 1922 and early 1923.[83] The tone of the discussions was set by the board chairman, H. G. Cook, who expressed the hope that the honorary staff would receive rather more consideration in the future than they had in the past, extracting an admission from Principal Trow, who had been invited to attend the deliberations, that 'he was now coming to the view that the students should come into contact with all the members of the honorary staff, and not only the units'. It was left to Professors Sheen and Kennedy (in one of his rare attendances) to outline what the teaching duties of the honorary staff would entail. In addition to regular bedside teaching they would be expected to give occasional lectures, perhaps one a month for the surgeons, once every three weeks for the physicians. For this they would receive the honorary university title of recognized clinical teacher.

The proposed title was not one in general use by the medical schools of the United Kingdom, where the title routinely awarded to honorary physicians and surgeons in recognition of their teaching responsibilities was lecturer or clinical lecturer. In some schools the assistant physicians and surgeons were also styled 'lecturer', though in others, such as Birmingham, the prefix 'assistant' was added. The title of tutor was widely conferred upon those clinicians who had organizational duties, but not at Cardiff, where such duties fell upon the academic staff of the professorial units. The title of recognized clinical teacher first emerged at Cardiff in the summer of 1922 during discussions over recognition of its clinical course by the London licensing bodies. Its validity as a title could only have been confirmed in the mind of the school authorities by the content of a letter, received from the dean of the Bristol Medical School in the autumn, which, among other things, stated that his institution did award the title of recognized teacher, albeit to relatively junior members of the clinical staff.[84] Since the clinical staff of the King Edward VII Hospital were doing virtually no teaching at the time, and the school intended to use the title of lecturer for those who would be expected to organize and provide clinical teaching in specialist areas such as children's diseases, dermatology and psychiatry, it seemed by no means unreasonable to confer what might be regarded as the slightly inferior title of recognized clinical teacher on their hospital colleagues, physicians, surgeons and their assistants alike.

Although the honorary clinical staff raised no objection to the title, this was not considered to be sufficient reward in itself. It will be recalled that they received no remuneration at all for working in the hospital, in contrast to members of the professorial units, who were remunerated as either full-time or part-time members of the college, the average part-time salary being £200 per annum. Tenison Collins, an honorary gynaecologist, articulated the general mood among the honorary staff. Rather self-righteously for someone who had never been much of a friend of the medical school, he proclaimed that had their services been solicited properly, and not ignored, they would have been given readily and voluntarily, but since everyone else was being paid for teaching, so should they.

In fact, the payment of the honorary clinical staff of the hospital for undergraduate clinical teaching ought not to have been a contentious issue, for this was standard practice in provincial medical schools at this time. In the old days medical students had paid their fees in respect of the tuition received during the clinical years direct to the participating hospitals, which had seen to the remuneration of the clinical staff involved. With the introduction of state funding for medical education before the First World War, Whitehall had decreed that such casual arrangements should cease, to be replaced by arrangements under which the universities collected the clinical fees, paying the hospital staff appropriate fees for their teaching contribution. As the UGC explained to Bristol University in 1921,

> The University should not expect the Final subjects in [the Faculty of Medicine] to be taught free of charge to the University, and paid for out of the fees of the students. The expenses of the Final Medical subjects teaching must always be expected to exceed the fees that students can pay, and should always rank among the objects to which University Funds should be devoted.[85]

The precise arrangements varied from place to place. The University Clinical Board at Birmingham devised a highly elaborate system of remuneration which combined a range of flat fees given to clinicians responsible for the day-to day organization of the clinical course, with variable payments made on the basis of the number of compulsory classes, lectures and demonstrations undertaken, weighted according to the seniority of the clinical teachers involved. During the 1922/3 session nearly £4,000 was spent rewarding the honorary staff of the Birmingham teaching hospitals, with many of the senior physicians receiving honoraria ranging between £130 and £195, and the senior surgeons attracting substantially more.[86] Liverpool too operated a scheme under which payments were based on the amount of teaching given, though the level of payment made to individuals tended, on the whole to be less.[87] At Bristol the honorary clinical staff, physicians, assistant physicians and the like, received a standard honorarium of £20 per year for bedside teaching, with additional payments varying from £20 to £50 being made to those providing courses of lectures.[88]

When Professor Kennedy spoke to the Medical Board on the question of payments it is not surprising that he cited Bristol, with its relatively uncomplicated scheme and modest honoraria, as an example of practice elsewhere.[89] Having secured an annual sum of £500 from the University Council to pay honoraria to the school's recognized clinical teachers, the Board of Medicine, in consultation with the hospital's Medical Board, devised a scheme for its distribution. The sum of £400 would be divided equally among the honorary physicians, surgeons and their assistants, eleven in all, with the remaining £100 being divided among the non-professorial members of the units. While Cardiff's honorary clinical staff fared less well than their counterparts in some parts of the country, they appeared to be treated as generously as their nearest neighbours across the Severn Estuary, and for the time being they were content. After all, the clinical course at Cardiff was still in its infancy compared with courses elsewhere in the United Kingdom. As time passed and student numbers increased the question of payment could be reviewed.

The question of increasing the number of medical beds in the hospital proved even more challenging. Some of the honorary clinical staff resented being dictated to by the external licensing bodies – the number of beds in the hospital should be based on 'the needs of the locality' – and the decision of the Medical Board, in October 1922 to take the matter further was only passed by a vote of ten to three, the professor of medicine being absent.[90] Given the financial circumstances of the hospital the only way of solving the problem was by a reallocation of existing beds within the hospital, mainly to the disadvantage of the surgeons, as William Martin, one of their number, bitterly complained:

> The primary object of the [hospital] is to provide for the surgical and medical requirements of Cardiff and district and no-one can deny that the predominant requirement is for surgical beds. If more beds are required *for the purpose of the Medical School* those who are so anxious for that Medical School should provide new beds.[91]

Nevertheless, at its meeting on 24 July 1923 (from which, needless to say, Professor Kennedy was absent) the Medical Board of the Cardiff Royal Infirmary (the hospital's new name since obtaining a royal charter in the spring) resolved to reallocate twenty-seven beds to the medical firms, Dr Cyril Lewis, one of the three hospital physicians, agreeing to take a smaller increase so that Mitchell Stevens and, more importantly, Professor Kennedy, could each have thirty. Only the inevitable bureaucratic paperwork in London would now delay the Welsh National School of Medicine's recognition by the London licensing bodies, recognition by London University arriving in March 1924, and by the Conjoint Board three months later.

Happily coinciding with good news from London University was an appearance at the medical school by Ramsay MacDonald, the prime minister, as part of a wider visit to Cardiff. Speaking to the medical staff and students in the Institute of Physiology, he set them two challenges to address, namely how to work effectively for twenty-four hours without a stop, and (this problem was clearly one that concerned him personally) how to enjoy dinner at a public function and still manage to deliver a coherent speech afterwards: 'In the interest of future prime ministers I hope you will devote the undoubted brain-power that you have to the solving of these two problems.'[92]

THE SCHOOL'S EXPANDING CLINICAL TEACHING BOUNDARIES

Although the priority of the external licensing bodies was to ensure the adequacy of the clinical teaching facilities at the Cardiff Royal Infirmary, this did not mean that other hospitals were excluded from the undergraduate clinical teaching programme. Indeed, the use of centres outside the main teaching hospital was very much regarded as good practice at this time, as Sir George Newman reported: 'In London, Glasgow, Manchester, Bristol, Birmingham and elsewhere, poor-law hospital accommodation is now for the first time being used for educational purposes, and on the whole, with excellent results to both patient and student.'[93]

From the 1922/3 session, the Cardiff City Lodge Hospital (a hospital administered by the Cardiff Board of Guardians, and later to be known as St David's Hospital) was used for the teaching of medicine (240 beds), diseases of children (46 beds) and dermatology (30 beds), with Dr Alfred Howell and Dr James Beatty, already members of the staff of the Infirmary, being appointed in 1923 as part-time lecturers in children's diseases and dermatology respectively, each commanding an honorarium of £50 a year. Professor Kennedy, awarded an honorary clinical contract at the hospital, would, given half a chance, have established a substantial academic centre there, divorcing himself even more from his difficult clinical colleagues at the infirmary.[94] The Cardiff City Council also agreed to provide facilities for the teaching of mental diseases to medical students at the Cardiff City Mental Hospital. This hospital (which would be renamed Whitchurch Hospital in 1948) had been established in 1908, its title earning the strong approval of Dr G. Arbour Stephens, a leading commentator on Welsh health matters. In his review of hospital provision in Wales immediately before the First World War he deplored the use of the term 'asylum' as a 'disgrace to any nation calling itself civilised, and to Cardiff be all praise for having designated their institution the "Mental Hospital"'. In fact the credit was chiefly due to Dr Edwin Goodall (1863–1944), the hospital's admirable medical superintendent from the time of its opening until his retirement in 1929. He stoutly resisted the adoption of the title 'Cardiff Asylum', firmly believing that the hospital should be a place for treatment, not simply custodial care. In his determination to establish the principle of a close relationship between psychiatry and general medicine, he created a psychiatric out-patient department at the Cardiff Royal Infirmary, and arranged for specialists in medicine, surgery, gynaecology and otology to visit his mental hospital. In July 1922 he was appointed part-time lecturer in mental diseases in the medical school, also with an honorarium of £50 a year.[95]

In the autumn of 1923, the school's sphere of influence widened still further when it received a letter from the secretary of the Prince of Wales Hospital, offering to 'place the beds, departments and the personnel of the Prince of Wales Hospital at the disposal of the Welsh National School of Medicine so that facilities might be given for the students in the teaching of Orthopaedic Surgery'. This hospital, established during the war as a centre catering for the needs of limbless soldiers, mainly through the efforts of Sir John Lynn-Thomas, was expanded into a complete orthopaedic hospital after the war, with Stanley Alwyn Smith (1882–1931), a highly regarded trainee of Sir Robert Jones, appointed as surgeon-in-chief. The hospital's offer was immediately accepted and Alwyn Smith was appointed part-time lecturer in orthopaedics, with the usual honorarium of £50.[96] The same meeting of the Board of Medicine in December 1923 saw the appointment of the medical school's first female member of the academic staff, Miss Erie Evans, part-time lecturer in venereal diseases at an annual honorarium of £25. She would have special responsibility for instructing the women students, while Owen Lewellin Rhys, the infirmary's radiologist, was appointed to teach the men, also for £25 a year. During the early 1920s Dr Evans briefly served as vice-president of the Western and South Wales branch of the Medical Women's Federation. She was also one of the proud daughters of Griffith Evans (1835–1935), the great Welsh medical pioneer who, before Robert Koch and Louis Pasteur, had established the link between micro-organisms and disease.[97] After his death she deposited her father's voluminous papers with the National Library of Wales.

The appointment of Miss Evans to teach venereal diseases to women is significant as the only example of the separate provision of classes for men and women students at Cardiff. Although the presence of women in anatomy and other classes had been a problem for some medical schools in earlier years,[98] such considerations had never been an issue in the Cardiff Medical School. From the outset, men and women appear to have enjoyed equal access to all classes. As Professor Hepburn proclaimed to the Haldane Commission, at Cardiff there was absolutely no distinction of sex, and nowhere, either in the minutes of the relevant college and school committees or in the pages of the student magazines of the time, is there any evidence to the contrary. While one can appreciate the particular sensitivities surrounding a subject such as venereal diseases, it is worth pointing out that not all medical schools were so fastidious. St Mary's Hospital Medical School, for one, set its face against separating the sexes for instruction in venereal diseases, or indeed any other subject, although, as Carol Dyhouse has shown, tensions existed there and elsewhere during the 1920s.[99] Of course, outside the teaching sphere, in Cardiff as elsewhere separate facilities were provided for women students, such as female halls of residence, women's common rooms and the like.

Of all the hospitals used as part of the undergraduate teaching programme, the farthest from Newport Road were Glan Ely Hospital, near St Fagans, and Cefn Mably Hospital, between Cardiff and Newport, both of which were available to final-year students wishing to take an optional course in tuberculosis. The facilities in Swansea were not used at this time, despite an enquiry from the authorities of the Swansea General and Eye Hospital in the autumn of 1922 'as to the exact position that Hospital occupies in connection with the Welsh National School of Medicine and also how far the Swansea Hospital may take part in the clinical and pathological instruction of medical students'. Dean Hepburn was asked to seek some information from the hospital 'with a view to submitting the whole matter of the relationship of Swansea General Hospital with the School, to the University'.[100] There is nothing recorded in the minutes of either the school's Faculty of Medicine, or of the University Council at this time, to indicate what, if anything, transpired, and there is no evidence to suggest that Swansea was used by the school for clinical teaching during the 1920s. Certainly Dr Tom Davies, the historian of the Swansea General and Eye Hospital, makes no claims in this respect, though he reminds us that the hospital was recognized by the Conjoint Board as a suitable place where students registered for its examinations could do some of their clinical training. One such student was J. W. Tudor Thomas, who spent six months there as a surgical dresser during the First World War.[101] Though, under the provisions of the Nurses' Registration Act (1919), the Royal Gwent Hospital became in the early 1920s a complete training school for nurses, it too had no involvement in the Welsh National School of Medicine's clinical teaching programme during the inter-war years. Apart from any logistical issues, this was due, no doubt in part, to the fact that it was not until the 1930s that

> The medical status of the hospital changed enormously, in that the Honorary Staff, instead of being manned by general practitioners became almost entirely a staff of consultants – a very important thing for the status of the hospital, as it brought the Royal Gwent into line with the big hospitals up and down the country.[102]

THE SHAPE OF THE MEDICAL COURSE AND THE QUALITY OF ITS PRODUCT

In one respect, the Welsh National School of Medicine was fortunate in initiating its full six-year curriculum at the beginning of the 1920s, just at the time when the General Medical Council itself was introducing revised regulations for the medical curriculum, with effect from 1 January 1923. This meant that staff and students at the school were not confronted with the sort of challenges faced by those in other medical schools, where the curricular arrangements were of longer standing. Where changes were necessary, particularly in relation to the first three years of the course, the school's Faculty of Medicine was committed to implementing them. 'The Faculty are alive to the need for the integration of parts of the preliminary sciences into the later years of the curriculum, and the Faculty are taking steps to carry this into effect so far as the teaching of the elements of Bacteriology is concerned.'[103] However, in some respects, the Welsh National School of Medicine would be regarded as in the vanguard of curricular development. Its adoption of the 'clinical unit' system could be regarded in that light, and Sir George Newman, in his review of recent advances in medical education, referred, with obvious approval, to the progressive approaches adopted by Professor Graham Brown and by Professor Ewen Maclean to the teaching of physiology and obstetrics and gynaecology, respectively, at Cardiff.[104] Moreover, the new emphasis in the GMC's revised regulations on the place of preventive medicine in the medical curriculum aroused no concern in the Welsh National School of Medicine. Professor Collis, in addition to securing time in the fifth-year timetable for a systematic course of lectures and practical demonstrations in hygiene and public health, managed to secure the support of the Faculty of Medicine for the concept that 'Preventive medicine may be styled as a horizontal stratum into which all branches of clinical medicine dip … Indeed preventive medicine today should permeate to an ever increasing extent the whole of clinical teaching. It cannot and should not be pigeon-holed as an isolated subject.'[105]

In essence, the shape of the school's medical curriculum during the 1920s was as follows. Of six years' duration, the first three years prepared students for a B.Sc. degree of the University of Wales, an essential prerequisite for those wishing to take the university's medical degrees, but not for students opting to work for the Conjoint Board or London University qualifications. As during the pre-full medical school era, the first year was devoted to the preliminary subjects of physics, chemistry, botany and zoology, and the second and third years were mainly spent studying organic chemistry, human anatomy and physiology.

It was the intention of the GMC that the main preclinical subjects should be taught so as to demonstrate their relevance to future clinical practice. As Keir Waddington has written with regard to the London scene at that time, 'To achieve this, emphasis was placed on practical classes, which ran in tandem with systematic lectures.'[106] If anything, the approach adopted in Cardiff went further, as Professor Kennedy, then dean of the medical school, explained in a memorandum to the Rockefeller Foundation in 1923.[107] In the anatomy department 'the method of teaching is Demonstrative and Practical. There is no such thing as a formal lecture or oration, but wherever possible every fact is illustrated by specimens, models, diagrams and lantern slides.' As advocated by the GMC the applied anatomy classes involved instruction on the living subject. Students spent most of their time however in the dissecting room (up to fifteen hours a week for six terms) under the close supervision of the teaching staff:

> No student is permitted to advance from one stage of his dissection to another until the teacher has been satisfied that the work has been satisfactorily performed,

the structures clearly displayed, and an intelligent understanding acquired of the structures as displayed by the actual dissection, as distinguished from the mere memorising of the printed statements of their books By such methods [Kennedy concluded] the student is guided and encouraged to cultivate technique, the habit of personal observation, the collection of his own facts, the description of his observations in his own language, reliance upon his own judgement in weighing the value of his observations. In other words, he is acquiring not only the method of Research, but the principles out of which a diagnosis is evolved in clinical practice.

As far as the teaching of physiology was concerned, the number of systematic lectures, regarded by the professor of physiology as outmoded, was being reduced in favour of a system of tutorial reading classes in which students' reading was supervised and directed by the academic staff. The main teaching consisted in practical instruction in all the main subsections of physiology, some involving the performing of experiments, in order, as Kennedy explained, that the students 'obtain a development of knowledge by the experimental method'.

During the second and third years the students were also given instruction, by way of lectures, tutorials and practical classes in materia medica and pharmacology, including practical pharmacy and therapeutics. However, although students of the University of Wales could not proceed into the fourth (first clinical) year of the course until they had satisfied the examiners in the preliminary and preclinical subjects, the examinations in pharmacology were held over until the clinical phase.

Although, prior to 1923, the GMC had laid down that medical courses in the United Kingdom should be of at least five years' duration, the dividing-line between the preclinical and clinical phases had lacked precision, comparing one university with another. The new GMC regulations were quite clear, for the first time, that the period of clinical studies following completion of the courses in anatomy and physiology should be of three years' duration. In Cardiff students spent their fourth year attending courses of instruction in medicine, surgery, pathology and bacteriology, obstetrics and gynaecology and vaccination, and, during the summer term, held appointments as medical clerks and surgical dressers. During the fifth year students continued to act as medical clerks and dressers, while holding clinical appointments in obstetrics and gynaecology, during which time they were expected to conduct at least twenty cases of labour. They also attended courses in forensic medicine, public health, mental diseases, diseases of children, anaesthetics and the main surgical sub-specialties, instruction which would carry over into the sixth year. In addition to further periods of clinical practice in medicine, surgery and obstetrics and gynaecology, sixth-year students had a range of optional clinical attachments to pursue, in disciplines such as tuberculosis, orthopaedics, ophthalmology and oto-rhino-laryngology, as well as classes in a range of special subjects including radiology, venereal disease and dermatology. Running throughout the session were further courses in pathology and bacteriology.[108]

In all the major clinical disciplines priority was placed on the self-development of the students themselves. Certainly courses of lecture/demonstrations were provided on the principles and practice of the various subjects, but great emphasis was placed throughout, on the students' own participation. In pathology, for example, all students were required to attend twenty post-mortems and carry out the duties of a post-mortem clerk for a period of three months. In surgery, students acted as surgical dressers for several months over a period of three years, involving work on the wards and in the operating theatres, in the out-patient and casualty departments of the hospital, and in the clinical pathology laboratory. In medicine, particular stress was placed on the laboratory as an essential feature of good clinical practice. In the medical unit's laboratory, students were taught how to examine blood, urine, sputum and gastric contents, and during their service as clinical clerks they were expected to carry out, under supervision, such laboratory investigations as might be indicated. Such an approach was just what Sir George Newman was looking for in the ideal clinical unit, when he wrote: 'Not every student can undertake research, but every student should be imbued with its spirit, its methods, its results.'[109]

Although initially comprising only seventeen beds and two cots, scattered over three wards of the hospital (the facilities were expanded and to some degree consolidated later), there was no shortage of what is euphemistically called 'good clinical material' for students to observe in the medical unit. This is known because among the archives of Cardiff University are five bound copies of 'Reports', or contemporary case notes. These concern several hundreds of in-patients dealt with in the medical unit during the first three years of its existence. The first dozen listed cover a wide spectrum of medical conditions ranging from infants admitted with 'cough and vomiting', through adolescents with pneumonia, anaemia and myelogenic leukaemia, to adults with heart failure, gastritis, stomach cancer with secondary tumours in the liver, chorea, diabetes and severe back strain (this acquired by an assistant colliery repairer from Maerdy who had been attempting to lift a derailed wagon full of coal). The home conditions of the patients are often described, with small, damp, overcrowded dwellings with no inside bathrooms and outside toilets. One woman, aged forty-four and married for twenty-four years, had produced nine children, only four of whom had survived, the other five having died of 'convulsions' as infants. In short, the learning opportunities for the students were excellent, especially if one bears in mind that the length of stay of patients in the 1920s was substantially greater than it is today, ranging from a few weeks to some months or longer.

In 1926, the Education Committee of the GMC conducted a nationwide survey to determine the extent to which its new resolutions regarding the medical curriculum were being implemented. In general, the council was able to report broad compliance, while at the same time drawing attention to variations, particularly in respect to study in the preliminary subjects, whether they were studied prior to university entry or, as in the University of Wales, as part of the first year of medical studies. The GMC's verdict on the University of Wales medical course was that its regulations 'are in general accordance with the Resolutions of the Council'. Not all medical courses were given such a clean bill of health, a number of relatively minor omissions being highlighted in the degree programmes at Bristol, Cambridge, Leeds, Liverpool and St Andrews. The Senatus at St Andrews was particularly indignant that its medical course had been criticized by the GMC: 'When the comments of the [Education] Committee are answered one by one it will be seen that in no important point have the recommendations of the Council been neglected.'[110]

All the necessary curricular changes, introduced by the school in response to the GMC's recommendations, were reflected in revised regulations for the degrees of MB B.Ch. of the University of Wales, adopted by the University Council in June 1923. In the regulations, initially compiled before the war, were arrangements for the award of the degrees with first- or second-class honours. In order to be awarded a degree with first-class honours a student had to negotiate three hurdles; first, complete his course of study in the minimum time of six years; secondly, be awarded distinctions in five subjects, including medicine, surgery, either obstetrics and gynaecology or pathology and bacteriology, and either human anatomy or physiology; thirdly, be successful, first time, in all the university examinations. To achieve a degree with second-class honours a student had to gain distinctions in four subjects. It is unlikely that the drafters of the regulations could have foreseen how formidable these hurdles were to prove, even to the most gifted of students. None of the first sixty-four medical graduates of the University of Wales, who obtained their degrees between 1916 and 1931, achieved honours status, hardly a surprising outcome in view of the fact that during that period only five distinctions were awarded in obstetrics and gynaecology, three in medicine and none at all in surgery. Indeed, in an exhaustive study of the examination performance of the school's medical students between 1933 and 1948, its author made absolutely no reference to the award of honours degrees at all, suggesting that the concept continued to be extremely elusive throughout the whole of the inter-war period.[111]

It should, however, be stressed that the Welsh National School of Medicine was not wholly out of line with practice elsewhere in the United Kingdom, where the award of medical degrees with honours remained a relatively rare occurrence. The annual statistical returns made by universities to the UGC are of some help here, for they show that in five sample years, the four sessions from 1925/6 to 1928/9 and the session 1930/1, the number of honours degrees awarded in medicine and surgery was fifty-five, fifty, forty-seven, thirty-seven and twenty-five, respectively. It is impossible to arrive at an exact percentage figure as at that time the number of medical and dental graduates each year was not shown separately, but a figure of 5 *per cent* may be considered a reasonable estimate.[112] A sample of nearly 1,000 holders of the English FRCS reveals that fewer than forty (under 5 per cent) are recorded as having qualified with honours from one of the universities of the United Kingdom, roughly the same proportion as graduated with honours from Liverpool University between 1921 and 1924, where six (including Henry, later Lord Cohen of Birkenhead) obtained first-class honours and twenty second-class. At Bristol, between 1921 and 1930, four students graduated with first-class honours and twenty-one with second-class, with half the cohort gaining honours in 1922, an exceptional year. The fact that students obtained honours at all very much depended on the flexibility of the degree regulations, which were certainly less prescriptive at Liverpool and Bristol than they were at the Welsh National School of Medicine.[113]

In one respect, however, the medical degree regulations of the University of Wales appeared to be rather more generous to its students than those of other universities. Almost uniquely among medical schools in the United Kingdom students taking the University of Wales qualification were not required to take the three subjects of the final examination (medicine, surgery, obstetrics and gynaecology) all at the same time, Wales finding itself in the company of the Society of Apothecaries, the English and Irish Conjoint Boards, the Apothecaries Hall, Dublin, and the Universities of St Andrews and Dublin. The Examination Committee of the GMC surveyed the regulations in force throughout the United Kingdom in 1927, but while noticing that there were certainly variations in practice, it did not then recommend that arrangements should be standardized.[114] In a report submitted at the time to the Birmingham Faculty of Medicine by Leonard Gamgee, the University of Birmingham's representative on the GMC, he commented that while it might seem desirable to introduce uniformity of practice, 'The Council favours as much individuality as possible in the examination methods of the various Licensing Bodies.'[115] The effect of the University of Wales regulation was that of the sixty-four students who graduated with the MB B.Ch. of the University of Wales between 1916 and 1931, only fourteen passed all three subjects in the final examination at the same sitting, six of them in 1924. Many students, taking advantage of the fact that the instruction in obstetrics and gynaecology was completed during the penultimate year of the course, chose to take the final examination in that subject at the end of the fifth year, twelve months in advance of the other two subjects.[116] Other students employed different strategies. The arrangements caused some unease among the external assessors of the GMC who visited Cardiff in 1930 to inspect the conduct of the final University of Wales examination in surgery and obstetrics and gynaecology. They took the view that the division of the final qualifying examination into two or three parts was contrary to the spirit, if not the letter, of the Medical Amendment Act (1886), which defined a qualifying examination as 'an Examination in Medicine, Surgery and Midwifery'. They further noted that, despite GMC guidance, there was no University regulation which required completion of all subjects within a period of nineteen months.[117] While the medical school took no immediate action, it was clear that it could not continue to allow one-fifth of its students to take two years or more to complete their final examinations, and finally in 1933 the University regulations were amended to comply with the expectations of the GMC in respect of the nineteen-month time limit.[118]

Final recognition, in 1924, by the University of London and the Conjoint Board of the Wales medical course, a mark of academic respectability, could hardly have come at a better time, as it more or less coincided with the first degree ceremony of the University of Wales at which medical and surgical degrees were conferred on students who had pursued some or all of their clinical training in Cardiff. This historic ceremony took place on 17 July 1924 at the University College of North Wales, Bangor, when eight students were presented by Professor William Sheen to the Congregation, two of whom had pursued all their clinical training in London. The 'Cardiff Six' included Daniel Thomas Davies (1889–1966), born in Pontycymmer, the son of a Congregationalist minister, who, much later, when consultant physician at the Royal Free Hospital, became physician to King George VI and Aneurin Bevan and was probably the first doctor to diagnose Addison's Disease in the young John Fitzgerald Kennedy. He was knighted in 1951.[119] It should be noted that it continued to be possible, under the regulations of the Conjoint Board, to qualify for its diploma after two years of clinical study, and Davies and two other Wales degree students who had started the clinical course in 1921 obtained the MRCS LRCP qualification in 1923.

Of the eight medical graduands at the ceremony three were women, two of whom, Constance Walters and Edith Margaret Davies, had trained in Cardiff throughout the course. Constance Walters went on to specialize in ophthalmology, pursuing a career as an assistant medical officer in Leicestershire, while Edith Davies, after a spell in Devon, returned to Cardiff where she too would work as an assistant medical officer with the Cardiff City Council. At exactly the same time that most of the London medical schools were terminating what was referred to as 'the great experiment' of admitting women students,[120] the University of Wales was setting an altogether better example. Of the sixty-four medical graduates of the University of Wales between 1916 and 1931, no fewer than twenty-two (34 per cent) were women, an outcome which undoubtedly gave much satisfaction to Daniel Lleufer Thomas and his General Committee for the Promotion of Medical Training of Women, established by the University of Wales, as has already been noted, during the First World War. By 1923 Thomas's committee had given financial assistance to fifteen students, nine of whom had already qualified as doctors, and at that year's annual meeting the chairman, quoting from the annual report, gave a flavour of the ethos of the committee:

> The report shows that great care is taken to make grants and loans to those students only whose work is of a high quality, and who are likely to be successful in a medical career. We have pleasure in acknowledging the loyal co-operation of the students

themselves, and of the readiness with which they inform us of any improvement in financial circumstances which makes assistance from the committee less necessary.

He proceeded to outline the sort of work that these excellent ladies were particularly well equipped to pursue, well away, some might muse, from the consulting rooms of Cardiff. 'A great sphere of activity awaited medical women in the East, where millions of women regarded it as an outrage to be examined and treated by men. Women trained in the Welsh National School of Medicine would find a wide missionary field in India and China. (Hear, hear).'[121] At the eighth annual general meeting in 1924, it was reported that altogether some £2,000 had been awarded to deserving students, a figure which, by June 1929, had risen to £2,432. By then twenty students had benefited from the scheme, with Mabel Howell, the secretary to the committee, observing, with obvious approval, that 'Only one, Enid Powell, has married. I don't know whether she continues to work.' Among the two score or so annual subscribers to the committee's funds at this time (£66 12s. 6d. was donated in 1928/9) were Gwendoline and Margaret Davies of Llandinam, Mary Rathbone, the Bangor philanthropist, and Sir William James Thomas.[122]

The summer degree congregation of 1924 was the first occasion at which Welsh graduands in medicine formally subscribed to the Hippocratic Oath before the ceremony. The arrangement had been narrowly approved at the meeting of the University Court the previous July by a vote of thirty-five to thirty-two, in the teeth of opposition from Daniel Lleufer Thomas and others who had taken the view that it was the University's job to acknowledge academic achievement, not to impose tests such as the Hippocratic Oath, which was the province of the professional bodies. The actual wording of the declaration, as approved by the University Council in November 1923, and which was subscribed to by every graduand in medicine of the University of Wales up until January 2002, when a new affirmation for a new millennium was introduced, reads as follows:

> I pledge myself and promise that I will exercise the science of Medicine to the best of my powers and in accord with the laws of honour and probity; that I will work for the benefit of all, whosoever shall seek my service, without distinction of great and small, of rich or poor, of youth and age, of good and bad; that I will hold my knowledge in trust for the benefit of the common weal; that I will revere my teachers who have given me this knowledge, and give to those that follow me the gift of knowledge which I have myself received; and whatever I shall see or hear in the lives of men, so be it improper to disclose, that will I not disclose.

In June 1988 a Welsh version of the declaration, provided by the distinguished physician and medical historian Dr Emyr Wyn Jones, was introduced into the medical degree ceremony for the first time.

ONLY A MEDICAL SCHOOL?

The medical school did not confine its ambitions to the training of women doctors at this time, for there was much concern in the land about the quality of nurse training, which was then a totally female preserve.[123] As has already been noted, the school had provided successful annual courses of lectures in midwifery for trainee midwives for nearly twenty years, led by Ewen Maclean, attracting between eighty and ninety students a year in most years.[124] That great benefactor, Sir William James Thomas, created three nursing medals, gold, silver and bronze, in 1917 (the year when he married the Infirmary's deputy matron), to be awarded annually to those Cardiff nurses who performed best in their final professional examinations. At the inaugural ceremony, attended by Sir Isambard Owen, Colonel Bruce Vaughan declared that the medals 'will be an award of merit, and an incentive for all time to every nurse who enters our hospital as a probationer to become a thoroughly efficient and highly-skilled nurse'.[125] Ewen Maclean wanted to go further, and at the end of 1921, he became actively involved in discussions regarding the possibility of providing nurse training in the medical school itself. In May 1922, Dean Hepburn, addressing a meeting of the Cardiff branch of the College of Nursing, declared that the University of Wales was seriously considering the establishment of a Diploma in Nursing, similar to one recently introduced at Leeds University, with a course of study being offered by the medical school.[126] In fact, nothing came of this in the short term, though the midwifery training offered by the school was given greater recognition in 1925, when it was brought formally under the aegis of the academic Department of Obstetrics and Gynaecology.[127] The establishment, later in the decade, of a course for health visitors, in the Department of Public Health, will be noted in the next chapter.

Veterinary medicine was another area which briefly claimed the attention of the medical school in the early 1920s. Mary Rathbone, an active lay member of the University of Wales, had been keen on the idea during the First World War, linking such a venture with the medical school: 'Our veterinary surgeons are for the most part very unsatisfactory and must at present take their training outside Wales at great expense.'[128] The Haldane Commission considered the matter, concluding, however, that there was insufficient demand for another veterinary school, especially as the University of Liverpool lay within easy reach of Wales.[129] Nevertheless, David Hepburn certainly included this discipline on the school's 'wish-list' during a wide-ranging interview to the *South Wales News* in December 1921:

> Because of the number of diseases which are transmissible from the lower animals to man, it is of the utmost importance that a Veterinary Department be added to the School of Medicine so that in the Veterinary Hospital the sick and injured animals of the farmer may be cared for and treated more effectively than under existing condi-

tions, and such diseases as are transmissible to man may be subject to study and research.[130]

The pressure of competing priorities meant that the issue was not again raised until the autumn of 1923, when the Denbighshire County Council chose to urge the University of Wales to 'give consideration to the importance of providing facilities in the Principality for the fuller training of students in Veterinary Medicine'. The matter was referred to the School of Medicine, the Faculty of Medicine of which prepared a well-researched report on the subject. Having reviewed the content of existing veterinary courses elsewhere in the United Kingdom the faculty believed that 'the course of instruction, although shorter, closely resembles that given to medical students', and concluded: 'The University of Wales with its National School of Medicine is well placed for organising a course of instruction in Veterinary Medicine and for following the example of London, Edinburgh and Liverpool in establishing degrees and diplomas of its own.' Brimming with self-confidence, the faculty proposed, as a way of assessing demand for such training (Bristol having expressed the view that there was none), that students should be admitted to the first, science-based year ('the medical curriculum in Chemistry, Physics, Botany and Zoology is generally wider than what is needed, although it will require a few minor alterations'). The faculty report continued: 'Subsequently if the number of students justify further development, steps could be taken to complete the course using the courses of instruction now given to medical students after their first year, as the basis upon which to work.'[131] The university, advised by the Academic Board, was sufficiently supportive of this development to encourage University College, Cardiff to invite the Royal College of Veterinary Surgeons to recognize a training scheme leading to the RCVS's first professional examination in veterinary sciences. A year was to elapse before the Royal college introduced a sense of reality into the proceedings, refusing to accede to the request because the College had not put together a credible scheme for the provision 'of a complete course of instruction in Veterinary Medicine and Surgery as contemplated by Section 4 of the Veterinary Surgeons Act, 1881'.[132] There the matter rested for many years, the issue not being raised again until after the Second World War.

However, the medical school spent more time over the issue of veterinary science during the early 1920s than it did over dental education, for on 15 February 1922, the Faculty of Medicine resolved: 'That the National Dental Association be informed that it is not possible, at present, to make arrangements for the inauguration of courses of instruction for the LDS qualification.' Many years were to elapse before dental education was given any sort of priority in Wales. Challenged about this during the annual dinner of the British Dental Association in Cardiff in 1931, the principal of University College, Cardiff, J. F. Rees, admitted that there were many in the room who could recall the pain caused during the squalling infancy of the Welsh National School of Medicine and they had been disinclined to embark on another experiment of that kind at that time.[133] However, in its final report, published in 1946, the Inter-departmental Committee on Dentistry, chaired by Lord Teviot, stated:

> We have formed the impression that favourable consideration would be given to the establishment at Cardiff of complete courses of training for a degree in dentistry … We gather that on account of the shortage of teaching staff and accommodation it may be some years before a school could be established in Cardiff; nevertheless we have no hesitation in recommending that the matter should be explored as soon as possible.[134]

A further twenty years would elapse before a dental school opened in Cardiff. It is, however, worth noting that University College, Cardiff had always provided limited facilities for students seeking careers as dentists. There had been, over the years, a regular flow of students who, having registered with the college for one year's preliminary instruction in the basic sciences, had gone elsewhere for their preclinical and clinical dental training. Between 1903 and 1920 some forty-three such students had passed through the science corridors of Cardiff in this way.

THE WELSH LANGUAGE

One issue not so far touched on in this book is that of the Welsh language. Given that the Welsh National School of Medicine was intended to have an all-Wales role, to what extent did people expect it to embrace the Welsh language in the fulfilment of its mission? The short answer is that the School of Medicine was not expected to perform such a role. It is certain that, from the outset, a substantial number of the school's medical students had Welsh as their mother tongue, though in those days the school authorities made no attempt to record this fact. Occasionally, bruised sensitivities received a public airing, such as when, in 1907, at a meeting of the Cardiff and District Educational Society, Professor John Berry Haycraft rather unwisely suggested that it was a waste of time to learn Welsh which, in his view, was of no commercial value. Haycraft was, in fact, reflecting one side of a fairly bitter argument which had been raging for some time over the teaching of Welsh in the schools of Cardiff. With the Cymmrodorion Caerdydd calling for Welsh to be made a compulsory subject, and the Chamber of Commerce and the 'British League of Cardiff' taking the optionalist position, a bitterly divided Cardiff City Council resolved in March 1907 to make Welsh an optional subject in schools.[135] The controversy did not die down immediately, and Haycraft's intervention in the debate not only attracted some barracking from medical students attending his lectures ('Wales for ever', 'Who ran down the Welsh?') and some critical comment in the local press, but also earned a rebuke from the Council of the college.[136] By contrast, when Edwin Goodall, born in Calcutta, the son of an English solicitor, applied, from his psychiatric post in Yorkshire, for the position of medical superintendent of the Joint Counties Asylum at Carmarthen, he learned Welsh in six months in order to fit himself for the post. Moreover, as his obituarist recorded, 'He produced his first annual report in such classical language that his local critics, who spoke only colloquial Welsh, could not understand it.'[137]

Apart from Goodall, few of the academic staff of the medical school, knew much, if any Welsh. Alfred Hughes, the school's first professor of anatomy and a native of Merionethshire, certainly did, and so did Ivor Davies, for some years first assistant in the medical unit. Among the staff of the infirmary John Lynn Thomas was a Welsh-speaker, as was Philip Rhys Griffiths. There may well have been others, but the fact was that it did not matter. Despite grumbles from zealots like William George, the University of Wales, between the wars, did not set itself up as a champion of the Welsh language. As Professor Gwynn Williams has pointed out, 'English was its official language, all its proceedings were in English,'[138] though, after pressure from the students the degree congregations were conducted in Welsh from 1921. At the end of the decade a debate was stimulated in the University by the proposition that students should be permitted to take their examinations either in Welsh or English; during the course of the debate the views of the several subject faculties were sought. The view of the Faculty of Medicine (and indeed that of most of the others) was short and to the point. The proposal was 'impracticable'.[139]

In 1928, having failed in the previous year through lack of interest, a female medical student in her second year, Winifred Acraman (later Llewhelyn-Acraman), again attempted to form a Welsh medical society (cymdeithas Cymraeg feddygol) in the school. As a gesture of support the medical students' magazine, *The Leech*, by now two years old, immediately proclaimed itself to be, henceforth, a bilingual journal: 'What is more fitting than that the language of our country should find an honoured place in our magazine?'[140] Not only did the Welsh medical society fail to get off the ground; in the five years that followed only one article (on the physicians of Myddfai) and one poem written in Welsh would appear in the magazine. It is perhaps interesting to note that it was not until April 1975 that Y Gymdeithas Feddygol, the society of Welsh doctors which conducted its affairs through the medium of Welsh, was established under the presidency of Dr Emyr Wyn Jones.[141]

6

Postgraduate Medical Education and Research

Although the primary role of the Cardiff Medical School and of its successor, the Welsh National School of Medicine, was to train medical students, particularly Welsh medical students, its contributions to postgraduate medical education and research were, at the very least, respectable. The work of the Department of Tuberculosis, for instance, carried the reputation of the school into distant corners of the British Empire, while such statistics as are available suggest that during the 1920s Cardiff's research performance bore comparison with that of several of the longer-established medical schools of provincial England. A few individuals, notably Professor Graham Brown, J. W. Tudor Thomas, Edwin Goodall and Lambert Rogers, attracted special acclaim from their peers, while the securing of a substantial grant from the Rockefeller Foundation, reward for its adoption of the clinical unit system, represented a significant milestone in the progress of the Welsh National School of Medicine towards maturity and credibility. Unfortunately, the manner in which the school implemented the clinical unit system also contributed to tensions with the Cardiff Royal Infirmary, which undoubtedly hampered its research effort. They caused, among other things, the loss of two professors of pathology in quick succession and of the medical unit's first full-time assistant, Daniel Thomas Davies, arguably the finest prospect produced by the Welsh National School of Medicine during the 1920s.

POSTGRADUATE MEDICAL EDUCATION

In the autumn of 1925 the Council of University College, Cardiff set up a committee of inquiry to consider certain allegations made by Mitchell Stevens, the senior physician at the Cardiff Royal Infirmary, concerning the way in which the Welsh National School of Medicine was being run. The main issues addressed by the committee will be discussed in a later chapter, but more than once, during the course of his evidence, Mitchell Stevens referred, with ill-disguised contempt, to certain 'fancy departments' which, in his opinion, held far too much sway in the affairs of the medical school.[1] He was referring specifically to the academic Departments of Public Health and

156

Tuberculosis, headed by Professor Leigh Collis and Professor Lyle Cummins, and in a particularly forceful statement to the committee he spoke as follows:

> You have got these fancy departments and these men are on your Faculty of Medicine. These men are running your place, Cummins and Collis, and they have more to say than the men who are doing the real work at the hospital. There is no reason why they should be on the Faculty of Medicine. They are not necessary departments for the medical course. I mean they are luxuries.

It has to be said that these churlish words were expressed by a man motivated, at least in part, by personal bitterness, and did not represent a fully rounded analysis of the nature of medical schools at that time. It is true that academic departments of public health and tuberculosis were few and far between (the only other department of tuberculosis was at Edinburgh), but their existence in Cardiff was the result of endowments given to the college by generous benefactors whose philanthropy the college authorities would have been extremely unwise to spurn. As the Faculty of Medicine itself stated in the autumn of 1922, in response to the report of the special committee charged with the task of assessing the medical school's financial health, not only were the disciplines of public health and tuberculosis areas of importance in themselves: 'These are the only two endowed Chairs in the National School, and the action recommended by the [special] Committee, were it to be followed, would undoubtedly discourage benefactors in the future.'[2] Moreover, the academic Departments of Public Health and of Tuberculosis provided virtually the whole of the Welsh National School of Medicine's output in the field of postgraduate medical education during the 1920s.

Postgraduate medical education in the sense that we understand it today, with a plethora of formal training schemes, covering all phases of a doctor's post-qualification career, only came into force after the Second World War, following the publication of the Report of the Inter-departmental Committee on Medical Schools (1944), popularly known as the Goodenough Report. Nevertheless, what the *British Medical Journal* referred to as 'post-graduation study' was a well-accepted concept before the First World War, as that journal proclaimed in its educational number for the 1910/11 session:

> The value, and in some circumstances even the necessity, of post-graduation study is now so generally recognized that there is no occasion to dilate upon it here. The need for some means of acquiring direct knowledge of the technique of the new branches which are constantly springing up is indeed so generally felt among otherwise experienced practitioners, that several institutions designed for their benefit have been at work now for some years ... Beyond this it need merely be said that in most medical centres it is now exceptional for one or more courses for qualified men not to be held once or more often during the year ... Hospitals make special arrangements for the

needs of qualified men desirous of studying work of the kind undertaken within their wards.[3]

Nor should it be forgotten that one of the prime objects of the many medical societies throughout the United Kingdom was to engage in the postgraduate education of its members, as the published proceedings of the meetings of the Cardiff Medical Society over many years bear witness.[4]

Before the First World War the provision of postgraduate courses leading to a limited range of diplomas was commonplace among the universities of the United Kingdom.[5] The London and Liverpool Schools of Tropical Medicine, and the University of Edinburgh offered courses leading to diplomas in the subject, while most of the universities in the United Kingdom provided courses leading to the Diploma in Public Health, awarded either by their own university or by the Conjoint Board. The other developing area in postgraduate medical education at this time was psychological medicine, confirming Sir Brian Windeyer's observation that it was the growth of specialization that aroused an increasing interest in postgraduate educa-tion.[6] By 1921, diplomas in psychiatry or psychological medicine were available from the universities of Cambridge, London, Durham, Edinburgh, Leeds, Manchester and the National University of Ireland, and from the Conjoint Board. It will be recalled that, at the instigation of Dean Hepburn, the Medical Board of the University of Wales had itself toyed with the idea of establishing a postgraduate diploma in psychological medicine in 1912, only to shelve the idea. By then, however, the University of Wales had set up (in 1908) a postgraduate diploma in public health, in line with most other British universities, adding a second postgraduate diploma, in tuberculosis, to its portfolio in 1921. In this respect, the Welsh National School of Medicine could certainly be regarded as 'pulling its weight' in the development of medical education, whatever disaffected critics like Mitchell Stevens might say.

Despite the fact that the standard history of education in public health makes no reference to the work of Professor Leigh Collis or his Department of Public Health and Institute of Preventive Medicine,[7] the University Diploma in Public Health devel-oped, after a slow start, into a well-regarded postgraduate qualification. Being a qualification registrable with the General Medical Council, the diploma's examina-tion arrangements were subject to periodic inspection by the council, and such an inspection took place on one occasion during the period under review, in June 1920. The inspector, R. Bruce Low, observed the conduct of both parts, one and two, of the examination and, notwithstanding a few minor criticisms, declared that the diploma examination was 'carried out generally in a satisfactory manner and requires from candidates a high standard of knowledge in the various branches of Sanitary Science and Preventive Medicine'.[8] In his report the inspector stated that since its inception, in 1910, fifteen candidates had taken part one of the diploma examination, ten of whom had been successful. During the same period thirteen had taken part two, ten obtaining the diploma. There had been no candidates from 1912 to 1916, a situation partly explained by the absence, on war service, of Professor Emrys-Roberts, a key lecturer and examiner. As the 1920s progressed, the number of students obtaining the diploma remained steady, as table 6.1 shows:

Table 6.1 Students obtaining the diploma

1921	6	1927	–
1922	–	1928	4
1923	1	1929	1
1924	2	1930	2
1925	2	1931	3
1926	1		

The course, to which several members of the local public health departments as well as Leigh Collis contributed (notably Ralph Picken, Cardiff's medical officer of health, and future provost of the school), undoubtedly met an important training need. Of the ten candidates successful in the second part of the examination between 1928 and 1931, at least six were former students of the Welsh National School of Medicine. Almost without exception the holders of the Wales diploma secured employment in one of the principality's public health departments, some making a considerable mark in their chosen field, including Arthur Culley, who became MOH for Glamorgan and medical member at the Welsh Board of Health, and William Morgan Lloyd, sometime MOH for Carmarthenshire.

The school's Department of Public Health also ran annual courses leading to the Joint Testamur in Sanitary Science for local sanitary inspectors, attracting classes ranging between a dozen and twenty-five.

In the 1929/30 session, as if further to demonstrate his department's relevance to the health-care needs of the local community, Professor Collis, assisted by several members of the staff of the Cardiff and Glamorgan public health authorities, established a six-months' full-time course of training for health visitors. Formally approved by the Ministry of Health, the course attracted sixteen candidates in its first year and fourteen in the next, and would continue to form an important part of the medical school's training portfolio for over fifty years. It is probable that Professor Collis's most important contributions to the health of the people of south Wales were in his studies on pneumoconiosis, and, as a member of the Central Miners' Welfare Committee, in his efforts to improve the working conditions of the miners, with the development of pithead baths, canteens and recreational schemes. With others he also produced a number of influential reports for the MRC on miners' mystagmus (an eye disease causing oscillation of the eyeballs), and on mining injuries caused by the overuse of certain joints such as the knee, hand and elbow. He acquired an international reputation in the field of industrial hygiene and was much in demand as a speaker at overseas conferences, particularly in the United States and Canada.[9]

Professor Stevenson Lyle Cummins made an equally significant contribution to the work and reputation of the school during the 1920s, like Professor Collis, doing much to promote its existence overseas. Though his department had an involvement in the undergraduate clinical course, his main focus was the provision of the postgraduate Diploma in Tuberculosis. For most of the decade laboratory aspects of the course were arranged in temporary accommodation in the Department of Anatomy, with clinical experience being obtained at the Glan Ely Hospital for Tuberculous Diseases, Fairwater Road, Cardiff and at other residential institutions of the Welsh National Memorial Association. Candidates for the diploma could also offer relevant experience in other approved medical schools, hospitals and tuberculosis dispensaries in the United Kingdom that were recognized by the University of Wales. Five of the six candidates taking the examination for the first time in 1923 were successful. In the following year, according to the report of the vice-chancellor on the degree, certificate and diploma examinations, 1924:

> Two examinations for the Tuberculous Diseases Diploma were held, one in January and one in June. In the first there were two candidates, one of whom, from South Africa [Johan Fredrik Wicht], was successful. In June, the unsuccessful candidate of the January examination, an Australian [Hilary Joseph Roche], was successful; the other candidate at the June examination failed.[10]

It is noteworthy that the vice-chancellor made much of the fact that the successful candidates were from overseas. Certainly this marked the beginning of a long and successful history of overseas involvement in the diploma course. It has been suggested that the diploma carried little weight in the United Kingdom, even in Wales. Certainly its possession was by no means a requirement for those in Wales seeking appointment as tuberculosis officers and assistant tuberculosis officers, the ability to speak Welsh being regarded as a much more relevant qualification.[11] The fact remains that throughout the 1920s the course attracted a respectable number of students, usually between five and ten a year, from all over the Empire, particularly from India, and as Cummins's obituarist would later observe, 'These students returned to their own countries to take prominent parts in the campaign against tuberculosis.'[12] In a report submitted to the Welsh National Memorial Association in 1928, Cummins himself observed:

> The large number of Indians who attend these courses is of special interest. Tuberculosis appears to be one of the most menacing and important problems of public health in India at the present time. The steady increase in industrial employment and the drawing in of village populations into industrial centres has been

associated in India, as elsewhere, with a marked increase of tuberculosis and the process appears likely to increase in the near future. It is, therefore, a source of special satisfaction to me that Indian medical men are making use of the courses of instruction in Cardiff to qualify themselves the better for coping with what is to them a National danger.[13]

Among the most eminent of the Indian medical men was Perakath Verghese Benjamin, a Christian from Travancore who, having qualified from Madras, came to Cardiff in 1930 to study for the diploma. Returning to India, he became recognized as the country's leading authority on the disease, becoming technical adviser to the Tuberculosis Association of India and to the government itself, and he established the National Tuberculosis Institute in Bangalore.[14]

Apart from the contributions of the 'fancy departments', the school provided little in the way of postgraduate medical education during the 1920s. In this respect it lagged behind many other, and it must be said longer-established, medical schools in London and the provinces. Birmingham, for instance, had initiated a scheme for post-graduate instruction based at the two main teaching hospitals, in 1906, offered free of charge to the local medical practitioners, apart from a registration fee of 5 shillings to cover the cost of printing notices and postage. The courses, which took the form of clinical demonstrations in medicine, surgery and ophthalmology, continued until the war, regularly attracting attendances of between eighty and one hundred doctors. The war had an adverse effect on this sort of postgraduate activity everywhere, but in April 1919, largely at the instigation of Sir William Osler, a meeting was held at the Royal Society of Medicine, with the intention of establishing a nationwide scheme of postgraduate medical education, locally organized but centrally co-ordinated. In his opening remarks, Osler

> emphasised the importance of post graduate teaching in general, and in particular the greatly increased demand for it on account of the large number of Colonial and American medical men now in this country. He drew attention to the fact that war conditions now made Berlin and Vienna, hitherto attractive centres for post graduate work, no longer available.

Sir George Newman was present at the meeting, and in support of the proposal, added that 'Organised post graduate teaching might make it possible to lighten the undergraduate curriculum, which would be a great advantage to the medical student.'[15] Though the idea of a national Postgraduate Association failed to get off the ground (Sir William Osler died within a few months of the meeting), the initiative undoubtedly stimulated postgraduate activity in the provinces. In Birmingham, for instance, the University Clinical Board took on the responsibility of organizing highly structured courses of postgraduate instruction for local doctors, covering almost every conceivable medical speciality and delivered by senior members of the medical school and associated hospitals. By 1924, several other provincial medical schools, including Bristol, Cambridge, Edinburgh, Glasgow, Leeds, Manchester and Newcastle upon Tyne (University of Durham), were offering clinical attachments and courses on recent advances in medicine to their local practitioners; Bristol actually had a director of postgraduate studies.[16]

The Welsh Consultative Council of Medical and Allied Services in Wales, established by the minister of health in 1919 as part of the general post-war reconstruction of health services in the United Kingdom, had the opportunity to promote the cause of postgraduate medical education in Wales too. The remit of the council was 'to consider and make representations as to the scheme or schemes required for the systematic provision in Wales of such forms of medical and allied services as should, in the opinion of the Council, be available for the inhabitants of a given area'.[17] Chaired by Sir Edgar Jones, MP for Merthyr Tydfil, the council included amongst its members Professor David Hepburn, in his capacity as dean of the Cardiff Medical School, and Ewen Maclean, shortly to become the school's professor of obstetrics and gynaecology. In its second report, published in 1921, the council proposed a new framework for the provision of health services to the people of Wales. General hospital services would be given in hospitals organized through a hierarchy of 'health institutes', small-scale health institutes in most parts of Wales, four larger health institutes based at Bangor, Wrexham, Swansea and Newport, and, at the head of the pyramid, a National Health Institute of Wales, associated with the Welsh National School of Medicine, which would also serve as the central health institute for the immediate area. This structure, involving much co-ordination of services, would, it was envisaged, also provide a framework for the systematic provision of postgraduate medical education, with the larger health institutes housing 'medical institutes'. These would afford facilities 'for each medical practitioner to be brought into close contact with his fellow practitioners in team work, and keep himself abreast with developments in medical science and practice'.[18] At the pinnacle of this structure stood the Welsh National School of Medicine, and it was not unreasonable to suppose that it would take the lead in the provision of postgraduate educational facilities for the practitioners of the Cardiff area, and, indeed, further afield.

Unfortunately nothing came of the council's perhaps grandiose plan. Certainly it was far too radical for the Ministry of Health, and the Welsh Consultative Council itself was formally abolished in 1926, 'all but forgotten', in Charles Webster's words.[19] Ewen Maclean had some cause to be grateful for the existence of the council however, for, having succeeded Sir Edgar Jones as its chairman, he secured a knighthood in 1923.

In 1924 Cardiff's Faculty of Medicine did look into the possibility of providing 'special courses for medical practitioners', going so far as to secure the agreement of the authorities of the Cardiff Royal Infirmary that no fee would be charged for the use of their facilities. Plans to run a course in the autumn term 1924/5 failed to materialize and, increasingly preoccupied with a number of contentious issues as the decade progressed, it was not until 1929/30 that the medical unit began to provide special intensive courses for medical practitioners from rural districts in Wales at the request of the Welsh Board of Health, with eight enrolments in June 1930 and fifteen in the following year. In the 1930/1 session the medical school, in co-operation with their hospital colleagues, organized postgraduate courses for local general practitioners, in the form of clinical demonstrations.[20]

MODEST PROGRESS IN ESTABLISHING A RESEARCH PORTFOLIO

As has already been noted in chapter 2, pressure of other commitments and a lack of resources and, indeed, of inclination kept the research activity of the Cardiff Medical School at a fairly low level before the war. Edward Emrys-Roberts, of whom much was expected, was a relatively recent arrival, and the only person with an established reputation was John Berry Haycraft, but, as Professor Graham Brown later suggested, his best years were behind him following the serious illness that had fallen upon him in middle age. He did, however, live to see his vision of a state-of-the-art Institute of Physiology become a reality. 'Few who have dreamt such dreams have seen their fulfilment, and the Physiology Institute at Cardiff will be Haycraft's memorial.'[21] The fact remains that Haycraft made no more of an impact on the pre-war national scene in respect of research in his discipline than most other academic physiologists in the provincial English medical schools, with the exception of Charles Sherrington at Liverpool. Stella Butler has compiled a table showing the institutional affiliation of contributors to the *Journal of Physiology* between 1900 and 1914. The overwhelming majority of contributions came from Cambridge, London, Oxford, Edinburgh and Glasgow. Twenty-seven came from Liverpool, two from Cardiff, one from Bristol and none from the other provincial medical schools.[22] The annual reports of the Medical Research Committee, established by the government in 1913 to promote the advancement of medical knowledge, not surprisingly revealed the amount of medical research in Cardiff considered worthy of financial support from the committee to be very small. It was largely confined to a handful of individuals such as Professor Emrys-Roberts in pathology and T. H. Burlend and J. H. Shaxby in the Department of Physiology, and even this support was suspended as the staff concerned became involved in wartime pursuits. It is ironic to note that the one person who managed to attract some research funding from the committee for the duration of the war was Captain Harold Scholberg, who had tried in vain to secure the chair of pathology at Cardiff in 1910.[23]

However, those promoting a full medical school in Cardiff were quite clear that such a school should have a strong research role. Their memorandum on the 'Proposed completion of the Medical School', submitted to Lloyd George in 1914, went so far as to proclaim that 'The complete scheme for medical education will also embrace an independent Department for Research, which, though closely associated with the teaching units, will allow absolute intellectual freedom for those engaged on this important work.' Unfortunately, no explanation was provided for the remit of this department, nor any costing attempted, and when the full medical school came into being in October 1921, the facilities available to prosecute research were poor, to say the least. The special committee, set up by the University Council in the summer of 1922 to review the needs of the new Welsh National School of Medicine, and chaired by the Hon. W. N. Bruce, was, rather surprisingly, non-committal about the school's research needs. As far as the committee was concerned the school's immediate priority was to train medical students:

> The prior claim upon available income must be for the adequate maintenance of those departments which are strictly necessary for the development of the course on the lines proposed, and that, until these are fully provided for, none of the essential departments should be developed out of proportion to the others, nor should new expenditure be incurred for departments which are not of primary importance for the initiation of the system.

Notwithstanding the recent opening of the Institute of Physiology, that department was considered to be over-resourced for its teaching role. While noting that the laboratory facilities of the Department of Tuberculosis were 'meagre and primitive, and quite unsuitable for the development of a vigorous department', neither that department, nor the School of Preventive Medicine, could justify additional university resources at the present time of financial stringency. Moreover, as far as the committee was concerned, secretarial staff were a luxury and should certainly not be expected to provide 'assistance to the Professor in dealing with papers and matters which are his individual concern and are not essential to the discharge of the duties of his Chair'.

Needless to say, the Faculty of Medicine was dismayed at the lack of sympathy shown by the report's authors in relation to the school's research role, particularly as, only a few months earlier, the Welsh Consultative Council, in its second report, had identified the Welsh National School of Medicine as a central component of Wales's future health service. As such, it would lead a network of medical institutes throughout Wales, which would not only provide facilities for postgraduate medical education, but also for research, including laboratories and libraries.[24] In a robust rejoinder to the authors of the report of the special committee, the Faculty of Medicine referred to its national dimension, which laid upon it 'a responsibility over and above that imposed by its high ideal of medical education'. The Faculty went on:

> Such a School as ours must aim at becoming a centre of medical culture and research, that it may be fitted to act in an advisory manner in connexion with the great prob-

lems of national health in Wales. This desirable position, foreseen by those who planned the School, necessitates the maintenance and pursuance of research in all subjects and participation in many organisations of national welfare. The Principality itself presents opportunity and necessity for research into its own problems of health as distinct from those of the United Kingdom as a whole. Wales does not yet enjoy that number of special institutions for treatment, teaching and research which, in the larger centres of medical education and national activity, may be called upon for advice. This aspect of the National School should be kept in sight for, while such a School elsewhere might confine itself to teaching duties, in Wales it will fail in its duty should it so restrict its activities.

As far as the special committee's observations on the role of secretaries were concerned, the faculty was dismissive: 'A whole-time Professor publishes research papers as part of the duties of his Chair, and such papers cannot be regarded as matters merely of his individual concern.' Overall, the faculty expressed itself disappointed in the tenor of the special report, which 'gives little guidance for future development'.[25] It was fortunate, therefore, that the Rockefeller Foundation should choose that moment to take an interest in the affairs of the Welsh National School of Medicine.

THE ROCKEFELLER FOUNDATION AND THE REFORM OF MEDICAL EDUCATION

Why should the greatest medical charity in the world turn its attention to the newest medical school in the United Kingdom? It was because the Welsh National School of Medicine had nailed its colours to the 'clinical unit' mast. As has already been mentioned in chapter 3, the origins of the 'clinical unit' system can be traced back to the establishment, in 1893, of the Johns Hopkins School of Medicine in Baltimore, where, 'deeply influenced by the clinics and laboratories in which they had trained in Germany',[26] the foundation professors ushered in a new era of medical education and research. Scientific method, the linking of the hospital clinic with the laboratory, was harnessed in the advancement of medical diagnosis and treatment, and in the student teaching programme bedside instruction was allied to the conduct of laboratory tests, examining secretions, blood and excreta and the like. The most influential of the foundation professors, William Osler, later commended the Johns Hopkins model, which, by the end of the first decade of the twentieth century, was being adopted elsewhere in the United States, to the Haldane Commission on London University. A major factor in the advance of the Johns Hopkins model in America was the establishment in New York of the Rockefeller Institute for Medical Research in 1901, the year when John D. Rockefeller, the world's wealthiest man, grieving for a grandson who had died from scarlet fever, was persuaded to channel, in a systematic way, some of his surplus millions into the war against disease. His main persuader, Frederick T. Gates, one of his senior advisers, was a great admirer of William Osler, and had read his book, *Principles and Practice of Medicine* (1897), perhaps, in the words of Christopher Lawrence, 'the most accessible guide to the new scientific medicine, embracing as it did germ theory, the latter being seen as one of the great triumphs of laboratory-based medicine'.[27] Nine years after the establishment of the institute came the building, next door, of the Rockefeller Hospital, dedicated to the furtherance of clinical research along Johns Hopkins principles, notably the employment of full-time clinical staff not otherwise diverted by the pursuit of private clinical practice. In the same year Abraham Flexner, the brother of the institute's first director, Simon, published an immensely influential report, *Medical Education in the United States and Canada*, which reinforced the case for the general adoption of the Johns Hopkins model in America, with its emphasis on the role of the laboratory sciences and the clinical unit system in medical education and research. He, like Osler, grasped the opportunity of appearing before the Haldane Commission with both hands, and, as has already been noted, his evidence greatly coloured the report's subsequent conclusions.

Neither did Rockefeller and Gates confine their philanthropic horizons within the United States. In 1913 the Rockefeller Foundation was incorporated to fund their worldwide ambitions, 'the promotion of the cause of human betterment through science and education'.[28] Though active in various relief activities during the First World War, the foundation came into its own once hostilities had ceased, as part of a general American mission to export advancement and modernity to the rest of the world – whether the rest of the world wanted it or not. In less developed parts of the world the foundation's strategy was to introduce measures to improve public health and the eradication of certain endemic diseases. In other parts of the world the Rockefeller mission was to reform medical education by introducing what William Bynum has referred to as 'the American Way'[29] into medical schools in centres as widely scattered as Beirut, São Paulo and Beijing, as well as in Europe.

The foundation's reform programme was spearheaded by its Division of Medical Education, established in 1919 in order to survey medical education outside the United States and to offer support to centres that would serve as models for reform elsewhere. Its director was Richard Pearce, a Harvard graduate and sometime professor of pathology at the University of Pennsylvania.[30] According to the minutes of the foundation, 'The program of the Division of Medical Education in Great Britain has for its object the encouragement of two distinct efforts in medicine, (a) Aid for the development of the laboratory side of medicine … [and] (b) The stimulation of academic clinics in medicine, surgery and obstetrics.'[31]

In order to assess where its assistance could best be offered, the division sent two senior academics from the United States to conduct a survey of universities and medical schools during the autumn of 1922. Their findings were fairly negative overall. Even in London, where the clinical unit system was in place, they found the quality of clinical training to be much inferior to that adopted in the United States, and everywhere, in London and the provinces, in the harnessing of the laboratory to the clinic in teaching and patient care, much remained to be done.[32] In parallel with this survey, Richard Pearce initiated his own review of medical education in the United Kingdom during the second half of 1922, enlisting the assistance of Sir Walter Fletcher, secretary of the Medical Research Council.

Fletcher, a Cambridge-trained physiologist, was an enthusiast for the mission of the Rockefeller Foundation. We have already noted how the Medical Research Committee, initially established in 1913 to fund tuberculosis research, had broadened its remit in order to address wider health problems thrown up by the First World War, and by the time of its reconfiguration as the Medical Research Council in 1920, it was committed to supporting medical research, pure, clinical and laboratory-based, across a wide spectrum, reflecting Fletcher's own research philosophy.[33] At Fletcher's memorial service in 1934 Frederick Gowland Hopkins, the eminent Cambridge biochemist, attested to his friend's determination to support medical research in all its aspects, while giving special encouragement to those wishing to devote all their time to the conduct of clinical research.[34] An early beneficiary of this policy was Thomas Lewis who, in 1916, became the MRC's first full-time investigator, heading the Department of Clinical Research at University College Hospital.

As a strong supporter of the clinical unit system, which he, like Pearce, considered the most effective way of advancing the cause of laboratory-based clinical research, Fletcher was only too pleased to assist Richard Pearce in his review of British medical education by co-ordinating the foundation's initial data-gathering exercise. In the autumn of 1922, Fletcher wrote to the deans of all the medical schools. 'I think all the schools will respond', he observed to Sir Wilmot Herringham, the medical member of the UGC, 'if only with an eye to possible dollars; if any do not respond that is their funeral, and it cannot be helped.'[35] Though most medical deans did respond, some did so with greater care than others, who did little more than submit various printed documents, calendars, prospectuses, annual accounts and the like. W. F. Haslam, dean of the Birmingham medical school, covered, at least to his own satisfaction, the information sought by the Foundation via Fletcher's letter, on one side of A4 paper.

Armed with a mass of documentation of varying relevance, Pearce visited several medical schools early in 1923 to assess their suitability as leaders in the Rockefeller reform movement. In Christopher Lawrence's words, the foundation's strategy was 'to identify what it saw as far-sighted institutions and individuals whose leadership, research and teaching could be expected to follow American lines'.[36] On the basis of what he read, saw and heard (paying particular attention to Fletcher's own advice), Pearce concluded that Oxford, Cambridge, Edinburgh and some of the London medical schools, those which had adopted the clinical unit system – University College Hospital, St Bartholomew's, the London and St Thomas's – were worthy of the foundation's support, all being centres which, in Pearce's judgement, 'should in the long run influence medical work in the empire'.[37] However, Pearce did not confine his plaudits to centres in England and Scotland, for he considered that the Welsh National School of Medicine in Cardiff was equally deserving of the foundation's support.

THE ROCKEFELLER FOUNDATION COMES TO CARDIFF

Like all the other medical school deans, Professor A. M. Kennedy compiled a response to the Foundation's request for information, and it is fair to say that Kennedy's submission, tailor-made for the purpose, was well presented and supported by a positive covering letter addressed to Fletcher:

> As you are aware, this is a young school whose final years of study have only just been instituted. It has high ideals; a six years' course is insisted upon for the Welsh Degree – the students take the BSc first, and 'units' have been established for the final teaching. I am sure we would all welcome a visit from Dr Pearce and give him every facility for investigating the School.[38]

Kennedy's submission, which consists of much factual information about the Welsh National School of Medicine, its size, structure and finances, the nature of the medical course – to which reference has already been made in chapter 5 – and accommodation, is included in a file on the school held at the Rockefeller Archive Centre, New York.[39] In the file is a report, apparently prepared for Richard Pearce by the Home Office, which, among other things, stated: 'All the available funds have to be devoted to the immediate necessities for teaching, leaving none available for research work, without which university standards cannot long be maintained.' There is also an assessment by Pearce of how the foundation might be able to help the school, and an interesting memorandum 'prepared at short notice' by the professor of surgery. In it Professor Sheen outlined his vision (not to be realized for many years) of a brand-new university hospital to replace the existing King Edward VII Hospital which, as he wrote in an illuminating covering letter, did not satisfy the needs of the school:

> The methods and 'vested interests' of a hospital staff totally unaccustomed to the work and the aspirations of a teaching hospital naturally produce difficulties. I believe that a first-rate University Hospital could be established and developed on almost ideal lines and I am enthusiastic for its formation.

Sheen clearly believed that this was the sort of thing that the Rockefeller Foundation, committed to the successful development of the professorial unit system throughout the world, wanted to hear and act upon.

Kennedy's submission 'ticked all the right boxes', to use a modern expression:

> The School is unique amongst the medical schools of the United Kingdom in that it possesses a very definite national character. It is the only school of medicine in Wales. Those who planned the School were largely guided by the advice of the late Sir William Osler. The policy adopted was to combine the best features of the great American and British Universities. The course of instruction was to be one of *six years'* duration; the first three years were to be spent in study for a degree in science, the last three years were to be spent in study for the medical degrees under the guidance of full-time professors. This plan, largely based on the models presented by the Johns Hopkins University, Baltimore, and the universities of Oxford and Cambridge, is now enforced. Had it not been that financial difficulties postponed the completion of the School, it would have been the first in the United Kingdom to institute the 'Unit' system of teaching in the final studies; and it is now the only School in this country which adopts the 'Unit' system in the final years while enforcing an initial degree in Science.

Any statement which managed to mention Sir William Osler, the Johns Hopkins Medical School and the unit system could hardly fail to attract Richard Pearce's attention, particularly if it also enjoyed the blessing of Sir Walter Fletcher. As has already been noted, Fletcher was well disposed to the Welsh National School of Medicine, having been an important player in the establishment of the chair of tuberculosis in Cardiff. Professor Kennedy was quite clear about Fletcher's influence with the Foundation. As he later wrote to the secretary of the MRC, 'We fully appreciate that it was due solely to your great interest and influence that Rockefeller came to consider us.'[40]

Pearce visited Cardiff on 30 and 31 January 1923, when, as he recorded in his diary, 'I was able to get a fair insight into the School and King Edward VII Hospital and the problems of both.'[41] He subsequently secured outside views during a visit to London in March. Professor Thomas R. Elliott, professor of medicine and director of the medical unit at University College Hospital, was rather lukewarm in his support for giving Wales any money at all, his views formed 'rather on the basis of the general footlessness of the Welsh than on the needs of Wales medically' (as Pearce recorded in his diary). On the other hand, Sir George Newman, the chief medical officer at the Ministry of Health, was much more positive, particularly if the Welsh National School of Medicine became independent of the Cardiff College. Although Pearce observed on one occasion to Professor Collis that it would be a 'great help' were this to happen, the foundation never made this a condition of its support. It was, in any case, most impressed with the way that the Welsh local authorities appeared to be contributing to the funding of the school through the rate system, a clear indication that the school was, truly, an all-Wales institution.

Having satisfied himself that the Welsh National School of Medicine was worthy of support, Pearce had to decide how best it should be provided. Professor Sheen's utopian vision of a new University Hospital, 'the focus of medical work in Wales, entering into liaison with all other hospitals, with medical institutions and practitioners setting an example of the highest class of work and helping everywhere in treatment and research',[42] was never a practical option for the foundation to consider. On the basis of what he had seen and heard, Pearce concluded that the cause of the unit system in Cardiff, the only centre outside London where it was in operation, could best be served by strengthening the medical unit. Indeed, writing to Professor Collis in May 1923, he observed: 'Without some effort on the part of the authorities to put this unit on its feet immediately, one must view with concern the future of your school.' Learning this from Richard Pearce, Professor Kennedy, who, according to a colleague of Pearce's, tended to pity himself a good deal, was much cheered. 'It has been very depressing for me here without any possibility for continuing my research work but your letter has given me renewed interest in life again.' In fairness to Kennedy, it should be noted that in his previous appointment at the University of Glasgow, he had enjoyed a good reputation as a research worker in the field of ante-natal pathology, earning the thanks of the MRC on his relocation to Cardiff: 'He has carried out the work with ability and enthusiasm and the Council regret that they are losing his services.'[43]

At Pearce's request Kennedy spent the summer months working on a plan for submission to the foundation. Two main components were to emerge. First, Kennedy needed good laboratory facilities to replace a small clinical laboratory set up in an unused operating theatre, 'unsatisfactory in every way' in the professor's opinion. The new laboratories would serve the separate, though related, functions of undergraduate teaching and research. However, in order for the objects of a clinical unit as generally understood to be achieved the laboratories needed to be located as conveniently as possible to Kennedy's wards. The plan that emerged, and which was ultimately accepted by the foundation, involved erecting a self-contained five-storey block off the main hospital corridor and adjacent to the ward block in which the medical unit beds were housed.[44] The first floor would be offices and laboratory space for the professor and his staff, the ground, third and fourth floors would provide substantial research accommodation, including clinical pathology, bacteriology and biochemistry. The second floor of the unit would comprise two teaching laboratories for the clinical students, one devoted to biochemistry, the other to clinical pathology and bacteriology. Direct access would be provided from this floor to the second component of Kennedy's plan, a new ward for the medical unit. Kennedy needed this ward for two reasons. It would enjoy direct access from his teaching laboratories. It would also add to his complement of beds, thereby satisfying the demands of the University of London and the Conjoint Board. Unfortunately the space in question was being used as a dining room for nurses, and the hospital did not have funding available to convert it into anything else. Richard Pearce indicated that as part of its support for the school, the foundation would provide funding to enable the hospital to relocate the nurses' dining facilities elsewhere.

Satisfied that the school now had plans in hand to place thirty beds under the direct control of the medical unit, the London licensing bodies agreed to recognize the Wales course, and having obtained the assurance of the hospital authorities that they would accept the revenue implications of the extra medical beds, Richard Pearce was able to place a funding package before the board of the Rockefeller Foundation. 'This plan', wrote Pearce to George E. Vincent, president of the foundation, 'ensures clinical and laboratory facilities for the medical unit, and I am prepared to urge it upon the Board as essential.' On 5 December 1923, shortly after it had granted £50,000 to Edinburgh University to provide new clinical laboratory facilities, the Rockefeller Foundation agreed to make a grant of £14,000 to the Welsh National School of Medicine to aid the development of the medical unit. In a letter to Lord Kenyon (who, as Pearce happened to note in the survey file, was the grandson of the Lord Kenyon after whom Kenyon College, Ohio had been named), Dr Pearce expressed the foundation's pleasure in being able to assist the school

> in carrying out the plans which you have so wisely developed. The suggested aid covers contributions towards the cost of building a laboratory and caring for part of its initial equipment (building £10,000: equipment £2,000 and also the sum of £2,000 to be used in connection with the authorities of the Royal Infirmary for the improvement of clinical facilities.

The *Western Mail* was delighted with the Rockefeller's decision. The foundation took great care in determining who should benefit from its largesse: 'To be ranked in the same company as the greater medical schools of the world is a sufficient justification of the wisdom of its founders; and those who have the academic control of the school are to be congratulated upon the reward of their labours.'[45] Edgar Leigh Collis expressed his satisfaction in a letter to Sir Walter Fletcher: 'We are all very grateful for the gift and for the blessing that goes with it. One and all of us know that we have to thank you for being the prime mover in the whole matter.'[46]

The early months of 1924 were spent negotiating the practicalities locally, agreeing the plans for a five-storey building in the very heart of the hospital (when the Medical Board considered the sketch plans on 7 March, Professor Sheen was there but, as usual, Professor Kennedy was not) and settling the financial details. The hospital undertook to continue to maintain the thirty beds for the medical unit provided the College Council would assume full responsibility for the maintenance, equipment, staffing and management of the medical unit and its new laboratories. At one point (as Professor Graham Brown, who had succeeded Kennedy as dean in April 1924, reported to Pearce) the hospital authorities were expressing concern about being left with accommodation in the middle of the Infirmary 'which would not be directly useful for healing the sick', in the event of the school becoming insolvent. Brown's letter earned the following despairing rebuke from Pearce:

> Is it not possible to educate your Hospital authorities to the point of view that in these days laboratory effort is perhaps one of the most important features in connection with the 'healing of the sick'? I should think that any hospital would be only too glad to have an addition to its laboratory facilities. Knowing the paucity of laboratory facilities of Cardiff Infirmary I am rather surprised to find any difficulty arising on that score.

Finally in mid-June the hospital authorities received the financial assurances they had been hoping for from the college, enabling them to confirm that work on the laboratories could now proceed. Having received Lord Kenyon's confirmation that all hurdles had now been successfully negotiated the foundation released the promised funds.[47]

The hospital, pleased to have been associated with the venture, took the view that 'The recognition of the Rockefeller Foundation has already enhanced the prestige of the School, and given it an international status.'[48] The grant from the Rockefeller Foundation was undoubtedly the first important milestone on the school's road to maturity and credibility and three years later the Rockefeller building opened for business, in the autumn of 1927. The event was well covered by *The Lancet* which, among other things, displayed the detailed layout of the second, third and fourth floors.[49] According to the accompanying article, written by A. M. Kennedy:

> A special feature of the laboratory block is its close proximity to the medical unit wards. A doorway from the internal staircase of the laboratory opens on to the top floor corridor of the hospital and is within twelve yards of the medical unit wards.

Kennedy admitted his guarded optimism to Richard Pearce:

> I'm sure you will be satisfied when you see the new laboratories. My trouble now is to get them humming with industry. It's a slow process, particularly with one of my temperament. But I would rather go slow, a step at a time, and build a medical unit on sound lines than found a sham department that could not stand scrutiny.[50]

An article similar to the one that had appeared in *The Lancet*, but this time illustrated not only by an isometric projection of the laboratories but by several photographs, appeared in *Methods and Problems of Medical Education* (eighteenth series), published by the Rockefeller Foundation in 1930, under the authorship of Professor Kennedy.[51] It is probably unnecessary to observe that neither article acknowledged the contribution made by the hospital authorities to the laboratories' erection and by the college and university authorities to its ongoing maintenance.

Dependent as he was, for most of the decade, on poor facilities, Kennedy's research output during the 1920s was fairly modest. Apart from the articles on the medical unit laboratories, it was confined to a handful of papers on clinical subjects and a textbook, *Medical Case-Taking: A Guide for Clinical Clerks* (1926). However, reflecting improvements in the research facilities in both the medical unit and the Department of Pathology, the year 1930 saw the product of collaborative research with academic colleagues in the latter department, with two publications in the *Journal of Pathology and Bacteriology*. To be sure, no research grants came his way from the MRC, though during the 1930/1 session, once the Rockefeller Unit was up and running, a newly appointed junior assistant, Duncan Leys, received a grant to support his studies on the lactic acid content of capillary and venous blood. Unfortunately, no sooner had the grant been awarded than Leys moved on to the University of Birmingham.

For a short while the Unit's research prospects appeared to be greatly enhanced by the appointment, in the autumn of 1927, of Daniel Thomas Davies as its first full-time assistant at a salary of £500 per annum. Davies, the first person to obtain the MD of the University of Wales, in 1927, had, since graduation in 1924, worked for more than two years as assistant to Professor (later Sir) Charles Dodds in the biochemistry department at the Bland Sutton Institute of the Middlesex Hospital. There he became immersed in the application of chemical pathology to clinical medicine, expertise which was exactly what the new Rockefeller laboratories in Cardiff needed. Unfortunately, however, disillusioned with the antagonism that was bedevilling relationships between the school and the infirmary at this time, Davies resigned from his post at the end of 1928, with no publications to show for his short stay, and returned to London. There he resumed his association with Professor Dodds at the newly opened Courtauld Institute, where he investigated gastric and liver function, before going on to establish himself as one of the country's most eminent physicians. Britain's gain was undoubtedly Cardiff's loss. Professor Kennedy's other assistants during the 1920s, Ivor Davies and Herbert Evans, were, because of a lack of funds, part-timers with substantial clinical loads at the infirmary and elsewhere, and therefore had limited opportunities to pursue research. Nevertheless, Davies, the first practitioner from south Wales to be elected as a member of the Association of Physicians of Great Britain, did make some useful contributions to the pages of *The Lancet* and the *British Medical Journal*.[52]

RESEARCH IN THE SURGICAL UNIT

Although William Sheen's utopian vision for academic surgery in Cardiff failed to attract funding support from the Rockefeller Foundation, the surgical unit did enjoy the patronage of the MRC.

The Council's annual budget, voted by Parliament, £125,000 in 1919/20, rising to £148,000 in 1930/1 was utilized in three ways, a sum varying between £7,800 and

£10,000 for administrative costs; between £40,000 and £50,000 for the National Institute for Medical Research; and the remainder, between £60,000 and £86,000, to fund long-term research in certain clinical units in London and the provinces, and specific research projects in universities and hospitals all over the country.[53] The main clinical units were located in London, the most celebrated being the Department of Clinical Research at University College Hospital Medical School, under the direction of Sir Thomas Lewis, the Cardiff Medical School's most distinguished alumnus.Other clinical units in London attracting support from the MRC, included the medical units at the London, St Bartholomew's, Guy's and St Thomas's Hospitals. Outside London, the centres favoured by the MRC for long-term support were the University and Royal Infirmary at Edinburgh, the James Mackenzie Institute for Clinical Research at St Andrews, and the University and Royal Infirmary, Sheffield, where the pharmacologist, Edward Mellanby, established a research unit which came to be regarded, in the judgement of Sir Thomas Lewis, as 'very much one of the bright spots in recent years in British Medicine'.[54]

However, for the first time, in the 1927/8 annual report of the MRC, reference was made to the award of a grant to the Welsh National School of Medicine's surgical unit. The award was made to Professor Sheen's first assistant, Lambert Rogers, the circumstances of whose appointment will be referred to in chapter 8; suffice it to say here that Rogers was appointed on a full-time basis and, apart from the professors, the first member of the units in Cardiff to enjoy this status. Though not ideal, the research laboratory was close to the wards and there was ready access to the animal facilities of the Department of Physiology, as required. The work initially supported by the MRC was on the effects of sympathectomy in human surgery. Further MRC funding soon followed to support collaborative studies with Professor C. M. West of the Department of Anatomy of the foramina of the human brain, in relation to the pathology of hydrocephalus.[55] Indeed, a feature of Rogers's work at this time was the extent to which he collaborated with colleagues elsewhere in the school, not only in the Department of Anatomy, but also in the Departments of Physiology (where he used the animal facilities) and Medicine. Lambert Rogers was widely recognized in the research community as a 'high flier', and in September 1928 he was elected a fellow of the American College of Surgeons, a rare distinction in the United Kingdom at that time.

In terms of research activity, Sheen was determined that his department should have 'strength in depth'. Sheen himself, despite his several other commitments, had a more than respectable research record himself, publishing extensively on the surgery of the spleen, the subject of his Hunterian Lecture to the Hunterian Society of London in March 1929, a year before his election as the society's president for the 1929/30 session. His part-time assistant colleagues were also encouraged to develop their own special research interests, T. E. Hammond in urological subjects, Geary Grant in diseases of the pancreas, and J. B. Haycraft in abdominal surgery. Sheen (in 1915 and

1919) and his three part-time assistants all served as presidents of the Cardiff Medical Society, Grant in 1931, Hammond in 1936 and Haycraft in 1941. William Sheen's vision was to see the establishment in Cardiff of an Institute of Surgery, comparable to the medical unit's Rockefeller Institute, where research would be pursued on the prevention of disease. As he explained in his annual report for 1929/30 to the College Council,

> The Unit, while giving of its best to the patients, would face each clinical problem not only with the enquiries 'What is it?' and 'What shall I do?' but also 'Why is it?' and 'How can I prevent it in others?' This development is an ideal and has not, so far, taken place in this country. It is to be found, to some extent, on the Continent, and in North America, and I sketch it briefly here in the hope of its realisation in the future.

Although Sheen would never realize his ambition, he deserves credit for striving to make the concept of the clinical unit a reality although, as will be seen in a later chapter, his vision was not always shared by his hospital colleagues.

While not claiming that the introduction of the clinical unit system in Cardiff had transformed the quality of patient care at the Infirmary, Sheen was proud of the contribution made by his unit during its early years. In an address to the Cardiff Medical Society in January 1926 on 'Some aspects of three and a quarter years' work of the surgical unit', Sheen gave a detailed analysis of the 1,807 admissions into the unit between 1 October 1921 and 31 December 1924, and drew various conclusions from his findings. While conceding that it was the job of units such as his to compile and interpret case records, Sheen maintained that others should learn from his example.[56] It was hardly a matter of pure coincidence that a few months later, as we shall see, the hospital published a pioneering Annual Clinical Record for the first time, classifying the conditions according to the Official Nomenclature of Diseases (1918) as recommended by Sheen in his talk.

Commenting, in the spring of 1934, on a favourable report on the achievements of the clinical unit system in some of the London medical schools, Dr Edward Mellanby, who had succeeded Sir Walter Fletcher as secretary of the MRC, wrote as follows:

> From the point of view of research [the clinical unit system] has been a joke, and I don't see how anything else could be expected. The heads of the units were not picked because they had ever given reason to believe that they were distinguished in this respect, except probably as regards Elliott, but they were placed in charge of a laboratory and wards and told to research. The same result might be expected if you picked out a few players from a Queen's Hall orchestra and told them to compose symphonies.[57]

Mellanby, who, it has to be said, had benefited from the introduction of a version of the clinical unit at Sheffield, was commenting specifically on what he perceived to be the position in London, and on the whole Keir Waddington, in rather more measured terms, has confirmed Mellanby's verdict. Even in St Bartholomew's Hospital, where the units' research endeavour was better than that elsewhere in London, 'Work in the professorial units was diluted by routine clinical duties, funding problems, and the culture of private practice that made working in a voluntary hospital and medical school possible.'[58]

It is not claimed here that the introduction of the unit system in Cardiff made a sensational impact either. The medical and surgical units were certainly mentioned by George Newman in his *Recent Advances in Medical Education in England*, but other than a clipping of William Sheen's talk to the Cardiff Medical Society in 1926, the otherwise substantial UGC file on 'Clinical units, 1920–29', kept in the National Archives, contains absolutely no references to developments in Cardiff during the 1920s. Nor, it is fair to say, do recent works dealing with medical education in the early decades of the twentieth century dwell upon, or even mention, the unit system in Cardiff. The fact remains that, although the unit system caused no little turbulence in relationships between the Welsh National School of Medicine and the Royal Infirmary during the 1920s, the Rockefeller Foundation would not have given the school a moment's thought without its introduction in Cardiff. The unit system set Lambert Rogers on course for a distinguished academic career. It also helped to ensure that the school was fairly well regarded by those walking the corridors of power in the Medical Research Council.

THE MRC AND RESEARCH IN CARDIFF

All medical schools in the country succeeded in attracting research funding from the MRC during the 1920s, either for long-term research programmes or for specific research projects. Some indication of their relative success can be obtained by comparing the number of references to universities, their medical schools and associated hospitals, cited in the index of the annual reports of the MRC published during the 1920s. This evidence suggests that in research terms the Welsh National School of Medicine and associated hospitals acquitted themselves honourably during the 1920s, performing as well, if not better, than several longer-established institutions in the English provinces. Although the amount of funding allocated by the MRC to support research at the various universities and associated hospitals was not published at this time, the committee did, at the request of the UGC, supply figures showing the sums provided to each research centre at the beginning of the 1928/9 financial year. This information has enabled table 6.2 to be compiled:[59]

Table 6.2 Universities, their medical schools and associated
hospitals: MRC funding at 1 April 1928 (£)

London		43,583
English provinces		
Birmingham	2,365	
Bristol	50	
Cambridge	15,347	
Durham	50	
Leeds	1,280	
Liverpool	400	
Manchester	2,203	
Oxford	4,417	
Sheffield	4,869	30,981
Wales		
Aberystwyth	400	
Cardiff	910	1,310
Scotland		
Aberdeen	846	
Edinburgh	2,631	
Glasgow	4,737	8,214
	Total	84,088

Though the committee always stressed that its policy was to fund good research wherever it was prosecuted, and not institutions *per se*, further updates during the early 1930s showed that, in respect of MRC funding, the Welsh National School of Medicine and the preclinical departments at the Cardiff College were maintaining their standing in relation to other provincial schools. In 1933 researchers in Cardiff received £1,057 from the MRC, compared with £4,289 in Sheffield (where the professor of pharmacology, Edward Mellanby, had been in receipt of a substantial programme grant for some years), £1,185 in Manchester, £955 in Leeds, £800 in Liverpool, £400 in Birmingham, £350 in Durham, and only £18 in Bristol.[60]

In its funding allocations the MRC was advised by a number of 'investigative committees for special subjects', several members of which were drawn from the academic staff of WNSM. Although for much of the decade the research facilities available to Professor Edgar Leigh Collis were sparse his expertise was heavily drawn upon by the council, which made him a member of four committees dealing with occupational health issues, the industrial fatigue research board, industrial health statistics, miners' nystagmus and the incidence of phthisis in relation to occupation. Throughout the 1920s Professor Lyle Cummins, whose appointment to his chair was much influenced by the secretary of the MRC, served as a member of the council's committee on the bacteriology of tuberculosis, while, until his untimely death in 1924, Professor Emrys-Roberts received a grant from the MRC to act as secretary and organizer of a committee set up jointly by the council and the Pathological Society of Great Britain and Ireland to investigate *Status Lymphaticus* and causes of unexplained death. Emrys-Roberts's successor in the Cardiff chair of pathology, Edgar Hartley Kettle (1882–1936), continued to serve on the council's committee on radiology, a position to which he had been appointed while at St Mary's Hospital, London. Finally, a new committee was set up in 1927/8, on the physiology of hearing. The staff of the medical school's Department of Physiology was prominently represented by J. H. Shaxby and, as the committee's chairman, by Professor Graham Brown, who had just been elected a fellow of the Royal Society, a clear demonstration of the esteem in which he was held in the scientific community.

There were several lines of Cardiff-based research which attracted favour and funding from the MRC during the 1920s.[61] Reference has already been made to Lambert Rogers's work in the surgical unit. The Department of Obstetrics and Gynaecology also enjoyed the support of the MRC at this time. The establishment of this academic unit did not cause the same turbulence in the hospital as the medical and surgical units had done. It had simply been set up by designating the senior member in the speciality as a part-time professor; no existing vested interests were threatened and Ewen Maclean worked hard to ensure that no gulf developed between him and his clinical colleagues in the Infirmary. Nevertheless, he took his academic responsibilities seriously, his personal contribution to the department's teaching load being substantial. He also regarded his department's research role as important, making several noteworthy contributions on clinical subjects to journals such as the *British Medical Journal* and the *Journal of Obstetrics and Gynaecology*. However, it was the research of Gilbert Strachan, which particularly attracted the attention and consequently the funding of the MRC. During the early 1920s, as part of a multi-centre MRC study also involving workers in London, Liverpool, Edinburgh and Glasgow, Strachan, initially as research pathologist at the King Edward VII Hospital, then as part-time first assistant to Professor Maclean, received council funding to study the causes of child death at and before birth, in collaboration with H. A. Scholberg. Strachan's main research interest during the 1920s, also funded by the MRC, was an investigation into the effects of radium on uterine carcinoma, a field in which he was acknowledged as a pioneer.

The two departments which benefited most from the MRC's munificence were the Departments of Tuberculosis and Physiology. Although it has been suggested that the MRC showed relatively little interest in research into tuberculosis at this time,[62] it has to be said that from the moment of his appointment to the chair at Cardiff, Stevenson

Lyle Cummins was given sufficient council funding to enable his department to pursue a wide range of research themes, both general and specific to Wales, which were recorded with approval in successive annual reports of the MRC. To be sure, Cummins was in the fortunate position of heading one of the only two departments of tuberculosis in the United Kingdom (the other being at Edinburgh); he also enjoyed the patronage of the widely respected Welsh National Memorial Association. Nevertheless, despite the paucity of his facilities for much of the decade, Cummins, supported by a number of talented MRC-funded research assistants, strove with great determination to make his mark. Until 1927, in addition to his academic responsibilities Cummins held the post of principal medical officer of the association, but in that year, the duties of this post becoming too onerous to be performed on a part-time basis, Dr D. A. Powell was appointed to the post on a full-time basis, with Cummins taking the title of director of research. In this capacity he was required to submit an annual report to the trustees of the association, and his research report for 1927/8 provides an interesting flavour of the range of his research activities during this period, involving bench work, animal experimentation, clinical trials and epidemiological studies:

> The greater part of the time which I have been able to devote to personal research has been spent in the investigation of problems connected with sanocrysin. This gold compound has given decidedly promising results in my hands in the selected cases treated and yet its use is fraught with danger owing to the tendency to serious reaction which is never separate from this form of treatment. It has been my aim by experiments on animals and by careful observations on cases in hospital to elucidate further the factors which make for safety and otherwise in the use of this preparation. I may say that I have had considerable success with the treatment of experimental tuberculosis in rabbits but I have completely failed to obtain arrest or cure of experimental tuberculosis in guinea-pigs. I have devoted a great deal of time to attempting to improve the methods of standardising tubercle bacillary emulsions in order to obtain more accurately comparable types of disease in experimental animals. Much of my work has been of a preparatory nature in order to make possible more conclusive experiments at a future time.
>
> In addition to research of this kind, I have been enabled in conjunction with my colleagues of the Welsh National Memorial Association to obtain valuable records of the reactions of different types of cases to tuberculin given by the intradermal method. It is my opinion that the most urgent need at the present time is for some method of curing tuberculosis in its earliest stages. Such a method if available would go far to neutralize the dangers of this disease which on account of social factors is so difficult to deal with from the preventive point of view. For this reason I propose during the coming year to continue working at sanocrysin and allied types of metallic therapy. Although none of these methods is as yet perfect, they appear to me

to provide a first step in the direction of a curative technique in tuberculosis and I consider them more important than any other line of research.

A further research which is contemplated during the coming year is with reference to the effects of coal-dust upon the human lung. It has been held in the past that coal-dust is innocuous or, perhaps, even beneficial. Whether this be true or not, it has recently been established that certain coal-miners develop silicosis, this being confined to the men who work in hard headings where they are exposed to silicon dust. This fact is now recognised by those in authority and before long miners with silicosis will be able to claim compensation under the Refractory Industries Act. It appears, however, that many coal-miners who have never worked in silica dust develop radiological appearances which are difficult to distinguish from those of silicosis and this effect of coal-dust may in the future lead to a great abuse of the compensation scheme. It is, therefore, exceedingly important to learn how to differentiate the radiological appearances produced by pure coal-dust from those produced by silica. As Director of Research to the Association, I have drawn up with Dr D. A. Powell a scheme of investigation on this subject to be undertaken by selected members of the Medical Staff, and I have been so fortunate as to obtain the co-operation of my colleague, Professor E. L. Collis, who is an authority on industrial diseases and who will be able to help greatly in this matter.[63]

Cummins's research interest in silico-tuberculosis among the south Wales miners led to his appointment in 1926 as adviser to the South African Institute for Medical Research, which was investigating tuberculosis among South African natives working in the mines of the Witwatersrand. His request, in the spring of 1929, to have six months' leave of absence from the medical school to complete his work in South Africa caused David Davies some concern. He felt that as his association's director of research, Cummins ought to be spending his time in Wales rather than South Africa. Fortunately, D. A. Powell, and F. J. (later Sir Frederick) Alban, general secretary of the association, were strongly supportive of Cummins's request:

Colonel Cummins has been, in our opinion, a great asset to the Association, not only because of the actual work done by him but also because he has been an indispensable link with the Medical Research Council, and with the leading scientific workers in Tuberculosis all over the world. The unique position provided for him in Wales and the facilities given him in his work have linked his name very closely with that of the Association, and in the scientific world the Association enjoys a reputation which has been materially enhanced by Colonel Cummins' connection with it. Moreover, in the epidemiological study of Tuberculosis, in which Colonel Cummins is particularly interested and in which he is a recognised authority, there are better opportunities for investigation in the relatively virgin stocks of South Africa than anywhere else, and we feel that Colonel Cummins is carrying out the spirit of his appointment irrespective of the venue of his work.[64]

In 1924, Cummins's department benefited from the establishment of the Cecil Prosser Research Scholarship, endowed by Ernest Prosser in memory of his son. Awarded triennially by the University of Wales to promote research into tuberculosis, this scholarship, with an annual value of £250, proved to be a most worthwhile addition to the department's resources, enabling Cummins to be innovative in his research strategy. The first holder of the post was Emrys George Bowen, an anthropologist by background, who pursued a comparative study of tuberculosis in the old lead-mining industry in Cardiganshire and in a coal-mining district in south Wales. Working with Cummins, Professor H. J. Fleure, professor of anthropology and geography at the University College of Wales, Aberystwyth, and Dr Charles Lloyd, the tuberculosis officer for Cardiganshire, Bowen had, according to Cummins's report to the Memorial Association, 'brought many interesting points to light as to the bearing of racial, cultural and industrial factors on tuberculosis'.[65] This scholarship placed Bowen on an academic ladder which would later secure for him the post of Gregynog professor of geography and anthropology at Aberystwyth, which he occupied with great distinction from 1946 to 1968.[66] In accordance with Cummins's aim to appoint someone with a laboratory, rather than an epidemiological, background to the scholarship on the next occasion, Enid Mary Williams, a medical graduate of the University of Wales, took up the scholarship in 1930. Her studies, also part-funded by the MRC, led to her becoming, in 1932, the first woman to obtain the Doctorate of Medicine of the University of Wales for 'an investigation into the health of old and retired coalminers in South Wales', the same year that she was appointed assistant in the Department of Tuberculosis. She was later awarded a prestigious MRC Dorothy Temple Cross Research Fellowship intended for those seeking a career in the field of tuberculosis.

Cummins's reputation undoubtedly helped to attract scientists of high calibre to the principality. In 1922, William Howard Tytler (1885–1957), having been a successful research fellow in the Rockefeller Institute and a well-regarded member of the MRC's central laboratories at the National Institute of Medical Research, moved to Cardiff to become chief bacteriologist at the central tuberculosis laboratory of the Welsh National Memorial Association. With the title of recognized teacher he immediately became a valuable member of the Department of Tuberculosis teaching and research staff, continuing to secure project funding from the MRC, and serving on the council's investigation committee on tuberculin. His main problem as a researcher was that he was too much of a perfectionist. According to his obituarist, the results of his experiments, conducted in a cluttered laboratory containing 'a forest of apparatus and equipment mostly constructed by himself', were 'never consistent enough to satisfy him, and a vast amount of valuable work consequently remained unpublished'. In 1938, Tytler would succeed Cummins as professor of tuberculosis. He devoted much of his time to running the diploma course, in relation to which 'He built up a reputation as a teacher, perhaps better known abroad than in this country, but he also did much to enhance the reputation of the Welsh National School of Medicine throughout the Commonwealth.'[67]

Indeed, the department's reputation at home during the 1930s was perhaps less exalted. The efficacy of sanocrysin, a product with a gold content of 37 per cent, trialled with some optimism by Cummins during the 1920s, had become largely discredited by the mid-1930s because of adverse side-effects. Furthermore, from 1928 much of the funding for the department's research programme, which had hitherto been provided by David Davies himself, began to be obtained from the Welsh local authorities, which did not always share the priorities of the Welsh National Memorial Association. As one prominent Cardiff councillor observed in 1937, 'Money proposed to be spent on research could be better spent on practical measures of prevention such as by improving the nutrition and other living conditions of the people'.[68] For, despite the efforts of the Memorial Association and the Department of Tuberculosis during the inter-war years, the incidence of tuberculosis remained significantly higher in Wales than elsewhere in Britain, largely because, having received good treatment in the sanatoria of the principality, people were expected to return to the bad social and economic conditions prevalent in their home communities. It was only from the late 1930s, for the first time, that the Memorial Association chose to allocate some of its budget for the after-care of patients who had been discharged from the sanatoria. It is noteworthy that, considering the substantial involvement of the MRC in the establishment and early development of the Department of Tuberculosis, a senior officer of the council would claim in 1943 that there were no departments of tuberculosis worth mentioning in the British Isles.

It is hardly surprising that the Department of Physiology attracted solid funding from the MRC. The council had a high regard for the discipline of physiology, a science which, until the First World War, had been regarded as largely irrelevant to developments in clinical medicine. However, 'During the war, the pressing need for bringing the best physiological knowledge to the aid of sailors, soldiers, and workers in their exposure to every kind of violence, hardship and physical stress, brought the physiologists increasingly to their proper place within the fields of preventive and curative medicine.' The MRC was pleased to observe that this trend had continued after the war, 'and it may be said with confidence that the various schools of physiology have been shewing a keener interest and a growing usefulness in work immediately directed to medical problems'.[69]

Working in arguably the most handsome department of physiology of the time, all the academic staff at Cardiff were gifted research workers, five of whom attracted research funding from the MRC. Professor Graham Brown's main research interest was the physiology of the nervous system, where he used 'the relatively new technique of cinematography to record the limb movements of cats and pigeons'.[70] Although Lord Adrian later observed, with obvious regret, that, despite the FRS, Brown never quite fulfilled his early promise, his publication output falling off markedly after 1927 as his passion for mountaineering loomed larger among his priorities,[71] nevertheless Brown remained a substantial figure, heading a department of accomplished scientists. John Pryde, appointed lecturer in physiological chemistry in 1922, who would, in 1956, become the first professor of biochemistry at University College, Cardiff, pursued basic research on the chemical structure of sugars. During the mid-1920s he was supported in this work by J. M. Peterson, assistant lecturer and demonstrator in the department until his departure to the University of Aberdeen in 1929. Returning to the department in 1935, Peterson would succeed Graham Brown as professor of physiology in 1947. J. H. Shaxby, lecturer in special sense physiology, secured MRC funding for, among other things, an investigation of the way light was absorbed by human skin of various colours, and studies on the physiology of sound-localization, with special reference to the qualities required in listeners. As the MRC reported in its annual report for 1929/30, the council had 'under consideration the selection and training of listeners for Anti-Aircraft Defence' and to that end Shaxby was making observations 'on binaural stimulation, produced under different conditions, by pure tones of varying intensity and frequency', a good example of the way the department's research was addressing practical issues.[72] A. Hemingway, lecturer in experimental physiology from 1927 (who later became professor of physiology at Leeds University), collaborated with Lambert Rogers in his MRC-funded sympathectomy studies. Although Hemingway's predecessor at Cardiff, Ivan de Burgh Daly, appointed as lecturer in experimental physiology in 1923, does not appear to have received MRC support for his research on the regulation of blood pressure, his work was sufficiently distinguished to earn him the chair of physiology at Birmingham in 1927 (where he was immediately appointed to the university's Joint Research Committee). In 1933 he was appointed to the chair in Edinburgh, where he was elected a fellow of the Royal Society in 1943 and in 1948 he became the first director of the Agricultural Research Council's Institute of Animal Physiology, Babraham, Cambridge.

Arguably the department's greatest contribution to medical progress during the 1920s was in providing facilities for J. W. Tudor Thomas, honorary assistant ophthalmologist at the Cardiff Royal Infirmary, to engage in pioneering work, again supported by the MRC, on corneal transplantation, involving the making of hundreds of grafts on rabbits before the technique was perfected. The annual report of the MRC for 1930/1 described progress as follows:

> Mr J. W. Tudor Thomas, working with an expenses grant in Professor T. Graham Brown's department at Cardiff, has continued his experiments on the grafting of healthy corneal tissue on the eye to replace tissue that has become opaque through disease or accident. Study has been made of the conditions necessary to secure the growth of a graft that will unite and at the same time retain its transparency. Much work yet remains to be done, but the experiments – of which accounts have been published – give hope of a radical cure by surgical means of blindness due to opacity of the cornea.[73]

Less than three years later, the *Western Mail* under the heading 'Eye Surgeon's Amazing Operation – Sight Restored to Man', reported how 'doctors all over the world' had been astonished by 'a brilliant operation' performed on a man from Newcastle upon Tyne by Tudor Thomas, called in by the authorities of the Royal London Ophthalmic Hospital as the only surgeon capable of the task. As the news-paper observed, 'Today the patient is walking about with the cornea of another man's and another woman's eye grafted on to his own, and is gradually getting back his sight.' Meanwhile, doctors from America, India and the Continent had been visiting the hospital to admire Thomas's achievement.[74] In 1931 he had been elected Hunterian professor of the Royal College of Surgeons of England, a rare accolade, which in 1934 would be conferred upon Lambert Rogers.

To judge by the annual reports of the MRC, the amount of research into mental disorders at this time was relatively small, invariably covered in no more than a couple of pages, and confined in the main to a few centres of activity: the University of Cambridge; the University of London (the Maudsley Hospital and the National Hospital, Queen's Square); the University of Birmingham, notable for the existence of a Joint Board of Research in Mental Disease in association with the City of Birmingham; the University of Manchester, linked to the Lancashire Mental Asylum, Rainhill; the Scottish Western Asylums Research Institute, Glasgow; and, by no means least, the City Mental Hospital, Cardiff. It is interesting to note that, although under-graduate instruction in mental diseases in Cardiff was firmly the responsibility of the Department of Medicine, and Edwin Goodall held the title of lecturer in that depart-ment, Professor Kennedy never chose to associate the research work of the City Mental Hospital with his department, despite being given the opportunity to do so from time to time. The fact remains that the hospital was much favoured by the MRC during the inter-war years. Edwin Goodall, the medical superintendent, hailed by his obituarist as 'a pioneer in the scientific study and treatment of mental disorders',[75] established a biochemical laboratory which, under his direction (and with support from the pathologist Harold Scholberg and R. V. Sandford, a research chemist), pursued a range of scientific studies into such issues as the relationship between cholesterol levels and epileptic fits, the treatment of neurosyphilis and the association of the cerebro-spinal fluid and blood plasma in mental disorders. Goodall's work on the pathology of the psychoses, and his advanced views on the treatment of mental illness – he was, as has already been noted, a strong advocate of the integration of the psychiatric clinic within the general hospital – brought him many distinctions. Elected a fellow of the Royal College of Physicians in 1903, he gave the Croonian Lectures on the pathology of mental disorders in 1914, and for two years served on the council of the college. At different times he served as president of the Section of Neurology and Psychiatry at annual conferences of the BMA, of the Section of Psychiatry of the Royal Society of Medicine and of the Royal Medico-Psychological Association. In 1927, two years before his retirement, he gave the Maudsley Lecture on the pathology of insanity. Following Goodall's retirement, his successor, P. K. McCowan, working in particular with a highly regarded biochemist, J. H. Quastel, maintained the hospital's reputation as an important provincial centre for psychiatric research, continuing to attract MRC funding during the next decade.

THE MRC AND RADIOTHERAPEUTIC RESEARCH IN CARDIFF

If the activities of Tudor Thomas represented one manifestation of the way that the Welsh National School of Medicine and the hospital clinicians could work together, developments in the general field of radiotherapy were another.

In 1920 the Ministry of Munitions transferred to the keeping of the MRC a substantial quantity of radium, collected from the parts of a wide range of war implements, 'in order to maintain its employment for research purposes, and especially for research into its value for the treatment of malignant disease'.[76] The council arranged for quantities of radium to be assigned to a small number of centres in the United Kingdom, five in London, together with the General Hospital, Birmingham and the Council for Public Health in Ireland, in Dublin. A year later the council was able to report that two further hospitals had been added to this select group, the Royal Infirmary, Aberdeen and the King Edward VII Hospital in Cardiff – important external recognition of the hospital's potential as a significant centre in the area of malignant disease.

It must be said that Cardiff's first steps in this new environment were somewhat halting. Initially the local management arrangements in relation to this prized commodity were perhaps slacker than was desirable. A radium subcommittee, reporting to the Medical Board, was set up under the secretaryship of Professor Emrys-Roberts, who was looking after the material. Although some rough documentation had been drafted by the subcommittee, it is apparent that no one had thought to alert the hospital authorities formally that radium existed in the hospital, and, at a meeting of the Medical Board in January 1922 concern was expressed about the liability of members of the clinical staff in the event of any mishap. 'It was pointed out that no member of the staff was likely to accept responsibility for the safe-keeping of so valuable a metal when in clinical use which might be used for very many hours consecutively.' Within a week of this meeting the hospital's Board of Management agreed that it would assume responsibility for the safe custody of the radium loaned to the hospital by the MRC

> provided every reasonable care is taken by those making use of it; further that it be an instruction from the Board that the radium be kept in the official care of the Medical Superintendent, and that the Emergency and Reference Committee are hereby authorised to draw up and approve regulations as to the use and the custody of the radium.[77]

Formal management arrangements having been established, the radium subcommittee, composed of senior clinicians from the school and the hospital, operated effectively thereafter, particularly under the control of Professor Sheen, who had assumed the secretaryship on the death of Emrys-Roberts. The preparation of annual reports to the MRC was efficiently undertaken by Sheen, who, when necessary, would co-ordinate the collection of specimens to be referred elsewhere at the request of the MRC. Suitable facilities were provided for the safe storage of radium, whether in use or not, in a lead safe, approved by the MRC, and detailed guidance was issued to medical and nursing staff on safe handling procedures.

Early in 1929, in response to pressure from the MRC and elsewhere, the government established a new body, the National Radium Commission, to co-ordinate and enhance the use of radium in treatment and research. The commission's priority was, in the words of the MRC, 'to concentrate the new supplies of radium at centres where adequate facilities of all kinds for its use, and proper safeguards against its dangers, can be guaranteed'.[78] As a first step, the commission approached all centres known to be using radium and invited them to apply for recognition as a national radium centre, success to be rewarded by additional supplies of radium. The questionnaire, completed in respect of Cardiff by Tudor Thomas, secretary to the Medical Board, for submission to the commission, provided a comprehensive statement of the hospital and medical school's clinical and research work in the field of malignant disease at this time. It stated that all forms of malignant disease were treated by radium at the infirmary, and that the members of the honorary staff had acquired 'both by their own experience and by the literature published, and by visits made by several of them to other Radium Centres, much theoretical and practical knowledge of the subject'. The infirmary's pathological department, linked to the medical school, had 'ample facilities for routine and research laboratory work bearing on the treatment of malignant disease by radium'. If the hospital's submission proved successful, thereby enhancing the radium-related activity in the hospital, it was recognized 'that the whole-time services of a responsible and capable person may have to be enlisted' to ensure the safe custody of the radium. The statement concluded with a list of publications concerning radium which had been written by staff from the hospital and medical school. Ten articles were listed, seven written by Gilbert Strachan, the others by members of the surgical staff. In support of the hospital's submission the Cardiff College registrar added a letter commending 'the claims of the Cardiff Royal Infirmary as a National Radium Centre, and assures the Commission that, as representing the Welsh National School of Medicine [the Faculty of Medicine] will be glad to support the Infirmary in any way possible'.[79] The hospital's submission to the National Radium Commission was approved in the spring of 1930, subject to the strengthening of supervisory arrangements. Thus it was that Richard Glyn Maliphant (1900–78), one of Cardiff's outstanding preclinical students during the immediate post-war years, returned to Wales as the infirmary's first radium registrar, before establishing himself as one of Cardiff's most distinguished obstetricians and gynaecologists.

Among the documents included with the submission to the National Radium Commission were copies of the Cardiff Royal Infirmary's annual clinical record. The publication was introduced for the first time in 1926, ostensibly on the initiative of the resident registrar of the time, and so interesting and useful did it prove to be that, in the words of the chairman of the Medical Board, writing in the 1927 issue, 'One wishes it had been started years ago.' William Martin was pleased to add: 'Interest in the Clinical Record of the Cardiff Royal Infirmary has not been confined to South Wales. The Registrar has been congratulated on his work by one of the large London Hospitals and asked for particulars of his method.' The publication comprised not only a complete statistical table of the patients under treatment in the wards of the hospital in any given year; it also included several short clinical case notes written by members of the hospital staff, thereby giving them an opportunity to disseminate the fruit of their labours to a wider community of practitioners than would otherwise have been the case. Indeed, William Martin was always dismissive of the concept that clinical research could only flourish within the unit system. He took the view that 'a doctor looked upon every case as an opportunity for research',[80] and he undoubtedly felt that the appearance of the annual clinical record endorsed his attitude. Martin conveniently chose to overlook the fact that the foundations of the project had been laid by the surgical unit, which had been assiduously tabulating and interpreting its patient data since its inception.

RESEARCH IN ANATOMY, PHARMACOLOGY AND PATHOLOGY

For much of the decade the research contribution of the departments of anatomy, materia medica and pharmacology and pathology was less than prolific. In the thirteen years between 1910 and 1927 the only published work emanating from the Department of Anatomy was a revision by Professor Hepburn of his entry on 'Arthrology' in Cunningham's *Text Book of Anatomy* and a section on 'Anatomy' in Chambers' *Encyclopaedia*. Hepburn's successor, Cecil McLaren West (1893–1951), who had joined the department from his position as university anatomist at Trinity College, Dublin, was rather more research-minded. Despite a heavy teaching load, he was able to find time to collaborate with Lambert Rogers in a number of studies, as well as to pursue his own research into the development of the human embryo and to write a study of the comparative anatomy of the mandibular fossa, as well as contributing to some of the standard textbooks. Nevertheless, a later professor of anatomy at Cardiff, Professor J. D. Lever, characterized anatomy during the inter-war years as essentially 'a scalpel and forceps subject'.[81]

Given the paucity of the accommodation available to the Department of Materia Medica and Pharmacology – it lacked a pharmacological laboratory of its own – and the fact that the head of department was a part-time lecturer with substantial clinical and other commitments, it was not surprising that the department made little contribution to the school's research endeavour. However, a part-time lecturer, James Beatty, who doubled up as the hospital's dermatologist, did publish a few articles, including one with the formidable title 'Iodine therapy in arterial disease – can arterial diseases (including those of old age) be prevented, or if inevitable their onset delayed, or if present can their progress be arrested or retarded by medicinal measures?' It would take the appointment of a full-time lecturer, Dr (later Professor) R. St A. Heathcote, to head the department in 1933, and the provision of new laboratories in the following year, to improve the situation.[82]

The most disappointing academic department from the research point of view during the 1920s was Pathology and Bacteriology, especially as the school's first professor of pathology, Edward Emrys-Roberts, was well regarded in MRC circles. However, in contrast, for example, with the situation at Cambridge, where the professor of pathology, Henry Roy Dean, regarded his discipline as a preclinical subject, and strove to avoid taking on a service role,[83] the academic department in Cardiff shared clinical responsibilities with Harold Scholberg, the hospital's senior pathologist. This arrangement was belatedly acknowledged in 1924 when, following Emrys-Roberts's untimely death after a long illness, his successor was appointed at the same salary as the professors of medicine, surgery and public health. Although H. R. Dean once observed that 'The duties of a pathologist to a great hospital and a teacher in a large medical school leave little time for original research,'[84] Emrys-Roberts's successor, Edgar Hartley Kettle, came to Cardiff from St Mary's Hospital with a high reputation for his work on silicosis and its relation to pulmonary tuberculosis, and more generally on the effect of dust on infection and resistance. These interests neatly complemented those of Edgar Leigh Collis and Stevenson Lyle Cummins, but although they collaborated, Kettle's research impact during his three years in Cardiff was certainly less than he had hoped. Only three articles emerged from his time in Cardiff, one in the *Journal of Industrial Hygiene* on experimental silicosis, one on aspects of inflammation and infection in *The Lancet*, the third on miners' phthsis in an obscure South African journal. Based in the Cardiff Royal Infirmary and subjected to the unsettling presence of Harold Scholberg, a far from easy colleague, Kettle was less than happy with the facilities he had inherited, as he admitted in his head of department's annual report of 1925/6 to the College Council:

> The limitations of the Department are such that it is impossible to offer facilities for postgraduate work. Indeed, the instruction of the undergraduates is more or less

restricted to formal teaching. Similarly, facilities for research are practically non-existent. It is hoped that with the completion of the Laboratories in the new Institute of Preventive Medicine and an increase in the staff, a wider scope may be given to the activities of the department.

The Institute for Preventive Medicine, funded by Sir William James Thomas, finally opened in January 1927. Initially intended exclusively to support the academic areas of preventive medicine and public health, the faculty realized by the end of 1925 that the accommodation was rather more extensive than had once been envisaged and it was decided to use some of the building for other purposes too. A report commissioned by the Board of Medicine confirmed that the Department of Pathology and Bacteriology was grossly under-accommodated, and it was agreed that, while ultimately the department deserved to be housed in an institute on a par with the Institute of Physiology, for the time being it should have space in the Institute of Preventive Medicine. The third floor was set aside for the department, comprising laboratories for research staff, medical students, and for clinical purposes, together with an office for the professor and his secretary, facing the Parade and the Grove. On this floor were also two bedrooms and a bathroom set aside for the caretaker of the building. The needs of the Department of Tuberculosis, at the time squatting in the Institute of Physiology, were served by the allocation of space on the fourth floor, which also housed a small lecture theatre and an animal house available for the use of the Departments of Tuberculosis, Pathology and Bacteriology and the School of Preventive Medicine, to be located on the second floor. The first floor would provide self-contained laboratory accommodation for the public health work of the city and county, in relation to which the school had no managerial responsibility. Apart from the heating apparatus for the whole building, and a private sitting room for the caretaker, the basement floor was to serve as a museum for all three departments. Lest people might think that the plans simply represented an opportunist attempt to solve a number of separate problems, inconsistent with the original intentions of the donor, the report of the faculty, endorsed by the Board of Medicine, said this:

> The concentration in one Institute of Pathology, Tuberculosis and Preventive Medicine, if the work carried out is of mutual interest, as often occurs, need not divert the Institute widely from its original purpose. For instance, the subject of miner's phthisis or silicosis is one to which the Professor of Preventive Medicine and of Pathology have already devoted considerable attention, while it is of no less interest to the Professor of Tuberculosis. Further research into this subject is contemplated directly the laboratories are available.[85]

Edgar Kettle had done much to plan the detailed arrangements in the institute, but he had become weary of the constitutional problems engulfing the school, described in more detail in the next chapter – suffice it to say here that they created financial problems for the school in general, and for Kettle's work in particular. As Lord Kenyon ruefully observed in a letter to Sir Thomas Lewis,

> The finances of the school are much suffering by the withholding of £7,000 by the University Grants Commission [*sic*] and by the non-payment of the special rate by certain Authorities, amounting to some £1,600 p.a. Consequently we ... have had great difficulty in giving Kettle the assistance he requires.[86]

Although he was able to expand his department with some excellent new appointments during his last year in Cardiff, he had also become tired of the tensions between the school and some of the hospital clinical staff, and of trying to reach a *modus vivendi* with the tedious Harold Scholberg. As his obituarist would later observe,

> These disputes provided, it is true, a great opportunity for Kettle's kindliness, tact and capacity for organisation, but both diplomacy and hard work were needed to establish friendly relationships and to obtain the supplies of pathological material which were needed for research and teaching.

When the invitation came for him to take up the chair of pathology at St Bartholomew's Hospital in 1927, he left Cardiff with a spring in his step, 'looking forward to new opportunities and the realisation of greater hopes and ambitions'.[87] After a brief hiatus, when the fort was held by the departmental lecturer, Kettle's successor, James Henry Dible (1889–1971), joined Cardiff from the London School of Medicine for Women in 1928 at a bad time. His obituarists cover Dible's Cardiff career in two sentences: 'At this time, unfortunately, the Cardiff School was suffering from severe internal difficulties that hampered its work and threatened its closure. So when, in 1929, Dible received an invitation from the University of Liverpool to the Chair of Pathology he had no hesitation in accepting.'[88]

Fortunately, by the end of the decade, sanity had returned to the school and the pathological facilities in the new institute were such as to enable good research to be pursued, some in collaboration with the medical unit. The work of one of the assistant lecturers, Jethro Gough, on 'Mitrochondia' was rated particularly highly by John Bright Duguid, his acting head of department in his annual report to the College Council for 1929/30:

> Dr Gough's work is of outstanding importance to biology, for not only has it brought to light many facts regarding the structure and function of intracellular bodies, but, by providing a new and superior technical method, it has also much facilitated the further study of this subject.

Gough's research secured for him the MD degree of the University of Wales in 1930, and in due course he would succeed Duguid as head of the department.

Approved by the University of Wales in 1925, the postgraduate research degrees of Doctor of Medicine and Master of Surgery were available to medical graduates of the University of Wales during or subsequently to the third year after obtaining their primary qualification, and involved not only the submission of a thesis incorporating original research but also a clinical examination.[89] The first person to obtain either higher qualification was Daniel Thomas Davies, who obtained the University of Wales MD in 1927, three years after gaining his MB B.Ch. His subject was 'Gastric acidity in health and disease'. The second, two years later, was James William Tudor Thomas, who obtained an MD on the subject 'Miners' nystagmus and incapacity for work'. The first person to obtain the Mastership in Surgery (M.Ch.) of the University of Wales was Thomas Geraint Illtyd James, a graduate of 1925 who, in 1933, submitted a thesis on the subject 'Some observations on the surgery of the sympathetic nervous system'.

LIBRARY FACILITIES

In an attempt at least partly to remedy a glaring deficiency in the medical school's facilities for research, as well as undergraduate and postgraduate teaching, the nucleus of a general school library was created on the second floor of the Institute of Preventive Medicine in 1927. The report of the special committee, set up in 1922 to review the needs of the full medical school, had stated clearly: 'Proper library provision for the Medical School has still to be made.' Noting that small, barely adequate libraries existed within the academic departments, the report had called for the establishment of a central medical library, ideally by the transfer of the medically related holdings of the National Library of Wales (NLW) to Cardiff. In September 1922, recognizing the unwillingness of the NLW simply to hand over its holdings to another body, the Faculty of Medicine had formally asked the University of Wales to approach the authorities of the NLW 'with a view to the establishment, in connection with the Welsh National School of Medicine, of a Medical Branch of the National Library under such control, and with the provision of such accommodation, as shall be satisfactory to the authorities of the National Library'. Unfortunately, nothing came of this, or of subsequent approaches made from time to time during the following decades. The main concern was that by making a concession to one institution the library would be faced with similar claims from other institutions or special interests which might eventually lead to the destruction of the coherence of the National Library of Wales.[90]

For most of the decade, therefore, staff and students of the school had to make do with the facilities of the College Drapers' Company Library, augmented by departmental libraries, which held textbooks, periodicals and standard works. Limited access was also available to the library of the Cardiff Medical Society, for some years housed in the Institute of Physiology. The opening of a general school library in the

Institute of Preventive Medicine was undoubtedly a step in the right direction. It was mainly stocked by 4,000 medical books obtained, after being inspected by the dean, from the library of a Dr Lloyd Roberts of Manchester. Purchased for the total sum of £39 15s. 3d. including packing and carriage, the collection was, unfortunately, soon dismissed as being virtually useless.[91] However, two encouraging developments took place at the end of the decade. At the instigation of the newly established Board of Clinical Studies, chaired by Mitchell Stevens and dominated by the honorary staff of the hospital, agreement was reached on the creation of a medical library within the precincts of the Cardiff Royal Infirmary.[92] Secondly, in the 1930/1 session the medical section of the college's main library was transferred on loan, to the medical school. Therefore, while far from being ideal, the school's library facilities at the turn of the decade were at least tolerable – better for the staff than the students – judging by a report submitted to the Court of the University of Wales in December 1932, little more than a year after the Welsh National School of Medicine had achieved its independence:

> The Council of the Welsh National School of Medicine begs to inform the Court that the Library provision of the School consists of a Central Library in the Institute of Preventive Medicine, of Departmental Libraries in the various School Departments, and of a Library conducted by the Board of Clinical Studies.
>
> A. Central Library
> The books in this Library, while considerable in number, are mostly obsolete works of no historical value, and bound volumes of old periodicals. The Library of the Cardiff Medical Society is, by arrangement, housed in the Central Library, and the books are both modern and useful. The Central Library throughout, is available for reference to staff and students.
>
> B. Libraries of Departments and of the Board of Clinical Studies
> In these Libraries there are approximately 1,200 books and sixty periodicals, which are all useful. The Libraries are at the disposal of staff, both for reference and borrowing. Students are only allowed access to the majority of these Libraries by special application and are not usually allowed to borrow books. Free access to these Libraries is rendered difficult through the impossibility, so far, of providing continuous supervision.[93]

Bearing in mind that the number of books in the various libraries of the school, admittedly of variable quality, totalled 5,000 or more, and that the holdings of the Cardiff Medical Society, some 3,000 volumes,[94] were available for consultation, the total number of books in the school compared not unfavourably with the number of bound volumes in the general and departmental libraries at most of the London medical schools at that time. Apart from those at University College Hospital, the Middlesex and St Bartholomew's Hospital Medical Schools, all of the other holdings comprised fewer than 6,000 volumes. The number of bound volumes in the libraries at St George's Hospital, for instance, totalled 5,800, while those at St Thomas's, St Mary's and Westminster Hospitals numbered fewer than 4,000.[95]

Even so, the less than helpful attitude of the authorities of the National Library of Wales towards the needs of the Welsh National School of Medicine still continued to rankle, particularly in the light of evidence that the medical holdings at Aberystwyth were hardly if ever consulted.[96] The library's intransigence caused at least one leading figure in Welsh public life, Sir Henry Stuart-Jones, principal of the University College of Wales, Aberystwyth, to write, despairingly, to the *Western Mail* in 1934:

> It is hard to believe that Sir John Williams, the president and chief benefactor of the National Library and a medical man of the highest eminence, would not have welcomed the idea of co-operation between the institution he so generously endowed and the National School of Medicine had it then been in existence.[97]

Constitutional Wrangles

For nearly five years the future of the Welsh National School of Medicine was the subject of sharp controversy involving the University of Wales, the University College of South Wales and Monmouthshire, Whitehall, the medical press and anyone else professing an interest in the future of medical education in Wales. It will be recalled that, with some reluctance, the government had, in the face of stout resistance from the Cardiff College authorities, decided not to insist on the implementation of the main recommendations of the Haldane Commission concerning the constitutional position of the medical school. Whitehall's decision, at the beginning of 1923, to revive Haldane's recommendations, created a period of often bitter conflict within higher education in Wales which only abated at the end of 1927 when the warring parties reached a compromise by which the Welsh National School of Medicine would be split into two parts. This judgement was hardly based on sound academic criteria, for expert opinion had firmly advised against it; the outcome was chiefly determined by financial realities and war-weariness.

It was a tribute to the dedication and commitment of the staff of the Welsh National School of Medicine that, despite the distractions created by this debilitating wrangle, high-quality teaching and research continued unabated for most of the 1920s. On one occasion Sir Thomas Lewis, who, despite his eminent position in the world of medicine, took a keen interest in the affairs of the school, was pleased to pass on to Lord Kenyon the observation of a recent external examiner, that 'So far as the Physiological Institute is concerned, its management and teaching, he has nothing but high praise.' What concerned Lewis was that Professor Graham Brown, tired of all the bickering, and indeed of the personal vendetta aimed at him by senior members of the Science Faculty during the early months of 1926, might decide to leave.[1] To his credit Brown resisted the temptation, choosing to vent any pent-up frustration on the mountain slopes of Europe. In fact, until 1928, the only senior member of the school to go elsewhere was Edgar Kettle; the others 'got on with the job'. Professor Graham Brown, writing to Sir Thomas Lewis in the summer of 1927, seemed to sum up the general mood fairly well:

> If the University and the College can agree to a proper constitution for the Medical School, it should be possible to get on with education. I still believe that there is a magnificent opportunity here, although the way things have gone have made it more difficult to develop the school than it should have been.[2]

WHITEHALL HAS SECOND THOUGHTS ON THE STATUS OF THE MEDICAL SCHOOL

The enactment of a supplementary charter for the University of Wales in September 1920, to which reference has been made in chapter 4, meant that the University College of South Wales and Monmouthshire, like the other constituent colleges of the University, had to submit draft supplemental charters themselves to the Privy Council. On 9 February 1922 the Cardiff Court of Governors approved a draft supplemental charter for the College, which defined the position of the Welsh National School of Medicine in Article XIV. Apart from spelling out the membership of the Faculty of Medicine the article stated: 'The Council of the College shall be the academic and administrative authority of the School.'

It took the Privy Council a year to deliberate over the draft and deliver its response to the Cardiff College authorities, partly because the UGC, whose views had been sought as part of the consultation process, admitted that it would take 'longer than usual' to supply its comments: 'The whole business of the so-called National School of Medicine is complicated and indeed critical.'[3] However, on 1 February 1923 Sir Almeric Fitzroy, clerk to the Privy Council, delivered what Lord Kenyon called 'a thunderbolt' by way of response.[4] He informed the college authorities that their lordships, on reflection, now believed that the recommendations of the Haldane Report concerning the status of the medical school should be implemented. Just over a month later, Fitzroy detailed the Privy Council's reasons to a baffled college. Their lordships, noting the prime aim of the Welsh National School of Medicine to become 'a first rate centre of medical teaching and research' operating at an all-Wales dimension, considered that this aspiration would be hampered by the cumbersome machinery of government now in place. Moreover, separation would not only be good for the school; it would be good for the college too, enabling it to become 'free to concentrate on the development of its important and growing body of work in the Faculties other than Medicine'. Finally, the clerk referred to the Privy Council's belief that much of Welsh opinion, which had initially opposed Haldane's recommendations, was now changing its mind.[5]

Who had persuaded Their Lordships that the views of Wales were changing? There was no evidence at that time that the local authorities were pledging one-eighth of a penny rate to the Welsh National School of Medicine on condition that it became free of University College, Cardiff (though one or two, notably Swansea, did raise the issue later). The south Wales correspondent of the leading Welsh-language newspaper, *Baner ac Amserau Cymru*, observed:

> The question of the moment is, who put the idea into the minds of the members of the Privy Council? It is agreed that someone or other (possibly someone in close connection with the college or school of medicine) brought the matter before the

> Privy Council and persuaded that authority to advocate the separation of school from college, [thereby] stumbling over a hornet's nest.[6]

It has to be said that neither the Privy Council nor the rest of Whitehall needed much persuasion that the Haldane Commission's recommendations concerning the status of the Welsh National School of Medicine should be implemented. Faced with Lloyd George's reluctant decision not to force the issue in the face of apparently resolute Welsh opposition in 1920, Whitehall – which, after all, had advised the prime minister on this course of inaction – had had to accept the position at that time, though it had never been reconciled to the permanent incorporation of the medical school in the Cardiff College. Nothing had happened since 1920 to convince the doubters that this institution had the medical school's best interests at heart. Sir Alfred Davies, permanent secretary of the Welsh Department of the Board of Education and a consistent advocate of independence for the medical school, more than once cited the appointment of William Sheen as professor of surgery in 1921 as one example of 'the unfortunate effect of giving local management [to a body] intended to be a national institution'.[7] The UGC, as well as influential men such as Thomas Lewis, had been dismayed by the haste with which the full medical school had come into being in the autumn of 1921, in the face of the anxieties of some of its own professors and an uncertain financial future. Moreover, the decision of the college to launch an appeal to fund developments in Cathays Park at precisely the same moment that an appeal was being launched to stabilize the finances of the infant medical school caused much eyebrow-raising at the time.

Whitehall's main concern was that the convoluted framework within which the medical school was expected to operate was unworkable. In fairness to the Cardiff College, the framework had only been in operation since the summer of 1921, so there was precious little hard evidence available to vindicate this view. Fortunately, Lord Kenyon was as unhappy with existing arrangements as were the men from Whitehall,[8] and he was instrumental in persuading Jenkin James, the university secretary, to provide a statement setting out some of the problems inherent in the existing constitutional status of the medical school as he saw them:

> The machinery has been carefully drawn up and elaborated, but experience has shown that it does not work smoothly and efficiently. The procedure is too cumbrous, much valuable time is lost in proceeding from one stage to another, and there are too many opportunities for friction to arise between the bodies concerned.[9]

Though thin on detail, this sort of evidence was quite sufficient for the UGC finally to advise, in December 1922, that Cardiff's draft charter be rejected by the Privy Council, a course of action which could safely be taken without embarrassing David

Lloyd George, who had fallen from power two months earlier. Writing to Sir Almeric Fitzroy, A. H. Kidd set out the UGC's considered position:

> The general complexity of the scheme, and the division of functions between the University Council, the Advisory Board of Medicine of the University, the University College Council and the College Board of Medicine, though sufficiently intelligible from the past history of this difficult matter, will undoubtedly make the task of efficient and harmonious administration most difficult, and may prove a serious impediment to the development of the National School of Medicine.[10]

The UGC's advice was to revert 'to the much simpler plan recommended by the Royal Commission'. Although Sir Almeric Fitzroy was in cordial agreement with this view, bearing in mind that the Haldane recommendations had previously been thwarted by Welsh opposition it was essential for Whitehall to satisfy itself that Welsh opinion would now be more receptive. Writing to Fitzroy, Lord Kenyon offered what reassurance he could: 'At the time of the Commission's report Griffiths worked us all up to support him in keeping the School subordinate to the College, and I think many of the authorities may have changed their views.'[11] According to a senior official in the Board of Education, Kenyon also succeeded in satisfying Sir William McCormick, chairman of the UGC, that the plan recommended by the Royal Commission 'would now be favoured by the majority opinion in the University Council and in Wales generally. Even Cardiff opinion is more divided on the matter than it was when the present arrangement was set up.'[12]

As university pro-chancellor, Lord Kenyon was undoubtedly in a good position to assess feeling in Wales, but what evidence had he of a division in Cardiff? As far as the authorities of the King Edward VII Hospital were concerned, they really had no strong feelings in the matter either way. However, with the retirement of John Berry Haycraft in 1919, and the introduction of a full clinical course, the whole complexion of the medical school was altering. New professors were appointed, most of whom had not been nurtured in the traditions of pre-war Cardiff. This was certainly what Dr (later Sir) David Rocyn Jones observed. A product of Lewis School, Pengam, University College, Cardiff and London University, medical officer of health for Monmouthshire, and a member of both the Board of Medicine and the Cardiff College Council, he once remarked, rather intemperately, that the medical school, established and endowed by local benefactors, was now in the hands of 'alien professors'.[13] To be sure, a number of them were less than impressed with the way in which the authorities of University College, Cardiff were managing the affairs of the school (the views of Professors Brown and Collis have already been noted). Although it was not until April 1923 that the Faculty of Medicine first publicly expressed its support for separation from the Cardiff College, it could surely not have produced such a clear statement of its views so quickly unless it reflected fairly deeply held sentiments. By then, Professor Hepburn, throughout his career a strong supporter of the school's integration with the college, was no longer dean of medicine, having been succeeded, after a continuous reign of nineteen years, by Professor Kennedy in 1922. Indeed, Mitchell Stevens, another member of the 'old guard', always claimed that Hepburn had been removed from the deanship by intrigue 'and from that day the School has been run by the separatists'.[14] Lord Kenyon, as chairman of the Board of Medicine, and indeed William Bruce, as a member, were both in a good position to gauge the mood of members of the medical school, and for his meeting with Sir William McCormick in December 1922, Lord Kenyon had been accompanied by one of the medical school professors.[15] Certainly, when referring to the Privy Council's change of mind in an address to the University Council in September 1924, William Bruce would explain that the Privy Council had had 'some inkling of a new feeling, especially in medical circles on the subject'.[16] However, in answer to the question of the *Baner ac Amserau Cymru* correspondent who asked who had persuaded the Privy Council at the beginning of 1923 to propose the separation of the medical school from the Cardiff College, the response must be 'Nobody.' The Privy Council, indeed the whole of Whitehall, wanted to take the matter forward anyway, but, as Principal Trow and Daniel Brown were to suggest in their history of University College, Cardiff, written ten years later,[17] they were fortunate to find, particularly in the persons of Lord Kenyon and William Bruce, powerful allies in the University of Wales and much support in the medical school itself.

A MIXED RESPONSE

Though understandably upset by the decision of the Privy Council to reopen the question of the constitutional position of the Welsh National School of Medicine, the authorities at University College, Cardiff were disinclined to make a hasty response. Indeed, it was not until 15 July 1924 that the college formally wrote to the Privy Council declining to accept the terms of its letter of 1 February 1923 and submitting revisions in its draft charter which, in essence, restated the college's supremacy over the affairs of the medical school. In the meantime the college authorities had obtained a wide range of opinions. The position of the medical school was overwhelmingly in favour of separation. In May, as Lord Kenyon reported to Fitzroy, the Board of Medicine voted in favour, *nem. con.*: 'There were two or three opponents but they realised that the other side were too strong and they did not vote.'[18] Moreover, 'I hear the students to a man are in favour of it.'[19] David Hepburn remained a supporter of continued integration with the college but, since standing down from the deanship in 1922, he had become increasingly disaffected, failing to attend a single one of forty meetings of the Faculty of Medicine in the next two years, preferring to keep in touch with proceedings by writing querulous letters to Daniel Brown, the faculty secretary, from time to time. The most authoritative indication of faculty opinion was expressed in a statement prepared by Professor Kennedy (then dean of the faculty) and Professor Graham Brown, and formally approved by the Faculty of Medicine on 17 July 1923. This asserted that, as a national institution, the medical school 'would be more likely to appeal to the people of Wales if it is established as a separate entity within the University of Wales than if it is carried on as a subordinate institution under the control of the local Cardiff College'. The endorsement of Professor Graham Brown, professor of physiology, who would succeed Kennedy as dean of medicine in 1924, was of particular importance in response to those who asserted that it would be academic nonsense to separate the preclinical sciences from the college's other scientific disciplines. William Sheen also questioned the ability of the college authorities truly to promote the best interests of the school. 'There are some thirty medical men on the school staff, and their head is the principal of the college who – not being a medical man himself – naturally cannot guide and govern them and interpret and give effect to their aspirations.'[20]

Outside the Faculty of Medicine, however, the concept of separation met with much hostility. The Academic Board of the University of Wales, the university's supreme advisory body on academic matters, resolved (with the two medical school representatives, Professors Brown and Kennedy dissenting) that 'on academic and educational grounds' the Welsh National School of Medicine should continue to be part of 'a constituent college providing teaching and carrying on research in other than medical subjects'.[21] As far as the Senate of University College, Cardiff was concerned, if the existing administrative arrangements for governing the medical school were unnecessarily cumbersome, the remedy was simple; the school should be fully integrated in the college, like the other faculties.[22] The professor of botany at Cardiff, R. C. McLean thought that the medics were being selfish. The college had created the school and had carried it forward 'at a cost of much sacrifice by other departments'. The whole institution was organically one and should continue to be so.[23] Mabel Howell, one of Cardiff's leading lay members, and a member of the Board of Medicine, was able to refer to a letter she had received from Dr J. Kay Jamieson, dean of medicine at Leeds University. He had dismissed those seeking independence for the Welsh National School of Medicine as motivated simply by 'vanity'. In his medical school

> We attach the highest value to the fact that we work in association with the members engaged in the fundamental sciences and even in departments very remote from medicine, such as the leather and agricultural departments, in which there are problems common to them and the medical faculty.[24]

The difference, of course, between Leeds and Cardiff was that the former did not have a wider national dimension to grapple with, but it came as little surprise that the Council of University College, Cardiff on 13 June 1924 voted, with three dissentients, to oppose the separation of the medical school. This position was confirmed by the Court of the college, a month later, by a vote of fifty-nine to nine, after what the *Western Mail* reporter called a good-tempered debate.[25] The most powerful speech in favour of separation came from Percy Watkins, one-time registrar of the college, who said that any attempt to graft a national on to a local institution was doomed to failure, akin to making the National Museum of Wales an integral part of the administration of the Cardiff City Council (a comparison against which Lord Pontypridd uttered what the reporter described as 'a mild protest'). Undoubtedly the most powerful spokesman against separation was Sir Isambard Owen, who, to the surprise of those who only recalled his evidence to the Haldane Commission and not his subsequent backtracking, urged the college to fight hard to maintain its position. Eleven days later, the college authorities informed the Privy Council of their considered position, and resubmitted a draft charter for the college which incorporated the medical school firmly within it.

THE UNIVERSITY OF WALES JOINS THE FRAY

For over a year, the University Council had managed to escape involvement in the controversy, arguing that it needed to have the formal views of University College, Cardiff before it could deal with the matter. The Council could no longer bury its head in the sand; it now knew where Cardiff stood, and moreover the Privy Council sent the college's response to the university for comment. At its meeting on 25 September 1924, the Council decided to set up a high-powered committee to consider the arguments for and against separation, chaired by Lord Kenyon and including the principals of the four constituent colleges of the university, together with Alderman William George and Professor Joseph Jones, lecturer in New Testament Greek and exegesis at the Brecon Memorial College. The only condition imposed upon the committee by the Council was that, if the committee concluded that independence was the best solution, the medical school had to be a constituent 'school', not a 'college', within the federal university. The committee did a thorough job in the time available, commissioning individual members to prepare papers on the main issues at stake. Sir Harry Reichel, Bangor's principal, was charged with the task of drafting a possible charter for an independent medical school. As an independent medical school would not be granted parity of status with the other constituent institutions, it would be inappropriate for the title 'principal' to be conferred on the chief executive of the medical school. Another title was needed, and Reichel, for no recorded reason, settled on the designation of 'provost'. There is no evidence to suggest that the views of senior members of the medical school were canvassed on this, or indeed on any matter being discussed by the special committee.

The committee met on three occasions,[26] and, by a vote of three to two (the minority consisting of Principal Trow and Professor Jones), reached the conclusion that 'Complete independence of the School as a School of the University is the only satisfactory solution.' Apart from this being the best solution in terms of the school's national dimension, the report noted how, during the previous three years, the balance of the medical school's finances had shifted from the Cardiff College to the university, indicating 'the necessity of shifting the control, and points inevitably in the direction of giving the school a status independent of the College'. As far as some of the practical implications of separation were concerned, 'It is maintained that the question of endowments presents no serious difficulty and that the allocation of buildings, though it will undoubtedly be troublesome at first, presents no difficulties that are insuperable or likely to be permanent.' By a vote of ten to four (with one abstention) the University Council, at its meeting on 10 December 1924, decided to adopt the report of its special committee, and to inform the Privy Council that in its opinion 'The National School of the University be constituted as a School of the University.'

Sir Maurice Hankey, who had succeeded Sir Almeric Fitzroy as clerk to the Privy Council in 1923, formally advised the lord president of the Council (Lord Parmoor) that the University Council's conclusion be endorsed. Hankey had received a strong letter of support from the UGC, a comprehensive briefing from his deputy, Colin Smith, and had discussed the matter with Thomas Jones in the Cabinet Office, 'who has an exceptional knowledge of Welsh University matters, and was in close touch with Mr Lloyd George when the Welsh National School of Medicine was taking shape'. In Hankey's opinion,

> In following this course we shall have behind us the Board of Education, the University Grants Committee, the Majority Report of the Council of the Welsh University, to say nothing of the School of Medicine itself and *The Lancet*. The only opposition is the interested opposition of the Cardiff College.[27]

Meanwhile, back in Cardiff, a war of words between supporters and opponents of the proposal broke out in the local press. The most persuasive contribution from the opponents of separation came from Dr George Adami, vice-chancellor of Liverpool University, who argued that the proposal to separate the Welsh National School of Medicine from its Cardiff parent was quite contrary to current thinking: 'Throughout the English-speaking world for the last fifty years and more the movement has been most pronounced in the direction of fusing hitherto independent and autonomous schools of medicine into the university.' He cited Manchester, Liverpool and Leeds as examples in the United Kingdom, McGill University in Canada, and Sydney, Melbourne and Brisbane in Australia: 'Indeed in none of the Dominions is there nowadays a Medical School that is not intimately associated with a University.'[28]

However, as a writer in the *British Medical Journal* wearily observed, 'One story is good until another is told.'[29]

What Adami chose not to admit was that the position in Wales, because of the wider national dimension, was not strictly analogous to the relationship between an English medical school and its associated university. Sir Charles Sherrington, president of the Royal Society, professor of physiology at Oxford (and previously Professor Graham Brown's chief at Liverpool), was rather better informed in this matter. He had served as an external examiner in Cardiff and had been a good friend of the medical school for many years. He denied that what was being proposed was 'separation' at all in the way that Adami and others claimed. The Welsh National School of Medicine would be linked to the whole academic community of Wales, while retaining close links with Cardiff. Under the proposed arrangements the medical school 'will carry on its work in complete harmony with the University College at Cardiff, functioning, however, as a unit of the university rather than as a department of a constituent college'. Furthermore,

> The University of Wales occupies a unique position among the universities of Great Britain, not only on account of its federal character but also by reason of the fact that it is a national university in a sense which is not true of any other British university. It is a single expression of the ideals and aspirations of a whole nation.[30]

On 28 February 1925, readers of the *South Wales News* were greeted with the bold headline 'DECISION AT LAST', over an account of a meeting of the University of Wales Council held (as they often were in those days) in London on the previous day. At the meeting Lord Kenyon had presented a letter from the Privy Council stating that their lordships had decided, in the light of all the evidence, that the Welsh National School of Medicine should be constituted as a school of the university. They believed that the Cardiff College's scheme, submitted the previous July was 'not one which offers any reasonable prospect of providing adequately for the unfettered development of the School as a national centre of advanced medical education and research'. While the newspaper acknowledged that the college would not welcome the Privy Council's verdict, it did reflect majority Welsh opinion:

> We trust, therefore that the decision will be accepted with good grace and instead of attempting to prolong the controversy, all concerned should make an effort to ensure that the progress and success of the School are promoted without injury, loss or inconvenience to the College.

Sir George Newman, who was still following the fortunes of the Welsh National School of Medicine with interest, congratulated Colin Smith on the Privy Council's decision, adding, however, 'that a little bird tells me that they [the Cardiff College] propose to disregard your letter. If they do, what action do you propose to take? Like you, I am getting very weary of the continual vacillations and monkey tricks down at Cardiff'. In reply, Smith said that they just had to persevere, admitting that, in reality, it was 'by no means easy to impose the will of the Privy Council upon a recalcitrant body'.[31]

Sir George's 'little bird' had been well informed. First the Council, then the Court of University College, Cardiff rejected the verdict of the Privy Council, only three members of the Court voting in support, at its meeting on 4 June 1925. Faced with such intransigence the University Council had no alternative but to arrange for a special meeting of the University Court to be held in the autumn to settle the constitutional status of the Welsh National School of Medicine, once and for all. Or so it was hoped.

Meanwhile, the local authorities were becoming restive. It will be recalled that by the end of 1924 agreement had been reached with all the local authorities of Wales that they would contribute one-eighth of a penny rate towards the income of the medical school. However, this commitment was fragile and already, on 25 March 1925, the Swansea town council had suspended payment because of the resistance of the Cardiff College to the secession of the medical school. In the view of the *British Medical Journal*, 'It seems likely that the rest of Wales will follow Swansea's lead – no national school, no national contributions,'[32] and within a matter of weeks Breconshire became the second authority to suspend its contribution. Merthyr Tydfil and, more seriously, Wales's largest local authority, the Glamorgan County Council, came out publicly in support of the separationist camp, its chairman, Alderman William Jenkins warning of the financial disaster which would envelop a Welsh National School of Medicine which, if linked to the Cardiff College, would be denied not only local authority support, but that of the Treasury too.[33]

None of this dampened the resolve of the Cardiff authorities. Indeed, hints were beginning to surface that some among them, frustrated by the attitude of the university authorities, were giving serious thought to leaving the university and setting up as a university in its own right. A reporter for the *South Wales News* had, in February, noted a feeling among some partisans of the college that 'Cardiff should strike out on its own and separate itself from the federal University of Wales.'[34] Speaking to the Cardiff Rotarians at the end of June, Principal Trow went so far as to assert that the college was already a university in all but name, adding his opinion that the day was not far distant when the city would have a university of its own.[35] This sort of thing was often said when the college and university authorities fell out, but Captain David Brynmor Anthony (1886–1966), who had succeeded Mortimer Angus as university registrar in 1921, was sufficiently alarmed to seek the views of his predecessor. Angus shared Anthony's concern:

> I quite agree with what you say as to the breaking up of the University. It will be a great pity if Cardiff secedes and I don't think it's quite fair for Cardiff to entertain the

idea now. It has obtained much that it wanted by the new Charter and having been a party in promoting it, it should honourably abide by the conditions laid down, at least till the new state of things has been fairly tried. I think it not only unwise but dishonourable to talk of further independence. But to say so might only tend to widen the rift.

However, even if Cardiff was determined to secede, it could not expect to take the medical school with it. 'I don't think Cardiff can fairly claim to retain a National institution if it becomes a local University.'[36]

THE UNIVERSITY COURT DELIVERS ITS VERDICT

The university authorities approached the special meeting of the University Court, scheduled for 16 October 1925, with some nervousness. Not trusting the university to present their case adequately the Cardiff authorities sent a comprehensive, if partisan, dossier to all members of the Court beforehand.[37] Appended to a covering letter from the principal were the replies of the college to various letters from the Privy Council, the college's own constitutional proposals for the status of the medical school, selective academic views about the dangers of separation, a statement claiming to demonstrate the substantial additional costs associated with separation and, finally, the well-thumbed statement by the vice-chancellor of Liverpool University. The dossier contained nothing new, and its presentation of the views of the Faculty of Medicine was brief and misleading: 'The Faculty of Medicine has indeed voted for separation, but the difference of opinion within the Faculty is acute.'

It was vital that the university case was well presented at the meeting. The original plan was to get Alderman William Jenkins to propose the separatist motion, but he thought that a north Wales member of the Court would be better. So Alderman William George, David Lloyd George's brother, was asked to take on the task. George was a substantial figure in the public affairs of Wales. He was chairman of the Caernarfonshire Education Committee and of the Central Welsh Board (the body responsible for the examination arrangements in Welsh schools), a passionate defender of Welsh life and culture, and surely the ideal person to promote the claims of the medical school as a great national institution. William George agreed, though he had some concerns:

I am still of opinion that it is in the interests of the School it should be independent of the College. It is difficult to see how otherwise it could be regarded as a National School. But an equally important consideration, I think, is that the School should be conducted in the National Spirit – and from everything that I can gather this is not now the case. According to all accounts, the doctors in charge of this institution at present quarrel together like cats and dogs, and I for one have not much stomach for a fight to give greater powers of control to fellows who are apparently unable to control themselves. Cannot something be done to remove this personal equation out of the question? The other point I have in mind is with reference to the S.W. College. I must confess to an uneasy feeling that we as a council have not done as much as we might to meet the difficulties and to soothe the *amour propre* of the College authorities in reference to this matter.[38]

William George had, a few days earlier, read in the *Western Mail*, a paper he only very occasionally saw, about a public argument that had broken out between Mitchell Stevens and the medical school and Cardiff College authorities, and which had led Alderman George to conclude 'that things are apparently getting from bad to worse with the Medical School'.[39] The nature of this argument will be examined in the next chapter. What is important now is to note that the university registrar, in a series of persuasive letters, managed to allay William George's main concerns, assuring him that the squabbles among members of the medical school were not as bad as they appeared, and setting out, very effectively, the main arguments in favour of separation.[40]

To some, however, the time for argument was already at an end. Writing to Captain Anthony, Lord Kenyon reported: 'I have seen Kidd [secretary to the UGC] today. He said argument is quite useless as the Govt. has made up its mind to have a separate School.'[41] Nevertheless, whatever the government may have been saying behind the scenes, the stage was set for what the *South Wales News*, on 16 October, the day of the Court meeting, proclaimed as 'a first-class Welsh contest, one which promises (or threatens) to be the keenest in the academic annals of Wales'. After passing a resolution to send hearty greetings to the university chancellor, the Prince of Wales, on his return from visits to South America and South Africa, the Court received an important communication from Sir William Diamond, chairman of the Board of Management of the Cardiff Royal Infirmary, who was unable to attend the meeting in person. He confirmed the hospital's support 'for some form of separation which would enable the School to free itself from the cumbersome machinery which had been set up'. He emphasized the importance of co-operation and smooth working between the authorities of the school and the hospital: 'Under existing arrangements this is, in my opinion, impossible.' The fact was that, during the months and years leading up to the meeting of the Court, virtually nothing had been heard from the hospital authorities concerning the constitutional position of the school, about which the hospital was, in essence, indifferent. Indeed, Mitchell Stevens would later claim that Lord Kenyon had persuaded Sir William Diamond to write at the last minute, and without the authority of the hospital, in order that his letter would create the maximum impact at the meeting.[42]

William George then proposed the motion, that the Court:

Is of the opinion that, with a view to providing for the full development of the School of Medicine as a national centre for medical education and research in Wales, the best interests of the School will be served by constituting it an independent School in the University. The University Court therefore hereby resolves, on the recommendation of the University Council, to submit a humble petition to His Majesty in Council for a Charter incorporating the School as an independent School of the University of Wales.

In a conciliatory speech he acknowledged that in its own proposals University College, Cardiff was seeking to reflect the national dimension of the school, but he believed that the University Council's approach was more likely to achieve that objective. He was also mindful of the serious financial consequences for the school if separation was not agreed. The motion was seconded by Alderman Frank Treharne James of Merthyr Tydfil, solicitor and art connoisseur, but who, by his own admission, was not an expert on higher education, notwithstanding the fact that his daughter Alice was the wife of the great Sir Thomas Lewis. In agreeing to participate he had confessed to the university registrar: 'I should have thought that Lord Kenyon would have found someone with a more intimate knowledge of the working of the Cardiff and South Wales University College and University affairs generally than myself.'[43] He was, however, prominent in Welsh public life and, as a governor of both the National Library and the National Museum of Wales (where his bust, by Sir William Goscombe John, may be seen), he had a good appreciation of what the all-Wales dimension meant.

Principal Trow and Sir Isambard Owen led those opposing the motion. Trow's contribution was particularly animated. Having deployed the usual academic arguments, he pursued another line of attack. What was being proposed by the university, he claimed, 'put bluntly, was confiscation of a part of the property of Cardiff College, the appropriation of the whole of moral property in the reputation of the School and of certain trust funds now vested in the College'.

It is worth pausing at this point, to ponder the force of Principal Trow's words, for as if in desperation, all other arguments having failed, he was advancing an argument which had not been deployed as strongly as perhaps it should have been. As we have seen, during the many months of debate that had preceded this historic meeting of the University Court, the issue had, it is fair to say, mainly revolved around the main contestants' view about the best way to provide medical education in the principality. Those favouring separation had argued that independence would not only be good for medical education but also for University College, Cardiff, which had enough on its agenda already, coping with the other disciplines. Separation would entail the disentanglement of some assets, but that could be sorted out, given good will on all sides. Those taking the side of the college argued the educational benefits of having medical education given in a multi-faculty environment, as happened elsewhere.

There was no reason why a subject like medicine, which had an all-Wales dimension, could not be taught from one of the constituent colleges of the university; after all, there was only one school of law, and that was part of Aberystwyth. However, Principal Trow and others were also infuriated by what they viewed as the sheer unfairness of the situation. Not only was Cardiff being expected to forgo an activity which it had itself set up and nourished; it was also being expected to surrender some of its physical and financial assets in a process which the college's memorandum to the Court described as 'the dismemberment and spoliation of [the university's] largest and most prosperous College'. The minutes of the University Council during 1926/7 demonstrate the dominant position of Cardiff among the Welsh colleges at that time. Of the Cardiff College's income, nearly 29 per cent (over £25,000) was associated with the Welsh National School of Medicine, and nearly 19 per cent of the undergraduates were medical students. It was little wonder that Principal Trow was so passionate in his defence of the college's interests when he addressed the University Court.

Table 7.1 College incomes and student numbers

	Estimates of income	Undergraduate students
Aberystwyth	£57,429	537
Bangor	£46,798	364
Cardiff	£88,065	780
Swansea	£45,471	341

Of the other speeches for and against the motion the most important was that by William Sheen. He was able to refute an allegation which had been disseminated by the Cardiff authorities that the medical school was seriously upset that the university was planning to downgrade the proposed institution from 'constituent College' to 'School'. As far as he was concerned, separation was the important thing, separation from a college which had never really welcomed the medical school's presence. Though he held Principal Trow in high regard, he did not think it possible for him to be an effective head of the medical school, given all his other onerous duties.

Before the main resolution was put to the meeting, Professor Joseph Jones of the Brecon Memorial College, and a leading layman on the Cardiff College Council, moved an amendment that a final vote be deferred while discussions continued. Professor Lyle Cummins spoke against this delaying tactic, but it was a measure of the unease that many members of the Court felt that the amendment was only narrowly defeated, by a vote of sixty-two to fifty-four. Then came the substantive motion, which was carried by a vote of seventy-one to forty-one, the margin of victory no doubt influenced by William George's assurance that the principle of separation was that day's issue, with the fine detail left for separate agreement. Indeed, on the motion of

Lleufer Thomas, the Court's final act was to agree that the University and Cardiff Councils should meet to deal with the necessary paperwork.[44]

A few days after the meeting, Alderman Frank James wrote a private letter to his son-in-law. Sir Thomas Lewis had been a consistent supporter of independence for the Welsh National School of Medicine since before its establishment in 1921, warning Sir George Newman, in March of that year, that 'No local body of men could be sufficiently acquainted with the modern needs of medical education to conduct a new school upon lines along which it would develop soundly.'[45] He had refused an invitation to represent the University of Wales on the Board of Medicine because he was out of sympathy with the constitutional arrangements then in place,[46] and, a few days before the crucial meeting of the University Court, he had made, in the *Western Mail*, an impassioned appeal in support of an independent medical school: 'Unfetter this child of the College.'[47] Alderman James's purpose in writing was to offer Sir Thomas, on behalf of Lord Kenyon, the position of principal of the Welsh National School of Medicine: 'You would be able to continue your research work and would not be tied down to delivering lectures etc; in fact, you would have a free hand.'[48] Whom Lord Kenyon had consulted before allowing this offer to be made is not known. What is known is Lewis's response, briefly noted at the head of James's letter: 'Saw Kenyon and refused, Nov. 1925.'

CARDIFF REMAINS DEFIANT

The *Western Mail* welcomed the Court's decision, and hoped that all the wrangling was now over:

> The vast number of Welsh people who are keenly interested in the educational affairs of the Principality will, we are sure, be practically unanimous in hoping that the prolonged controversy regarding the status of the National Medical School in Cardiff will be ended by the decision of the University Court.[49]

Opinion throughout Wales, as recorded in the columns of the newspaper in the days that followed, was positive. *The Lancet* was equally content: 'We are of opinion that only by the constitution proposed by the University of Wales will the School undergo proper development and become not only a national, but an international institution for medical education and research.'[50]

However, the *South Wales News* took a different view entirely: 'The decision of the University Court in favour of separation of the Medical School from the Cardiff College cannot be accepted as final. It must be resisted by every possible means.'[51] And this is precisely what the Cardiff authorities proceeded to do. Far from acting in such a way as to ease the process of separation, within days of the University Court's resolution the College Senate decided that henceforth it, rather than the Faculty of Medicine, would be responsible for appointing internal examiners in the departments of anatomy and physiology. Graham Brown, still dean of the medical faculty, wrote in despair to Sir Thomas Lewis, urging him to raise the matter with Lord Kenyon. Lewis, though unwilling to become its principal, remained interested in the school's welfare and duly wrote to Kenyon: 'This transference of power may not itself be important, though it obviously forms a slight to the Faculty. Its importance lies in its clearly indicating the line which the College proposes to pursue. It is an unprovoked move and clearly has a political purpose behind it'. 'I had heard of this latest irritant,' Kenyon wearily replied. 'I have no illusion that the College will accept defeat.'[52]

This was just as well for, in two joint conferences with representatives of the University Council, during the early months of 1926 the Cardiff authorities steadfastly refused to contemplate the medical school's secession. Their only concession was to propose that the head of the school, whether designated provost, warden or master, should be a permanent appointment, thereby relieving the college principal of a great deal of heavy work. For as Trow sourly observed, 'The medical school gave him more work than the rest of the college put together.'[53] Under no circumstances however would the head of the medical school be responsible for the departments of anatomy and physiology.

At its meeting on 11 April 1926, the University Council, frustrated by the attitude of the Cardiff College, decided to proceed with drafting a Petition and Charter for the establishment of an independent school of medicine for submission to the Privy Council. Jenkin James, the university secretary, wrote to A. H. Kidd, for advice on presentation. Kidd's reply provides further evidence of Whitehall's determination to see the establishment of an independent Welsh National School of Medicine:

> I am very glad to hear that you are now able to go ahead with the preparation of a Petition and Draft Charter. It is clear that there is no use in continuing negotiations with people who have no intention of meeting you on any essential point, and that the time has come to bring things to a definite issue …
>
> As regards Petition Mr Colin Smith [Privy Council] could not provide me with anything of real value … He agreed with me that your Petition should set out plainly and forcibly the history of the matter which has led to the deadlock; this is the kind of thing that Mr Bruce would do admirably if you can get him to take it in hand. The main emphasis would, I suppose, be laid on the desire for a really National School, and the proved impossibility of devising any scheme of government that will give the School a fair chance except on some independent lines as the University is now proposing. This has been the burden of practically every official utterance on the subject from the Report of the Departmental Committee in 1914 onwards, and the University Court, representing the interests of Wales as a whole, has now declared unmistakeably in the same sense. I should think that the Petition might fairly touch

on the financial relation of the School to the central University authority, and to the harmful effect of the present uncertainty upon the School's work and prestige.[54]

Whether or not the school's work and reputation was suffering, there is no doubt that its funding was being harmed by the 'present uncertainty'. The payment by the UGC of £5,000 a year, dependent on the committee's approval of the school's status, was as far off as ever, and at its meeting in May, the University Finance Committee reported that five local authorities were now withholding their annual contributions to the school (Breconshire, Cardiganshire, Monmouthshire, Radnorshire and Swansea). Unabashed, the June meeting of the Cardiff College Council passed a revised version of Article XIV of its draft charter. It proposed that the Welsh National School of Medicine 'shall be a distinct unit of the College', under 'the immediate academic and administrative supervision called the Master/Warden/Provost'. The ownership of the land, buildings and equipment 'shall remain vested in the College', and 'The Council of the College shall continue the administration of all its trusts and endowments, both present and future, without diminution or reservations.' Furthermore, the second clause of Article XIV specifically excluded the departments of anatomy and physiology from membership of the medical school. The draft charter was, of course, intended as a blueprint for the future. However, at its meeting on 9 July the College Council took a decision of more immediate significance; henceforth the departments of anatomy and physiology would, for administrative purposes, be put under the aegis of the college's Faculty of Science. While the heads of the two departments would, as we shall see, continue to involve themselves in the affairs of the Faculty of Medicine (indeed, Professor Graham Brown greatly resented the college's action), the determination of the college to keep a firm grip on the two departments was forcefully underlined.

Meanwhile, the drafting committee set up by the University Council got on with its task, meeting on four occasions between April and October 1926 (Principal Trow withdrawing from membership at an early stage).[55] Using as a starting-point Sir Harry Reichel's draft constitution for an independent school of medicine drawn up in the autumn of 1924, the committee sought advice not only from bodies directly interested, such as the Faculty of Medicine, the Cardiff Senate and the University Academic Board, but also from outside experts. The committee was particularly interested in three issues.

The first was whether the honorary clinical staff of the infirmary should be represented on what was being proposed as the supreme academic body of the school, the Professorial Board. Neither the Cardiff Senate nor the Academic Board had an opinion on the matter, but the Faculty of Medicine, some of whose members were, as we shall see later, in dispute with their hospital colleagues, were not in favour of their inclusion. While two of the external experts consulted, Sir Humphrey Rolleston, president of the Royal College of Physicians, and Sir John Rose Bradford, senior physician at

University College Hospital, believed that liberal representation should be given to the hospital clinicians, Sir Charles Sherrington took the side of the faculty, arguing that school business would be discharged more efficiently if the board consisted of heads of departments, 'undiluted with other teachers less directly cognizant of and responsible for laboratory direction'.

The second issue related to the danger, as some perceived it, of an independent medical school deciding to set up its own basic science departments (chemistry, physics, botany, zoology) in wasteful duplication of what already existed at University College, Cardiff. While the Cardiff Senate saw the danger, no one else did. As the Faculty of Medicine commented, all that was needed was a clause in the charter forbidding such a development 'so long as adequate provision for such courses of instruction is made by the University College of South Wales and Monmouthshire'.

The third, and by far the most important issue concerned the position of the Departments of Anatomy and Physiology. Though by no means conceding the possibility of an independent medical school, the authorities of the Cardiff College were adamant that under no circumstances could these two departments be detached from the college. The views of the external experts initially consulted by the university diverged, much to the embarrassment of Lord Kenyon, as he admitted to Sir Thomas Lewis:

> I am afraid that in calling in Rose Bradford [we] called in the wrong man and he seemed to me to be rather out of date. Anyway, the suggestions he made did not please Graham Brown and Co. I asked him what position he would assign to Anatomy and Physiology in the School of Medicine ... His reply was that they should be in the College. This, of course, upsets all our schemes and gives immense pleasure to Cardiff. I therefore got the Committee, and the Council eventually, to agree that we should ask three physiological experts, Sir Walter Fletcher, Sir Charles Sherrington and Dr Pearce of the Rockefeller Trust. I have not much doubt what their answer will be.[56]

As expected, these three, and others consulted by the university, Sir Berkley Moynihan, president of the Royal College of Surgeons of England, Sir George Newman and Sir Donald MacAlister, president of the GMC, all provided the answer sought by the university, Sir Donald going so far as to say: 'If the National School of Medicine does *not* include Departments of Anatomy and Physiology as integral parts of its equipment, the General Medical Council will be moved to oppose the Charter before the Privy Council.' It is worth giving a flavour of some of the other replies as they give a good indication of contemporary thinking about the place of the preclinical disciplines within universities. In Sir Charles Sherrington's view:

The interrelation between, on the one hand, Anatomy and Physiology, and, on the other hand, the further studies of the Medical course naturally embraced in the School of Medicine is so close that any circumstance which tends to prejudice their prosecution alongside one of another is to the disadvantage of the student and to the detriment of the School as a seat of medical education, learning and science. It is true that the above referred to 'further subjects' of the medical curriculum are, by universal custom based on long experience, taken by the student subsequently to his entering on Anatomy and Physiology. This fact is, however, no cogent argument for placing the study of these latter two subjects outside the School itself. The sequence of the curriculum from Anatomy and Physiology onward to the other studies of the School is but the natural outcome and expression of the fact that those other subjects of the curriculum are properly intelligible only after some knowledge of these two has been acquired. This very circumstance of itself instances the close intimacy, both in theory and practice, binding these subjects with the rest.

For Sherrington, the presence of anatomy and physiology within the medical school also benefited the other subjects with which they naturally interrelated: 'The prosperity of the School as a seat of activity pursuing the rapid advances of Medical Science' could only be enhanced by the inclusion of the preclinical subjects within the school.

Given his well-known interest in fostering the closest possible partnership between the laboratory and the clinic, it was not surprising that Richard Pearce, medical director of the Rockefeller Foundation, favoured the inclusion of anatomy and physiology within the medical school: 'It is only by such an arrangement that common interest of laboratory and clinical men, closely associated in one group, can be brought to bear on the important problem of medical teaching, research and practice.' Sir Walter Morley Fletcher concurred:

Anatomy and Physiology are not to be regarded only as sciences which are a necessary preliminary to medicine, and useful only to the student at an early stage. They are this, but they should be much more besides. At every stage in his professional education, whether in Pathology or in Clinical Surgery or Medicine, the student should be kept in close touch with those sciences and especially with the experimental study of function provided in Physiology. It is the experience of all progressive schools in England and America, and especially during the years which have followed the war, that continuous co-operation and intercourse is highly desirable between the clinician and the physiologist, whether in the work of the teachers or in that of the students. A student cannot intelligently follow the modern developments of scientific Clinical Medicine and Surgery without continual reference to the underlying Anatomical and Physiological principles.

Fletcher acknowledged that anatomy, and particularly physiology were important scientific disciplines in their own right, with close affinities with the other natural sciences. These could be sustained by 'appropriate representation of these departments in the Faculty of Science, without any prejudice to their position in the School of Medicine', an arrangement which worked well in Cambridge.[57]

In the light of all the evidence, the university's drafting committee produced a petition and draft charter that proposed the establishment of an independent Welsh National School of Medicine, including departments of anatomy and physiology, but which would 'not conduct courses of instruction in the Pure Science subjects of Chemistry, Physics, Botany and Zoology'. There would be no representation of the recognized clinical teachers of the infirmary on the Professorial Board. However, the draft charter proposed the establishment of two faculties within the medical school, of pure medical science and of applied medical science, and left it to statutes to determine the composition of these bodies. At its meeting on 11 December 1926, the University Council resolved to submit the petition and draft charter, together with the Cardiff College's revised Article XIV, to a special meeting of the University Court, to be held on 14 February 1927.

On the day before the meeting the *Western Mail* published a letter from Sir Isambard Owen to Principal Trow, regretting that he would not be present at the Court as he was in Paris visiting his sick daughter. He repeated his oft-stated arguments against separation in general (including the harmful effects on medical students, divorced from the other college students), and, in particular the separation of the preclinical subjects from the basic sciences: 'I should be sorry to see a great and growing science like physiology, the importance of which to public policy is beginning to be recognised, relegated in Wales to the position of a subordinate department of a professional school.'[58]

At the meeting of the Court, W. N. Bruce, the proposer of the motion in favour of separation, dismissed Owen's intervention. As far as he was aware, the relations between the medical students and the others were not particularly close at the present time; what was important to the medical students was the best possible education, which was what the university's proposals aimed to achieve. Alderman George, seconding the motion, confessed to being influenced by the weight of expert opinion. No one else was called upon to speak in favour of the motion, not even Professor Sheen, who by now had become dean of medicine. Perhaps the university authorities were confident of success without a contribution from him. This was before Principal Trow, in the words of the *Western Mail* reporter, 'sprung upon the Court a series of replies by eminent counsel [to legal points put to him by the college authorities] that compelled everyone present, as it were, to "sit up and listen"'.

First, counsel (Mr Alexander Grant KC) asserted that the university was not empowered by its charter to become a teaching as well as an examining body, which would be its role if the medical school became directly responsible to it. Secondly (and this is when the audience really began to sit up) the university was not entitled to confiscate the rights and property of the Cardiff College, which would be the effect of the university's proposal. In the view of counsel, 'No power or authority whatever existing, is authorised to carry out the suggested scheme, except, of course, that Parliament, being under the British Constitution omnipotent, could, if it so pleased, take anything from anybody.' Thirdly, bearing in mind that some of the funding of the federal university came from the Cardiff College, the college would be within its rights to take out an injunction against the university to prevent it from acting against Cardiff's interests. Principal Trow assured members of the Court that his college had every intention of going to law to protect its interests in this matter. Despite the intervention of the vice-chancellor, Sir Harry Reichel, who said that the GMC would oppose Cardiff's own proposal, and a plea from the Privy Council (in a letter to Lord Kenyon) that there should be no further delay, Principal Trow's amendment to the motion, that the proposal be referred back to the University Council for further consideration, was narrowly carried, by fifty-three to forty-eight votes. In the words of Professor Gwynn Williams, 'The Court had wavered because it had little time to digest the legal opinion with which it had been starkly confronted.'[59] As far as Lord Kenyon was concerned, the result was 'most annoying and disappointing'.[60]

The Privy Council despaired at the situation. A few days after the meeting, Colin Smith wrote privately to Lord Kenyon, thanking him for the press cuttings which made 'decidedly unpleasant reading'. The barrister's views on the legality of what the University was trying to do gave real cause for concern:

> If Alexander Grant's opinion is correct nothing but an Act of Parliament would meet the difficulty. I do not know how far this aspect of the matter has been put before the Standing Counsel of the University of Wales, but if he has not yet been asked to consider this point his opinion should, in my view, be sought, for it would be necessary for us at the Privy Council to take the opinion of the Law Officers upon any draft Charter upon the validity of which doubts have been cast by an eminent legal authority.[61]

Principal Trow, however, who had led the defence of Cardiff's interests with much skill, was elated by the outcome. One of his first actions was to write to Sir Isambard Owen, thanking him for his invaluable support and expressing optimism about the eventual outcome:

The decision was a narrow one – a majority of five only (53 to 48) – but Counsel's opinion is very strong and is completely consistent with the view that you, and I too, have held for a long time and must carry weight further afield. The University will no doubt seek Counsel's opinion on their own account and if that agrees with the one already to hand, we shall be in a much stronger position and I cannot but believe that we shall ultimately arrive at a decision which will prove acceptable, if not agreeable to both parties.[62]

Sadly, Sir Isambard never saw this letter, for on the very day of the meeting of the Court he suffered a stroke at his daughter's home in Paris, and within a few hours he was dead. The worlds of medicine and of higher education were shocked. Tributes were immediately spoken or written about his great contributions to public life, though those appearing in the *British Medical Journal* and *The Lancet* disappointingly dwelt more on his impact on the university's early years than on his ongoing contributions to the University of Wales and its medical school. The *Western Mail* was more balanced, and Principal Trow's own tribute was particularly generous in relation to Owen's recent involvement in the affairs of the University:

It is eminently noteworthy that as he first attained fame in Wales as an administrator in the sphere of higher education, so also his very last effort appears to have been in his attempt to lead Wales in the right path in a sphere where his expert guidance was much needed. In addition to the letter published in the *Western Mail* last week, I received from him last Friday, addressed to the meeting-place of the Court, Shrewsbury, a letter on the same question, written with no sign of impending failure, in his clear and careful style, which I shall preserve as a memorial of his life-long fidelity to the best interests of Wales.[63]

Sir Isambard Owen was a man of great stature, who had made a major impact on the development of medical education in Wales. He had been involved in every significant milestone in the early history of the Cardiff Medical School from the 1890s to the 1920s. He had played his part in the initial fund-raising efforts and in advising on the establishment of the chairs of anatomy and physiology; in the securing of medical degree-awarding powers by the university during the Edwardian period; in determining the location of the Institute of Physiology in close proximity to the hospital; and there can be no doubt that his advice to the Haldane Commission was crucial in setting the school on the road to independence. He set in motion a train of thought that could never be completely contained, despite his own later efforts to convince people that he had been misunderstood. Though it is doubtful, Trow's kindly comments notwithstanding, that Owen's opposition to separation was ever decisively influential, bearing in mind the equally eminent voices on the other side of the argument, he deserves much credit for staying in the fray to the end, and retaining the respect of all sides: 'What a splendid life!' wrote Principal Trow. 'How enviable a death! To be called to the other side while still in harness and pulling his full weight.'

THE SEARCH FOR A COMPROMISE SOLUTION

For several months the impasse between the college and university authorities continued, with one, and then another joint meeting failing to achieve a breakthrough. Only towards the end of July did the first signs of compromise emerge. Before the meeting of the University Court at Aberystwyth were proposals from Cardiff which seemed to offer, in the words of Captain Anthony, 'a happy solution to the Medical School problem'.[64] In essence, the college was still insisting that the Departments of Anatomy and Physiology should be located within its own Faculty of Science, but proposed that the heads of those departments be 'neutralized' by becoming Crown appointments akin to the regius professorships in Oxford and Cambridge. Cardiff 'would put no obstacle in the way of the constitution of the Clinical Departments as a separate School of Medicine under a Charter of their own'. Arrangements would be made to ensure effective liaison between the two institutions. The Court was only too glad to allow the various parties to work out the details and report back in the autumn.

A number of factors contributed to a softening of attitudes. The university authorities had sought the views of their own lawyers on the opinion of Mr Alexander Grant, and the fact that they were never made public suggests that the legal position of University College, Cardiff was stronger than the university had hoped or expected. The law officers of the Crown, whose views Lord Kenyon regarded as crucial, clearly took the same view.[65] The serious illness of Lord Kenyon, shortly after the July meeting of the University Council, was a blessing in disguise. Although the pro-chancellor had been a consistent advocate of independence for the Welsh National School of Medicine, he had continued to enjoy respect from all sections of the higher education community for his fairness in conducting the often difficult affairs of the university. However, there is evidence to suggest that his prominent role in the dispute over the medical school was now becoming a wasted asset. He was coming under attack in the editorials of the *Western Mail* as a partisan north Walian, 'employing preposterously specious' arguments in an underhand way,[66] and he was beginning to react badly to criticism. He was particularly upset by editorials in the *South Wales News*, which seemed to impugn his impartiality in chairing business, and he wrote a letter of complaint to the editor. The reply of T. A. Davies was, or ought to have been, disarming:

> Your services to Wales in so many spheres are such that we hesitate to differ from you on any question. On the subject of the Medical School we are forced to be at vari-

ance, but it is far from our desire to introduce any personal consideration into the discussion.

This was not good enough for Lord Kenyon, as he complained to the University registrar: 'I am not thin skinned but I resent being accused of partiality in the Chair for the advantage of the side I happen to favour.' He wanted the matter raised at the meeting of the Court, but not by him.[67] In the event he was absent and nothing was said. Lord Kenyon was only sixty-two when he eventually died in November 1927, and Sir Harry Reichel later expressed his opinion that Kenyon had been worn out by the 'acrimonious vehemence with which the *perfervidum ingenium Celtorum* is apt to pursue controversies'.[68] His enforced retirement from the fray at a critical time in the negotiations may well have eased the process.

Although Principal Trow had demonstrated a dogged stubbornness in defending Cardiff's position, he had good reason to seek a compromise by the second half of 1927, for the medical school, and therefore the college, was facing a serious financial crisis at this time. Although the Treasury had adjusted the annual grant payable to the school in the event of a satisfactory conclusion to the discussions from £5,000 to £7,000,[69] Whitehall had clearly had enough, and the possibility of cancelling this commitment was seriously being considered. Among the papers of Dr Thomas Jones, at the time deputy secretary to the Cabinet, is a remarkably frank memorandum written by the secretary of the UGC. The memorandum appears in full among the appendices, but this is some of what A. H. Kidd wrote:

> The principal point of practical interest to us at the moment is that if no satisfactory scheme emerges, we shall save £7,000 a year, for which we can find very good use elsewhere. The matter is now one mainly of local interest and reduces itself to the question 'does Wales want a first rate National School of Medicine?' When the idea was first mooted over ten years ago the School was going to be a pioneer institution wholly organised on a 'unit' basis, but since then the London medical schools have gone ahead very fast. For instance, University College Hospital School is now complete with units in Medicine, Surgery and Obstetrics under full-time directors and the total number of units in London is 11. The experiment in Wales is therefore now no longer of anything like such general interest and importance to the national Government.

As Kidd observed, the Treasury was already contributing £10,000 a year to the running of the Welsh National School of Medicine: '£17,000 a year is more than we give to the largest medical school on our whole list with about three times as many students, and of incomparably superior value to medical science and the nation'.[70]

Meanwhile the Welsh local authorities were reviewing their own financial commitment to the school. Six out of eighteen (Breconshire, Cardiganshire, Swansea,

Monmouthshire, Merthyr Tydfil and Radnorshire) had already ceased to contribute to the medical school appeal fund, and two more, Flintshire and the Rhondda, had given notice of their intention to do likewise. Glamorgan, by far the largest contributor, was beginning to ask questions. The minutes of the meeting of the University Finance Committee, held on 27 September 1927, made gloomy reading. Instead of a potential annual income from local authorities of some £6,870 the medical school could realistically expect no more than £4,340. The UGC's supplemental annual contribution remained a mirage. The medical school's budget for 1927/8 showed an estimated increase in expenditure of £2,085 and a decrease in income of £1,534, as compared with 1926/7. An overall medical school deficit for the year of nearly £9,000 was estimated, a figure which the appeal fund and University grants could not cover.[71]

At the same time the Welsh National School of Medicine was facing some unavoidable commitments. The new Institute of Preventive Medicine finally opened on the Parade in January 1927. As has already been noted, this provided new, long-awaited and much-needed accommodation for the School of Preventive Medicine, and the Departments of Pathology and Bacteriology and Tuberculosis. However, although the capital costs of the building had been donated by Sir William James Thomas, the running costs were the responsibility of the school, at a time when money was short. The year 1927 also saw the opening in the autumn of the new and very much state-of-the-art laboratories of the medical unit in the Royal Infirmary. Again, although the capital costs had been met by the Rockefeller Foundation, this had been conditional on the Cardiff College and the university meeting the running costs. The growing medical school was facing other cost pressures. For example, £915 was needed to provide additional accommodation for the medical school in the Royal Infirmary, the conversion of the male students' common room into a classroom for the surgical unit, the relocation of the common room to the carpenters' workshop, and the conversion of the porters' room into a staff and student refectory. The money was found by digging deep into the medical school reserve fund.

It is therefore not surprising that by late 1927 financial considerations were driving all parties towards a settlement of a dispute which had, according to W. N. Bruce, already lasted longer than the siege of Troy![72]

The crucial meeting took place in Cardiff on 6 October, between representatives of the councils of the Cardiff College and the university. At this meeting, the main features of what was finally agreed some months later were laid down. The clinical parts of the college would form a separate Welsh National School of Medicine. While formally remaining in the college, the Departments of Anatomy and Physiology would be 'neutralized' in the sense that the heads of these departments would be appointed by a joint committee of the college and the university. Furthermore, the academic relationship between the college and the medical school in relation to the first three years of the medical course would be governed by a Joint Standing Academic Committee, chaired by the provost of the medical school. Adequate financial provision would be made for the departments of anatomy and physiology. Finally, an agreement would be entered into between the college and the university concerning the use of buildings by the school. While not divulging the details to his Court of Governors later in the day, Principal Trow felt sufficiently confident to proclaim: 'We cannot now, without ill-will at some point or another, go wrong.'[73]

The University Council, meeting on 24 October, endorsed the recommendations of the joint meeting of 6 October and set up a committee to draft a charter for the Welsh National School of Medicine. Not everyone was impressed, least of all the *South Wales News*, which considered the proposed agreement as 'little short of a monstrosity' which should be absolutely rejected.[74] Newspapers, then, as now, were entitled to their views, but to others fell the responsibility of taking hard decisions. Exhausted by an often bitter campaign lasting over four years and undoubtedly anxious about the future, everyone shared a desire to see the whole lengthy business settled. No one could claim victory, but in a very British compromise, everyone had cause for some satisfaction. Cardiff would retain that part of the medical school to which it felt most entitled both legally and historically, while the rest would become an independent clinical school with, hopefully, an all-Wales mission to perform.

What did members of the Welsh National School of Medicine think of it all? There is no evidence that the dean, Professor Sheen, was formally consulted, either by the college or university authorities, about the main features of the scheme, though it is surely inconceivable that his opinion on the chairmanship of the Joint Standing Advisory Committee, for instance, would not have been sought. The fact remains that never, throughout the 1927 calendar year, did either the college or the university formally seek the views of either the Faculty of Medicine or the Board of Medicine on the future of the school. Indeed, the only occasion when the issue came up at all was on 4 July, when, at a meeting of the Board of Medicine, Lord Kenyon referred to a letter he had received from Cornelius Griffiths, senior surgeon at the infirmary, Mitchell Stevens and Professor David Hepburn, making suggestions about the future of the school.

No action was taken after receipt of this letter. It is now mainly of interest as the last intervention in the affairs of the school by David Hepburn as professor of anatomy prior to his final departure from the college in September 1927 after twenty-four years in post, the last three beyond the normal retirement age. Though he had ploughed a rather solitary furrow in latter years, his commitment to his subject remained undiminished, and it is noteworthy that the first article in the first issue of the new medical students' journal, *The Leech*, published in October 1926, was by him. His subject was 'The importance of anatomy' and, after three pages of erudite discussion, he triumphantly concluded: 'Anatomy is the foundation upon which the whole structure of medical education is supported.'[75] On his retirement *The Leech* paid him a handsome tribute, including the following words:

> The solidarity of character, quiet dignity, unassuming manner and sincerity of purpose which Dr Hepburn displayed at all times could not fail to grip the imagination of his students and to play an important part in moulding their characters. Few teachers can hope to win and retain so completely the confidence and warm affection of their students as he has done.[76]

As the result of a gift made to Hepburn by past students of the Department of Anatomy between the years 1903 and 1927, the David Hepburn Medal was endowed, to be awarded annually to the best medical student in the degree examination in human anatomy, anthropology, embryology and histology.

David Hepburn was succeeded as professor of anatomy by Cecil McLaren West, aged thirty-four, previously university anatomist and chief demonstrator in anatomy at Trinity College, Dublin. Hepburn's position as the representative of the University of Wales on the GMC, held without a break since 1912, was taken by William Sheen, dean of the Faculty of Medicine.

Although the essential framework for the independent Welsh National School of Medicine had been agreed by the autumn of 1927, it took nearly another four years for the new institution to sail from harbour, on 1 July 1931. Had Sheen realized how difficult the next few years would be for him he might have asked someone else with a little more time to take on the GMC. For the medical school was poised to embark upon the most painful episode in its relatively brief history, a matter which nearly brought the school to destruction. How fitting were the sorrowful words of the *Western Mail*, written at the end of October 1927: 'Complication follows complication in the efforts to lift the Welsh National School of Medicine from the arena of controversy.'[77]

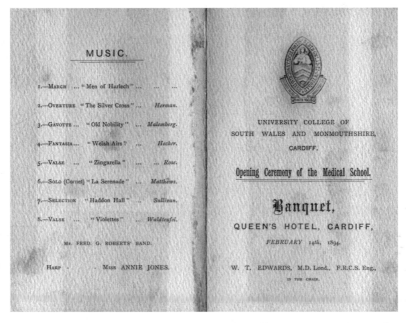

MUSIC.

1.—MARCH ... "Men of Harlech" ... ...

2.—OVERTURE "The Silver Cross" ... *Herman.*

3.—GAVOTTE ... "Old Nobility" ... *Malemberg.*

4.—FANTASIA... "Welsh Airs" ... *Hecker.*

5.—VALSE ... "Zingarella" ... ... *Rose.*

6.—SOLO (Cornet) "La Serenade" ... *Matthews.*

7.—SELECTION "Haddon Hall" ... *Sullivan.*

8.—VALSE ... "Violettes" ... *Waldteufel.*

MR. FRED. G. ROBERTS' BAND.

HARP - - MISS ANNIE JONES.

UNIVERSITY COLLEGE OF
SOUTH WALES AND MONMOUTHSHIRE,
CARDIFF.

Opening Ceremony of the Medical School.

Banquet,

QUEEN'S HOTEL, CARDIFF,

FEBRUARY 14th, 1894.

W. T. EDWARDS, M.D. Lond., F.R.C.S. Eng.,
IN THE CHAIR.

1 Menu card of the banquet celebrating the official opening of Cardiff Medical School on 14 February 1894. Owing to the numbers attending, the venue was changed to the Town Hall.

2 Dr William Thomas Edwards (left) and Mr Alfred Sheen in 1894.

3 The University College of South Wales and Monmouthshire in 1905, the departments of anatomy and physiology being located on the top floor. Until 1883 the buildings had served as the Glamorganshire and Monmouthshire Infirmary and Dispensary.

4 Thomas Lewis as an undergraduate student at University College, Cardiff.

5 Memorial to Professor Alfred Hughes, founder professor of anatomy at the Cardiff Medical School, erected beside the main Dolgellau–Machynlleth road above Corris and officially unveiled on 9 September 1905.

6 John Lynn Thomas (left), honorary surgeon at the Cardiff Infirmary, and William Osler, regius professor of medicine, Oxford University, at the opening of the new outpatients department, Cardiff Royal Infirmary, May 1908.

7 The staff and students of Cardiff Medical School in 1908. On the second row from the front are John Berry Haycraft (fifth from left) and David Hepburn (sixth from left). The lady in between is Dorothy Logan, a third year student. To Hepburn's left is Dr John Evatt.

8 A memorial to Donald Rose Paterson, designed by Sir William Goscombe John, in the main corridor of the Cardiff Royal Infirmary.

9 Professor Edward Emrys-Roberts, professor of pathology and bacteriology, 1910–24.

10 Professor David Hepburn, professor of anatomy 1903–27 and dean of the medical school, 1903–22.

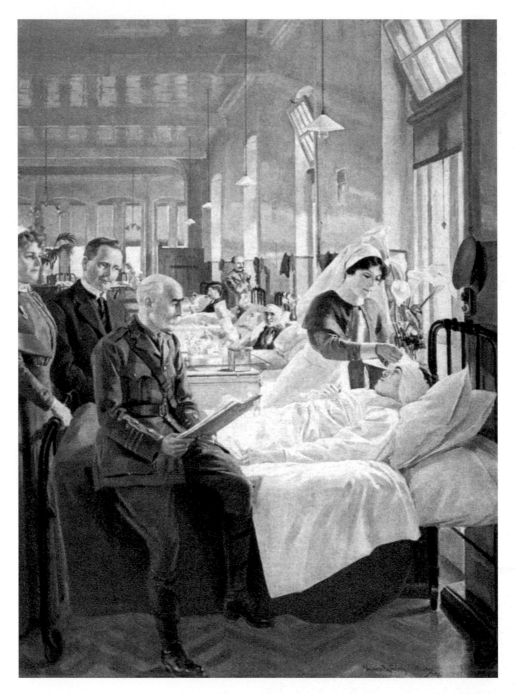

11 Painting by Margaret Lindsay Williams of Lieut. Col. Hepburn, commanding officer of the Third Western General Hospital, Matron Montgomery Wilson and Sir William James Thomas (who had commissioned the work) in a ward full of wounded soldiers at the King Edward VII Hospital in 1916.

12 Visit of the Haldane Commission to Cardiff in June 1916. Those attending include, from the left, Principal E. H. Griffiths (first), Sir William Osler (second), John Lynn Thomas (fourth), A. H. Kidd (fifth), Lieut. Col. E. M. Bruce Vaughan (sixth), D. J. A. Brown (ninth), David Hepburn (tenth) and the Hon. W. N. Bruce (twelfth). Seated are Lord Aberdare (president of University College, Cardiff), Lord Haldane and Emily Penrose (principal of Somerville College, Oxford).

13 Lord Haldane and Sir Isambard Owen at the opening of the Institute of Physiology, 8 June 1921.

14 Newport Road during the 1920s, showing the new Institute of Physiology.

15 The staff and students of the Welsh National School of Medicine at the main entrance of the Institute of Physiology in 1921/22, its first year as a full medical school. Those seated on the third row from the front include, from the left, T. Graham Brown (seventh), William Sheen (ninth) and David Hepburn (tenth).

16 Aerial view of the Cardiff Royal Infirmary, 1923.

17 Professor Alexander Mills Kennedy.

18 Professor William Sheen.

19 Sir Ewen Maclean.

20 Visit of the prime minister, Ramsay MacDonald, to
the school in March 1924.

21 A group of final-year medical students in 1924:
W. E. C. Thomas and Daniel T. Davies (above) and E. C.
James, Emrys Owen and Illtyd James (below).

22 Staff and students of the Welsh National School of Medicine, 1925. Those seated on the front row
include (from the left) William Sheen (ninth), Sir Ewen Maclean (tenth), Mrs Cornelius Griffiths
(eleventh), Cornelius Griffiths (twelfth), Gilbert Strachan (thirteenth) and Lambert Rogers (fourteenth).

23 Front cover of the first issue of 'The Leech', October 1926.

24 Portrait of Cornelius Griffiths, senior surgeon at the Cardiff Royal Infirmary and past-president of the Medical Students' Club, vandalized by disaffected medical students, September 1928.

25 Sir William James Thomas, honorary treasurer, and Sir William Diamond, chairman of the Cardiff Royal Infirmary, 1933.

26 Three members of the Cardiff Royal Infirmary Council, 1933: H. J. Smith (chairman of the Finance Committee), D. R. Paterson (chairman of the Nursing Committee) and William Mitchell Stevens (senior physician).

27 The Institute of Preventive Medicine, the Parade, 1929. The Institute became the home of the independent Welsh National School of Medicine in 1931.

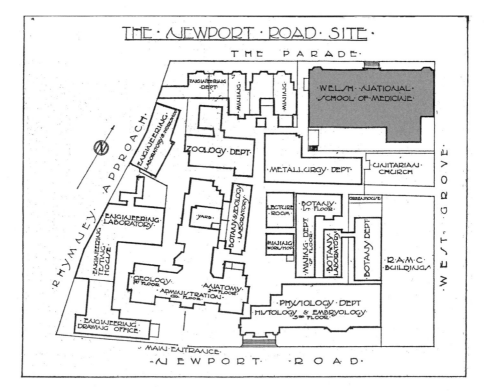

28 Plan of the Newport Road site in 1933, showing the Institute of Preventive Medicine (shaded) on the Parade. The Cardiff Royal Infirmary was about 200 yards to the east on the other side of Newport Road.

8

The Infirmary in Revolt

As if the constitutional wranglings described in the previous chapter were not enough for the infant Welsh National School of Medicine to cope with, differences between the school and hospital staff grew to the point where relations finally broke down altogether during the spring and summer of 1928. Tensions between clinical academic staff and their hospital colleagues are not unknown at the interface between hospitals and medical schools. As Dr Malcolm Parsons, a historian of the medical scene in Leeds, has observed, 'The friction between university and clinical staff seems to be universal – when Allbutt, our most distinguished physician moved to a chair in Cambridge it was eight years before he got any beds in Addenbrookes.'[1] It has already been noted in chapters 5 and 6 how the issue of the introduction of clinical units in London and the provinces during the 1920s created tensions between medical schools and their associated hospitals.

Nowhere, however, did relations between them deteriorate to the point of collapse as occurred in Cardiff. Ralph Picken, on the verge of retirement as provost of the Welsh National School of Medicine in 1955, tried hard to be fair to everyone involved. While acknowledging the 'uncompromising whole-hoggery of the professors and doctors', he wrote:

> I would like to record that I found much that was admirable in the partisans of both sides of this battle. While, of course, personal interests did figure, there was in several quarters a quite disinterested desire to do what was best for the University and for medical education. Indeed, some of the finest men I knew in Cardiff were on the side which I would not have favoured if I had been called upon to take any active part in this affair. I am still not quite sure which administrative structure was or would have been best for the University or for medical education in Wales; but I am quite certain of this, that one of the main issues, viz. whole-time professional clinical units versus part-time Chairs, was decided in the right way. Our experience amply confirms it, and since then many other universities have followed suit.

Even so, Picken did take the view that 'It took us a good many years to live down the sad reputation we, as a school, acquired both in and outside of Wales, through very little fault of our own.'[2] In fact, once a settlement had been reached between the school and hospital authorities, business returned to normal pretty quickly. Nevertheless,

Professor Gwynn Williams is surely right to describe the dispute as 'a disgraceful episode'.[3]

THE STEVENS COMMITTEE OF INQUIRY

On 1 July 1925, the *South Wales News* carried a short report about the senior physician at the Cardiff Royal Infirmary, W. Mitchell Stevens, who had apparently resigned his appointment as a recognized clinical teacher a few weeks earlier. No reason was given and the report stated that the Board of Medicine had asked Stevens to explain his action. On 3 September Stevens's letter of explanation was given prominent coverage by the *Western Mail*. Stevens himself always denied being the source of the leak; whatever the truth of the matter, the letter caused a sensation. After outlining the history of the Cardiff Medical School, with a 'reputation second to none in the Kingdom', up to 1921, Stevens proceeded to pour scorn on its subsequent development under the control of 'a small clique of inexperienced professors' who had made no attempt to work with their hospital colleagues in carrying out the teaching programme, and had excluded them from participating in the Faculty of Medicine. Neither the college nor the hospital authorities had heeded their sense of frustration, and Stevens had had enough, deciding to sever his connection with the clinical teaching. He ended his letter with a quotation from Abraham Lincoln: 'You can fool all the people some of the time, some of the people all the time, but not all the people all the time.'

What could have provoked such an outburst by Dr Stevens, at the very time when the future status of the Welsh National School of Medicine was coming under intense scrutiny? It is hardly surprising that Alderman William George was privately expressing some doubt to the university authorities about the ability of the school to manage itself properly. It has already been noted that Stevens was an opponent of the separation of the medical school from the college, so that his intervention in the summer of 1925 was hardly a matter of pure coincidence. However, it would be a mistake simply to dismiss his attack on those responsible for running the affairs of the medical school as merely an opportunist manoeuvre in the separatist debate.

We have already noted how relationships between the clinical staff of the infirmary and senior members of the medical school and the college were less than comfortable during the early 1920s. Although arrangements had been made to involve the hospital staff in the teaching programme, thereby securing its recognition by the Conjoint Board and London University, the clinical staff remained unhappy. For two years they continued to grumble about the teaching remuneration scheme because the level of payment depended on the number of teachers involved, and discriminated between the honorary physicians and honorary surgeons on the one hand and the assistants on the other. Finally in 1925 a new scheme was introduced under which all recognized clinical teachers, whatever their hospital status, would receive the same fixed annual honorarium of £40. This was by no means a fortune but, as the college insisted, 'Such payment could not be really "adequate" in the strict sense of payment for services rendered, but was rather in the nature of a recognition for those services.'[4]

There was, however, a far more serious bone of contention. Although the honorary staff were expected to participate in the clinical teaching programme, they were excluded from membership of the Faculty of Medicine, the body formally responsible for determining all matters relating to the conduct of the course. As part-time head of the Department of Materia Medica and Pharmacology, Mitchell Stevens was a member of the Faculty of Medicine but since Professor Hepburn had ceased to be dean Stevens had stopped attending himself. In any case he was not there to represent the recognized clinical teachers. The matter of their representation on the Faculty of Medicine was first raised at a meeting of the hospital Medical Board in September 1923. The college authorities referred the matter to the Board of Medicine, who deferred consideration until the views of the Faculty of Medicine were known. The faculty finally pronounced in March 1924. After pointing out that this was an inopportune time to raise the matter as the whole constitutional position of the medical school was currently under review, it added that it was inappropriate to have on an academic body of the university 'one or more persons over whom the University can exercise no academic authority'.[5] This view, which seems ungenerous now, was subsequently endorsed, without apparent comment, by the Board of Medicine and the College Council.

The Medical Board, frustrated by the negative response, decided to ask the hospital authorities to send a direct appeal to the Privy Council in London, 'praying that any Charter that may be granted for the governance of the Welsh National Medical School, shall contain provision for the representation of the Recognised Clinical Teachers on the Faculty of Medicine'.[6] The hospital authorities took up the matter again with the College Council, but, again to no avail. Nothing could be done until the college's revised charter was approved.[7] Certainly nothing had been done by the time Stevens, who had become chairman of the Medical Board in March 1924, decided to relinquish the title of recognized clinical teacher, and it is clear from his letter that this remained a contentious issue.

However, his letter had also alluded to the dictatorial way in which the school authorities were running its affairs, and there was one particular incident, early in 1925, affecting Stevens himself, which suggests that matters were becoming distinctly personal. Two final-year clinical students, R. J. Rankin and T. J. Lloyd, having failed their Conjoint Board clinical examinations in January, sought access to the hospital for revision purposes without re-registering as Cardiff students, and paying what Stevens happened to consider exorbitant revision fees. They approached Mitchell Stevens who, regarding them as excellent students, indicated his willingness to have them in attendance on his ward, but advised them to obtain permits from the hospital authorities – which were issued. As far as Stevens was concerned, the Conjoint Board rules fully allowed such an arrangement. All the board needed for re-examination purposes was a note from a responsible consultant in a recognized hospital to say that the students had undertaken remedial instruction. The dean, Graham Brown, no friend of Stevens at the best of times, regarded the situation where unregistered students could obtain clinical tuition in the infirmary for external examinations without the school's approval to be unacceptable. Indeed the Faculty of Medicine approved the wording of a note to be issued to all teachers in the medical school:

> All students who are entitled to attend clinics or classes, etc., are provided with cards of admission, signed by the Dean and countersigned by the Secretary. All Teachers are asked to assist the administration of the School by inspecting the cards of admission at the beginning of each term, and to restrict their tuition to students who possess such cards, in respect of the period in question.

In terms of student discipline, the dean's attitude was quite reasonable and he secured the Conjoint Board's undertaking not to examine Cardiff students unless their entry form had been signed either by the dean or the school secretary.[8] Needless to say, Stevens was outraged by what he regarded as medical school interference in his own business and in the general affairs of the hospital, and on 19 May 1925, the Board of Medicine received Stevens's resignation as a recognized clinical teacher with effect from the end of June. It has to be said that Stevens had a point; so did the dean. What this episode clearly shows is that the transition of an old-style voluntary hospital into a teaching hospital with obligations to bodies other than itself was not easy to manage, least of all when some of the leading actors on the stage were particularly combative characters.

It was not until 2 October that the Board of Medicine formally considered Mitchell's letter of 21 August. After deploring the premature publication of the letter in the press, the board recommended to the College Council that the presidents of the Royal Colleges of Physicians of London and Surgeons of England be asked to inquire into Mitchell's allegations. This recommendation was not accepted, the Council, meeting on 9 November, preferring, in the first instance, to establish an internal committee of inquiry to determine whether there was a prima-facie case to submit to external experts. As the chairman of the committee, Hugh Ingledew, was later to observe, the Council wished, if at all possible, to avoid 'washing any dirty linen in public'. The committee comprised eight members, four Council representatives (the Ven. Archdeacon David Davies, Hugh Ingledew, D. Lleufer Thomas and the principal, and four representatives of the Board of Medicine (Alderman T. H. Morris, Sir William James Thomas, Councillor Peter Wright and Principal T. F. Sibly of Swansea, who was never able to attend). The committee met on seven occasions between 2 December 1925 and 16 April 1926, with Mitchell Stevens appearing before them three times and Professor Graham Brown twice.

Although the proceedings were held in private, a verbatim account was kept, a copy of which is preserved in the Cardiff University archives.[9] This provides a quite unique picture of the tensions which existed in the mid-1920s, both within the Welsh National School of Medicine and between members of the school and their hospital colleagues, not least Mitchell Stevens. The main stages in the inquiry may be summarized as follows. After a preliminary meeting on 2 December, the committee met Mitchell Stevens on 14 December. Having noted Stevens's objection to the composition of the committee, seven of the eight members being members of the Board of Medicine of which he was critical, and, much to Stevens's disappointment, deciding for the time being not to invite evidence from the students, the committee got down to business. Stevens devoted much time to the way the school authorities on the one hand interfered with the business of the hospital, citing the recent dispute over the presence of unregistered students, while on the other hand failing to collaborate with the hospital over the co-ordination of teaching. Stevens gave an illustration:

> To give you an example of co-ordination – my time of visiting is eleven to one. About five minutes to twelve the students say, 'We have got to go now – lecture.' They lecture in the middle of the day. That obviously interferes with the ward work; it is not a bit of good to take any students who have to attend lectures in the middle of the day.
>
> During the last two years there has never been once a meeting of the staff together at the hospital where any attempt has been made to co-ordinate. Although we came on as recognized teachers, certain people were inclined to treat us as though we did not exist.

The chairman sought to explore the matter further.

> Chairman: During the last two or three years since the time when the Conjoint Board recognized the college there have been no steps taken at all between the dean and the Faculty of Medicine and the professors of the Medical School to come together and co-ordinate with the medical staff. Is that so?
>
> Dr Stevens: Yes – one of the gravest things that ought to be remedied. The so-called Faculty of Medicine – a more ridiculously constituted body I never heard of – why – in the first place it is composed of fourteen members. There is the principal and thirteen professors, and one of them – a lecturer – myself. Three are professors from outside constituent colleges. There is not a single man on that faculty representing the hospital as such. Now, that is a point raised by my colleagues.

Stevens criticized the quality of the teaching given to the students by the staff of the medical unit before they arrived on the wards:

> Three of the men are part-time assistants. There are some who have no idea of teaching. My statement applies to three out of the four. There is one who I think is really a good teacher. I should be very pleased to get any students through Abel Evans's hands.

Stevens had absolutely no time for Professor Kennedy. Indeed he had opposed his appointment. Kennedy never attended the meetings of the Medical Board and treated the board with disdain:

> When we appoint HPs or HSs [house physicians or surgeons] we always bring our names before the Medical Board and give our reasons for selection. He [Kennedy] never dreams of doing that – the name is usually handed to us and no trouble is taken by him to report, an ordinary act of courtesy.

Stevens was equally critical of the dean, Professor Graham Brown, whom he accused of neglecting his duties, both as administrator and as teacher. This statement caused Principal Trow to sit up. 'I would suggest that since we have heard so many times the statement that the Head of the Department of Physiology does no teaching at all we must probe that, and the proper way is to ask him whether he does any teaching or not'.

At the next meeting of the committee, on 19 January 1926, Mitchell Stevens renewed his attack on the leading members of the Faculty of Medicine, which, according to him, was now in the hands of a separatist cabal, who had turned Professor Hepburn out of the deanship in 1922 'by low intrigue'. He was kindest towards Professor Sheen: 'Sheen is a very hard-working man but has no experience of teaching. He does his level best.' Others were treated more harshly. He condemned the professor of physiology for empire-building to no good effect in either research or teaching:

> I don't think he has done any teaching for over eighteen months or so. He does very little work as dean. That is left to his clerk. Also I know that he cannot be lecturing when I meet him in Queen Street during an hour at which, according to timetable, he should be lecturing.

Stevens would ask his pharmacology students about their knowledge of physiology: 'The students simply howl with laughter and I have to teach them the elementary principles of Physiology myself.' He regarded Kennedy as 'absolutely useless' and was scathing about the professor's lack of the membership or fellowship of the Royal College of Physicians, a situation which would preclude his appointment to a junior position in the hospital. He finished the meeting with a fierce attack on the professors of preventive medicine and of tuberculosis: 'You have got these fancy departments and these men are on your Faculty of Medicine. These men are running your place, Cummins and Collis, and they have more to say than the men who are doing the real work at the Hospital … They are luxuries.' Meanwhile the honorary staff were excluded from membership of the faculty.

At the meeting held on 25 January the committee, by now somewhat weary of the bombardment of negative criticism, were looking to Stevens for some positive proposals. He had several. First, he would scrap the unit system, which had proved to be a 'perfect farce'. Secondly, he would keep the medical school as part of the college. Thirdly, he would divide the school into two separate faculties, of preclinical and clinical medicine. As far as representation on the clinical faculty was concerned, he would appoint two professors in each of the departments of medicine and surgery, one, more junior, who would be responsible for teaching the fundamentals of the subject, the other, who would be professor of clinical medicine, or clinical surgery, appointed from among the senior members of the honorary staff of the hospital. There would also be a professor of obstetrics and gynaecology and of pathology and bacteriology. In addition the clinical faculty would include representation from the honorary staff. As far as he was concerned he would exclude the research professors, men like Collis and Cummins, heads of what Stevens dismissed as 'fancy departments. University College, London has not got a Tuberculosis Department. There is only one place that has, and that is Edinburgh.' Sir William James Thomas took some exception to all this: 'Therefore you think that the block of buildings I am erecting will be useless.' Stevens hurriedly responded, 'Oh, no. I think the block will be exceedingly useful. They are very fine buildings and will be very useful for other work as well as for preventive medicine.' After criticizing Sir William Diamond for sending what he regarded as a misleading letter to the meeting of the University Court at Llandrindod Wells, Stevens completed his bravura performance, leaving the committee to sort out some dates to interview Professor Graham Brown.

Brown met the committee on 11 and 23 March. He was in no mood to be conciliatory in the face of Stevens's criticisms. He admitted that there was little or no formal dialogue between the school and the hospital regarding the timetabling of the course, though there was frequent intercommunication between the professors and the clinical staff. He did, however, accept that once the medical school had achieved separation there would be room for representation of the recognized clinical teachers within the committee structure. Stevens's objection to the unit system was based on self-interest, as Stevens held the belief that on its demise he would become the professor of clinical medicine. He also reminded the committee that although Stevens had resigned as a recognized clinical teacher he had not resigned his part-time appointment as head of the Department of Materia Medica and Pharmacology, a far more lucrative post. As far as his own teaching role was concerned, he did lecture twice a week, but in any case the idea that one could deliver the medical course via lectures was old-fashioned; book-reading, supported by tutorials, was the way of the future.

Having heard Stevens and Brown, the committee decided they had heard enough. They chose not to interview Professor Kennedy or any of the students, preferring to wrap up the inquiry as painlessly as possible. In their brief report, which was adopted by the Board of Medicine on 18 May 1926, the committee concluded that it was neither necessary nor desirable to seek further advice from outside experts and that in everybody's best interests the questions raised by Mitchell Stevens in his letter 'should now be allowed to drop'. The committee had been 'greatly impressed by the acute difference of opinion' expressed by Stevens and Brown, not least with regard to the continuance of the unit system. However,

> Your Committee do not feel that this broad question of principle is one upon which they can usefully express any opinion, either within the scope of the reference to them or consistently with the fact that the present constitution based upon the Unit system had so far had too short an experience to justify any safe conclusion upon so complex and controversial a subject.

In other words, the committee, and the Board of Medicine, stuck their collective heads firmly in the sand. What the committee had heard in private ought to have caused the college authorities much more alarm than it did. While there is no doubt that Stevens had some personal axes to grind, he was also articulating long-standing concerns felt by the honorary staff, and the impression is gained that the response of the Board of Medicine was inadequate.

THE DEANSHIP CHANGES HANDS

In May 1926, at the insistence of Professor G. H. Livens, professor of mathematics, the Senate of the college did set up a committee 'to enquire into the conduct of the Professor of Physiology in order to ascertain whether adequate grounds existed for proceeding with a notion to Senate proposing the dismissal of Professor Graham Brown'. There is no doubt that Brown did not fulfil the image of a conventional academic. His obituarist many years later would describe him as 'essentially a man's man, short of stature, and with tremendous physical and mental energy' whose abiding passion was mountaineering, a pursuit in which he was an undoubted expert, indeed one of the leading practitioners in Europe.[10] Despite Brown's vigorous advocacy of a modern approach to teaching medicine, one that relied less than hitherto on formal instruction, there remained a strong belief that Brown was rather neglecting his teaching duties in favour of the slopes of the French Alps. Chaired by the Fulton professor of economics and political science, Professor W. J. Roberts, the committee asked Professor Brown to provide detailed information on the amount of teaching and examination he and his staff had given to the students over the previous three years. Professor Hepburn was invited to meet the committee to give evidence, and the registrar was asked to provide other evidence of Brown's neglect of his duties. Professor Hepburn asked to be excused from attending. 'My health is giving me some cause for at least walking carefully, if not anxiously and I find it very difficult to attend meetings in addition to giving attention to my classes. My medical adviser (Dr Herbert Evans) warns me against undertaking extras.'[11] However, Hepburn had taken the trouble to write to over a dozen former students of the Department of Physiology to gather evidence against Brown ('It is hoped that conditions for present and future students will be improved as the result of this enquiry') and he submitted the replies from seven of them. In general, they confirmed that Brown gave relatively few lectures, though it is clear that at least some of those approached by Hepburn were known to be ill disposed towards the dean. As we have already noted, the conduct of Reginald J. Rankin had been the cause of conflict between Brown and Mitchell Stevens, so that it was hardly surprising that Rankin could find few good words for Brown in his letter to Hepburn.

> Unfortunately my memory does not serve me as to the number of lectures given, though I distinctly remember that as time went on they became fewer and fewer... The most damning thing about the man however is that to me he never seems to behave himself as a gentleman, and has an unfortunate manner of attempting to treat one as a child.

Rankin also accused Brown of trying to exclude him from demonstrations 'purely because I was taking Conjoint, not Welsh', omitting to mention that the real reason for his exclusion was that he had not paid his revision fees to the school. Most of the other students felt that the teaching they had received from the Department of Physiology had been adequate, if not from Brown, then from the other members of staff. Brown denied that he had been negligent in responding to college requests for information for the prospectus and other purposes; it was simply that he chose to work through the Faculty of Medicine rather than the Faculty of Science (the Departments of Anatomy and Physiology being members of both). When asked 'whether he has been present to enter students at the beginning of each session since he has been Dean of the Faculty of Medicine', he replied, 'I have been present or close at hand.' In short, the proceedings of the inquiry were inconclusive. There really was not enough evidence to support the efforts of some members of the Faculty of Science, notably Professor Livens, to have him dismissed, though Brown's decision, in May, to relinquish the deanship at the end of the session, a year early, was prudent, indeed inevitable under the circumstances.

It has to be said, however, that Brown was more highly regarded by his peers than some cared to recognize. As has already been noted, he was to be elected a Fellow of the Royal Society in 1927, no mean accolade. Nevertheless, Ronald Eccles has provided an interesting glimpse of Brown's rather unconventional lifestyle, one that would not have made him instantly endearing to everyone:

> He continued to reside in the department for many years after his retirement [in 1947], when he was forced to leave his bachelor quarters in the Park Hotel. All his personal belongings were moved into his room in the department and he slept on a small camp bed, with his breakfast and tobacco brought to him each morning by a technician.[12]

Graham Brown's decision to relinquish the deanship (to be succeeded by Professor A. W. Sheen from 1 October 1926) did not cause Stevens to reconsider his own decision to resign from the position of recognized clinical teacher, despite efforts by Sir William James Thomas and others to persuade him to do so. Stevens did, however, agree that his beds could be used for teaching by his clinical colleagues on those days when he was not himself in attendance. On the strength of this, letters were sent to the University of London and the Conjoint Board, who had been made aware of the local problems by Stevens himself, to brief them of the situation. The Conjoint Board were comfortable with what had been arranged but wished to be kept informed.[13] No immediate response was received from the University of London. When it finally came, some months later, it would prove to be less than helpful.

In terms of maintaining good relations between the medical school and the infirmary, the previous two deans had been little short of disastrous. Alexander Mills Kennedy, prone to self-pity (an observation once made by an officer of the Rockefeller Foundation) and feeling himself unwanted among his hospital colleagues, had determined to have as little to do with them as possible. Even during his deanship, between 1922 and 1924, he had hardly ever attended meetings of the Medical Board. His whole attitude exasperated Sir William Diamond, the hospital chairman, who once bitterly observed: 'Professor Kennedy's views are not ascertainable, as he keeps aloof from our meetings and from any personal association with our considerations.'[14] We have already noted how Professor Graham Brown was regarded by Mitchell Stevens and some of his university colleagues. Lord Adrian's obituary of him depicted Brown as by nature a combative rather than a conciliatory character: 'He was a formidable opponent and did not always conceal his pleasure in the fight and the victory.'[15] Furthermore, although Brown was medically qualified, as professor of physiology he lacked clinical status within the infirmary and was not a member of the Medical Board, even during the period of his deanship.

Ideally Brown's successor as dean should have been blessed with tact and conciliation skills, gifts that the two previous incumbents had manifestly lacked. However, though respected, even admired by the students, Professor William Sheen could also be difficult. His obituarist would later describe him as 'not a good listener', and in possession of 'a rather brusque, dictatorial manner'.[16] How, then, was he elected dean, a decision which, again according to his obituarist, astonished Sheen at the time? In truth, there were no credible alternatives. Professors Collis and Cummins were regarded by many as peripheral to the core business of the school, while Sir Ewen Maclean, easily the most amenable and distinguished of the senior members of the school, had too many other interests, including (as a part-time professor) a substantial private practice. So William Sheen became dean, to enjoy annual reappointment every year until 1931. This rather insensitive man was also, of course, director of the surgical unit, and it was in that capacity that he managed to upset his surgical colleagues in the hospital to such an extent that a sequence of events was triggered off which led to the closure of the infirmary to all students in September 1928.

THE HOSPITAL STAFF TAKE THE OFFENSIVE

It has already been noted how the school's practice, as an economy measure, of appointing part-time rather than full-time assistants to the medical and surgical units had been a bone of contention among the honorary clinical staff. At last, in 1925, to the satisfaction of all concerned, the school found enough money to appoint its first full-time assistant in the surgical unit. Ten applications were received and three candidates were interviewed by the Faculty of Medicine. Two were graduates of the school, who had pursued the whole course in Cardiff. The third was an Australian product of the Middlesex Hospital, described in the report subsequently submitted to the Board of Medicine as having 'the longest experience, being a few years older than the others. He has had a good training and already has published several papers on surgical and other subjects.' It was inevitable that one of the local candidates, T. G. Illtyd James, 'a very capable student of our school and a good resident in the Cardiff Royal Infirmary', was offered the post, but he turned it down for unexplained private reasons. The other local candidate was no longer available, so the Board of Medicine, on the faculty's advice, appointed the Australian. Thus it was that Lambert Charles Rogers (1897–1961), later to become one of the giants of Welsh medicine, came to Cardiff in the spring of 1926.[17]

Little more than a year later, out of the blue, Professor Sheen announced that Lambert Rogers was changing his contract from full-time to part-time, in order to take up a part-time appointment at the Prince of Wales Hospital, which was very short-staffed. As far as the honorary surgeons were concerned, that was not the point; the professor of surgery appeared to be reverting to a policy of having part-time assistants in his unit, with absolutely no consultation with them. Sheen upset his colleagues further by announcing that he was adjusting the academic commitments of another of his part-time assistants, T. E. Hammond, changing his honorary college title and reducing his salary from £200 to £50 a year. Hammond, who had not been consulted beforehand, was naturally upset by this high-handed action. When confronted by his hospital colleagues, Sheen's general defence was that as director of the surgical unit he was entitled to run his unit's affairs more or less as he saw fit, claiming this to be the essence of the clinical unit system as he understood it, and quoting practice elsewhere in the United Kingdom.[18] On other occasions at this time Sheen attracted the honorary surgeons' displeasure by failing to keep them properly informed about arrangements he made for covering his clinical duties during absences from the hospital. They contended that in the interests of patient care they should be consulted; as far as Sheen was concerned, he was fully entitled to make appropriate arrangements within the surgical unit. It is fair to say that Professor Kennedy, though regarded as a thoroughly difficult colleague in most respects, was at least given credit for adhering to the rules. As the hospital chairman once conceded, Professor Kennedy was 'careful at all times to get into touch with and carry out all the regulations of the hospital meticulously and faithfully'.[19]

Neither Professor Kennedy nor Professor Sheen earned much praise from their honorary clinical colleagues for the way they were used in the clinical teaching programme. Indeed, this was a constant grumble from the honorary staff who argued that if they were used properly then the professorial units would not need to employ so many assistants. We have already seen what Mitchell Stevens thought about the way Kennedy organized the medical teaching. Sheen denied that he was excluding the honorary surgeons from the clinical teaching programme: 'The difficulty was to get them to do anything. There was a great want of co-operation on their part.' He did not add that because of inadequate liaison between the professors and the honorary staff, some of the clinical teaching was scheduled at times when the recognized clinical teachers were away from the hospital. Moreover, even when the honorary staff were involved in clinical teaching, the professorial units appeared to have no systematic arrangements in place for assessing students' attendance and performance on the wards.[20] It is little wonder that the honorary clinical staff felt more than a little unappreciated.

All these matters were debated furiously at a series of meetings of the infirmary's Medical Board during May and June 1927, when Professor Sheen (unsupported by Professor Kennedy who was, as usual, absent) did his best to defend the position of the school in general, and the unit system in particular. Unconvinced, the three honorary surgeons, William Martin, Cornelius Griffiths and Geary Grant (who had been elevated to the position of honorary surgeon on the retirement of H. G. Cook), threatened to resign as recognized clinical teachers because, in their view, the school's undertakings to the Conjoint Board and the University of London were not being carried out, a view shared by the University of London which, rather inconveniently, chose this moment to give its opinion on the Mitchell Stevens controversy. Alarmed, on the advice of the Board of Medicine the College Council agreed to remedy a long-standing grievance of the infirmary by adding five representatives of the hospital's honorary clinical staff to the Faculty of Medicine, and decided not to allow Professor Sheen's plans to restructure the surgical unit to proceed. Lambert Rogers therefore continued to be a full-time assistant in the unit, while Hammond continued in post, 'without any alteration in his title, status or duties'. Flushed with success the honorary clinical staff, including Mitchell Stevens, undertook to continue to act as recognized clinical teachers.[21] Professor Graham Brown's perspective on these developments, as described in a letter to Sir Thomas Lewis, is interesting:

> The internal position is extremely bad. The recent action of the University of London in again raising the question of recognition on the fact of Mitchell Stevens' refusal to act as a teacher was at once followed by the resignation of other recognised teachers. A pistol was held at our heads and these gentlemen told us that they would consent to be recognised again as teachers if the Hospital Staff were given five seats in the Faculty of Medicine. As Mitchell Stevens and Ewen Maclean already are members of the Faculty, this virtually means that the Hospital Staff would have control of the School. The Faculty of Medicine has not been consulted in the matter – nor will it be consulted. The College Council have surrendered to the staff of the Hospital. Unless the University vetoes the proposal, the next meeting of the Faculty will be largely dominated by the Hospital staff, with all that that implies.[22]

The honorary staff strengthened their position further in October 1927 when they succeeded in changing the hospital regulation which required them to retire at the age of sixty. The clinical academic staff were not subject to such a rule and the hospital staff took the view that they should not be either. Only one clinician, Ivor Davies, first assistant in the medical unit, opposed the proposition and referred to the matter in his memoirs:

> I had been fifteen years in outpatients when I should have been moved up to the wards on my 'senior' reaching the age of sixty. I was again bunkered, for three seniors reached the age of sixty together and avoided retirement through the decision of the Council [of the Infirmary] and the Board of Management to extend the retiring age to sixty-five. I did all in my power to defeat the proposal but failed owing to the combined action of the seniors in pushing the proposal through the controlling bodies.[23]

By his own admission, Davies's opposition to changing the regulation was based mainly on self-interest, though in his memoirs he also observed: 'This retrograde step led to the Medical School crisis for if the age limit had remained at sixty, the senior members in opposition to the School would have left the staff.' Although, throughout most of Britain, the 'sixty-year rule' was the norm, in reality, given the local circumstances, the change of rule was inevitable, and simply brought the arrangements for the honorary staff into line with those of the clinical staff of the college. Nevertheless, as a matter of fact, Davies was right. Had the regulation not been changed, the school's most persistent critics during the looming crisis, Mitchell Stevens and Cornelius Griffiths, would have retired or been on the verge of doing so.

Instead, led now by William Martin, honorary surgeon, another long-standing critic of the unit system, who had succeeded Mitchell Stevens as chairman of the Medical Board, the honorary staff, having secured some concessions from the college, were determined to keep up the pressure. At a crowded meeting of the Medical Board on 1 November (though without the benefit of Professor Kennedy's presence) H. A. Scholberg, the hospital's senior pathologist, and by no means a friend of the school, proposed:

> That the Medical Board is of opinion that the clinical work and teaching of the Welsh National School of Medicine, at the Cardiff Royal Infirmary, should be reorganised and the duties of the Professorial Units and the Honorary Staff defined, in order to promote the efficiency of the Hospital and Medical School.[24]

On the following day, the Faculty of Medicine, now substantially enlarged by the presence of several representatives of the honorary clinical staff of the hospital, endorsed the motion and proposed the establishment of a joint committee of the Faculty of Medicine and the Medical Board to take the matter further. Since three of the six faculty representatives on the committee were members of the honorary staff of the hospital it was inevitable that the report, produced after eight meetings, would be controversial, to say the least. The report, in effect, turned existing arrangements upside down. Instead of a Faculty of Medicine there should be a Medical School Committee as the academic authority of the Welsh National School of Medicine. The committee would comprise twenty members, twelve of whom would represent the honorary staff of the infirmary. This committee would 'make arrangements with the Cardiff Royal Infirmary as to clinical teaching and other matters'. The committee would set up subcommittees to oversee the running of the professorial units, though the duties of the assistants would be governed by the Medical School Committee itself. Although the professors of medicine and surgery should have general control of the systematic teaching of the principles of their discipline, 'The clinical instruction of the students should be carried out mainly by the Honorary Staff of the hospital.' There was no need for the school to have a provost. Instead, there should be a dean, appointed annually by and from the Medical School Committee. The report of the joint committee concluded with some general observations. It criticized the professor of medicine for not seeing his way to attending any of the meetings. It took the view that the proposals therein, modelled on arrangements in place at University College

Hospital, London, supplied 'the basis of a satisfactory settlement, and they hope that the authorities will accept the proposals in all their educational and financial implications'. The report ended with the threat that unless its recommendations were accepted the members of the honorary staff of the hospital would reconsider their position as recognized clinical teachers with effect from 28 June 1928.

Whatever may be said for this report, it did not represent the coming together of the views of the medical school and the honorary staff of the hospital. The report was the handiwork of the school's tormentor-in-chief, Mitchell Stevens, whose views on medical education were shaped by the conviction that whatever was done at University College Hospital, London was exemplary. He had said so, almost *ad nauseam*, at the college committee of inquiry held two years earlier, and now was his chance to get his blueprint adopted in Cardiff. Needless to say, the report of the joint committee was not even accepted by all its members. Professor Kennedy had totally dissociated himself from the proceedings; indeed, his main preoccupation at this time was an argument with the officers of the Cardiff Medical Society over a trivial procedural matter which led to his resignation from membership.[25] Dr Donald Rose Paterson, a universally respected member of the honorary staff, now on the verge of retirement, who had, to much local acclaim, obtained the still relatively rare accolade of fellowship of the Royal College of Physicians of London a few weeks earlier, chose to abstain. Professor Sheen voted against. Eight members of the honorary staff voted in favour, together with one senior member of the school, Sir Ewen Maclean.[26]

Sir Ewen's position was not particularly surprising, for he was very much his own man. By 1928, he was arguably the most prominent member of the medical profession in Wales, enjoying an international reputation which, two years before, had secured him an honorary fellowship from the American College of Surgeons. The summer of 1928 would see him elected president of the British Medical Association at the annual meeting in Cardiff. Since his appointment as 'professor extraordinary' (what would now be called a personal chair) in 1921, he had played a full part in the affairs of the medical school, serving as an active member of the Board of Medicine, its finance committee and the Faculty of Medicine. In 1926 he presented the school with £3,000 in order to endow the Ewen Maclean Research Scholarship to promote research in the field of midwifery. Yet he had never alienated himself from the honorary staff of the hospital whence he had come. He was a regular attender at meetings of the Medical Board, of which he would soon become vice-chairman. Once, when asked why his department had managed to avoid all the controversy swirling around the medical and surgical professorial units, Sir Ewen modestly replied that 'this was not due to any merit on his part but he was in an entirely different category because the setting up of his department disturbed no vested interest and his colleagues were fitted into his department.'[27] This was undoubtedly true. He was also a fine man, as his obituarist much later testified: 'Nobody could meet Maclean without being impressed by his courtesy and dignity, which did not conceal from his friends a very kindly heart.'[28]

The proposals of the so-called joint committee were immediately shelved (by a vote of six to five, the representatives of the honorary staff being in the minority) by the Faculty of Medicine. What else could the faculty do about a report which in effect sought to remove control of the medical school from the academic authorities and place it in the hands of the hospital doctors? Needless to say, the university authorities, who had done their best to distance themselves from what they chose to regard as a local squabble of little consequence, became concerned as it appeared that the hospital clinicians were seeking to overturn the whole structure of the Welsh National School of Medicine, which had only recently secured the endorsement of the University Council. At the meeting of the University Court in December 1927, the acting pro-chancellor, W. N. Bruce undertook to meet the authorities of the Cardiff Royal Infirmary 'to get to a termination of this almost endless discussion'.[29]

Several meetings took place between representatives of the University Council (including the acting pro-chancellor, the vice-chancellor and the dean of medicine) and of the Royal Infirmary during the first half of 1928 and, in truth, they got nowhere. As far as the authorities of the infirmary were concerned, they admitted that they had never held strong views as to whether the medical school should be part of University College, Cardiff or should be an independent entity. Writing on behalf of the infirmary in May 1928, the hospital secretary, L. D. Rea, stated: 'the attitude of the Infirmary all along has been one of detachment, as it did not seem greatly to matter by which body the School was managed.' The hospital authorities had accepted the decision of the university authorities, considering that 'it was not proper to oppose an arrangement by which its interests were not affected'.[30] What mattered to the infirmary was the issue of representation of the hospital and its clinical staff on the governing bodies of the school. In the draft of the charter of the new, independent Welsh National School of Medicine it was being proposed that the infirmary should have three representatives on the school Council, and that the honorary clinical staff should have three representatives on the Senate. Persuaded by the formidable Mitchell Stevens, what the infirmary sought was not the university scheme (with a provost, a Council and a Senate), but rather a medical school with an annually elected dean, a Council with five or six hospital representatives, and, instead of a Senate, a Medical School Committee as the chief academic authority of the school, on which the honorary clinical staff would have a decisive majority. As the discussions proceeded the infirmary's proposals became increasingly unrealistic. Dominated by Mitchell Stevens, they went so far as to propose a structure for medical education in Wales that replicated the relationship between University College, London (Stevens's alma mater) and the University of London.[31]

The details of Stevens's proposals need not detain us. The important thing to note was that the university, increasingly irritated by the obtuse demeanour of the infirmary authorities, dismissed the infirmary's proposals out of hand. Apart from the fact that it was now far too late to start unscrambling the draft charter of the medical school, the university representatives considered that the infirmary's scheme totally failed to take into account the all-Wales context within which the Welsh National School of Medicine was expected to operate. This was an extremely sensitive issue in the early months of 1928, as four more local authorities (Merionethshire, Denbighshire, Flintshire and Montgomeryshire), frustrated by the delay in sorting out the future of the medical school, joined the growing ranks of those deciding to withhold their annual subscriptions in support of its work. It took much persuasion from the chairman of the Glamorgan County Council to prevent his own authority going the same way.[32]

Moreover, the infirmary's scheme, particularly the creation of a Medical School Committee, 'would effectively transfer the academic control of the School to the part-time clinical staff, over whom the University could exercise no control, and such a constitution would be wholly unacceptable to the University, the University Grants Committee and the Local Educational Authorities'.[33] As an alternative, the university representatives proposed the creation of a new committee within the medical school structure, a Board of Clinical Studies, made up of the honorary staff and tasked with advising the school authorities on a range of matters concerned with the teaching of the medical course, including 'the setting and co-ordination of timetables of Infirmary and School work having regard to the welfare of patients, the courses of study required, and the commitments – Infirmary and other – of teachers'.[34] This seemed a good idea to Sir William Diamond, the hospital chairman, who was becoming concerned at the apparent intransigence of his clinical colleagues, and he privately urged them to give the university's proposal full consideration, 'without bias or prejudice'.[35] Unfortunately, they did not heed his plea, rejecting the university's proposal because the Board of Clinical Studies would only have advisory powers. In other words, the honorary staff would not be able to dictate to the school how it should conduct its teaching responsibilities.

NOTICE TO QUIT

By now, many of the senior clinicians in the hospital, led by Mitchell Stevens, were in open revolt. At the beginning of May 1928 the school authorities were informed that unless the report of the joint committee was adopted by 30 June ten of the school's recognized clinical teachers would relinquish their teaching responsibilities. Those involved, apart from Mitchell Stevens, were Cornelius Griffiths, the senior surgeon; D. Leighton Davies, honorary ophthalmic surgeon; Alfred Howell and Herbert Evans, assistant physicians; J. O. D. Wade, D. J. Harries and T. E. Hammond, assistant surgeons; Garfield Evans, physiotherapist; and James Beatty, dermatologist. Several wrote to the college registrar, Daniel Brown, placing the blame squarely upon the Faculty of Medicine for not having accepted the report of the joint committee, thereby confirming how little they understood about the *raison d'être* of the Welsh National

School of Medicine. D. J. Harries demonstrated the limit of his own vision when he observed that several of the Welsh counties had withdrawn their financial support, 'and this to me appears to express the attitude of the People of Wales towards the so-called Welsh National Medical School. The title is obviously a misnomer.'[36]

At this time of impasse the medical school was presented with a golden opportunity to try to conciliate its most persistent critic, Mitchell Stevens, who had never come to terms with the clinical unit system as it operated in Cardiff. In most medical schools in the United Kingdom, the senior physician was given the title of professor of clinical medicine, responsible for organizing the ward-based teaching in the discipline. Stevens, as the senior physician at the infirmary, resented the fact that the Cardiff College had failed to give him the recognition he felt he richly deserved, particularly as he regarded the accredited professor, Kennedy, with total contempt. Moreover, although he had been part-time head of the Department of Materia Medica and Pharmacology since 1906, this had always been at the grade of lecturer. However, in October 1927, in a valedictory letter to the College Council on his retirement (though he managed to retain membership of the Board of Medicine until his death as a nominee of the Cardiff and County Public Health Committee), David Hepburn had drawn the college's attention to what he considered a serious oversight through its failure to confer a professorship on Mitchell Stevens. He urged the Council to 'take early steps to rectify this anomalous condition of affairs, and so remove a real blot from the medical curriculum, as well as an unintentional but long-standing injustice to a distinguished member of the Faculty of Medicine'. If they had wished, the Council could have rectified an undoubted anomaly by giving Stevens a personal chair; they had done this in Ewen Maclean's case after all. Instead the Council referred the matter to the Faculty of Medicine, which set up a subcommittee composed of the dean and Stevens's greatest enemies, Professors Graham Brown and Kennedy. The subcommittee decided to devise a substantial questionnaire for their long-standing and distinguished, if prickly, colleague to complete, covering teaching and research commitments, staff and non-staff resources and accommodation. Needless to say, despite two written reminders, Stevens, affronted by this approach, resolutely refused to respond, resulting in a report from the subcommittee which concluded that, from the information obtained from other sources, there appeared to be 'no exceptional circumstances' which would justify the award of a professorship to Mitchell Stevens.[37] It is impossible to say whether a different approach would have mollified Stevens; perhaps not, given the depth of the animosity on all sides by the late spring of 1928. What is certain is that the Faculty of Medicine's response to Hepburn's (possibly mischievous) initiative was unlikely to improve the atmosphere.

Though distinctly uncomfortable with the militancy of his medical colleagues, Sir William Diamond had spoken so often in the past of his determination to protect the reputation of his honorary staff that he was not going to stand against them now. As he wrote privately to the college registrar, 'Whatever the view may be of these good people there can be no doubt that the Clinical Teachers regard the present position very seriously indeed.'[38] At its meeting on 31 May, under pressure from the honorary staff, the infirmary's Board of Management was persuaded to terminate, with one month's notice, the existing agreement entered into between the infirmary and University College, Cardiff in 1921, which defined the basis on which clinical teaching was undertaken. The stage was set by Cornelius Griffiths, who provided an illuminating insight into the way most of the honorary staff viewed the unit system. He likened the chairman of the hospital to a host in his own home:

> The guest, the Medical School, was invited to come into the house, in which there was already a large family, and the members of the family were asked if they would co-operate in entertaining the guest. All the family promised to do so. They gave up their best rooms to the guest, who became established among them. The guest very soon began to assert himself; he began to make things very uncomfortable for the family, who had occupied the house for a considerable number of years before he came. The family put up with it for a long time, and they were gradually being crowded and frozen out into small spaces in the building. Still they put up with it. Then came the time when the last shred of their patience was absolutely worn out.[39]

The hospital authorities offered to enter into discussions either with the College or with 'another competent Authority, which would enable the Medical School to be carried on with the satisfaction and efficiency which can only come from the complete harmony and co-operation of all the authorities concerned'.[40]

The authorities of the infirmary had taken a momentous step. The essential features of the 1921 agreement were that the hospital would, as far as it reasonably could, give such facilities as the college might require for the teaching, examining and research purposes of the school; and that the agreement would last for an initial period of five years, to continue thereafter 'until altered by agreement between the parties'. While the hospital might claim that it had become increasingly displeased with the conduct of the school and college authorities, and while the honorary staff might, and did indeed, argue that they had, in January, stated their intention to stop teaching at the end of June unless their demands had been met, the fact remained that the college and hospital had not agreed to change the agreement. In effect, what the infirmary authorities were doing was 'illegal' and at the meeting of the Board of Management Professor Sheen told them so. The infirmary's actions were roundly condemned by most other well-informed observers. The *Western Mail* was appalled:

> The incredible has happened, and the board of management of the Cardiff Royal Infirmary has decided to withdraw from co-operation with the Welsh National

Medical School, leaving the latter stranded and helpless, incapable of giving to its pupils that clinical experience which is essential to the training of a doctor.[41]

Sir William James Thomas, who had invested years of his life and much of his fortune in the medical school and the infirmary, viewed the current impasse with total dismay: 'If my life is shortened it will be because of this controversy.'[42]

Others were becoming increasingly alarmed by the turn of events. Sir Walter Fletcher wrote a despairing letter to Sir Wilmot Herringham, still the medical member on the UGC:

> I have no doubt you know all about the scandals and disasters in the medical world at Cardiff. Do you see any way of effectively healing the situation from some broad national point of view? Is the UGC taking any action? The present deadlock has even an international flavour because the Rockefeller money already there seems to be in danger of being lost, and by breach, if not of formal contract, at least of honourable understanding.
>
> Cardiff has been given wonderful opportunities in recent years, in the excellent School of Physiology, in the liberally endowed chair of Preventive Medicine, in the well endowed Chair of Pathology, in the special resources for tuberculosis work in the Medical Unit supplied by the Foundation, and it has other good assets as well. Almost all these have in effect been thrown away by the recent disturbances and squabbles.[43]

This letter is of interest for a number of reasons. It confirms the generally high regard in which the medical school was held by the secretary of the Medical Research Council in the late 1920s. It hints at alarm being felt by the medical school's most influential international supporter, the Rockefeller Foundation, because of the difficulties with the hospital authorities. Indeed, documents in the Rockefeller Archive demonstrate the efforts made by Professor Kennedy at this time to reassure Richard Pearce that all would eventually be well. They also include an assessment by Pearce's deputy, Dr Alan Gregg, after visiting the school, that, despite the hospital staff 'trying to gain their way by threats and bluffing', it was now far too late for the Foundation to turn its back on a scheme which, after all, provided a firm, 'perhaps the best', foothold for the school within the hospital.[44] The letter is also interesting for the impact it made on the UGC – none whatsoever. The minutes of the UGC show that absolutely no discussion was held, at least formally, about the crisis threatening to overwhelm the Welsh National School of Medicine, at any of the meetings of the Committee in 1927 and 1928. The harsh reality was that, as A. H. Kidd's memorandum of 5 March 1927, referred to in chapter 7, demonstrated, the UGC, which, at the beginning of the decade, had taken such a close interest in the affairs of the school, had become weary of all the controversy which seemed to dog its every halting step. Furthermore, as the

UGC's change of attitude over the question of clinical units exemplified, the committee appeared to be taking an increasingly 'hands off' approach to matters of policy as the decade progressed. Fletcher's suggestion, made at the end of his letter to Sir Wilmot Herringham, that Lord Balfour, the former prime minister, now lord president of the Council in Baldwin's cabinet, might 'order a special inquiry from the point of view of the Privy Council' also came to naught.

Meanwhile, totally frustrated by the infirmary's intransigence, the University Council on 15 June decided to delete all references to the Cardiff Royal Infirmary in the draft charter of the medical school, substituting the words 'the Governing Body or Bodies of recognised Clinical Institutions'. While, in reality, the infirmary was the only significant clinical institution associated with the school, apart from the wise principle of keeping the wording in charters as general as possible, there was no harm in sending out a message that the infirmary was perhaps not quite as important as it professed to be.

Such messages meant little to the likes of Mitchell Stevens, who was being singled out in the local press as the villain of the piece, a description in which he revelled:

> He had been told that he was an extremist and a crank. He was glad to be an extremist and a crank in that instance because what was meant by it was that he placed the interests of the hospital before the interests of the school ... certainly the worst school in Great Britain.[45]

Stevens's intemperate observation immediately lost him any of the respect he might once have enjoyed among the clinical students, fifty-one of whom (out of fifty-eight) signed a letter of protest, addressed to William Martin, chairman of the Medical Board. They viewed Stevens's statements with 'great indignation', they demanded reasons for such 'outrageous remarks' and an explanation from the clinical staff of their current actions.[46] No reply was forthcoming.

In view of later events, it is important to note here that the Cardiff College never accepted the validity of the infirmary's decision to terminate the 1921 agreement. In the opinion of Trevor Harris, the college solicitor,

> Probably the legal position can be stated that the Agreement is perpetual unless either (a) a revised Agreement is made, or (b) a reasonable notice to terminate is given. The notice given is not, in my opinion reasonable and no attempt has been made to enter into a revised Agreement. In these circumstances the College should not accept the Infirmary's letter of June 1st as notice to terminate, and care should be taken in all communications not to accept it as such ... It should be made clear that the letter is not accepted as a notice to terminate on 30th June or on any date, and that revision [of the agreement] can only be taken on that understanding.

The College Council readily accepted this view, which was immediately communicated to the hospital secretary, with an offer to enter into early discussions regarding a revision of the terms of the agreement. Leonard Rea, in his response, a fortnight later, while welcoming the opportunity of entering into discussions about a new agreement, wished to make it equally clear that the hospital authorities

> do not admit that the notice contained in our letter of 1st June is not valid. It is their opinion that such notice is valid, and I am directed to say that the negotiations contemplated can only be undertaken by them on the understanding that the validity of such notice is not in question.[47]

EFFORTS TO REACH A COMPROMISE

Whether or not the college accepted the validity of the notice, it could certainly not ignore it, particularly in view of the contents of the report of a committee set up by the Board of Medicine to consider the grievances of the recognized clinical teachers. The committee, though small, was high-powered, including amongst its members not only the principal of the college as chairman, and the chairman of the hospital board of management, but also Dr David Llewelyn Williams, the chief medical officer of the Welsh Board of Health and Revd Hugh M. Hughes, minister of Ebenezer Independent chapel, Cardiff and a senior member of the Cardiff College Council imminently to be elevated to the position of vice-president. They met on three occasions and heard evidence from the professors of medicine, surgery and obstetrics and gynaecology, and from those among the clinical teachers – mainly the assistant surgeons – who chose to appear before them. Little was heard about the alleged shortcomings of the unit system *per se*, which was perhaps a little surprising in view of the criticism it aroused in the local press during the month of June. In an article written by an anonymous, though well-informed 'correspondent' for the *South Wales News*, the unit system was attacked as an 'alien system' introduced from abroad (Germany and America) 'and very few British medical schools of repute have adopted it'. T. E. Hammond, one of the disaffected members of the clinical staff, condemned the concept of full-time professors in the *Western Mail*, claiming that such appointments would inevitably 'attract those who have no experience of private practice, so that the teaching would tend to become more academic and less practical'.

Although a member of the committee, Sir William Diamond appeared, from the outset, to assume the role of chief prosecutor. He criticized not so much the unit system as a matter of principle, but rather the manner in which the professors of medicine and surgery had implemented the system in Cardiff, signally failing to carry their hospital colleagues with them. He accused the professors of acting as dictators, treating the honorary medical staff with contempt. 'That', asserted Diamond, 'was the fundamental cause of all the trouble.' He deplored the way in which Professor Kennedy treated his colleagues with disdain. 'He had attended only one meeting of the Honorary Medical Board of the Infirmary since his appointment nearly six years ago', and emphasized that the only way of getting success was by co-operation. He accused Professor Sheen of ignoring the regulations of the infirmary by running his unit without reference to his surgical colleagues or the management.

> Whenever a Senior who was in charge of beds absented himself he had to report to the Medical Superintendent and suitable arrangements had to be made to carry on in his absence. Professor Sheen had failed to report to the Medical Superintendent on several occasions. He told his assistant, Mr Lambert Rogers, to carry on and ignored their Honorary Members.

Confronted with such allegations, Sheen simply denied them, while Kennedy accused his clinical colleagues of having ostracized him from the time of his appointment, though he did admit that 'the committees had got on his nerves'.

Whether or not Sir William Diamond's assessment of the situation was entirely fair, the evidence given by the clinical teachers added weight to his analysis. Both of the professors were accused of arranging the teaching programmes without taking account of the clinical teachers' other commitments, not having proper arrangements in place to record the attendance and conduct of students attached to units other than the professorial units, and, as far as the professorial surgical unit was concerned, of failing to treat his part-time assistants with respect. T. E. Hammond accused William Sheen of showing undue favouritism to his full-time assistant, Lambert Rogers, while implying that the part-time assistants were a nuisance, being unavailable for teaching when required because of 'the exigencies of private practice and the necessity of attending court for compensation cases'. In reply, Sheen did admit that his 'difficulty was to get them to do anything. There was a great want of co-operation on their part.'

Nothing that the committee heard was really new. Complaints about the way the professors conducted themselves in their dealings with their clinical colleagues stretched back to the earliest weeks of the full medical school. The senior clinical staff chose not to attend the meetings at all, considering the exercise pointless, and at the end of the third meeting on 18 June the committee decided they could do no more.

Approved by the Board of Medicine on 22 June 1928, the committee's report concluded that the difficulties were 'rather of a personal than of a constitutional character' but unless the personal difficulties were quickly resolved 'the closure of the Clinical Section of the School cannot be long delayed.'[48]

Although a few students were already making arrangements to 'desert the sinking ship',[49] there were early grounds for optimism. At a joint conference held on 4 July between representatives of the college and the infirmary under the chairmanship of Sir William Diamond, it was agreed that in order to make progress, both sides would reserve their rights with regard to the validity of the notice. The conference then proceeded to agree certain propositions as a basis for discussion, including acceptance of the right of the infirmary 'to the control and direction of all the internal arrangements of the institution', and the requirement that 'The University professors in the discharge of their clinical duties shall conform to all the rules and regulations laid down by the Infirmary.' Moreover, 'The College shall make an agreement with the Members of the Honorary Staff of the Infirmary for the teaching arrangements in the Infirmary.' To that effect it was proposed that the clinical staff should work out a scheme, and in the meantime the dissident clinicians were urged to continue as recognized clinical teachers for the next twelve months. The local press was encouraged by the outcome of the conference. 'Public feeling in Wales will be greatly relieved by the conciliatory spirit that prevailed,' observed the *Western Mail*, while even the *South Wales News*, which had consistently defended the actions of the honorary clinical staff, reported 'a favourable turn' with a way paved for settlement.[50] The clinical students were, naturally, encouraged too. In a statement to the press, having confirmed their unanimous support for the unit system, 'the best possible method by which a University can train its students', they expressed their concern if the discussions were to end in failure. They emphasized the severe financial implications of having to relocate elsewhere, which might cause some students to terminate their studies, as well as the adverse impact on the good name of the university. However, the students remained convinced that 'With good will on both sides, a satisfactory solution can be worked out very quickly.'[51]

Unfortunately, good will and good sense were lacking in several of the dissidents, for whom the outcome of the conference had not been nearly good enough. At a meeting of recognized clinical teachers on 6 July (also 'gatecrashed' by the clinical professors, to the annoyance of some), D. J. Harries, James Beatty, T. E. Hammond and Garfield Evans expressed their willingness to serve as teachers while discussions continued. Six refused to do so, including Mitchell Stevens, Cornelius Griffiths and Leighton Davies. For them the continuance of the unit system was an insuperable obstacle. Their refusal immediately jeopardized continuing recognition of the school's clinical course by the authorities of London University and the Conjoint Board, which required that students pursuing their qualifications should have access to all the beds of the infirmary for teaching purposes.

Despite the fact that the school was in the middle of the greatest crisis in its history, the advent of the long vacation at the beginning of July meant that no meetings of the Faculty of Medicine and the Board of Medicine were scheduled to be held until the end of September. A body known as the Vacation Committee was created to deal with the day-to-day management of the school and its problems.[52] Chaired by the dean, and including the college principal and the professors of anatomy, medicine, obstetrics and pathology, the committee's immediate task was to respond to the fact that one-third of the recognized clinical teachers were refusing to participate in the teaching programme. The continuation of the first three preclinical years was never in doubt. However, the committee immediately realized that, in such a situation, although the school could provide clinical teaching to those students who were pursuing the Wales degree, it would struggle to provide suitable facilities for the others, a conclusion confirmed following a visit to London by Professors Sheen and Kennedy. With regret the committee reported this conclusion to the College Council on 13 July, and immediately thereafter the college registrar, as a precautionary measure, sent a letter to all existing and prospective students of the school, part of which stated:

> Students preparing for the Degrees of MB B.Ch. of the University of Wales who desire to pursue the Second Part of the Scheme of Study for those degrees … will, under present circumstances, be admitted as usual; but Students preparing for the Examinations of other Bodies in any of the foregoing [clinical] subjects cannot be accepted as students until more complete arrangements have been made between the Hospital and the College Authorities.[53]

The college authorities had not yet given up hope. A further joint meeting between representatives of the college and the hospital, held on 12 July, had agreed that the recognized clinical teachers should go away and come up with their own scheme for the organization of teaching at the infirmary, and, anticipating a satisfactory conclusion the College Council had authorized the registrar to reappoint all the recognized clinical teachers for the 1928/9 session.

The responses from the honorary staff were mostly positive, even friendly.[54] J. W. Tudor Thomas, honorary assistant ophthalmologist (and at the time secretary of the Medical Board), was prepared to accept the title of recognized clinical teacher: 'I hope that the difficulties in connection with the School will be faced by all in a spirit of earnest endeavour to build up and maintain a School of which we may all be proud.' The splendid Dr Cyril Lewis, who had to be sent a letter of reminder, was most apologetic: 'I am very sorry I did not reply to your letter of 17th July as I supposed I took it for granted that you would know that I should do all in my power to assist the Welsh National School of Medicine.' It is easy to forget that there were three honorary physicians at the Infirmary during the 1920s, Mitchell Stevens, Alexander Kennedy (known as 'Sandy' or 'Jock' to his friends) and Cyril Lewis. It will be recalled that Lewis had been very accommodating during the process of reallocating the medical beds in 1923, and had generally maintained a low profile during this period while Stevens and Kennedy were busy squabbling. Many years later, his obituarist, none other than Professor Kennedy himself, would recall Lewis with generosity, as a kind, thoughtful and courteous colleague.[55] Mitchell Stevens's reply to Daniel Brown was less positive: 'I need scarcely say that I am not prepared under present circumstances to accept the appointment referred to. At the meeting last week I made it perfectly clear what my position was.' Cornelius Griffiths, Herbert Evans and J. O. D. Wade wrote back in similar terms. The sharpest response came from D. Leighton Davies, the senior ophthalmologist:

> The fact that the Council have re-appointed me as a recognised clinical fills me with amazement. Have the Council not yet realised that I, with others of my colleagues resigned our position as clinical teachers owing to the scandalously inefficient way in which the Medical School is being conducted? And are they aware that no efficient steps have yet been taken, or it seems to me are likely to be taken to meet our criticisms. Until such changes as we consider necessary have been made and not merely talked about in the management of the Medical School I decline to allow my name to appear on the syllabus as a clinical teacher.

William Martin, chairman of the Medical Board, was only slightly more conciliatory: 'As no satisfactory settlement has yet been arrived at I cannot at present accept the appointment for a year, but for the benefit of the present students I am willing to act for the first three months of the year.'

To digress for a moment, the replies to the registrar provide interesting information about the addresses of the honorary staff of the infirmary during the 1920s. D. Leighton Davies, Cornelius Griffiths and Herbert Evans all lived in Newport Road. J. O. D. Wade and Cyril Lewis were near neighbours in Park Place, while Windsor Place was full of doctors, surgeons William Martin, Geary Grant and T. E. Hammond, physicians Ivor Davies and Alfred Howell, gynaecologists Gilbert Strachan and B. K. Tenison Collins and F. R. Cresswell, the ophthalmic surgeon. Mitchell Stevens was at 21 St Andrew's Crescent. In other words they not only lived close to the infirmary; as Hilary Wade, one of J. O. D. Wade's four doctor sons, once pointed out, 'It was essential for the consultant to live reasonably close to the railway stations, because practically all their patients from outside Cardiff came in by train.' One or two doctors, James Beatty and J. W. Tudor Thomas, were based in Cathedral Road, but this area only became popular with the medical profession during the 1930s with the development of motor transport. Wade also told a cautionary tale about William Martin:

> He was a Scot and had a very thriving practice from his home in Windsor Place. However he decided to move to Marine Parade in Penarth and his practice rapidly deteriorated. My father used to tell this story to give dire warning to us boys on the importance of a consultant living over his shop.

In his memoirs Owen Wade, another of J. O. D. Wade's sons, has described how 'In our house … the telephone, an ancient upright model which had its earphone hanging on a little Y-shaped lever at its side, dominated our lives.'[56]

With five, perhaps six, of the honorary staff, including the senior physician and the senior surgeon, still digging in their heels, the prospects for an early resolution of the dispute were poor. The last thing that the local medical community needed at this juncture was for the whole of the medical world to converge on the city for the annual conference of the British Medical Association during the last week of July, for the first time since 1885. However, under the benign presidency of Sir Ewen Maclean, the event proved to be a great success.[57] Certainly, during the public sessions no one, least of all Sir Ewen, made any reference to the local difficulties. The Marquess of Bute hosted a garden party and a banquet. The National Museum of Wales put on what the *British Medical Journal* called 'an interesting little exhibition', including the Laws of Hywel Dda and the text of the 'Meddygon Myddfai' (the Physicians of Myddfai), to whom Sir Ewen Maclean had referred during his presidential address. The City Hall, much admired by all, was used for the major plenary sessions, while most of the business sessions were hosted by the college, earning the praise of the *British Medical Journal*: 'Many members from other parts of the country will henceforth take a livelier interest in the progress of higher education in the Principality.' The college library was used as a pathological museum where several specimens from the departments of pathology and surgery and elsewhere were displayed, with pride of place being given to a collection of memorabilia of Joseph, first Baron Lister, pioneer of antiseptic surgery, presented to the medical school by the Wellcome Historical Museum after negotiations involving Professor Sheen and Lord Kenyon.[58] The University of Wales also contributed to the success of the conference by conferring honorary degrees on six distinguished members of the medical profession, including Sir Thomas Lewis, at a special degree ceremony at the City Hall, an event enlivened, according to the *Western Mail*, by 'good-humoured interjections, song and whistling' by the Cardiff students attending to receive their BA, B.Mus. and B.Sc. degrees.[59] However, much to the disappointment of the BMA officers, who had wanted to make him an honorary member of the Association, the chancellor of the university, the Prince of Wales, was not in attendance.[60] Otherwise the meeting was deemed to be a great success, with the delegates going home blissfully unconcerned, even perhaps unaware, that the whole future of medical education in Wales seemed to be hanging in the balance.

The authorities of the University of Wales were certainly not disposed to allow the irritating dispute between some of the doctors at the Infirmary and the College to divert them from their immediate objective, that of securing final agreement over the terms of the charter for an independent Welsh National School of Medicine, shorn of its preclinical departments. Invited by the university to comment on the draft, the Faculty of Medicine expressed no opinion on the main issues and simply offered some textual amendments.[61] The Cardiff Court, having heard Principal Trow express regret at the outcome, nevertheless voted, by forty-seven to twenty-two, to accept what he now regarded as 'the only practical solution'.[62] A week later, at Bangor, the University Court itself approved the final draft of the charter and authorized its submission to the Privy Council, much to the amazement of its deputy clerk: 'So great has been the pugnacity and animosity shown that I can only marvel that agreement or compromise of any description has at length been reached.'[63]

Meanwhile, the honorary clinical staff of the infirmary, charged by the joint conference on 12 July to devise a scheme for the provision of clinical teaching at the hospital, were making extremely slow progress. On 28 July they decided to adjourn their discussions until early September and, despite appeals from Sir William Diamond to expedite matters, it was not until the end of that month that they reassembled to give preliminary consideration to the proposals they had formulated.[64] By then the situation had deteriorated dramatically. Aware, in the middle of September, that several of the honorary staff were still refusing to teach the clinical students, the Conjoint Board and the University of London formally withdrew their recognition of the Welsh National School of Medicine as an institution suitable to train students seeking to take their qualifications. The *Western Mail* was appalled by the spinelessness of the hospital authorities for not summarily dismissing the dissident doctors and replacing them with other private practitioners who would have been more than happy to assume their duties. The newspaper also proposed that the retirement age of the honorary staff should be brought back to sixty, thereby eliminating the ringleaders of the dispute at a stroke.[65] Neither suggestion was likely to achieve an immediate settlement.

THE INFIRMARY CLOSES THE DOOR

By mid-September, most medical students who had expected, under normal circumstances, to progress to the fourth, fifth and sixth years of the course in the autumn of 1928, were making arrangements to secure clinical places elsewhere. Not only were London and Conjoint students doing this but also several Welsh degree students (most of whom were in any case registered for other qualifications too), who regarded the prospect of staying in Cardiff as unattractive, notwithstanding the extra costs they would undoubtedly face by leaving. The London medical schools, while not wishing to get involved in what they regarded as a local dispute, expressed great sympathy for the students and made it clear that they would do what they could to help.[66] Even so, the school authorities were still confident that, given the good will of sufficient of their clinical colleagues at the infirmary, they could offer a clinical course to those Welsh degree students who remained. While the college was not in a position to issue a medical school prospectus for the 1928/9 session following the usual format, a short pamphlet was produced for the attention of existing and prospective students (of whom there would be well over a hundred in the first three years in any event) which provided basic information about the school, its general regulations and fees payable. On its front page the pamphlet stated that whereas students preparing for qualifications other than those of the University of Wales could not be accepted for clinical training 'until more complete arrangements have been made between the Hospital and College Authorities', students preparing for the degrees of MB B.Ch. of the University of Wales and who wished to spend the fourth, fifth and sixth years in Cardiff 'will, under present conditions, be admitted as usual'.

The conditions changed dramatically on the evening of 25 September when an unknown number of medical students still in Cardiff caused a disturbance in their common room at the infirmary, during the course of which they vandalized a portrait of Cornelius Griffiths, ex-president of the Medical Students' Club, which had been presented to the club by the senior surgeon's wife. Across the lower part of the muti-lated portrait the word 'Traitor' had been chalked, as a photograph in the *Western Mail* clearly showed. Whether the culprits were students soon to be leaving for London or elsewhere, or from the handful of students still hoping to remain in Cardiff, was never established, but the affray was attributed to a group who were disgruntled with the rupture between the hospital and the school. One student interviewed by the *Western Mail* stated that feelings were running high: 'Owing to this dispute we have been driven from our native land to seek education elsewhere. Some of us cannot afford the extra expense, so the outlook is very black in those cases.'[67] Most students, at least in public, professed to deplore the act of vandalism perpetrated on what, as a matter of fact, was their own property, but the honorary staff and the hospital authorities were outraged. Writing to Daniel Brown on 27 September, Leonard Rea notified the college that

> The Infirmary Authorities cannot permit Students to have access to the Infirmary precincts after 30th instant, until some arrangement has been arrived at between the two Authorities ... Recent disturbances emphasise the expediency of ensuring that the Students shall not be admitted except under defined conditions.

Two days later Rea sent another letter, adding that the infirmary's ban applied 'not only to the Students but to the Welsh National School of Medicine as a whole'.[68]

The college authorities were stunned by the turn of events. Though Leonard Rea attempted to justify the infirmary's action on the grounds that, in accordance with is letter of 1 June, the agreement had now lapsed, the fact was that the college had never accepted the validity of the notice. All the college's subsequent actions, taken with the full knowledge of the infirmary, had been based on the assumption that a clinical course of some sort, albeit with far fewer students than had been expected, would be offered in 1928/9. To use the student fracas as a pretext for closing the doors of the Infirmary to the school, 'until some arrangement has been arrived at between the two Authorities', was quite unacceptable. Fairly positive conferences had already been held between representatives of the infirmary and themselves at the highest level and there was, in the college's view, every prospect of a successful outcome. The fact that the clinical teachers, after nearly three months, had not yet formulated proposals for another joint conference to consider was no fault of the College.

After a flurry of telegrams and hurried meetings involving senior officers of the medical school and the college, Daniel Brown's response to Rea was carefully couched in sorrowful rather than angry terms. No reference was made to the apparent exclusion from the hospital premises of the school staff. The college registrar chose to place most emphasis on the harmful effect of the infirmary's action upon the small group of medical students still remaining in Cardiff, most, if not all of whom, Brown reminded Rea, had already paid in advance for the hospital tickets which granted them access to the infirmary's facilities: 'The College may be under some obligation to students whom the Infirmary refuses to admit. If this is so, the College is of opinion that the Infirmary must be held responsible for any loss which the College sustains.'[69]

Simultaneously Brown wrote to the students affected, explaining the position and asking whether, in the circumstances, it was still their intention to enrol for the fourth, fifth or sixth years of the Welsh degree course: 'The College is not accepting the validity and the effect of the notice given by the Cardiff Royal Infirmary, and will take every possible step to make adequate provision for its students.'[70] Eight students, undoubtedly those whose personal (including financial), circumstances made a move from Cardiff particularly difficult, indicated their wish to remain in the school. In the biting words of the *Western Mail*,

> Most of the students have, owing to the unfortunate dispute between the Medical School and the Infirmary board of management, already taken their departure for more hospitable and congenial homes of medical study, and it is the few who remain who are the victims of the latest exhibition of hostility.[71]

The school's Vacation Committee, which had been kept in being to deal with the crisis, urgently reviewed possible options. One seriously considered involved a significant extension of teaching to the City Lodge Hospital, a step which would have required the appointment of Professor J. H. Dible, who had succeeded Edgar Kettle as professor of pathology and bacteriology in May 1928, as honorary pathologist to that hospital. The other involved the school departments simply calling the bluff of the Infirmary authorities. This option was much favoured by the pugnacious Principal Trow, who was more than happy 'to accept the responsibility of advising the heads of departments concerned at the Infirmary to carry on their work at the infirmary unless or until they were prevented from doing so'.[72]

The College Council, on 2 October, having unanimously expressed its regret about the offences committed in the students' common room at the infirmary, resolved that a final appeal be sent to the hospital. Surely common sense might still prevail, even at this late stage. Unfortunately, a well-attended special meeting of the Infirmary Council, held on 4 October, simply dithered, deciding to do nothing until the college and the infirmary had produced proposals for the future conduct of clinical teaching at the hospital, and refusing to do anything for the handful of medical students still in Cardiff. As usual during this time the *Western Mail* was scathing in its criticism of the Infirmary Council:

> A great calamity had already befallen the Medical School by the withdrawal of recognition on the part of London University and the Conjoint Board. That calamity cannot be repaired in a day, but the position of the remaining students, who should have continued their clinical training for the term 1928/9, can be rectified immediately. Why was this duty left unfulfilled at yesterday's meeting of the Infirmary Council? Why is it that a body of business men has failed to deal with this issue in a businesslike manner? Why is it that the Council of the Infirmary are cherishing the humiliation which they have brought upon themselves, and why are they still exposing Cardiff to the contempt of the rest of Wales?[73]

Why indeed! In his history of the infirmary, Arnold Aldis referred to 'misunderstandings and some personality problems' on both sides, causing otherwise small irritations to become magnified into major problems, with attitudes hardening and positions becoming more entrenched.[74] None of this should have led to the action taken by the infirmary authorities. However, condemned on all sides for their lack of judgement and perspective and, frankly, intimidated by an irreconcilable group of powerful doctors in the hospital, including the senior physician and the senior surgeon, the beleaguered chairman and his colleagues demonstrated that they were totally out of their depth. We have already noted how, on more than one occasion, Sir William Diamond, while clearly unhappy with the way things were going, failed to show leadership, an unexpected failure in a man who had served as president of the Engineers' and Shipbuilders' Employers' Association throughout the First World War, earning a knighthood for his efforts. However, he himself, described at the time by a local weekly newspaper as 'a genial, great-hearted, accessible individual' with 'a directness of speech, bordering on bluntness',[75] would admit that he had made grave mistakes. 'I came into the job without hospital experience and I had to take advice from people around me', surely a reference to the senior members of the honorary staff. As a businessman, he confessed he did 'not understand the academic mind'.[76] Even the resignation in late September (the news was suppressed for some days) of Lord Aberdare as honorary treasurer of the infirmary because of 'the recent decision of the [Infirmary] Council not to co-operate with the Medical School', had not caused the members of the Infirmary council to think again.[77]

The outcome, of course, was calamitous. On 5 October the college had no alternative but to inform the remaining medical students that there was no immediate hope of their continuing their studies in Cardiff and that they should make other arrangements.[78] The following Sunday evening witnessed the sad sight of four medical students bidding farewell to the congregation of Pembroke Terrace Calvinistic Methodist church, of which they were members, before finally leaving for London to complete their studies.[79] Under normal circumstances there should have been sixty students pursuing clinical studies in Cardiff in 1928/9, nineteen in the fourth year, twenty-three in the fifth and eighteen in the sixth. As a result of the actions of the infirmary there were none. Apart from a handful whose personal circumstances precluded their relocation, all the students managed to secure admission to other medical schools. Half a dozen went to Bristol; the rest went to London. The majority of these found places at University College Hospital, though quite a few went to Charing Cross Hospital, and others, in ones and twos, joined Guy's, Mary's, Westminster, the Middlesex and the Royal Free Hospitals.[80] Ninety-two per cent of the students ultimately qualified, two-thirds of them 'on time'.

One was the writer's uncle, David Glanville Evans, son of the chief inspector at the Welsh Board of Health. Educated at Cardiff High School, Glanville Evans entered the Welsh National School of Medicine in 1924 and occupied himself during the General Strike by serving as a volunteer conductor on one of the tramways of the Cardiff Corporation, being awarded a souvenir brochure 'in recognition of his faithful adherence to the ideals of true citizenship' by the lord mayor of Cardiff at a civic reception. With the closure of the infirmary he entered the penultimate year at University College Hospital, graduating with the medical degrees of both Wales and London in 1930. During his time in Cardiff, Glanville Evans (dubbed 'Cyclone' by his contemporaries because of his sporting prowess – he captained the Medics First XV in 1927/8) had become acquainted with Margaret Emma Williams of New Tredegar in the Rhymney Valley, a medical student in the year below. Though she went to Bristol to pursue her clinical studies, they would subsequently marry and go into practice together in Pwllheli in the mid-thirties. 'Dr Margaret', as she was affectionately known, was the first, and for many years the only woman medical practitioner in the Llŷn peninsula. Idris Jones, who, at the time of the infirmary 'lock-out' was also due to begin the fourth year, spent his clinical years at Guy's Hospital, later working in partnership with Glanville and Margaret Evans at the Pwllheli practice.

9

The Students

It is perhaps with some relief that the trials and tribulations of the Welsh National School of Medicine are, for a moment, put to one side. Some consideration should be given to aspects of the student experience during the first forty or so years of the medical school's existence: how many were there, what was their background, how did they spend their time, and what happened to them after graduation? Of all the facts presented in this chapter, arguably the most striking in the light of the bitter debates about the constitutional position of the school is the tiny proportion of students who hailed from the six counties of north Wales, less than 3 per cent of the total, compared with over 80 per cent from the counties of Glamorgan and Monmouthshire. In this respect the Welsh National School of Medicine was, throughout the period, rooted in south Wales and it was little wonder that the Cardiff College fought so hard, for so long, to keep control of it, and that, after an initial commitment generated by the enthusiasm of Gwilym Hughes, most of the Welsh local authorities proved to be so reluctant to subscribe to the school's finances. People from north Wales looking for medical role models, rather than look south, would look across to Liverpool, where great Welsh doctors like Sir Robert Jones were establishing an international reputation.

THE 'ADMIN'

In recent decades, entry into medical school has largely been dictated by government-imposed quotas. This was not the case during the period covered by this volume. In Cardiff as elsewhere, the number of entrants fluctuated from one year to the next. Even when, immediately after the First World War, the numbers soared, causing, as we have seen, some concern to the college authorities, the principal expressed his aversion to the idea of turning appropriately qualified students away. Writing to Colonel Bruce Vaughan in January 1919, Professor Trow stressed the importance of having the new physiology building finished and available for use as soon as possible as 'I am very anxious that we should not refuse any medical student on the grounds of insufficient accommodation.'[1] It would not be until the early 1930s, beyond the boundaries of the present study, that regulations were introduced by the college which were designed to restrict the number of medical students in the first three years of the course.

Until then, how did the students gain admission? Most students probably consulted the special educational issues of *The Lancet* and the *British Medical Journal*, which appeared in late August or early September each year, and which gave basic details about the several medical schools available for consideration. There could be found the name of the relevant contact person, usually the dean of medicine. By 1927 the concept of pursuing a medical career had become sufficiently well established in the United Kingdom for the General Medical Council to publish, for potential students to consult, a pamphlet, *Memorandum by the Registrar on the Procedure to be Adopted by those who Desire to Enter the Profession of Medicine, with Notes on Cost and Prospects*.[2]

They would also obtain copies of the medical school prospectuses, as they do today, though in all likelihood they would focus their attention on one school, probably with economic considerations uppermost in their minds, or, more likely, in the minds of their parents. We shall come back to this. Inside the front cover of the prospectus of the Welsh National School of Medicine during the 1920s was the following statement:

> Information regarding the School of Medicine, and advice regarding the courses of study, may be obtained on application by letter to the Dean of the Faculty of Medicine, who will be pleased to meet intending Students, or their parents, at the Welsh National School of Medicine, University College, Newport Road, by appointment, at the beginning of each term.

Having made themselves known to the dean, students intending to pursue their studies in Cardiff were required to complete a blue 'Form for new students desiring to enter the College' which, having been filled in, was to be taken to the 'Dean of the Faculty in which it is proposed to study'. The form asked for basic information (name, address, date of birth, school or college last attended) and details of relevant entrance examinations passed. Testimonials from head teachers or other appropriate people were required. Provided the applications were accepted, the students in question were expected to arrive at the beginning of the autumn term (though it was, for most of the period, possible to enrol at the beginning of the spring and summer terms and a few did so), and formally register in the college's registration record books. These are still preserved in the archives of Cardiff University and provide a superb source for compiling a profile of the sort of boys and girls who wished to become doctors during the early decades of the twentieth century.

After the registration process had been completed, the dean of medicine compiled an annual 'Index of medical students' enrolled in the college, and these are also preserved in the Cardiff University archives. For nearly twenty years it was Professor Hepburn himself who, in peace and war, wrote up the entries painstakingly in the index in his neat handwriting, with scarcely an error (though he was weak on hyphenated surnames), and if some of the relevant information was missing (such as student registration numbers), he would send urgent notes to his clerk, requesting the missing details so that his index could be completed. Such was the importance that Dean Hepburn placed on ensuring that the medical students were properly enrolled at the beginning of the session that it was no wonder that he bitterly complained at having to attend a meeting of the Haldane Commission during the first week of the autumn term in 1916. A. H. Kidd, the secretary to the commission, did what he could to reassure the registrar of University College, Cardiff: 'I am sure that the Commission will do all they can to detain Professor Hepburn no longer than is necessary but you will of course understand that I cannot give a definite undertaking that the Commission will finish with him that evening.'[3] According to Dr Mitchell Stevens, Professor Graham Brown, when dean, took a more strategic, or in the modern parlance, hands-off, approach to his duties as dean. Much of the day-to-day administration 'is left to his clerk'. Brown's obituarist in *The Lancet* seemed to confirm this when he referred to his impatience with 'the details of academic routine'.[4] If further evidence is required to demonstrate the dedication of Hepburn to his duties as dean, in comparison with those who succeeded him in the role, Professors Kennedy and Brown, Dr J. Eilir Thomas provides it. In August 1925 he wrote the following letter to Professor Hepburn:

I am a candidate for the post of Assistant Schools' Medical Officer for Carmarthenshire and I feel that a reference from you to the effect that I studied under you for 3 years while you were Dean would be of inestimable value in my candidature. My qualifications are BSc. MRCS LRCP. I suppose the correct thing for me to do would be to apply to the present Dean [T Graham Brown] for a testimonial. That I have not the slightest intention of doing. I have to thank this particular professor and the one who followed you when you resigned your office as Dean for the most perfect example of mismanaging a career as it is possible to conceive.

After graduating BSc in 1922 (I entered in Oct. 1919) I entered the Infirmary as student, believing all the wonderful things said of the Welsh National School of Medicine. I was soon disillusioned. The Professor of Medicine had no registers of attendance and no method of teaching. If in doubt as to attendance at lectures he would have to fall back on the students' testimony – and he generally refused to believe them.

Then came another Dean – and this time, although the Professor of Physiology was appointed, the real Dean was the clerk. The great man himself was too interested in monkeys to have time for students.

I think it is a disgrace that the studies of those people entering upon their final years in Cardiff should be entrusted to such fools.

Forgive me, Sir, for taking such liberties. In the years I spent with you as Dean I found you always ready to sympathise with a student's grievance, otherwise I would not dare write this letter. Whether you decide to give me a reference or not I shall be glad to have given you an idea of what is the students' opinion generally.[5]

From what has already been written it is clear that, particularly in the 1920s when the full medical school was in being, the administrative staff played an important part in the day-to-day running of its affairs, as was only to be expected. The head of the administration was the college registrar, Daniel James Arthur Brown, who also served as secretary to the Welsh National School of Medicine and its main committees, the Board of Medicine, its Finance Committee and the Faculty of Medicine. Bearing in mind his wider responsibilities to the college as a whole, he was a diligent, hard-working and extremely well-organized administrator, who was awarded a well-deserved honorary MA by the University of Wales on the occasion of University College, Cardiff's Golden Jubilee, in July 1933. The citation, read by Cardiff's principal, J. F. Rees, included the following:

> An official who is never officious. A servant who has served the College with unswerving loyalty for nearly forty years. The *fidus Achates* of three successive Principals, nothing would induce him to compare their merits or reveal their faults. Cautious in counsel, scrupulous in judgement, sound in finance; ever ready at any hour to take on tasks, however onerous or humble, and not only to perform them to the full but to efface himself in the interests of the institution. Generations of students have found that behind the formal façade of the office, perhaps at first forbidding, they have a friend with a sympathetic ear and a kindly heart.

What the citation did not mention was that, before taking up a career in university administration, Brown had taught accountancy and bookkeeping in local technical schools, and was the author of the textbook *Elementary Practical Book-keeping*, and joint author of *Investment and Loan Societies Accounts*. His dedication to duty was, no doubt, partly due to his strong Nonconformist convictions. His father had, for many years, been the pastor of a Congregationalist chapel in Leominster, and Brown himself was an active member of New Trinity Congregationalist chapel, in Cowbridge Road, Cardiff. During the First World War, when not engaged in college affairs, he undertook voluntary service with the Red Cross, and he was frequently to be seen on the Cardiff railway platform supervising the conveyance of wounded soldiers to various local hospitals. In appreciation of his services he was made honorary commander of the Glamorgan Red Cross, Detachment No. 77. When he finally retired from the college, in 1936, a year before his death at the age of sixty-six, he left behind, in the words of Sir Percy Watkins, 'a most fragrant memory among all who knew him, as well as a record of quiet, effective and wise service of which any man might well be proud'.[6] A scrutiny of some of the registrar's files, still stored among the Cardiff University archives, demonstrates how meticulous he was in the preparation of committee papers and briefing notes for the college principal and other senior officers with whom he dealt on a regular basis. It is clear from his correspondence and other evidence that he commanded widespread trust, in the College, in the wider university community, and in the Cardiff Royal Infirmary, no mean achievement considering the difficult events in which he was involved, particularly during the 1920s.

However, able though he was, Brown could not do everything himself, and one of the first actions taken by the principal, the dean and the registrar, once the full medical school had come into being, was to appoint a clerk, in the office of its secretary, to manage the day-to-day running of the school. Frederick G. Hartland, who had previously worked at St George's Hospital, London, was appointed with effect from 1 December 1921, at an initial annual salary of £200 (about one-third of what the registrar earned). By the time of Hartland's resignation as chief clerk, early in 1931, there had also been appointed a second and third clerk. It is quite clear from the testimonies of Mitchell Stevens and J. Eilir Thomas, that Hartland was highly thought of, and it was to him that anxious students and their parents appeared to turn in times of trouble. For example, it was to Hartland that Mrs A. M. Farrington wrote, no doubt at the suggestion of her son, in November 1928:

> I am sorry to bother you, but if you could let me know if the trouble with the Infirmary is settled yet, and if Merlyn will be able to resume his studies in Cardiff in Jan., I should be very much obliged. He is working here in Bristol and likes it alright, but prefers Cardiff. So if you could just drop me a line I should be very glad.

As any prudent administrator would do in such circumstances, Hartland left it to Brown to dispatch a rather pessimistic reply to Merlyn's mother.[7]

STUDENT NUMBERS AND QUALIFICATIONS

The excellent sources referred to above tell us much about the medical students enrolled with University College, Cardiff until 1931. First, as to numbers, it has already been noted that in the inaugural year of the Cardiff Medical School, in 1893/4, there were a dozen students. Ten years later, in 1903/4, there was a total of forty-three students enrolled for the three years of the Cardiff course. Table 9.1 gives the full picture from that date up to the time when clinical training began in Cardiff.

Table 9.1 shows that numbers were fairly static until the later years of the First World War when they soared, causing, as we have seen in earlier chapters, considerable pressure on the school's facilities, and the new Institute of Physiology came not a moment too soon. Although, throughout its existence, the medical school proclaimed its commitment to the training of women medical students, these figures also show that the proportion of women students only reached a significant level during the war. The final column serves as a reminder that throughout the period there was a regular flow of students through the basic science departments of the college, for one year, before going elsewhere (usually London), to take preclinical and clinical training in dentistry.

Table 9.1 Cardiff student numbers, 1903–1921

	Year 1	Year 2	Year 3	Total (incl. women)		'Dental'
1903/4	20	13	10	43	(3)	4
1904/5	15	14	13	42	(2)	2
1905/6	21	17	13	51	(3)	–
1906/7	25	17	14	56	(2)	2
1907/8	17	24	15	56	(2)	1
1908/9	25	13	25	63	(3)	4
1909/10	21	19	13	53	(1)	5
1910/11	16	21	19	56	(2)	5
1911/12	11	19	17	47	(3)	3
1912/13	10	17	15	42	(6)	1
1913/14	18	6	13	37	(5)	2
1914/15	25	8	4	37	(4)	2
1915/16	35	23	8	64	(8)	1
1916/17	45	24	6	75	(21)	1
1917/18	41	41	14	95	(32)	1
1918/19	89	49	27	165	(37)	–
1919/20	124	78	46	248	(44)	9
1920/21	85	94	73	252	(42)	8

In October 1921, the Welsh National School of Medicine added clinical, as well as preclinical training, to its portfolio, as table 9.2 shows.

According to returns made to the UGC in 1930,[8] the total number of full-time women medical (including dental) students attending university institutions in England, Scotland and Wales during the second half of the decade was as shown in table 9.3. Apart from the last two years, disrupted by difficulties between the college and the Cardiff Royal Infirmary, the number of women students in Wales remained fairly stable during the 1920s, in contrast with the situation in England and Scotland where there was a steady decline throughout the decade. On average, women students in Wales represented some 15–18 per cent of the medical student body, compared with about 12 per cent in Great Britain as a whole. Indeed, many of the London medical schools still did not admit women students. There is no obvious reason why the percentage of girl students should be slightly higher in Cardiff than in the English provincial medical schools other than the natural inclination of Welsh girls to stay close to home, though the efforts of Daniel Lleufer Thomas and his colleagues may also have made a difference.

Table 9.2 Cardiff student numbers, 1921–1931

	Year 1	Year 2	Year 3	Year 4	Year 5	Year 6*	Total
1921/2	63	54	102	22			241
1922/3	52						208
1923/4	53						210
1924/5	52						200
1925/6	46	35	53	16	27	10	187
1926/7	43	25	46	19	27	13	173
1927/8	61	30	43	22	20	20	196
1928/9	28	47	46	–	–	–	121
1929/30	41	24	61	22	2	14	164
1930/1	68	26	38	28	22	10	192

Notes: a) Data for the years 1922/3, 1923/4 and 1924/5 incomplete.
  b) *Includes 'revision' students.

Table 9.3 Women medical and dental student numbers

	1924/5	1925/6	1926/7	1927/8	1928/9	1929/30
England	1,197	1,059	930	862	824	842
Wales	32	30	32	30	14	19
Scotland	431	313	274	254	270	275
Total	1,660	1,402	1,236	1,146	1,108	1,136

In terms of size, how did the Welsh National School of Medicine rank among UK medical schools in the 1920s? Table 9.4 shows the number of medical and dental students attending the provincial universities of England and Wales in selected years.

Unfortunately, the returns made by universities to the UGC at that time did not separate medical from dental students, and all but three institutions in the table (Cambridge, Cardiff and Oxford) had dental schools. One conclusion is, however, clear. Though the youngest medical school on the list, Cardiff was, in terms of medical student numbers, larger than Bristol, Oxford (most of whose medical students spent their clinical years in London) and Sheffield. None of the provincial medical schools approached the largest London schools in size – Guy's and St Bartholomew's Hospitals both exceeded 600 medical students – while Glasgow had over 800 medical and dental students, and Edinburgh, the largest school in the country, had over 1,000. At the other end of the Scottish spectrum came St Andrews, where medical student enrolments barely exceeded 100.[9]

Table 9.4 Medical and dental students (provincial universities)

	1925/6	1927/8	1930/1
Birmingham	298	289	298
Bristol	195	192	190
Cambridge	419	357	396
Cardiff	197	193	192
Durham	301	245	305
Leeds	335	319	347
Liverpool	460	382	464
Manchester	372	367	472
Oxford	98	129	131
Sheffield	103	99	112

In the Special Collections Department of the Cardiff University Library is a handwritten file entitled 'Register of students who are qualified', compiled in the late 1930s by staff in the medical school office. The contents of the file show whether or not those students who commenced their studies at University College, Cardiff during the First World War and subsequently succeeded in obtaining a medical qualification, and if so, in which year. The names of all students are recorded, both those who completed their clinical studies in Cardiff and those who did so elsewhere. The information contained in the file, when linked to the data in table 9.2, enables a broad conclusion to be drawn about student success rates in the 1920s. First, the number of students enrolled in the first year of the course between the 1921/2 and 1929/30 sessions totalled 439. However, it is known that, on average, only about 80 per cent of students in the first year were new, the other one-fifth repeating the year following examination failure. In other words, the actual number of individual students who participated in the first-year course during the 1920s came to some 350. Of these 294 are known to have obtained a registrable medical qualification following clinical training at Cardiff or elsewhere, usually in the form of the Conjoint Board diploma but often a university degree from either London or Wales as well. This suggests an ultimate 84 per cent pass rate. It should be noted, however, that for students to secure a medical qualification in the minimum possible space of time was far from usual, as an authoritative article in the *British Medical Journal* explained in September 1931:

> It must be remembered that the period of five years is a minimum; more is often required, even by the man of good abilities and reasonable industry, and some of the universities prescribe a longer period. Besides these qualities a student, to obtain a registrable qualification in the minimum period of five years, or fifty-seven months, must have a considerable amount of good luck; in other words, he must keep in

good health through every turn, and never fail at a single examination … It is thus exceedingly easy for a student to fail to qualify in five years, and, as a fact, the majority of students take longer.[10]

For instance, of the forty-three first-year Cardiff students in 1921/2 who eventually qualified, only six secured a registrable qualification (the Conjoint Board diploma) in the minimum period of time. One of them was Jethro Gough, the most brilliant undergraduate student in his cohort, who was awarded the MRCS LRCP in October 1926 (and who obtained the Wales MB B.Ch. in 1927, again in the minimum time possible). Twenty students took an extra year to qualify, six took two extra years, the remaining eleven students taking even longer, with one man finally obtaining the Conjoint Board diploma in 1933, before settling down to work for many years as a general practitioner in Cardiff. As was noted in chapter 5, one of the main contributory factors was the flexibility built into the degree regulations of the University of Wales – and in those of the Conjoint Board – whereby students could choose to take their final examinations all at once or, more commonly, one or two at a time, with no time limit imposed.

As table 9.2 shows, even in a normal year (and the 1928/9 session was by no means a normal year), a substantial number of students, having completed their preclinical training in Cardiff, chose to pursue their clinical training in London or elsewhere, and they included sons of people who were otherwise well disposed towards the Welsh National School of Medicine. Such a person was Arthur Goronwy Watkins, who started in Cardiff in the same year as Jethro Gough, but who took four years to complete his preclinical studies. He was the son of Percy Watkins, sometime registrar of University College, Cardiff and assistant secretary at the Welsh Insurance Commission who, in 1925, succeeded Sir Alfred Davies as permanent secretary at the Welsh Department of the Board of Education. Watkins referred to his son's medical education in his memoirs:

> We had been much concerned as to whether he should remain at Cardiff for the last three years of his course or move to one of the big medical schools of London. My prospective removal from Cardiff to London the following April disposed of that problem for us, and when we were settled in London he became a student at University College Hospital, and was able to live at home with us until he had completed the remaining three years of his course.[11]

It was Watkins's clear inference that in the eyes of many, the clinical training given in the metropolis was superior to that given in Cardiff (and, perhaps, other provincial centres too). Nevertheless, the data for 1927/8 and 1930/1 suggest that as the clinical school settled down, a larger proportion of preclinical students were choosing to complete the course in Cardiff.

However, not all of those who chose to pursue their clinical training in Cardiff intended to sit for the medical qualification of the University of Wales. Many still preferred to take the London and Conjoint Board examinations instead of, or as well as, those leading to the MB B.Ch. (Wales). This would not have come as a surprise to Sir Isambard Owen who, in a memorandum to Colonel Bruce Vaughan early in 1919, had made the following prediction:

> The majority of students of the School, one may hope, will aim at the degrees of the University of Wales; but doubtless for some years to come, an appreciable number, for various reasons, good or bad, will, or be desired by their parents, to take the degrees of the University of London, the requirements of which are in some respects rather less exacting. A further contingent of the less ambitious students will probably aim only at the Conjoint Board diplomas.[12]

Table 9.5 summarizes the intentions of those students who studied in the fourth, fifth and sixth years of the Cardiff course during the 1925/6, 1926/7 and 1927/8 sessions:

Table 9.5 Examination intentions of Cardiff medical students

	1925/6	1926/7	1927/8	Total
Wales	5	11	11	27
London	1	4	2	7
Conjoint	21	21	13	55
Wales & London	–	4	7	11
Wales & Conjoint	23	16	21	60
Wales/Conj./Lond.	1	2	2	5
London & Conjoint	–	1	3	4
Camb. & Conjoint	1	–	–	1
LSA	1	–	1	2

In other words, some 40 per cent of these clinical students were studying for medical qualifications other than the University of Wales degrees, and fewer than 16 per cent were working for the University of Wales degrees alone. One reason for this was that, uniquely in the United Kingdom, the University of Wales final examinations in medicine, surgery and obstetrics and gynaecology were only held once a year, in the summer. This placed Wales degree students, already pursuing (at six years) the longest degree course in the United Kingdom, at a disadvantage compared with those working for other registrable qualifications. A subcommittee of the Faculty of Medicine, chaired by Professor Kennedy during the autumn of 1925, found that 'A number of the Welsh degree students who are preparing also for the other medical qualifications complete the latter owing to the more frequent opportunities for doing so, and do not proceed to complete the Welsh degrees.' In December 1925 the Faculty resolved that the final examinations for the Wales degree be held twice a year, an arrangement which was eventually introduced two years later, thereby bringing the Wales degree into line with those elsewhere in the country.[13]

DOMICILIARY, EDUCATIONAL AND SOCIAL BACKGROUND

As Percy Watkins inferred in his above-quoted memoirs, the overriding reason why students were attracted to a particular medical school in the late nineteenth and early twentieth centuries was its proximity to home. This was certainly the case as far as Cardiff was concerned, at least in respect to preclinical training. Indeed, as we have already noted, the primary motive of Dr W. T. Edwards, its founder, was to provide every Welsh boy with 'the fullest opportunity to study medicine at home'.[14] All but one of the dozen preclinical students enrolling at Cardiff in 1893 had been domiciled in the south-eastern corner of Wales, and this pattern continued throughout the period covered by this book, as the following statistical samples show.

The home addresses of seventy-seven students registered in the first three years of the medical course in Cardiff during the 1908/9, 1909/10 and 1910/11 sessions are known. The home addresses of a further sixty-six students, registered during the 1917/18 session, are also known, while the University of Wales archive at the National

Table 9.6 Home addresses of Cardiff medical students

County of domicile	1908–10	1917/18	1923/4	1929/30	Total	Percentage
Glamorgan	44	38	124	115	321	64.8
Monmouthshire	13	8	39	19	79	16.0
Carmarthenshire	11	6	15	7	39	7.9
Breconshire	3	3	8	2	16	3.2
Cardiganshire	3	0	6	5	14	2.8
Caernarfonshire	0	1	1	3	5	1.0
Montgomeryshire	0	1	1	0	2	0.4
Denbighshire	0	2	0	0	2	0.4
Merionethshire	0	1	3	0	4	0.8
Pembrokeshire	0	0	2	1	3	0.6
Anglesey	0	0	1	0	1	0.2
Flintshire	0	0	0	0	0	0
Radnorshire	0	0	0	0	0	0
England	3	0	0	3	6	1.2
Elsewhere	0	0	0	3	3	0.6

Library of Wales contains details of the domiciliary status of all medical students registered in 1923/4 and 1929/30.[15] The findings are presented in table 9.6.

The general conclusion is quite clear. Whatever its aspirations as the national medical school for the whole of Wales, the fact was that the Welsh National School of Medicine was overwhelmingly the school of choice for the boys and girls of south-east Wales, attracting very few students from the north and west of the country. It was hardly surprising that Gwilym Hughes, the tireless fund-raiser for the Welsh National School of Medicine Appeal Fund, always regarded the north of Wales as his greatest challenge. 'In North Wales the County Councils feel that the medical students from that area may, for some years, as in the past, proceed to medical schools in Dublin, Liverpool and Manchester, which are more conveniently situated in North Wales than Cardiff,' he wrote in 1923.[16] Indeed, when a north Walian, and a girl at that, presented herself as a candidate for admission to Cardiff, even when she did not, strictly speaking, possess all the matriculation requirements, the registrar of the University of Wales himself got involved to ease her passage. In October 1918, Dr Angus wrote to Professor Hepburn about a Miss Ceinwen Evans, the daughter of a retired engineer from Llanwnda, who was seeking admission to the first year of the medical course:

> Miss Evans is exceptionally good as entering a course for MB. She was the top pupil in Science in Carnarvonshire and I understand that in 3 out of her 4 Intermediate Sci. courses she has already covered the ground at school, which will give her a good start, and an advantage over the many girls who find 4 Science courses too heavy a first year's work. I hope she can be admitted without difficulty.[17]

It seems that Miss Evans's misfortune had been to offer Welsh rather than French in her Central Welsh Board senior examination, but she was eventually accepted, the matter having been taken to the University Court as a special case.

The data for 1929/30 show that three students hailed from 'Elsewhere', two from Africa (one of whom came from Egypt), and one from the Irish Free State. In truth, the number of what would now be called overseas students admitted to the undergraduate medical course during the 1920s was very small. The school's policy in relation to the admission of students of 'non-European extraction' had been debated in the autumn of 1922, with the involvement of the hospital authorities. The consensus reached within the Board of Medicine then had been that while there could be no objection 'to the principle of admitting such students …very great care should be taken in admitting them' and the number of students pursuing courses of study in the hospital should be limited.[18] In reality, despite periodic enquiries from bodies such as the Indian High Commission and the Egyptian Educational Mission, applications from overseas students were almost invariably rejected by the Faculty of Medicine during this period 'owing to lack of facilities'.

In general, students wishing to study medicine were required to satisfy the examiners in one (or more) of the university entrance examinations recognized by the General Medical Council. The annual prospectus of University College, Cardiff listed the main ones, the matriculation examinations of the Universities of Wales, of London, Oxford, Cambridge, of certain English provincial universities, and of the Scottish or Irish universities. Alternatively, aspiring medical students could sit for the examinations offered by the College of Preceptors, which organized examinations in Cardiff and other large towns twice a year. Success in the Senior and Honours Examination of the Central Welsh Board (CWB) was also an acceptable entrance qualification before the First World War, but most of those offering the CWB certificate also held one of the other qualifying certificates. In the cohort of students between 1908 and 1910 whose records have been scrutinized, nearly half (twenty-nine) had only passed the London matriculation examination (typically in English, mathematics, Latin, history and chemistry), eighteen had acquired the College of Preceptors' qualification, and most of the remainder had the CWB qualification, usually together with another diploma. J. W. Tudor Thomas, exceptionally, held only the Senior CWB examination, passing in English, history, Welsh, Latin, French, geometry, algebra, arithmetic and physics.

By 1917/18, the emphasis was changing, with those offering the London qualification alone (fourteen) coming second to intending entrants holding the CWB qualification alone (seventeen), while the College of Preceptors qualification was far less popular. In other words, people in Wales seemed to be developing greater confidence in the worth of their own examination board, moving away from the assumption that longer-established examination boards across Offa's Dyke enjoyed a monopoly on quality. As was entirely permissible, one or two Cardiff students entered the second year of the course, having taken the first, premedical year in another Welsh college. The records show, for instance, that Sarah Evans, a farmer's daughter from Llanwrda, Carmarthenshire, registered at Cardiff in October 1917, armed with a testimonial from Principal T. F. Roberts himself, having spent a year studying the basic sciences at Aberystwyth.

As has already been noted, the original medical students of 1893 hailed from the middle classes, being overwhelmingly the sons of merchants and professional men, and the parental occupational profile remained much the same in the ensuing decades, though the categories had broadened a little. The general picture can be seen in table 9.7.

Of the parents' professional group, doctors and dentists were the commonest, with eighteen in the period 1908–10 and six in 1917/18, which made up 20 per cent of the fathers of all the students included in this survey. Nine of the fathers were ministers of religion and eight were teachers (one of whom was David Hepburn, professor of anatomy). The table shows that, outside the professions, the shopkeepers predominated, with confectioners, drapers, ironmongers, provision merchants and a jeweller

Table 9.7 Two cohorts of students classified according to parental occupation

	1908–10	1917/18
Professions	34	19
Managerial	4	6
Manufacturing/engineering	4	7
Farmers	5	3
Shopkeepers/merchants	17	13
Artisans	4	5
Navy	2	–

among them. Not surprisingly, artisans were less well represented in this sample of Cardiff's medical students, and included a smith, a cooper, a tinplate worker, a monumental mason, a miner and a coal trimmer (whose son actually transferred to the Faculty of Science within a fortnight of starting on the medical course).

None of this comes as much of a surprise. The previous schooling of Cardiff's medical students was no less predictable. Most had attended the local grammar or intermediate school nearest to their home though about a third had had the privilege of a public school education, not at Eton or Harrow, but at lesser, though eminently respectable establishments such as Llandovery College, Christ College, Brecon and Queen's College, Taunton (the three most popular), with places like Rossall, Malvern College and Mill Hill featuring from time to time. Lest it be thought that the public schools were filled with the sons of doctors and dentists and other members of the elite professions, it should be said that of the twelve students recorded as having attended the colleges at Taunton, Llandovery and Brecon between 1909 and 1911, the fathers of only two were in the medical profession, the remainder being ministers of religion, shopkeepers, farmers and a schoolteacher. In fact, the majority of doctors' sons attended intermediate and secondary schools in Cardiff.

In dealing with their place of residence during their time as undergraduates, a distinction must be made between the male and female students. Apart from the few who were able to live at home, the women had no choice in the matter, as the Welsh National School of Medicine prospectus for 1929/30 made clear:

> Women students not residing with their parents or guardians are required to reside at Aberdare Hall, or in other buildings under the control of the Council of the Hall, or in a College Hostel under the control of the Council of the College. In case Women Students cannot be accommodated at the Hall, or in such other buildings as aforesaid, or in a College Hostel, they will be required to reside with some person or persons appointed by the parents or guardians and approved by the College.[19]

In the University of Wales, it was only at Bangor that hostel accommodation for males was provided, so that all male Cardiff students had to find their own lodgings. By examining the term-time addresses of sample cohorts of students before and during the First World War, it can be concluded that about one-third of the men students lived at home, at least during the first year or two of their studies, a few travelling by train to the college from as far afield as Newport, Barry, Penarth and even Treorchy. At the turn of the century, Thomas Lewis would cycle each day from his home at Tynant, Taff's Well to Newport Road, an invigorating round trip of several miles, though whether he was then the heavy smoker that he later became is not recorded.[20] The majority of students used to live in 'digs' in the warren of streets within a mile or two of Newport Road.

MONEY MATTERS

For all students, whether living at home or not, the objective was to minimize living expenses as much as possible, for the costs of medical education during the early years of the twentieth century, as now, were not inconsiderable. In truth, despite the fact that the full medical course in Cardiff was longer by between six months and a year than most other medical degree schemes in the United Kingdom during the late 1920s, the costs of medical education in the Welsh National School of Medicine were somewhat lower than the average. This may be seen in table 9.8, compiled from information collected, and published by the GMC.[21]

Writing in 1923, just before a modest increase in the fees for the preclinical years of the course at the Welsh National School of Medicine was approved, it was certainly David Hepburn's view that, at least as far as the first three years were concerned, 'There can be no doubt that medical education in Cardiff is offered for exceedingly small rates and it would still be very cheap in comparison with other Schools if increased by 50 %.' However, that would have to be a matter for the College Council, 'who should understand the public opinion of Wales upon the costs of Education better than I do', to decide.[22] As Professor Gwynn Williams has written: 'When fees were revised in the University of Wales it was with a heavy heart,'[23] it being the deliberate policy of the University of Wales to keep the level of student fees to an absolute minimum at this time, in deference to the relative lack of affluence of the people of Wales, compared with their English neighbours.

During their clinical years, medical students throughout Britain were also required to pay hospital fees to cover the costs incurred by the hospitals in the provision of teaching facilities. These varied from school to school, ranging from a total fee of £16. 16s. 0d. at Glasgow to £67. 13s. 0d. at Durham to cover clinical teaching at the Newcastle hospitals, and as much as £90 at Belfast, which was otherwise the least expensive medical school in the United Kingdom in the 1920s. The cost of a 'hospital

Table 9.8 Medical training costs in the 1920s

Med. school	Course (yrs)	Total tuition fees	Total exam fees	Graduation fees	Books/ instruments etc.
Belfast	5	£105 0s. 0d.	£12 12s. 0d.	£10 10s. 0d.	N/a
Birmingham	5	£164 10s. 6d.	£22 10s. 0d.	£2 2s. 0d.	About £50
Bristol	6	£215 5s. 0d.	£21 0s. 0d.	£3 12s. 6d.	£75 max.
Durham	5	£140 0s. 0d.	£33 3s. 0d.	£13 2s. 0d.	£50
Edinburgh	5	£223 0s. 0d.	£34 13s. 0d.	£1 0s. 0d.	£50 to £100
Glasgow	5	£178 10s. 0d.	£35 13s. 0d.	£1 0s. 0d.	N/a
Leeds	5½	£255 0s. 0d.	£18 0s. 0d.	£1 0s. 0d.	£46
Liverpool	5	£227 1s. 6d.	£15 0s. 0d.	£6 0s. 0d.	£53
Manchester	5½	£239 18s. 6d.	£33 12s. 0d.	£8 8s. 0d.	£35
NUI, Dublin	5	£160 13s. 0d.	£10 0s. 0d.	£11 0s. 0d.	£40
Sheffield	5	£190 0s. 0d.	£18 0s. 0d.	–	£40
WNSM	6	£200 0s. 0d.	£23 5s. 0d.	£1 1s. 0d.	£30 min.
Barts	5½	£231 0s. 0d.	£31 10s. 0d.	–	£50
St Mary's	5½	£200 0s. 0d.	£31 10s. 0d.	–	£30 to £40
UCL/H	5½	£263 0s. 6d.	£31 10s. 0d.	–	£35 to £40

ticket' in Cardiff was extremely reasonable, either £5. 5s. 0d. a year for the last three years of the course, or as little as £12. 12s. 0d. by one payment at the beginning of the fourth year of study. At first, when introduced in 1921, the purpose of the fee was not entirely clear to anyone, including the authorities of the King Edward VII Hospital, as the college registrar noted at the time, following a meeting with Leonard Rea, the general superintendent of the hospital: 'I stated that I thought it might cover the provision of ordinary furniture for student rooms, lighting and heating etc. He [Rea] was quite in the dark as to what it was intended to cover.' Shortly afterwards, Rea wrote to Brown, informing the school of the hospital authority's conclusions:

> The fee is intended to cover what is generally called 'Hospital practice', and which includes attendance at the services of the hospital. We shall provide the wards with chairs without relation to the hospital fee, while it is not regarded as covering furniture and equipment, but my committee are agreed that it should cover lighting and heating services, and cleaning.[24]

Over and above the various fees directly related to their studies, those medical students not living at home incurred costs for board and lodgings. The GMC memorandum provided guidance for students in this sphere too. The maintenance costs quoted for each school were an estimate, supplied by the institutions themselves, 'which will enable a student to take a fair share in student activities, without extravagance, but on the other hand without undue hardship. There is no doubt that in cases of necessity the student can manage on a smaller sum.' Some medical schools gave an annual estimate, between £200 and £250 in Oxford, £200 in Edinburgh, £150 in London and Belfast, £100 in Leeds, a little more in Liverpool. Others gave a weekly estimate, up to £3 per week in Durham and Glasgow, £2. 5s. 0d. in Birmingham and £2 per week in Sheffield and Cardiff. In this respect as well, therefore, the Welsh National School of Medicine emerged relatively favourably.

Even so, the financial implications of studying medicine in Cardiff were considerable and, as it was a relatively new establishment, the range of scholarships available to worthy students was not as great as in many other schools.[25] There was the Samuel Bros. (of Cardiff) Scholarship, established in 1897 through an endowment of £500 by a local business, with an annual value of about £15, and awarded on the results of the work during the first year of the medical course. Tenable for one year, the scholarship was held by some of the school's most distinguished students over the years, including Thomas Lewis, Laura Powell and Jethro Gough. In terms of financial reward, the Dr Price Prize, established at the end of the war, was better, having an annual value of £50. This prize was also awarded on the basis of first-year performance, and its first holder, in 1920, Richard Glyn Maliphant, would, in later years, achieve recognition as one of Cardiff's most distinguished obstetricians and gynaecologists. The Alfred Sheen Prize, established in 1906, in memory of the father of the school's dean of medicine, was worth somewhat less (the interest on an endowment of £100), but was undoubtedly the most prestigious in the school, being awarded on the basis of excellence in the preclinical examinations. Winners included Charles Jennings Marshall (1908), J. W. Tudor Thomas (1912), Francis Davies (1919) and Jethro Gough (1923). Though having no monetary value the Alfred Hughes Memorial Medal, established in 1902, and awarded for excellence in the anatomy course, was much sought after. Holders included Abel Evans (1909), Clement Price Thomas (1919), Richard Glyn Maliphant (1922) and Rolf Ström-Olsen (1925).

For clinical medical students working for the MB B.Ch. of the University of Wales, four prizes were established during the 1920s, to be awarded by the university. The John Maclean Prize was endowed by Professor Sir Ewen Maclean in 1923 in memory of his father, for excellence during the course in obstetrics and gynaecology. It consisted of a silver medal and bound books to the value of £2. 10s., selected by the prizewinner. Early winners included Jethro Gough (1926) and Rolph Ström-Olsen (1927). Three Willie Seager Prizes were endowed by G. Leighton Seager, a member of the Cardiff ship-owning family, in memory of his brother, who had been killed in action at Neuve Chapelle during the First World War. Each prize consisted of a gold medal and books to the value of £4, and was awarded each year to the clinical students who had shown the greatest proficiency in the university examination in medicine, surgery and pathology and bacteriology respectively. The standards set by the examiners were high. Initiated in 1926/7, the pathology gold medal was awarded only once during the first five years, the medicine gold medal only twice (William Phillips, the recipient in 1930, later achieved legendary status as 'Billy Pink', the infirmary's senior physician), and the surgery gold medal on three occasions.

Cardiff medical students very occasionally secured scholarships available to the college students at large, such as the Craddock Wells Exhibitions, which covered college fees for periods of two or three years, and the Caroline Williams Scholarship, worth £25 a year and tenable by women students resident in Aberdare Hall. A few medical students were successful in obtaining County Free Scholarships offered by the Glamorgan and Monmouthshire County Councils and the Cardiff City and Newport Borough Councils. That their number was relatively small can be seen in table 9.9, compiled from information in the student records of the time, kept in the Cardiff University archives.

With the increase in medical students following the establishment of a full medical school in 1921, the number of award-holders, still relatively small, was a little larger, as table 9.10 shows.

Until 1924, a handful of medical students benefited from an arrangement whereby the fees of children of members of staff at the Cardiff College were waived. However,

Table 9.9 County/city/borough scholarships

Year	Number of awards to medical students
1903/4	8
1904/5	5
1905/6	4
1906/7	3
1907/8	1
1908/9	1
1909/10	4

Table 9.10 Numbers of award holders, 1922–1927

	Glam. Schol.	Mon.	Cardiff	Craddock Wells	Car. Wms.	Other	Total
1922/3	15	6	1	1	1	3	27
1924/5	9	3	1	1	1	6	21
1926/7	7	3	1	–	–	4	15

in that year, the practice was discontinued on the insistence of the University of Wales Council, making Cardiff fall in line with the other colleges.[26]

THE MEDICAL STUDENTS AND COLLEGE LIFE

To some extent the financial burden on medical students could everywhere be mitigated by the availability of good library facilities. As has already been outlined in chapter 6, in this respect the situation in Cardiff, especially for the students, was less than ideal, notwithstanding the improvements introduced in the late 1920s, including the creation of a library in the Cardiff Royal Infirmary. Apart from the benefits afforded to the clinical students, this latter initiative was significant for two other reasons. First, it was a good indication of the extent to which the Cardiff Royal Infirmary was beginning to acknowledge its role and responsibilities as a 'teaching hospital' after years of arid dispute. Secondly, the development would reinforce the generally held conviction that the medical students of the college were truly a distinct body of men and women.

This had not always been the case, at least not entirely so. In fact, the first three holders of the post of president of the Cardiff Students' Representative Council were all medical students. The first, Benjamin Gregory Fiddian, the son of a Cardiff doctor and himself a keen sportsman – he represented the college at rugby and athletics – served as president during the 1896/7 session, before proceeding to Charing Cross Hospital for his clinical training. The second, Herbert Septimus Ward, the council's first secretary, was president during the 1997/8 session and, like Fiddian, was very much an all-rounder, involved in every aspect of college life. According to a contemporary tribute in the college student magazine:

> He could sing, act, and play Cricket and Rugby well. He obtained his 'dragon' in Cricket twice, '97 and '98, and in Rugby '96–7, while he also dabbled with fair success in 'Soccer', Tennis and Hockey. He was our most versatile entertainer, doing the light parts in the dramatics so well that everybody thought it would be no good trying to get up a piece after he had gone. His songs from Comic Opera were always a feature of our Soirees. But we could not recognize the Ward of 'Chin-Chin-Chinaman' and 'The Tin Soldier' in the second President of our SRC. He fulfilled his duties here with dignity and despatch, and made a model chairman.[27]

After passing his preclinical examinations, Ward spent his clinical years at St Bartholomew's Hospital, before qualifying with the London MB BS in 1901. Within a year he was dead, struck down by a mystery illness contracted in hospital, 'perhaps the most startling and deplorable event which has taken place in the history of the students of the Cardiff University College since its foundation', in the view of the student magazine.[28] The third student president, James W. Evans (1898/9), was, during his preclinical years, acknowledged as an outstanding member of the college's Literary and Debating Society and a prime mover in the establishment of the Tennis Society. His clinical years at Charing Cross Hospital were full of academic achievement, and his untimely death in 1906, a few months after qualifying, cut short a promising medical career.

During the early years of the school, other medical students played an active part in the wider life of the college. Several took their places on the Student Representative Council, representing the medical students, while others served as the medical students' nominees on bodies such as the Women's Common Room Club. The formidable H. S. Clogg was a stalwart of the college Cricket First XI during the mid-1890s. Leigh Richmond Roose, having passed a number of science examinations at the University College of Wales, Aberystwyth in the summer of 1899, spent the 1899/1900 session at Cardiff – an episode that seems to have eluded chroniclers of his life. There he studied for the University of London preliminary science (MB) examination in biology with the intention of continuing his medical training in the metropolis. During his time at Cardiff, Roose turned out for the Rugby XV as a forward from time to time and received his colours in polo and swimming. However, as a member of Aberystwyth Town FC, he was also one of the outstanding British goalkeepers of his generation and, while a Cardiff student, obtained the first of twenty-four caps for Wales, against Ireland, in February 1900. Roose did proceed to King's College, London to continue his medical studies, but football and other distractions took over his life and he never completed his medical training. He was killed in action on the Somme in 1916. His body was never found and his name (wrongly spelt as Rouse) is recorded on the memorial at Thiepval.[29]

Despite the contribution made to college life by the aforementioned students, there is also evidence to suggest that, even before the turn of the century, the medical students were regarded as a little remote by their contemporaries. Some blamed the college authorities for 'raising a barrier between the general body of men students and the Medicals'. As one anonymous student complained in the pages of the student magazine,

> Not only does the College, as was pertinently and pointedly shewn in your last issue, provide the Medicals with an inaugural lecture, while the College *qua* College has to be without one, but in order, as it were, to further emphasise the Medicals as a distinct Sect apart from the Gentiles and Barbarians, a separate Common Room is rented out to them. It will at once, I know, be remarked that the general Common Room is already too small. This I admit. But why not make the two Common Rooms open to all? … That I am not fighting a bogey of my own creation will be clear to anyone who is in the habit of attending the general societies, of which the Literary and Debating Society is the chief. Will you, Mr Editor, make a calculation of the

number of Medicals who have taken any part in the L D & S and the Christian Union this term up to and including November 24th? Is there more than one?[30]

The phenomenon described by this anonymous complainant would certainly not have been a matter of surprise to such a seasoned observer of medical matters as Sir Isambard Owen. Despite his later assertions, during the mid-1920s, that the separation of the medical students from those in other faculties would be harmful for all concerned, it was Sir Isambard Owen himself who, in a report to the college authorities early in 1913, wrote: 'There is a general tendency in our modern Universities for the students of a technical faculty to keep themselves rather to themselves, forming their own especial clubs and societies, and holding more or less aloof from others.'[31] This was certainly the experience of Clement Price Thomas, a first-year medical student in Cardiff just before the First World War:

> I remember we considered ourselves to be rather an exclusive lot. We had our own common room into which students of other faculties were admitted only by invitation; we also had an unwritten law which was faithfully obeyed, that no medical student ever wore a gown. This I found to my cost for the undergraduate gown I had purchased before entering the School was solemnly and ritually burned before my eyes on the common room fire. We were, however, a very happy crowd, and although we made every pretence at not working, it was strange that our failure rate was very low.[32]

That this state of affairs continued in Cardiff after the war is confirmed in an illuminating letter, written in 1924 to the *Western Mail*, by someone else who was in a good position to know the facts. Alistair Livingston Gunn, who would serve as chairman of the Medical Students' Club in 1926/7 before going on to obtain the MB B.Ch. of the University of Wales in 1928, its MD in 1932 and ultimately an address in Harley Street, wrote as follows:

> The medical students number about 200, about one-fifth of the total strength of the college. They are compelled to make an annual subscription of 27s. to the funds of the Students' Representative Council, and there their contribution ceases. The medical students have neither the time nor the inclination to join in the social life of the college. Out of 200 one medical student is a member of the College Christian Union, while the Literary and Debating Society, the Political Union, and the Choral Society cannot muster two 'medicals' between them. The medical students *do* join in the sport of the college. Over a period of years the medical students have occupied at least half of the places in the college teams. That in some measure explains the apathetic attitude of the college students towards their athletic teams – they are largely represented by people who are complete strangers to them.[33]

How distinctive the medical students were regarded by others can be seen in an article appearing in *Cap and Gown* about a mock election being conducted in the Students' Union in 1928. Everything ran fairly smoothly until the medical students decided to turn up *en masse* and disrupt the proceedings. 'Some excitement was caused by the entry of the medical students. Their presence was soon realised, particularly when they remembered that they were due at their "smoker". They left before the close, but not without some slight token of remembrance.'[34]

THE MEDICAL STUDENTS' CLUB

The main focus for the social life of the medical students was the Cardiff Medical Students' Club. Established in the autumn of 1894, the club's intention had not been to isolate the medical students from the rest of the college, but to further what the college student magazine at the time referred to as 'the distinctive and peculiar interests which unite medical students'.[35] This was essentially the same motive which had already led to the establishment of the Engineering Society, restricted to students of engineering and mining, in 1891/2, and would later lead to the formation of other student societies, such as the 'Frogs' Society (for classicists) in 1899/1900, the Chemical and Physical Society in 1900, the Philosophical Society in 1900/1, and the Geological and Mining Society in 1903/4.[36]

Membership of the Medical Students' Club was not automatic, requiring those wishing to join to pay an entrance fee of 2 shillings and an annual subscription of 3 shillings (the same as that for the Engineering Society but sixpence more than members of the Philosophical Society were expected to pay to join their society). After initially struggling to attract recruits from the first, preliminary science year, the club made good progress, so that by the autumn of 1898, the membership totalled fifty men and five women. In 1909 the numbers exceeded seventy-five, comprising all, or nearly all the students, together with several members of staff. Indeed, from the outset, the academic staff of the school, and local luminaries, gave the club their strong and active support. The first two presidents of the club were John Berry Haycraft and Alfred Hughes, and others to hold the position before the First World War included Tatham Thompson, consulting ophthalmic surgeon, and William Sheen. Two annual events were awaited with particular eagerness by the club members, the rugby match against the Bristol Medicals, and the annual 'smoker'. The rugby match, played home and away in alternate years, invariably generated great excitement, as much in the post-match festivities as during the contest itself. In November 1898 after losing a hard match by two goals to one try, 'our defeat being due, chiefly, to the weaknesses of our three-quarter line', both teams, and their supporters, made their way to the centre of Bristol. After a dinner characterized by much good fellowship, all made their way, 'with much singing', to the Tivoli Music Hall where 'Welsh airs were rendered with fine feeling.' At 9.30 p.m. the students adjourned to a 'smoking' concert, where each party took turns in entertaining the other. Finally, after an emotional rendering of 'Hen Wlad fy Nhadau', the Cardiff contingent rushed for their train, arriving back in Cardiff at five minutes past three in the morning. As far as the author of the article (which subsequently appeared in the student magazine) was concerned, 'We all regard the day's outing as one of the pleasantest and most enjoyable in the course of our years at Cardiff.'[37] The annual Smoking Concerts (or 'smokers') were equally successful. Initially held in the anatomy dissecting room under the watchful eyes of the professors of anatomy and physiology (on the instructions of the Senate),[38] they soon went off campus, to one of the local hotels, the Queen's, the Royal, the Park or the Philharmonic. Attended not only by a large number of students, but by many of the local medical fraternity, these proved to be highly convivial events, dominated by tobacco, refreshments and a varied programme of music and song performed by club members, though D. J. Harries, a preclinical student in 1903, later recalled that he had found the speeches rather tedious:

> The beauty of this event was marred by the number of speeches the members of staff insisted on delivering. These interfered with the calm and philosophic quenching of one's thirst; although they seemed to have a salutary effect on the speakers, as they invariably had one or two as soon as their efforts were over.[39]

By 1910 the club had achieved sufficient maturity for formal by-laws to be drawn up for the first time, and the years immediately before the war saw an expansion of the club's activities, with the introduction of golf into the sporting calendar and an annual dance into the social diary. Indeed, as the medical club became acknowledged as the prime focus of the medical students' attention, discussions were initiated with the college's Student Representative Council (SRC) in 1911, with a view to reducing the amount of the annual amalgamation fee paid by the medical students into central funds in order to augment the funds available to the medical students' club. Not surprisingly the SRC refused to countenance such a proposition and, as A. L. Gunn indicated in his previously quoted letter to the *Western Mail*, relationships between the medical students' club and the SRC continued to be somewhat uneasy during the 1920s. By then the annual fee for membership of the medical students' club had risen to 1 guinea, so that the requirement for medical students also to have to pay an annual amalgamation fee of £1. 17s. 6d. to the SRC (known as the Students' Union Society from 1927) was resented. All attempts by the medical students to persuade the College Council to reduce the amalgamation fee were rebuffed save that, with the creation, in 1924, of hospital-based common room clubs for men and women, attracting membership fees of 5 shillings a year, the annual amalgamation fees for students in their clinical years were mitigated by that amount.[40]

The establishment of the Welsh National School of Medicine as a full medical school in 1921 was regarded as a sufficiently important milestone for the medical students' club to invite David Davies MP, of Llandinam, to become its president for one year, in succession to Sir William James Thomas. Davies was concerned about what such a commitment would entail, until D. W. Evans, the general director of the Welsh National Memorial Association, of which Davies was president, was able to write a reassuring letter to his assistant. 'This is quite a good organisation and has been in existence for many years. I strongly advise the Chief to accept the position.' A month later, having spoken to Davies himself, Evans was even more reassuring:

> I told the Chief that no financial responsibility would be involved and the medical students, through their Chairman and Secretary, have since assured me that this is so. They do not expect anything but would of course gladly accept anything that the Chief would give. Sir William James Thomas, the President of the Club last year, did give them a 'feed'; that does not at all follow the Chief is to do the same. The students unanimously appointed the Chief as President in this, the first year of the complete Medical School; they thought he was the only person entitled to do it, especially in regard to his having founded the Chair of Tuberculosis and the coming among the students of Colonel Cummins.[41]

In subsequent years the medical students tended to confer the presidency of the club upon popular members of the staff of the school and the Royal Infirmary, including Cornelius Griffiths (1922/5), Professor Sir Ewen Maclean (1926/7), Geary Grant (1927/8) and Gilbert Strachan (1930/1). The advantage of choosing local men was that they could usually be relied on to attend the various functions of the club, though Sir Ewen Maclean's term of office was interrupted by frequent absences on other business; his other handicap was the lack of a wife. The election of his successor, Geary Grant, was welcomed in *The Leech* with particular enthusiasm: 'For many years, Mr Grant has taken a great and practical interest in Club affairs while Mrs Grant has also done much to brighten the somewhat monotonous lives of students by her enjoyable social evenings'.[42]

During the 1920s, each academic session invariably began with the freshers' social and dance, the first part of the evening being devoted to that excellent ice-breaker, a whist drive. The club organized regular dances during the autumn and spring terms in several local hotels, with the annual 'Med Club Ball' usually taking place shortly before Christmas at the Cardiff City Hall. Reading the accounts of these events in the pages of *The Leech*, the impression is gained that the organizers were sometimes striving hard in the face of a degree of apathy among the student body at this time. The report of the annual medical ball held in December 1927, contains the following paragraph:

As we encircled the room to such haunting tunes as Hallejulah and Charmaine we couldn't help noticing the comparative infrequency with which one encountered fellow medical students. It surely seems a great pity that a function of this sort should be mainly supported by outsiders.

The more serious tastes of the medical students were catered for by the Literary and Scientific Section of the club, which organized meetings during the winter months. The range of topics was impressive. The programme for 1926/7, for instance, was:

15 October: 'Medical Literature and Medical Life' by Sir Squire Sprigge, editor of *The Lancet*.
Chairman: Professor A. W. Sheen.

15 November: 'A Doctor's Mental Equipment' by Sir Thomas Horder, Physician to HM The King.
Chairman: Professor A. M. Kennedy.

28 January: 'Some Impressions of America' by Sir Ewen Maclean.
Chairman: Professor A. W. Sheen.

4 February: 'Spiritualism' by Professor Boycott, University College Hospital.
('Equally interesting but not so well attended').
Chairman: Professor E. H. Kettle.

25 February: 'Medical Work in the Congo' by Dr H. C. Gilmore.
Chairman: Dr Ivor Davies.

It is clear, from the tributes paid by the contributors to *The Leech*, that the extent to which the various social and cultural events were successful was largely due to the input of the school, and indeed hospital, staff, who offered suggestions for the programmes, acted as chairmen at the meetings, and attended dances and similar events (accompanied by their wives), even when the students themselves were conspicuous by their absence. The support given to the club by Professor Sheen, 'father-confessor and friend, a guide and helper', was particularly appreciated by the students at this time, as the following tribute, written in April 1932, conveys:

He is devoted to his beloved School and his worth in this respect will never be fully enough assessed. From the standpoint of the Club he has been its corner stone. He is a great figure, zealous of our traditions, proud of our achievements, and worthy of our cheers. For many years too, Mrs Sheen has followed very sympathetically the varying fortunes of our School and club. Her interests are still and will always be unabated.[43]

There is no doubt that *The Leech* provided a good insight into the life and work of the Cardiff medical students during the late 1920s. Under the initial editorship of Rolf

Ström-Olsen, a fifth-year student who went on to become the medical superintendent of a psychiatric hospital in Essex, the first issue appeared, with the blessing of the Faculty of Medicine, in October 1926, priced at 1 shilling. Its purpose was explained in the first editorial:

> The present status of the Welsh National School of Medicine is such that it promises to become one of the leading institutions in the country; but it is important for students to realise that it will never reach the front ranks unless they do their bit and have an adequate share in its development. During the last four or five years, when so many epoch-making changes have taken place in our school, the need of a channel in which to express the general sentiments and ideas of the student body as a whole has especially been felt, while at the same time a journal which should be educating and useful has been sorely missed … We hope that the magazine has come to stick in the manner of *Hirudo Medicinalis* after which it has been named.

The first issue of the journal was well received in the local and medical press.[44] In the opinion of the *Western Mail*, The Leech 'has made an excellent start', while the *South Wales News* considered it to be 'equal to any of its contemporaries'. Apart from pointing out some typographical errors, *The Lancet* felt that the format was pleasing and 'the subject matter well planned, both serious and frivolous matter finding a place'.

With the appearance of the sixth issue in May 1928 *The Leech* officially proclaimed its existence as a bilingual journal. 'The very name of the School proclaims our nationality and what is more fitting than that the language of our country should find an honoured place in our magazine?' Soon afterwards, for unrelated reasons, the journal ceased production for two years, being one of the casualties of the crisis that overwhelmed the Welsh National School of Medicine at that time, only to reappear in December 1930:

> In 1928 our Club was buried in lava. The site of the eruption was uncertain; its manifestations plain to all. In the flash of light pillars of reputed gold were seen to be feet of clay; and in the heat of the explosion our Club, our stroma, liquefied. Now we are born again: we have struggled towards the light: we have been 'inspected, palpitated and concussed' and given a clean bill, so that we have but to find our lost voice to show how much alive we are.

As might be expected, several pages of each issue of *The Leech* during this period were devoted to the club's sporting activities, specifically soccer, rugby and hockey, all exclusively male pursuits at this time. None of the teams were conspicuously successful, the pool of eligible students being relatively small, particularly after the best medical students had been creamed off to play for the main college teams. It is probable that the most proficient sportsman among the medical students during the late 1920s was Morgan David Arwyn Evans, one of the sons of the aforementioned professor of music at the Cardiff College. He represented not only the college but Wales itself at hockey until the autumn of 1928. At that point, he was forced to go to University College Hospital to complete his clinical studies, before returning to Cardiff, where he was to achieve great distinction as an obstetrician and gynaecologist.

One of the teams' problems, until the 1926/7 season, was the lack of a ground where they could play home matches on a regular basis. However, in that year the club was granted the use of an athletic field at Ty-to-Maen, St Mellons, by the Cardiff Royal Infirmary. As *The Leech* recorded at the time, 'This was fitted up so that a complete programme of Rugby, Soccer and Hockey fixtures could be arranged for the season. The three teams have been playing regularly, and although the results have been varied there has been a steady improvement, which is encouraging.'[45] Sadly the reported 'steady improvement' was not sustained. The most successful of the teams in 1927/8 was the rugby XV, which played thirteen matches, winning five, losing five and drawing three. Probably the highlight of their season was to win again, as it usually did, the Inter-faculty Cup, beating the Faculty of Arts by a try to nil. The early optimism of the soccer XI was not justified by events, the team winning four times, losing six times and drawing once, against Treorchy Junior Athletic Club, on a gravel pitch. The team's charabanc journey home, after a heavy defeat against St David's College, Lampeter was described by *The Leech* reporter:

> The return journey to Cardiff was started at about 6.30. We had rather an exciting time coming over Brecon Beacons for a very thick mist had gathered and our progress was very slow for many miles. On one occasion the driver pulled up within two feet of some mountain ponies which had strayed on to the road. We were very glad to see the lights of Cardiff again at about 10.30 pm.[46]

The hockey team, shorn of Arwyn Evans and other talented club members, had a particularly poor season, winning only one of ten matches. For the *Leech* reporter, independence for the School of Medicine could not come soon enough.

> Now that a separation between the University College and the National School of Medicine is in sight we look forward to the time when M. D. A. Evans, E. V. Evans and Dr Isaac will be able to play for us. With their aid we would have a team which would be very difficult to defeat.[47]

With the resumption of 'normal service' in 1930, only the rugby XV had survived and its performance during the 1930/1 session was undistinguished. Of twenty games played only two were won and three drawn, the medics' greatest disappointment being their defeat against the Faculty of Arts in the first round of the Inter-faculty Cup.

A cricket team had performed briefly during 1927, but the competing pressures of summer examinations always made its continuing existence extremely fragile, and the team apparently played no further games until 1932.

It may be inferred from the foregoing that such sporting activity as existed at this time was exclusively a male preserve. To be sure, there were not many women in evidence, being not more than 15 per cent of the medical student population. In any case, as a *Leech* editorial noted in December 1930, the women members of the Student Club had other roles to perform:

> They seem to have a marvellous power of dancing on one foot while cutting sandwiches with the other, while at the same time they are pleasant to see in the landscape. All this is done without fuss, without hysteria, and, best of all, almost without money. Iechyd da![48]

OUT INTO THE WIDE WORLD

Having qualified, what became of the sixty-four medical students who graduated from the University of Wales between 1916 and 1931? We can answer that question in respect of sixty of them. As the *British Medical Journal* explained in its education issue of 1931, the normal starting-point for medical graduates at that time was as house physicians, house surgeons or casualty officers in a hospital.[49] In this regard the Wales graduates were no different from the rest, most taking up appointments at the Cardiff Royal Infirmary and at other hospitals in south Wales, though some of those who had completed their clinical training in London, particularly before 1924 and between 1928 and 1931, secured positions in one of the teaching hospitals of the metropolis. The *BMJ* added that some might subsequently choose to see something of the world by obtaining a short-term appointment as ship's surgeons. At least one distinguished graduate of the University of Wales, Charles Langmaid (1913–97), later to become a consultant neurosurgeon at the Cardiff Royal Infirmary, is known to have done this. Commencing his student career in 1929, he qualified in 1935, and after working as a house surgeon at the infirmary for a few months he became, with the encouragement of Lambert Rogers, ship's surgeon on the MV *Glengarry* on a hundred-day round trip to the Far East. To judge by a letter he sent *en route* to his family, the duties were not particularly onerous:

> After breakfast at about 9 am I see any patients that are to be seen. There are usually not more than two or three. They have such picturesque names as Chang Ming Tsai, Wong Mai Ching, Wong Sue Chong, Tso Ah Nee etc but for convenience of reference on board they all have numbers. Mostly cut fingers, sore legs, coughs, etc are the things which one sees but so far I have done two dental extractions.[50]

The *BMJ* maintained that three-quarters, at least, of those who passed out of the medical schools became general practitioners, or 'family doctors', sooner or later. In fact only some fifteen of the sixty Wales graduates whose careers are known appear to have pursued this particular path, eight in Wales, seven elsewhere. They included, however, some remarkable characters, not least Bryneilen and Rosentyl Griffiths (both of whom graduated in 1929). As children in Merthyr Tydfil they had been introduced into the world of medicine by their mother Martha, a well-known 'healer', especially of skin cancer; Daniel James, 'Gwyrosydd', author of the great Welsh hymn 'Calon lân', was 'cured' by her. Inseparable throughout their lives, they worked for six decades as family doctors in private practice in Cardiff. They chose not to join the NHS in 1948, fearing that, as part of the state system, they would have insufficient time to treat their patients properly. To the Griffiths sisters time was of the essence, time to talk, time to get to know the patients and their families as people, in order to make the correct diagnosis.[51] Four graduates became academics, three at the Welsh National School of Medicine: Jethro Gough (who graduated in 1927) as professor of pathology, the first medical graduate of the University of Wales to obtain a chair in his alma mater; Arwyn Evans (1930) as first assistant to Gilbert Strachan in the Department of Obstetrics and Gynaecology; and Enid Williams (1928) as assistant lecturer in the Department of Tuberculosis. The fourth, Charles Victor Harrison (1929), after working in the school's Department of Pathology during the early 1930s, eventually became professor of pathology at the British Postgraduate Medical Federation in London. Fourteen graduates of the University of Wales entered the area of public health in its various forms, eight working for one or other of the Welsh local authorities, five in England and one, Watcyn Rendel Williams (1931), based in Sierra Leone as a health officer in the Colonial Medical Service.[52] Another extensive traveller during the course of his career was Arthur Richards Culley (1927). Having served as medical officer of health for Glamorgan during the 1940s, he became the medical member of the Welsh Board of Health in 1948, with the responsibility of implementing Aneurin Bevan's National Health Service scheme in Wales. During his seventeen years' tenure of this post he made over 1,000 train journeys from Cardiff to London. He was awarded the CBE in 1959 and three years later was appointed honorary physician to the queen (QHP).[53]

The largest proportion of Wales graduates, nearly half (twenty-seven), worked in the hospital service. Three became consultants at the Cardiff Royal Infirmary, J. W. Tudor Thomas (1916) specializing in ophthalmology, David Ioan-Jones (1923) in surgery, and William Phillips (1930) as a physician, while four prospered in London. Daniel Davies (1924) became senior physician at the Royal Free Hospital and physician to the household of King George VI, and T. G. Illtyd James (1925) became senior surgeon at the Central Middlesex Hospital. Alistair Gunn (1928) combined duties as a consultant obstetrician and gynaecologist at Lewisham and Bromley Hospitals with a successful private practice in Harley Street. Martha Griffith (1924) held the position of senior anaesthetist at the London Homeopathic Hospital. Of the remaining twenty, twelve ended their careers holding appointments at district hospitals in Wales, four as surgeons, four as physicians, two as chest physicians and one each in pathology and psychiatry. Eight held a variety of posts at general and psychiatric hospitals in England. One was Thomas Percy Rees (1924), who, during his tenure as medical superintendent at Warlingham Park Hospital, pioneered the doctrine of 'the unlocked door' in the treatment of mental patients, earning him the OBE and the freedom of the County Borough of Croydon. In 1956, the year of his retirement, he was elected president of the Royal Medico-Psychological Association.[54] A few combined service in hospital with other medical activities, such as general practice and factory work. Such a person was David John Davies (1926), who was, by the early 1950s, not only a general practitioner, but also a surgeon at St Joseph's Hospital, Preston, a medical officer with the Lancashire Fire Service, a medical referee for some insurance companies and the chairman of the local medical committee.

Of the sixty Wales graduates included in this brief survey, thirty-four (57 per cent) eventually settled down to pursue a career in Wales, fifteen (25 per cent) settled in the English provinces, and nine (15 per cent) in London. As was noted in chapter 2, the number of Cardiff's pre-war preclinical students who eventually settled down to practise in Wales had been about 50 per cent, the post-war improvement being at least partly attributable to the number of students who were spending all of their medical training in Cardiff.

Although it was not obligatory, between the wars, for those seeking to pursue specialist careers to obtain postgraduate qualifications, it was advisable to do so. Certainly 55 per cent of Wales graduates surveyed obtained at least one, the great J. W. Tudor Thomas acquiring no less than four, the FRCS (Eng.) in 1925, the London MS and the Wales MD in 1929 and the Wales D.Sc. in 1931. Assuming that the MRCOG and the FRCOG counted as two separate qualifications (though the fellowship was obtained by election rather than examination), Alistair Gunn and Arwyn Evans also held four qualifications, the other two being the Wales MD and the FRCS. In fact, the most common postgraduate qualification among Wales graduates was the Wales MD, held by fourteen (another held the surgical equivalent, the M.Ch.), followed by the DPH, held by almost all of those working in the public health service either as medical officers of health or as school medical officers. Ten possessed the FRCS of England or Edinburgh, or, in one case, both.

Whether they reached the very heights of their profession, like Sir Daniel Davies, or settled for satisfying if less spectacular careers serving their local communities in a variety of ways, the graduates of the University of Wales could, with some justification, feel that their medical school had prepared them well for their working lives. Certainly Lord Horder of Ashford, the greatest clinician of his day, held the Welsh National School of Medicine and its graduates in high regard, as he proclaimed during the school's opening-of-session ceremony in October 1933: 'When I meet a graduate in medicine of the University of Wales, my attitude is one of entire respect.'[55]

Admittedly, it was unlikely that Horder would have set out to offend his hosts on such a special occasion. Nevertheless, his words could only have given pleasure to past students who heard them, or read them in the medical journals, including, no doubt Dr Marjorie Speirs (née Duggan) who, having qualified in 1926, had become, in the following year, the first woman to hold a full-time academic appointment in the school, as demonstrator in the Department of Pathology. In 1931 she went to Canada to work as a bacteriologist at the University of Alberta, returning to Wales in 1932 to become assistant bacteriologist with the Welsh National Memorial Association. To widespread regret she died in January 1934 at a relatively early age.[56] Happily, as we have seen, all her near-contemporaries were to be more fortunate in that respect.

Parting of the Ways

All good dramas have a denouement in which the loose ends are neatly tied. In a real sense this chapter meets expectations. The debilitating conflict between the school and hospital authorities and staff was finally resolved to general relief, with the clinical staff of the hospital achieving what, more than anything, they had always demanded, a real involvement in the planning and administration of the undergraduate clinical course. Despite some last-minute blustering by the Cardiff College and infirmary authorities, a final agreement satisfactory to the Privy Council and the UGC was reached on the terms on which the Welsh National School of Medicine, albeit somewhat truncated, would become an independent constituent institution within the University of Wales. The division of assets, staff and non-staff, between college and school was conducted without controversy and rancour, a rare achievement given all that had gone before. To be sure, Mitchell Stevens behaved with characteristic ill humour at the final meeting of the Board of Medicine in May 1931. However, as William Sheen and his colleagues no doubt reflected, Stevens was nearing the time when retirement would mercifully intervene, allowing the infant Welsh National School of Medicine to embrace the challenges of independence with optimism, guarded perhaps in view of recent history, but real enough.

BUSINESS AS USUAL FOR THE DEPARTMENTS OF ANATOMY AND PHYSIOLOGY

'I want you to realize that we now have no Welsh National School of Medicine.' So said Dr David Llewelyn Williams, chief medical officer of the Welsh Board of Health, to the members of the University of Wales Court, meeting at Newport in December 1928. However, this statement was not entirely accurate. While the clinical course was undoubtedly in abeyance, the course for the first three years was proceeding more or less as normal. As Principal Trow reported to the College Council, 'Most of the departments included in the Faculty of Medicine remain, comparatively speaking, unaffected and their growth and development has not been appreciably handicapped,' though, as we shall see, not all were equally well favoured.[1] In 1928/9 there were 121 students in attendance, though the number in the first year, twenty-eight, was roughly half the usual first-year figure, reflecting an understandable degree of nervousness by prospective students and their parents about the future stability of medical training in Cardiff.

While tensions had been growing among the clinicians, the question of the appropriate division of available teaching hours during the second and third years, traditionally a bone of contention in medical schools everywhere, was amicably settled during 1927 as in table 10.1.[2]

Table 10.1 Division of teaching hours, second and third years

Pharmacology	228
Organic chemistry	224
Anatomy	726
Histology and embryology	268
Physiology	514

It will be noted that 'Biochemistry' did not exist as a distinct discipline in Cardiff at that time, and only after the Second World War did it gain official recognition at University College, Cardiff as an academic department in its own right. However, as has been noted in chapter 2, the essential elements of what was later understood by the term 'biochemistry' had been taught by the Department of Physiology from its inception, being given special recognition in 1910 with the designation of R. L. Mackenzie Wallis as lecturer in physiological chemistry. John Pryde, lecturer in physiological chemistry from 1922, would later become the college's first professor of biochemistry.[3]

Some of the preclinical timetables were tidied up at the same time in the interests of academic and administrative efficiency. As far as possible instruction would be organized in terms, so that, for instance, senior chemical physiology would be concentrated in one particular term, thereby simplifying the procurement of fresh materials. Physiology practical classes would normally be held in the mornings rather than in the afternoons because of the length of time it took 'the laboratory boys' (the lowest form of technician life, earning wages of £26 per year) to clean up afterwards, ideally commencing at the same hour of the day. However, they would no longer be held on Saturday mornings 'on account of the impossibility of obtaining the necessary fresh organic materials from the public slaughter house on that day of the week'.

Although the Department of Anatomy made the largest single contribution to the preclinical course in terms of hours, its facilities and resources were, throughout the 1920s, markedly inferior to those available to the Department of Physiology. As Professor J. D. Lever, a more recent head of the Department of Anatomy, observed half a century later, this disparity reflected 'different technical requirements but probably also the fact that until the late 1920s little or no research was in progress in Anatomy, while a substantial amount of original work poured forth from Physiology'.[4] Certainly, when in 1922 the sum of £6,014 had been earmarked for the purchase of urgent items of equipment for teaching, whereas physiology had been allocated £2,544, surgery £1,040 and pathology £805, anatomy had received £500 (to buy display cases and specimens for its museum), the same amount as that given to medicine and obstetrics and gynaecology.[5] Although the Department of Anatomy, housed in the main Old College building, did benefit from some reallocation of accommodation with the opening of the Institute of Preventive Medicine in 1927 and the transfer of the Physics Department to Cathays Park, lack of funds prevented the immediate refurbishment of the new space. As Professor C. McLaren West, David Hepburn's successor, complained in his annual report to the College Council, for the 1928/9 session, 'The Department is cramped for want of room and money; nothing has been able to be done with the rooms vacated by the Physics department, there is no money to furnish and equip the rooms which thus lie idle.' Moreover, 'The roof of the Dissecting Room still leaks and there is still no electric light; this must be unique in Departments of Anatomy.' Fortunately, in the following year, West was able to report that most of the department's physical deficiencies had been rectified, though he was still not in a position to create an X-ray room in which 'students might learn the appearance of the various bones, joints and certain of the internal organs of the living'. The staff resources available to him remained scarcely adequate. The professor gave all the anatomy lectures himself: in the 1927/8 session these amounted to sixty-five in the junior year and ninety-three in the senior, a substantial load. Practical classes and work in the dissecting room were shared between the professor and a couple of demonstrators, a category of staff which West found difficult to recruit and retain because the pay was so poor. Until 1928, when a laboratory 'boy' was appointed, the department's only laboratory attendant was the indestructible Alick MacIntosh, a man in his mid-seventies, who had faithfully served the medical school from its commencement in 1893. Fortunately West's good relationships with his professional colleagues helped him to ease some of his difficulties. He secured the teaching skills of Lambert Rogers and R. V. Cooke, the full-time assistants in the Department of Surgery, and persuaded his friend, Professor J. C. Brash, head of the Department of Anatomy at the University of Birmingham, to provide him with cadavers for the dissecting room when his own sources of supply were proving to be inadequate.[6]

During the 1920s the Department of Physiology, thanks to Sir William James Thomas housed in its state-of-the-art institute, was the largest academic department in the Welsh National School of Medicine, as table 10.2 shows.[7]

Large though the Department of Physiology was, compared with most of the others, Professor Graham Brown still felt aggrieved that his department was not being properly resourced. In successive annual reports to the University Council at the end of the decade he claimed that the teaching staff 'is still much smaller than the staffs of other modern Departments of Physiology of similar size', and drew particular atten-

Table 10.2 Estimate of expenditure by academic departments for the year ending 30 June 1929 (£)

	Academic staff	Support staff	Non-staff	Dept. library	Total
Anatomy	2301	481	80	90	2952
Physiology	3550	1145	700	100	5495
Materia Medica	600	110	40	25	775
Pathology & Bact.	3500	791	470	75	4836
Medicine	2450	338	150	35	2973
Surgery	2700	602	140	50	3492
Obs. & Gynae.	1075	125	125	60	1385
Public Health	2425	104	110	20	2659
Tuberculosis	1250	343	27	10	1630

tion to the fact that 'No adequate sum was ever provided for the equipment of the Physiology Institute, and (that) much of the actual structure was left more or less unfinished and has never been completed.'[8] His letter to the university registrar in the spring of 1931 offers an interesting glimpse into the realities of running an academic department at that time:

> The staff of the laboratory and myself have spent considerable sums on furnishings and equipment. In this connection we have supplied comfortable chairs (comparable to chairs supplied by the College in some other departments); much research apparatus of various sorts; books (including valuable sets of complete journals); teaching diagrams; and so forth. While some of these items (such as the pictures we have supplied) could not under any circumstances be regarded as a fair charge against any funds for teaching and research, many of the items supplied (I give as an instance the complete set of the Journal of Physiology) are not only legitimate ones, but should have been considered essential. In view of the very inadequate sums with which the Department has been supplied for equipment and so forth, we have faced many of these expenses ourselves. Much of the furniture – such as storage cupboards and so forth – with which other departments have been supplied out of equipment grants, have been made personally by the technical staff of the department. In addition to the above apparatus and fittings either supplied by members of the department or made by the technical staff, a certain amount of special research equipment in the department has been supplied personally to the members of the staff by such bodies as the Royal Society. By these means the Department has been able to carry on its work in spite of the very inadequate sums given for equipment *but the Department is almost completely lacking in the major kinds of service apparatus* which are too expensive for our private purses and are never supplied by bodies

such as the Royal Society. As a single instance the room designed originally in the building as a refrigerator room has never been fitted with its proper plant.[9]

Despite all this, Brown consistently refused to believe that his department would be better served as part of University College, Cardiff. For as long as he could, he campaigned for the preclinical departments to remain within the Welsh National School of Medicine, on one occasion appealing in vain to Sir Walter Fletcher to use his influence with the UGC to maintain the status quo: 'If the Charters are granted in their present form the position here will be a bad one, and I cannot but believe that the University Grants Committee must know that this is the case.'[10] Brown even went so far as to submit, on his own behalf, a futile petition to the Privy Council to protest against the separation of the departments of anatomy and physiology from the school, earning him the private wrath of the Cardiff principal, J. F. Rees, who accused him of gross disloyalty.[11]

The final outcome of the debate about the future affiliation of the Departments of Anatomy and Physiology certainly did not diminish the involvement of their heads in the affairs of the Faculty of Medicine at this time. The attendances at the meetings of the Faculty of Medicine of McLaren West and Graham Brown (the latter no doubt revitalized by ascending the south side of Mont Blanc in September 1927 by a route hitherto considered unclimbable),[12] were exemplary and put the attendance record of certain other members of the Faculty, representing the all-Wales dimension of the Welsh National School of Medicine, to shame (see table 10.3).

Table 10.3 Attendance at Faculty of Medicine meetings

| | 1927/8 | | 1928/9 | |
	Actual	Possible	Actual	Possible
Professor Graham Brown	10	13	12	16
Professor C. M. West	13	13	15	16
Professor R. C. McLean (Botany, Cardiff)	8	13	5	16
Professor J. E. Coates (Chemistry, Swansea)	0	13	0	16
Professor T. C. James (Chemistry, Aberystwyth)	0	13	0	16
Professor K. J. P. Orton (Chemistry, Bangor)	1	13	0	16

It is hardly surprising that the honorary staff of the infirmary had long resented their exclusion from membership of the Faculty of Medicine in view of the deplorable attendance of the Aberystwyth, Bangor and Swansea representatives, none of whom had managed to put in an appearance in 1926/7 either.

SCHOOL AND HOSPITAL FEEL THEIR WAY TOWARDS A RECONCILIATION

Although, for a brief moment, the authorities of the infirmary had seemed to signal their intention to exclude all members of the school, staff as well as students, from its precincts, wisely no attempt was made to prevent the academic staff from conducting such business as they could within the hospital. Ivor Davies's observation was surely correct. 'Perhaps the acceptance of the Rockefeller bequest of the medical unit buildings accounted for this dispensation.'[13] At all events, he and his academic colleagues were able to carry on with their clinical duties unhindered – though on one occasion Professor Sheen was accused of diverting one of Mitchell Stevens's patients to his own unit[14] – and most continued to attend meetings of the Medical Board. Despite understandable impatience from some quarters (even *John Bull*, a fairly sober magazine since the downfall of Horatio Bottomley, having condemned the infirmary authorities for their 'disgraceful blunder', called for the resumption of 'a normal working routine without delay'),[15] neither side was inclined to make a settlement in haste, particularly now that all the clinical students had disappeared. It was not until 12 October 1928, after three months' deliberation, interrupted by their summer holidays, that the clinical teachers finally produced a draft scheme for the future organization of teaching in the infirmary which most (sixteen out of twenty four) were prepared to support.

The scheme was considered by the third joint conference between representatives of the infirmary and University College, Cardiff on 22 October. The centrepiece of the clinical teachers' scheme was the establishment of a Board of Clinical Studies composed of the clinical teachers and the professors of medicine, surgery, obstetrics and gynaecology and pathology. This board would 'be responsible for organising and arranging the clinical teaching of the non-professorial clinics at the Royal Infirmary and shall co-ordinate this teaching with that of the professorial clinics'. As it stood, this wording represented a concession by the clinical teachers, or at least a majority of them, in that the autonomy of the professorial units in the organization of teaching was maintained. On the other hand the scheme proposed that the board would report direct to the Board of Medicine, a proposal which reflected the honorary staff's long-standing antipathy to the Faculty of Medicine. The scheme also addressed, in detail, some of their main grievances against the school authorities. Their other commitments would be taken into account when the teaching timetables were compiled; they would henceforth have a formal role in reporting to the medical school on the attendance, performance and conduct of the students attached to them; 'As far as practicable, all the clinical facilities in the Infirmary, and all Departments in the Infirmary should be available for teaching students of the School.'

The college representatives had no problem with any of the proposals except one, that the Board of Clinical Studies should report direct to the Board of Medicine (or Council under the draft charter of the future Welsh National School of Medicine), thereby bypassing the Faculty of Medicine (Senate). Albert Trow, still college principal, his retirement having been deferred for a year, proposed that on receipt of reports from the Board of Clinical Studies the Board of Medicine would be expected to seek the advice of the Faculty of Medicine before taking any action. As if in retaliation the infirmary representatives proposed that the broad terms of reference of the Board of Clinical Studies be modified so as to 'be responsible for organising and arranging the clinical teaching at the Infirmary', in other words ending the special status of the professorial units. It was clear that final agreement on the clinical teachers' scheme would not be reached on 12 October, and it was resolved that the infirmary authorities should reflect on the discussion and prepare a draft agreement, incorporating proposals for a Board of Clinical Studies, for the College Council to consider in due course.[16] This would take time, but William Sheen, for one, did not mind. As he privately confided to Daniel Brown, he was determined that negotiations should lead to a lasting solution, one that ensured that the school could never again be held to ransom by the likes of Mitchell Stevens. The infirmary should give undertakings to this effect. Indeed 'There should be a clear understanding with the Infirmary that if members of the staff won't teach they must go.'[17]

In fact, it took the authorities of the infirmary a further two months and six internal committee meetings to produce a draft agreement for the college to consider. They looked at everything, what should be the role of the Board of Clinical Studies, how far it should control the work of the professorial units and their staff, whether indeed the unit system should continue at all, whether the agreement drawn up between the infirmary and the university regarding the Rockefeller grant was valid (counsel's opinion confirming that it was) and even questioning whether any agreement between themselves and the college was needed at all. They wrote to ascertain practice in England: 'There appeared in almost every instance to be no Agreement or written understanding between the Hospital and the Medical School. It was suggested that the absence of anything written accounted for the friendly understanding existing between the Hospitals and the Medical Schools.'[18] Only on 20 December did the infirmary deliver a new agreement for the college to consider.

Meanwhile the affairs of the school had taken several turns for the worse. First, the college began to receive claims for compensation from the parents of several clinical students who were experiencing financial hardship owing to their enforced removal from Cardiff. Although one or two students had managed to secure scholarships from the London medical schools, and some local authorities, notably Glamorgan, had agreed to continue to meet the fees of and provide maintenance grants to those students they had hitherto supported in Cardiff, by the middle of November claims had been received in respect of eleven medical students.[19] There were one or two pleas of a general nature, arguing that, whatever may have been the legal niceties, the college had a moral obligation to do something. The father of a fifth-year student, already suffering hardship 'owing to acute trade depression', invited Principal Trow to inform him as to what you consider the responsibilities of the College in this matter, and whether any financial help will be available as a set off against the expense required to be gone to as a consequence of conditions arising which are contrary to what was represented in the Prospectus.[20]

Most claimants sought reimbursement to cover the extra costs incurred by living in London, estimated at between £2 and £2. 10s. 0d. per week, while a few wanted reimbursement for the cost of a now useless infirmary hospital ticket. One medical student, now in his final year at University College Hospital, had gone so far as to issue a writ against the college claiming damages for breach of contract.

The college sought counsel's opinion as to its liability in respect of the claims. The opinion was clear:

> The College is not now able to provide Hospital instruction for medical students, and this prevents some students from continuing their studies at the College. In the case of students who are in compliance with conditions on their part to be performed, and for whom hospital instruction is now necessary, the failure on the part of the College constitutes a breach of contract, and such students will probably be able to prove damages from the fact that they have to proceed elsewhere to complete their studies.

However, it was also counsel's opinion that the infirmary could not evade its own responsibility for the present situation:

> Although the Agreement [between the College and the Infirmary] was not permanent, reasonable notice was necessary before it could be brought to an end. Notice could only be considered reasonable which enabled existing contracts to be performed. The Hospital did not give such notice. The Hospital has been paid fees for Hospital Tickets which entitle students to attend for three years, and the Hospital has prevented attendance during that period. Further, the differences which have arisen are not such as to entitle the Hospital to contend that it was impossible to carry out its obligations. For these reasons, in my opinion the College will have a right of action against the Hospital for damages which it suffers through the action of the Hospital authorities.[21]

Fortified by this opinion the Cardiff registrar invited the infirmary authorities to indicate how they wished to proceed, whether they would wish the college to handle the claims and seek reimbursement later or 'whether the Infirmary would prefer to take over the claims and proceedings and settle or defend the same at its discretion'. The infirmary's response was swift and unambiguous, that the matter was nothing to do with them and that the college should act as it saw fit. The University Council was equally keen to distance itself from the problem, resolving 'that the matter be left to the discretion of the College'.[22] As will be seen later, several months would elapse before the issue of compensation was amicably resolved.

Meanwhile, there was growing concern about the medical school's financial position. It was estimated that during 1928/9 there would be a reduction in income of some £3,000, about 10 per cent of annual turnover, half through a loss of student fees and half through a reduced grant from the University of Wales appeal fund, owing to the fact that only two local authorities (Newport and Montgomeryshire) had paid their annual subscription to the fund for the year 1928/9. Advised by its Finance Committee, the Board of Medicine managed, by the end of December, to find savings of £1,600 from the clinical academic departments (none being sought from the Departments of Anatomy and Physiology which were working as normal).[23] While some of the savings were easy to make, there being no immediate requirement to pay honoraria to the recognized clinical teachers, other savings were painful, arising as they did from the resignation of key members of the academic staff which the beleaguered school could ill afford to lose.

There was Professor J. H. Dible, the school's third professor of pathology and bacteriology in the space of four years. Following the untimely death of Edward Emrys-Roberts early in 1924, Edgar Kettle had occupied the chair for three years, during which time he had supervised the relocation of the academic department to the new Institute of Preventive Medicine,[24] had reached a *modus vivendi* with H. A. Scholberg, the prickly head of the pathology service at the infirmary, and, after a period of frustrating financial stringency, had finally secured sufficient funds to recruit some excellent colleagues to his department. In 1926 Dr John Bright Duguid (1895–1981), an Aberdeen graduate, had joined from the University of Manchester as lecturer, and Dr John Mills had come from Cambridge to be assistant lecturer, and one of Kettle's last acts, before leaving Cardiff for St Bartholomew's Hospital in the autumn of 1927, had been to appoint two recent graduates of the school, Miss Marjorie Maisie Duggan (1926) and Jethro Gough (1927), as demonstrators. The students wished Kettle well. 'We are sorry he has gone – for we liked him – and he has left behind pleasant memories and a live department.'[25] After several months' interregnum, during which John Duguid had acted as head of department, J. H. Dible joined the school from a chair at the Royal Free Hospital in May 1928, and for some months proved to be an active member of both the Faculty of Medicine and of the hospital's Medical Board. He gave every indication that he intended to settle down in Cardiff – he had bought a house locally – when, to everyone's surprise, he tendered his resignation in December in order to take up the chair of pathology at Liverpool, where he felt his services could be better employed. Once again, John Duguid was appointed as acting head of department with effect from 1 April 1929, with the unusual title of acting professor and a special honorarium of £150 per annum to supplement his annual salary of £750.

The dispute with the infirmary was the direct cause of the resignations of three other members of the academic staff. The Department of Pathology saw the departure of Dr Mills, to a non-university appointment in Reading, while the brilliant Jethro Gough left for a junior post at Manchester University. 'I deeply regret the circumstances which have led me to take this step, but I feel that I can make better progress elsewhere.'[26] The fourth to resign within the space of a few weeks before Christmas was Daniel Thomas Davies, the first, and at that time the only, holder of the MD of the University of Wales. After qualifying from the school in 1924, Davies had spent six months as resident house physician to Professor Kennedy before spending two years in the biochemical department of the Middlesex Hospital under Professor E. C. Dodds. Davies's return to Cardiff in 1927 as assistant in Professor Kennedy's medical unit was regarded as a feather in the school's cap, and the decision of this talented young Welshman to go back to London after no more than a year, frustrated by the collapse of the clinical school, was a grievous blow indeed.

> One may wonder [observed the *Western Mail*] how far the process of impoverishment will continue and what hope there is of securing, in the future, the services of well-qualified teachers. Continuity of work and security of tenure are of the essence of the case, and if Wales cannot offer them in the medical branch of its university system the evil which has been wrought will be most difficult to repair.[27]

When it was finally deposited with the college authorities just before Christmas, the draft agreement was received with some disappointment, especially as the hospital authorities had seemed to be taking a conciliatory attitude towards the medical school. There were a small number of students who, though based elsewhere, had sought permission to return to Cardiff in December, to take the final professional examinations leading to the medical degrees of the University of Wales. Not only did the hospital agree to the school's overtures in this respect, enabling two students to graduate; it was at pains to make it clear that Sir Ewen Maclean's midwifery students had never been subject to a ban at all. Writing to the college registrar, Maclean considered that the signs were encouraging:

> It seems to me that the content of the Medical Superintendent's letter, written under the authority of Sir William Diamond may, with sympathetic handling, very well lead to a useful degree of continuance of the machinery of the medical school on its clinical side, pending the issue of the comparatively favourable negotiations now proceeding.[28]

Sir Ewen, as always leaning over backwards to be fair to everyone, misread the runes. The hospital's draft agreement, twenty-nine clauses in all, made no real concessions to meet the previously expressed concerns of the school. The agreement still demanded that the new Board of Clinical Studies, overwhelmingly composed of the honorary clinical staff, should have total control over the teaching arrangements in the infirmary, including those within the professorial units. Moreover, it was proposed that the board should not report to the Faculty of Medicine, but direct to the Board of Medicine (the Council, within an independent Welsh National School of Medicine), thereby arrogating to itself the status of a Senate. The agreement would be valid for five years, subject to termination or amendment by either side, with one year's notice. Meeting on 30 January 1929, the Faculty of Medicine declared substantial parts of the draft agreement to be quite unacceptable. Furthermore, the faculty required clarification of the future role and status of the assistants in the professorial units, and, probably most important of all, it wanted cast-iron guarantees from the infirmary authorities that the school would never again be held to ransom by a small group of disaffected clinicians. The faculty's views, endorsed by the College Council, were sent back to the hospital.[29]

The *Western Mail* was extremely disturbed by the lack of progress:

> Negotiations for a restoration of co-operation between the infirmary and the school have been proceeding in a most leisurely fashion during the past seven months, and there is still no indication of the approach of a settlement in spite of the fact that the time is due, if not overdue, for completing arrangements for the academic courses which should commence after the summer holidays.[30]

So was Principal Trow. In a valedictory address to the Cardiff College Court in February, while weighing his words carefully, he attributed the continuing impasse to petty and personal considerations (by implication, among the clinical staff of the infirmary) and he warned his audience that unless agreement was soon reached, the clinical school would end, with Cardiff students once again going to London to complete their training as in the past.[31]

It took another three and a half months for a settlement to be achieved. Three factors intervened to make this possible. One was the decision, in March, by the student who had issued a writ against the college claiming damages for breach of contract, to join the Cardiff Royal Infirmary as co-defendants. In a private and confidential letter to Principal Trow, Hugh Ingledew, an influential member of the Cardiff College Finance Committee, conveyed the gist of a talk he had just had with Henry J. Smith, apart from the chairman, the leading layman on the hospital board of management.

> Sir William [Diamond] feels now that the action of the Infirmary in giving notice and closing the School to the students was perhaps ill-advised and that he has now realised that the Infirmary may be involved in substantial claims. I have told Mr

Smith that there may be a total liability of £3,000 to £4,000 and possibly if litigation goes on and is taken to higher Courts an even higher figure … There appears to be now a definite agreement on the part of the Infirmary that it is in the interests of everybody that these claims shall be dealt with and settled on the best terms possible without litigation and with a view to limiting and keeping as low as possible whatever liability has to be dealt with by the person or persons on whom it eventually falls. It seems to me that this action by [the student]'s solicitors gives an opportunity for a definite move being made on our part to try and settle this and other claims without further litigation and without incurring further costs.[32]

The authorities of the college and the infirmary, in a long-overdue act of co-operation, decided to work together to settle the student's claim. He thought he deserved £200. The solicitors for the college and the infirmary initially suggested £160. Finally, a settlement was reached whereby the student accepted £125 together with sixty guineas costs and an undertaking by the hospital that, when a satisfactory settlement was reached between the college and the infirmary, the student would be 'entitled to enjoy the same privileges of visiting the hospital as he would have been entitled to had the difficulties between the College and the Infirmary not arisen'.[33] Having settled this claim the college and hospital authorities went on to consider how they might together deal with the others which would undoubtedly follow. At a series of meetings during April, it was agreed that a joint bank account should be opened, into which each body would pay an initial sum of £500, and that a small joint committee of hospital and college officers and laymen be set up to consider claims as they were submitted. At one of the meetings H. J. Smith reminded his hospital colleagues that the sooner clinical teaching recommenced at the infirmary the less would be the ultimate financial damage to all concerned.

Indeed, the active role of Henry J. Smith OBE was the second crucial factor in the eventual settlement of the dispute. He had been an influential member of all the important infirmary committees for several years (he was chairman of its finance committee) and, having recently retired as manager of the National Provincial and Union Bank of England, St Mary's Street, Cardiff, he had the time to spare to make a difference. The ill health and enforced absence, during crucial weeks in March and April, of Sir William Diamond, who had shown himself to be weak in confronting his senior clinicians, gave Smith the opportunity to take the lead. The hospital clinicians had been found wanting and, as far as he was concerned, it was time for others to engage in serious negotiations with the college authorities.

There was some urgency in the matter. The third factor influencing a resolution of the dispute was the school's financial position. Principal Trow was now openly stating that, unless a settlement was reached by 30 June, the medical school would probably have to close down through lack of funds, the University Finance Committee having in March having already invited the college to consider the implications of retaining a skeleton staff only in the medical school. In a series of meetings with the principal and other senior college officers (but, perhaps significantly, excluding the dean, or any other member of the medical school), during April and early May, the hospital negotiating team, led by Smith, went carefully through the initial draft agreement, concentrating in particular on the clauses offensive to the school.[34] Smith personally rewrote the clauses dealing with the role of the Board of Clinical Studies, so as to confine its remit to organizing the clinical teaching *outside* the professorial units. While, with some reluctance, the college authorities indicated their willingness to agree that the board would report direct to the Board of Medicine, Smith committed the hospital authorities to accept that this board could refer the reports of the Board of Clinical Studies to the Faculty of Medicine, for comment. The position of the assistants in the professorial units was settled. Provided that the hospital played a proper role in their appointment, they would be afforded status and rights within the clinical structure of the hospital appropriate to their grade. However, in acknowledgement of the well-known sensitivities of the hospital clinicians, it was agreed that the assistants should hold full-time, not part-time appointments. Finally, agreement was reached on arrangements to ensure the future stability of clinical teaching in the hospital. In this matter, H. J. Smith had every sympathy with the sentiments of the college, suggesting to his hospital colleagues at one point that he would withdraw as a member of the negotiating team unless the college's legitimate concerns were addressed. Early in May, the university authorities were brought into the negotiations, in recognition of the fact that within a relatively short time, the Cardiff College would relinquish its responsibilies in respect of the Welsh National School of Medicine. 'About time too', would have undoubtedly been the observation of a senior layman on the College Council who had never understood why the college was still involved in the negotiations at all.

> There was some reason in our doing so when the crisis arose, because there was a possibility of making some provisional arrangement whereby the work of the School need not be interrupted. Now that the work has been interrupted and the suggestion has been made that there should be a five year agreement, it seems to me that the parties between whom there should be negotiations are the Infirmary on the one hand and the University on the other.[35]

The initial draft of the new agreement, prepared by the honorary clinical staff during the previous autumn, had contained twenty-nine clauses. By the middle of May 1929 only fourteen had survived unscathed, the remainder either deleted or substantially rewritten in response to the college's concerns. Formally endorsed by the College Council on 22 May, the agreement was received by the Faculty of Medicine, as a matter of information only, on 23 May. On the following day a special meeting of the University Council itself formally approved the agreement. The

Council also resolved that urgent approaches be made to the Welsh local authorities to resume their subscriptions in support of the Welsh National School of Medicine and, hopefully, to settle their arrears, as the finances of the school were now in a parlous state.

All eyes now turned to the Cardiff Royal Infirmary, where some of the senior clinicians were fighting a rearguard action, particularly regarding clause 19 of the draft agreement. This stated: 'The Infirmary shall hold all its beds at the disposal of the School for the purpose of clinical teaching.' As far as the medical school was concerned, this was the assurance that it required that never again would they be held to ransom by a few disaffected members of the honorary staff. Passed by twelve votes to three (Stevens, Griffiths and Martin) in one of the infirmary's sub-committees, the draft agreement went before a crowded meeting of the infirmary's supreme authority, the Board of Management, on 29 May. In front of more than eighty members, the chairman, Sir William Diamond, was uncharacteristically magisterial in reminding the honorary clinical staff that they, 'like all others were subject to the discipline and control of the Infirmary Council and Board of Management'. No department, 'not even their medical board', could be allowed to dominate the situation. While giving general support to the draft agreement, Cornelius Griffiths voiced his opposition to clause 19 which, in his view, stated in effect 'that the infirmary honorary staff must teach under compulsion. They were perfectly ready to teach and carry on the school as voluntary workers, but not with a pistol at their heads.' He proposed an amendment, that the clause be removed. In response, H. J. Smith told the meeting that his negotiating committee had been told definitely by the college authorities that they would not enter into an agreement that did not contain such a clause and, speaking for himself, he thought it entirely reasonable 'that the school should be protected in future in the event of two or three men getting into a bad temper and declining to teach'. He added that the existence of clause 19 would ensure the re-accreditation of the school with the Conjoint Board and London University.

Put to the vote, Cornelius Griffiths's amendment was heavily defeated, attracting only seven votes, the motion to approve the draft agreement being then carried *nem. con.* Mitchell Stevens, realizing that the mood of the meeting was against him, was magnanimous in defeat: 'We have fought the fight and I abide by the result.' Cornelius Griffiths spoke in similar vein, at which point, in a dramatic intervention, Sir William James Thomas sprang to his feet:

> This ending to our day's programme is simply beautiful. [Applause.] But I would like to see the Agreement accepted absolutely unanimously. Some of you gentlemen refrained from voting. Shall we now have the resolution put again in order to carry it absolutely unanimously? [Hear, hear.] Our chairman has been through a hell of a time, but tonight he will sleep a happy man.

The motion was again put and, in the words of the *Western Mail* reporter, 'It was carried amidst an extraordinary scene of enthusiasm, all present voting in favour.'[36]

So ended the worst few months in the short history of the Welsh National School of Medicine, a crisis unparalleled in the modern history of medical education in the United Kingdom. Given enough mutual good will the crisis could have been avoided, but personal enmity, combined with a lack of understanding of what was expected of a teaching hospital, ensured that a generation of Cardiff medical students was, at least, seriously inconvenienced. Fortunately, there is no evidence to indicate that lasting damage was caused to the students caught up in the unhappy dispute, virtually all of them qualifying as doctors and most returning to Wales to pursue their medical careers. The direction of some careers was, however, changed for ever, not least that of Daniel Davies who, despairing of the situation in Cardiff during the autumn of 1928, chose to put down his roots in London, never again to work in Wales.

The medical press was greatly relieved by the outcome, both the *British Medical Journal* and *The Lancet* hailing the new agreement as a worthy compromise, on the one hand guaranteeing for the honorary staff a proper role in the formulation of the curriculum and the organization of teaching, while on the other ensuring that the medical school could never again be blown off course by the actions of some of the clinicians. The *British Medical Journal* was particularly impressed by the role of the lay members of the hospital in securing the school's position, noting that at the meeting of the board of management

> There appeared somewhat disquieting indications that the medical members were still unwilling to assent to the principle that a staff appointment should carry with it an obligation to teach. The lay members, however, were emphatic upon this point, and it was laid down quite clearly that the clause in the agreement which places all the Infirmary beds at the disposal of the school must also be taken to mean that every member of the staff shall co-operate in the work of the school.[37]

BACK TO BUSINESS

If the school was to reopen fully for business in October 1929, there was much to do. Undoubtedly the college's first priority was to secure the future allegiance of the honorary staff of the infirmary, to which end the registrar wrote to all those eligible, re-engaging them as recognized clinical teachers or part-time lecturers as appropriate. All (including Mitchell Stevens and Cornelius Griffiths) accepted, though Alfred Howell briefly attempted to exploit a delicate situation to his own advantage. For some years he had held both a part-time lectureship in the diseases of children, for which he was paid, and, as an honorary assistant physician, an appointment as a recognized clinical teacher, for which he was not paid, in accordance with an arrangement agreed in 1925. Howell now informed the registrar that unless he was paid in this latter role, he would not accept appointment, thereby throwing the robustness of the new agreement between the college and the infirmary into doubt. D. J. A. Brown anxiously wrote to Sir William Diamond: 'The Principal considers that it would be a great pity that anything should now endanger the re-opening of the School in October next,' and it was hoped that the chairman would persuade Howell not to pursue matters at this time. Though it took a fortnight to do so, Howell was finally persuaded to accept re-appointment as a recognized clinical teacher in accordance with his previous contract (but a year later, exceptionally, he was granted an honorarium for his services as a recognized clinical teacher). In an impressive act of pragmatism demonstrating its anxiety to avoid needless controversy at a sensitive time, the college conferred the title of recognized clinical teacher on Dr H. A. Scholberg, the hospital's senior pathologist. Strictly speaking, he was not entitled to the title as he made no contribution to the teaching programme, but he wished to be a member of the Board of Clinical Studies and the new agreement largely confined membership to those with the title of recognized clinical teacher. The last thing that the college wanted was to give anybody, particularly the difficult Dr Scholberg, an excuse to challenge the agreement now, so he was given the title of recognized clinical teacher – and an honorarium of £40, despite the fact that Principal Trow had initially told Scholberg that the college could not afford to pay him anything![38]

Having ensured that all the recognized clinical teachers, and therefore their beds, were 'on board', the college immediately sought renewed accreditation for its clinical course from the Conjoint Board and the University of London. Both bodies were understandably cautious, demanding not only copies of the agreement but also firm evidence as to the total number of beds available for teaching, personally vouched for by the dean of medicine. However, on 18 July, the responses anxiously awaited by the college were received, both the Conjoint Board and the University of London granting the recognition sought with effect from 1 October 1929.[39]

By now, urgent steps had been taken to strengthen the clinical staff of the school, which had been seriously depleted during the previous autumn, the opportunity being taken to implement, as far as was affordable, clause 14 of the agreement, dealing with the staffing of the professorial units. The clause stated that in each of the professorial units there should henceforth be two grades of assistants, senior and junior. The senior assistants, who should be appointed according to the same procedures as applied to clinical professors, involving external assessors and representatives of the Infirmary,

> shall be recognised by the hospital as qualified and authorised to take charge of the Wards in the absence of the professor, to take full charge of the Out-Patient Department, and to have responsibilities and obligations similar to those of the Assistant Surgeons or Assistant Physicians in the Infirmary.

The junior assistants, on the other hand, would be appointed by the college, but only after the name of the successful candidate had been endorsed by the election committee of the hospital. Their duties were more circumscribed, the junior assistants working under the close supervision of the professor or, in his absence, the senior assistant. Not only were the duties and privileges of the assistants made absolutely clear for the first time; it was further stated that 'All assistants in the professorial clinics shall be normally full-time officers of the School.' Clause 14 therefore went a long way to addressing some of the greatest concerns of the honorary staff.

However, recognizing that the appointment of full-time assistants in all three professorial units at the same time was unaffordable, the Board of Medicine, at a special meeting held on 14 June, approved the recommendation of the Faculty of Medicine that a start be made in the surgical unit, an approach endorsed by the election committee of the hospital five days later. After Lambert Rogers was duly appointed, without advertisement, as senior full-time assistant in the professorial surgical unit (following consultation with a panel which included Lord Moynihan and Cornelius Griffiths), the post of junior assistant was advertised, much to the disgust of T. E. Hammond. Honorary assistant surgeon in the hospital and hitherto one of the surgical unit's part-time assistants, he found himself displaced, without so much as a word of warning, from Professor Sheen. 'Whether it is malice on the part of Professor Sheen or merely a want of tact I cannot say,' he complained to Principal Trow, adding rather plaintively that if finance was the problem, 'I will undertake the work for nothing provided my status in the Unit is upheld.'[40] The fact is that Professor Sheen had been trying to manoeuvre 'Tommy' Hammond, once described by Hilary Wade as 'extremely eccentric',[41] out of his unit for some little time, and the new agreement gave him the opportunity he sought. Following advertisement, which generated a good field of applicants, R. V. Cooke, a Bristol graduate with substantial clinical and academic experience in three teaching hospitals, was appointed as junior assistant in the surgical unit.

With Ivor Davies agreeing to be appointed, as a temporary measure, as senior assistant in the medical unit on a part-time basis, the college proceeded to fill the new full-time post of junior assistant. The successful candidate, Dr Duncan Leys, a prizeman at Balliol, had already published a book on diseases of the lung, and was regarded by all as the best qualified of all the candidates. It is interesting to note that the runner-up was Alan Trevor Jones, some twenty-five years later to achieve his ambition to work for the Welsh National School of Medicine, though in a different capacity. As far as the Department of Obstetrics and Gynaecology was concerned, it was agreed, on account of the financial stringency, that the three existing part-time assistants, Gilbert Strachan, B. K. Tenison Collins and Miss M. I. Adams, be continued in post for a further year (all part-time assistants still being subject to annual review).

The other significant new appointment made in the school during the summer of 1929 was in the Department of Pathology, where the post of assistant lecturer had been vacant since the previous autumn. Though all five applicants were worthy of consideration, one was outstanding. Jethro Gough (1903–79), after briefly holding an appointment in Manchester, wanted to return to his alma mater. The report of the selection committee to the Faculty of Medicine could not have been more favourable:

> His work while on the staff of the Pathology Department of this School was charac-
> terised by such originality and promise as to stamp him a man of outstanding merit
> and one who will go far; thus confirming the indications given by his brilliant under-
> graduate career. During the time he worked in Cardiff and in Manchester it is
> reported by the head of the department that he had carried out work on a difficult
> technical subject with results that are destined to be far reaching. On the grounds of
> his distinguished academic career and subsequent research combined with his
> teaching experience in our own School, the Faculty recommends that Mr Gough be
> appointed.[42]

The most important matter arising out of the new agreement was, pursuant to clause 15, the establishment of the Board of Clinical Studies, a body which, it was hoped, would herald a new and harmonious relationship between the school and the infirmary. Membership consisted of 'all the recognised clinical teachers and part-time lecturers who are members of the honorary medical staff of the Royal Infirmary, and the lecturers in radiology and anaesthetics, together with the professors of medicine, surgery, obstetrics and gynaecology, and pathology'. Its role was 'to organise and arrange the clinical teaching of the non-professorial units at the Royal Infirmary ... and as a joint body co-ordinate this teaching with that of the professorial clinics, having due regard to the commitments of members of the Board'. The board would be responsible for arranging an equitable allocation of clerkships and dresserships in the various clinics, allowing, as far as was possible, student freedom of choice, and for ensuring that proper records were kept of student performance, attendance and discipline throughout the hospital. The board was required to elect its own chairman annually, and at its first meeting, on 5 July 1929, Mitchell Stevens was elected as chairman with Cornelius Griffiths as vice-chairman, an inevitable outcome given the difficulties of previous months and the spirit of reconciliation now said to prevail. Although no minute books of the board have survived prior to the mid-1930s,[43] appended to the minute books of both the Board of Medicine and Faculty of Medicine are regular reports submitted by the board. These reveal that Mitchell Stevens and his colleagues were by no means hesitant in generating business for the school to consider, so much so that H. F. Pegler, the second clerk in the medical school office, was awarded the sum of £20, additional to his salary of £100 per year, in recognition of the extra work falling on his desk.

Counted among the board's earliest achievements was agreement first, that its membership be prominently displayed in the school's annual prospectus, and secondly, that, where appropriate, part-time assistant physicians and surgeons, with the new title of 'clinical tutor', be appointed to non-professorial hospital firms for teaching duties. This was a clear attempt by Mitchell Stevens and his colleagues to erode the special position of the professorial units. It was a move that the school was disinclined to resist, having made it clear that no payment was available to the clinical tutors. However, the Faculty of Medicine did wryly point out that the part-time appointments now being proposed were analogous to those which had given rise to 'much misunderstanding' in the past. In fact, the two men appointed by the Board of Medicine in March 1930 were old friends of the school, J. B. Haycraft and Abel Evans, appointed as clinical tutors to Cornelius Griffiths and Mitchell Stevens respectively. In response to the disturbance in the male students' common room in the hospital, new disciplinary rules, drawn up by the medical superintendent, were approved by the board. The board, however, was less successful in abolishing the courses of systematic lectures for medical students (defined as those in which cases, specimens or apparatus were not demonstrated) organized by the professorial units, which some, at least, of the recognized clinical teachers considered to be a waste of valuable time. 'They are of opinion that teaching should be of a practical nature, as the time at the disposal of the student for learning is so limited.' The Faculty of Medicine asserted that, whether or not such courses were given in London, they were a universal feature of the curricula in the provincial medical schools. Probably the two most important developments initiated by the board, in partnership with members of the Faculty of Medicine, prior to the independence of the school in the summer of 1931, were the establishment of library facilities in the infirmary, and the provision of weekly courses of postgraduate instruction for local general practitioners, taking the form of clinical demonstrations, both briefly referred to in chapter 6.

The new spirit of co-operation generally displayed in the Board of Clinical Studies was also shown in the way that the hospital and college authorities worked together in the matter of compensation for the students affected by the closure of the infirmary. By May 1930 the joint committee had met on seven occasions, considering fifty-two claims for compensation, each of which had been deemed eligible. Though the total amount sought had come to £5,473, the total awarded was £2,573. 14s. 11d., with one claim still being dealt with. In addition there were various legal costs to be met. When the joint committee had been set up no assumption had been made regarding the respective liabilities of the two bodies involved, but by the time its work had come to an end it had been unanimously agreed, 'especially having regard to the future success of the school', that the final costs should be divided equally between them. At its meeting in July 1930, the University Council approved the recommendation of its finance committee that the college's costs be met from the University Appeal Fund.[44]

It will have been noted that neither of Mitchell Stevens's 'fancy departments' had been included in membership of the Board of Clinical Studies, as they did not use the resources of the infirmary for undergraduate clinical teaching. Indeed, there were some in the Board of Medicine who believed that the contribution of the Department of Public Health to undergraduate education was not as great as it should be. In a slightly weary memorandum to the Board of Medicine in July 1930, Professor Collis, determined to demonstrate his credentials as a dedicated academic and his commitment to the all-Wales profile of the school, recalled how, at the instigation of the University Court, he had, during the 1924/5 and 1925/6 sessions, conducted a series of lectures on health topics to the students and staff of all four colleges in the University of Wales, to which members of the general public had also been invited. Each lecture had been fixed well in advance, with the co-operation of the local student organization. However, this imaginative, and perhaps pioneering, excursion in the field of what is now called interprofessional education (IPE) was a less than resounding success:

> At Cardiff the attendance at the first lecture was *nil*, which did not encourage any effort to continue the course. At Aberystwyth, Bangor and Swansea the first lecture was given in 1924/5, and the second in 1925/6. But the attendances were sparse, and obviously consisted of persons whipped up to attend out of compliment to the visiting lecturer. No sign was forthcoming of any keenness or desire for acquaintance with the subject. Hence the lectures were discontinued in 1926/7. Apparently they have not been missed, as no word as to any desire for their continuance has ever reached the lecturer from any of the colleges.

Having reviewed the syllabus during the preclinical years, Collis saw no reason to 'interfere' with existing arrangements, while he was satisfied with his department's input into the clinical course. Indeed he referred to a recent survey of the teaching of public health at the various medical schools of the United Kingdom, conducted by the Society of Medical Officers of Health: 'The teaching in the Welsh school was found to compare favourably with that given elsewhere.'

ALL OUTSTANDING ISSUES RESOLVED AND THE BASIS FOR THE SCHOOL'S INDEPENDENCE AGREED

With the re-engagement of the recognized clinical teachers, the renewal of recognition by the University of London and the Conjoint Board, the appointment of new academic staff, and the establishment of the Board of Clinical Studies, enough had been done to ensure that the full medical school would reopen for business in October 1929. While scarcely a handful of Cardiff's displaced clinical students returned to complete their studies in Wales, twenty-two preclinical students entered the fourth year and, to the relief of all, the number of first-year students enrolling for in 1929, forty-one, showed a marked increase over the previous year, a sure sign of returning optimism, certainly among the students and their parents. The university pro-chancellor, W. N. Bruce, had been as relieved as anyone that the dispute between the Cardiff College and the infirmary was over, but he was careful to avoid euphoria, as he confessed to his old friend Sir John Herbert Lewis: 'I believe we have reached a respectable settlement of that terrible School of Medicine controversy but we have still to face the Univ. Grants Committee and to win back the confidence of the LEAs, the majority of whom have withdrawn their contributions, and no wonder.'[45] In reality the finances of the school in the summer of 1929 were, according to the statement of need submitted by the university authorities to the University Grants Committee, 'in a most precarious position', caused partly through a loss of student fees, but primarily through a decrease in the contributions of the local education authorities, as table 10.4 shows.

Table 10.4 Contributions by local education authorities

1924/5	£6204 14s. 4d.
1925/6	£4988 3s. 8d.
1926/7	£4920 5s. 8d.
1927/8	£3538 6s. 1d.
1928/9	£736 7s. 6d.

At the same time the school faced unavoidable new commitments, including a recurrent sum of £2,000 per year to maintain the new Rockefeller laboratories, and additional funds to meet the staffing implications of the new agreement between the college and the infirmary relating to the professorial units.

> It is evident, therefore, that the current year, viz. 1929/30, will be one of peculiar difficulty and anxiety, and the University sincerely hopes that in the special circumstances, the University Grants Committee will see its way to make a non-recurrent grant to help to tide over the immediate difficulties.[46]

The response of A. H. Kidd on behalf of the UGC was sympathetic. While not yet in a position to give long-term assurances regarding the finances of the school, the UGC, he said,

> have observed with pleasure that for the first time in the history of this difficult question local opinion in Wales is united in favour of a scheme of organisation for its National School of Medicine, which appears to mark a decided advance upon earlier schemes. They feel, therefore, that the Medical School has been re-opened this session under really hopeful auspices, and that it would be most unfortunate if, at the inauguration of a new epoch in the history of the School serious financial difficulties were allowed to hamper progress.

The UGC were therefore prepared to pay to the university an additional non-recurrent grant of £5,000, without delay, to meet the school's immediate financial pressures, on the assumption that the Welsh local education authorities would resume their own contributions to the school.[47] In fact, by the time of Kidd's letter, in November 1929, half of the eighteen local authorities had pledged to contribute, most also undertaking to meet their arrears, and by the following April only two authorities, Flintshire and Merionethshire, were still categorically refusing to resume their payments despite much pressure from senior members of the university. Even Swansea, finally assured that the school of medicine, or at least most of it, was breaking free of Cardiff College, had agreed, not only to resume its annual contribution, but to pay five years' arrears, over £2,000 in total.[48]

In order to reassure the UGC that the affairs of the Welsh National School of Medicine were back on an even keel, and that good progress was being made towards its establishment as an independent body, the university authorities had, a few weeks prior to the submission of the statement of need, sent to the Privy Council copies of the draft charter of the Welsh National School of Medicine, as more or less agreed by the University Court in July 1928, and of the agreement signed by the Cardiff College, the Royal Infirmary and the university. As Pro-Chancellor Bruce explained to the university registrar,

> Without this evidence that the demand of the Government for a satisfactory scheme of administration for the School of Medicine is on the way to be met the representatives of the University would be at a serious disadvantage in discussing with the Grants Committee the needs of the School of Medicine for the ensuing quinquennium.[49]

The Cardiff College authorities were furious. Not only had the university, in its desire to demonstrate progress, broken a previous undertaking that the final version of the draft charter of the school would be submitted to the Privy Council at the same time as the draft supplemental charters of the college and the university; the version of the school charter submitted by the university had omitted clauses that the college had wished to be included, and had excluded any reference to an agreement, not yet finalized, between the university, the college and the School of Medicine, dealing with the terms of the separation of the school from the college. The Cardiff College thereupon lodged a petition with the Privy Council against the granting of the school charter until various outstanding matters had been settled.[50]

Emboldened by the action of the college, the authorities of the infirmary decided to air their own grievances regarding aspects of the draft school charter. They had been disappointed that, instead of the six representatives of the infirmary on the Board of Medicine, there would only be three on its successor body, the School Council. Furthermore, strictly speaking, the three would be nominated, not specifically by the infirmary but by the governing bodies of clinical institutions recognized by the university, a form of words which had reflected the extreme irritation felt by the university authorities towards the hospital during the spring of 1928. In addition, representation by the honorary clinical staff on the Council was not guaranteed.[51] As has already been noted, a third petition against the granting of the school charter was submitted to the Privy Council by the professor of physiology.

The Privy Council referred everything back to the university authorities to sort out. W. N. Bruce had already learned that the UGC itself (whose views on the draft charter had been sought by the Privy Council) was supporting the infirmary's contention that one of the three representatives of the recognized clinical institutions should be a member of the honorary clinical staff, and he was more than happy to commend this to the University Court.[52] The UGC's other main observation was not so easily resolved. Article I, clause 5 of the draft charter had included the sentence: 'The School shall not institute Departments in Chemistry, Physics, Botany, Zoology, Anatomy or Physiology *or in any sub-division of these sciences.*' The concern of the UGC was that this sentence would prevent the school from establishing departments such as biochemistry or biophysics, with direct relevance to clinical studies, a point immediately endorsed by the Faculty of Medicine, when invited to comment by the University Council. The faculty, after mischievously suggesting that the departments of anatomy and physiology should be deleted from the clause in question, proposed that the following sentence be added: 'But nothing herein provided shall preclude the School from establishing Departments dealing with the application of these subjects to medicine.' The College Council finally came up with a form of words which proved to be acceptable to the University Court and which met the concerns of the UGC, by adding to the relevant sentence of clause 5 the crucial words 'The School shall not institute Departments *open to students in the preclinical years of study* in Chemistry ...'. As Cardiff principal J. F. Rees reassured Pro-Chancellor Bruce:

> The clause now suggested by the Council attempts more or less successfully to make it clear that the College is only concerned with the preclinical years of study and that as long as developments in the National School of Medicine do not trespass upon the work of these years the College has no kind of objection to them.[53]

At a special meeting of the University Court, held on 28 March 1930, all the contentious issues relating to the draft charter of the school, and the supplemental charters of Cardiff College and the university were finally resolved. The college's main concerns were addressed. Not only did its version of clause 5 secure acceptance; a recital was added to the school's draft charter, referring to the establishment of the Joint Academic Committee of the school and the college, to oversee the day-to-day management of the first three years of the medical course, and to the future arrangements for appointing the college's professors of anatomy and physiology. Moreover, the infirmary's demand for representation of the honorary clinical staff on the School Council was conceded. The tripartite agreement between the university, the college and the infirmary had been in place since 1 July 1929, and its main provisions had already been implemented. The outcome of the meeting came as a great relief to the *Western Mail*:

> The friends of higher education in Wales will breathe more freely when they learn, from the report of yesterday's meeting of the University Court, that all outstanding questions relating to the status and organisation of the National Medical School have been settled.[54]

Writing on behalf of the UGC, A. H. Kidd wearily advised the Privy Council to accept the situation and finally approve the various charters, particularly the one in respect of the new Welsh National School of Medicine:

> The constitution of a National School of Medicine for Wales has now been under active and often acrimonious discussion for over fifteen years, and the Committee are inclined to think that if the scheme now put forward, which appears to represent a substantial measure of agreement between the University, the University College and the Royal Infirmary, were to fall through, the prospects of medical education in Wales are likely to remain precarious for a good many years more, since the local dissensions and jealousies which have held up progress for so long, are by no means extinct, though at present somewhat diminished in intensity.
>
> In view of this, the Committee are disposed to look rather to what is reasonably practicable than to the requirements of an ideal organisation, and to pass over without comment features of the scheme which could only have been improved, if the various parties concerned had been able to disregard past history and to approach the problem with unprejudiced minds.
>
> Taking all the relevant circumstances into account, the Committee do not propose to offer objections to the organisation proposed for the Welsh National School of Medicine.[55]

PREPARING FOR SEPARATION

In view of the agreement reached at the University Court, the Welsh National School of Medicine was on course for independence by the summer of 1931, a timescale projected by Principal Trow in the summer of 1929. There was, however, one major issue to be settled, the 'division of the spoils' between the college and the school. In truth, the school had no 'spoils' over which to haggle. Everything legally belonged to the college, of which the school was a part. There was no dispute that the school, once independent, should enjoy full use of the Institute of Preventive Medicine. After all, Sir William James Thomas had paid for the building with this aim in mind. However, the fact remained that the building belonged to the college and stood unambiguously on college land, and for nearly three years discussions took place between the college and university authorities, to decide the basis on which the school could continue to occupy the building and use its facilities.[56] The arrangement finally agreed in the spring of 1931, after much expenditure of expensive lawyers' time, was enshrined in two legal documents, a rather clumsily entitled deed, 'Agreement for a lease of the Institute of Preventive Medicine and the transfer of certain Medical Departments of the College to the School of Medicine', and 'Lease of the Institute of Preventive Medicine situate in the Parade in the City of Cardiff'.[57] Taken together these documents asserted the institute, its existing fixtures and fittings, apparatus and equipment, and even its library books and periodicals, to be the continuing property of the college. The institute would be leased to the Welsh National School of Medicine for a period of sixty years, to be used 'solely for the purpose of a School of Medicine' and not 'for any other purpose whatsoever'. For the first thirty years the college would receive an annual rental payment of £244, a figure that would reduce to £1 a year during the next thirty years. The school would be obliged to insure the building and contents, to maintain the facilities in good order and to meet all the running costs, and to allow the college authorities to inspect the premises 'at all reasonable times', to ensure that the terms of the lease were being honoured. The agreement also required the school to vacate, unless otherwise agreed, any college property other than the institute, within three months of independence. This would not, in practice, cause a serious problem. Arrangements were made to transfer the medical school office from the main building into space loaned by Professor Collis at the institute. Otherwise, apart from a few scattered rooms occupied by the Department of Materia Medica and Pharmacology, the school departments not already housed in the institute were accommodated in the infirmary in accordance with arrangements not affected by the school's establishment as an independent body. So far as the Department of Materia Medica and Pharmacology was concerned the College Council agreed, in July 1931, that the school could continue to occupy the rooms in the college used by that department for one year from 1 July 1931, at an inclusive rental of £25 per annum, the position to be reviewed in a year's time. At the same meeting the Council agreed to grant facilities to the professor of surgery to give instruction in operative surgery in the Department of Anatomy.[58]

The college also managed trust funds created at various times in the past for the benefit of medical education in Wales. Since most had dated from the pre-war period, had been applied for purposes relating to the preclinical course, and the Departments of Anatomy and Physiology were remaining within the college, it was counsel's clear opinion that 'The College will be entitled to retain the corpus of all funds now vested in it.'[59] The funds involved were the Hughes Anatomical Medal and Museum Funds, the W. Price Estate, the Dr W. T. Edwards Legacies, the Samuel Brothers Scholarship and the Alfred Sheen Prize. Two trust funds were regarded differently. The Mansel Talbot Professorship in Preventive Medicine, and the David Davies Chair of Tuberculosis, were clearly intended to be held within the new School of Medicine and the trust deeds were suitably modified to enable this to happen.[60]

It was obviously important that the new Welsh National School of Medicine, when up and running, should not be saddled with any debts carried over from the time when it had been part of the college. The auditors of the university and the college, charged with the task of arriving at a figure, concluded that the accumulated deficit attributable to the school, as at 30 June 1931, was £4,905, an amount that the University Council, on 24 April 1931, undertook to meet from the university's Sinking Fund.[61] From the school's point of view it was even more important to receive some reassurance from the UGC concerning its long-term financial situation. The crucial information it needed was that the additional annual grant of £7,000, so long promised by the UGC but never paid, would now be forthcoming. Jenkin James, the university secretary, wrote to the secretary of the UGC in mid-March pointing out that the Privy Council had finally approved the charter of the school, effective from 5 February 1931,[62] and that the school was on course to becoming operational with effect from 1 July. This was not enough for the cautious A. H. Kidd, who wished to know 'how far effective steps have been taken by the three bodies concerned [the university, Cardiff College, and the school of medicine] to bring the new order of things into operation'. The university secretary's response was as thorough as it could be:

> The terms of an Agreement for a lease of the Institute of Preventive Medicine and the transfer of certain medical departments of the College to the School were finally agreed upon on 20th inst., and it is proposed to convene a special meeting of the court of the University on 7th May in order to set up a Council of the School and to make other necessary arrangements under the new Charter. The authorities of the University College of South Wales and Monmouthshire on their part are taking steps to set up a Joint Academic Committee in accordance with the terms of the Agreement arrived at between the College and the University.[63]

Having finally satisfied Whitehall that everything was well in hand, the University Council, at its meeting on 9 June, was pleased to note that the additional sum of £7,000 from the UGC, earmarked for the school of medicine, would be included in the university grant in the following month.

The special meeting, on 7 May, of the University Court, which would, within a matter of weeks, in accordance with the charter of the school, also become the Court of the Welsh National School of Medicine, began sombrely, with its members conveying their sympathy to the relatives of Emeritus Professor David Hepburn. He had died, perhaps fittingly, on 9 March, before seeing the school attain its independence, a development for which he had never much cared. The remainder of the meeting was reasonably businesslike, involving the appointment of the two officers who had to be in place on the first day of the new school. The university authorities proposed as president Sir Arthur Lyulph Stanley KCMG, fifth Baron Stanley of Alderley, scion of a prominent north Wales landowning family, a man of some distinction (he served as governor of the Australian state of Victoria from 1914 to 1920), but in poor health and enjoying no obvious connection with the Welsh National School of Medicine. A not insignificant number of Court members (nineteen against forty-one) immediately called for the election to be postponed until the availability of Sir William James Thomas had been ascertained, but, responding to the chairman's appeal to proceed as time was short, the Court finally resolved (with three dissentients) that Lord Stanley be elected as the school's first president. On the face of it nothing would have been more appropriate than to have chosen the school's greatest benefactor to serve as its first president. The explanation for his lordship's appointment was given in the *Western Mail*'s editorial. Apart from any personal qualities Lord Stanley of Alderley would bring to the position, his appointment

> will serve a useful purpose in establishing a new link between the School, which originated as a South Wales institution, and the northern half of the Principality. The people of the whole of Wales may be assured that the fortunes of the School are in wise and competent keeping.[64]

Unfortunately, Lord Stanley was given no time to prove his worth, expiring in August 1931. He was succeeded by Gilbert Cunningham Joyce, bishop of Monmouth, whose academic and all-Wales credentials were good, as he had previously served as warden of St Deiniol's Library, Hawarden and as principal of St David's College, Lampeter. As for Sir William James Thomas, he became the school's honorary treasurer.

The second appointment made by the Court generated less controversy, with Professor William Sheen being elected as acting provost until more permanent arrangements were made. The Court also appointed several of its members to serve on the Council of the new school.

The Court had no role in appointing a chief administrative officer for the school. This would be a matter for its new Council to determine in due course, but for the time being Captain D. Brynmor Anthony, the university registrar, took on the responsibilities of acting secretary. For several weeks, he and D. J. A. Brown, who was having to cope without F. G. Hartland (who had resigned as chief clerk in the medical school office at the beginning of the year leaving some disgruntled office staff behind)[65] worked closely to ensure that the process of separation between the college and the school was handled as smoothly as possible. Files covering the busy weeks leading up to 1 July, held in the Cardiff University archives, bear witness to Brown's meticulous attention to detail.

There are schedules of those members of staff (eighty-two in total) whose contracts of employment had to be transferred to the new school of medicine; correspondence with the officers of the Federated Superannuation Scheme for Universities regarding the transfer of eligible staff; letters to the secretary of the Cardiff Royal Infirmary, to insurance companies, the Cardiff Corporation electricity department, the district manager of the post office telephones, the Cardiff Gas Company, and the providers of all manner of other services. He wrote to the heads of the departments in the new school advising them how to draw up departmental inventories of equipment, marking items 'WNSM' to distinguish them from newly acquired items, properly belonging to the new school, to be identified by the letters 'USM'. One letter drew a kind reply from Gilbert Strachan, who was responsible for compiling the inventory for the Department of Obstetrics and Gynaecology. 'I would like to say how much I regret that the severance of the School from the College will cause our association to discontinue. It has been a great pleasure to work with you and I venture to think that you also may have some regrets.' Brown was clearly touched by these words:

> Like you I much regret that our close association has necessarily to cease. The way in which you and others have so kindly helped me on many occasions during the past years has considerably lightened the burden which necessarily fell to some extent upon me.[66]

The final words of the last meetings of the Board of Medicine on 19 May 1931, and of the Faculty of Medicine on the following day, were expressions of thanks to Brown for his services to the medical school in recent years. Otherwise both meetings were suitably businesslike, approving matters that could be approved and referring to the first meetings of the Senate and Council of the Welsh National School of Medicine such matters as only those bodies were competent to deal with. Lest those present at the meeting of the Board of Medicine might be under the illusion that all the controversies of the past were now behind them, the formidable Mitchell Stevens disabused them in no uncertain terms. No doubt smarting from the school's shelving of his claim for an enhancement in status and salary, he accused it of treating the Board of Clinical Studies, of which he was chairman, with insufficient respect. At the end of a long letter of complaint to D. J. A. Brown he concluded:

> I foresee the probability of serious friction if the position of the Board of Clinical Studies is not made quite clear. I hope these points will be brought to the notice of the new body which is taking over the functions of the Board of Medicine at the earliest possible date as my colleagues and I are very desirous that there should be no misunderstandings as to what the taking over of the Agreement [with the Infirmary] really means.[67]

It is unlikely that Mitchell Stevens's mood would have been lightened by the content of a memorandum submitted by the Academic Board to the University Council on 9 June 1931, dealing with the question of the salaries of senior academic staff in the Welsh National School of Medicine. Having considered salary levels elsewhere, the Academic Board concluded that while the salary of the full-time professor of pathology, when filled (£1,500), was adequate, those of the professors of medicine and surgery should be increased to £2,000 per annum 'when circumstances permit'. As far as the part-time lecturer and head of the Department of Material Medica and Pharmacology was concerned, the board took the view that he was, if anything, over-paid compared with similar posts elsewhere. The holder had every opportunity to engage in lucrative private practice; indeed his university appointment gave additional status to the holder, 'leading to the increase of such practice'. The board therefore recommended that if, on retirement, he was succeeded on the same part-time basis, the salary 'should not exceed £250'. Poor Stevens would have gained little consolation from the board's view that the school's part-time professor of obstetrics and gynaecology was also overpaid.

FINAL THOUGHTS

The first phase of the history of the Welsh National School of Medicine was complete. The journey, from small beginnings as the Cardiff Medical School, with a dozen students, in 1893, to a full school of medicine, of over two hundred undergraduate and postgraduate students, and an all-Wales perspective, had been long and often painful. Had William Thomas Edwards, Alfred Sheen (the dean's father) or any of the other early pioneers in the development of the school been invited to speculate on the shape of their vision at the beginning of the 1930s, it is unlikely that they would have predicted the eventual outcome. It is tempting to suggest that they would have expected the Cardiff Medical School to develop into a faculty of medicine, with clinical as well as preclinical departments, to be sure, but integrated into a broadly based university institution, along the same lines as the medical schools in the English provinces, schools which, it should be remembered, had scarcely embraced the professorial unit system by this time. They would undoubtedly have been dismayed by the friction between the academic and hospital authorities during the 1920s, a state of affairs without parallel anywhere else in Britain at that time.

What was it about Cardiff and Wales that ensured that the organization and provision of medical education here developed along different lines from the rest of Britain, particularly the English provinces, during the first three decades of the twentieth century? First, compared with the rest of the country, medical education was a new development in Cardiff at the start of the twentieth century, and it was probably inevitable that, when thinking about the way clinical training might be organized, those in Cardiff who were reflecting on such matters, would be attracted by new ideas. It is no coincidence that the new medical schools of today are in the vanguard in embracing the new approaches to the delivery of medical education in the new millennium. So it was in pre-war Cardiff, where the great Sir William Osler, the most advanced medical thinker of his day, was a regular and most welcome counsellor to influential local men such as Colonel Bruce Vaughan and John Lynn Thomas. It was Osler, more than anyone else, who was responsible for the adoption, by the Cardiff medical school, of the clinical unit system, and had not the First World War intervened, it is quite possible that Cardiff, rather than St Bartholomew's Hospital, would have been the first centre in the country to introduce this innovative concept. However, the very newness of the Cardiff medical school, and the lack of any tradition of working with its local hospitals, ensured that the immediate introduction, in 1921, of the clinical unit system into a hospital with no real understanding of its new role was bound to create conflict. Whether the events of 1928 were therefore inevitable is another matter. Had the personalities been different, it is possible that the outcome might also have been different.

One may infer from the above that the introduction of the clinical unit system was less than a complete success. Certainly very few other medical schools were tempted to follow suit during the inter-war years. However, the unit system did have some influence on the school's approach to clinical teaching, and there is no denying the fact that had it not been introduced in Cardiff, there is no way that the Rockefeller Foundation would have invested any of its funds in the Welsh National School of Medicine.

If Sir William Osler was one of the key figures in the development of the school, Sir Isambard Owen was another. Despite his later protestations, it was he, more than anyone else, who planted in the minds of influential people in Whitehall and in the University of Wales the idea that the Welsh National School of Medicine should be an independent institution within the University of Wales. Prior to his evidence in 1916 to the commission, the chairman of which was the chancellor of the university of which Owen was vice-chancellor (Bristol), no one, inside or outside Wales, had seriously thought of such an idea. Certainly many people, not least David Lloyd George, had been anxious to ensure that the school of medicine should have an all-Wales remit, but the general assumption had always been that the medical school would be an integral part of the University College of South Wales and Monmouthshire. Sir Isambard set a hare running, which could never be completely ensnared. On the positive side, the concept of a truly national medical school, affiliated to none of the existing colleges, was increasingly attractive to many who looked for an institution which truly expressed a growing sense of Welsh national identity. On the negative side, the idea of separating the medical school from University College, Cardiff was immensely appealing to those in Wales, particularly those from centres such as Swansea, who resented Cardiff's pre-eminent position in the principality. Whitehall's stance in favour of independence for the Welsh National School of Medicine as the 1920s proceeded was influenced by both strands of thinking. It found the idea of an independent medical school with an all-Wales dimension attractive and cost-effective; it was equally alarmed that a medical school tied to University College, Cardiff would not attract from the rest of Wales the income deemed necessary to keep it solvent.

Perhaps some principals of University College, Cardiff would have given in to the seemingly inexorable march of events, preferring to take the advice of many, not least in Whitehall, and concentrate on building up the rest of their institution. However, Principal E. H. Griffiths, and even more so Principal A. H. Trow, were made of sterner stuff. Trow strove hard to keep the medical school within the fold as long as he could, employing not only academic arguments, the sort of arguments that would be well understood in the provincial medical schools of England, but also rather more selfish ones. Cardiff created and developed the medical school. What right had the University of Wales, the government or anyone else to take it from them? Faced with the prospect of sterile litigation and reprisals from an increasingly offended government, the warring parties chose compromise, and divided the medical school in two. Whether, in the long run, the compromise reached was sensible in academic terms, time alone would tell. The *Western Mail* took a deep breath: 'The terms of the compromise may not accord with all the academic ideals as interpreted by every person qualified to interpret them, but they do provide a working basis and as such must be accepted.'[68]

The last word should go to the Council of University College, Cardiff, which passed the following generous resolution a few months before the Welsh National School of Medicine, or at least most of it, went its own way:

> That this Council taking notice of the grant of the Charter of the Welsh National School of Medicine and the new Charter of this College as affecting such School desires to place on record and as a guide to those of its staff who may be affected thereby, its firm resolve that whether the Welsh National School of Medicine shall remain a separate and distinct institution or whether it shall hereafter revert to its former position as an integral part of this College, this Council will co-operate to the fullest extent possible in giving to such School both in word and deed its cordial and whole-hearted support.[69]

Appendix 1

CERTAIN SENIOR OFFICERS OF THE UNIVERSITY OF WALES, OF THE CARDIFF COLLEGE, AND MEDICAL SCHOOL HEADS OF DEPARTMENT

1 University of Wales
Senior deputy chancellor
Sir Isambard Owen, 1895–1910
Lloyd, fourth Baron Kenyon of Gredington, 1910–20

Pro-chancellor
Lloyd, fourth Baron Kenyon of Gredington, 1920–7
The Hon. William Napier Bruce, 1927–34

Vice-chancellor
John Viriamu Jones, 1895–6, 1898–1900
Sir Harry Reichel, 1896–7, 1900–1, 1905–7, 1911–13, 1917–21, 1926–7
Thomas Francis Roberts, 1897–8, 1901–3, 1907–9, 1913–15
Ernest Howard Griffiths, 1903–5, 1909–11, 1915–17
Albert Howard Trow, 1921–3, 1927–9
John Humphreys Davies, 1923–5
(Sir) Thomas Franklin Sibly, 1925–6
(Sir) Henry Stuart Jones, 1929–31

Registrar
Ivor James, 1895–1905
J. Mortimer Angus, 1905–21
D. Brynmor Anthony, 1921–45

Secretary
Jenkin James, 1921–45

2 University College of South Wales and Monmouthshire
Principal
J. Viriamu Jones, 1883–1901

E. H. Griffiths, 1901–18
A. H. Trow, 1918–29
(Sir) J. Frederick Rees, 1929–49

Registrar
Ivor James, 1883–95
J. Austin Jenkins, 1895–1910
(Sir) Percy Watkins, 1910–13
D. J. A. Brown, 1913–36 (secretary to the Board and Faculty of Medicine, 1921–31)

Dean of the Faculty of Medicine
John Berry Haycraft, 1895–8
Francis Dixon, 1898–1903
David Hepburn, 1903–22
A. Mills Kennedy, 1922–4
T. Graham Brown, 1924–6
A. W. Sheen, 1926–31

3 Medical School Heads of Departments

Anatomy
A. W. Hughes, 1893–7
A. F. Dixon, 1897–1903
D. Hepburn, 1903–27
C. McLaren West, 1927–51

Physiology
J. Berry Haycraft, 1893–1919
T. Graham Brown, 1920–47

Pathology and Bacteriology
E. Emrys-Roberts, 1910–24
E. H. Kettle, 1924–7
J. H. Dible, 1928–9
J. B. Duguid, 1929–32 (Acting Head)

Materia Medica and Pharmacology
D. R. Paterson, 1894–1906
W. Mitchell Stevens, 1906–33

Hygiene and public health
Edward Walford, 1900–19

Preventive Medicine and Public Health
E. L. Collis (Mansel Talbot professor of preventive medicine), 1919–33

Medicine
A. M. Kennedy, 1921–50

Surgery
A. W. Sheen, 1921–35

Obstetrics and Gynaecology
Sir Ewen Maclean, 1921–31

Tuberculosis
S. L. Cummins (David Davies professor of tuberculosis), 1921–38

Appendix 2

AGREEMENT BETWEEN THE UNIVERSITY COLLEGE OF SOUTH WALES AND MONMOUTHSHIRE AND THE KING EDWARD VII HOSPITAL, SIGNED ON 23 OCTOBER 1922

1. The hospital shall so far as it reasonably can give such facilities as the College may require for the teaching examination and research purposes of the Medical School in the present Hospital Building or in any extension thereof or additions thereto.

2. Any structural alterations or additions to the Hospital Buildings which may be necessary for the aforesaid purposes either present or future shall after approval by the College and the University Council be carried out by the Hospital and the cost thereof in so far as the same is for the sole benefit of the College shall be paid by the College and all such alterations and additions as aforesaid as are for the benefit or advisable in the interests of both the College and the Hospital shall be paid for by the two Bodies in such proportions as they may mutually agree upon and in default of agreement in such proportions as may be determined by arbitration as hereinafter provided.

3. For the purpose of interpreting the last clause of this agreement it is hereby agreed that the alterations or additions mentioned or referred to in Part 1 of the Schedule hereto are to be deemed to be for the sole benefit of the College, or referred to in Part II of the said Schedule are to be deemed to be for the benefit or advisable in the interests of both the College and the Hospital.

4. The College shall give the Hospital an inventory of the equipment which it considers to be necessary for the portion of the Hospital Building set apart for teaching and research purposes under the terms of this agreement. Such of the said equipment as cannot be provided by the College shall be provided by the Hospital at the expense of the College. Such equipment shall be the property of the College and shall be maintained by the Hospital at the expense of the College.

5. Any sum which the College may require from the University Council or His Majesty's Treasury by way of grant to the College in respect of special services rendered by the Hospital in connection with the teaching examination or research carried on by the National School of Medicine shall with the approval of the University Council be paid direct by the College to the Hospital.

6. Any student of the College desiring to utilise the Hospital shall pay a special Hospital fee to be agreed upon between the College and the Hospital to the College who will hand a ticket to the student which shall not be available until countersigned by the Secretary or other officer of the Hospital, the amount of such special Hospital fees shall be forthwith paid by the College to the Hospital.

7. Beds shall be allocated by the Hospital to the University Professors of the College who shall thereby become honorary members of the Hospital Staff as follows:-

> 20 to the Professor of Medicine
> 40 to the Professor of Surgery
> 8 to the Professor of Obstetrics and Gynaecology

8. In order to increase the teaching facilities of the said University Professors of the College they may with the consent of the Members of the Medical Staff of the Hospital concerned and for teaching purposes only have access to cases under the charge of the Honorary Physicians, Surgeons and Gynaecologists on the staff of the Hospital; provided always that the treatment of the said cases shall remain in the hands and under the sole control of such Physicians, Surgeons or Gynaecologists to whom the beds have been allocated by the responsible officers of the Hospital. The professor of Obstetrics and Gynaecology at the College shall also be entitled to take duty in turn at the Maternity Hospital.

9. In the event of additional beds at the Hospital becoming in the future available for medical surgical or gynaecological cases such additional beds shall be allocated to the said University Professors of the College and to the other members of the medical staff of the Hospital in the like proportions as under the present allocations, the total number of beds in the Hospital Building available for such cases at the present time being taken to be 244.

10. The determination by the College of any appointment made by it shall determine the rights of the appointee of the College under this agreement.

11. The College will appoint two persons nominated by the Hospital on any Joint Standing Committee of Selection to be set up in accordance with Article VIII of the Supplemental Charter of the University of Wales.

12. The parties hereto will use their best endeavours to secure the appointment of a member of the Council of the College to be nominated by the College to serve on the Board of Management of the Hospital and of one member of the said Board of Management to be nominated by the Hospital to serve on the Council of the College.

13. This present agreement shall be for a term of five years reckoned from the 1st day of October 1921 and after the expiration of the said term shall continue in force until revised by agreement between the College and the Hospital.

14. Every dispute difference or question which shall at any time arise between the College and the Hospital or their respective successors or assigns touching the

construction meaning or effect of these presents or any clause or thing therein contained or the rights or liabilities of the College or the Hospital or their respective successors or assigns under these presents shall be referred to the arbitration of some person to be nominated for the purpose by the Minister of Health and this shall be deemed to be a submission of Arbitration within the meaning of the Arbitration Act 1889 or any statutory modification or re-enactment thereof for the time being in force, the provisions whereof shall apply as far as applicable.

Appendix 3

MEMORANDUM ON THE WELSH NATIONAL SCHOOL OF MEDICINE, WRITTEN BY A. H. KIDD, SECRETARY OF THE UNIVERSITY GRANTS COMMITTEE, 5 MARCH 1927

1. The issue at present lies between the Privy Council and the Councils of the University and the Cardiff College. Our interest in the matter is comparatively remote except that we are always anxious to give in an unofficial way what help we can towards adjusting difficulties experienced by the institutions on our grant list. The principal point of practical interest to us at the moment is that if no satisfactory scheme emerges, we shall save £7,000 a year, for which we can find very good use elsewhere. The matter is now one mainly of local interest and reduces itself to the question 'does Wales want a first rate National School of Medicine?' When the idea was first mooted over ten years ago the School was going to be a pioneer institution wholly organised on a 'unit' basis, but since then the London medical schools have gone ahead very fast. For instance, University College Hospital School is now complete with units in Medicine, Surgery and Obstetrics under full-time directors and the total number of units in London is 11. The experiment in Wales is therefore now no longer of anything like such general interest and importance to the national Government.

2. Our position simply is this. About £10,000 a year of Treasury money is going to the Medical School as it now is, and we have offered another £7,000 a year, Provided that a satisfactory scheme can be devised. £17,000 is more than we give to the largest medical school on our whole list with about three times as many students, and of incomparably superior value to medical science and the nation. We should have no justification whatever for giving £17,000 a year to the school in Wales, if we did not feel reasonably secure that the school would be an outstanding success, and that in so elementary a matter as its management it would start under favourable conditions. The Privy Council have stated quite clearly that, with the exception of the proposal of virtual separation, the scheme so far sent forward would not give the school a chance, and we cannot help agreeing with the Privy Council on this point.

3. We do not want to take sides in a domestic controversy or to say what the precise status of the National School should be within the University. All that we should

say is that the School should be under a form of management that looks only to the interest of the School and of medical education, and that, moreover, Wales must be behind the School. If the School is to be virtually subject to the Cardiff College Council, and always to be considered in relation to other faculties of that College, with possible jealousies as to salaries, scales of staffing etc., the School cannot hope to make real or rapid progress.

4. We say that Wales as a whole must be behind the School. That means that it must not only give money, but that it must send its best students there. It is a very hard business to start a new medical school and to gain for it a reputation which will bear comparison with other schools of long standing and with great traditions. The prestige of the London schools is great and growing, and the units prove their merits, and their influence spreads throughout all departments. Liverpool is also an attraction for students from North Wales, and Bristol is waking up and as it develops its residential system may become increasingly attractive to students from South Wales. Moreover, apart from the question of students, it must be remembered that if the medical school in Cardiff continues to be known as an uncomfortable place to work in, filled with local strife and jealousy, first rate men will not want to go or stay there as teachers.

5. The interest of Cardiff City is surely to get a first rate school in its midst, irrespective of the question of domestic management etc. Whatever happens, the fact remains that the School actually is in Cardiff, and on a broad view the interest of Cardiff as a city, is to see the school as important and efficient as possible. If the school simply is one among a number of provincial medical schools, serving mainly Glamorgan and Cardiff, it is not likely to go very far. If, to take a very remote hypothesis, Cardiff should, in the distant future, succeed in breaking up the present University of Wales and become a separate University with its own medical school, it is quite possible that Swansea, which may, by then be as wealthy and populous a centre as Cardiff, may also want to start a medical school which would draw off potential students from the Cardiff school and prevent its ever being a very big thing. Cardiff being by then outside the federal University, would find it very difficult to prevent Swansea from realising an ambition of this kind.

6. We are not legal experts and what the University and the Privy Council can or cannot do is not our business; but it needs no legal knowledge to see what the alternatives are. If the College and the University can agree upon a really workable scheme, which satisfies the Privy Council as guaranteeing the school a genuine chance of developing into a first-rate national school of teaching and research, well and good. It should however be added even here, that any agreement of this kind must be accepted and worked with goodwill by all parties, for without this it will be wholly without the strong moral support which a new institution especially needs.

If however there is no agreement between the University and the College, the deadlock must be solved by a decision substantially either in favour of the College or of the University. Either (1) the College will win and will, in effect keep the school as its own, which will thus become just one more provincial medical school. Our extra £7,000 a year will not be forthcoming for we could not recommend the Treasury to put more money into a small provincial school of unproved merits than it does into the largest medical school in the country with a long record of splendid successes. Or (2) the University Council will win and its scheme or something like it will be imposed from above on the College. Whether this needs legislation or not, this will be a longish process. The progress of the school will be delayed and there will remain an atmosphere of dissension and controversy which must inevitably damage the school and keep the best students and teachers from going there.

(Source: The papers of Dr Thomas Jones, National Library of Wales, J, xv, 142.)

Appendix 4

AGREEMENT BETWEEN THE UNIVERSITY COLLEGE OF SOUTH WALES AND MONMOUTHSHIRE AND THE CARDIFF ROYAL INFIRMARY DATED 1 JULY 1929

1. The Agreement dated the Twenty-third day of October One-thousand Nine-hundred and Twenty-two and made between the College of the one part and Sir William Henry Diamond and Donald Rose Paterson acting on behalf of the then King Edward VII Hospital Cardiff of the other part shall be terminated as and from the date of these presents but without prejudice to the rights and remedies of either party thereto.

2. The Royal Infirmary shall, so far as it reasonably can, give such facilities as the College may require for the teaching, examination and research purposes of the Welsh National School of Medicine (hereinafter called 'The School') in the present Infirmary building or in any extension thereof or addition thereto, on the basis of the Unit system.

3. Any structural alterations or additions to the Royal Infirmary buildings which may be necessary for the aforementioned purposes, either present or future, shall, after approval by the College and the Council of the University of Wales, be carried out by the Royal Infirmary, and the cost thereof, in so far as the same is for the sole benefit of the College shall be paid for by the College, and all such alterations or additions as aforesaid as are for the benefit or advisable in the interests of both the College and the Royal Infirmary shall be paid for by the parties hereto in such proportions as they may mutually agree upon, and in default of agreement in such proportions as may be determined by arbitration as hereinafter provided.

4. The Royal Infirmary shall not admit any student until he shall have obtained a Hospital Ticket. Such Ticket shall be issued by the College on behalf of the Royal Infirmary to each student on payment of a special Hospital Fee to be agreed on between the College and the Royal Infirmary, and shall be countersigned by the Royal Infirmary. The Hospital Fee thus collected by the College shall be handed over forthwith to the Royal Infirmary. The Royal Infirmary may, in special circumstances, and with the express consent of the College, admit students of medicine other than students of the School.

5. Beds shall be allocated by the Royal Infirmary to the University Professors of the College, who shall thereby become Honorary Members of the Infirmary Staff, as follows:-

> Thirty to the Professor of Medicine.
> Forty-six to the Professor of Surgery.
> Eleven to the Professor of Obstetrics and Gynaecology.

The Professor of Obstetrics and Gynaecology at the College shall take duty in turn at the Maternity Hospital.

The Professor of Pathology on appointment shall become an Honorary Member of the Royal Infirmary Staff and an Honorary Pathologist to the Royal Infirmary. He shall be given reasonable facilities and responsibility for such pathological work at the Royal Infirmary as may be required for teaching purposes.

6. In the event of additional beds at the Royal Infirmary becoming in the future available for medical, surgical or gynaecological cases, such additional beds shall be allocated to the said University Professors of the College and to the other Members of the Medical Staff of the Royal Infirmary in the like proportions as under the present allocations, the total number of Beds in the Royal Infirmary building available for such cases at the present time being taken to be Three-hundred and Twenty-one.

7. The determination by the College of any appointment made by it shall determine the rights of the appointee of the College under this Agreement.

8. The College shall appoint two persons nominated by the Royal Infirmary on any Joint Standing Committee of Selection to be set up in accordance with Article XVIII of the Supplemental Charter of the University of Wales, in relation to appointments of Professors in Medicine, Surgery, Obstetrics and Gynaecology, and Pathology and Bacteriology, and in such other Departments as may be recognised for this purpose by the University of Wales on the recommendation of the School authorities.

9. This Agreement shall continue for a term of seven years from the date hereof and thereafter until determined by one year's notice, in writing, given by either party: the terms of this Agreement shall be re-considered at the end of the third year after the date on which it comes into operation, and if desired by either party, at the end of every fourth year thereafter.

10. Every dispute, difference, or question which shall at any time arise between the Royal Infirmary and the College or their respective successors or assigns touching the construction, meaning or effect of any of the clauses or things contained in this Agreement, or the rights or liabilities of the Royal Infirmary or the College or their respective successors or assigns hereunder shall be referred to arbitration pursuant to the Arbitration Act One-thousand Eight-hundred and Eighty-nine or any statutory modification or re-enactment thereof for the time being in force.

11. During the continuance of this Agreement, neither party hereto shall make any agreement with a third party on any matters contained in this Agreement without first submitting same to the other party.

12. Except in so far as provided in this Agreement, nothing herein contained shall in any way infringe the right of the Royal Infirmary to the full control and direction of all the internal arrangements of the Royal Infirmary, and the Royal Infirmary shall be advised, for sanction or otherwise, of any arrangements which may affect such control and/or direction that may be desired by the College.

13. The University Professors, whilst in the discharge of their clinical duties at the Royal Infirmary and in their capacity as Honorary Members of the Royal Infirmary Staff, shall be subject to the same rules and regulations as those laid down by the Royal Infirmary for the other Honorary Members of the Staff of the Royal Infirmary.

14. Each Professorial Unit or Clinic shall be considered and accepted as one of the Hospital Clinics or Firms, and shall be analogous to the other Hospital (non-professorial) Firms in its constitution, staffing, duties towards patients and obligations to the Royal Infirmary.

All Assistants in the Professorial Clinics shall be normally full-time Officers of the School.

In each Professorial Unit there shall be two grades of Assistants, Senior and Junior.

The method of appointment described under Clause 8 shall apply to Senior Assistants in the Units.

Such *Senior Assistants* shall be recognised by the Royal Infirmary as qualified and authorised to take charge of the Wards of the Royal Infirmary in the absence of the Professor and to take full charge of the Out Patient Department of the Royal Infirmary and to have responsibilities and obligations similar to those of the Assistant Surgeons or Assistant Physicians to the Royal Infirmary.

Junior Assistants in the Units shall be appointed by the College.

Such *Junior Assistants* shall be recognised by the Royal Infirmary as qualified and authorised to attend to patients: to carry out work under the supervision of the Professor or his Senior Assistants, and to render assistance to patients in case of emergency. The Professor, or in his absence a Senior Assistant, shall be responsible to the Hospital Authorities that Junior Assistants carry out their duties satisfactorily.

If, for any reason, it be not possible to obtain full-time Assistants, then, *as a temporary measure*, Members of the Honorary Staff of the Royal Infirmary in the corresponding Departments shall be invited to apply for such appointments as part-time Assistants.

All part-time Assistants shall be annual appointments.

All part-time Assistants shall be required to give adequate time to the hospital work of the Unit, and shall carry out such teaching and other school duties as may be reasonably required of them by the Professor. They shall be required to attend punctually at such times as may be arranged.

In the event of no Member of the Honorary Staff of the Royal Infirmary applying for any such appointment, under these conditions, part-time Assistants may be appointed who are not Members of the Honorary Staff of the Royal Infirmary but not more than one of these shall be a Senior Assistant in a Unit.

No candidate shall be appointed by the College to any Assistantship in the Units which involves the treatment of patients within the Royal Infirmary until after his application has been considered and approved by the Election Committee of the Royal Infirmary.

15. A Board of Clinical Studies shall be formed which shall consist of all the Recognised Clinical Teachers and part-time Lecturers who are Members of the Honorary Medical Staff of the Royal Infirmary, and the Lecturers in Radiology and Anaesthetics, together with the Professors of Medicine, Surgery, Obstetrics and Gynaecology, and Pathology, and such other Teachers as may be recommended by the Board of Clinical Studies and approved by the Authorities of the School.

16. The Board of Clinical Studies shall organise and arrange the clinical teaching of the non-professorial Clinics at the Royal Infirmary, to conform to the regulations and courses of study required for the degrees and qualifications of the University of Wales and other Licensing Bodies for which the School accepts students and shall, as a joint body, co-ordinate this teaching with that of the Professorial Clinics, having due regard to the commitments of Members of the Board.

17. The Board of Clinical Studies shall ensure:
    (a) That due records of the attendance and progress of students at such courses of clinical instruction be kept by those Recognised Clinical Teachers and part-time Lecturers concerned and reported to the competent authority of the School when required.
    (b) That each such Recognised Clinical Teacher and part-time Lecturer, shall, at the end of each term or period of instruction, certify to the competent authority of the School whether the students who have attended his course have done so regularly and have duly profited by the instruction given, and shall at the same time make a return of the number of such students.
    (c) That each such Recognised Clinical Teacher and part-time Lecturer shall enforce proper discipline amongst students attending his course of instruction.

18. The Board of Clinical Studies shall make arrangements for the equitable allocation of Clerkships and Dresserships in the various Clinics of the Royal Infirmary. If possible, and as far as practicable, students shall be permitted freedom of choice as

to the particular clinic in which they may desire to act as Clerk or Dresser, it being understood that each student shall be required to act in that capacity for a minimum period of three months in the Medical Professorial Clinic and for a similar period in the Surgical Professorial Clinic.

19. Pursuant to this Agreement, the Royal Infirmary shall hold all its Beds at the disposal of the School for the purpose of clinical teaching, except that if in the future the Royal Infirmary shall accept paying patients, the beds occupied by such patients shall be deemed to be outside the terms of this Agreement and not subject to any conditions contained therein.

20. The Board of Clinical Studies shall elect its own Chairman annually.

21. The Board of Clinical Studies shall have the right of appointing a representative to attend meetings of the Board of Medicine when matters affecting the Board of Clinical Studies are under consideration, but such representative shall not have the right to vote.

22. The Board of Clinical Studies shall have the right of direct access to the Board of Medicine and of submitting its reports directly to the Board of Medicine provided that the Board of Medicine shall, before taking any action thereon, submit such reports to the Faculty of Medicine for its consideration and report. Copies of reports of meetings of the Board of Clinical Studies shall be sent to the Secretary of the Royal Infirmary for information.

23. The Board of Clinical Studies may report to the Board of Medicine on any matter connected with the clinical teaching at the Royal Infirmary which they may deem of importance for the welfare of the School.

24. All students attending the Royal Infirmary shall be subject to the authority of the Medical Superintendent of the Royal Infirmary in respect of general discipline.

25. In the event of the School being constituted or incorporated as a body distinct from the College or in the event of any other body than the College taking over the School then and in either of such cases the obligations and liabilities of the College hereunder shall devolve upon and be undertaken by the School as so constituted or incorporated or such other body taking over the same as the case may be.

IN WITNESS WHEREOF the said parties hereto have respectively caused their common seals to be hereunto affixed the day and year first before written.

Notes

ABBREVIATIONS

Bangor	Bangor University Archives
BM	Minutes of the Board of Medicine of the Welsh National School of Medicine
BMJ	*British Medical Journal*
Cardiff	Cardiff University Archives
Chrimes (ed.)	S. B. Chrimes (ed.), *University College, Cardiff: A Centenary History, 1883–1983* (Cardiff, privately printed, 1983)
CRI	Cardiff Royal Infirmary Archives, Glamorgan Record Office
College Magazine	*The South Wales and Monmouthshire University College Magazine*
FM	Minutes of the Faculty of Medicine of the Welsh National School of Medicine
GMC	General Medical Council
NLW, Davies	National Library of Wales, Lord Davies of Llandinam Collection
NLW, Jones	National Library of Wales, Thomas Jones Collection
NLW, Lewis	National Library of Wales, Sir John Herbert Lewis Papers
NLW, Wales	National Library of Wales, University of Wales Archive
SWDN	*South Wales Daily News*
SWN	*South Wales News*
TNA	The National Archives
UCC, *Calendar*	*Calendar of the University College of South Wales and Monmouthshire*
Univ. Cncl.	Minutes of the Council of the University of Wales
Univ. Ct.	Minutes of the Court of the University of Wales
Williams	J. Gwynn Williams, *The University of Wales, 1893–1939*
W. Mail	*Western Mail*

Note: The name of the *South Wales Daily News* was changed to *South Wales News* on 9 April 1918. The *South Wales News* was suddenly absorbed by the *Western Mail* on 25 August 1928 and for the next few years the newspaper carried the masthead *Western Mail and South Wales News*. In the footnotes the abbreviation *W. Mail* is retained.

Chapter 1 – Origins of the Cardiff Medical School to 1893

1   T. N. Bonner, *Becoming a Physician: Medical Education in Britain, France, Germany and the United States, 1750–1945* (Oxford, 1995), chapter 9.
2   Keir Waddington, *Medical Education at St Bartholomew's Hospital, 1123–1995* (Woodbridge, 2003), p. 13.
3   F. F. Cartwright, *A Social History of Medicine* (London, 1977), p. 50.
4   Irvine Loudon, *Medical Care and the General Practitioner, 1750–1850* (Oxford, 1986), p. 14.
5   *W. Mail*, 30 July 1923.
6   Roy Porter, *The Greatest Benefit to Mankind: A Medical History of Humanity from Antiquity to the Present* (London, 1997), pp. 316–17.
7   Charles Newman, *The Evolution of Medical Education in the Nineteenth Century* (London, 1957), pp. 112–14.
8   Cartwright, *Social History*, p. 50.
9   W. J. Reader, *Professional Men* (London, 1966), p. 68.
10 B. T. Davis, 'The Queen's Hospital and William Sands Cox, 1840–1941', *Aesculapius*, 15 (1995).
11 J. Reinarz, 'Healthcare and the Second City: the development of the Birmingham teaching hospitals in the nineteenth century', *Birmingham Historian* (2004), 16–27.
12 W. S. Porter, *The Medical School in Sheffield, 1828–1928* (Sheffield, 1928), pp. 2–3; G. Grey Turner, *The Newcastle-upon-Tyne School of Medicine, 1834–1934* (Newcastle upon Tyne, 1934); S. T. Anning, 'Provincial medical schools in the nineteenth century', in F. N. L. Poynter (ed.), *The Evolution of Medical Education in Britain* (London, 1966), pp. 121–34.
13 Bonner, *Becoming a Physician*, p. 169.
14 Loudon, *Medical Care*, p. 225.
15 Bonner, *Becoming a Physician*, pp. 193–5.
16 S. J. Reiser, 'The science of diagnosis: diagnostic technology', in W. F. Bynum and Roy Porter (eds.), *Companion Encyclopaedia of the History of Medicine*, vol. 2 (London, 1993), p. 831.
17 Donald MacAlister, 'The General Medical Council: its powers and its work', *The Lancet*, 6 October 1906, pp. 915–21.
18 Loudon, *Medical Care*, p. 298.
19 Newman, *The Evolution of Medical Education*, pp. 74–80, 107–11, 211.
20 Ibid., p. 270.
21 Gerald L. Geison, *Michael Foster and the Cambridge School of Physiology: The Scientific Enterprise in Late-Victorian Society* (Princeton, 1978), p. 151.
22 Newman, *The Evolution of Medical Education*, p. 270.
23 Waddington, *Medical Education at St Bartholomew's Hospital*, p. 124.
24 David R. Jones, *The Origins of Civic Universities: Manchester, Leeds and Liverpool* (London, 1988), pp. 159–60; Michael Sanderson, *The Universities and British Industry, 1850–1970* (London, 1972), chapter 3; Stella V. F. Butler, 'A transformation in training: the formation of medical faculties in Manchester, Leeds and Liverpool, 1870–84', *Medical History*, 30 (1986), 115–32; T. Cecil Gray and Sally Sheard, *A Brief History of Medical Education in Liverpool* (Liverpool, 2001), pp. 6–7.
25 Stella V. F. Butler, 'Centres and peripheries: the development of British physiology, 1870–1914', *Journal of the History of Biology*, 21, 3 (1988), 473–500, p. 478.
26 C. Bruce Perry, *The Bristol Medical School* (Bristol, 1984), p. 19.
27 Waddington, *Medical Education at St Bartholomew's Hospital*, pp. 128, 186–7.
28 *The Lancet*, 6 October 1906, p. 919.
29 *BMJ*, 25 April 1885, p. 850.
30 P. H. Thomas, 'Medical men of Glamorgan: Thomas Williams of Swansea, 1815–1865', *Glamorgan Historian*, 9 (1973), 70–95.

31 *The Cambrian*, 8 July 1858, quoted in T. G. Davies, *Deeds Not Words: A History of the Swansea General and Eye Hospital, 1817–1948* (Cardiff, 1988), p. 57.

32 J. Gwynn Williams, *The University Movement in Wales* (Cardiff, 1993), p. 17.

33 John Davies, *A History of Wales* (London, 1993), p. 383.

34 C. B. Turner, '"A blot on any society": the development of public health in the south Wales valleys during the nineteenth century', in C. Baber and J. Lancaster (eds.), *Healthcare in Wales: An Historical Miscellany* (Cardiff, 2000), pp. 66–80.

35 Loudon, *Medical Care*, pp. 215–16.

36 T. W. Rammell, 'Report to the General Board of Health … into … the sanitary condition of Merthyr Tydfil' (1850), p. 12, cited in I. Gwynedd Jones, *Health, Wealth and Politics in Victorian Wales* (University College of Swansea, 1979), p. 15.

37 J. Gross, ' Hospitals in Merthyr Tydfil, 1850–1974', *Merthyr Historian*, 2 (1978), 78–92.

38 Gwyn A. Williams, 'Odd man in', in Gwyn Jones and Michael Quinn (eds.), *Fountains of Praise: University College, Cardiff, 1883–1983* (Cardiff, 1983), p. 6.

39 Martin Powell, 'What was Wales? Towards a contextual approach to medical history', in Pamela Michael and Charles Webster (eds.), *Health and Society in Twentieth-Century Wales* (Cardiff, 2006), table 9.1, p. 226.

40 R. G. Maliphant, 'Two famous Welsh obstetricians', *Proceedings of the Cardiff Medical Society* (1964/5), 53–62.

41 Emyr Wyn Jones, 'Syr William Roberts a penisilin', *Gwyddonydd*, 23 (Summer and Winter, 1985/6), 5–9, 78–82.

42 Emyr Wyn Jones, 'Sir John Williams (1840–1926): his background and achievement', in John Cule (ed.), *Wales and Medicine: An Historical Survey* (Llandysul, 1975), pp. 86–95.

43 *Dictionary of Welsh Biography down to 1940* (London, 1959), p. 562.

44 Ibid., p. 1028.

45 Ibid., p. 949.

46 Dean Powell, *Eccentric: The Life of William Price* (Llantrisant, 2005).

47 Nigel Naunton Davies, 'Two and a half centuries of medical practice: a Welsh medical dynasty', in John Cule (ed.), *Wales and Medicine*, pp. 216–21.

48 D. Geraint James, 'Dr Isambard Owen', ibid., pp. 96–106.

49 Neil McIntyre, 'Britain's first medical marriage: Frances Morgan (1843–1927), George Hoggan (1837–1891) and the mysterious Elsie', *Journal of Medical Biography*, 12 (2004), 105–14.

50 *SWDN*, 14 December 1910.

51 Edward Davies, *The North Wales Quarry Hospitals, and the Health and Welfare of the Quarrymen* (Caernarfon, 2003).

52 John Davies, *Cardiff* (Cardiff, 2002), p. 29.

53 Dennis Morgan, *The Cardiff Story* (Cowbridge, 1991), chapter 7; Davies, *Cardiff*, chapter 2.

54 Neil Evans, 'The Welsh Victorian city: the middle class and civic and national consciousness in Cardiff, 1850–1914', *Welsh History Review*, 12, 3 (1985), 350–87.

55 Morgan, *The Cardiff Story*, pp. 186–8.

56 Neil Evans, 'The first charity in Wales: Cardiff Infirmary and south Wales society, 1837–1914', *Welsh History Review*, 9, 3 (1979), 319–46; Neil Evans, 'Urbanisation, elite attitudes and philanthropy: Cardiff, 1850–1914', *International Review of Social History*, 27, 3 (1982), 290–323.

57 John Surtees and Alan Trevor Jones, *The Medical Teaching Centre, Cardiff* (Cardiff, 1971), p. 9.

58 A. W. Sheen, 'The history of the Cardiff Medical Society', *Proceedings of the Cardiff Medical Society* (1938/9), 3–15.

59 Quoted by T. E. Hammond in his presidential address, 'The purpose of a medical society', ibid., 23–4.

60 Evans, 'The first charity in Wales', p. 327.

61 Steven Thompson, 'To relieve the sufferings of humanity, irrespective of party, politics or creed? Conflict, consensus and voluntary hospital provision in Edwardian south Wales', *Journal of the Society for the Social History of Medicine*, 16, 2 (2003), 247–62, p. 250.

62 Ray Earwicker, 'Miners' medical services before the First World War: the south Wales coalfield', *Llafur*, 3, 1 (1981), 39–52; Steven Thompson, 'A proletarian public sphere: working-class provision of medical services and care in south Wales, c. 1900–1948', in Anne Borsay (ed.), *Medicine in Wales, c. 1800–2000: Public Service or Private Commodity?* (Cardiff, 2003), pp. 87–8.

63 Davies, *The North Wales Quarry Hospitals*, chapter 3.

64 D. T. W. Price, *A History of Saint David's University College Lampeter*, vol. 1: *To 1898* (Cardiff, 1977), pp. 44–5.

65 Williams, *The University Movement in Wales*, p. 41.

66 Davies, *A History of Wales*, pp. 439, 447.

67 For a full account of the aftermath of the Aberdare Report see G. W. Roderick, 'A new college for South Wales. Cardiff versus Swansea: a battle of the sites, 1881–83', *Transactions of the Honourable Society of Cymmrodorion*, n.s., 6 (2000), 90–103.

68 Davies, *Deeds Not Words*, p. 105.

69 For the Cardiff memorial see 'University College for South Wales and Monmouthshire: Memorial of the Cardiff Corporation', 13 February 1882, Local Studies Department, Cardiff Central Library, 948.2 (398.1).

70 Roderick, 'A new college for South Wales', 94.

71 Williams, 'Odd man in', p. 10.

72 G. W. Roderick, 'Education in an industrial society', in R. A. Griffiths (ed.), *The City of Swansea: Challenge and Change* (Stroud, 1990), pp. 186–7.

73 This account of the origins of the University College of South Wales and Monmouthshire is largely based on A. H. Trow and D. J. A. Brown, *A Short History of the University College of South Wales and Monmouthshire, Cardiff, 1883–1933* (Cardiff, 1933), pp. 12–13; Williams, *The University Movement in Wales*, chapters IV and V.

74 Davies, *Cardiff*, p. 51.

75 Vanessa Cunningham and John Goodwin, *Cardiff University: A Celebration* (Cardiff, 2001), pp. 15–16.

76 Minutes of the Council of UCC, 9 July 1883.

77 Trow and Brown, *A Short History*, p. 13.

78 P. H. Thomas, 'Medical men of Glamorgan: William Thomas Edwards (1821–1915)', *Glamorgan Historian*, 7 (1971) and 8 (1972).

79 Minute book of the Cardiff Medical Society, 1877–95, Glamorgan Record Office, DCMS/2.

80 The minute book of the South Wales and Monmouthshire branch of the British Medical Association, 1871–9, held at the Glamorgan Record Office (DBMA/1), indicates that no reference was made to the need to establish a medical school in south Wales during the 1870s. Unfortunately no minute books have survived for the crucial 1880s.

81 *BMJ*, 2 May 1885, p. 914.

82 'Education number, Session 1895/6', *BMJ*, 7 September 1895, pp. 591–8.

83 *SWDN*, 14 December 1910.

84 *BMJ*, 1 August 1885, p. 185.

85 Included in Appendix F of the memorial of the Court of governors of the University College of South Wales and Monmouthshire and others, presented to the lord president of the Council in April 1886, Cardiff, 'Medical School miscellaneous cuttings file, 1890'.

86 A. W. Sheen, 'The history of the Cardiff Medical Society', *Proceedings of the Cardiff Medical Society* (1938/9), 3–15; *BMJ*, 29 December 1906, p. 1891.

87 For the correspondence between Alfred Sheen and Sir William Thomas Lewis see Cardiff, 'Medical School miscellaneous cuttings file, 1890'.
88 Minutes of the Council of UCC, 10 March 1886.
89 *SWDN*, 15 April 1886; *BMJ*, 24 April 1886, pp. 795–6.
90 Williams, *The University Movement in Wales*, p. 106.
91 Minutes of the Council of UCC, 7 March 1888.
92 *BMJ*, 15 February 1890, p. 374.
93 *SWDN*, 28 June 1890.
94 The handwritten notes of the meetings, probably kept by Alfred Sheen, are in Cardiff, 'Medical School miscellaneous cuttings file, 1890'. They record a suggestion made at the first meeting on 1 July 1890, 'that it might be possible for the anatomy and physiology professors, when appointed, to give courses of lectures at Swansea in connection with the medical school. The suggestion was discussed and it was the general feeling that such an idea was impracticable.'
95 Letter from Owen to Sheen, 11 July 1890, Cardiff, 'Medical School miscellaneous cuttings file, 1890'.
96 Ibid. At a special meeting of the Welsh of London, convened at the Royal Medical and Chirugical Society, Hanover Square in July 1890, the proposal to establish a Department of Medical Sciences in Cardiff was moved by Sir William Roberts, censor of the Royal College of Physicians, one-time professor of medicine at Owen's College, Manchester and one of the most eminent medical scientists of his day. *W. Mail*, 29 July 1890.
97 *W. Mail*, 15 January 1891.
98 *SWDN*, 13 October 1891.
99 *W. Mail*, 13 October 1892.
100 *SWDN*, 13 October 1892.
101 Williams, *The University Movement in Wales*, p. 186.
102 Ibid., p. 115.
103 Williams, p. 13.
104 K. O. Morgan, *Wales in British Politics, 1868–1922* (Oxford, 1963), pp. 102–3, 129–32.
105 Williams, *The University Movement in Wales*, p. 185.
106 Ibid., p. 150.
107 *W. Mail*, 23 March 1893.
108 For an account of the debate over the proposed charter of the University of Wales see Williams, *The University Movement in Wales*, chapter VI.
109 Minutes of the Council of UCC, 7 December 1892.
110 Williams, p. 37.
111 *SWDN*, 16 March 1893.
112 *The Lancet*, 25 March 1893, p. 673.
113 Minutes of the Senate of UCC, 5 October 1886.
114 'Former students of the College who have become qualified', UCC *Calendar* (1909/10), pp. 336–41; *The Medical Directory*, 1914 and 1919 editions.
115 'Educational number, Session 1895/6', *BMJ*, 7 September 1895, pp. 573–84.
116 *W. Mail*, 4 May 1893.
117 UCC, *Calendar* (1895/6), p. 216.
118 *College Magazine*, VI, 1 (December 1893).
119 Minutes of the Council of UCC, 4 October 1893.
120 UCC, *Calendar* (1895/6), p. 246.
121 M. Sanderson, *The Universities and British Industry, 1850–1970*, chapter 5.
122 Minutes of the Council of UCC, 29 September 1893.

Chapter 2 – The Cardiff Medical School

1   *W. Mail*, 9 January 1925.
2   *BMJ*, 21 October 1893, p. 913.
3   *W. Mail*, 5 October 1893.
4   The content of this paragraph is based on the Cardiff principal's annual reports published in the college *Calendars* for 1895/6 and 1896/7, cited in Alan J. Parsons's thesis, 'The origin and subsequent development of the Cardiff Medical School into the Welsh National School of Medicine, 1894–1971' (1979), submitted as part of the requirements for the degree of M.Ed. of the University of Wales; also on material contained in 'University College SW & M Matriculation Book' covering student registrations in the Cardiff college between 1883/4 and 1894/5, stored in the Cardiff University Archives.
5   Carol Dyhouse, *No Distinction of Sex? Women in British Universities, 1870–1939* (London, 1995), pp. 12–13: J. S. Garner, 'The great experiment: the admission of women students to St Mary's Hospital Medical School, 1916–1925', *Medical History*, 42 (1998), 68–88, p. 73.
6   *BMJ*, 28 September 1895, p. 809.
7   UCC, *Calendar* (1909/10), p. 339; *W. Mail*, 14 July 1917.
8   *W. Mail*, 15 February 1894.
9   P. H. Thomas, 'Medical men of Glamorgan: Dr Donald Rose Paterson (1862–1939)', *Glamorgan Historian*, 5 (1968), 38–60.
10   Minutes of the Council of UCC, 5 December 1894.
11   A number of other professors of physiology, all full-time appointees, served as deans of provincial medical schools during this period, Arthur Gamgee at Manchester, A. de Burgh Birch at Leeds and Francis Gotch at Liverpool. Stella V. F. Butler, 'Centres and peripheries: the development of British physiology, 1870–1914', *Journal of the History of Biology*, 21, 3 (1988), 473–500, p. 493.
12   *BMJ*, 7 September 1895, p. 573.
13   Bonner, *Becoming a Physician*, pp. 285–7.
14   This, and other descriptions of the Cardiff curriculum, are taken from the college *Calendar*, 1897/8, pp. 205–23.
15   *College Magazine*, VIII, 1 (December 1910), 43.
16   J. Grigg, *Lloyd George, War Leader, 1916–1918* (London, 2002), pp. 146–8; *The Lancet*, 6 September 1947, p. 313.
17   Bonner, *Becoming a Physician*, p. 260.
18   S. Sturdy, 'The political economy of scientific medicine: science, education and the transformation of medical practice in Sheffield, 1890–1922', *Medical History*, 36 (1992), 115–32, p. 130.
19   J. Reinarz, 'The age of museum medicine: the rise and fall of the medical museum at Birmingham's School of Medicine', *Social History of Medicine*, 18, 3 (2005), 419–37, p. 420.
20   M. Weatherall, *Gentlemen, Scientists and Doctors: Medicine at Cambridge, 1800–1940* (Woodbridge, 2000), p. 221.
21   Minutes of the Council of UCC, 5 December 1894.
22   Minutes of the Senate of UCC, 21 November 1899.
23   Sir Clement Price Thomas, 'The Sheens and the Welsh National School of Medicine', *Proceedings of the Cardiff Medical Society* (1965/6), 56–7.
24   Waddington, *Medical Education at St Bartholomew's Hospital*, pp. 224–5.
25   Sir Garrod Thomas (1853–1931) and his wife contributed £5,000 towards the erection of the hospital on its new site in 1901, and in 1912 he was awarded a knighthood in recognition of his public services. He was chiefly responsible for the present name of the hospital, the Royal Gwent Hospital, conferred in 1913. He served briefly as Liberal MP for South Monmouthshire during the First World War. *BMJ*, 14 February 1931, p. 288; T. B. Jones and W. J. T. Collins, *History of the Royal Gwent Hospital* (Newport, 1948), pp. 29–34.

26 *SWDN*, 15 October 1896.

27 Katherine Viriamu Jones, *Life of John Viriamu Jones* (London, 1915), pp. 179–80.

28 *College Magazine*, IX, 3 (June 1897).

29 Chrimes (ed.), p. 69.

30 *SWDN*, 5 January 1896.

31 *BMJ*, 27 August 1898, p. 522.

32 Jones, *Life of John Viriamu Jones*, p. 15.

33 *SWDN*, 26 November 1900.

34 *W. Mail*, 21 June 1902. William Goscombe John was later commissioned to design and sculpt a memorial to Alfred Hughes beside what is now the main A487 road, overlooking Corris. The memorial was unveiled, amidst much ceremony, on 9 September 1905. D. Jones, *Corris through the Eye of the Camera* (Cardiff, 2002), p. 43.

35 *W. Mail*, 22 December 1903, 27 November 1901.

36 T. G. Davies, *Ernest Jones, 1879–1958* (Cardiff, 1979), p. 21.

37 Ernest Jones, *Free Associations: Memories of a Psychoanalyst* (New Brunswick and London, 1990) pp. 45–7.

38 Arthur Hollman, *Sir Thomas Lewis, Pioneer Cardiologist and Clinical Scientist* (London, 1997), pp. 5–7; Ivor J. Davies, *Memories of a Welsh Physician* (Aberystwyth, 1959), pp. 16–17.

39 Chrimes (ed.), p 324.

40 *Cap and Gown*, n.s. 1, 2 (December 1903). In 1903 this became the new name of the publication previously entitled *The South Wales and Monmouthshire University College Magazine*.

41 *BMJ*, 21 March 1931, p. 517.

42 *BMJ*, 13 January 1923, p. 86. For a critique of Haycraft's Milroy Lectures see T. G. Davies, 'Some early Glamorgan contributors to medical journals', *Morgannwg*, 51 (2007), 19–41.

43 Cunningham and Goodwin, *Cardiff University: A Celebration*, p. 26.

44 Hollman, *Sir Thomas Lewis*, pp. 10, 12.

45 Chrimes (ed.), p. 328; R. E. Kohler, *From Medical Chemistry to Biochemistry: The Making of a Biomedical Discipline* (Cambridge, 1982), pp. 40–1.

46 *SWDN*, 14 December 1910.

47 Details of the women students listed here were verified by Neil McIntyre, emeritus professor of medicine at the Royal Free and University College of Medicine, who is writing a history of the Royal Free Hospital School of Medicine (originally the London School of Medicine for Women).

48 *College Magazine*, XII, 3 (February 1900), p. 120.

49 Ibid., XIV, 1 (November 1901), p. 26.

50 Ibid, XII, 3 (February 1900), p. 119.

51 Ibid., XI, 3 (February 1899), p. 107.

52 Ibid., XII, 5 (June 1900), p. 223. Brenda Maddox, in her biography of Ernest Jones, *Freud's Wizard: The Enigma of Ernest Jones* (London, 2006), pp. 22–5, includes an account of Jones's student days in London, when, with John Jennings and Herbert Ward – 'The Holy Trinity' – he would regularly visit Speakers' Corner in Hyde Park and engage in lively debate with groups such as the anti-vaccinators and anti-vivisectionists.

53 *College Magazine*, XIII, 3 (February 1901), p. 116.

54 Thomas Lewis to his mother, 19 October and 1 December 1902, Sir Thomas Lewis Papers, Wellcome Library, PP/LEW/B2. Sir Victor Horsley was professor of clinical surgery at University College Hospital, London.

55 A. J. P. Taylor, *English History, 1914–1945* (Oxford, 1965), p. 38.

56 Kate Adie, *Corsets to Camouflage: Women at War* (London, 2003), chapter 7.

57 Minutes of the Medical Board, 12 December 1914, CRI, D/D HC 32.

58   *The Lancet*, 13 March 1915, p. 563.

59   *BMJ*, 1 July 1916, p. 24; J. S. Garner, 'The great experiment *etc.*', *Medical History*, 42 (1998), 66–88.

60   *W. Mail*, 14 February 1917.

61   Among the papers of Sir Daniel Lleufer Thomas are items relating to his work with the General Committee for the Promotion of the Medical Training of Women between 1916 and 1941, NLW, D. Lleufer Thomas Papers, C 1/7.

62   *W. Mail*, 19 December 1916.

63   For the obituary of Sir Clement Price Thomas see *BMJ*, 31 March 1973, p. 807. The letter of 21 July 1914 from the director of education of Merthyr Tydfil to the young Francis Davies, informing him of his appointment as a pupil teacher at Georgetown Boys' School, where he would receive 'training in the art of teaching' (D/DX 359/6/1–2), is included in the rather disappointing collection of Francis Davies Papers, deposited in the Glamorgan Record Office; for his obituary see *The Lancet*, 27 March 1965, pp. 714–15. For Ivor Lewis see *The Lancet*, 2 October 1982, p. 779.

64   A. S. Aldis, *Cardiff Royal Infirmary, 1883–1983* (Cardiff, 1984), pp. 24–5. Aldis's book contains the illustration of a fine oil painting of Lieutenant Colonel Hepburn and Matron Montgomery Wilson in one of the wards of the hospital during the First World War. The painting, by the celebrated Cardiff artist, Margaret Lindsay Williams, was commissioned by Sir William James Thomas, who is also depicted therein. The painting is currently located at the Queen Alexandra's Royal Army Nursing Corps Museum, Aldershot.

65   *W. Mail*, 3 January 1917.

66   *BMJ*, 7 September 1918, p. 269, Leah Leneman, *In the Service of Life. The Story of Elsie Inglis and the Scottish Women's Hospital* (Edinburgh, 1994), *passim*.

67   *W. Mail*, 27 December 1916.

68   E. H. Griffiths to D. Hepburn, 11 March 1918, Cardiff, box 21.

Chapter 3 – Towards a Full Medical School

1   *W. Mail*, 7 July 1898.

2   Jones, *The Origins of Civic Universities*, p. 161

3   Morgan, *The Cardiff Story*, p. 182.

4   For the response of the Cardiff port authorities see Neil Evans, '"Sea wall against disease": port health in Cardiff, 1850–1950', in Michael and Webster (eds.), *Health and Society in Twentieth-Century Wales*, pp. 78–97.

5   *W. Mail*, 24 March 1897.

6   *SWDN*, 3 December 1896.

7   *BMJ*, 28 August 1900, p. 496; *The Lancet*, 17 March 1900, p. 798.

8   *SWDN*, 13 June 1904; *BMJ*, 3 September 1904, p. 516, 15 October 1904, p. 1041; City of Cardiff, *Annual Report of the Medical Officer of Health*, 1908–14.

9   Sir Isambard Owen to Sir Francis Knollys, 24 February 1902, Bangor, General Collection, 6274.

10   Sir Isambard Owen to Sir Arthur Bigge, 6 May 1904, Bangor, General Collection, 6276.

11   *SWDN*, 14 May 1904.

12   GMC, *Minutes*, XLIV (1907), pp. 88–9. The relevant statutes are quoted in full on pp. 199–202.

13   Sir Isambard Owen to J. M. Angus, 21 October 1910, NLW, Wales, LU 1/1.

14   Sir Isambard Owen to J. M. Angus, 13 October 1910, NLW, Wales, CG 5/6.

15   J. M. Angus to Lord Kenyon, 4 December 1911, NLW, Wales, CG 5/4.

16   GMC, *Minutes*, XLIX (1912), p. 3.

17   For the minute book of the University Medical Board, 1908–19, see NLW, Wales, LU 1/1. In fact, Sir John Williams never attended meetings of the board and, despite being arguably Wales's most eminent doctor, his involvement in the development of medical education in the principality at this

time was, at best, sporadic. An inspection of Sir John's papers, held in the National Library of Wales, confirms this. While undoubtedly of interest in other respects, the papers contain nothing of significance in relation to the history of the Cardiff Medical School and the Welsh National School of Medicine.

18 E. H. Griffiths to J. Lynn Thomas, 22 October 1915, Cardiff, box 21.

19 *BMJ*, 7 February 1976, p. 345.

20 Information compiled from the annual reports of the Court of the University of Wales, held at the University of Wales registry, Cathays Park, Cardiff.

21 The students were particularly enthusiastic about the teaching of J. H. Sugden, part-time lecturer in hygienic chemistry and a member of the Cardiff City and County Public Health Laboratory. 'His exposition of a difficult subject, his patience, and his kindly manner in dealing with us, have left nothing to be desired. Individually we have been trained in different [medical] schools, and have consequently been under various teachers, and we are unanimously agreed that Mr Sugden is one of the best teachers we have ever had'. Testimonial from the chemistry laboratory, University College, Cardiff, 6 December 1910, signed by John Dodd, Laura Powell and six others, Cardiff, box 21.

22 N. C. King to J. M. Angus, 7 June 1912, NLW, Wales, CG 21/4/1.

23 Minutes of meetings of the University Medical Board, 27 April 1912, 18 October 1913, NLW, Wales, LU 1/1.

24 For the early history of the Cardiff Royal Infirmary see Aldis, *Cardiff Royal Infirmary*, pp. 7–11.

25 *Dictionary of Welsh Biography, 1941–1970* (London, 2001), pp. 268–9.

26 *W. Mail*, 15 November 1905.

27 Ibid., 21 May 1908. At the opening ceremony, Osler was presented with a golden key, a replica of a key of the Charles I period, by the architect, Edwin Seward. The key is now preserved among the archives of Cardiff University, Heath Park campus. Osler's uncle had worked as a hospital surgeon in Swansea during the 1820s, a fact commemorated in 1911 when Sir William Osler unveiled a brass tablet at the Swansea General Hospital 'To the memory of Edward Osler, MRCS, FLS, House Surgeon of this Hospital in 1825'. John Cule, 'Sir William Osler and his Welsh connections', *Postgraduate Medical Journal*, 64 (1988), 568–74.

28 Aldis, *Cardiff Royal Infirmary*, p.19.

29 See 'Note by Dr MacAlister on the Faculty of Medicine' in *The Report of the Committee on the University of Wales and the Welsh University Colleges* (London, HMSO, 1909), Cd. 4571, pp. xxxii–xxxiii. For a copy of the report see NLW, Lewis, D 37.

30 Aldis, *Cardiff Royal Infirmary*, p.10.

31 For details of the Southern *v.* Lynn Thomas and Skyrme case, particularly the retrial at the King's Bench Division in November and December 1906, see the *Western Mail* at that time and several issues of *The Lancet* during 1908, including that of 21 March, pp. 871, 879–81. For Sir John Lynn-Thomas's obituary notices see *BMJ*, 30 September 1939, pp. 708–9; *The Lancet*, 7 October 1939, p. 808. The National Library of Wales also holds a substantial archive of files, press cuttings and correspondence relating to the career of Sir John Lynn Thomas (NLW, MSS 13723–36). In particular there is a scrapbook on the Southern *v.* Lynn Thomas and Skyrme case, containing many letters of support from outraged members of the medical profession, including Dr Hugh Jones (NLW, MS 13725E). It should be noted that on receipt of his knighthood Sir John's middle name and surname became hyphenated.

32 P. H. Thomas, 'Medical men of Glamorgan: Dr Donald Rose Paterson (1862–1939)', *Glamorgan Historian*, 5 (1968), 38–60. For Paterson's obituary see *The Journal of Laryngology and Otology*, 54 (1939), 437–40.

33 P. H. Thomas, 'Medical men of Glamorgan: the Vachells of Cardiff', *Glamorgan Historian*, 4 (1967), 136–161.

34   *Lives of the Fellows of the Royal College of Physicians of London, 1826–1925*, compiled by G. H. Brown (London, 1955), p. 539: minutes of the Senate of UCC, 29 May 1908.

35   P. H. Thomas, 'Medical men of Glamorgan: P. Rhys Griffiths (1857–1920)', *Glamorgan Historian*, 6 (1969), 174–200.

36   Sir Clement Price Thomas, 'The Sheens and the Welsh National School of Medicine', *Proceedings of the Cardiff Medical Society* (1965/6), 53–63. Though formally referred to as 'A. W.' Sheen, he often signed his name 'William' and, according to Price Thomas, his younger colleagues called him 'Bill'.

37   *BMJ*, 24 October 1953, pp. 941–3.

38   For this account of the relationship between the Cardiff Medical Society and members of the Cardiff Medical School before the First World War, see the minute books of the society at the Glamorgan Record Office, DCMS/2 (1877–95), DCMS/3 (1895–1905) and DCMS/4 (1905–22).

39   Minutes of the Medical Board, 1 July 1913, CRI, D/D HC 32.

40   *W. Mail*, 7 November 1913.

41   Ibid., 15 November 1913.

42   Ibid., 21 May 1908. For Bruce Vaughan generally, see the article on him in the Eminent Chairmen series in *The Hospital*, 29 July 1911; also G. R. Orrin, *Church Building and Restoration in Victorian Glamorgan* (Cardiff, 2004), *passim*; Carole Winn, 'A biographical dictionary of Cardiff architects, c. 1850–1920' (unpublished dissertation for the University of Wales College, Cardiff, 1991); Evans, 'The first charity in Wales', *Welsh History Review*, 9 (1979), no. 3, pp. 337–40.

43   *W. Mail*, 13 November 1913.

44   A copy of the printed memorandum, 'University of Wales: proposed completion of the medical school', undated but written in January 1914, is contained in Cardiff, box 21.

45   This account of the Haldane Commission on the University of London is taken from G. Graham, 'The formation of the medical and surgical professorial units in the London teaching hospitals', *Annals of Science*, 26 (1970), 1–22; Waddington, *Medical Education at St Bartholomew's Hospital*, pp. 160–6; Sir Brian Windeyer, 'University education in the twentieth century', in Poynter (ed.), *The Evolution of Medical Education in Britain*, pp. 219–27. For Haldane's overall contribution in the field of education, see Eric Ashby and Mary Anderson, *Portrait of Haldane at Work on Education* (London, 1974).

46   Waddington, *Medical Education at St Bartholomew's Hospital*, pp. 168–72.

47   *BMJ*, 10 January 1920, p. 67.

48   *W. Mail*, 26 November 1913.

49   'Memorandum 1', Departmental Committee on the Medical School at Cardiff, 1914, TNA, UGC, 5/4.

50   Graham, 'The formation of the medical and surgical units', 3.

51   'Memorandum on clinical units in medical schools' (UGC, April 1920).

52   *Appendix to the First Report of the Commissioners: Minutes of Evidence* (London: HMSO, 1917), Cd. 8507, 1388–91.

53   *W. Mail*, 19 October 1906; Chrimes (ed.), p. 68, note 87.

54   Printed record of the interview between the chancellor of the Exchequer and the deputation from the University of Wales, 3 March 1904, NLW, Lewis, D 37; see also TNA, ED 24/570.

55   W. F. Bynum, 'Sir George Newman and the American way', in V. Nutton and R. Porter (eds.), *The History of Medical Education in Britain* (Amsterdam, 1995), p. 42.

56   For the events surrounding the establishment of the Raleigh Committee see Williams, pp. 37–44.

57   For the full report of what was called 'The Welsh Colleges Committee', including MacAlister's report on the situation in Cardiff, see NLW, Wales, D 37.

58   George Newman, *Recent Advances in Medical Education in England* (London: HMSO, 1923), p. 6.

59   E. A. Heaman, *St Mary's: The History of a London Teaching Hospital* (London, 2004), p. 148.

60   Bynum, 'Sir George Newman', p. 42.

61   W. D. Foster, *Pathology as a Profession in Great Britain and the Early History of the Royal College of Pathologists* (London, 1982), p. 15.
62   For developments in academic pathology during the late nineteenth and early twentieth centuries see Weatherall, *Gentlemen, Scientists and Doctors: Medicine at Cambridge, 1800–1940* (Woodbridge, 2000), chapter 6; Waddington, *Medical Education at St Bartholomew's Hospital*, chapters 4 and 5.
63   Butler, 'A transformation in training', p. 131.
64   *BMJ*, 25 September 1909, p. 909.
65   *The Lancet*, 2 November 1940, p. 574.
66   Minutes of the Medical Board, 1 March 1910, CRI, D/D HC 32.
67   For Edward Emrys-Roberts see the obituary in *BMJ*, 26 January 1924, pp. 174–5.
68   Minutes of the Medical Board, 7 November 1911, CRI, D/D HC 32.
69   Davies, *Memories of a Welsh Physician*, p. 60.
70   Ibid. For details of the process of appointing the professor of pathology and bacteriology see the minutes of the Senate of UCC, 7 March and 2 May 1910, and of the Council, 8 June and 13 July 1910.
71   *W. Mail*, 10 February 1911.
72   Ibid., 26 October 1910.
73   G. R. Jones, 'The King Edward VII Welsh National Memorial Association, 1912–1948', in J. Cule (ed.), *Wales and Medicine*, pp. 30–41; Linda Bryder, 'The King Edward VII Welsh National Memorial Association and its policy towards tuberculosis, 1910–1948', *Welsh History Review*, 13, 2 (1986), 194–216; E. L. Ellis, *T J: A Life of Dr Thomas Jones, CH* (Cardiff, 1992), pp. 137–8; J. Davies, *A History of Wales*, p. 495. For details of the Shrewsbury conference and of a follow-up meeting held on 20 June 1911, see NLW, Records of the Welsh National Memorial Association, box 39.
74   *W. Mail*, 3 June 1912.
75   *BMJ*, 26 January 1924, p. 174.
76   Williams, pp. 84–8; Trow and Brown, *A Short History*, pp. 35–6; Cunningham and Goodwin, *Cardiff University: A Celebration*, pp. 133–5.
77   Dewi-Prys Thomas, '"A quiet dignity …" William Douglas Caröe and the quiet presence', in Jones and Quinn (eds.), *Fountains of Praise*, p. 54.
78   E. H. Griffiths to E. M. Bruce Vaughan, 9 July 1912, Cardiff, box 21.
79   Chrimes (ed.), p. 77.
80   *W. Mail*, 14 June 1911.
81   Ibid., 14 October 1911.
82   Ibid., 25 June 1912.
83   Undated memorandum, 'Accommodation for the Department of Physiology and the comparative claims of other departments', Cardiff, box 21.
84   E. H. Griffiths to Dr T. H. Morris, 26 July 1912, ibid.
85   'Site of the Medical School', a memorandum written by Principal Griffiths in preparation for the meeting of the Cardiff College Accommodation Committee, 4 November 1912, ibid.
86   W. J. Thomas to Percy Watkins, 11 December 1912, ibid.
87   Statement from Sir Isambard Owen to the Accommodation Committee, 18 January 1913, ibid.
88   E. H. Griffiths to Lord Merthyr, 25 February 1913, ibid.
89   Butler, 'A transformation of training', p. 131.
90   Stella V. F. Butler, 'Centres and peripheries: the development of British physiology, 1870–1914', *Journal of the History of Biology*, 21, 3 (1988), 473–500.
91   Memorandum by the professor of physiology to the principal, 23 July 1912, Cardiff, box 21.
92   E. H. Griffiths to Lord Merthyr, 26 March 1913, ibid.
93   Sir Percy Watkins, *A Welshman Remembers* (Cardiff, 1944), pp. 97–8.
94   E. H. Griffiths to Meredith Richards, 13 December 1913, Cardiff, box 21.

95 Printed memorandum, 'University of Wales: proposed completion of the Medical School' (undated), ibid.

96 E. M. Bruce Vaughan to E. H. Griffiths, 26 February 1914, Cardiff, box 35, R/File/M/1.

97 Annual report of the Council of UCC to the College Court, 1 October 1913 to 30 September 1914.

98 E. H. Griffiths to H. R. Thompson (UCC treasurer), 9 March 1914, Cardiff, box 21.

99 E. H. Griffiths to David Davies, 23 March, ibid.

100 For the minutes of the meetings of the departmental committee, and appendices recording relevant correspondence, see TNA, UGC 5/4: for copies of the interim and final reports of the committee see TNA, UGC 5/5.

101 Lord Kenyon to E. H. Griffiths, 4 August 1914, Cardiff, box 21: Griffiths to Kenyon, 6 August 1914, Cardiff, box 35, R/File/M/2.

102 E. M. Bruce Vaughan to D. J. A. Brown, 2 October 1914, Cardiff, box 35, R/File/M/2.

103 *Final Report of the Departmental Committee on the Medical School at Cardiff* (1914), p. 3, TNA, UGC 5/5.

Chapter 4 – Whose Medical School?

1 Newman, *Recent Advances in Medical Education*, p. 8.

2 *SWDN*, 14 December 1910.

3 Ibid., 19 May 1906.

4 J. Davies, *A History of Wales*, pp. 494–6.

5 Minutes of a meeting of the Departmental Committee on the Medical School at Cardiff, 14 July 1914, Appendix II, TNA, UGC, 5/3.

6 David Lloyd George was once reported as saying 'What's the use of being a Welsh Chancellor of the Exchequer if one can do nothing for Wales?' Williams, p. 155.

7 John Grigg, *The Young Lloyd George* (London, 1973), p. 206; John Grigg, *Lloyd George: The People's Champion, 1902–1911* (London, 1978), p.155.

8 Lord Kenyon to D. Hepburn, 17 January 1914, NLW, Jones, J, xv, 88; Lord Kenyon to Thomas Jones, 25 January 1914, NLW, Jones, J, xv, 92.

9 David Davies to Thomas Jones, 27 April 1914, NLW, Jones, xv, 101.

10 Memorandum No. 1, TNA, UGC 5/4.

11 Thomas Jones to David Davies, 30 June 1914, NLW, Jones, J, xv, 102.

12 E. H. Griffiths to D. J. A. Brown, 4 August 1914, Cardiff, box 21.

13 TNA, UGC 5/5.

14 Williams, pp. 119–21.

15 Sir T. L. Heath to J. M. Angus, 24 February 1915, TNA, ED 119/82.

16 Sir T. L. Heath to D. J. A. Brown, 18 March 1915, Cardiff, box 21.

17 Article on the laying of the foundation stone of the Welsh National School of Medicine, *BMJ*, 21 August 1915. Sir William Osler's speech was subsequently published as a pamphlet, NLW, Jones, J, xv, 119. University College, Cardiff also produced two pamphlets (kept in the Cardiff University archives) to commemorate the event. One, entitled 'New Physiological Buildings for the Welsh National School of Medicine (The Gift of Sir William James Thomas)' contained the programme of the stone-laying ceremony, an informative brief history of the School of Medicine, and a description of the new buildings.

> The front has been designed on severe lines well in keeping with its serious purpose. The centre and end blocks and the wide bays are of stone; it is true these have delicate carved panels of foliage, such as one sees on some of the chateaux of France, but the carving of the mouldings of the windows and deep portico are all subordinated to the stern lines of the building. The turrets

to the centre block rise undiminished in width to a height of over 100 feet, and are crowned with pierced tracery. Between the turrets the space is spanned by a pointed arch deeply recessed, and as it faces south this will throw broad shadows across the front and give it a beauty such as nothing else would do. The lower portion of the centre feature forming the portico is divided into three bays by massive columns surmounted by canopied niches, which will contain the statues of Hippocrates and Aesculapius, and the panels flanking them will contain portrait busts of Pasteur, Lister, Hunter and Jenner with figures in bas-relief in the background indicating the daily activities of these worthies.

Though now part of Cardiff University's Engineering Block, the front still remains, as described, in all its glory. The second pamphlet was entitled 'The Welsh National School of Medicine: inaugural proceedings at Cardiff, 15 August 1915'.

18   Williams, p. 122.
19   Sir T. F. Heath to the chairman of the Welsh University Education Conference of 1915, 21 September 1915, Cardiff, box 21.
20   Sir William James Thomas to E. H. Griffiths, 7 October 1915, ibid.
21   Memorandum on 'completion of the proposed Medical School Buildings at Cardiff', enclosed with a letter from J. Herbert Lewis to William Davies, 24 January 1916, NLW, Lewis, D 76.
22   R. McKenna to Sir William James Thomas, 23 February 1916, TNA, ED 119/82.
23   Memorandum from Sir George Newman to the chancellor of the Exchequer, 18 March 1916, ibid.
24   Sir William James Thomas to Sir George Newman, 18 March 1916, ibid.
25   R. McKenna to Sir William James Thomas, 19 April 1916, ibid.
26   Williams, p. 124.
27   A. H. Kidd to C. L. Stocks, 3 March 1916, TNA, ED 119/82.
28   *W. Mail*, 13 April 1916.
29   This, and the other quotations in this paragraph are found in Harvey Cushing, *Sir William Osler*, vol. 2 (Oxford 1925), pp. 524–5.
30   *W. Mail*, 29 June 1916.
31   *SWDN*, 22 June 1916.
32   The evidence of Sir Isambard Owen and the others referred to in the following paragraphs is taken from the *Appendix to the First Report of the Commissioners: Minutes of Evidence* (London, HMSO, 1917), Cd. 8507.
33   D. Hepburn to D. J. A. Brown, 29 June 1916, Cardiff, box 5, original précis of evidence file.
34   *Times Educational Supplement*, 7 June 1917.
35   *The Welsh Outlook* (August 1917). For information about this magazine, founded in 1914 by David Davies, MP, as a 'journal of national social progress', see the entry in Meic Stephens (ed.), *The New Companion to the Literature of Wales* (Cardiff, 1998), p. 775.
36   *SWDN*, 21 November 1917.
37   *W.Mail*, 17 January, 1 March 1917; *BMJ*, 3 March 1917, p. 315.
38   See note by Haldane in Cushing, *Sir William Osler*, vol. 2, p. 412.
39   R. G. Hetherington to Sir William Osler, 22 February 1918, Cardiff, box 26, R/File/M/25.
40   E. M. Bruce Vaughan to E. H. Griffiths, 25 February 1918, ibid.
41   *Royal Commission on University Education in Wales, Final Report* (London: HMSO, 1918), Cd. 8991, paras. 216–22.
42   *W. Mail*, 20 March, 29 October 1918.
43   *SWDN*, 20 March 1918.
44   H. M. Ingledew to D. J. A. Brown, 29 April 1918, Cardiff, box 5, RC on University Education in Wales, 18/56 file 1.

45 Cardiff, box 21, contains both Principal Griffiths's memorandum to the Senate and a dossier summarizing the resolutions of the Cardiff Senate and Councils, the King Edward VII Hospital, the Senate and Court of the University of Wales and the various county and city councils of south Wales, compiled in readiness for the university deputation to 10 Downing Street on 14 August 1918.

46 Quoted in Cushing, *Sir William Osler*, vol. 2, p. 412.

47 Sir William Osler to E. H. Griffiths, 28 May 1918 and Griffiths's reply on 3 June 1918, Cardiff, box 21.

48 Sir Isambard Owen to Lord Aberdare, 5 May 1918, Cardiff, box 5, RC on University Education in Wales, 18/56, file 1.

49 Sir Isambard Owen to D. J. A. Brown, 7 May 1918, ibid. Sir Isambard Owen's career has been recorded in an unpublished University of Wales MA thesis by G. A. Jones, 'The life and work of Sir Isambard Owen, with particular reference to his contribution to education in Wales' (1967). While the study is valuable in other respects it says little about Sir Isambard's contribution to the development of medical education in Wales.

50 *SWN*, 23 November 1918. It should be noted that the newspaper changed its name from *South Wales Daily News* to *South Wales News* with effect from 9 April 1918. Without prior warning, the newspaper ceased its independent existence on 24 August 1928, to be merged with the *Western Mail* which, for some years thereafter, incorporated the title of its long-standing rival into its own heading.

51 Grigg, *Lloyd George: War Leader*, pp. 574–5.

52 'Shorthand notes of a deputation to the prime minister from the University of Wales', a booklet printed following the meeting. Cardiff, box 5, RC on University Education in Wales, 18/56, file 2.

53 *SWN*, 23 November 1918.

54 *W. Mail*, 16 October 1918.

55 'Draft scheme for the constitution of the National School of Medicine as an integral part of the University College of South Wales and Monmouthshire', Cardiff, box 5, RC on University Education in Wales, 18/56. file 2.

56 Cunningham and Goodwin, *Cardiff University: A Celebration*, p. 54.

57 *SWN*, 23 November 1918.

58 Sir Harry Reichel to W. N. Bruce, 28 May 1919, TNA, ED 24/2027.

59 J. M. Angus to A. H. Kidd, 23 July 1919, ibid.

60 Memorandum from W. N. Bruce to A. H. Kidd, 30 May 1919, ibid.

61 Memorandum from A. H. Kidd to the president of the Board of Education, 18 June 1919, ibid.

62 H. A. L. Fisher to David Lloyd George, 15 August 1919, ibid.

63 Confidential memorandum 'The Welsh National School of Medicine', 15 February 1923, Cardiff, box 35, R/File/M/3.

64 N. C. King to D. J. A. Brown, 24 June 1920, and Brown's reply, 25 June 1920, Cardiff, box 26, R/File/M/26.

65 Waddington, *Medical Education at St Bartholomew's Hospital*, chapter 5.

66 Christopher C. Booth, 'Clinical research', in W. F. Bynum and Roy Porter (eds), *Companion Encyclopaedia of the History of Medicine*, vol. 1 (London, 1993), p. 216.

67 Christopher Lawrence, *Rockefeller Money, the Laboratory, and Medicine in Edinburgh, 1919–1930: New Science in an Old Country* (Rochester, 2005), p. 14.

68 Christopher Lawrence, 'Incommunicable knowledge: science, technology and the clinical art in Britain, 1850–1914', *Journal of Contemporary History*, 20 (1985), 503–20, p. 510.

69 Steve Sturdy and Roger Cooter, 'Science, scientific management, and the transformation of medicine in Britain, c. 1870–1950', *History of Science*, 36 (1998), 421–66, pp. 438–440.

70 D. Abse (ed.), *My Medical School* (London, 1978), p. 25.

71 Waddington, *Medical Education at St Bartholomew's Hospital*, pp. 172–6.

72 Information provided by Adrian Allan, archivist, University of Liverpool.

73 'Memorandum showing the action taken by the Board of Education in regard to University Education in Medicine', Minutes of the UGC, 10 December 1919, TNA, UGC 11/1.

74 S. T. Anning and W. K. J. Walls, *A History of the Leeds School of Medicine, 1831–1981* (Leeds, 1982), p. 103.

75 S. W. Sturdy, 'The political economy of scientific medicine', *Medical History*, 36 (1992), 140.

76 University of Bristol, *Calendar* (1922/3), p. 30.

77 Minutes of the University of Birmingham Clinical Board, 19 May 1911.

78 E. M. Bruce Vaughan to D. J. A. Brown, 27 December 1918, Cardiff, box 5, RC on University Education in Wales, 18/56, file 2.

79 Sir Isambard Owen to E. M. Bruce Vaughan, 4 January 1919, Bangor, General Collection, 5987.

80 Material relating to Sir Isambard Owen (DM 1149/ Box 5), in the Special Collections Department at the University of Bristol Health and Social Sciences Library, shows Owen's personal interest in the affairs of the Bristol Medical School despite all his other commitments as university vice-chancellor.

81 Minute Book of Committees, 1915–20, CRI, D/D HC 11.

82 E. M. Bruce Vaughan to Sir Isambard Owen, 14 April 1919, Bangor, General Collection, 5987.

83 For reports of Bruce Vaughan's death and funeral see *W. Mail*, 14 and 18 June 1919.

84 Ibid., 19 February 1920.

85 Ibid., 24 April 1920; *The Lancet*, 1 May 1920, p. 985.

86 Waddington, *Medical Education at St Bartholomew's Hospital*, pp. 273–5.

87 For details of the teaching hospitals cited in this paragraph see 'The student guide, 1921–22', *The Lancet*, 27 August 1921, pp. 428–54.

88 Minutes of the Emergency and Reference Committee, 12 January 1921, CRI, D/D HC 12.

89 *SWN*, 11 February 1921.

90 Waddington, *Medical Education at St Bartholomew's Hospital*, pp. 172–9.

91 Minutes of the Medical Board, 5 April 1921, CRI, D/D H/C 33.

92 Thomas Lewis to Sir George Newman, 23 March 1921, Sir Thomas Lewis Papers, Wellcome Library, PP/LEW/D.5/1.

93 *Univ. Cncl.*, 3 and 4 February 1921, 8.

94 Minutes of the Hospital Board of Management, 21 April 1921, CRI, D/D HC 12.

95 Minutes of Emergency and Reference Committee, 21 January 1921, ibid.

96 For the minutes of the meetings of the Joint Committee of the hospital and the college between 26 April and 11 July 1921 see ibid.

97 Minutes of Emergency and Reference Committee, 30 May 1921, ibid.

98 Report by the secretary of the Cardiff Royal Infirmary to a meeting of hospital clinical staff, 19 November 1928, CRI, D/D HC 14.

99 Minutes of the Revision of Rules Committee, 11 April 1921, CRI, D/D HC 12.

100 The final version of the agreement appears as appendix 2. NLW, Wales, CG 21/3/1.

Chapter 5 – A Full Medical School at Last

1 *SWN*, 21 March 1919, article entitled 'Unprecedented rush at Cardiff'.

2 A. H. Trow to E. M. Bruce Vaughan, 17 January 1919, Cardiff, box 21.

3 For a full account of the celebrations see *W. Mail*, 8, 9 and 10 June 1921. For details of Graham Brown see the obituary in *BMJ*, 13 November 1965, p. 1187.

4 Typescript report of a conference regarding the establishment of a School of Preventive Medicine and Department of Public Health, held on 15 March 1918, Cardiff, box 26, R/File/M/25.

5 The full text of Collis's lecture, 'The aims of the Welsh National School of Medicine, with special reference to preventive medicine', was published in *The Lancet*, 3 January 1920, pp. 6–11. For Collis see *W. Mail*, 11 December 1919, and his obituary in *BMJ*, 12 October 1957.

6   For the correspondence between Balfour, Sir William Osler and Colonel Bruce Vaughan in October 1918 see the Sir Andrew Balfour Papers, Wellcome Library, WA/BSR/BA/Isa/6 (The Talbot Professorship). Included in the file are pamphlets presumably given by Bruce Vaughan to Balfour to assist his understanding of developments at Cardiff. One is entitled 'Colonel Bruce Vaughan's speeches on the delay [in building the Institute of Preventive Medicine] and in reply to the Treasury letter dated 21st Sept. 1915' (Cardiff, 1916); the other 'Speeches on the delay and the case for the School, made at King Edward VII Hospital by Lieut. Col. Bruce Vaughan, VD, JP, 12 Jan. and 17 Feb. 1916'. It is little wonder that Whitehall had become tired of Bruce Vaughan's persistent campaigning during the autumn and winter of 1915/16.

7   *BMJ*, 10 January 1920, p. 67.

8   The table is taken from Jones, 'The King Edward VII Welsh National memorial Association, 1912–1948', in Cule (ed.), *Wales and Medicine: An Historical Survey*, p. 33. For the information in this paragraph see Linda Bryder, *Below the Magic Mountain: A Social History of Tuberculosis in Twentieth-Century Britain* (Oxford, 1988), Introduction and chapter 1; also Bryder, 'The King Edward VII Welsh National Memorial Association and its policy towards tuberculosis', *Welsh History Review*, 13 (1986), 194–216.

9   David Davies to D. W. Evans, 23 June 1919, NLW, Davies, D 12/1.

10 Linda Bryder, 'Tuberculosis and the MRC', in Joan Austoker and Linda Bryder (eds.), *Historical Perspectives on the Role of the MRC* (Oxford, 1989), pp. 1–6.

11 Résumé of the proceedings of the Advisory Committee on Research, held on 6 November 1919, NLW, Davies, D12/1.

12 Sir Walter Fletcher to David Davies, 13 July 1920, ibid. The records of the Welsh National Memorial Association held at the National Library of Wales include Box 71 with the promising title 'Files of correspondence and papers relating to the Welsh National School of Medicine and the Chair of Tuberculosis, 1920s to 1960s'. Unfortunately this box contains virtually no material of relevance to the present study.

13 Tuberculosis Committee, 3 July 1928, Cardiff, R/File/M/31.

14 Sir Alfred Davies to R. G. Mayor, 29 December 1922, TNA, ED 119/75; minutes of the Council of UCC, 22 June 1921.

15 Minutes of the Council of UCC, 15 July 1921. Mitchell Stevens's attitude to Kennedy's appointment was graphically outlined during his evidence to a committee of inquiry set up in 1925 by the UCC Council in connection with his relations with the Welsh National School of Medicine, Cardiff, R/File/M/16. However, there is nothing in the minutes of the Cardiff Medical Society of the period to suggest that the appointments, or indeed the adoption of the clinical unit system, were topics of discussion at the society's meetings.

16 *The Lancet*, 8 October 1960, p. 820.

17 *Univ. Cncl.*, 14 January 1921, 4.

18 G. Graham, 'The formation of the medical and surgical professorial units', *Annals of Science*, 26 (1970), 14.

19 Minutes of a special meeting of the Council of UCC, 26 May 1920.

20 *FM*, 7 October 1921, 55.

21 Report of the Academic Board to the University Council, meeting on 9 June 1921.

22 UGC, *Returns from Universities and University Colleges in receipt of Treasury Grant 1928/9* (London: HMSO, 1930), p. 54. Although an annual salary of £1,082 during the 1920s was eminently respectable, Sir Walter Fletcher, secretary of the MRC was by no means impressed. Writing on 2 May 1930 to compliment A. H. Kidd on the general excellence of the UGC's annual report for 1928/9, he found 'only one matter for regret. That is when the Committee accepts with such apparent calm the fact, given on p. 24, that the annual salary of British university professors is £1,082. The Committee

rather weakly say that this would be felt 'to fall somewhat short' of what picked men in the academic world ought to have. I think the fact is damnable. I do not think of the comfort of the men themselves, though indeed a professor ought to be able to travel abroad and to buy books. This level of salary makes it impossible for a professor to have children and to give them an adequate education. This is in the highest degree against the national interest, as it seems to me. (TNA, FD 5/12)

23   Guy Routh, *Occupation and Pay in Great Britain, 1906–1979* (London, 1980), pp. 63, 70, 101.

24   Minutes of CRI House Committee, 5 June 1923, CRI, D/D HC 13.

25   *Univ. Cncl.*, 23 September 1921, 8; and 10 November 1921, 26; *W. Mail*, 10 December 1921.

26   Minutes of the UGC, 10 December 1919, Appendix II ('Summary of aid by the Board of Education to Medical Schools', para. 8), TNA, UGC 11/1.

27   For correspondence between Thomas Lewis and Sir George Newman during March 1921, see the Sir Thomas Lewis Papers, Wellcome Library, PP/LEW/D.5/1.

28   Diaries of Sir George Newman, 1921–5, TNA, MH 139/4.

29   Minutes of the UGC, 20 October 1921, TNA, UGC 11/1.

30   *W. Mail*, 13 June 1924; *SWN*, 17 June 1924.

31   *BM*, 26 July 1921, 3.

32   *W. Mail*, 27 July 1921.

33   Minutes of the Emergency and Reference Committee, 5 October 1921, CRI, D/D HC 12.

34   *BMJ*, 8 October 1960, p. 1094.

35   *The Lancet*, 8 October 1921, p. 782.

36   W. B. Riddell to S. S. G. Leeson (Board of Education), 21 January 1922, TNA, ED 24/2027.

37   *Univ. Cncl.*, 23 September 1921, 4, and 10 November 1921, 35.

38   *The Lancet*, 7 January 1922, p. 47.

39   *Univ. Cncl.*, 10 November 1921, 34.

40   *W. Mail*, 6 December 1921.

41   The progress of the national appeal is covered in the minutes of successive meetings of the University of Wales Council between 1922 and 1924, and in the columns of the Welsh newspapers, for example *W. Mail*, 26 January, 22 July, 28 October 1922, 27 January, 6 March, 8 May 1923; *SWN*, 13 October 1922, 2 February 1923. Correspondence relating to the Merthyr campaign is located in NLW, Wales, CH 6/3. Altogether the University of Wales archive at the National Library of Wales contains Hughes's meticulous correspondence with nine Welsh local authorities and their members, Anglesey (CH 6/1), Glamorgan (CH 6/2), Merthyr Tydfil (CH 6/3), Monmouthshire (6/4), Montgomeryshire (CH 6/5), Newport (CH 6/6), Pembrokeshire (CH 6/7), Radnorshire (CH 6/8) and Swansea (CH 6/9).

42   Gwilym Hughes to Lloyd Davies, 6 January 1923, NLW, Wales, CH 6/6.

43   The federal University of Wales, as reconstituted in 1920, had two chief administrative officers of equal status and salary (£800 per annum), the registrar, Captain D. Brynmor Anthony, who commenced duties on 18 April 1921, and the secretary, Jenkin James, who had taken up his duties a month earlier. The secretary had particular responsibility for the work of the University Council and for the financial affairs of the university. Under the previous arrangements the registrar (J. M. Angus) had been the single chief administrative officer of the university, responsible for everything.

44   Gwilym Hughes to Jenkin James, 30 June 1923, NLW, Wales, CH 5/2.

45   Gwilym Hughes to Jenkin James, 7 July 1924, ibid.

46   The report of the Special Committee is appended to the minutes of the University Council, 19 July 1922.

47   For the report of the Faculty of Medicine upon the report of the Special Committee see *BM*, 4 December 1922; for subsequent discussions on the funding of the Welsh National School of Medicine see *Univ. Cncl.*, 14 December 1922, 19 and 20; 19 January 1923, 3; 15 June 1923, 19.

48 *SWN*, 28 December 1921.

49 'Memorandum on clinical units in medical schools' (UGC, April 1920); Newman, *Recent Advances in Medical Education*, chapter 9.

50 Lawrence, *Rockefeller Money*, p. 17.

51 I am grateful to Professor John Pickstone for allowing me to quote from a paper presented by Roger Cooter, Caroline Murphy and himself on 'Exploring clinical research: academic medicine and the clinicians in early twentieth century Britain' to the conference 'Science in modern medicine' at Manchester, April 1985.

52 Lawrence, *Rockefeller Money*, p. 36.

53 Sturdy and Cooter, 'Science, scientific management, and the transformation of medicine in Britain, *c.* 1870–1950', 444; Waddington, *Medical Education at St Bartholomew's Hospital*, pp. 193–202.

54 C. Bruce Perry, *The Bristol Medical School*, pp. 21–2.

55 Sturdy, 'The political economy of scientific medicine', 147–50.

56 Bonner, *Becoming a Physician*, p. 331.

57 Minutes of the University of Birmingham Faculty of Medicine, 17 June 1920, 16 November 1928.

58 T. Kelly, *For Advancement of Learning: The University of Liverpool, 1881–1981* (Liverpool, 1981), p. 247.

59 A. H. Kidd to Sir George Newman, 2 December 1922, UGC file on Clinical Units, 1920–9, TNA, UGC 7/1064.

60 Sir Wilmot Herringham to A. H. Kidd, 19 June 1924, ibid.

61 Sir Walter Fletcher to Sir George Newman, 16 December 1929, TNA, FD 5/12.

62 Andrew Hull, 'Hector's house: Sir Hector Hetherington and the academicization of Glasgow hospital medicine before the NHS', *Medical History*, 45 (2001), 207–42.

63 Helen Valier, 'The politics of scientific medicine in Manchester, c. 1900–1960' (unpublished Ph.D. thesis, University of Manchester, 2002), 205–10.

64 *Report of the Inter-departmental Committee on Medical Schools* (London, 1944), p. 17.

65 In fact, Durham's first full-time professor of medicine, F. J. Nattrass, had been appointed in 1944, followed shortly thereafter by F. H. Bentley (surgery) and James Spence (the country's first full-time professor of child health). Elsewhere full-time appointments were made as follows: Liverpool, Charles Wells (surgery, 1945) and Norman Jeffcoate (obstetrics and gynaecology, 1945), the first full-time professor of medicine, Cyril Clarke not being appointed until Lord Cohen's retirement in 1965; Leeds, Andrew Claye (obstetrics and gynaecology, 1945), Ronald Tunbridge (medicine, 1946), J. C. Goligher (surgery, 1954); Manchester, Robert Platt (medicine, 1945), A. Boyd (surgery, 1946), W. I. C. Morris (obstetrics and gynaecology, 1949); Birmingham, Melville Arnott (medicine, 1946), F. A. R. Stammers (surgery, 1946), Hilda Lloyd (obstetrics and gynaecology, 1946), J. M. Smellie (child health, 1946); Sheffield, C. Stuart Harris (medicine, 1946), C. S. Russell (obstetrics and gynaecology, 1950), R. P. Jepson (surgery, 1954); Belfast, Professor Macafee (obstetrics and gynaecology, 1945), Harold Rogers (surgery, 1947), Graham Bull (medicine, 1951). In addition to several colleagues whose assistance has been acknowledged in the Preface, the following publications have been helpful in compiling this information: John Walton and Miles Irving (eds), *100 years of the RVI, 1906–2006* (Newcastle upon Tyne Hospitals NHS Trust, 2006); O. L. Wade, 'The legacy of Richard Burdon Haldane: the university clinical units and their future', *Ulster Medical Journal*, 45 (1976), 146–56.

66 *SWN*, 11 June 1928.

67 *Univ. Cncl.*, 16 February 1922, 5.

68 *SWN*, 11 June 1928. In a partisan article at the height of the conflict between the school authorities and the hospital clinician 'A Correspondent' wrote: 'When a professor describes himself as a "Director of a Unit", his adoption of a military title shows that he has lost the sense of being a "guest" introduced into the hospital for the purpose of acting as a tutor supervising the theoretical studies of the students'.

69 Sturdy, 'The political economy of scientific medicine', 146–7.

70 Valier, 'The politics of scientific medicine in Manchester', chapter 3.

71 Lawrence, *Rockefeller Money*, p. 114.

72 Waddington, *Medical Education at St Bartholomew's Hospital*, p. 194.

73 Minutes of the Medical Board, 16 January 1922, CRI, D/D HC 33.

74 Ibid., 4 April 1922.

75 Ibid., 7 March 1922.

76 Professor Kennedy reported this in 1928 at a meeting of the committee set up by the Board of Medicine to investigate a dispute between the recognized clinical teachers of the hospital and the UCC authorities, Cardiff, R/File/M/17.

77 For Geary Grant, Haycraft and Strachan see, respectively, *BMJ*, 8 November 1947, p. 750; *BMJ*, 1 March 1969, p. 582; *The Dictionary of Welsh Biography, 1941–1970* (London, 2001), p. 252.

78 GMC, *Minutes*, vol. LVIII (1921), pp. 131–2.

79 This correspondence, and details of discussions between the medical school and the hospital over the next few months, is contained in the minute books of the Board of Medicine, the Faculty of Medicine and the Board of Medicine committees.

80 'Memorandum on clinical units in medical schools' (1920).

81 G. Newman, *Recent Advances in Medical Education* (London, 1923), appendix C (abstracts of the organization of university clinics).

82 Minutes of the Medical Board, 2 January 1923, CRI, D/D HC 33.

83 Ibid., 7 and 28 November, 6 December 1922, 26 February 1923.

84 E. Fawcett to A. M. Kennedy, 22 September 1922, Letter Books of Deans of Medicine, University of Bristol, 15 February to 29 November 1922 (DM 1148).

85 Minutes of the Bristol University Council, 12 May 1922.

86 Minutes of the University of Birmingham Clinical Board, 19 November 1923.

87 Minutes of the University of Liverpool Board of Clinical Studies, 2 July 1928.

88 Minutes of the Bristol University Council, 12 May 1922.

89 Minutes of the Medical Board, 6 December 1922, CRI, D/D HC 33.

90 Ibid., 30 October 1922.

91 W. Martin to H. G. Cook, 2 September 1923, letter affixed to the minutes of the Medical Board held on 4 September 1923, ibid.

92 *SWN*, 17 March 1924.

93 Newman, *Recent Advances in Medical Education*, para. 114.

94 In a report about the City Lodge Hospital, considered by the Board of Medicine on 15 June 1922, Kennedy observed: 'There is, in his opinion, ample material and scope for teaching medicine at City Lodge, and that at comparatively small expense the place could be equipped in such a way as to form a most admirable adjunct to the Medical Unit of the Medical School. Amongst the things to be provided by the Medical School would be laboratory accommodation, cloak-rooms etc. This could be accomplished by the erection of a suitable hut within the grounds of City Lodge.'

95 For a brief history of Whitchurch Hospital, in celebration of its seventy-fifth anniversary, see Hilary M. Thomas, *Whitchurch Hospital, 1908–1983* (Cardiff, 1983); see also Goodall's obituary in *The Lancet*, 23 December 1944, p. 837; G. Arbour Stephens, *The Hospitals of Wales* (Swansea, 1912), p. 16.

96 *FM*, 7, 21 and 29 November 1923, 48. For Stanley Alwyn Smith see *BMJ*, 7 March 1931, pp. 425–6. For an account of the early history of the Prince of Wales Orthopaedic Hospital, Cardiff, see Robert Phelps, *The Prince and the Pioneers* (Cardiff, 1993).

97 In his memoirs, Ivor Davies referred to the time when, addressing a meeting of the Cardiff Medical Society, Sir William Osler enquired, to a blank-looking audience, about Dr Griffith Evans. 'Surely you must know the first man to see a trypanosome?' Erie Evans, who was in the audience, intro-

duced herself to him, much to Sir William's delight (Davies, *Memories of a Welsh Physician*, pp. 110–11). The Medical Women's Federation was founded in 1916 'to safeguard and promote the professional interests of medical women'. In April 1923 the Western and South Wales Association of the Federation was established, with an initial membership of twenty-four, Erie Evans being appointed vice-president. During the early years the meetings were sporadic in their incidence because of the wide area from which the members were drawn. When held, the meetings invariably took place in Bristol or another English venue in the area, and the number of members from south Wales at this time was very small. Until 1934 any members of the federation based in north Wales belonged to the Liverpool and District Association. In that year two new associations were created, one for north Wales and one for south Wales. The papers of the Medical Women's Federation, including its *Newsletter*, are held at the Wellcome Library.

98 Anning and Walls, *A History of the Leeds School of Medicine*, pp. 96–8. Dr Jonathan Reinarz, in his forthcoming history of the medical school and teaching hospitals in Birmingham, describes how, in Birmingham during the Edwardian period, separate classes were organized for men and women students, in the medical school and on the wards.

99 Garner, 'The great experiment', *Medical History* (1998), 42, p. 85; C. Dyhouse, 'Driving ambitions: women in pursuit of a medical education, 1890–1939', *Women's History Review*, 7, 3 (1998), 321–41.

100 Davies, *Deeds Not Words*, p. 172.

101 Ibid., pp. 156, 172.

102 Jones and Collins, *History of the Royal Gwent Hospital*, pp. 69–70. For a more recent account of this hospital, and its later involvement in undergraduate medical education, see W. D. Peeling, *The Royal Gwent and St Woolos Hospitals: A Century of Service in Newport* (Abertillery, 2004).

103 Report of the Faculty of Medicine on the report of the Special Committee (November 1922), p. 12, para. 44.

104 Newman, *Recent Advances in Medical Education*, paras. 50 and 162.

105 *FM*, 6 February 1924, 103; *BMJ*, 1 September 1923, p. 354.

106 Waddington, *Medical Education at St Bartholomew's Hospital*, p. 206.

107 The memorandum is included in R. M. Pearce, 'Medical Education in Wales' (Survey report, revised 1926, unpublished manuscript), Rockefeller Archive Centre Library, RG1.1, series 407A (Wales), box 1, folder 5.

108 Unless otherwise indicated, details of the curriculum have been compiled from the prospectus of the Welsh National School of Medicine

109 Newman, *Recent Advances in Medical Education*, p. 91. For the Medical Unit see the memorandum referred to in footnote 107.

110 GMC, *Minutes*, vol. LXIII (1927), Appendix XIV, and vol. LXIV (1928), Appendix VII.

111 E. Lewis-Faning, *Report of the Examination Performance of Medical Students, 1933–1948* (Welsh National School of Medicine, 1950).

112 UGC, *Returns*, 1925/6, 1926/7, 1927/8, 1928/9 and 1930/1.

113 E. H. Cornelius, *Lives of the Fellows of the Royal College of Surgeons of England, 1974–1982* (London, 1988); University of Bristol, *Calendar* (1930/1); University of Liverpool, *Calendar* (1924/5, 1929/30).

114 GMC, *Minutes*, vol. LXIII (1927), Appendix XX.

115 Minutes of the University of Birmingham Faculty of Medicine, 13 January 1928.

116 University of Wales, *Calendar* (1920/1 to 1931/2).

117 GMC, *Minutes*, vol. LXVIII (1932), addendum: Inspection of examinations, 1930–2.

118 Minutes of the Senate of the Welsh National School of Medicine, 1 March 1933, 323; 3 May 1933, 372.

119 John S. Morris, 'Sir Daniel Davies: a Welshman in London', *Journal of Medical Biography*, 9 (2001), 7–11.

120 Garner, 'The great experiment', 68–88; Waddington, *Medical Education at St Bartholomew's Hospital*, pp. 303–6.

121 *SWN*, 17 November 1923.

122 *BMJ*, 6 December 1924, p. 1073; Mabel Howell to D. Lleufer Thomas, 7 February 1930, NLW, D. Lleufer Thomas Papers, C 1/7.

123 See Sara Brady, 'Public service and private ambitions: nursing at the King Edward VII Hospital, Cardiff during the First World War', in Borsay (ed.), *Medicine in Wales, c. 1800–2000*, pp. 108–27.

124 The enrolments, as recorded in selected editions of the UCC *Calendar*, were:
    1911/12 81
    1912/13 80
    1914/15 90
    1918/19 67
    1919/20 92

125 *SWN*, 21 November 1917.

126 *W. Mail*, 6 May 1922.

127 *FM*, 11 March 1925, 367.

128 M. F. Rathbone to Thomas Jones, 10 September 1916, NLW, Jones, J, i, 25.

129 Haldane, *Report*, para. 243.

130 *SWN*, 28 December 1921.

131 The report of the Faculty of Medicine subcommittee appointed to examine the possibility of providing instruction in veterinary science at the medical school is included with the minutes of the Faculty, 20 February 1924.

132 *FM*, 4 November 1925, 513.

133 B. E. D. Cooke, *The History of the University of Wales Dental School from 1961 to 1982* (Cardiff, 1997), p. 6.

134 *Final Report of the Inter-departmental Committee on Dentistry* (London: HMSO, 1946), Cd. 6727, para. 65.

135 N. Evans, 'The Welsh Victorian city', *Welsh History Review*, 12, 3 (1985), pp. 378–80.

136 *Evening Express and Evening Mail*, 27 November 1907; *W. Mail*, 5 December 1907.

137 *The Lancet*, 23 December 1944, p. 837.

138 Williams, p. 363.

139 Report of the Academic Board presented to the University Council, 18 July 1929; *FM*, 6 December 1928, 436.

140 For Miss Acraman's appeal to her fellow students and *The Leech*'s announcement of its bilingual status see vol. II, 3 (May 1928).

141 *Welsh Medical Gazette* (Spring, 1980).

Chapter 6 – Postgraduate Medical Education and Research

1 'Notes taken at the committee appointed to report on the letter from Dr W. Mitchell Stevens, meeting held on 19 January 1926', Cardiff, R/File/M/16.

2 Report by the Faculty of Medicine upon the report presented by the Special Committee, 22 November 1922, p. 15.

3 *BMJ*, 10 September 1910, p. 712.

4 See D'Arcy Power (ed.), *British Medical Societies* (London, 1939); for A. W. Sheen's account of the Cardiff Medical Society see chapter XIX.

5 *BMJ*, 10 September 1910, pp. 712–19.

6 Sir Brian Windeyer, 'University education in the twentieth century', in Poynter (ed.), *The Evolution of Medical Education in Britain*, p. 222.

7 Elizabeth Fee and Roy M. Acheson (eds.), *A History of Education in Public Health* (Oxford, 1991).

8 GMC, *Minutes*, vol. LVIII (1921), addendum: Inspection of examinations 1920/1, p. 878.

9 The statistics for the DPH examinations are taken from the annual *Calendars* of the University of Wales; details of the other courses are contained in the annual reports of the heads of departments,

communicated by the principal to the Council of UCC. For Collis's wider contribution see his obituary in *BMJ*, 12 October 1957, p. 886; *The Lancet*, 12 October 1957, p. 750; Anne Borsay and Sara Knight (eds.), *Medical Records for the South Wales Coalfield, c.1890–1948: An Annotated Guide to the South Wales Coalfield Collection* (Cardiff, 2007), pp. 11–12, 56, 235. See also Ministry of Health file on health visitors' training courses, 1929–69, TNA, MH 96/2330.

10 Report presented to the University Court meeting on 10 December 1924.

11 Linda Bryder, *Below the Magic Mountain: A Social History of Tuberculosis in Twentieth-Century Britain*, p. 73; NLW, Records of the Welsh National Memorial Association, box 71 (ii).

12 *BMJ*, 11 June 1948, p. 1054.

13 'Report by the David Davies professor of tuberculosis to the sub-committee, summer term 1928', Cardiff, R/File/M/31.

14 Harley Williams, *Requiem for a Great Killer: The Story of Tuberculosis* (London, 1973), pp. 111–12.

15 The origins of postgraduate medical education in Birmingham and details of national developments in 1919 were described by Professor Douglas Stanley, professor of therapeutics and pharmacology at the University of Birmingham, in reports included in the minutes of the University of Birmingham Faculty of Medicine, 6 October 1919 and 17 February 1921.

16 *BMJ*, 6 September 1924, p. 435.

17 Ministry of Health, *First Report of the Welsh Consultative Council of Medical and Allied Services in Wales* (London, 1920), Cmd. 708, p. 4..

18 Ministry of Health, *Second Report of the Welsh Consultative Council of Medical and Allied Services in Wales* (London, 1921), Cmd. 1448, p. 15.

19 Charles Webster, 'Devolution and the health services in Wales, 1919–1969', in Michael and Webster (eds.), *Health and Society in Twentieth-Century Wales*, p. 245.

20 *FM*, 7 May 1924; UCC, *Reports of the Heads of Departments Communicated by the Principal*, 1929/30, 1930/1.

21 T. Graham Brown, 'John Berry Haycraft, MD, D.Sc.', *Proceedings of the Royal Society of Edinburgh* (1922/3), 265.

22 Stella V. F. Butler, 'Science and the education of doctors in the nineteenth century: a study of British medical schools with particular reference to the development and uses of physiology' (unpublished Ph.D. thesis, University of Manchester, 1981), 212.

23 MRC, *Annual Reports* (1914/15 to 1918/19), *passim*

24 Ministry of Health, *Second Report of the Welsh Consultative Council of Medical and Allied Services in Wales*, p. 15.

25 For the Report of the Special Committee and the Faculty of Medicine's response, see the appendices to the bound minutes of the University of Wales Council, 1920/2, 1922/3.

26 Christopher C. Booth, 'Clinical research', in W. F. Bynum and Roy Porter (eds.), *Companion Encyclopaedia of the History of Medicine*, vol. 1 (London, 1993), p. 210.

27 Lawrence, *Rockefeller Money*, p. 19.

28 Ibid., p. 28.

29 Bynum, 'Sir George Newman and the American way', in Nutton and Porter (eds.), *The History of Medical Education in England*, chapter 2.

30 For Richard Pearce and the work of the Division of Medical Education see W. H. Schneider, 'The men who followed Flexner: Richard Pearce, Alan Gregg, and the Rockefeller Foundation Medical Divisions, 1919–1951', in W. H. Schneider (ed.), *Rockefeller Philanthropy and Modern Biomedicine* (Bloomington, 2002), pp. 7–59.

31 Lawrence, *Rockefeller Money*, p. 45.

32 Ibid., pp. 34–42.

33 For a general review of the work of the MRC during this period see Christopher Booth, 'Clinical research', in Austoker and Bryder (eds.), *Historical Perspectives on the Role of the MRC*, chapter 10.

34 Weatherall, *Gentlemen, Scientists and Doctors*, pp. 168–9.

35 Sir Walter Fletcher to Sir Wilmot Herringham, 8 October 1922, TNA, FD 5/138. This file, dealing with the MRC's association with the Rockefeller Foundation, contains Fletcher's correspondence with the deans of the British medical schools during 1922 and 1923.

36 Lawrence, *Rockefeller Money*, p. 31.

37 Ibid., p. 44. For Pearce's investigations in London and Edinburgh see in particular chapter 3 of Lawrence's book.

38 A. M. Kennedy to Sir Walter Fletcher, 13 January 1923, TNA, FD 5/138.

39 R. M. Pearce, 'Medical education in Wales' (Survey report, revised 1926, unpublished manuscript), Rockefeller Archive Centre Library, RG 1.1, series 407A (Wales), box 1, folder 5.

40 A. M. Kennedy to Sir Walter Fletcher, 22 December 1923, TNA, FD 5/138.

41 Unless otherwise referenced, the paragraphs relating to the award of the Rockefeller grant to the Welsh National School of Medicine, including extracts from Pearce's diary, and correspondence between Pearce and A.M. Kennedy, E. L. Collis, G. E. Vincent, Lord Kenyon and Professor T. Graham Brown, are based on documents held at the Rockefeller Archive Centre, New York, particularly a comprehensively referenced essay on Cardiff, 1923–8, by C. Lewerth et al., 'Source history of the Rockefeller Foundation', vol. xx, pp. 4164–93 (unpublished manuscript), Rockefeller Archive Centre Library.

42 R. M. Pearce, 'Medical education in Wales' (Survey report).

43 MRC, *Annual Report 1920/1* (1921), p. 62.

44 The details of the Medical Unit laboratories appeared in an article written by Kennedy in *The Lancet*, 5 November 1927, pp. 994–5.

45 *W. Mail*, 21 December 1923.

46 E. Leigh Collis to Sir Walter Fletcher, 21 December 1923, TNA, FD 5/138.

47 Minutes of a meeting of the hospital Rockefeller Grant Sub-committee, 9 July 1924, CRI, D/D HC 14.

48 CRI, *Annual Report of the Board of Management* (1923), p. 23.

49 *The Lancet*, 5 November 1927, pp. 994–5.

50 C. Lewerth et al., 'Source history of the Rockefeller Foundation', vol. xx, p. 4186.

51 This article may be consulted in the National Library of Wales.

52 The dates of Daniel T. Davies's employment in the years immediately following graduation as given in *Munk's Roll* and elsewhere are incorrect; see *FM*, 27 June 1927, for the circumstances of his appointment to the Medical Unit. For Ivor Davies see his *Memories of a Welsh Physician*, p. 55.

53 The information on which this paragraph is based is contained in successive numbers of the MRC *Annual Report*.

54 Quoted in Sturdy, 'The political economy of scientific medicine', 150.

55 MRC, *Annual Report 1927/8* (1929), p. 63, and *Annual report 1930/1* (1932), p. 71.

56 *BMJ*, 30 January 1926, p. 217. The report of the University of London's inspectors, following a visit to its medical schools in 1933, while commenting in great detail about the working of the unit system in London's medical schools, made no reference to any specific benefits bestowed on the quality of clinical care. However, the report made the following observation, thereby endorsing Professor Sheen's own experience in Cardiff: 'It is an important fact that much of the information collected by the Units could only have been obtained by such organisations. The recording and examination of observations require a considerable amount of time and could not be performed by workers employed other than full-time. Material obtained by carefully-organised Follow-up Departments has shown itself to be of very great value, and the follow-up system which has been organised in some hospitals might well be adopted at others where such work is left to individual initiative and is mainly unorganised.' The London Report was appended to a letter from an officer at the UGC to the secretary of the MRC, 29 March 1934, TNA, FD 5/12.

57 E. Mellanby to John Beresford (of the UGC), 4 April 1934, ibid.

58 Waddington, *Medical Education at St Bartholomew's Hospital*, pp. 201–2.

59 For correspondence from Sir Walter Fletcher and A. Landsbrough Thomson to A. H. Kidd in December 1928 see TNA, FD 5/12.

60 A. Landsbrough Thomson to A. H. Kidd, 8 January 1934, ibid.

61 Unless otherwise referenced, the material in the following paragraphs is mainly drawn from the annual reports of the MRC, 1919/20 to 1930/1, and the annual reports submitted by the school heads of department to the College Council.

62 Linda Bryder, 'Tuberculosis and the MRC', in Austoker and Bryder (eds.), *Historical Perspectives on the Role of the MRC*, p. 13.

63 'Report by the David Davies professor of tuberculosis to the sub-committee, summer term 1928', Cardiff, R/File/M/31.

64 D. A. Powell and F. J. Alban to David Davies, 16 February 1929, NLW, Davies, D 12/4.

65 Cardiff, R/File/M/31.

66 For E. G. Bowen see Harold Carter and K. Davies, *Geography, Culture and Habitat: Selected Essays (1925–1975) of E. G. Bowen* (Llandysul, 1976).

67 For J. B. Duguid's obituary of W. H. Tytler see *Journal of Pathology and Bacteriology*, 78 (1959), pp. 297–301.

68 Bryder, 'The King Edward VII Welsh National Memorial Association and its policy towards tuberculosis', *Welsh History Review*, 13, 2 (1986), 203. Apart from this article the material in this paragraph is drawn from Bryder, *Below the Magic Mountain*, pp. 73, 193, K. O. Morgan, *Rebirth of a Nation: A History of Modern Wales* (Oxford, 1998), pp. 234–5: Steven Thompson, 'A social history of health in inter-war south Wales' (Ph.D. thesis, University of Wales, 2001), chapter 6.

69 MRC, *Annual Report 1923/4* (1924), pp. 12–13.

70 R. Eccles, 'Physiology', in Chrimes (ed.), p. 334.

71 Lord Adrian, 'Thomas Graham Brown', in *Biographical Memoirs of Fellows of the Royal Society*, vol. 12 (London, The Royal Society, 1966), pp. 23–33.

72 MRC, *Annual Report 1929/30* (1931), p. 99.

73 MRC, *Annual Report 1930/1* (1932), p. 71.

74 *W. Mail*, 3 February 1934.

75 *BMJ*, 16 December 1944, p. 803.

76 MRC, *Annual Report 1919/20* (1920), p. 79.

77 Minutes of the Medical Board, 3 January and 7 February 1922, CRI, D/D hc 33.

78 MRC, *Annual Report 1928/9* (1930), p. 31.

79 A copy of the CRI's submission to the National Radium Commission is appended to the minutes of a special meeting of the Faculty of Medicine, 19 November 1929.

80 *W. Mail*, 1 June 1928.

81 J. D. Lever, 'Anatomy', in Chrimes (ed.), p. 324. For C. M. West's obituary see *BMJ*, 4 August 1951, p. 303.

82 *W. Mail*, 13 October 1934.

83 Weatherall, *Gentlemen, Scientists and Doctors*, pp. 167–73.

84 See H. R. Dean's obituary of E. H. Kettle, *Journal of Pathology and Bacteriology*, 44 (1934), p. 496.

85 The reports of the committees set up to consider the accommodation needs of the Department of Pathology and Bacteriology, and on the uses to which the new Institute of Preventive Medicine might be put, are appended to the minutes of the meeting of the Board of Medicine held on 19 January 1926. See also Cardiff, R/File/M/27.

86 Lord Kenyon to Sir Thomas Lewis, 19 June 1926, Sir Thomas Lewis Papers, Wellcome Library, BB/LEW/D.5/1.

87 See Kettle's obituary, *Journal of Pathology and Bacteriology*, 44, p. 495.
88 *Journal of Pathology*, 111 (1973), p. 65.
89 *FM*, 11 March 1925, 363.
90 David Jenkins, *A Refuge in Peace and War: The National Library of Wales to 1952* (Aberystwyth, 2002), p. 228.
91 *FM*, 10 May 1927, 159; 1 June 1927, 178; 27 June 1927, 188; 12 October 1927, 211.
92 *BM*, 20 January 1931, 19.
93 *Univ. Ct.*, 15 December 1932.
94 Sir D'Arcy Power (ed.), *British Medical Societies*, p. 170.
95 UGC, *Returns*, 1928/9.
96 *W. Mail*, 26, 27 and 29 October 1934.
97 Ibid., 30 October 1934.

Chapter 7 – Constitutional Wrangles

1   Sir Thomas Lewis to Lord Kenyon, 18 June 1926, Sir Thomas Lewis Papers, Wellcome Library, PP/LEW/D.5/1.
2   T. Graham Brown to Sir Thomas Lewis, 15 July 1927, ibid.
3   W. B Riddell to Sir Almeric Fitzroy, 8 June 1922, TNA, PC 12/76.
4   Lord Kenyon to Sir Almeric Fitzroy, 17 February 1923, ibid.
5   Sir Almeric Fitzroy to Trevor Harris, 1 February and 14 March 1923, ibid.
6   Quoted in *W. Mail*, 20 February 1923.
7   Departmental memorandum, 19 January 1925, TNA, ED 119/75.
8   Lord Kenyon to Sir Thomas Lewis, 5 May 1922, Sir Thomas Lewis Papers, Wellcome Library, PP/LEW/D.5/1.
9   Private and confidential memorandum on the status, organization etc. of the Welsh National School of Medicine, by Jenkin James (December 1922), TNA, PC 12/76.
10 A. H. Kidd to Sir Almeric Fitzroy, 11 December 1922, ibid.
11 Lord Kenyon to Sir Almeric Fitzroy, 3 December 1922, ibid.
12 R. G. Mayor to the permanent secretary of the Board of Education, 3 January 1923, TNA, ED 119/75.
13 *SWN*, 2 September 1925.
14 'Notes taken at the committee appointed to report on a letter by Dr W. Mitchell Stevens, meeting on 19 January 1926', Cardiff, R/File/M/16.
15 Minutes of the UGC, 7 December 1922, TNA, UGC 11/1. The identity of the professor was not stated; it was probably the dean of medicine, Professor Kennedy.
16 Verbatim typescript report of W. N. Bruce's speech to the University Council, 25 September 1924, NLW, Wales, CG 21/3/2.
17 Trow and Brown, *A Short History*, p. 62.
18 Lord Kenyon to Sir Almeric Fitzroy, 8 May 1923, TNA. PC 12/76.
19 Lord Kenyon to Sir Almeric Fitzroy, 18 March 1923, ibid.
20 *W. Mail*, 6 June 1924.
21 Report of the Academic Board to the University Council, meeting on 14 November 1923.
22 Minutes of the Senate of UCC, 23 November 1923.
23 *W. Mail*, 17 June 1924.
24 *SWN*, 2 July 1924.
25 *W. Mail*, 5 July 1924.
26 Appended to the minutes of the meeting of the University Council held on 20 December 1924 are copies of the various reports submitted to it, together with Sir Harry Reichel's draft constitution of the Welsh National School of Medicine.

27 Memorandum by Sir Maurice Hankey to the Lord President of the Council, 18 February 1925, TNA, PC 12/76.

28 *W. Mail*, 8 January 1925.

29 *BMJ*, 17 January 1925, p. 135.

30 *W. Mail*, 7 February 1925.

31 Sir George Newman to Colin Smith, 6 March, and Smith's reply, 10 March 1925, TNA, PC 12/76.

32 *BMJ*, 13 June 1925, p. 1095; *Univ. Cncl.*, 22 May 1925, 3.

33 *SWN*, 17 September 1925.

34 Ibid., 28 February 1925.

35 Ibid., 30 June 1925.

36 J. M. Angus to D. B. Anthony, 29 August 1925, NLW, Wales, CG 21/3/2.

37 Cardiff, box 35, R/File/M/3, 'D. J. A. Brown, Medical School papers'.

38 William George to Lord Kenyon, 22 September 1925, NLW, Wales, CG 21/4/6. For William George see *The Dictionary of Welsh Biography, 1941–1970*, pp. 79–80.

39 William George to D. B. Anthony, 24 September 1925, ibid.

40 D. B. Anthony to William George, 26 September, 9 October 1925, ibid.

41 Lord Kenyon to D. B. Anthony, 15 September 1925, ibid.

42 'Notes taken at the committee appointed to report on a letter by Dr W. Mitchell Stevens, meeting held on 25 January 1926', Cardiff, R/File/M/16.

43 F. T. James to D. B. Anthony, 5 October 1925, NLW, Wales, CG 21/3/2. For James's biography see *The Dictionary of Welsh Biography, 1941–1970*, p. 107.

44 *SWN*, 17 October 1925.

45 Thomas Lewis to Sir George Newman, 8 March 1921, Sir Thomas Lewis Papers, Wellcome Library, PP/LEW/D.1/1.

46 Thomas Lewis to Jenkin James, 8 April 1922, NLW, Wales, CH 5/1.

47 *W. Mail*, 13 October 1925.

48 Frank T. James to Sir Thomas Lewis, 25 October 1925, Sir Thomas Lewis Papers, Wellcome Library, PP/LEW/B.6.

49 *W. Mail*, 17 October 1925.

50 *The Lancet*, 31 October 925.

51 *SWN*, 17 October 1925.

52 Sir Thomas Lewis to Lord Kenyon, 7 November, and Kenyon's reply, 9 November 1925, Sir Thomas Lewis Papers, Wellcome Library, PP/LEW/D.5/1.

53 *W. Mail*, 12 March 1926.

54 A. H. Kidd to Jenkin James, 15 April 1926, NLW, Wales, CG 21/2/3.

55 Minutes of the University Council , 10 June, 19 July and 15 October 1926.

56 Lord Kenyon to Sir Thomas Lewis, 19 June 1926, Sir Thomas Lewis Papers, Wellcome Library, PP/LEW/D.1/1. Ivor Davies regarded Sir John Rose Bradford, whose wife was the Welsh-speaking niece of the eminent physician, Sir William Roberts, as 'the greatest clinical teacher in general medicine of his day'. Ivor J. Davies, *Memories of a Welsh Physician*, p. 131.

57 This correspondence is kept in NLW, Wales, CG 21/2/3. The letters from Sir Charles Sherrington, Sir Walter Morley Fletcher, Sir Humphrey Rolleston, Dr Richard Pearce and Sir John Rose Bradford, were also appended to the minutes of the meeting of the University Council held on 16 October 1926.

58 *W. Mail*, 13 January 1927.

59 Williams, p. 179.

60 Lord Kenyon to Colin Smith, 16 January 1927, TNA, PC 12/76.

61 C. Smith to Lord Kenyon, 25 January 1927, NLW, Wales, CG 21/4/7.

62   A. H. Trow to Sir Isambard Owen, 15 January 1927, Bangor, General Collection, 5990 A.

63   *W. Mail*, 17 January 1927.

64   D. B. Anthony to Lord Kenyon, 27 July 1927, NLW, Wales, CG 5/4.

65   Lord Kenyon to Colin Smith, 26 January 1927, TNA, PC 12/76.

66   *W. Mail*, 16 June 1927.

67   T. A. Davies to Lord Kenyon, 11 July 1927, and Lord Kenyon to D. B. Anthony, 12 July 1927, NLW, Wales, CG 5/4. The irritability of Lord Kenyon at this time can also be noted in his response to a letter from Sir Thomas Lewis, the year before, about the low morale of the medical school professors. 'I did not need to know the condition of things in the Medical School. Graham Brown, and indeed all the professors, confide their woes to me frequently'. Lord Kenyon to Sir Thomas Lewis, 19 June 1926, Sir Thomas Lewis Papers, Wellcome Library, PP/LEW/D.5/1.

68   *North Wales Chronicle*, 25 October 1929.

69   Minutes of the UGC, 25 June and 9 July 1925, TNA, UGC 11/1.

70   'Memorandum on the Welsh National School of Medicine' written by A. H. Kidd, 5 March 1927, NLW, Jones, J, xv, 142.

71   *Univ. Cncl.*, 24 October 1927 (report of the Finance Committee).

72   *W. Mail*, 15 January 1927.

73   Ibid., 7 October 1927.

74   *SWN*, 25 October 1927.

75   *The Leech*, I, 1, October 1926, pp. 2–5.

76   Ibid., I, 3, May 1927, p. 6.

77   *W. Mail*, 26 October 1927.

Chapter 8 – The Infirmary in Revolt

1   Letter from Dr Malcolm Parsons to the author, 25 April 2006; Sir Humphry Rolleston, *Life of Sir Clifford Allbutt* (London, 1929), pp. 110–12.

2   R. M. F. Picken, 'The growth of a medical school', *Proceedings of the Cardiff Medical Society* (1954/5), 27–37.

3   Williams, p. 181

4   Minutes of the meeting of a joint conference between representatives of the Board of Medicine and the Medical Board, 16 June 1925, CRI, D/D HC 33; *BM*, 30 June 1925, 119.

5   *FM*, 5 March 1924, 134.

6   Minutes of the Medical Board, 6 May 1924, CRI, D.D HC 33.

7   D. J. A. Brown to L. D. Rea, 14 June 1924, ibid., 1 July 1924.

8   This issue is addressed in the minutes of the meetings of the Faculty of Medicine held on 4, 11 and 18 March, 20 May and 3 June 1925, and by Mitchell Stevens in his evidence to the committee of inquiry referred to in note 9 below.

9   Notes (slightly amended) taken at the committee appointed to report on the letter from Dr W. Mitchell Stevens, meetings held on 14 December 1925, 19 and 25 January, 11 and 23 March 1926, Cardiff, R/File/M/16.

10   *BMJ*, 13 November 1965, p. 1187.

11   Relevant papers and correspondence relating to the committee of inquiry are kept in Cardiff, R/File/Phys/3.

12   R. Eccles, 'Old man of the mountains: T. Graham Brown', in G. Jones and M. Quinn (eds.), *Fountains of Praise*, p. 106.

13   *BM*, 18 January 1927, 228.

14   Sir William Diamond to Jenkin James, 27 March 1928, *Univ. Cncl.*, 16 April 1928, Appendix A.

15 Lord Adrian, 'Thomas Graham Brown', in *Biographical Memoirs of Fellows of the Royal Society*, vol. 12 (London, 1966), p. 26.
16 *The Lancet*, 14 April 1945, p. 485.
17 *BM*, 17 November 1925, 135, and 14 January 1926, 149.
18 The substantial dossier of evidence submitted by Professor Sheen to the Board of Medicine was included among the papers for a conference of representatives of the Board of Medicine and the Cardiff Royal Infirmary, held on 4 July 1927, *Minute Book of Board of Medicine Committees* (October 1926–September 1930).
19 Evidence given to a committee established by the Board of Medicine to consider the grievances of the recognized clinical teachers, 11 June 1928, Cardiff, R/File/M/17.
20 Evidence given by Professor Sheen, T. E. Hammond and D. J. Harries to the Board of Medicine's committee of inquiry, ibid.
21 *Minute Book of Board of Medicine Committees* (October 1926–September 1930).
22 T. Graham Brown to Sir Thomas Lewis, 15 July 1927, Sir Thomas Lewis Papers, Wellcome Library, PP/LEW/D.5/1.
23 Davies, *Memories of a Welsh Physician*, p. 56.
24 Minutes of the Medical Board, 1 November 1927, CRI, D/D HC 33.
25 See in particular the minutes of a meeting of the Executive Committee of the Cardiff Medical Society held on 13 December 1927, Glamorgan Record Office, DCMS/6 (1912–48).
26 Minutes of the meeting of the committee of representatives of the Faculty of Medicine and the Medical Board of the Infirmary, held on 5 January 1928, *Minute Book of Board of Medicine Committees* (October 1926–September 1930).
27 See note 19 above.
28 *BMJ*, 24 October 1953, p. 942.
29 *W. Mail*, 8 December 1927.
30 L. D. Rea to Jenkin James, 25 May 1928, *Univ. Cncl.*, 15 June 1928, Appendix A.
31 H. Hale Bellot, *University College, London, 1826–1926* (London, 1929), pp. 404–5.
32 *Univ. Cncl.*, 16 April, 4 and 15 June 1928, 15; *SWN*, 16 March 1928; *W. Mail*, 9 May 1928.
33 *Univ. Cncl.*, 23 February 1928, 13 (report of a conference between representatives of the university and the infirmary, held on 16 February 1928).
34 Draft proposals for a Board of Clinical Studies were received by the University Council on 15 June 1928.
35 Letter from Sir William Diamond to William Martin, 28 April 1928, reported to the Medical Board on 7 May 1928, CRI, D/D HC 33.
36 For the correspondence between D. J. A. Brown and the recognized clinical teachers during May 1928, see Cardiff, R/File/M/17.
37 Professor Hepburn's letter and details of the subsequent work of the subcommittee, were appended to the minutes of the Board of Medicine meeting on 15 May 1928.
38 Sir William Diamond to D. J. A. Brown, 27 May 1928, Cardiff, R/File/M/17.
39 *SWN*, I June 1928. For Cornelius Griffiths (1865–1955) see *BMJ*, 21 May 1955, p. 1284; *The Lancet*, 28 May 1955, p. 1130.
40 L. D. Rea to D. J. A. Brown, 1 June 1928, Cardiff, R/File/M/19.
41 *W. Mail*, 1 June 1928.
42 *SWN*, 1 June 1928.
43 Sir Walter Fletcher to Sir Wilmot Herringham, 5 July 1928, TNA, FD 5/12.
44 C. Lewerth et al., 'Source History of the Rockefeller Foundation', vol. xx, pp. 4191–3.
45 *SWN*, 1 June 1928.
46 *W. Mail*, 9 June 1928; Cardiff, R/File/M/18.

47 The letter from T. Harris to D. J. A. Brown, 8 June 1928 and the exchange of correspondence between Brown and Rea on 8 and 26 June 1928 are in Cardiff/File/M/19.

48 'Report of the committee appointed to consider and report on the situation which has arisen in regard to the recognised clinical teachers', appended to the minutes of the Board of Medicine, 22 June 1928. For documentation and correspondence relating to the work of the committee see Cardiff, R/File/M/17. Also *SWN*, 11 June 1928; *W. Mail*, 16 June 1928.

49 For instance, Athel Sayce, a fourth-year student registered for the University of Wales degrees, formally applied to transfer to the London School of Medicine for Women on 21 June 1928, her application form being countersigned by Professor Sheen. This information was provided by Victoria Rea of the Royal Free Hospital Archives Centre.

50 *W. Mail*, 5 July 1928; *SWN*, 5 July 1928.

51 *W. Mail*, ibid.

52 For the minutes of the meetings of the Vacation Committee held during the long vacation see *Minute Book of Board of Medicine Committees* (October 1926–September 1930).

53 *Annual Report of the Council of UCC to the College Court* (1927/8), p. 12.

54 For the correspondence between the registrar and the honorary clinical staff see Cardiff, R/File/M/22.

55 *BMJ*, 16 January 1954, pp. 160–1.

56 Presidential address by Hilary Wade on 'Surgeons as past presidents of the Cardiff Medical Society', to the Cardiff Medical Society, 9 October 1979; O. L. Wade, *When I Dropped the Knife* (Bishop Auckland, 1996), p. 10.

57 The meeting was extensively covered in *BMJ*, 28 July 1928, pp. 139–43, 4 August 1928, pp. 212–16.

58 Lord Kenyon to the director of the Wellcome Historical Museum, 20 April 1927, NLW, Wales, CG 5/4.

59 *W. Mail*, 25 July 1928. In addition to Sir Thomas Lewis, those honoured by the University of Wales were: Henry Britten Brackenbury, a prominent general practitioner and chairman of the council of the BMA; Sir Robert Philip, professor of tuberculosis at the University of Edinburgh and past president of the BMA; Professor Walter Chipman, professor of obstetrics and gynaecology at McGill University, Montreal and past president of the American College of Surgeons; Sir George Syme, president of the College of Surgeons of Australasia and vice-president of the BMA; Mr Franklin Martin, president-elect of the American College of Surgeons.

60 D. B. Anthony to Lord Kenyon, 4 October 1927, NLW, Wales, CG 5/4.

61 *FM*, 21 June 1928, 382.

62 *W. Mail*, 19 July 1928.

63 Colin Smith to Sir George Newman, 2 August 1928, TNA, PC 12/76.

64 For a typescript summary of events between July and early October 1928, prepared by the registrar for Principal Trow, see Cardiff, R/File/M/19.

65 *W. Mail*, 18 and 19 September 1928.

66 Ibid., 19 September 1928.

67 Ibid., 27 September 1928.

68 L. D. Rea to D. J. A. Brown, 27 and 29 September 1928, Cardiff, R/File/M/19.

69 D. J. A. Brown to L. D. Rea, 2 October 1928, ibid.

70 D. J. A. Brown to Welsh Degree students, 29 September 1928, ibid.

71 *W. Mail*, 2 October 1928.

72 Minutes of the Vacation Committee, 1 October 1928.

73 *W. Mail*, 4 October 1928.

74 Aldis, *Cardiff Royal Infirmary*, p. 35.

75 *The Critic* ('No spleen, always keen'), 9 March 1929.

76 *W. Mail*, 13 October 1928.

77 Ibid., 9 October 1928.

78 A useful typescript 'Summary history of conditions which led to the closing of the Infirmary', commencing in May 1925, and compiled by D. J. A. Brown from the minutes of relevant committees in the medical school and UCC, may be found in Cardiff, R/File/M/20.

79 *W. Mail*, 9 October 1928.

80 This information is based on a confidential typescript schedule prepared by the Cardiff registrar in April 1929, 'Particulars relating to students who should have been pursuing fourth, fifth, and sixth year courses of study in the School during the Session 1928/9', Cardiff, R/File/M/20.

Chapter 9 – The Students

1 A. H. Trow to E. M. Bruce Vaughan, 17 January 1919, Cardiff, box 21.

2 *Memorandum by the Registrar on the Procedure to be Adopted by those who Desire to Enter the Profession of Medicine, with Notes on Cost and Prospects* (General Medical Council, July 1927).

3 A. H. Kidd to D. J. A. Brown, 29 September 1916, Cardiff, box 9, R. C. on University Education in Wales, file 16/56, no. 2.

4 *The Lancet*, 6 November 1965, p. 958.

5 J. E. Thomas to D. Hepburn, 2 August 1925, Cardiff, box 12, R/File/Phys/3.

6 Sir Percy Watkins, *A Welshman Remembers*, p. 98. For a good obituary of D. J. A. Brown see *Cardiff Times*, 18 September 1937.

7 A. M. Farrington to F. G. Hartland, 28 November 1928, and D. J. A. Brown to Mrs. Farrington, 3 December 1928, Cardiff, R/File/M/19.

8 *BMJ*, 5 September 1931, p. 453.

9 The information in this paragraph is drawn from the annual returns made by universities to the UGC, held at the National Archives (TNA, UGC 3). The slight discrepancy between the figures given for Cardiff in the UGC returns and in the annual, and more detailed, reports presented to the Faculty of Medicine and shown in the earlier table, is explained by the time in the year when the figures were compiled.

10 *BMJ*, 5 September 1931, p. 421.

11 Sir Percy Watkins, *A Welshman Remembers*, p. 123.

12 Sir Isambard Owen, 'Notes and amendments on draft scheme of the organisation of the Medical School' (1919), Bangor, General Collection, 5987.

13 *FM*, 16 December 1925, 560 and appendix III.

14 *SWDN*, 14 December 1910.

15 Cardiff, 'University College, Cardiff, registration and record book no. 5, student register, 1906–10'; 'Registration forms, sessions of 1916/17 and 1917/18'; T. Graham Brown to J. James, 10 May 1924, NLW, Wales, CH 5/2; NLW, Wales, CG 21/3/2. (Note that the 1929/30 statistics, compiled during the autumn term, provisionally showed 158 students in attendance during that session. The final figure for the session was 164.)

16 Gwilym Hughes to Dr Lloyd Davies, 6 January 1923, NLW, Wales, CH 6/6.

17 J. M. Angus to D. Hepburn, 14 October 1918, Cardiff, letter interleaved in the 1918/19 manuscript register of medical students.

18 *BM*, 5 February 1823, 157 (report of the Special Joint Committee of the School of Medicine and the King Edward VII Hospital). The attitude of the medical school and hospital authorities to the admission of Jewish refugees from Europe during the 1930s was rather more sympathetic. See Paul Weindling, 'The Jewish medical refugee crisis and Wales, 1933–1945', in Michael and Webster (eds.), *Health and Society in Twentieth-Century Wales*, pp. 183–200.

19   For a brief history of Aberdare Hall, see the essay by Barbara How, 'A residence for young women', in Jones and Quinn (eds.), *Fountains of Praise*, pp. 43–50.

20   Hollman, *Sir Thomas Lewis*, p. 5.

21   'Table of fees and cost of tuition and examinations for a primary qualification in medicine, surgery and midwifery and an estimate of the cost of maintenance for the duration of the curriculum', appended to *Memorandum by the Registrar*.

22   Letter from D. Hepburn to D. J. A. Brown, 30 January 1923, appended to *FM*, 7 February 1923.

23   Williams, p. 272.

24   For D. J. A. Brown's note of a conversation with L. D. Rea, held on 12 October 1921, and Rea's subsequent letter to Brown, of 21 October 1921, see Cardiff, R/File/M/19.

25   The information on which this paragraph is based has been compiled from issues of the Cardiff College *Calendar* and medical school prospectuses of the period.

26   Minutes of the Council of UCC, 19 February 1924.

27   *College Magazine*, XII, 4 (March 1900), 158. The article, 'SRC presidents' discussed the contributions of the first four SRC presidents.

28   Ibid., XV, 2 (December 1902), 43.

29   Spencer Vignes, *Lost in France: The Remarkable Life and Death of Leigh Richmond Roose, Football's First Playboy* (Stroud, 2007), pp. 30–3; *Dictionary of Welsh Biography down to 1940*, p. 890; UCC *Calendar* (1900/01); *College Magazine*, XII, 4 (March 1900), 179.

30   Article on 'College sects' by 'Reg. No. 0025', *College Magazine*, XII, 2 (December 1092), 60.

31   Report by Sir Isambard Owen to the Cardiff College Accommodation Committee, 18 January 1913, Cardiff, box 21.

32   Sir Clement Price Thomas, 'The Sheens and the Welsh National School of Medicine', *Proceedings of the Cardiff Medical Society* (1965/6), 60.

33   *W. Mail*, 25 June 1924.

34   'The Mock Election', *Cap and Gown*, XXV, 1 (March 1928), 20.

35   *College Magazine*, VII, 2 (March 1895), 30.

36   UCC, *Students' Handbook* (1903/4).

37   *College Magazine*, XI, 2 (December 1898), 90.

38   Minutes of the Senate of UCC, 19 November 1895. The activities of the Medical Students' Society before the war were covered from time to time by the *College Magazine* and its successor, *Cap and Gown* (established in 1903).

39   D. J. Harries (president of the Medical Students' Club), 'The Leech, the Club and the School', *The Leech*, 1, 1 (March 1939), 13.

40   *FM*, 27 June 1924, 229; 2 June 1926, 669; 28 June 1926, 701.

41   D.W. Evans to Harri Williams, 22 October and 14 November 1921, NLW, Wales, Davies, D 12/2.

42   *The Leech*, II, 1 (November 1927), 16.

43   Ibid., IV, 1 (April 1932), 4.

44   *W. Mail*, 1 November 1926; *SWN*, 2 November 1926; *The Lancet*, 6 November 1926.

45   *The Leech*, I, 2 (January 1927), 24.

46   Ibid., II, 2 (February 1928), 29.

47   Ibid., II, 1 (November 1927), 27.

48   Ibid., III, 1 (December 1930), 5.

49   *BMJ*, 5 September 1931, p. 416.

50   Charles Langmaid to his brother, 5 January 1937. This letter, and Langmaid's detailed diary of his experiences as ship's surgeon on the MV *Glengarry*, are included in Langmaid's papers, in the possession of the family.

51   I am grateful to Dr Bethan Jones, secretary of Minny Street Welsh Congregational chapel, Cardiff, for

providing information on Drs Bryneilen and Rosentyl Griffiths, faithful members of the chapel for many years.

52 The information on which this and subsequent paragraphs are based is mainly contained in issues of the *Medical Directory*, particularly those for 1940 and 1953.
53 *BMJ*, 29 January 1983, p. 405.
54 Ibid., 15 June 1963, p. 1615.
55 *W. Mail*, 7 October 1933.
56 Ibid., 17 January 1934.

Chapter 10 – Parting of the Ways

1   Report by the principal to the Council of UCC for the 1927/8 session.
2   *FM*, 10 May 1927, 160.
3   Chrimes (ed.), pp. 329–32; Jones and Quinn (eds.), *Fountains of Praise*, p. 180.
4   Chrimes (ed.), p. 324.
5   *BM*, 4 December 1922, 150.
6   Annual report of the head of the department of anatomy to the Council of UCC, 1927/8.
7   *FM*, 1 June 1929, appendix.
8   Annual report of the head of the department of physiology to the Council of UCC, 1929/30.
9   T. Graham Brown to D. B. Anthony, 7 May 1931, NLW, Wales, CH 5/3.
10 T. Graham Brown to Sir Walter Fletcher, 19 May 1930, TNA, FD 5/12. By this time it was too late to change minds. Everyone else, including the UGC, being weary of argument, was relieved that, within Wales, general agreement had been reached on a way forward. Inspection of the minutes of meetings of the UGC during the late 1920s (TNA, UGC 11/1) can only lead readers to the conclusion that the problems of the University of Wales were by no means at the top of the committee's agenda. Indeed, meetings of the UGC were by no means frequent at this time, only two being held in 1928 and one in 1929.
11 *Univ. Ct.*, 28 March 1930. For the petition in full see NLW, Wales, CG 21/2/4. In a memorandum to the Privy Council, dated 12 February 1930, Rees wrote: 'I had a long conversation with [Brown] yesterday in which I tried to convince him that he was crying for the moon and that he was allowing his supposed grievances to make him thoroughly disgruntled and quite disloyal to the Institution he is serving.' TNA, PC 12/76.
12 *The Leech*, II, 1 (November 1927), 8–10. The following summer found Brown and his climbing companion, F. B. Smythe, ascending Mont Blanc by yet another new route. *The Times* of 18 August 1928 carried an account of their achievement, 'the greatest climb of our lives', written by Smythe, accompanied by a photograph of Brown taken during the ascent.
13 Davies, *Memories of a Welsh Physician*, p. 62.
14 Minutes of the Medical Board, 9 April 1929, CRI, D/D HC 33.
15 *John Bull*, 3 November 1928.
16 Minutes of the joint conference between representatives of the council of the Cardiff Royal Infirmary and the Council of University College, Cardiff, held on 22 October 1928, *Minute Book of Board of Medicine Committees* (October 1926–September 1930).
17 Typescript memorandum of a conversation between D. J. A. Brown and Professor Sheen, Cardiff, R/File/M/19.
18 For the minutes of the six meetings of the Infirmary representatives, held between 30 October and 10 December 1928 see CRI, D/D HC 14.
19 Minutes of the Finance Committee of UCC, 15 November 1928; 'Particulars relating to students who should have been pursuing fourth, fifth and sixth year courses of study in the School during the Session 1928/9', Cardiff, R/File/M/20.

20   Letter to A. H. Trow, 17 September 1928, Cardiff, R/File/M/17.
21   Counsel's Opinion, provided to UCC, by T. W. Langman, Cardiff, 16 October 1928, Cardiff, R/File/M/19.
22   Minutes of a special meeting of the Finance Committee of UCC; *Univ. Cncl.*, 30 November 1928, 5.
23   Minutes of the Finance Committee of the Board of Medicine, 20 December 1928; minutes of the University of Wales Finance Committee, 7 February 1929, approved by the University Council, 22 February 1929.
24   'Report of the further development of Pathology in the Welsh National School of Medicine', appended to *BM*, 18 January 1926.
25   *The Leech*, II, 1 (November 1927), 15.
26   Jethro Gough to D. J. A. Brown, 29 January 1929, Cardiff, R/File/M/20
27   *W. Mail*, 17 January 1929.
28   Sir Ewen Maclean to D. J. A. Brown, 4 December 1928, Cardiff, R/File/M/19.
29   *FM*, 30 January 1929, 451; *W. Mail*, 4 and 5 February 1929.
30   *W. Mail*, 15 February 1929.
31   Ibid.
32   H. M. Ingledew to A. H. Trow, 19 March 1929, Cardiff, R/File/M/20.
33   For correspondence involving the college, the infirmary, and the solicitors acting for the student see Cardiff, ibid.
34   Ibid.
35   C. G. Brown to A. H. Trow, 10 December 1928, Cardiff, R/File/M/19.
36   *W. Mail*, 30 May 1929.
37   *BMJ*, 8 June 1929, p. 1049; *The Lancet*, 8 June 1929, p. 1208.
38   For correspondence between the Cardiff registrar and the honorary staff of the infirmary in connection with the terms of their re-engagement, see Cardiff, R/File/M22.
39   For correspondence between the Cardiff registrar and officers of the Conjoint Board and London University, see Cardiff, R/File/M/21.
40   T. E. Hammond to A. H. Trow, 16 June 1929, ibid.
41   Hilary Wade, 'Surgeons as past presidents of the Cardiff Medical Society', *Proceedings of the Cardiff Medical Society* (1979/80).
42   For details of the appointments to the professorial units and the Department of Pathology, see appendices to *FM*, 20 July 1929.
43   The minute book of the Board of Clinical Studies covering the period 1935 to 1945 is kept in the archives of Cardiff University. The material on which this paragraph and the next are based is contained in the minutes of the Board of Medicine and the Faculty of Medicine between October 1929 and June 1931. Details of H. F. Pegler's salary are contained in the papers submitted to the first meeting of the Council of the independent Welsh National School of Medicine, held on 29 May 1931, Cardiff, R/File/M/13.
44   Minutes of the Council of the Cardiff Royal Infirmary, held on 22 May 1930, CRI, D/D HC 15; *Univ. Cncl.*, 10 July 1930.
45   W. N. Bruce to Sir John Herbert Lewis, 31 May 1929, NLW, Wales, Lewis, A1, 358.
46   'Statement for consideration by the University Grants Committee in connection with the quinquennial re-assessment of grants' (12 September 1929), appended to the minutes of the University Council, 14 October 1929.
47   A. H. Kidd's letter, dated 22 November 1929, to the university authorities is reproduced in *Univ. Cncl.*, 28 November 1929, 16.
48   See the relevant minutes of the University of Wales Finance Committee, included in the minutes of the University Council, 14 October and 28 November 1929, 27 February and 8 May 1930.

49   W. N. Bruce to D. B. Anthony, 6 September 1929, NLW, Wales, CG 21/4/8.

50   For correspondence between officers of UCC and the University of Wales see Cardiff, R/File/M/9.

51   For correspondence between D. B. Anthony and L. D. Rea, secretary of the Cardiff Royal Infirmary in this matter see NLW., Wales, CG 21/4/2.

52   W. N. Bruce to D. B. Anthony, 23 January 1930, ibid., CG 21/4/8.

53   J. F. Rees to W. N. Bruce, 27 January 1930, ibid.

54   *W. Mail*, 29 March 1930.

55   A. H. Kidd to the clerk of the Privy Council, 26 March 1930, TNA, PC 12/76.

56   Cardiff, R/File/M/6.

57   The terms of the deed and the lease were appended to the minutes of the University Council, 24 April 1931.

58   Letters from D. J. A. Brown to D. B. Anthony, 18 July 1931, Cardiff, R/File/M/12.

59   Counsel's opinion, provided by W. J. Whittaker, 31 January 1930, Cardiff, R/File/M/12.

60   Cardiff, R/File/M/30 and R/File/M/32.

61   For correspondence regarding the deficit see Cardiff, R/File/M/11; *Univ. Cncl.* 24 April 1931, 11.

62   The Cardiff College's supplemental charter had been granted on 21 January 1931, and the supplemental charter of the University of Wales would be granted on 27 November 1931, Chrimes (ed.), p. 94.

63   A. H. Kidd to Jenkin James, 17 March, and James to Kidd, 23 March 1931, NLW, Wales, CH 5/3.

64   *W. Mail*, 8 May 1931.

65   In a letter to D. J. A. Brown, dated 8 March 1931, H. F. Pegler, second clerk in the medical school office, unsuccessfully requested a pay increase from £100 to £160 per annum. 'Owing to the resignation of the late Chief Clerk I am looked upon as the one who knows most of the work in the office and nearly all enquiries, directly or indirectly, come to me for reply and this thereby *throws a great deal of responsibility upon my shoulders*', Cardiff, R/File/M/11.

66   G. I. Strachan to D. J. A. Brown, 11 June, and Brown to Strachan, 13 June 1931, Cardiff, R/File/M/13.

67   W. Mitchell Stevens to D. J. A. Brown, 16 May 1931, Cardiff, R/File/M/14.

68   *W. Mail*, 29 March 1930.

69   *Univ. Cncl.*, 24 April 1931, 3.

Bibliography

A. UNPUBLISHED PRIMARY SOURCES

Cardiff University, Main Building, Cathays Park: Archives Store-Room

Welsh National School of Medicine minute books (bound volumes)

- Board of Medicine (4 vols: July 1921–July 1923; Sept. 1923–Sept. 1926; Oct. 1926–Sept. 1930; Oct. 1930–June 1931)
- Board of Medicine Committees (2 vols: July 1921–Sept. 1926; Oct. 1926–Sept. 1930)
- Faculty of Medicine (4 vols: July 1921–Sept. 1923; Oct. 1923–Sept. 1926; Oct. 1926–Sept. 1930; Oct. 1930–June 1931)
- Senate, 1932/3

University College of South Wales and Monmouthshire minute books

- Council 1883–1931
- Senate 1883–1931

Medical School correspondence, June 1912–July 1921 (box 21)

Registrar's correspondence files
  R/File/M/1 (box 35), 'Medical School buildings'
  R/File/M/2 (box 35), 'Medical School (new)'
  R/File/M/3 (box 35), 'Medical School Papers'
  R/File/M/6 (box 35), 'Conferences between representatives of the College and the University, June-October 1927'
  R/File/M/9 (unnumbered box), 'Recent correspondence with University of Wales and papers relating to School of Medicine Charter and Petition of College Against'
  R/File/M/11 (unnumbered box), 'Agreement: University of Wales, UCSW&M, WNSM'
  R/File/M/12 (unnumbered box), 'University of Wales, UCSW&M, WNSM, correspondence June-Sept. 1931'

R/File/M/13 (unnumbered box), 'Supplemental Charter (WNSM), transferred departments, inventory etc., general matters'

R/File/M/14 (unnumbered box), 'Board of Medicine, final meeting'

R/File/M/16 (unnumbered box), 'Dr. Mitchell Stevens' committee'

R/File/M/17 (unnumbered box), 'Board of Medicine Committee re Recognised Clinical Teachers'

R/File/M/18 (unnumbered box), 'Cardiff Royal Infirmary: Termination of Agreement in regard to Medical School'

R/File/M/19 (unnumbered box), 'Medical School, College and Infirmary, I'

R/File/M/20 (unnumbered box), 'Medical School, College and Infirmary, II'

R/File/M/21 (unnumbered box), 'Medical School, College and Infirmary, III'

R/File/M/22 (unnumbered box), 'Medical School, College and Infirmary, IV'

R/File/M/24 (box 26), 'Summary history of conditions which led to closing of Infirmary'

R/File/M/25 (box 26), 'National School of Preventive Medicine'

R/File/M/26 (box 26), 'National School of Preventive Medicine'

R/File/M/27 (box 26), 'New Preventive Medicine and Public Health Building in the Parade, 1926/7'

R/File/M/29 (box 26), 'Mansel Talbot Professorship, 1921'

R/File/M/30 (box 26), 'Transfer to the School of Mansel Talbot Professorship, 1931'

R/File/M/31 (box 26), 'Tuberculosis Committee, 3 July 1928'

R/File/M/32 (box 26), 'Professor of Tuberculosis'

R/File/Phys/3 (box 12), 'Investigation into Professor Graham Brown, 1926'

Royal Commission on University Education in Wales
'Original precis of evidence' (box 5)
'18/56 file 1' (box 5)
'18/56 file 2' (box 5)
'16/56 file 2, July–Sept. 1916' (box 9)
'16/56 file 3, Oct.–Dec. 1916' (box 9)
'Bound Royal Commission Reports' (box 23)

Files of newspaper cuttings, 1883–1931
'Medical School miscellaneous cuttings file, 1890'
Student records
'University College SW&M Matriculation Book, 1883/4 to 1894/5'
'University College, Cardiff, Registration and Record Book No.5, Student Register 1906–10'
'Registration Forms, Sessions of 1916/17 and 1917/18'
'Cardiff Medical School Record Book 1919–1922'
'WNSM: Lists of students, session 1915/16 to session 1926/27'

'Register of students who are qualified' (handwritten file, compiled in the late 1930s)

Medical Unit Reports (case notes), 1922/4 (5 volumes)

Glamorgan Record Office

British Medical Association, South Wales and Monmouthshire branch, minute book, 1871–9

Cardiff Medical Society, minute books, 1877–95, 1895–1904, 1904–23, 1923–40

Cardiff Medical Society, Executive Committee, minute book, 1912–48

Cardiff Royal Infirmary archives

Minute Books of Committees

D/D HC 11 1915–20

D/D HC 12 1920–1

D/D HC 13 1922–4

D/D HC 14 1924–8

D/D HC 15 1929–31

Medical Board minutes

D/D HC 32 1908–21

D/D HC 33 1921–30

Francis Davies Papers

The National Archives, Kew

Diaries of Sir George Newman (MH)

Records of the Board of Education (ED)

Records of the Medical Research Council (FD)

Records of the Ministry of Health (MH)

Records of the Privy Council Office (PC)

Records of the University Grants Committee (UGC)

The National Library of Wales

Lord Davies of Llandinam Collection

Thomas Jones Collection

Sir John Herbert Lewis Papers

Sir Daniel Lleufer Thomas Papers

Sir John Lynn-Thomas Papers

Sir John Williams Papers

Records of the Welsh National Memorial Association

University of Wales Archive

CG 5 Registrar's correspondence with senior University officers, 1899–1983

CG 21/2 WNSM: Registrar's subject files, 1916–76

CG 21/3 Registrar's general correspondence, 1911–36

CG 21/4 Registrar's correspondence with specific individuals and institutions, 1906–67

CH 5 Secretary of Council: WNSM correspondence and papers, 1921–50

CH 6 LEA grants-in-aid to WNSM, 1921–61

LU 1 Medical Board of the University, 1908–19

Rockefeller Archive Centre, Sleepy Hollow, New York

C. Lewerth et al., 'Source history of the Rockefeller Foundation', vol. xx, pp. 4164–93 (unpublished manuscript)

R. M. Pearce, 'Medical education in Wales' (survey report, revised 1926; unpublished manuscript)

Bangor University

General Collection (papers of Sir Isambard Owen)

University of Birmingham Library, Special Collections Department

Minutes of the Faculty of Medicine, 1919–28

Minutes of the University of Birmingham Clinical Board, 1911–30

University of Bristol Health and Social Sciences Library, Special Collections

Letter books of deans of medicine, University of Bristol, 1922 (DM 1148)

Material relating to Sir Isambard Owen (DM 1149/ box 5)

Minutes of the Bristol University Council, 1921/2

University of Liverpool Library

Minutes of the University of Liverpool Board of Clinical Studies, 1927/8

University of Wales Registry

University of Wales Council minutes, 1921–31

University of Wales Court minutes, 1921–32

The Wellcome Library, Euston Road, London

Papers of Sir Thomas Lewis

Papers of Sir Andrew Balfour

Papers of the Medical Women's Federation

Privately owned

Papers of Charles Langmaid

B. OFFICIAL PAPERS

Report of the Committee on the University of Wales and the Welsh University Colleges (London: HMSO, 1909), Cd. 4571

Interim and Final Reports of the Board of Education Departmental Committee on the Medical School at Cardiff (August and December 1914)

Final Report of the Royal Commission on University Education in Wales (London, 1918), Cd. 8891

Appendix to the First Report of the Commissioners: Minutes of Evidence (London, 1917), Cd. 8507

Ministry of Health, *First Report of the Welsh Consultative Council of Medical and Allied Services in Wales* (London, 1920), Cd. 708

Ministry of Health, *Second Report of the Welsh Consultative Council of Medical and Allied Services in Wales* (London, 1921), Cd. 1448

Report of the Inter-departmental Committee on Medical Schools (London, 1944)

Final Report of the Inter-departmental Committee on Dentistry (London: HMSO, 1946), Cd. 6727

C. OTHER PUBLISHED PRIMARY SOURCES

Cardiff Royal Infirmary, *Annual Reports of the Board of Management*, 1923–31

City of Cardiff, *Annual Reports of the Medical Officer of Health*, 1908–14

General Medical Council, *Minutes*, 1907–31

King Edward VII Hospital, *Annual Reports of the Board of Management*, 1914–22

Medical Research Committee, *Annual Reports*, 1914/15 to 1919/20

Medical Research Council, *Annual Reports*, 1920/1 to 1931/2

University Grants Committee, *Returns from Universities and University Colleges in Receipt of Treasury Grant*, 1921/2 to 1930/1

University College of South Wales and Monmouthshire, *Calendar*, 1893–1931

University College of South Wales and Monmouthshire, *Faculty of Medicine Prospectus*, 1910–21

University of South Wales and Monmouthshire, *Students' Handbook*, 1903/4

University of Birmingham, *Calendar*, 1920–31

University of Bristol, *Calendar*, 1921–31

University of Liverpool, *Calendar*, 1921–31

University of Wales, *Calendar*, 1920–32

Welsh National School of Medicine, *Prospectus*, 1921–31

D. PAMPHLETS, REPORTS AND PRINTED MEMORANDA

'University College for South Wales and Monmouthshire: Memorial of the Cardiff Corporation' (13 February 1882)

'Memorial of the Court of Governors of the University College of South Wales and Monmouthshire, and Others, Presented to the Lord President of the Council' (1886)

'University of Wales: Proposed Completion of the Medical School', memorandum submitted to the chancellor of the Exchequer (1914)

'New Physiological Buildings for the Welsh National School of Medicine (The Gift of Sir William James Thomas)' (Cardiff, 1915)

'The Welsh National School of Medicine: Inaugural Proceedings at Cardiff, 15 August 1915' (Cardiff, 1915)

'Colonel Bruce Vaughan's Speeches on the Delay, and in Reply to the Treasury Letter Dated 21 September 1915' (Cardiff, 1916)

'Speeches on the Delay and the Case for the School, made at King Edward VII Hospital by Lieut. Col. Bruce Vaughan, 12 January and 17 February 1916' (Cardiff, 1916)

University Grants Committee, 'Memorandum on Clinical Units in Medical Schools' (1920)

University of South Wales and Monmouthshire, 'Reports of the Heads of Departments Communicated [to the Council] by the Principal', 1925/6 to 1930/1

General Medical Council, 'Memorandum by the Registrar on the Procedure to be Adopted by those who Desire to Enter the Profession of Medicine, with Notes on Cost and Prospects' (July 1927)

E. NEWSPAPERS AND PERIODICALS

British Medical Journal
Cap and Gown
Cardiff Times
The Critic
Evening Express and Evening Mail (Cardiff)
John Bull
Journal of Laryngology and Otology
Journal of Pathology
Journal of Pathology and Bacteriology
The Lancet
The Leech
North Wales Chronicle
The South Wales and Monmouthshire University College Magazine

South Wales Daily News
South Wales News
The Times
The Times Educational Supplement
Welsh Medical Gazette
Welsh Outlook
Western Mail

F. WORKS OF REFERENCE

Brown, G. H. (ed.), *Lives of the Fellows of the Royal College of Physicians of London, 1826–1925* (London, 1955)

Cornelius, E. H. and S. F. Taylor, *Lives of the Fellows of the Royal College of Surgeons of England, 1974–1982* (London, 1988)

Cule, J. H., *Wales and Medicine: A Source-List of Printed Books and Papers showing the History of Medicine in relation to Wales and Welshmen* (Aberystwyth, 1980)

Dictionary of Welsh Biography down to 1940 (London, 1959)

Dictionary of Welsh Biography, 1941–1970 (London, 2001)

The Medical Directory

Power, Sir D'Arcy and W. R. Le Fanu, *Lives of the Fellows of the Royal College of Surgeons of England, 1930–51* (London, 1953)

Ross, Sir James Paterson and W. R. Le Fanu (eds.), *Lives of the Fellows of the Royal College of Surgeons of England, 1965–1973* (London, 1981)

Stephens, Meic (ed.), *The New Companion to the Literature of Wales* (Cardiff, 1998)

Trail, R. R. (ed.), *Munk's Roll, 5: Lives of the Fellows of the Royal College of Physicians of London, continued to 1965* (London, 1968).

Wolstenholme, G. (ed.), *Munk's Roll, 6: Lives of the Fellows of the Royal College of Physicians of London, continued to 1975* (Oxford, 1982)

G. BIOGRAPHICAL WORKS

Ashby, Eric and Mary Anderson, *Portrait of Haldane at Work on Education* (London, 1974)

Cushing, Harvey, *Sir William Osler*, vol. 2 (Oxford, 1925)

Davies, Ivor J., *Memories of a Welsh Physician* (Aberystwyth, 1959)

Davies, T. G., *Ernest Jones, 1879–1958* (Cardiff, 1979)

Ellis, E. L., *T. J.: A Life of D. Thomas Jones, CH* (Cardiff, 1992)

Geison, G. L., *Michael Foster and the Cambridge School of Physiology: The Scientific Enterprise in Late-Victorian Society* (Princeton, 1978)

Grigg, J., *The Young Lloyd George* (London, 1973)

Grigg, J., *Lloyd George: the People's Champion, 1902–1911* (London, 1978)

Grigg, J., *Lloyd George: War Leader, 1916–1918* (London, 2002)

Hollman, Arthur, *Sir Thomas Lewis, Pioneer Cardiologist and Clinical Scientist* (London, 1997)

Jones, Ernest, *Free Associations: Memories of a Psychoanalyst* (New Brunswick and London, 1990)

Jones, Katherine Viriamu, *Life of John Viriamu Jones* (London, 1915)

Leneman, Leah, *In the Service of Life: the Story of Elsie Inglis and the Scottish Women's Hospital* (Edinburgh, 1994)

Maddox, Brenda, *Freud's Wizard: The Enigma of Ernest Jones* (London, 2006)

Powell, Dean, *Eccentric: The life of William Price* (Llantrisant, 2005)

Rolleston, Sir Humphry, *Life of Sir Clifford Allbutt* (London, 1929)

Vignes, Spencer, *Lost in France: The Remarkable Life and Death of Leigh Richmond Roose, Football's First Playboy* (Stroud, 2007).

Wade, O. L., *When I Dropped the Knife* (Bishop Auckland, 1996)

Watkins, Sir Percy, *A Welshman Remembers* (Cardiff, 1944)

H. OTHER BOOKS

Abse, D. (ed.), *My Medical School* (London, 1978).

Adie, Kate, *Corsets to Camouflage: Women at War* (London, 2003)

Aldis, A. S., *Cardiff Royal Infirmary. 1883–1983* (Cardiff, 1984)

Anning, S. T. and W. K. J. Walls, *A History of the Leeds School of Medicine, 1831–1981* (Leeds, 1982)

Austoker, Joan and Linda Bryder (eds.), *Historical Perspectives on the Role of the MRC* (Oxford, 1989)

Baber, C. and J. Lancaster (eds.), *Healthcare in Wales: An Historical Miscellany: A Collection of Papers in Celebration of the National Health Service in the New Millennium* (Cardiff, 2000)

Bellot, H. Hale, *University College, London, 1826–1926* (London, 1929)

Bonner, T. N., *Becoming a Physician: Medical Education in Britain, France, Germany and the United States, 1750–1945* (Oxford, 1995)

Borsay, Anne (ed.), *Medicine in Wales, c.1800–2000: Public Service or Private Commodity?* (Cardiff, 2003)

Borsay, Anne and Sarah Knight (eds.), *Medical Records for the South Wales Coalfield, c. 1890–1948: An Annotated Guide to the South Wales Coalfield Collection* (Cardiff, 2007)

Bryder, Linda, *Below the Magic Mountain: A Social History of Tuberculosis in Twentieth-Century Britain* (Oxford, 1988)

Bynum, W. F. and Roy Porter (eds.), *Companion Encyclopaedia of the History of Medicine*, vols 1 and 2 (London, 1993)

Carter, Harold and K. Davies, *Geography, Culture and Habitat: Selected Essays (1925–1975) of E. G. Bowen* (Llandysul, 1976)

Cartwright, F. F., *A Social History of Medicine* (London, 1977)

Chrimes, S. B. (ed.), *University College, Cardiff: A Centenary History, 1883–1983* (privately published, 1983)

Cooke, B. E. D., *The History of the University of Wales Dental School,1961–1982* (Cardiff, 1997)

Cule, J. H. (ed.), *Wales and Medicine: A Historical Survey from Papers given at the Ninth British Congress on the History of Medicine* (Llandysul, 1975)

Cunningham, Vanessa and John Goodwin, *Cardiff University: A Celebration* (Cardiff, 2001)

Davies, Edward, *The North Wales Quarry Hospitals, and the Health and Welfare of the Quarrymen* (Caernarfon, 2003)

Davies, John, *A History of Wales* (London, 1993)

Davies, John, *Cardiff* (Cardiff, 2002)

Davies, T. G., *Deeds Not Words: A History of the Swansea General and Eye Hospital 1817–1948* (Cardiff, 1988)

Dyhouse, Carol, *No Distinction of Sex? Women in British Universities, 1870–1939* (London, 1995)

Ellis, T. I., *The Development of Higher Education in Wales* (Wrexham, 1935)

Evans, D. Emrys, *The University of Wales, A Historical Sketch* (Cardiff, 1953)

Fee, Elizabeth and Roy M. Acheson (eds.), *A History of Education in Public Health* (Oxford, 1991)

Foster, W. D., *Pathology as a Profession in Great Britain and the Early History of the Royal College of Pathologists* (London, 1982)

Gray, T. Cecil and Sally Sheard, *A Brief History of Medical Education in Liverpool* (Liverpool, 2001)

Griffiths, R. A. (ed.), *The City of Swansea: Challenges and Change* (Stroud, 1990)

Heaman, E. A., *St. Mary's: The History of a London Teaching Hospital* (Liverpool, 2004)

Jenkins, David, *A Refuge in Peace and War: The National Library of Wales to 1952* (Aberystwyth, 2002)

Jenkins, G. H., *The University of Wales: An Illustrated History* (Cardiff, 1993)

Jones, D., *Corris Trwy Lygad y Camera / Corris through the Eye of the Camera* (Cardiff, 2002)

Jones, D. R., *The Origins of Civic Universities: Manchester, Leeds and Liverpool* (London, 1988)

Jones, G. and M. Quinn (eds.), *Fountains of Praise: University College, Cardiff 1883–1983* (Cardiff, 1984)

Jones, I. Gwynedd, *Health, Wealth and Politics in Victorian Wales* (University College of Swansea, 1979).

Jones, T. B. and W. J. T. Collins, *History of the Royal Gwent Hospital* (Newport, 1948)

Kelly, T., *For Advancement of Learning: The University of Liverpool 1881–1981* (Liverpool, 1981)

Kohler, R. E., *From Medical Chemistry to Biochemistry: The Making of a Biomedical Discipline* (Cambridge, 1982)

Lawrence, Christopher, *Rockefeller Money, the Laboratory, and Medicine in Edinburgh, 1919–1930: New Science in an Old Country* (Rochester, 2005)

Loudon, Irvine, *Medical Care and the General Practitioner, 1750–1850* (Oxford, 1986)

Michael, Pamela and Charles Webster (eds.), *Health and Society in Twentieth-Century Wales* (Cardiff, 2006)

Morgan, Dennis, *The Cardiff Story* (Cardiff, 1991)

Morgan, K. O., *Wales in British Politics, 1868–1922* (Oxford, 1963)

Morgan, K. O., *Rebirth of a Nation: A History of Modern Wales* (Oxford, 1988)

Morgan, Prys, *The University of Wales, 1939–1993* (Cardiff, 1997)

Newman, Charles, *The Evolution of Medical Education in the Nineteenth Century* (London, 1957)

Newman, George, *Recent Advances in Medical Education in England* (London: HMSO, 1923)

Nutton, V. and R. Porter (eds.), *The History of Medical Education in Britain* (Amsterdam, 1995)

Orrin, G. R., *Church Building and Restoration in Victorian Glamorgan* (Cardiff, 2004)

Peeling, W. B., *The Royal Gwent and St Woolos Hospital: A Century of Service in Newport* (Abertillery, 2004)

Perry, C. Bruce, *The Bristol Medical School* (Bristol Branch of the Historical Association, Bristol, 1984).

Phelps, Robert, *The Prince and the Pioneers* (Cardiff, 1993)

Porter, Roy, *The Greatest Benefit to Mankind: A Medical History of Humanity from Antiquity to the Present* (London, 1997)

Porter, W. S., *The Medical School in Sheffield, 1828–1928* (Sheffield, 1928)

Power, D'Arcy (ed.), *British Medical Societies* (London, 1939)

Poynter, F.N.L. (ed.), *The Evolution of Medical Education in Britain* (London, 1966)

Price, D. T. W., *A History of Saint David's University College, Lampeter*, vol. 1: *To 1898* (Cardiff, 1977)

Reader, W. J., *Professional Men* (London, 1966)

Routh, Guy, *Occupation and Pay in Great Britain, 1906–1979* (London, 1980)

Sanderson, Michael, *The Universities and British Industry, 1850–1970* (London, 1972)

Schneider, W. H. (ed.), *Rockefeller Philanthropy and Modern Biomedicine* (Bloomington, 2002)

Stephens, G. Arbour, *The Hospitals of Wales* (Swansea, 1912)

Surtees, J. and Alan Trevor Jones, *The Medical Teaching Centre, Cardiff* (Cardiff, 1971)

Taylor, A. J. P., *English History, 1914–1945* (Oxford, 1965)

Thomas, Hilary M., *Whitchurch Hospital, 1908–1983* (Cardiff, 1983)

Trow, A. H. and D. J. A. Brown, *A Short History of the University College of South Wales and Monmouthshire, Cardiff, 1883–1933* (Cardiff, 1933)

Turner, G. Grey, *The Newcastle upon Tyne School of Medicine, 1834–1934* (Newcastle upon Tyne, 1934)

Waddington, K., *Medical Education at St Bartholomew's Hospital, 1123–1995* (Woodbridge, 2003)

Walton, John and Miles Irving (eds.), *100 Years of the Royal Victoria Infirmary* (Newcastle upon Tyne, 2006)

Weatherall, Mark, *Gentlemen, Scientists, and Doctors: Medicine at Cambridge, 1800–1940* (Woodbridge, 2000).

Williams, Harley, *Requiem for a Great Killer: The Story of Tuberculosis* (London, 1973)

Williams, J. Gwynn, *The University Movement in Wales* (Cardiff, 1993)

Williams, J. Gwynn, *The University of Wales, 1893–1939* (Cardiff, 1997)

I. ARTICLES

Adrian, Lord, 'Thomas Graham Brown', in *Biographical Memoirs of Fellows of the Royal Society*, vol. 12 (London: The Royal Society, 1966)

Anning, S. T., 'Provincial medical schools in the nineteenth century', in F. N. L. Poynter (ed.), *The Evolution of Medical Education in Britain*

Booth, Christopher, 'Clinical research', in Joan Austoker and Linda Bryder (eds.), *Historical Perspectives on the Role of the MRC*

Booth, Christopher, 'Clinical research', in W. F. Bynum and Roy Porter (eds.), *Companion Encyclopaedia of the History of Medicine*, vol. 1

Brown, T. Graham, 'John Berry Haycraft, MD, DSc', *Proceedings of the Royal Society of Edinburgh* (1922/3)

Bryder, Linda, 'The King Edward VII Welsh National Memorial Association and its policy towards tuberculosis, 1910–1948', *Welsh History Review*, 13, 2 (1986)

Bryder, Linda, 'Tuberculosis and the MRC', in Joan Austoker and Linda Bryder (eds.), *Historical Perspectives on the Role of the MRC*

Butler, Stella V. F., 'A transformation in training: the formation of medical faculties in Manchester, Leeds and Liverpool, 1870–94', *Medical History*, 30 (1986)

Butler, Stella V. F., 'Centers and peripheries: the development of British physiology, 1870–1914', *Journal of the History of Biology*, 21, 3 (1988)

Bynum, W. F., 'Sir George Newman and the American way', in V. Nutton and R. Porter (eds.), *The History of Medical Education in Britain*

Collingwood, Frances, 'The Welsh National School of Medicine', *History of Medicine*, 2, 2 (Summer 1970)

Cule, J. H., 'Sir William Osler and his Welsh connections', *Postgraduate Medical Journal*, 64 (1988)

Cule, J. H., 'The Welsh National School of Medicine', in C. Baber and J. Lancaster (eds.), *Healthcare in Wales: An Historical Miscellany*

Davies, N. Naunton, 'Two and a half centuries of medical practice: a Welsh medical dynasty', in J. H. Cule (ed.), *Wales and Medicine: An Historical Survey*

Davies, T. G., 'Some early Glamorgan contributors to medical journals', *Morgannwg*, 51 (2007).

Davis, B. T., 'The Queen's Hospital and William Sands Cox, 1841–1940', *Aesculapius*, 15 (1995)

Dyhouse, Carol, 'Driving ambitions: women in pursuit of a medical education, 1890–1939', *Women's History Review*, 7, 3 (1998)

Earwicker, Ray, 'Miners' medical services before the First World War: the South Wales coalfield', *Llafur*, 3, 1 (1981)

Eccles, Ronald, 'Old man of the mountains: T. Graham Brown', in G. Jones and M. Quinn (eds.), *Fountains of Praise*

Evans, Neil, 'The first charity in Wales: Cardiff Infirmary and South Wales society, 1837–1914', *Welsh History Review*, 9, 3 (1979)

Evans, Neil, 'Urbanisation, elite attitudes and philanthropy: Cardiff, 1850–1914', *International Review of Social History*, 27, 3 (1982)

Evans, Neil, 'The Welsh Victorian city: the middle class and civic and national consciousness in Cardiff, 1850–1914', *Welsh History Review*, 12, 3 (1985).

Evans, Neil, '"Sea wall against disease": port health in Cardiff, 1850–1950', in Pamela Michael and Charles Webster (eds.), *Health and Society in Twentieth-Century Wales*

Garner, J. S., 'The great experiment: the admission of women students to the St Mary's Hospital School of Medicine', *Medical History*, 42 (1998)

Graham, G., 'The formation of the medical and surgical professorial units in the London teaching hospitals', *Annals of Science*, 26 (1970)

Gross, J., 'Hospitals in Merthyr Tydfil, 1850–1974', *Merthyr Historian*, 2 (1978).

Hammond, T. E., 'The purpose of a medical society', *Proceedings of the Cardiff Medical Society*, 1938/39

How, Barbara, 'A residence for young women', in G. Jones and M. Quinn (eds.), *Fountains of Praise*

Hull, Andrew, 'Hector's House: Sir Hector Hetherington and the academicization of Glasgow hospital medicine before the NHS', *Medical History*, 45 (2001).

James, D. Geraint, 'Dr Isambard Owen (1850–1927)', in J. H. Cule (ed.), *Wales and Medicine: An Historical Survey*

Jones, A. Trevor, 'The new medical centre and the development of medical education in Wales', in J. H. Cule (ed.), *Wales and Medicine: An Historical Survey*

Jones, Emyr Wyn, 'Sir John Williams (1840–1926): his background and achievement', in J. H. Cule (ed.), *Wales and Medicine: An Historical Survey*.

Jones, Emyr Wyn, 'Syr William Roberts a penisilin', *Gwyddonydd*, 23 (1985/6)

Jones, G. R., 'The King Edward VII Welsh National Memorial Association, 1912–1948', in J. H. Cule (ed.), *Wales and Medicine: An Historical Survey*

Kennedy, A. M., 'Medical unit laboratories, Welsh National School of Medicine (University of Wales)', in *Methods and Problems of Medical Education*, eighteenth series (The Rockefeller Foundation, New York, 1930)

Lawrence, Christopher, 'Incommunicable knowledge: science, technology and the clinical art in Britain, 1850–1914', *Journal of Contemporary History*, 20 (1985)

Maliphant, R. G., 'Two famous Welsh obstetricians', *Proceedings of the Cardiff Medical Society* (1964/5)

McIntyre, Neil, 'Britain's first medical marriage: Frances Morgan (1843–1927), George Hoggan (1837–1891) and the mysterious Elsie', *Journal of Medical Biography*, 12 (2004)

Morris, J. S., 'Sir Daniel Davies: a Welshman in London', *Journal of Medical Biography*, 9 (2001)

Picken, R. M. F., 'The growth of a medical school', *Proceedings of the Cardiff Medical Society* (1954/5)

Powell, Martin, 'What was Wales? Towards a contextual approach to medical history', in Pamela Michael and Charles Webster (eds.), *Health and Society in Twentieth-Century Wales*

Reinarz, J., 'Healthcare and the Second City: the development of the Birmingham teaching hospitals in the nineteenth century', *Birmingham Historian* (2004)

Reinarz, J., 'The age of museum medicine: the rise and fall of the medical museum at Birmingham's School of Medicine', *Journal of the Society for the Social History of Medicine*, 18, 3 (2005)

Reiser, S.J., 'The science of diagnosis: diagnostic technology', in W. F. Bynum and Roy Porter (eds.), *Companion Encyclopaedia of the History of Medicine*, vol. 2

Roberts, A. W., '"A great school and hospital so skilfully combined": the origins and development of the medical teaching centre concept, 1922–1971', in C. Baber and J. Lancaster (eds.), *Healthcare in Wales: A Historical Miscellany*

Roberts, A. W., 'A short history of academic medicine in Wales', *Welsh Paediatric Journal*, 21 (2004)

Roderick, G. W., 'Education in an industrial society', in R. A. Griffiths, *The City of Swansea: Challenges and Change* (Stroud, 1990)

Roderick, G. W., 'A new college for south Wales. Cardiff versus Swansea: a battle of the sites, 1881–83', *Transactions of the Honourable Society of Cymmrodorion*, n.s., 6 (2000)

Schneider, W. H., 'The men who followed Flexner: Richard Pearce, Alan Gregg, and the Rockefeller Foundation Medical Divisions, 1919–1951', in W. H. Schneider (ed.), *Rockefeller Philanthropy and Modern Biomedicine*

Sheen, A. W., 'The history of the Cardiff Medical Society', *Proceedings of the Cardiff Medical Society* (1938/39)

Sturdy, S. W., 'The political economy of scientific medicine: science, education and the transformation of medical practice in Sheffield, 1892–1922', *Medical History*, 36 (1992)

Sturdy, S. W. and Roger Cooter, 'Science, scientific management, and the transformation of medicine in Britain, c. 1870–1950', *History of Science*, 36 (1998)

Thomas, Sir Clement Price, 'The Sheens and the Welsh National School of Medicine', *Proceedings of the Cardiff Medical Society* (1965/6)

Thomas, Dewi-Prys, '"A Quiet Dignity ...": William Douglas Caroe and the visual presence', in G. Jones and M. Quinn (eds.), *Fountains of Praise*

Thomas, P. H., 'Medical men of Glamorgan: the Vachells of Cardiff', *Glamorgan Historian*, 4 (1967)

Thomas, P. H., 'Medical men of Glamorgan: Dr Donald Rose Paterson (1862–1939)', *Glamorgan Historian*, 5 (1968)

Thomas, P. H., 'Medical men of Glamorgan: P. Rhys Griffths (1857–1920)', *Glamorgan Historian*, 6 (1969)

Thomas, P. H., 'Medical men of Glamorgan: William Thomas Edwards (1821–1915)', 2 parts, *Glamorgan Historian*, 7 (1971), and 8 (1972)

Thomas, P. H., 'Medical men of Glamorgan: Thomas Williams of Swansea (1815–1865)', *Glamorgan Historian*, 9 (1973)

Thompson, Steven, 'To relieve the sufferings of humanity, irrespective of party, politics or creed?: Conflict, consensus and voluntary hospital provision in Edwardian south Wales', *Journal of the Society for the Social History of Medicine*, 16, 2 (2003)

Thompson, Steven, 'A proletarian public sphere: working-class provision of medical services and care in south Wales, c. 1900–1948', in Anne Borsay (ed.), *Medicine in Wales, c. 1800–2000: Public Service or Private Commodity?*

Turner, C. B., '"A blot on any society": the development of public health in the south Wales Valleys during the nineteenth century', in C. Baber and J. Lancaster (eds.), *Healthcare in Wales: A Historical Miscellany*

Wade, O. L., 'The legacy of Richard Burdon Haldane: the university clinical units and their future', *Ulster Medical Journal*, 45 (1976)

Webster, Charles, 'Devolution and the health services in Wales, 1919–1969', in Pamela Michael and Charles Webster (eds.), *Health and Society in Twentieth-Century Wales*

Weindling, Paul, 'The Jewish medical refugee crisis and Wales, 1933–1945', in Pamela Michael and Charles Webster (eds.), *Health and Society in Twentieth-Century Wales*

Williams, G. A., 'Odd man in', in G. Jones and M. Quinn (eds.), *Fountains of Praise*

Windeyer, Sir Brian, 'University education in the twentieth century', in F. N. L. Poynter (ed.), *The Evolution of Medical Education in Britain*

J. UNPUBLISHED THESES

Butler, Stella V. F., 'Science and the education of doctors in the nineteenth century: a study of British medical schools with particular reference to the development and uses of physiology' (Ph.D., University of Manchester, 1981)

Jones, G. A., 'The life and work of Sir Isambard Owen, with particular reference to his contribution to education in Wales' (MA, University of Wales, 1967)

Parsons, A. J., 'The origin and subsequent development of the Cardiff Medical School into the Welsh National School of Medicine, 1894–1971' (M.Ed., University of Wales, 1979)

Thompson, Steven D., 'A social history of health in inter-war South Wales' (Ph.D., University of Wales, 2001)

Valier, Helen, 'The politics of scientific medicine in Manchester, c. 1900–1960' (Ph.D., University of Manchester, 2002)

Winn, Carole, 'A biographical dictionary of Cardiff architects, c.1850–1920' (dissertation for the University of Wales College, Cardiff, 1991)

Index